Data Structures Using Java

Data Structures Using Java

D. S. Malik
P. S. Nair

THOMSON

COURSE TECHNOLOGY

Australia • Canada • Mexico • Singapore • Spain • United Kingdom • United States

Data Structures Using Java

by D. S. Malik and P. S. Nair

Managing Editor:
Jennifer Muroff

Editorial Assistant:
Christy Urban

Cover Designer:
Steve Deschene

Development Editor:
Susan Gilbert, Edex

Production Editor:
Aimee Poirier

Compositor:
GEX Publishing Services

Associate Product Manager:
Janet Aras

Associate Product Marketing Manager:
Angie Laughlin

Manufacturing Coordinator:
Laura Burns

TO

Sadhana Malik

and

Suseela Nair

Contents

BRIEF

TABLE OF
Contents

2. Inheritance and Exception Handling   75

3. Array-Based Lists   169

6. Stacks   365

8. Search Algorithms   485

11. Graphs   671

APPENDIX F Java for C++ Programmers   773

Preface

Welcome to *Data Structures Using Java*. Designed for a second Computer Science (CS2) Java course, this text will provide a breath of fresh air for you and your students. The CS2 course typically completes the programming requirements of the Computer Science curriculum. This text is a culmination and development of our classroom notes throughout more than fifty semesters of successfully teaching programming and data structures to computer science students.

This book is a continuation of the work started in the CS1 book, *Java Programming: From Problem Analysis to Program Design*, published by Course Technology. The approach taken in this book to present the material is similar to the one used in the CS1 book and, therefore, is driven by the students' demand for clarity and readability. The material was written and rewritten until the students felt comfortable with it. Most of the examples in this book resulted from student interaction in the classroom.

This book assumes that the reader is familiar with the basic elements of Java such as data types, control structures, functions and parameters, and arrays. However, if you need to review these concepts, or you have taken C++ as a first programming language, you will find the relevant material in Appendix F quite helpful. If you need to review the CS1 topics in more detail than given in Appendix F, refer to the Java programming book by the authors listed in the preceding paragraph and also in Appendix G. In addition, some adequate mathematics background such as college algebra is required.

APPROACH

Intended as a second course in computer programming, this book focuses on data structures as well as object-oriented design (OOD). The programming examples given in this book effectively use OOD techniques to solve and program a particular problem.

Chapter 1 introduces the software engineering principles. After describing the life-cycle of software, this chapter discusses why algorithm analysis is important and introduces the Big-O notation used in algorithm analysis. There are three basic principles of OOD—encapsulation, inheritance, and polymorphism. Encapsulation in Java is achieved via the use of classes. The second half of this chapter discusses user-defined classes. If you are familiar with how to create and use your own classes, you can skip this section. This chapter also discusses a basic OOD technique to solve a particular problem.

Chapter 2 continues with the principles of OOD and discusses inheritance and exception handling. This chapter explains how to extend the definitions of classes via the principle of inheritance. When you execute a Java program, several things can happen. For example, an inadvertent attempt to divide by 0, trying to tokenize a string that does not exist, and an array index that goes out of bounds; these types of errors are called exceptions in Java. Java provides extensive support for handling exceptions in a program. In addition to explaining how to use existing Java exception classes, this chapter also explains how to construct your own exception classes.

Chapter 3 discusses how data is organized and manipulated in an array. In addition to explaining how to develop your own code, this chapter also illustrates how the Java **class Vector** works.

Chapter 4 discusses linked lists. This chapter first describes the basic properties of linked lists such as item insertion and deletion, and how to construct a linked list. This chapter then develops a generic code to process data in a single linked list. Chapter 4 also discusses doubly linked lists. Moreover, this chapter introduces linked lists with header and trailer nodes and circular linked lists.

Chapter 5 introduces recursion and gives various examples to show how to use recursion to solve a problem, as well as think in terms of recursion.

Chapters 6 and 7 discuss stacks and queues. In addition to showing how to develop your own generic code to implement stacks and queues, these chapters explain how the Java **class Stack** works. These chapters also discuss applications to stacks and queues.

Chapter 8 describes the searching algorithms. After analyzing the sequential search algorithm, it discusses the binary search algorithm and provides a brief analysis of this algorithm. After giving a lower bound on comparison-based search algorithms, this chapter discusses hashing.

Sorting algorithms such as the selection sort, insertion sort, quick sort, merge sort, and heap sort are introduced and discussed in Chapter 9. Chapter 10 introduces and discusses binary trees. Chapter 11 introduces graphs and discusses graph algorithms such as the shortest path, minimal spanning tree, and topological sorting.

Appendix A lists the reserved words in Java. Appendix B shows the precedence and associativity of the Java operators. Appendix C lists the ASCII (American Standard Code for Information Interchange) and EBCDIC (Extended Binary Code Decimal Interchange) character sets. Appendix D shows how user-defined classes can be used in a Java program. Appendix E describes the Java classes used in this book. Appendix F provides a quick review of the basic elements of Java. It also compares the basic concepts such as data types, control structures, functions and parameters, and arrays of the languages C++ and Java. Therefore, if you have taken C++ as a first programming language, Appendix F helps familiarize you with these basic elements of Java. Appendix G provides a list of references for further study and where to find the additional Java topics not covered in Appendix F. Appendix H gives the answers to selected exercises in the text.

HOW TO USE THIS BOOK

The main objective of this book is to teach data structure topics using Java as well as OOD to solve a particular problem. To do so, the book discusses data structures such as linked lists, stacks, queues, and binary trees. Java also provides the necessary code to implement some of these data structures. However, our emphasis is to teach you how to develop your own code. At the same time, we also want you to learn how to use professionally written code.

Chapter 5 discusses recursion. However, Chapter 5 is not a prerequisite for Chapters 6 and 7. If you read Chapter 5 after these chapters, then you can skip the section "Removing Recursion" in Chapter 6 and read this section after reading Chapter 5. Even though Chapter 5 is not required to study Chapter 8, ideally, Chapters 8 and 9 should be studied in sequence. Therefore, we recommend that you should study Chapter 5 before Chapter 8. The following diagram illustrates the dependency of the chapters.

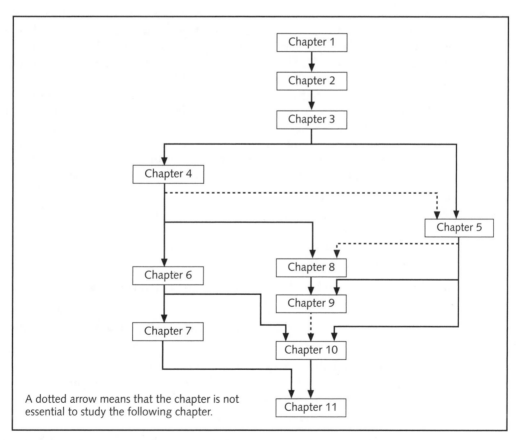

Figure 1   Chapter dependency diagram

FEATURES

This book includes the following features in every chapter. These features are both conducive to learning and make it possible for readers to learn the material at their own pace.

- *Learning objectives* offer an outline of the Java programming concepts that are discussed in detail within the chapter.

- *Notes* highlight important facts regarding the concepts introduced in the chapter.

- Visual diagrams, both extensive and exhaustive, illustrate the difficult concepts. The book contains over 375 figures.

- Numbered *Examples* within each chapter illustrate the key concepts with relevant code. Each line of the programming code in these examples is numbered. Every program, illustrated through a sample run, is then explained line-by-line. The rationale behind each line is discussed in detail.

 - *Programming Examples* are programs featured at the end of each chapter. These examples contain the accurate, concrete stages of Input, Output, Problem Analysis and Algorithm Design, and a Program Listing. Moreover, the problems in these programming examples are solved and programmed using OOD. These case studies form the backbone of the book and are highlighted with an icon in the margin. The programs are designed to be methodical and user-friendly. Beginning with the Problem Analysis, the Programming Example is then followed by the Algorithm Design. Every step of the algorithm is then coded in Java. In addition to teaching problem-solving techniques, these detailed programs show the user how to implement concepts in an actual Java program. We strongly recommend that students study the Programming Examples very carefully in order to learn Java effectively.

- *Quick Review* sections at the end of each chapter reinforce learning by summarizing the concepts covered within the chapter. After reading the chapter, readers can quickly walk through the highlights of the chapter and then test themselves using the ensuing Exercises. Many readers refer to the Quick Review as a way to quickly review the chapter before an exam.

- *Exercises* further reinforce learning and ensure that students have, in fact, learned the material.

- *Programming Exercises* challenge students to write Java programs with a specified outcome.

From beginning to end, the concepts are introduced at a pace that is conducive to learning. The writing style of this book is simple and straightforward. Before introducing a key concept, we explain why certain elements are necessary. The concepts introduced are then explained using examples and small programs.

All source code and solutions have been written, compiled, and quality assurance tested with Sun Java JDK 1.4.0.

TEACHING TOOLS

The following supplemental materials are available when this book is used in a classroom setting. All of the teaching tools available with this book are provided to the instructor on a single CD-ROM.

Electronic Instructor's Manual. The Instructor's Manual that accompanies this textbook includes:

- Additional instructional material to assist in class preparation, including suggestions for lecture topics.

- Solutions to all the end-of-chapter materials, including the Programming Exercises.

ExamView®. This textbook is accompanied by ExamView, a powerful testing software package that allows instructors to create and administer printed, computer (LAN-based), and Internet exams. ExamView includes hundreds of questions that correspond to the topics covered in this text, enabling students to generate detailed study guides that include page references for further review. The computer-based and Internet testing components allow students to take exams at their computers, and also save the instructor time by grading each exam automatically.

PowerPoint Presentations. This book comes with Microsoft PowerPoint slides for each chapter. These are included as a teaching aid for classroom presentations, either to make available to students on the network for chapter review, or to be printed for classroom distribution. Instructors can add their own slides for additional topics that they introduce to the class.

Distance Learning. Course Technology is proud to present online courses in WebCT and Blackboard, as well as at MyCourse.com, Course Technology's own course enhancement tool, to provide the most complete and dynamic learning experience possible. When you add online content to one of your courses, you're adding a lot: self tests, links, glossaries, and, most of all, a gateway to the 21st century's most important information resource. We hope you will make the most of your course, both online and offline. For more information on how to bring distance learning to your course, contact your local Course Technology sales representative.

Source Code. The source code is available at `www.course.com`, and also available on the Teaching Tools CD-ROM. The input files needed to run some of the programs are also included with the source code. However, the input files should first be stored on a floppy disk in drive `A:`.

Solution files. The source code for all the programming exercises is available at `www.course.com`, and also available on the Teaching Tools CD-ROM. The input files needed to run some of the programming exercises are also included with the source code. However, the input files should first be stored on a floppy disk in drive `A:`.

ACKNOWLEDGEMENTS

There are many people that we must thank who, one way or another, contributed to the success of this book. We owe a great deal to the following reviewers who patiently read each page of every chapter of the current version and made critical comments to improve on the book: Ted Bangay, Sheridan College; Ron Davidson, Highline Community College; Connie Elder, Cuyamaca College; Craig Murray, Indiana University; and Marguerite Nedreberg, Youngstown State University. The reviewers will recognize that their criticisms have not been overlooked and, in fact, made this a better book. Thanks to Development Editor Susan Gilbert for carefully editing each chapter. All this would not have been possible without the planning of Managing Editor Jennifer Muroff. Our sincere thanks to Jennifer as well as to Production Editor Aimee Poirier, and also to the QA department, especially to Vitaly Davidovich, of Course Technology for carefully testing the code.

We are thankful to our parents for their blessings.

Finally, we are thankful to the support of our wives, Sadhana and Suseela, to whom this book is dedicated and especially our daughters, Shelly and Meera. They cheered us up whenever we were overwhelmed during the writing of this book.

We welcome any comments concerning the text. Comments may be forwarded to the following e-mail addresses: `malik@creighton.edu` or `psnair@creighton.edu`.

D. S. Malik
P. S. Nair

SOFTWARE ENGINEERING
PRINCIPLES AND JAVA CLASSES

In this chapter, you will:

♦ Learn about software engineering principles

♦ Discover what an algorithm is and explore problem-solving techniques

♦ Become aware of structured design and object-oriented design programming methodologies

♦ Learn about user-defined classes

♦ Learn about `private`, `protected`, and `public` members of a class

♦ Explore how classes are implemented

♦ Become aware of Unified Modeling Language (UML) notation

♦ Examine constructors and destructors

♦ Learn about the abstract data type (ADT)

♦ Explore how classes are used to implement ADT

M ost everyone working with computers is familiar with the term "software." Software are computer programs designed to accomplish a specific task. For example, word-processing software is a program that enables you to write term papers, create impressive looking résumés, and even write a book. This book, for example, was created with the help of a word processor. Students no longer type their papers on typewriters or write them by hand. Instead, they use word-processing software to complete their term papers. Many people maintain and balance their checkbooks using personal finance software.

Powerful, yet easy-to-use software has drastically changed the way we live and communicate. Terms, such as the Internet, which were unfamiliar just a few years ago, are very common today. With the help of computers and the software running on them, you can send letters to, and receive letters from, loved ones within seconds. You no longer need to send a résumé by mail to apply for a job; in many cases, you can simply submit your job application via the Internet. You can watch how stocks perform in real time, and instantly buy and sell them. Students in elementary school regularly "surf" the Internet and use computers to design their classroom projects.

Without software a computer is of no use. It is the software that enables you to do things that were, perhaps, fiction a few years ago. However, software is not created overnight. From the time a software program is conceived until it is delivered, it goes through several phases. There is a branch of computer science, called software engineering, that specializes in this area. Most colleges and universities offer a course in software engineering. This book is not concerned with the teaching of software engineering principles. However, this chapter briefly describes some of the basic software engineering principles that can simplify program design.

SOFTWARE LIFE CYCLE

A program goes through many phases from the time it is first conceived until the time it is retired, called the life cycle of the program. The three fundamental stages a program goes through are: **development**, **use**, and **maintenance**. Usually a program is initially conceived by a software developer because a customer has some problem that needs to be solved, and the customer is willing to pay money to have it solved. The new program is created in the software development stage. The next section describes this stage in some detail.

Once the program is considered complete, it is released for the users to use. Once users start using the program, they most certainly discover problems or have suggestions to improve it. The problems and ideas for improvements are conveyed to the software developer, and the program goes through the maintenance phase.

In the software maintenance process, the program is modified to fix the (identified) problems and/or to enhance it. If there are serious or numerous changes, typically, a new version of the program is created and released for use.

When a program is considered too expensive to maintain, the developer might decide to **retire** the program and no new version of the program is released.

The software development phase is the first and perhaps most important phase of the software lifecycle. A program that is well developed is easy and less expensive to maintain. The next section describes this phase.

SOFTWARE DEVELOPMENT PHASE

Software engineers typically break the software development process into the following four phases:

- Analysis
- Design
- Implementation
- Testing and debugging

The next few sections describe these four phases in some detail.

Analysis

Analyzing the problem is the first and most important step. This step requires you to do the following:

- Thoroughly understand the problem.

- **Requirement analysis:** Understand the problem requirements. Requirements can include whether the program requires interaction with the user, whether it manipulates data, whether it produces output, and what the output looks like.

  For example, suppose that you need to develop a program to make an automated teller machine (ATM) operational. In the analysis phase, you determine the functionality of the machine. Here you determine the necessary operations performed by the machine such as allow withdrawals, deposits, and transfers, provide account balances, and so on. During this phase, you also talk to potential customers who will use the machine. To make it user-friendly, you must understand their requirements and add any necessary operations.

- If the program manipulates data, the programmer must know what the data is and how it is represented. That is, you need to look at sample data. If the program produces output, you should know how the results should be generated and formatted.

- If the problem is complex, divide the problem into subproblems, analyze each subproblem and understand each subproblem's requirements.

Design

After you carefully analyze the problem, the next step is to design an algorithm to solve the problem. If you broke the problem into subproblems, you need to design an algorithm for each subproblem.

Algorithm: A step-by-step, problem-solving process in which a solution is arrived at in a finite amount of time.

Structured Design

Dividing a problem into smaller subproblems is called **structured design**. The structured design approach is also known as **top-down design**, **stepwise refinement**, and **modular programming**. In structured design, the problem is divided into smaller problems. Each subproblem is then analyzed, and a solution is obtained to solve the subproblem. The solutions of all the subproblems are then combined to solve the overall problem. This process of implementing a structured design is called **structured programming**.

Object-Oriented Design

In object-oriented design (OOD), the first step in the problem-solving process is to identify the components called **objects**, which form the basis of the solution, and determine how these objects interact with one another. For example, suppose you want to write a program that automates the video rental process for a local video store. The two main objects in this problem are the video and the customer.

After identifying the objects, the next step is to specify for each object the relevant data and possible operations to be performed on that data. For example, for a video object, the data might include the movie name, starring actors, producer, production company, number of copies in stock, and so on. Some of the operations on a video object might include checking the name of the movie, reducing the number of copies in stock by one after a copy is rented, and incrementing the number of copies in stock by one after a customer returns a particular video.

This illustrates that each object consists of data and operations on the data. An object combines data and operations on the data into a single unit. In OOD, the final program is a collection of interacting objects. A programming language that implements OOD is called an **object-oriented programming (OOP)** language. You learn about the many advantages of OOD in later chapters.

OOD has the three basic principles:

- Encapsulation—The ability to combine data and operations in a single unit

- Inheritance—The ability to create new (data) types from existing (data) types

- Polymorphism—The ability to use the same expression to denote different operations

In Java, encapsulation is accomplished via the use of the data types called classes. The way classes are implemented in Java is described later in this chapter. Chapter 2 discusses inheritance and polymorphism.

In object-oriented design, you decide which classes you need and what are their relevant data members and methods. You then describe how classes interact with each other.

Implementation

In the implementation phase, you write and compile programming code to implement the classes and methods that were discovered in the design phase.

This book uses the OOD technique (in conjunction with structured programming) to solve a particular problem. It contains many case studies, called Programming Examples, to solve real-world problems.

The final program consists of objects and methods. Methods are designed to accomplish a specific task. Some methods are part of the main program; others are used to implement various operations on objects. Objects interact with each other via method calls.

In order to use a method, the user needs to know only how to use the method and what the method does. The user should not be concerned with the details of the method, that is, how the method is written. Let us illustrate this with the help of the following example.

Suppose that you want to write a method that converts a measurement given in inches into equivalent centimeters. The conversion formula is 1 inch = 2.54 centimeters. The following method accomplishes the job:

```
double inchesToCentimeters(double inches)
{
      if(inches < 0.0)
      {
          System.err.println("The given measurement "
                            + "must be nonnegative");
          return -1.0;
      }
      else
          return 2.54 * inches;
}
```

 The object `System.err` corresponds to the unbuffered standard error stream. Unlike the object, `System.out` (whose output first goes to the buffer), the output of `System.err` is immediately sent to the standard error stream, which is usually the screen.

If you look at the body of the method, you can recognize that if the value of inches is less than 0, that is, negative, the method returns −1.0; otherwise, the method returns the equivalent length in centimeters. The user of this method does not need to know the specific details of how the algorithm that finds the equivalent length in centimeters is implemented. However, the user must know that in order to get the valid answer, the input must be a nonnegative number. If the input to this method is a negative number, the program returns −1.0. This information can be provided as part of the documentation of this method using specific statements, called preconditions and postconditions.

Precondition: A statement specifying the condition(s) that must be true before the method is called.

Postcondition: A statement specifying what is true after the method call is completed.

The precondition and postcondition for the method `inchesToCentimeters` can be specified using commented statements as follows:

```
//Precondition: The value of inches must be nonnegative
//Postcondition: If the value of inches is < 0, the method
//               returns -1.0; otherwise, the method returns
//               the equivalent length in centimeters;
double inchesToCentimeters(double inches)
{
      if(inches < 0.0)
      {
          System.err.println("The given measurement "
                            + "must be nonnegative");
          return -1.0;
      }
```

```
        else
            return 2.54 * inches;
}
```

The preceding form of the method `inchesToCentimeters` returns `-1.0` if the value of the formal parameter is less than `0.0`. Rather than return the value `-1.0`, the method can throw an exception and force the user to deal with the exception. Suppose that there is a `class` that throws a `NumberOutOfRangeException` if the number is negative. You can write the definition of the `inchesToCentimeters` method as follows:

```
//Precondition: The value of inches must be nonnegative
//Postcondition: If the value of inches is < 0, the method
//               throws NumberOutOfRangeException;
//               otherwise, the method returns the equivalent
//               length in centimeters;
double inchesToCentimeters(double inches)
                                 throws NumberOutOfRangeException
{
        if(inches < 0.0)
            throw new NumberOutOfRangeException("Negative inches");

        return 2.54 * inches;
}
```

As you can see, the same method can be implemented differently by different programmers. Because the user of a method need not be concerned with the details of the method, the preconditions and postconditions are specified with the method heading. That is, the user is given the following information:

```
double inchesToCentimeters(double inches)
  //Preconditions: The value of inches must be nonnegative
  //Postconditions: If the value of inches is < 0, the method
  //               returns -1.0; otherwise, the method returns
  //               the equivalent length in centimeters;
```

As another example, to use a method that searches a list for a specific item, the list must exist before the method is called. After the search is complete, the method returns `true` or `false` depending on whether the search was successful:

```
boolean search(int []list, int listLength, int searchItem)
  //Preconditions: The list must exist
  //Postconditions: The method returns true if searchItem is in
  //                list; otherwise, the method returns false
```

Testing and Debugging

The term *testing* refers to testing the correctness of the program; that is, making sure that the program does what it is supposed to do. The term *debugging* refers to if errors exist, then finding and fixing the errors.

After a method or an algorithm is written, the next step is to verify that it works properly. However, in a large, complex program, errors almost certainly exist. Therefore, to increase the reliability of the program, errors must be discovered and fixed before the program is released to the user.

You can certainly prove this by using some (perhaps mathematical) analysis of the correctness of a program. However, for large, complex programs, this technique alone might not be enough because errors can be made in the proof. Therefore, you should also rely on testing to determine the quality of the program. In the testing phase you would run the program through a series of specific tests, called **test cases**, in an attempt to find problems.

A test case consists of a set of inputs, user actions, or other initial conditions, and the expected output. Because a test case can be repeated several times, it must be properly documented. Typically, a program manipulates a larger set of data. It is, therefore, impractical (although possible) to create test cases for all possible inputs. For example, suppose that a program manipulates integers. Clearly, it is not possible to create a test case for each integer. You can categorize test cases into separate categories, called equivalence categories. An **equivalence category** is a set of input values that are likely to produce the same output. For example, suppose that you have a method that takes an integer as input and returns `true` if the integer is nonnegative, and `false` otherwise. In this case, you can form two equivalence categories: one consisting of negative numbers and the other consisting of nonnegative numbers.

There are two types of testing: **black-box testing** and **white-box testing**.

In *black-box* testing, you do not know the internal working of the algorithm or method. You know only what the method does. Black-box testing is based on inputs and outputs. The test cases for black-box testing are usually selected by creating equivalence categories. If a method works for one input in the equivalence category, it is expected to work for other inputs in the same category.

Suppose that the method `isWithInRange` returns a value `true` if an integer is greater than or equal to 0 and less than or equal to 100. In black-box testing, the method is tested on values that surround and fall on the boundaries, called **boundary values**, as well as general values from the equivalence categories. For the method `isWithInRange`, in black-box testing, the boundary values might be –1, 0, 1, 99, 100, and 101; therefore the test values might be –500, –1, 0, 1, 50, 99, 100, 101, and 500.

White-box testing relies on the internal structure and implementation of a method or algorithm. The objective is to ensure that every part of the method or algorithm is executed at least once. Suppose that you want to ensure that an `if` statement works properly. The test cases must consist of at least one input for which the `if` statement evaluates to `true` and at least one case for which it evaluates to `false`. Loops and other structures can be tested similarly.

ALGORITHM ANALYSIS: THE BIG-O NOTATION

Just as a problem is analyzed before writing the algorithm and the computer program, after an algorithm is designed it should also be analyzed. Usually, there are various ways to design a particular algorithm. Certain algorithms take very little computer time to execute, while others take a considerable amount of time.

Consider the following problem. The holiday season is approaching and the gift shop is expecting sales to be double or even triple the regular amount. The shop has hired extra delivery persons to deliver packages on time. The company calculates the shortest distance from the shop to a particular destination and hands the route to the driver. Suppose that 50 packages are to be delivered to 50 different houses. The company, while creating the route, finds that the 50 houses are one mile apart and are in the same area. The first house is also one mile from the shop (see Figure 1-1).

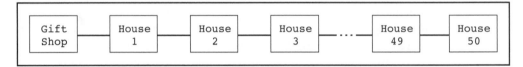

Figure 1-1   Gift shop and the 50 houses

To simplify this figure, we use Figure 1-2:

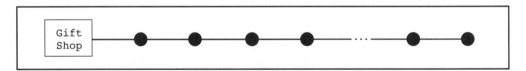

Figure 1-2   Gift shop and each dot representing a house

Each dot represents a house and the distance between houses, as shown in Figure 1-2, is 1 mile.

To deliver 50 packages to their destinations, one of the drivers picks up all 50 packages, drives one mile to the first house, and delivers the first package. Then he drives another mile and delivers the second package, drives another mile and delivers the third package, and so on. Figure 1-3 illustrates this delivery scheme.

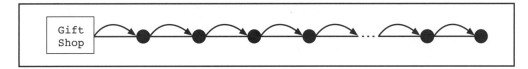

Figure 1-3 Package delivering scheme

It now follows that using this scheme, the distance the driver drives to deliver the packages is:

$1 + 1 + 1 + ... + 1 = 50$ miles

Therefore, the total distance traveled by the driver to deliver the packages and return to the shop is:

$50 + 50 = 100$ miles

Another driver has a similar route to deliver another set of 50 packages. The driver looks at the route and delivers the packages as follows: The driver picks up the first package, drives one mile to the first house, delivers the package, and then comes back to the shop. Next, the driver picks up the second package, drives 2 miles, delivers the second package, and then returns to the shop. The driver then picks up the third package, drives 3 miles, delivers the package, and comes back to the shop. Figure 1-4 illustrates this delivery scheme.

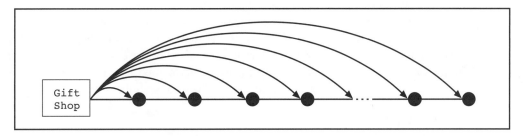

Figure 1-4 Another package delivery scheme

This driver delivers only one package at a time. After delivering a package, the driver comes back to the shop to pick up and deliver the next package. Using this scheme, the total distance traveled by this driver to deliver the packages and return to the store is:

$2 * (1 + 2 + 3 + ... + 50) = 2550$ miles

Now suppose that there are n packages to be delivered to n houses, and each house is one mile apart from each other as shown in Figure 1-4. If the packages are delivered using the first scheme, the following equation gives the total distance traveled:

$$\underbrace{1+1+1+...+1}_{n \text{ times}} + n = 2n \qquad (1\text{-}1)$$

If the packages are delivered using the second method, the distance traveled is:

$$2*(1+2+3+...+n) = 2*(\frac{n(n+1)}{2}) = n^2 + n \qquad (1\text{-}2)$$

In Equation 1-1, we say that the distance traveled is a function of n. Now consider Equation 1-2. In this equation, for large values of n, we find that the term consisting of n^2 becomes the dominant term and the term containing n is negligible. In this case, the distance traveled is a function of n^2. Table 1-1 evaluates Equations (1-1) and (1-2) for certain values of n. (Table 1-1 also shows the values of n, $2n$, n^2, and $n^2 + n$.)

Table 1-1   Values of n, $2n$, n^2, and $n^2 + n$

n	$2n$	n^2	$n^2 + n$
1	2	1	2
10	20	100	110
100	200	10000	10100
1000	2000	1000000	1001000
10000	20000	100000000	100010000

While analyzing a particular algorithm, we usually count the number of operations performed by the algorithm. We focus on the number of operations, not on the actual computer time to execute the algorithm. This is due to the fact that a particular algorithm can be implemented on a variety of computers and the speed of the computer can affect the execution time. However, the number of operations performed by the algorithm would be the same on each computer. Let us consider the following examples.

Example 1-1

Consider the following algorithm. (Assume that all variables are properly declared.)

```
System.out.print("Enter the first number: ");          //Line 1
System.out.flush();                                    //Line 2

num1 = Integer.parseInt(keyboard.readLine());          //Line 3
System.out.println();                                  //Line 4

System.out.print("Enter the second number: ");         //Line 5
System.out.flush();                                    //Line 6

num2 = Integer.parseInt(keyboard.readLine());          //Line 7
System.out.println();                                  //Line 8
```

```
if(num1 >= num2)                                          //Line 9
    max = num1;                                           //Line 10
else                                                      //Line 11
    max = num2;                                           //Line 12

System.out.println("The maximum number is: " + max);    //Line 13
```

Lines 3 and 7 each have 1 operation, =. Line 9 has 1 operation, >=. Either Line 10 or Line 12 executes; each has 1 operation, =. There is 1 operation, +, in Line 13. Therefore, the total number of operations executed in the preceding code is 1 + 1 + 1 + 1 + 1 = 5. In this algorithm, the number of operations executed is fixed.

Example 1-2

Consider the following algorithm. (In this algorithm, we assume that keyboard is a BufferedReader object initialized to the keyboard.)

```
System.out.println("Enter positive integers, one number per "
                + "line, ending with -1");                //Line 1

count = 0                                                  //Line 2
sum = 0;                                                   //Line 3

num = Integer.parseInt(keyboard.readLine());              //Line 4

while(num != -1)                                           //Line 5
{
    sum = sum + num;                                       //Line 6
    count++;                                               //Line 7
    num = Integer.parseInt(keyboard.readLine());          //Line 8
}

System.out.println("The sum of the numbers is: "
                + sum);                                    //Line 9

if(count != 0)                                             //Line 10
    average = sum / count;                                 //Line 11
else                                                       //Line 12
    average = 0;                                           //Line 13

System.out.println("The average is: " + average);         //Line 14
```

This algorithm has 4 operations (Lines 1 through 4) before the while loop. Similarly, there are 5 or 4 operations after the while loop, depending on whether Line 11 or Line 13 executes.

Line 5 has 1 operation, and there are 4 operations within the while loop (Lines 6 through 8). Thus, Lines 5 through 8 have 5 operations. If the while loop executes 10 times, these 5 operations execute 10 times plus one extra operation is executed at Line 5 to terminate the loop. Therefore, the number of operations executed is 51 from Lines 5 through 8.

If the `while` loop executes 10 times, the total number of operations executed is:

$10 * 5 + 1 + 4 + 5$ or $10 * 5 + 1 + 4 + 4$

that is,

$10 * 5 + 10$ or $10 * 5 + 9$

We can generalize it to the case when the `while` loop executes n times. If the `while` loop executes n times, the number of operations executed are:

$5n + 10$ or $5n + 9$

In these expressions, for very large values of n, the term $5n$ becomes the dominating term and the terms 10 and 9 become negligible.

Usually, in an algorithm, certain operations are dominant. For example, in the preceding algorithm, to add numbers, the dominant operation is in Line 6. Similarly, in a search algorithm, because the search item is compared with the items in the list, the dominant operations would be comparison, that is, the relational operation. Therefore, in the case of a search algorithm we count the number of comparisons. For another example, suppose that we write a program to multiply matrices. The multiplication of matrices involves addition and multiplication. Because multiplication takes more computer time to execute, to analyze a matrix multiplication algorithm, we count the number of multiplications.

This book not only develops algorithms, but also provides a reasonable analysis of each algorithm. In fact, if there are various algorithms to accomplish a particular task, the algorithm analysis allows you to choose between various options.

Suppose that an algorithm performs $f(n)$ basic operations to accomplish a task, where n is the size of the problem. Suppose that you want to determine whether an item is in a list. Moreover, suppose that the size of the list is n. To determine whether the item is in the list, there are various algorithms, as you will see in Chapter 8. However, the basic method is to compare the item with the items in the list. Therefore, the performance of the algorithm depends on the number of comparisons.

Thus, in the case of a search, n is the size of the list and $f(n)$ becomes the count function, that is, $f(n)$ gives the number of comparisons done by the search algorithm. Suppose that, on a particular computer, it takes c units of computer time to execute one operation. Thus, the computer time it would take to execute $f(n)$ operations is $cf(n)$. Clearly, the constant c depends on the speed of the computer, and therefore varies from computer to computer. However, $f(n)$, the number of basic operations, is the same on each computer. If we know how the function $f(n)$ grows as the size of the problem grows, we can determine the efficiency of the algorithm. Consider Table 1-2.

Table 1-2 Growth Rate of Various Functions

n	$\log_2 n$	$n\log_2 n$	n^2	2^n
1	0	0	1	2
2	1	2	2	4
4	2	8	16	16
8	3	24	64	256
16	4	64	256	65536
32	5	160	1024	4294967296

Table 1-2 shows how certain functions grow as the parameter n, that is, the problem size, grows. Suppose that the problem size is doubled. From Table 1-2, it follows that if the number of basic operations is a function of $f(n) = n^2$, the number of basic operations is quadrupled. If the number of basic operations is a function of $f(n) = 2^n$, then the number of basic operations is squared. However, if the number of operations is a function of $f(n) = \log_2 n$, the change in the number of basic operations is insignificant.

Suppose that a computer can execute 1 billion steps per second. Table 1-3 shows the time that computer takes to execute $f(n)$ steps.

Table 1-3 Time for $f(n)$ Instructions on a Computer that Executes 1 Billion Instructions per Second

n	$f(n) = n$	$f(n) = \log_2 n$	$f(n) = n\log_2 n$	$f(n) = n^2$	$f(n) = 2^n$
10	0.01μs	0.003μs	0.033μs	0.1μs	1μs
20	0.02μs	0.004μs	0.086μs	0.4μs	1ms
30	0.03μs	0.005μs	0.147μs	0.9μs	1s
40	0.04μs	0.005μs	0.213μs	1.6μs	18.3min
50	0.05μs	0.006μs	0.282μs	2.5μs	13 days
100	0.10μs	0.007μs	0.664μs	10μs	4×10^{13} years
1000	1.00μs	0.010μs	9.966μs	1ms	
10000	10μs	0.013μs	130μs	100ms	
100000	0.10ms	0.017μs	1.67ms	10s	
1000000	0.01s	0.020μs	19.93ms	16.7m	
10000000	0.10s	0.023μs	0.23s	1.16 days	
100000000	1.00s	0.027μs	2.66s	115.7 days	

In Table 1-3, 1μs $= 10^{-6}$ seconds and 1ms $= 10^{-3}$ seconds.

The remainder of this section develops a notation that shows how a function $f(n)$ grows as n increases without bound. That is, we develop a notation that is useful in describing the behavior of the algorithm, which gives us the most useful information about the algorithm. First, we define the term "asymptotic."

Let f be a function of n. By the term **asymptotic** we mean the study of the function f as n becomes larger and larger without bound.

Consider the functions $g(n) = n^2$ and $f(n) = n^2 + 4n + 20$. Clearly, the function g does not contain any linear term, that is, the coefficient of n in g is zero. Consider Table 1-4.

Table 1-4 Growth Rate of n^2 and $n^2 + 4n + 20$

n	$g(n) = n^2$	$f(n) = n^2 + 4n + 20$
10	300	360
50	2500	2720
100	10000	10420
1000	1000000	1004020
10000	100000000	100040020

Clearly, as n becomes larger and larger the term $4n + 20$ in $f(n)$ becomes insignificant, and the term n^2 becomes the dominant term. For large values of n, we can predict the behavior of $f(n)$ by looking at the behavior of $g(n)$. In the algorithm analysis, if the complexity of a function can be described by the complexity of a quadratic function without the linear term, we say that the function is of $O(n^2)$, called "Big-O of n^2."

Let f and g be real-valued functions. Assume that f and g are nonnegative.

Definition: We say that $f(n)$ is **Big-O** of $g(n)$, written $f(n) = O(g(n))$, if there exists positive constants c and n_0 such that

$$f(n) \leq cg(n) \quad \text{for all } n \geq n_0.$$

Table 1-5 shows some common Big-O functions that appear in the algorithm analysis. Let $f(n) = O(g(n))$, where n is the problem size.

Table 1-5 Some Big-O Functions that Appear in Algorithm Analysis

Function $g(n)$	Growth rate of $f(n)$
$g(n) = 1$	The growth rate is constant and so does not depend on n, the size of the problem.
$g(n) = \log_2 n$	The growth rate is a function of $\log_2 n$. Because a logarithm function grows slowly, the growth rate of the function f is also slow.
$g(n) = n$	The growth rate is linear. The growth rate of f is directly proportional to the size of the problem.
$g(n) = n * \log_2 n$	The growth rate is faster than the linear algorithm.
$g(n) = n^2$	The growth rate of such functions increases rapidly with the size of the problem. The growth rate is quadrupled when the problem size is doubled.
$g(n) = 2^n$	The growth rate is exponential. The growth rate is squared when the problem size is doubled.

Using the preceding notations, we can conclude that Equation (1–1) is of $O(n)$; Equation (1–2) is of $O(n^2)$. Moreover, the algorithm in Example 1-1 is of order $O(1)$, and the algorithm in Example 1-2 is of $O(n)$.

$$O(1) < O(\log_2 n) < O(n) < O(n * \log_2 n) < O(n^2) < O(2^n)$$

USER-DEFINED CLASSES

 The reader can skip this section, if the reader is familiar with how classes are implemented in Java.

Recall that in OOD, the first step is to identify the components called objects; an object combines data and the operations on that data in a single unit, called *encapsulation*. In Java, the mechanism that allows you to combine data and the operations on that data in a single unit is called a class. This section describes how to use classes in Java.

A **class** is a collection of a fixed number of components. The components of a **class** are called the **members** of the **class**.

The general syntax for defining a **class** is

```
modifier(s) class ClassIdentifier modifier(s)
{
    classMembers
}
```

where **modifier(s)** are used to alter the behavior of the class, and, usually, **classMembers** consists of variable declarations and/or methods. That is, a member of a **class** can be either a variable (to store data) or a method. Some of the commonly used modifiers are `public`, `private`, and `static`.

- If a member of a class is a variable, you declare it just like any other variable.

- If a member of a class is a method, you define it just like any other method.

- If a member of a class is a method, it can (directly) access any member of the class—data members and method members. That is, when you write the definition of the member method, you can directly access any data member of the class without passing it as a parameter.

In Java, `class` is a reserved word, and it defines only a data type; no memory is allocated. It announces the declaration of a class. In Java, the data members of `class` are also called **fields**.

The members of a `class` are usually classified into three categories: `private`, `public`, and `protected`. This chapter mainly discusses the first two types—`private` and `public`.

Following are some facts about `public` and `private` members of a class:

1. If a member of a class is `private`, you cannot access it outside the class.

2. A `public` member is accessible outside the `class`.

 A package is collection of related classes. Later in this chapter, in the section titled "Creating Your Own Packages," you learn how to create your own packages. If a `class` member is declared or defined without any modifier, then that `class` member has packagewide access; that is, that member can be accessed anywhere in the package.

In Java, `private`, `protected`, and `public` are reserved words.

Suppose that we want to define the `class Clock` to implement the time of day in a program. Furthermore, suppose that the time is represented as a set of three integers: one to represent the hours, one to represent the minutes, and one to represent the seconds. We also want to perform the following operations on the time:

1. Set the time.

2. Return hours.

3. Return minutes.

4. Return seconds.

5. Print the time.

6. Increment the time by one second.

7. Increment the time by one minute.

8. Increment the time by one hour.

9. Compare the two times for equality.

10. Copy the time.

11. Return a copy of the time.

In order to implement these 11 operations, we write algorithms, which we implement as methods. Thus, we need 11 methods to implement these 11 operations. So far, the `class Clock` has 14 members: 3 data members and 11 method members. Suppose that the three data members are `hr`, `min`, and `sec`, each of the type `int`.

Some members of the `class Clock` will be `private`; others will be `public`. Deciding which member to make `public` and which to make `private` depends on the nature of the member. The general rule is that any member that needs to be accessed outside the class is declared `public`; any member that should not be accessed directly by the user should be declared `private`. For example, the user should be able to set the time and print the time. Therefore, the members that set the time and print the time should be declared `public`.

Similarly, the members to increment the time, and compare the time for equality, should be declared `public`. On the other hand, to control the *direct* manipulation of the data members `hr`, `min`, and `sec`, we declare them `private`. Furthermore, note that if the user has direct access to the data members, methods such as `setTime` are not needed.

The data members for the `class Clock` are:

```
private int hr;  //store hours
private int min; //store minutes
private int sec; //store seconds
```

The (non-`static`) data members of a `class` are called **instance variables**. Therefore, the variables `hr`, `min`, and `sec` are the instance variables of the `class Clock`.

Suppose the 11 methods to implement the 11 operations are (method headings are also specified):

1. `setTime`—To set the time to the time specified by the user. The method heading is:

   ```
   public void setTime(int hours, int minutes, int seconds)
   ```

2. `getHours`—To return hours. The method heading is:

   ```
   public int getHours()
   ```

3. `getMinutes`—To return minutes. The method heading is:

   ```
   public int getMinutes()
   ```

4. `getSeconds`—To return seconds. The method heading is:

   ```
   public int getSeconds()
   ```

5. `printTime`—To print the time in the form `hh:mm:ss`. The method heading is:

   ```
   public void printTime()
   ```

6. `incrementSeconds`—To increment the time by one second. The method heading is:

   ```
   public void incrementSeconds()
   ```

7. `incrementMinutes`—To increment the time by one minute. The method heading is:

   ```
   public void incrementMinutes()
   ```

8. `incrementHours`—To increment the time by one hour. The method heading is:

   ```
   public void incrementHours()
   ```

9. `equals`—To compare the two times whether they are equal. The method heading is:

   ```
   public boolean equals(Clock otherClock)
   ```

10. `makeCopy`—To copy the time of one object into another object. The method heading is:

    ```
    public void makeCopy(Clock otherClock)
    ```

11. `getCopy`—To return a copy of the time. A copy of the object's time is created and a reference of the copy is returned. The method heading is:

    ```
    public Clock getCopy()
    ```

The methods of a class are called the **instance methods** of the class.

 In the definition of the `class Clock`, all data members are `private` and all method members are `public`. However, a member method can also be `private`. For example, if a member method is used only to implement other member methods of the class, and the user does not need to access this method, you make it `private`. Similarly, a data member of a `class` can also be `public`.

Notice that we have not yet written definitions of the methods of the `class Clock`. (You will learn to write them in the section "Definitions of the Constructors and Methods of the `class Clock`.") Also, notice that the method `equals` has only one parameter, although you need two things to make a comparison. Similarly, the method `makeCopy` has only one parameter. The section "Implementation of Member Methods" later in this chapter presents an example to help explain this point.

Before giving the definition of the `class Clock`, the following section introduces another important concept related to classes: constructors.

Constructors

In addition to the methods necessary to implement operations, every class has special types of methods, called constructors. Constructors are used to provide guaranteed initialization of the instance variables of the class to specific values.

There are two types of constructors: with parameters and without parameters. The constructor without parameters is called the **default constructor**.

Constructors have the following properties:

- The name of a constructor is the same as the name of the class.

- A constructor, even though it is a method, has no type. That is, it is neither a value-returning method nor a **void** method.

- A class can have more than one constructor. However, all constructors of a class have the same name.

- If a class has more than one constructor, the constructors must have a different formal parameter list.

- Constructors are automatically executed when a class object is instantiated. Because they have no types, they cannot be called like other methods.

- Which constructor executes depends on the type of values passed to the class object when the class object is instantiated.

For the **class Clock**, we include two constructors, the default constructor and a constructor with parameters. The default constructor initializes the instance variables to store hours, minutes, and seconds each to **0**. Similarly, the constructor with parameters initializes the instance variables to the values specified by the user. We will illustrate shortly how constructors are invoked. The headings of the two constructors are as follows:

The heading of the default constructor is:

```
public Clock()
```

The heading of the constructor with parameters is:

```
public Clock(int hours, int minutes, int seconds)
```

It now follows that the definition of the **class Clock** has 16 members: 11 methods, to implement the eleven operations, 2 constructors, and 3 instance variables to store hours, minutes, and seconds.

 If you do not include any constructor in a class, then Java *automatically* provides the default constructor. Therefore, when you create an object, the instance variables are initialized to their default values. For example, **int** variables are initialized to **0**. If you provide at least one constructor and do not include the default constructor, then Java *will not automatically* provide the default constructor. Generally, if a class includes constructors, we also include the default constructor.

Unified Modeling Language Diagrams

A class and its members can be described graphically using a notation known as **Unified Modeling Language (UML)** notation. For example, the UML diagram of the **class Clock** is shown in Figure 1-5.

```
                        ┌─────────────────────────────────┐
                        │              Clock              │
                        ├─────────────────────────────────┤
                        │ -hr: int                        │
                        │ -min: int                       │
                        │ -sec: int                       │
                        ├─────────────────────────────────┤
                        │ +Clock()                        │
                        │ +Clock(int, int, int)           │
                        │ +setTime(int, int, int): void   │
                        │ +getHours(): int                │
                        │ +getMinutes(): int              │
                        │ +getSeconds(): int              │
                        │ +printTime(): void              │
                        │ +incrementSeconds(): int        │
                        │ +incrementMinutes(): int        │
                        │ +incrementHours(): int          │
                        │ +equalTime(Clock): boolean      │
                        │ +makeCopy(Clock): void          │
                        │ +getCopy(): Clock               │
                        └─────────────────────────────────┘
```

Figure 1-5   UML diagram of the `class Clock`

The top box contains the name of the class. The middle box contains the data members and their data types. The last box contains the names of the member methods, the parameter list, and the return type of the method. A + (plus) sign in front of a member indicates that this member is a `public` member and a – (minus) sign indicates that this is a `private` member. The symbol (#) before the member name indicates that the member is a `protected` member.

Variable Declaration and Object Instantiation

Just as you can declare variables of primitive data types, you can also declare variables using a class. When you declare a variable using a class, that variable is called a reference variable of that class type. Moreover a variable is called a **reference variable** if it stores the address of a memory space.

The following statement declares `myClock` to be a reference variable of the type `Clock`:

```
Clock myClock;
```

The preceding statement *does not* allocate memory space to store hours, minutes, and seconds. Next we explain how to allocate memory space to store hours, minutes, and seconds, and how to access that memory space using the variable `myClock`.

The `class Clock` has three instance variables. In order to store hours, minutes, and seconds, we need to create a `Clock` object, which is accomplished by using the operator `new`. Every `Clock` object would have three instance variables.

The general syntax for using the operator **new** is

```
new className()                                        //Line 1
```

or

```
new className(argument1, argument2, ..., argumentN)    //Line 2
```

The expression in Line 1 is used to instantiate the object and initialize the instance variables of the object by using the default constructor. The expression in Line 2 is used to instantiate the object and initialize the instance variables using a constructor with parameters.

For the expression in Line 2:

1. The number of arguments and their type should match the formal parameters (in the order given) of one of the constructors.

2. If the type of the arguments does not match the formal parameters of any constructor (in the order given), Java uses type conversion and looks for the best match. For example, an integer value might be converted to a floating-point value with a zero decimal part. Any ambiguity results in a compile-time error.

For example, consider the following statements:

```
myClock = new Clock();                                 //Line 3
yourClock = new Clock(9,35,15);                        //Line 4
```

The statement in Line 3 allocates memory space for a **Clock** object, initializes each instance variable of the object to **0**, and stores the address of the object into **myClock**. The statement in Line 4 allocates memory space for a **Clock** object, initializes the instance variables **hr**, **min**, and **sec** of the object to **9**, **35**, and **15**, respectively, and stores the address of the object into **yourClock**. See Figure 1-6.

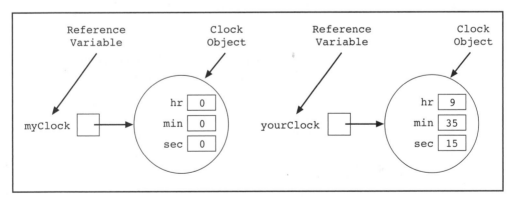

Figure 1-6 Variables **myClock** and **yourClock** and **Clock** objects

To be specific, we call the object that **myClock** points to the object **myClock** and the object that **yourClock** points to the object **yourClock**. See Figure 1-7.

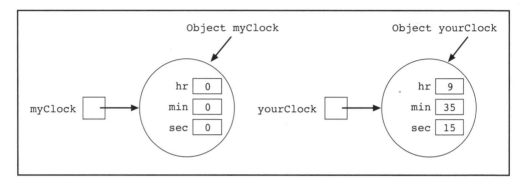

Figure 1-7 Objects **myClock** and **yourClock**

Of course, you can combine the statements to declare the variable and instantiate the object into one statement as follows:

```
Clock myClock = new Clock();   //declare and instantiate
                               //myClock
```

This statement declares **myClock** to be a reference variable of the type **Clock**, and instantiates the object **myClock** to store hours, minutes, and seconds. Each instance variable of the object **myClock** is initialized to **0** by the default constructor.

Similarly, the statement

```
Clock yourClock = new Clock(9,35,15);   //declare and
                                        //instantiate yourClock
```

declares **yourClock** to be a reference variable of the type **Clock** and instantiates the object **yourClock** to store hours, minutes, and seconds. The instance variables **hr**, **min**, and **sec** of the object **yourClock** are initialized to **9**, **35**, and **15**, respectively, by the constructor with parameters.

 When we use phrases such as "create an object of a **class** type," we mean (i) declare a reference variable of the **class** type; (ii) instantiate the **class** object; and (iii) store the address of the object into the reference variable declared. For example, the following statement creates the object **tempClock** of the **Clock** type:

```
Clock tempClock = new Clock();
```

The object **tempClock** is accessed via the reference variable **tempClock**.

Typically, a `class` object is called an **instance** of that `class`. Therefore, creating the object is called **instantiation**.

Accessing Class Members

Once an object is created, you can access the `public` members of the `class`. The general syntax to access a data member of a `class` object or a `class` method is

`referenceVariableName.memberName`

In Java, the dot, **.** (period), is an operator called the **member access operator**.

Example 1-3 illustrates how to access the members of a class.

Example 1-3

Suppose that the objects `myClock` and `yourClock` have been created as before. Consider the following statements:

```
myClock.setTime(5,2,30);
myClock.printTime();
yourClock.setTime(x,y,z);        //Assume x, y, and z are
                                 //variables of the type int

if(myClock.equals(yourClock))
.
.
.
```

These statements are legal; that is, they are syntactically correct. The following describes how these statements work:

- In the first statement, `myClock.setTime(5,2,30);`, the method `setTime` is executed. The values 5, 2, and 30 are passed as parameters to the method `setTime`, and the method uses the values to set the values of `hr`, `min`, and `sec` of the object `myClock` to 5, 2, and 30, respectively. Similarly, the second statement executes the method `printTime` and outputs the values of `hr`, `min`, and `sec` of the object `myClock`. In the third statement, the values of the variables `x`, `y`, and `z` are used to set the values of `hr`, `min`, and `sec` of the object `yourClock`.

- In the fourth statement, the method `equals` executes and compares the instance variables of the object `myClock` with the corresponding instance variables of the object `yourClock`. Because in this statement the method `equals` is invoked by the variable `myClock`, it has direct access to the instance variables of the object `myClock`. So it needs one more object, which in this case is the object `yourClock`, with which to compare. This explains why the method `equals` has only one parameter.

You can access only `public` members of the class. Thus, the following statements are illegal, because `hr` and `min` are `private` members of the `class Clock` and, therefore, cannot be accessed by `myClock` and `yourClock`:

```
myClock.hr = 10;              //illegal
myClock.min = yourClock.min;  //illegal
```

Built-In Operations on Classes

Most of Java's built-in operations do not apply to classes. You cannot use arithmetic operators to perform arithmetic operations on `class` objects. For example, you cannot use the operator `+` to add the values of two `Clock` objects. Also, you cannot use relational operators to compare two class objects for equality.

The built-in operation that is valid for classes is: reference variables can use the dot operator (`.`) to access a `public` member of the class, and classes can use the dot operator to access `static public` members.

The Assignment Operator and Classes: A Precaution

Suppose that the objects `myClock` and `yourClock` are as shown in Figure 1-8.

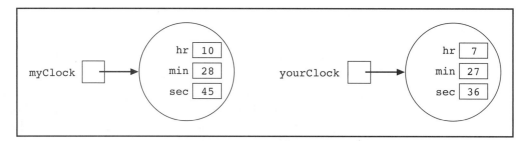

Figure 1-8 `myClock` and `yourClock`

The statement

```
myClock = yourClock;
```

copies the value of `yourClock` into `myClock`. After this statement executes, both `yourClock` and `myClock` refer to the same object. Figure 1-9 illustrates this:

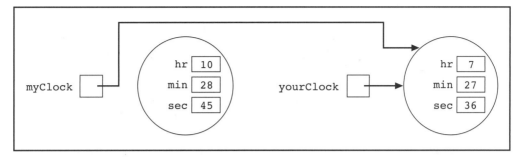

Figure 1-9   myClock and yourClock after the statement myClock = yourClock; executes

This is called shallow copying of data. More formally, in **shallow copying** two or more reference variables of the same type refer to the same object, as in Figure 1-9.

To copy the instance variables of the object **yourClock** into the corresponding instance variables of the object **myClock**, you need to use the method **makeCopy**. The following statement accomplishes this:

```
myClock.makeCopy(yourClock);
```

After the execution of this statement,

1. The value of **yourClock.hr** is copied into **myClock.hr**.

2. The value of **yourClock.min** is copied into **myClock.min**.

3. The value of **yourClock.sec** is copied into **myClock.sec**.

In other words, the values of the three instance variables of the object **yourClock** are copied into the corresponding instance variables of the object **myClock** as shown in Figure 1-10.

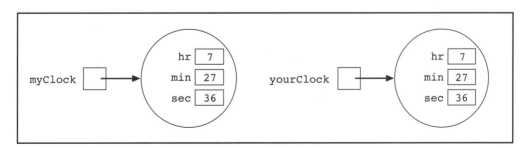

Figure 1-10   Objects myClock and yourClock after the statement myClock.makeCopy(yourClock); executes

This is called deep copying of data. More formally, in **deep copying** each reference variable refers to its *own* object, as in Figure 1-10, not the *same* object, as in Figure 1-9.

Another way to avoid shallow copying of data is to have the object being copied create a copy of itself and then return a reference of the copy. This is accomplished by the method `getCopy`. Consider the following statement:

```
myClock = yourClock.getCopy();
```

In this statement, the expression `yourClock.getCopy()` makes a copy of the object `yourClock` and returns the address, that is, a reference of the copy. The assignment statement stores this address into `myClock`.

 Both the methods `makeCopy` and `getCopy` are used to avoid shallow copying of data. The main difference between these two methods is the following: To use the method `makeCopy`, both the objects, the object whose data is being copied and the object that is copying the data, must be instantiated before invoking this method. To use the method `getCopy`, the object whose data is being copied must be instantiated before invoking this method, while the object of the reference variable that receives a copy of the data need not be instantiated. Also note that the methods `makeCopy` and `getCopy` are user-defined methods.

Class Scope

A reference variable has the same scope as other variables. A member of a class is local to the class. You access a `public class` member outside the `class` through the reference variable name (for non-`static` members) or the `class` name (for `static` members) and the member access operator (`.`).

Methods and Classes

Reference variables can be passed as parameters to methods and returned as method values. When a reference variable is passed as a parameter to a method, both the formal and the corresponding actual parameter point to the same object.

Definitions of the Constructors and Methods of the `class Clock`

We now give the definition of the methods of the `class Clock`, and then we will write the complete definition of this class. Before giving the definitions of the methods, let us note the following:

1. The `class Clock` has eleven methods: `setTime`, `getHours`, `getMinutes`, `getSeconds`, `printTime`, `incrementSeconds`, `incrementMinutes`, `incrementHours`, `equals`, `makeCopy`, and `getCopy`. It has three instance variables: `hr`, `min`, and `sec`.

2. The three instance variables, hr, min, and sec, are private to the class and cannot be accessed outside the class.

3. The methods setTime, getHours, getMinutes, getSeconds, printTime, incrementSeconds, incrementMinutes, incrementHours, equals, makeCopy, and getCopy can directly access the instance variables (hr, min, and sec). In other words, we do not pass instance variables or data members as parameters to member methods. Similarly, constructors directly access the instance variables.

Let us first write the definition of the method setTime. The method setTime has three parameters of the type int. This method sets the instance variables to the values specified by the user, which are passed as parameters to this method. The definition of the method setTime is as follows:

```
public void setTime(int hours, int minutes, int seconds)
{
    if(0 <= hours && hours < 24)
        hr = hours;
    else
        hr = 0;

    if(0 <= minutes && minutes < 60)
        min = minutes;
    else
        min = 0;

    if(0 <= seconds && seconds < 60)
        sec = seconds;
    else
        sec = 0;
}
```

Note that the definition of the method setTime checks for valid values of hours, minutes, and seconds. If these values are out of range, the instance variables hr, min, and sec are initialized to 0. Let us now explain how the member method setTime works.

The method setTime is a void method and has three parameters. Therefore,

1. A call to this method is a stand-alone statement.

2. We must use three parameters in a call to this method.

Furthermore, recall that, because setTime is a member of the class Clock, it can directly access the instance variables hr, min, and sec as shown in the definition of setTime.

Suppose that the object myClock is as shown in Figure 1-11.

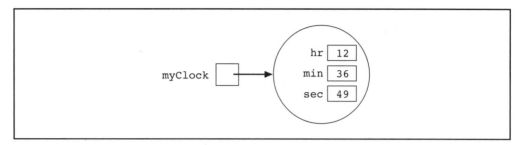

Figure 1-11   Object myClock

Consider the following statement:

```
myClock.setTime(3,48,52);
```

The variable **myClock** accesses the member **setTime**. In the statement **myClock.setTime(3,48,52);**, **setTime** is accessed by the variable **myClock**. Therefore, the three variables—hr, min, and sec—referred to in the body of the method **setTime** are the three instance variables of the object **myClock**. Thus, the values **3, 48,** and **52,** which are passed as parameters in the preceding statement, are assigned to the three instance variables of the object **myClock** by the method **setTime** (see the body of the method **setTime**). After the previous statement executes, **myClock** is as shown in Figure 1-12.

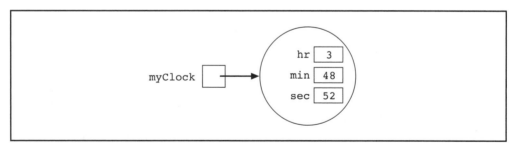

Figure 1-12   myClock after statement myClock.setTime(3, 48, 52); executes

Next, let us give the definitions of the other methods of the **class Clock**. The definitions of these methods are simple and easy to follow:

```
public int getHours()
{
    return hr;      //return the value of hr
}
```

```java
public int getMinutes()
{
    return min;    //return the value of min
}

public int getSeconds()
{
    return sec;    //return the value of sec
}

public void printTime()
{
    if(hr < 10)
       System.out.print("0");
    System.out.print(hr + ":");

    if(min < 10)
       System.out.print("0");
    System.out.print(min + ":");

    if(sec < 10)
       System.out.print("0");
    System.out.print(sec);
}

public void incrementHours()
{
    hr++;              //increment the value of hr by 1
    if(hr > 23)        //if hr is greater than 23,
       hr = 0;         //set hr to 0
}

public void incrementMinutes()
{
    min++;             //increment the value of min by 1
    if(min > 59)       //if min is greater than 59
    {
       min = 0;                //set min to 0
       incrementHours();       //increment hours
    }
}

public void incrementSeconds()
{
    sec++;             //increment the value of sec by 1
    if(sec > 59)       //if sec is greater than 59
    {
       sec = 0;                //set sec to 0
       incrementMinutes();  //increment minutes
    }
}
```

From the definitions of the methods `incrementMinutes` and `incrementSeconds`, it is clear that a method of a **class** can call other methods of the **class**.

The method `equals` has the following definition:

```
public boolean equals(Clock otherClock)
{
    return(hr == otherClock.hr
            && min == otherClock.min
            && sec == otherClock.sec);
}
```

Let us see how the member method `equals` works.

Suppose that `myClock` and `yourClock` are as shown in Figure 1-13.

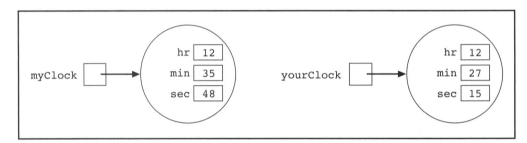

Figure 1-13   Objects `myClock` and `yourClock`

Consider the following statement:

```
if(myClock.equals(yourClock))
```

In the expression

```
myClock.equals(yourClock)
```

`myClock` accesses the method `equals`. The value of the parameter `yourClock` is passed to the formal parameter `otherClock`, as shown in Figure 1-14.

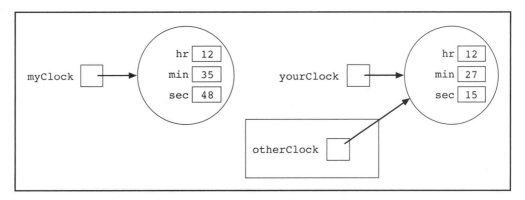

Figure 1-14   Object myClock and parameter otherClock

Note that **otherClock** and **yourClock** refer to the same object. Clearly, the instance variables **hr, min,** and **sec** of the object **otherClock** have the values 12, 27, and 15, respectively. In other words, when the body of the method **equals** executes, the value of **otherClock.hr** is 12, the value of **otherClock.min** is 27, and the value of **otherClock.sec** is 15. The method **equals** is a member of **myClock**. When the method **equals** executes, the variables **hr, min,** and **sec** in the body of the method **equals** are the instance variables of the object **myClock.** Therefore, the instance variable **hr** of the object **myClock** is compared with **otherClock.hr**, the instance variable **min** of the object **myClock** is compared with **otherClock.min**, and the instance variable **sec** of the object **myClock** is compared with **otherClock.sec**.

Once again, in the expression

```
myClock.equals(yourClock)
```

the method **equals** is invoked by **myClock** and the method **equals** compares the object **myClock** with the object **yourClock**. It follows that the method **equals** needs only one parameter.

The method **makeCopy** copies the instance variables of its parameter, **otherClock**, into the corresponding instance variables of the object referenced by the variable using this method. Its definition is:

```
public void makeCopy(Clock otherClock)
{
    hr = otherClock.hr;
    min = otherClock.min;
    sec = otherClock.sec;
}
```

Consider the following statement:

```
myClock.makeCopy(yourClock);
```

In this statement, the method makeCopy is invoked by myClock. The three instance variables hr, min, and sec in the body of the method makeCopy are the instance variables of the object myClock. The variable yourClock is passed as a parameter to makeCopy. Therefore, yourClock and otherClock refer to the same object, which is the object yourCopy. Therefore, after the preceding statement executes, the instance variables of the object yourClock are copied into the corresponding instance variables of the object myClock.

The method getCopy creates a copy of an object's hr, min, and sec and returns the address of the copy of the object. That is, the method getCopy creates a new Clock object, initializes the instance variables of the object, and returns the address of the object created. The definition of the method getCopy is:

```
public Clock getCopy()
{
    Clock temp = new Clock();              //Line 1

    temp.hr = hr;                          //Line 2
    temp.min = min;                        //Line 3
    temp.sec = sec;                        //Line 4

    return temp;                           //Line 5
}
```

The following illustrates how the method getCopy works. Suppose that yourClock is as shown in Figure 1-15.

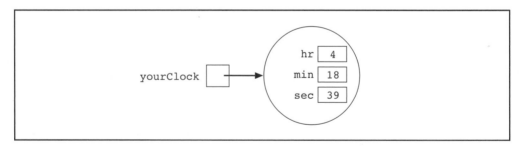

Figure 1-15 Object yourClock

Consider the following statement:

```
myClock = yourClock.getCopy();     //linespace A
```

In this statement, the method getCopy is invoked by yourClock. Therefore, the three variables hr, min, and sec in the body of the method getCopy are the instance variables of the object yourClock. The body of the method getCopy executes as follows. The statement in

Line 1 creates the **Clock** object **temp**. The statements in Lines 2 through 4 copy the instance variables of the object **yourClock** into the corresponding instance variables of **temp**. In other words, the object referenced by **temp** is a copy of the object **yourClock** (see Figure 1-16).

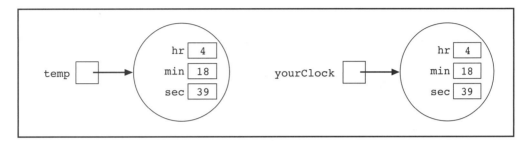

Figure 1-16   Objects **temp** and **yourClock**

The statement in Line 5 returns the value of **temp**, which is the address of the object holding a copy of the data. The value returned by the method **getCopy** is copied into **myClock**. Therefore, after the statement in Line A executes, **myClock** and **yourClock** are as shown in Figure 1-17.

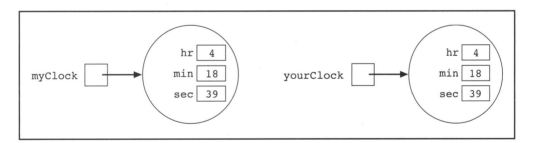

Figure 1-17   Objects **myClock** and **yourClock**

Next we give the definitions of the constructors. The default constructor initializes each instance variable to 0. Its definition is:

```
public Clock()
{
    hr = 0;
    min = 0;
    sec = 0;
}
```

You can also write the definition of the default constructor using the method `setTime` as follows:

```
public Clock()
{
    setTime(0,0,0);
}
```

The definition of the constructor with parameters is the same as the definition of the method `setTime`. It initializes the instance variables to the values specified by the user. Its definition is:

```
public Clock(int hours, int minutes, int seconds)
{
    if(0 <= hours && hours < 24)
        hr = hours;
    else
        hr = 0;

    if(0 <= minutes && minutes < 60)
        min = minutes;
    else
        min = 0;

    if(0 <= seconds && seconds < 60)
        sec = seconds;
    else
        sec = 0;
}
```

As in the case of the default constructor, you can write the definition of the constructor with parameters using the method `setTime` as follows:

```
public Clock(int hours, int minutes, int seconds)
{
    setTime(hours, minutes, seconds);
}
```

This definition of the constructor with parameters makes debugging easier as only the code of `setTime` needs to be checked.

Definition of the `class Clock`

Now that you have written the definition of the methods of the **class Clock**, next we show how to write the definition of this **class**.

The following describes how to write the complete definition of the **class Clock**:

```
public class Clock
{
    private int hr;  //store hours
    private int min; //store minutes
    private int sec; //store seconds

        //Place the definitions of the constructors and methods
        //as described in the preceding sections here.
}
```

 In a class definition, it is a common practice to list all of the instance variables, named constants, other data members, or variable declarations first and then list the constructors, followed by the methods.

The Copy Constructor

Suppose that you have the following statement:

```
Clock myClock = new Clock(8, 45, 22);        //Line 1
```

You can use the object **myClock** to declare and instantiate another **Clock** object. For example, consider the following statement:

```
Clock aClock = new Clock(myClock);           //Line 2
```

This statement declares **aClock** to be a reference variable of the type **Clock**, instantiates the object **aClock**, and initializes the instance variables of the object **aClock** using the values of the corresponding instance variables of the object **myClock**. However, to successfully execute the statement in Line 2, first you need to include a special constructor, called the **copy constructor**, in the **class Clock**. The copy constructor executes when an object is instantiated and initialized using an existing object.

The syntax of the heading of the copy constructor is

```
public ClassName(ClassName otherObject)     //copy constructor heading
```

For example, the heading of the copy constructor for the **class Clock** is

```
public Clock(Clock otherClock)
```

Furthermore, the definition of the copy constructor for the **class Clock** is:

```
public Clock(Clock otherClock)
{
    hr = otherClock.hr;
    min = otherClock.min;
    sec = otherClock.sec;
}
```

If you include this definition of the copy constructor in the **class Clock**, then the statement in Line 2 declares **aClock** to be a reference variable of the type **Clock**, instantiates the object **aClock**, and initializes the instance variables of the object **aClock** using the values of the instance variables of the object **myClock**.

The copy constructor is very useful and is included in most of the classes.

Classes and the Method toString

Suppose that **x** is an **int** variable and the value of **x** is 25. The statement

```
System.out.println(x);
```

outputs

```
25
```

However, the output of the statement

```
System.out.println(myClock);
```

is:

```
Clock@f617d64b
```

which looks quite strange. This is due to the fact that whenever you create a **class**, the Java system provides the method **toString** to the **class**. The method **toString** is used to convert an object to a **String** object. The methods **print** and **println** output the string created by the method **toString**.

The default version, that is, the definition of the method **toString**, creates a string that is the name of the object's **class** followed by the hash code of the object. For example, in the preceding statement, **Clock** is the name of the object **myClock**'s **class** and the hash code for the object referenced by **myClock** is **@f617d64b**.

The method **toString** is a **public** value-returning method. It does not take any parameters and it returns the address of a **String** object. More specifically, the heading of the method **toString** is

```
public String toString()
```

You can *override* the default definition of the method **toString** to convert an object to a desired string. For example, suppose that for the **class myClock** you want the method **toString** to return the string **hh:mm:ss**, that is, the string consists of the object's hour, minutes, seconds, and the colons as shown. In other words, the string returned by the method **toString** is the same as the string the method **print** of the **class myClock** outputs. You can easily accomplish this by providing the following definition of the method **toString**:

```
public String toString()
{
    String str = "";

    if(hr < 10)
        str = "0";
    str = str + hr + ":";

    if(min < 10)
        str = str + "0" ;
    str = str + min + ":";

    if(sec < 10)
        str = str + "0";
    str = str + sec;

    return str;
}
```

In the preceding code, `str` is a **String** variable used to create the required string.

Of course, the preceding definition of the method **toString** must be included in the **class Clock**. We can, after including the method **toString** in the **class Clock**, in fact, remove the method **print**. If the values of the instance variables **hr**, **min**, and **sec** of **myClock** are 8, 25, and 56, respectively, then the output of the statement

```
System.out.println(myClock)
```

is

```
08:25:56
```

Static Members of a Class

Java contains the **class Math**, which contains many useful mathematical methods. To use a method of the **class Math**, you do not need to create any object. You simply use the name of the class, the dot operator, and the method name. For example, to use the method **pow** of the **class Math**, you use expressions such as

```
Math.pow(5,3)
```

Can we do the same with the **class Clock**? The answer is no. And the reason is that the methods of the **class**es **Math** and **Character**, even though they are **public**, also are defined using the modifier **static**. For example, the heading of the method **pow** of the **class Math** is

```
public static double pow(double base, double exponent)
```

The modifier **static** in the heading specifies that the method *can* be invoked by using the name of the **class**. Similarly, if a data member of a **class** is declared using the modifier **static**, it *can* be accessed using the name of the **class**.

Example 1-4 further clarifies the effect of the modifier `static`.

Example 1-4

Consider the following definition of the `class Illustrate`:

```
public class Illustrate
{
    private int x;
    private static int y;
    public static int count;

    public Illustrate()
    {
        x = 0;
    }

    public Illustrate(int a)
    {
        x = a;
    }

    public void print()
    {
        System.out.println("x = " + x
                        + ", y = " + y
                        + ", count = " + count);
    }

    public static void incrementCount()
    {
        count++;
    }
}
```

Suppose that you have the following declaration:

```
Illustrate illusObject = new Illustrate();
```

The reference variable can access any **public** member of the **class Illustrate**.

Now, because the method `incrementCount` is **static** and **public**, the following statement is legal:

```
Illustrate.incrementCount();
```

Similarly, because the data member `count` is **static** and **public**, the following statement is legal:

```
Illustrate.count++;
```

Static Variables (Data Members) of a Class

Suppose that you have a **class**, say **MyClass**, with data members (**static** as well as non-**static**). When you instantiate objects of the type **MyClass**, only non-**static** data members of the **class MyClass** become the data members of each object. So what about the memory for the **static** data members of **MyClass**? For each **static** member of the **class**, the Java system allocates only one memory space. All **MyClass** objects refer to the same memory space. In fact, **static** data members of a **class** *exist* even when no object of the **class** type is instantiated. Moreover, **static** variables are initialized to their default values. Outside the **class**, you can access the **public static** data members of the class as explained in the previous section.

The following example further clarifies how memory space is allocated for **static** and non-**static** data members of a class:

Suppose that you have the **class Illustrate** as given in Example 1-4. Then memory space exists for the **static** data members **y** and **count**.

Consider the following statement:

```
Illustrate illusObject1 = new Illustrate(3);      //Line 1
Illustrate illusObject2 = new Illustrate(5);      //Line 2
```

The statements in Line 1 and Line 2 declare **illusObject1** and **illusObject2** to be reference variables of the **Illustrate** type and also instantiated objects (see Figure 1-18).

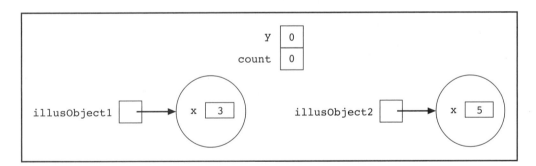

Figure 1-18   **illusObject1** and **illusObject2**

Now consider the following statements:

```
Illustrate.incrementCount();
Illustrate.y++;
```

The output of the statement

```
illusObject1.print();                              //Line 3
```

is

```
x = 3, y = 1, count = 1
```

Similarly, the output of the statement

```
illusObject2.print();                              //Line 4
```

is

```
x = 5, y = 1, count = 1
```

Finalizer

Like constructors, finalizers are also methods. However, a finalizer is a **void** method. More-over, a class can have only one finalizer, and the finalizer can have no parameters. The name of the finalizer is **finalize**. The method **finalize** automatically executes when the class object goes out of scope.

Creating Your Own Packages

Recall that a package is a collection of related classes. As you develop classes, you can create packages and categorize your classes. You can import your classes, just the same way you import classes from the packages provided by the Java system.

Usually, every SDK contains a directory where the compiled versions of the classes are stored. For example, if you are using JDK, then the name of this directory is **classes**. Both the compiler and the interpreter know the location of the directory. On JDK 1.4, the location of this directory is:

```
c:\j2sdk1.4.0-rc\jre\lib
```

You can check your SDK's documentation to find the directory where compiled codes of classes are stored.

To create a package and add a class to the package so that the class can be used in a program, we do the following:

- Define the **class** to be **public**. If the **class** is not **public**, it can only be used within the **package**.

- Choose a name for the **package**. To categorize your packages, you can create sub-directories within the directory that contain the compiled code of classes, which is explained later in this section. For example, the title of this book is "Data Structures Using Java." You can create the directory **dsuj**. Moreover, this is Chapter 1. To place classes of this chapter into one directory, you can create the directory **ch01** within the directory **dsuj**.

1

Suppose that you want to create a **package** to group classes implementing time. Let us call this **package clockPackage**. To add the **class Clock** to this package, you need to include the following statement in the file containing the **class Clock**. To place the package **clockPackage** within the subdirectory **ch01** of the directory **dsuj**, you include the following package statement:

```
package dsuj.ch01.clockPackage
```

This statement is put before the definition of the **class**. To be specific, the definition of the **class Clock** is:

```
package dsuj.ch01.clockPackage;

public class Clock
{
    //put instance variables and methods, as before, here
}
```

The name of the file containing the **package** statement and the definition of the **class Clock** is **Clock.java**. The next step is to compile the file **Clock.java**. The SDK you are using is most likely to have a compile command. You can use the compile command.

If you are using **jdk1.4**, which contains a command line compiler, you need to include the option **–d** to only compile the file **Clock.java** as follows:

```
javac -d c:\j2sdk1.4.0-rc\jre\lib Clock.java
```

If the directories **dsuj** and **ch01** do not exist, then the compiler automatically creates these directories.

After the **package** is created, you can use the appropriate **import** command in your program to make use of the **class**. For example, to use the **class Clock**, as created in the preceding steps, you use the following **import** statement in your program:

```
import dsuj.ch01.clockPackage.Clock;
```

In Java, **package** is a reserved word.

Multi-File Programs

In the preceding section, you learned how to create a **package**. Creating a **package** to group related classes is very useful if the classes are to be used again and again. On the other hand, if a class is to be used only in one program or you have divided your program so that it uses more than one class, rather than create a **package**, you can directly add the file(s) containing the classes to the program.

The Java SDKs, Forte for Java, J++ Builder, and CodeWarrior put the editor, compiler, and linker all into one program. With one command, a program is compiled and linked with the other necessary files. These SDKs also manage multiple-file programs in the form of a project. A **project** consists of several files, called the project files. These SDKs include a command that will allow you to add several files to a project. Also, these SDKs usually have commands like **build**, **rebuild**, or **make** (check your software's documentation) to automatically compile and link all files required to create the executable code. When one or more files in the project change, you can use these commands to recompile and relink the files.

Example 1-5 further illustrates how classes are designed and implemented. The `class` `Person` that is designed in Example 1-5 is very useful; we use this `class` in subsequent chapters.

Example 1-5

The most common attributes of a person are the person's first name and last name. The typical operations on a person's name are to set the name and print the name. The following statements define a `class` with these properties. (See Figure 1-19.)

```
public class Person
{
    private String firstName; //store the first name
    private String lastName;  //store the last name

        //Default constructor;
        //Initialize firstName and lastName to empty string
        //Postcondition: firstName = ""; lastName = "";
    public Person()
    {
        firstName = "";
        lastName = "";
    }

        //Constructor with parameters
        //Set firstName and lastName according to the parameters
        //Postcondition: firstName = first; lastName = last;
    public Person(String first, String last)
    {
         firstName = first;
         lastName = last;
    }
        //Method to return the first name and last name
        //in the form firstName lastName
    public String toString()
    {
        return (firstName + " " + lastName);
    }
```

```
    //Method to set firstName and lastName according to
    //the parameters
    //Postcondition: firstName = first; lastName = last;
public void setName(String first, String last)
{
    firstName = first;
    lastName = last;
}

    //Method to return the firstName
    //Postcondition: the value of firstName is returned
public String getFirstName()
{
    return firstName;
}

    //Method to return the lastName
    //Postcondition: the value of lastName is returned
public String getLastName()
{
    return lastName;
}
}
```

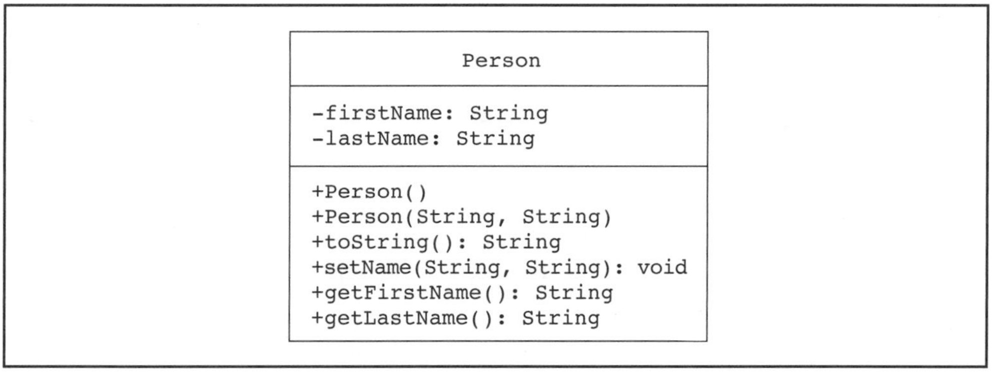

```
                    Person

-firstName: String
-lastName: String

+Person()
+Person(String, String)
+toString(): String
+setName(String, String): void
+getFirstName(): String
+getLastName(): String
```

Figure 1-19   UML diagram of the class Person

The following program tests the `class Person`:

```
import java.io.*;

public class TestProgPerson
{
    public static void main(String[] args)
    {
        Person name = new Person();                         //Line 1

        Person emp = new Person("Donald", "Doc");           //Line 2

        System.out.println("Line 3: name: " + name);        //Line 3

        name.setName("Sleeping", "Beauty");                 //Line 4
        System.out.println("Line 5: name: " + name);        //Line 5

        System.out.println("Line 6: emp: " + emp);          //Line 6

        emp.setName("Sandy", "Smith");                      //Line 7
        System.out.println("Line 8: emp: " + emp);          //Line 8
    }//end main
}
```

Output

```
Line 3: name:
Line 5: name: Sleeping Beauty
Line 6: emp: Donald Doc
Line 8: emp: Sandy Smith
```

The Reference `this`

In this chapter, we defined the **class Clock**. Suppose that **myClock** is a reference variable of the type **Clock**. Moreover, assume that the object **myClock** has been created. Consider the following statements:

```
myClock.setTime(5,6,59);        //Line 1
myClock.incrementSeconds();     //Line 2
```

The statement in Line 1 uses the method **setTime** to set the instance variables **hr**, **min**, and **sec** of the object **myClock** to 5, 6, and 59, respectively. The statement in Line 2 uses the method **incrementSeconds** to increment the time of the object **myClock** by one second. The statement in Line 2 calls the method **incrementMinutes** because after incrementing the value of **sec** by 1, it becomes 60, which would be set to 0 and the method **incrementMinutes** is invoked.

How do you think Java makes sure that the statement in Line 1 would set the instance variables of the object **myClock** and not of another **Clock** object? Similarly, how does Java make sure that when the method **incrementSeconds** calls the method **incrementMinutes**, the method `incrementMinutes` increments the value of the instance variable `min` of the object `myClock` and not of another `Clock` object?

The answer to these questions is that every object has access to a reference to itself. The name of this reference is `this`. In Java, `this` is a reserved word.

Java implicitly uses the reference `this` to refer to both the instance variables and methods of a class. Recall that the definition of the method `setTime` is:

```
public void setTime(int hours, int minutes, int seconds)
{
    if(0 <= hours && hours < 24)
        hr = hours;
    else
        hr = 0;

    if(0 <= minutes && minutes < 60)
        min = minutes;
    else
        min = 0;

    if(0 <= seconds && seconds < 60)
        sec = seconds;
    else
        sec = 0;
}
```

The statement

```
hr = hours;
```

in the method `setTime` is, in fact, equivalent to the statement

```
this.hr = hours;
```

In this statement, the reference `this` is explicitly used. You can explicitly use the reference `this` and write the equivalent definition of the method `setTime` as follows:

```
public void setTime(int hr, int min, int sec)
{
    if(0 <= hr && hr < 24)
        this.hr = hr;
    else
        this.hr = 0;

    if(0 <= min && min < 60)
        this.min = min;
    else
        this.min = 0;

    if(0 <= sec && sec < 60)
        this.sec = sec;
    else
        this.sec = 0;
}
```

Notice that in this definition of the method `setTime` the name of the formal parameters and the name of the instance variables are the same. In this definition of the method `setTime`, the expression `this.hr` means the instance variable `hr`, not the formal parameter `hr`, and so on. Because the code explicitly uses the reference `this`, the compiler can distinguish between the instance variables and the formal parameters. Of course you could have kept the name of the formal parameters as before and still used the reference `this`, as shown in the code.

Similarly, explicitly using the reference `this`, you can write the definition of the method `incrementSeconds` as follows:

```
public void incrementSeconds()
{
    this.sec++;
    if(this.sec > 59)
    {
        this.sec = 0;
        this.incrementMinutes(); //increment minutes
    }
}
```

Inner Classes

The classes that we have defined in this chapter until now are said to have file scope, that is, they are contained within a file, but not within another class. Classes that are defined within other classes are called **inner classes**.

An inner class can be either a complete class definition or an anonymous inner class definition. Anonymous classes are classes with no name.

One of the main uses of inner classes is to handle events.

ABSTRACT DATA TYPES

Historically, abstract data types (ADTs) were the first attempt towards abstracting the structure of the data from the data itself. To better understand this concept, consider the following seemingly unrelated items:

- A deck of playing cards
- A set of index cards with contact information
- Telephone numbers stored in your cellular phone

There is no structural difference among these three items. Note that all three have the following structural properties:

- Each one is a collection of elements.
- There is a first element.

- There is a second element, third element, and so on.

- There is a last element.

- Given an element other than the last element, there is a "next" element.

- Given an element other than the first element, there is a "previous" element.

- An element may be removed from the collection.

- An element may be added to the collection.

- A specified element may be located in the collection by systematically going through the collection.

In your programs, you may want to keep a collection of various elements such as addresses, students, employees, departments, projects, and so on. Thus, this structure appears quite commonly in various applications; it is worth studying in its own right. We call this organization a "list." A list is an example of an ADT.

There is a data type called `Vector` (discussed in Chapter 3) with basic operations such as the following:

- Insert an item.

- Delete an item.

- Find an item.

You can use the `class Vector` to create an address book. You need not write a program to insert an address into your address book; you need not write a program to delete an address from your address book, nor do you need to write a program to search your address book. Java also allows you to create new data types through classes.

An ADT is an abstraction of a commonly appearing data structure along with a set of defined operations on the data structure.

Abstract data type (ADT): A data type that specifies the logical properties without the implementation details.

In Java, ADT is accomplished through the use of classes.

As noted earlier in this section, historically, the concept of ADT came into the study of computer programming as a way of abstracting the common data structure and the associated operations. Along the way, ADT provided **information hiding**. That is, ADT kept the implementation details of the operations and the data from the users of the ADT. Users of ADT can use the operations on an ADT without knowing how the operation is implemented.

PROGRAMMING EXAMPLE: CANDY MACHINE

A common place to buy candy is from a candy machine. A new candy machine is bought for the gym, but it is not working properly. The machine sells candies, chips, gum, and cookies. You have been asked to write a program for this candy machine so that it can be put into operation.

The program should do the following:

1. Show the customer the different products sold by the candy machine.
2. Let the customer make the selection.
3. Show the customer the cost of the item selected.
4. Accept money from the customer.
5. Release the item.

Input   The item selection and the cost of the item

Output   The selected item

Problem Analysis and Algorithm Design

A candy machine has two main components: a built-in cash register and several dispensers to hold and release the products. Therefore, we need to define a class to implement the cash register, a class to implement the dispenser, and a class to implement the candy machine. First we describe the classes to implement the cash register and dispenser, and then use these classes to describe the candy machine.

Cash Register

Let us first discuss the properties of a cash register. The register has some cash on hand, it accepts the amount from the customer, and if the amount entered is more than the cost of the item, then, if possible, it returns the change. For simplicity, we assume that the user enters the exact amount for the product. The cash register should also be able to show the candy machine's owner the amount of money in the register at any given time. Let us call the class implementing the cash register `CashRegister`.

The members of the **class CashRegister** are (see Figure 1-20):

Instance Variables:

```
private int cashOnHand;
```

Methods:

```
public int currentBalance()
   //Method to show the current amount in the cash register
   //Postcondition: The value of the instance variable
   //               cashOnHand is returned
```

```
public void acceptAmount(int amountIn)
   //Method to receive the amount deposited by
   //the customer and updates the amount in the register.
   //Postcondition: cashOnHand = cashOnHand + amountIn

public CashRegister(int cashIn)
   //Constructor with parameters
   //Postcondition: cashOnHand = cashIn;

public CashRegister()
   //Default constructor with parameters
   //To set the cash in the register 500 cents
   //Postcondition: cashOnHand = 500;
```

```
              CashRegister

   -cashOnHand: int

   +CashRegister()
   +CashRegister(int)
   +currentBalance(): int
   +acceptAmount(int): void
```

Figure 1-20 UML diagram of the class CashRegister

Next, we give the definition of the methods to implement the operations of the class CashRegister.

The method currentBalance shows the current amount in the cash register. Its definition is:

```
public int currentBalance()
{
    return cashOnHand;
}
```

The method acceptAmount accepts the amount entered by the customer. It updates the cash in the register by adding the amount entered by the customer to the previous amount in the cash register. Essentially, the definition of this method is:

```
public void acceptAmount(int amountIn)
{
    cashOnHand = cashOnHand + amountIn;
}
```

The constructor with a parameter sets the value of the instance variable to the value specified by the user. The value is passed as a parameter to the constructor. The definition of the constructor with parameters is as follows:

```
public CashRegister(int cashIn)
{
    if(cashIn >= 0)
        cashOnHand = cashIn;
    else
        cashOnHand = 500;
}
```

Note that the definition of the constructor checks for valid values of the parameter cashIn. If the value of cashIn is less than 0, the value assigned to the instance variable cashOnHand is 500.

The default constructor sets the value of the instance variable cashOnHand to 500 cents. Its definition is:

```
public CashRegister()
{
    cashOnHand = 500;
}
```

Now that we have the definitions of all the methods necessary to implement operations of the class CashRegister, we can give its definition. (We have put this class in the package candyMachine.) Its definition is:

```
//class cashRegister

package dsuj.ch01.candyMachine;

public class CashRegister
{
    private int cashOnHand;    //variable to store the cash
                               //in the register

        //Constructor with parameters
        //To set the cash in the register to a specific amount
        //Postcondition: cashOnHand = cashIn;
    public CashRegister(int cashIn)
    {
        if(cashIn >= 0)
            cashOnHand = cashIn;
        else
            cashOnHand = 500;
    }
```

```
        //Default constructor with parameters
        //to set the cash in the register 500 cents
        //Postcondition: cashOnHand = 500;
    public CashRegister()
    {
        cashOnHand = 500;
    }

        //Method to show the current amount in the cash register.
        //Postcondition: The value of the instance variable
        //               cashOnHand is returned
    public int currentBalance()
    {
        return cashOnHand;
    }

        //Method to receives the amount deposited by
        //the customer and updates the amount in the register.
        //Postcondition: cashOnHand = cashOnHand + amountIn
    public void acceptAmount(int amountIn)
    {
        cashOnHand = cashOnHand + amountIn;
    }
}
```

Dispenser

The dispenser releases the selected item, if it is not empty. It should show the number of items in the dispenser and the cost of the item. Let us call the class implementing a dispenser `Dispenser`. The members necessary to implement the **class Dispenser** are (see Figure 1-21):

Instance Variables:

```
private int numberOfItems;    //variable to store the number of
                              //items in the dispenser
private int cost;        //variable to store the cost of an item
```

Methods:

```
public int getCount()
   //Method to show the number of items in the machine
   //Postcondition: The value of the instance variable
   //               numberOfItems is returned
```

```
public int getProductCost()
   //Method to show the cost of the item
   //Postcondition: The value of the instance
   //                 variable cost is returned

public void makeSale()
   //Method to reduce the number of items by 1
   //Postcondition: numberOfItems = numberOfItems - 1;

public Dispenser(int setNoOfItems, int setCost)
   //Constructor with parameters to set the cost and number
   //of items in the dispenser specified by the user
   //Postcondition: numberOfItems = setNoOfItems;
   //                 cost = setCost;

public Dispenser()
   //Default constructor to set the cost and number of
   //items to the default values
   //Postcondition: numberOfItems = 50; cost = 50;
```

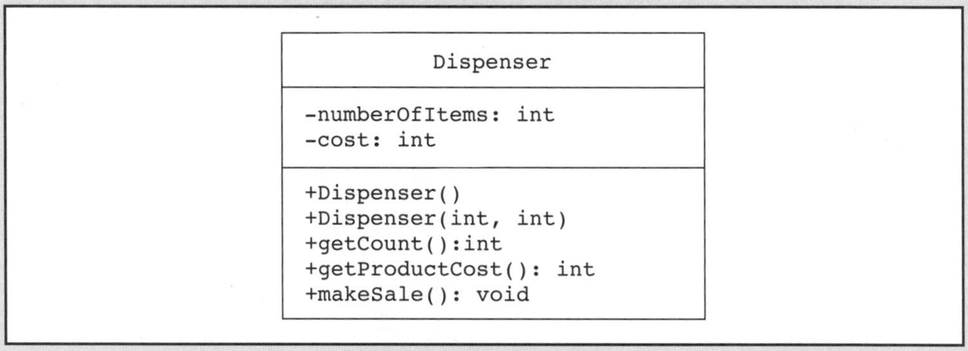

```
                      Dispenser

         -numberOfItems: int
         -cost: int

         +Dispenser()
         +Dispenser(int, int)
         +getCount():int
         +getProductCost(): int
         +makeSale(): void
```

Figure 1-21   UML diagram of the class Dispenser

Because the candy machine sells four types of items, we shall create four objects of the type Dispenser. The statement

Dispenser chips = new Dispenser(100,65);

creates the object chips, and sets the number of chip bags in this dispenser to 100 and the cost of each chip bag to 65 cents. (See Figure 1-22.)

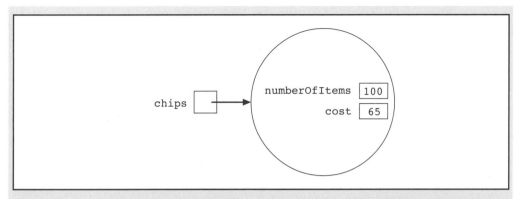

Figure 1-22   The object `chips`

Next, we discuss the definitions of the methods to implement the operations of the
class `Dispenser`.

The method `getCount` returns the number of items of a particular product. Because
the number of items currently in the dispenser is stored in the instance variable
`numberOfItems`, it returns the value of the instance variable `numberOfItems`. The
definition of this method is:

```
public int getCount()
{
    return numberOfItems;
}
```

The method `getProductCost` returns the cost of a product. Because the cost of a
product is stored in the instance variable `cost`, it returns the value of instance variable
`cost`. The definition of this method is:

```
public int getProductCost()
{
    return cost;
}
```

When a product is sold, the number of items in that dispenser is reduced by 1. Therefore, the method `makeSale` reduces the number of items in the dispenser by 1. That is,
it decrements the value of the instance variable `numberOfItems` by 1. The definition
of this method is:

```
public void makeSale()
{
    numberOfItems--;
}
```

The definition of the constructor checks for valid values of the parameters. If these values are less than 0, the default values are assigned to the instance variables. The definition of the constructor is:

```
    //constructor with parameters
public Dispenser(int setNoOfItems, int setCost)
{
    if(setNoOfItems >= 0)
       numberOfItems = setNoOfItems;
    else
       numberOfItems = 50;

    if(setCost >= 0)
       cost = setCost;
    else
       cost = 50;
}
```

The default constructor assigns the default values to the instance variables.

```
public Dispenser()
{
    numberOfItems = 50;
    cost = 50;
}
```

The definition of the **class Dispenser** is (we have put this **class** in the **package candyMachine**):

```
//class Dispenser

package dsuj.ch01.candyMachine;

public class Dispenser
{
    private int numberOfItems;   //variable to store the number of
                                 //items in the dispenser
    private int cost;     //variable to store the cost of an item

       //Default constructor to set the cost and number of
       //items to the default values
       //Postconditions: numberOfItems = 50;
       //                 cost = 50;
    public Dispenser()
    {
        numberOfItems = 50;
        cost = 50;
    }
```

```
        //Constructor with parameters to set the cost and number
        //of items in the dispenser specified by the user
        //Postconditions: numberOfItems = setNoOfItems;
        //                 cost = setCost;
    public Dispenser(int setNoOfItems, int setCost)
    {
        if(setNoOfItems >= 0)
           numberOfItems = setNoOfItems;
        else
           numberOfItems = 50;

        if(setCost >= 0)
           cost = setCost;
        else
           cost = 50;
    }

        //Method to show the number of items in the machine
        //Postconditions: The value of the instance variable
        //                 numberOfItems is returned
    public int getCount()
    {
        return numberOfItems;
    }

        //Method to show the cost of the item
        //Postconditions: The value of the instance variable
        //                 cost is returned
    public int getProductCost()
    {
        return cost;
    }

        //Method to reduce the number of items by 1
        //Postconditions: numberOfItems = numberOfItems - 1;
    public void makeSale()
    {
        numberOfItems--;
    }
}
```

 We create the package candyMachine and place the classes CashRegister and Dispenser in this package. The main program can import these classes from this package.

Main Program

When the program executes, it must do the following:

- Show the different products sold by the candy machine.
- Show how to select a particular product.
- Show how to terminate the program.

Furthermore, these instructions must be displayed after processing each selection (except exiting the program), so that the user need not remember what to do if he or she wants to buy two or more items. Once the user makes the appropriate selection, the candy machine must act accordingly. If the user opts to buy a product and if that product is available, the candy machine should show the cost of the product and ask the user to deposit the money. If the money deposited is at least the cost of the item, the candy machine should sell the item and display an appropriate message.

This discussion translates into the following algorithm:

1. Show the selection to the customer.
2. Get the selection.
3. If the selection is valid and the dispenser corresponding to the selection is not empty, sell the product.

We divide this program into three methods—`showSelection`, `sellProduct`, and `main`.

Method `showSelection` This method displays the necessary information to help the user select and buy a product. Essentially, it contains the following output statements. (We assume that the candy machine sells four types of products.)

```
*** Welcome to Shelly's Candy Shop ***"
To select an item, enter
1 for Candy
2 for Chips
3 for Gum
4 for Cookies
9 to exit
```

The definition of the method `showSelection` is:

```java
public static void showSelection()
{
    System.out.println("*** Welcome to Shelly's Candy Shop ***");
    System.out.println("To select an item, enter ");
    System.out.println("1 for Candy");
    System.out.println("2 for Chips");
    System.out.println("3 for Gum");
    System.out.println("4 for Cookies");
    System.out.println("9 to exit");
}//end showSelection
```

Next we describe the method `sellProduct`.

Method `sellProduct`   This method attempts to sell the product selected by the customer. Therefore, it must have access to the dispenser holding the product. The first thing that this method does is check whether the dispenser holding the product is empty. If the dispenser is empty, the method informs the customer that this product is sold out.

If the dispenser is nonempty, it tells the user to deposit the necessary amount to buy the product. If the user does not deposit enough money to buy the product, the method `sellProduct` tells the user how much additional money must be deposited. If the user fails to deposit enough money, in two tries, to buy the product, the method simply returns the money. (Programming Exercise 9 at the end of this chapter asks you to revise the definition of the method `sellProduct` so that it keeps asking the user to enter an additional amount as long as the user has not entered enough money to buy the product.) If the money deposited by the user is sufficient, it accepts the money and sells the product. Selling the product means to decrement the number of items in the dispenser by 1, and update the money in the cash register by adding the cost of the product. (Because this program does not return the extra money deposited by the customer, the cash register is updated by adding the money entered by the user.)

From this discussion, it is clear that the method `sellProduct` must have access to the dispenser holding the product (to decrement the number of items in the dispenser by 1 and to show the cost of the item) as well as the cash register (to update the cash). Therefore, this method has two parameters: one corresponding to the dispenser, and the other corresponding to the cash register.

In pseudocode, the algorithm for this method is

    a. If the dispenser is nonempty:

        i. Show and prompt the customer to enter the cost of the item.

        ii. Get the amount entered by the customer.

        iii. If the amount entered by the customer is less than the cost of the product:

            1.   Show and prompt the customer to enter the additional amount.

            2.   Calculate the total amount entered by the customer.

        iv. If the amount entered by the customer is at least the cost of the product:

            1.   Update the amount in the cash register.

            2.   Sell the product—that is, decrement the number of items in the dispenser by 1.

        v. Display an appropriate message.

        vi. If the amount entered by the user is less than the cost of the item, return the amount.

    b. If the dispenser is empty, tell the user that this product is sold out.

The definition of the method `sellProduct` is:

```
public static void sellProduct(Dispenser product,
                               CashRegister cRegister)
                                        throws IOException
{
    int amount;  //variable to hold the amount entered
    int amount2; //variable to hold the extra amount needed

    if(product.getCount() > 0)  //if dispenser is not empty
    {
        System.out.println("Please deposit "
                        + product.getProductCost()
                        + " cents");
        amount = Integer.parseInt(keyboard.readLine());

        if(amount < product.getProductCost())
        {
            System.out.println("Please deposit another "
                    + (product.getProductCost() - amount)
                    + " cents");
            amount2 = Integer.parseInt(keyboard.readLine());
            amount = amount + amount2;
        }

        if(amount >= product.getProductCost())
        {
            cRegister.acceptAmount(amount);
            product.makeSale();
            System.out.println("Collect your item at the "
                        + "bottom and enjoy.");
        }
        else
            System.out.println("The amount is not enough. "
                        + "Collect what you deposited.");
        System.out.println("*-*-*-*-*-*-*-*-*-*-*-"
                        + "*-*-*-*-*-*-*-*-*-*-*");
    }
    else
        System.out.println("Sorry, this item is sold out.");
}//end sellProduct
```

Method main The algorithm for the method main is as follows:

1. Create the cash register—that is, create and initialize a `CashRegister` object.
2. Create four dispensers—that is, create and initialize four objects of the type `Dispenser`. For example, the statement

```
Dispenser candy = new Dispenser(100, 50);
```

creates a dispenser object, **candy**, to hold the candies. The number of items in the dispenser is **100**, and the cost of an item is **50** cents.

3. Declare additional variables as necessary.
4. Show the selection; call the method **showSelection**.
5. Get the selection.
6. While not done (a selection of **9** exits the program):
    a. Sell the product; call the method **sellProduct**.
    b. Show the selection; call the method **showSelection**.
    c. Get the selection.

The definition of the method **main** follows:

```
public static void main(String[] args) throws IOException
{
    CashRegister  cashRegister = new CashRegister();     //Step 1
    Dispenser candy = new Dispenser(100,50);             //Step 2
    Dispenser chips = new Dispenser (100,65);            //Step 2
    Dispenser gum = new Dispenser(75,45);                //Step 2
    Dispenser cookies = new Dispenser(100,85);           //Step 2

    int choice; //variable to hold the selection         //Step 3

    showSelection();                                     //Step 4
    choice = Integer.parseInt(keyboard.readLine());      //Step 5

    while(choice != 9)                                   //Step 6
    {
        switch(choice)                                   //Step 6a
        {
        case 1: sellProduct(candy, cashRegister);
                break;
        case 2: sellProduct(chips, cashRegister);
                break;
        case 3: sellProduct(gum, cashRegister);
                break;
        case 4: sellProduct(cookies, cashRegister);
                break;
        default: System.out.println("Invalid Selection");
        }//end switch

        showSelection();                                 //Step 6b
        choice = Integer.parseInt(keyboard.readLine()); //Step 6c
    }//end while
}//end main
```

Main Program Listing

```java
// Program candy machine

import java.io.*;
import dswj.ch01.candyMachine.*;

public class CandyMachine
{
    static BufferedReader keyboard = new
              BufferedReader(new InputStreamReader(System.in));

    //Place the definition of the method main as given above here

    //Place the definition of the method showSelection as
    //given above here

    //Place the definition of the method sellProduct as
    //given above here
}
```

Sample Run: In this sample run, the user input is shaded.

```
*** Welcome to Shelly's Candy Shop ***
To select an item, enter
1 for Candy
2 for Chips
3 for Gum
4 for Cookies
9 to exit
1
Please deposit 50 cents
50
Collect your item at the bottom and enjoy.
*-*-*-*-*-*-*-*-*-*-*-*-*-*-*-*-*-*-*-*
*** Welcome to Shelly's Candy Shop ***
To select an item, enter
1 for Candy
2 for Chips
3 for Gum
4 for Cookies
9 to exit
3
Please deposit 45 cents
45
Collect your item at the bottom and enjoy.
*-*-*-*-*-*-*-*-*-*-*-*-*-*-*-*-*-*-*-*
```

```
*** Welcome to Shelly's Candy Shop ***
To select an item, enter
1 for Candy
2 for Chips
3 for Gum
4 for Cookies
9 to exit
9
```

IDENTIFYING CLASSES, OBJECTS, AND OPERATIONS

The hardest part of OOD is to identify the objects and classes. This section describes a common and simple technique to identify classes and objects.

We begin with a description of the problem and then identify all of the nouns and verbs. From the list of nouns we choose our classes, and from the list of verbs we choose our operations.

For example, suppose that we want to write a program that calculates and prints the volume and surface area of a cylinder. We can state this problem as follows:

Write a **program** to *input* the **dimensions** of a **cylinder** and *calculate* and *print* the **surface area** and **volume**.

In this statement, the nouns are bold and the verbs are italic. From the list of nouns—**program**, **dimensions**, **cylinder**, **surface area**, and **volume**—we can easily visualize **cylinder** to be a class—say, `Cylinder`—from which we can create many cylinder objects of various dimensions. The nouns **dimensions**, **surface area**, and **volume** are characteristics of a **cylinder**, and thus can hardly be considered classes.

After we identify a class, the next step is to determine three pieces of information:

- Operations that an object of that class type can perform
- Operations that can be performed on an object of that class type
- Information that an object of that class type must maintain

From the list of verbs identified in the problem description, we choose a list of possible operations that an object of that class can perform, or has performed, on itself. For example, from the list of verbs for the cylinder problem description—*write*, *input*, *calculate*, and *print*—the possible operations for a cylinder object are *input*, *calculate*, and *print*.

For the `Cylinder` class, the dimensions represent the data. The `center` of the base, `radius` of the base, and `height` of the cylinder are the characteristics of the dimensions. You can input data to the object either by a constructor or by a method.

The verb *calculate* applies to determining the volume and the surface area. From this you can deduce the operations: `cylinderVolume` and `cylinderSurfaceArea`. Similarly, the verb *print* applies to the display of the volume and the surface area on an output device.

Identifying classes via the nouns and verbs from the descriptions to the problem is not the only technique possible. There are several other OOD techniques in the literature. However, this technique is sufficient for the programming exercises in this book.

QUICK REVIEW

1. Software are programs run by the computer.

2. A program goes through many phases from the time it is first conceived until the time it is retired, called the life cycle of the program.

3. The three fundamental stages a program goes through are: development, use, and maintenance.

4. The new program is created in the software development stage.

5. In the software maintenance process, the program is modified to fix the (identified) problems or to enhance it.

6. A program is retired if no new version of the program will be released.

7. The software development phases are: analysis, design, implementation, and testing and debugging.

8. During the design phase, algorithm(s) are designed to solve the problem.

9. An algorithm is a step-by-step, problem-solving process in which a solution is arrived at in a finite amount of time.

10. Two well-known design techniques are: structured design and object-oriented design.

11. In structured design, a problem is divided into smaller subproblems. Each subproblem is solved, and the solutions of all subproblems are then combined to solve the problem.

12. In object-oriented design (OOD), a program is a collection of interacting objects.

13. An object consists of data and operations on those data.

14. The three basic principles of OOD are: encapsulation, inheritance, and polymorphism.

15. In the implementation phase, you write and compile programming code to implement the classes and methods that were discovered in the design phase.

16. A precondition is a statement specifying the condition(s) that must be true before the method is called.

17. A postcondition is a statement specifying what is true after the method call is completed.

18. During the testing phase, the program is tested for its correctness; that is, making sure the program does what it is supposed to do.

19. Debugging refers to finding if errors exist, then finding and fixing the errors.

20. To find problems in a program, it is run through a series of test cases.

21. A test case consists of a set of inputs, user actions, or other initial conditions, and the expected output.

22. There are two types of testing—black-box testing and white-box testing.

23. While analyzing a particular algorithm, you usually count the number of operations performed by the algorithm.

24. Let f be a function of n. The term asymptotic refers to the study of the function f as n becomes larger and larger without bound.

25. A `class` is a collection of a fixed number of components.

26. Components of a `class` are called the members of the class.

27. Members of a `class` are accessed by name.

28. In Java, `class` is a reserved word.

29. Members of a class are classified into one of three categories: `private`, `protected`, and `public`.

30. The `private` members of a class are not accessible outside the class.

31. The `public` members of a class are accessible outside the class.

32. By default, all members of a class are `private`.

33. The `private` members are declared using the modifier `private`.

34. The `public` members are declared using the modifier `public`.

35. A member of a class can be a method or a variable.

36. If any member of a class is a variable, it is declared like any other variable.

37. In Java, a `class` is a definition.

38. Non-`static` variables of a `class` are called instance variables of that `class`.

39. Member methods of a class are called instance methods.

40. Constructors guarantee that the data members are initialized when an object is declared.

41. The name of a constructor is the same as the name of the class.

42. A class can have more than one constructor.

43. A constructor without parameters is called the default constructor.

44. Constructors automatically execute when a class object enters its scope.

45. In a UML diagram, the top box contains the name of the class. The middle box contains the data members and their data types. The last box contains the names of the member methods, the parameter list, and the return type of the method. A + (plus) sign in front of a member indicates that this member is a `public` member, and a – (minus) sign indicates that this is a `private` member. The symbol (#) before the member name indicates that the member is a `protected` member.

46. In shallow copying two or more reference variables of the same type refer to the same object.

47. In deep copying each reference variable refers to its own object.

48. A reference variable has the same scope as other variables.

49. A member of a class is local to the class.

50. You access a `public class` member outside the `class` through the reference variable name or the `class` name (for `static` members) and the member access operator (`.`).

51. The copy constructor executes when an object is instantiated and initialized using an existing object.

52. The method `toString` is a `public` value-returning method. It does not take any parameters and returns the address of a `String` object.

53. The methods `print` and `println` output the string created by the method `toString`.

54. The default definition of the method `toString` creates a string that is the name of object's `class` name followed by the hash code of the object.

55. The modifier `static` in the heading specifies that the method can be invoked by using the name of the class.

56. If a data member of a class is declared using the modifier `static`, it can be invoked by using the name of class.

57. Finalizers automatically execute when a class object goes out of scope.

58. A `class` can have only one finalizer, and the finalizer has no parameters.

59. The name of the finalizer is `finalize`.

60. You can create your own packages using the `package` statement.

61. Java implicitly uses the reference `this` to refer to both the instance variables and methods of a class.

62. Classes that are defined within another class are called inner classes.

63. A data type that specifies the logical properties without the implementation details is called an abstract data type (ADT).

EXERCISES

1. Mark the following statements as true or false.

a. The life cycle of a software program refers to the phases from the point the software was conceived until it is retired.

b. The three fundamental stages of software are: development, use, and discard.

c. The order of the expression $4n + 2n^2 + 5$ is $O(n)$.

d. The instance variables of a class must be of the same type.

e. The method of a class must be `public`.

f. A class can have more than one constructor.

g. A class can have more than one finalizer.

h. Both constructors and finalizers can have parameters.

2. Consider the following method heading, which returns the square root of a real number:

```
double sqrt(double x)
```

What should be the preconditions and postconditions for this method?

3. Each of the following expressions represents the number of operations for certain algorithms. What is the order of each of these expressions?

a. $n^2 + 6n + 4$

b. $5n^3 + 2n + 8$

c. $(n^2 + 1)(3n + 5)$

d. $5(6n + 4)$

4. Consider the following method:

```
void funcExercise4(int x, int y)
{
        int z;

        z = x + y;
        x = y;
        y = z;
        z = x;
        System.out.println("x = " + x + ", y = " + y
                         + ", z = " + z);
}
```

Find the exact number of operations executed by the method `funcExercise4`.

5. Consider the following method:

```
int funcExercise5(int list[], int size)
{
        int sum = 0;

        for(int index = 0; index < size; index++)
            sum = sum + list[index];

        return sum;
}
```

a. Find the number of operations executed by the method `funcExercise5` if the value of `size` is 10.

b. Find the number of operations executed by the method `funcExercise5` if the value of `size` is n.

c. What is the order of the method `funcExercise5`?

6. Consider the following method heading:

```
int funcExercise6(int x)
```

The method `funcExercise6` returns values as follows: if $0 <= x <= 50$, it returns $2x$; if $-50 <= x < 0$, it returns x^2; otherwise it returns -999. What are the reasonable boundary values for the method `funcExercise6`?

7. Write a method that uses a loop to find the sum of the squares of all integers between 1 and n. What is the order of your method?

8. What is black-box testing?

9. What is white-box testing?

10. Find the syntax errors in the definitions of the following classes.

a.

```
public class AA
{
    private int x;
    private int y;

    public void print()
    {
        System.out.println(x + " " + y);
    }

    public int sum()
    {
        return x + y;
    }

    public AA()
    {
        x = 0;
        y = 0;
    }

    public int AA(int a, int b)
    {
        x = a;
        y = b;
    }
}
```

b.

```
public class BB
{
    private int one;
    private int two;
```

```
public boolean equal()
{
    return (one == two);
}

public print()
{
    System.out.println(one + " " + two);
}

public BB(int a, int b)
{
    one = a;
    two = b;
}
}
```

11. Consider the definition of the following class:

```
class CC
{
    private int u;
    private int v;
    private double w;

    public CC()                           //Line 1
    {
    }

    public CC(int a)                      //Line 2
    {
    }

    public CC(int a, int b)               //Line 3
    {
    }

    public CC(int a, int b, double d)     //Line 4
    {
    }
}
```

a. Give the line number containing the constructor that is executed in each of the following declarations:

(i) CC one = new CC();

(ii) CC two = new CC(5, 6);

(iii) CC three = new CC(2, 8, 3.5);

b. Write the definition of the constructor at Line 1 so that the instance variables are initialized to 0.

    c. Write the definition of the constructor at Line 2 so that the instance variable u is initialized according to the value of the parameter, and the instance variables v and w are initialized to 0.

    d. Write the definition of the constructor at Line 3 so that the instance variables u and v are initialized according to the values of the parameters a and b, respectively, and the instance variable w is initialized to 0.0.

    e. Write the definition of the constructor at Line 4 so that the instance variables u, v, and w are initialized according to the values of the parameters a, b, and d, respectively.

12. Write a Java statement that creates the object mysteryClock of the Clock type and initializes the instance variables hr, min, and sec of mysteryClock to 7, 18, 39, respectively.

13. Given the statements

```
Clock firstClock = new Clock(2,6,35);
Clock secondClock = new Clock(6,23,17);

firstClock = secondClock;
```

what is the output of the following statements?

```
firstClock.print();
secondClock.print();
```

14. Consider the following declarations:

```
public class XClass
{
    private int u;
    private double w;

    public void func()
    {

    }

    public void print()
    {

    }

    public XClass()
    {

    }
```

```
      public XClass(int a, double b)
      {

      }
   }
```

```
XClass x = new XClass(10,20.75);
```

a. How many members does **class XClass** have?

b. How many **private** members does **class XClass** have?

c. How many constructors does **class XClass** have?

d. Write the definition of the member method **func** so that u is set to 10 and w is set to 15.3.

e. Write the definition of the member method **print** that prints the contents of u and w.

f. Write the definition of the default constructor of the **class XClass** so that the instance variables are initialized to 0.

g. Write the definition of the constructor with parameters of the **class XClass** so that the instance variable u is initialized to the value of a and the instance variable v is initialized to the value of b.

h. Write a Java statement that prints the values of the instance variables of x.

i. Write a Java statement that creates the **XClass** object t, and initializes the instance variables of t to 20 and 35.0, respectively.

15. Explain shallow copying.

16. Explain deep copying.

17. Suppose that two reference variables, say **aa** and **bb**, of the same type point to two different objects. What happens when you use the assignment operator to copy the value of **aa** into **bb**?

18. Assume that the method **toString** is defined for the **class Clock** as given in this chapter. What is the output of the following statements?

```
Clock firstClock;
Clock secondClock = new Clock(6,23,17);

firstClock = secondClock.getCopy();

System.out.println(firstClock);
```

19. What is the purpose of the copy constructor?

20. How does Java use the reference `this`?

21. Suppose that you have created the **class Mystery**. Write the Java statement that puts this class into the **package strangeClasses** under the directory **ch01**.

22. Can you use the relational operator **==** to determine if two objects of the same **class** type contain the same data?

23. Consider the definition of the following **class**:

```
class TestClass
{

    private int x;
    private int y;

        //default constructor
        //initialize the instance variables to 0
    public TestClass()
    {
    }

        //constructors with parameters
        //initialize the instance variables to the values specified
        //by the parameters
        //Postcondition: x = a; y = b;
    TestClass(int a, int b)
    {
    }

        //return the sum of the instance variables
    public int sum()
    {
    }

        //print the values of the instance variables
    public void print()
    {
    }
}
```

a. Write the definitions of the methods as described in the definition of the **class TestClass**.

b. Write a test program to test various operations of the **class TestClass**.

PROGRAMMING EXERCISES

1

1. Write a program to test various operations of the **class Clock**.

2. Write a program that converts a number entered in Roman numerals to decimal. Your program should consist of a **class**, say **Roman**. An object of the type **Roman** should do the following:

   a. Store the number as a Roman numeral.

   b. Convert and store the number into decimal form.

   c. Print the number as a Roman numeral or decimal number as requested by the user.

      The decimal values of the Roman numerals are:

      ```
      M     1000
      D      500
      C      100
      L       50
      X       10
      V        5
      I        1
      ```

   d. Test your program using the following Roman numerals: MCXIV, CCCLIX, MDCLXVI.

3. Design and implement the **class Day** that implements the day of the week in a program. The **class Day** should store the day, such as **Sun** for Sunday. The program should be able to perform the following operations on an object of the type **Day**:

   a. Set the day.

   b. Print the day.

   c. Return the day.

   d. Return the next day.

   e. Return the previous day.

   f. Calculate and return the day by adding certain days to the current day. For example, if the current day is Monday and we add 4 days, the day to be returned is Friday. Similarly, if today is Tuesday and we add 13 days, the day to be returned is Monday.

   g. Add the appropriate constructors.

   h. Write the definitions of the methods to implement the operations for the **class Day** as defined in a–g.

   i. Write a program to test various operations on the **class Day**.

4. a. Example 1-5 defined the **class Person** to store the name of a person. The member methods that we included merely print the name and set the name of a person. Redefine the **class Person** so that in addition to what the existing **class** does, you can:

   i. Set the last name only.

   ii. Set the first name only.

   iii. Store and set the middle name.

   iv. Check whether a given last name is the same as the last name of this person.

   v. Check whether a given first name is the same as the first name of this person.

   b. Add the method **equals** that returns true if two objects contain the same first and last name.

   c. Add the method **makeCopy** that copies the instance variables of a **Person** object into another **Person** object.

   d. Add the method **getCopy** that creates and returns the address of the object, which is a copy of another **Person** object.

   e. Add the copy constructor.

   f. Write the definition of the methods of the **class Person** to implement the operations for this **class**.

   g. Write a program that tests various operations of the **class Person**.

5. a. Some of the characteristics of a book are the title, author(s), publisher, ISBN, price, and year of publication. Design the **class Book** that defines the book as an ADT.

   Each object of the **class Book** can hold the following information about a book: title, up to four authors, publisher, ISBN, price, and number of copies in stock. To keep track of the number of authors, add another instance variable.

   Include the member methods to perform the various operations on objects of **Book**. For example, the usual operations that can be performed on the title are to show the title, set the title, and check whether a title is the same as the actual title of the book. Similarly, the typical operations that can be performed on the number of copies in stock are to show the number of copies in stock, set the number of copies in stock, update the number of copies in stock, and return the number of copies in stock. Add similar operations for the publisher, ISBN, book price, and authors. Add the appropriate constructors and a finalizer (if one is needed).

   b. Write the definition of the member methods of the **class Book**.

   c. Write a program that uses the **class Book** and tests various operations on the objects of **class Book**. Declare an array of 100 components of type **Book**. Some of the operations that you should perform are to search for a book by its title, search by ISBN, and update the number of copies of a book.

6. In this exercise, you will design the **class Member**.

   a. Each object of **Member** can hold the name of a person, member ID, number of books bought, and amount spent.

b. Include the member methods to perform the various operations on the objects of **Member**—for example, modify, set, and show a person's name. Similarly, update, modify, and show the number of books bought and the amount spent.

c. Add the appropriate constructors and a finalizer (if one is needed).

d. Write the definitions of the methods of the **class Member**.

7. Using the classes designed in Programming Exercises 5 and 6, write a program to simulate a bookstore. The bookstore has two types of customers: those who are members of the bookstore and those who buy books from the bookstore only occasionally. Each member pays a $10 yearly membership fee and receives a 5% discount on each book bought.

For each member, the bookstore keeps track of the number of books bought and the total amount spent. For every eleventh book that a member buys, the bookstore takes the average of the total amount of the last 10 books bought, applies this amount as a discount, and then resets the total amount spent to **0**.

Write a program that can process up to 1000 book titles and 500 members. Your program should contain a menu that gives the user different choices to effectively run the program; in other words, your program should be menu driven.

8. Rational fractions are of the form a / b, where a and b are integers and $b \neq 0$. In this exercise, by "fractions" we mean rational fractions. Suppose a / b and c / d are fractions. Arithmetic operations on fractions are defined by the following rules:

$a / b + c / d = (ad + bc) / bd$

$a / b - c / d = (ad - bc) / bd$

$a / b \times c / d = ac / bd$

$(a / b) / (c / d) = ad / bc$, where $c / d \neq 0$.

Fractions are compared as follows: a / b op c / d if ad op bc, where op is any of the relational operations. For example, $a / b < c / d$ if $ad < bc$.

Design the **class Fraction** that can be used to manipulate fractions in a program. Among others, the **class Fraction** must include methods to add, subtract, multiply, and divide fractions. When you add, subtract, multiply, or divide fractions, your answer need not be in the lowest terms. Also override the method **toString** so that the fraction can be output using the output statement.

Write a Java program that, using the **class Fraction**, performs operations on fractions.

9. The method **sellProduct** of the Programming Example Candy Machine gives only two chances to the user to enter enough money to buy the product. Rewrite the definition of the method **sellProduct** so that it keeps prompting the user to enter the money as long as the user has not entered enough money to buy the product. Also, write a program to test your method.

2

INHERITANCE AND EXCEPTION HANDLING

In this chapter, you will:

♦ Learn about inheritance

♦ Learn about sub- and superclasses

♦ Explore how to override the methods of a superclass

♦ Examine how the constructors of super- and subclasses work

♦ Examine abstract classes

♦ Learn about composition

♦ Learn about exceptions

♦ Become aware of exception classes and their hierarchy

♦ Learn about checked and unchecked exceptions

♦ Learn how to handle exceptions within a program

♦ Examine `try/catch` blocks

♦ Discover how to throw and rethrow an exception

Chapter 1 introduced classes. By using classes, you can combine data and operations in a single unit, called encapsulation. Therefore, an object becomes a self-contained entity. Operations can directly access the data. The internal state of an object cannot be manipulated directly by the user.

In addition to implementing encapsulation, classes have other features. For instance, classes can create new classes from existing classes. This important feature encourages code reuse. In Java, you can relate two or more classes in more than one way. Two common ways to relate classes in a meaningful way are:

- **Inheritance** ("is–a" relationship)

- **Composition** ("has–a" relationship)

INHERITANCE

Suppose that you want to design a class, `PartTimeEmployee`, to implement and process the characteristics of a part-time employee. The main features associated with a part-time employee are the name, pay rate, and number of hours worked. In Example 1-5 (in Chapter 1), you designed the `class Person` to implement a person's name. Every part-time employee is a person. Therefore, rather than design the `class PartTimeEmployee` from scratch, we want to be able to extend the definition of the `class Person` (from Example 1-5) by adding additional members (data and/or methods).

Of course, we do not want to make the necessary changes directly to the `class Person`— that is, edit the `class Person`, and add and/or delete members. In fact, we want to create the `class PartTimeEmployee` without making any physical changes to the `class Person`, by adding only the members that are necessary. For example, because the `class Person` already has data members to store the first name and last name, we do not include any such members in the `class PartTimeEmployee`. In fact, these data members are inherited from the `class Person`. (We will design such a `class` in Example 2-3.)

In Chapter 1, we extensively studied and designed the `class Clock` to implement the time of day in a program. The `class Clock` has three data members (instance variables), to store the hours, minutes, and seconds. Certain applications, in addition to hours, minutes, and seconds, might also require us to store the time zone. In this case, we would like to extend the definition of the `class Clock` and create a `class`, `ExtClock`, to accommodate this new information. That is, we want to derive the `class ExtClock` by adding a data member—say, `timeZone`—and the necessary method members to manipulate the time (see Programming Exercise 1 at the end of this chapter). Every extended clock is a clock. In Java, the mechanism that allows us to accomplish this task is the principle of **inheritance**. Inheritance is an "is-a" relationship; for instance, "every employee is a person."

Inheritance lets us create new classes from existing classes. Any new class that we create from the existing classes is called a **subclass** or **derived class**; existing classes are called the **superclasses** or **base classes**. The subclass inherits the properties of the superclass. So rather than create completely new classes from scratch, we can take advantage of inheritance and reduce software complexity.

Inheritance can be viewed as a treelike, or hierarchical, structure wherein a superclass is shown with its subclasses. Consider the tree diagram in Figure 2-1, which shows the relationship between various types of shapes.

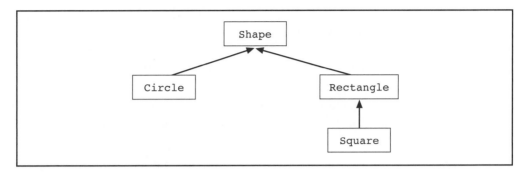

Figure 2-1   Inheritance hierarchy

In this diagram, Shape is the superclass. The classes Circle and Rectangle are derived from Shape, and the class Square is derived from Rectangle. Every Circle and every Rectangle is a Shape. Every Square is a Rectangle.

The general syntax of deriving a class from an existing class is:

```
modifier(s) class ClassName extends ExistingClassName modifier(s)
{
        memberList
}
```

In Java, extends is a reserved word.

Example 2-1

Suppose that we have defined a class called Shape. The following statements specify that the class Circle is derived from Shape:

```
public class Circle extends Shape
{
    .
    .
    .
}
```

Note the following about superclasses and subclasses:

1. The private members of the superclass are private to the superclass; hence, the members of the subclass cannot directly access them. In other words, when you write the definitions of the methods of the subclass, you cannot directly access the private members of the superclass.

2. The subclass can directly access the public members of the superclass.

3. The subclass can include additional data and/or method members.

4. The subclass can override, or redefine, the `public` methods of the superclass. That is, in the subclass, you can have a method with the same name, number, and types of parameters as a method in the superclass. However, this redefinition applies only to the objects of the subclass, not to the objects of the superclass.

5. All data members of the superclass are also data members of the subclass. Similarly, the methods of the superclass (unless overridden) are also the methods of the subclass. (Remember Rule 1 when accessing a member of the superclass in the subclass.)

Each subclass, in turn, becomes a superclass for a future subclass. Inheritance can be either single inheritance or multiple inheritance. In **single inheritance** the subclass is derived from a single superclass; in **multiple inheritance** the subclass is derived from more than one superclass. Java only supports single inheritance; that is, in Java a class can *extend* the definition of only one class.

The next sections describe two important issues related to inheritance. The first issue is using the methods of the superclass in the subclass. While discussing this issue, we will also address how to access the `private` (data) members of the superclass in the subclass. The second key inheritance issue is related to the constructor. The constructor of a subclass *cannot directly* access the `private` data members of the superclass. Thus, we need to ensure that the `private` data members inherited from the superclass are initialized when a constructor of the subclass executes.

Using Methods of the Superclass in a Subclass

Suppose that a `class SubClass` is derived from a `class SuperClass`. Further assume that both `SubClass` and `SuperClass` have some data members. It then follows that the data members of the `class SubClass` are its own data members, together with the data members of `SuperClass`. Similarly, in addition to its own methods, the subclass also inherits the methods of the superclass. It is possible for the subclass to give some of its methods the same name that is given by the superclass. For example, suppose that `SuperClass` contains a method, `print`, that prints the values of the data members of `SuperClass`. Now `SubClass` contains data members in addition to the data members inherited from `SuperClass`. Suppose that you want to include a method in `SubClass` that prints the data members of `SubClass`. You can give any name to this method. However, in the `class SubClass`, you can also name this method as `print`, (the same name used by `SuperClass`). This is called **overriding (redefining)** the method of the superclass.

To override a `public` method of the superclass in the subclass, the corresponding method in the subclass must have the same name, number, and types of parameters. In other words, the name of the method being overridden in the subclass must have the same name and the same set of formal parameters. If the corresponding methods in the superclass and the subclass have the same name but different sets of parameters, then this is method overloading in the subclass, which is also allowed.

Whether you override or overload a method of the superclass in the subclass, the question is how to specify a call to the method of the superclass that has the same name as used by a method of the subclass. This is illustrated with the help of the following example.

Consider the definition of the following class (see Figure 2-2):

```java
public class Rectangle
{
    private double length;
    private double width;

    public Rectangle()
    {
        length = 0;
        width = 0;
    }

    public Rectangle(double l, double w)
    {
        setDimension(l, w);
    }

    public void setDimension(double l, double w)
    {
        if(l >= 0)
            length = l;
        else
            length = 0;

        if(w >= 0)
            width = w;
        else
            width = 0;
    }

    public double getLength()
    {
        return length;
    }

    public double getWidth()
    {
        return width;
    }

    public double area()
    {
        return length * width;
    }
```

```
public double perimeter()
{
    return 2 * (length + width);
}

public void print()
{
    System.out.print("Length = "  + length
                          + "; Width = " + width);
}
}
```

```
                    ┌─────────────────────────────────────┐
                    │              Rectangle               │
                    ├─────────────────────────────────────┤
                    │ -length: double                     │
                    │ -width: double                      │
                    ├─────────────────────────────────────┤
                    │ +Rectangle()                        │
                    │ +Rectangle(double, double)          │
                    │ +setDimension(double, double): void │
                    │ +getLength(): double                │
                    │ +getWidth(): double                 │
                    │ +area(): double                     │
                    │ +perimeter(): double                │
                    │ +print(): void                      │
                    └─────────────────────────────────────┘
```

Figure 2-2   UML diagram of the `class Rectangle`

The `class Rectangle` has 10 members.

Now consider the definition of the following class (see Figure 2-3).

The `class Box`, given next, is derived from the `class Rectangle`.

```
public class Box extends Rectangle
{
    private double height;

    public Box()
    {
        //The definition is as given below
    }

    public Box(double l, double w, double h)
    {
        //The definition is as given below
    }
```

```
public void setDimension(double l, double w, double h)
{
    //Sets the length, width, and height of the box
    //The definition is as given below
}

public double getHeight()
{
    return height;
}

public double area()
{
    //Returns the surface area
    //The definition is as given below
}

public double volume()
{
    //Returns the volume
    //The definition is as given below
}

public void print()
{
    //Outputs length, width, and height of the box
    //The definition is as given below
}
}
```

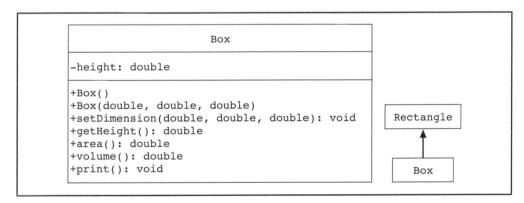

Figure 2-3   UML diagram of the class Box and the inheritance hierarchy

From the definition of the **class Box**, it is clear that the **class Box** is derived from the **class Rectangle**. Therefore, all **public** members of **Rectangle** are **public** members of **Box**. The **class Box** overrides the methods **print** and **area** and overloads the method **setDimension**.

In general, while writing the definition of the methods of a subclass to specify a call to a **public** method of the superclass we do the following:

- If the subclass overrides a **public** method of the superclass, then the subclass specifies a call to that **public** method of the superclass by using the reserved word **super** followed by the dot operator followed by the method name with an appropriate parameter list.

- If the subclass does not override a **public** method of the superclass, then the subclass can call that **public** method of the superclass by using the name of the method and an appropriate parameter list.

Next, let us write the definition of the method **print** of the **class Box**.

The **class Box** has three data members: **length**, **width**, and **height**. The method **print** of the **class Box** prints the values of these data members. To write the definition of the method **print** of the **class Box**, keep the following in mind:

- The instance variables **length** and **width** are **private** members of the **class Rectangle** and so cannot be directly accessed in the **class Box**. Therefore, when writing the definition of the method **print** of the **class Box**, we cannot directly access **length** and **width**.

- The instance variables **length** and **width** of the **class Rectangle** are accessible in the **class Box** through the **public** methods of the **class Rectangle**. Therefore, when writing the definition of the method **print** of the **class Box**, we first call the method **print** of the **class Rectangle** to print the values of **length** and **width**. After printing the values of **length** and **width**, we output the values of **height**.

As mentioned previously, to call the method **print** of **Rectangle** in the definition of the method **print** of **Box**, we must use the following statement:

```
super.print();
```

This statement ensures that we call the method **print** of the superclass **Rectangle**, not of the class **Box**.

The definition of the method **print** of the **class Box** is:

```
public void print()
{
    super.print();
    System.out.print("; Height = " + height);
}
```

Let us write the definition of the remaining methods of the **class Box**.

```
public void setDimension(double l, double w, double h)
{
    super.setDimension(l, w);

    if(h >= 0)
        height = h;
    else
        height = 0;
}

public double getHeight()
{
    return height;
}
```

The method **area** of the **class Box** determines the surface area of the box. To do so, we need to access the length and width of the box, which are declared as **private** members of the **class Rectangle**. Therefore, we use the method **getLength** and **getWidth** of the **class Rectangle** to retrieve the length and width, respectively. Because the **class Box** does not override the methods **getLength** and **getWidth**, we call these methods of the **class Rectangle** without using the reserved word **super**.

```
public double area()
{
    return  2 * (getLength() * getWidth()
              + getLength() * height
              + getWidth() * height);
}
```

The method **volume** of the **class Box** determines the volume of the box. To determine the volume of the box, you need to multiply the length, width, and height of the box or multiply the area of the base of the box with its height. Let us write the definition of the method **volume** by using the second alternative. To do so, you can use the method **area** of the **class Rectangle** to determine the area of the base. Because the **class Box** overrides the method **area**, to specify a call to the method **area** of the **class Rectangle** we use the reserved word **super** as shown in the following definition:

```
public double volume()
{
    return super.area() * height;
}
```

The next section discusses how to specify a call to the constructor of the superclass when writing the definition of a constructor of the subclass.

Constructors of the Superclass and Subclass

A subclass can have its own **private** data members, so a subclass also can have its own constructors. A constructor typically serves to initialize instance variables. When we instantiate a subclass object, this object inherits the instance variables of the superclass, but the subclass object cannot directly access the `private` instance variables of the superclass. The same is true for the methods of a subclass. That is, the methods of the subclass cannot directly access the `private` members of the superclass.

As a consequence, the constructors of the subclass can (directly) initialize only the instance variables of the subclass. Thus, when a subclass object is instantiated, to initialize the (`private`) instance variables it must also automatically execute one of the constructors of the superclass. A call to a constructor of the superclass is specified in the definition of a subclass constructor by using the reserved word `super`.

The preceding section defined the `class Rectangle` and derived the `class Box` from it. Moreover, we illustrated how to override a method of the `class Rectangle`. Let us now discuss how to define the constructor of the `class Box`.

The `class Rectangle` has two constructors and two instance variables. The `class Box` has three instance variables: `length`, `width`, and `height`. The instance variables `length` and `width` are inherited from the `class Rectangle`.

Next, we write the definitions of the constructors of the `class Box`.

First, let us write the definition of the default constructor of the `class Box`. Recall that, if a class contains the default constructor and no values are specified during object instantiaton, the default constructor executes and initializes the object. Because the `class Rectangle` contains the default constructor, when writing the definition of the default constructor of the `class Box`, we use the reserved word `super` with no parameters as shown in the following code. Moreover, a call to the (default) constructor of the superclass must be the first statement.

```
public Box()        //default constructor
{
    super();
    height = 0;
}
```

Next, we discuss how to write the definitions of constructors with parameters.

To specify a call to a constructor with parameters of the superclass, we use the reserved word `super` with appropriate parameters. Moreover, a call to the constructor of the superclass must be the first statement.

Consider the following definition of the constructor with parameters of the `class Box`:

```
public Box(double l, double w, double h)
{
    super(l, w);
    height = h;
}
```

In this definition, we specified the constructor of **Rectangle** with two parameters. When this constructor of **Box** executes, it triggers the execution of the constructor with two parameters of the type **double** of the **class Rectangle**.

We leave it as an exercise for you to write the complete definition of the **class Box**.

Consider the following statements:

```
Rectangle myRectangle = new Rectangle(5, 3);    //Line 1
Box myBox = new Box(6, 5, 4);                   //Line 2
```

The statement in Line 1 creates the **Rectangle** object **myRectangle**. Thus, the object **myRectangle** has two instance variables: **length** and **width**. The statement in Line 2 creates the **Box** object **myBox**. Thus, the object **myBox** has three instance variables: **length**, **width**, and **height**. See Figure 2-4.

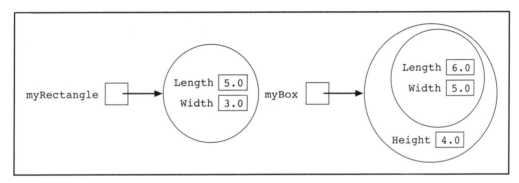

Figure 2-4   Objects **myRectangle** and **myBox**

Consider the following statements:

```
myRectangle.print();                            //Line 3
System.out.println();                           //Line 4
myBox.print();                                  //Line 5
System.out.println();                           //Line 6
```

In the statement in Line 3, the method **print** of the **class Rectangle** is executed; in the statement in Line 5, the method **print** associated with the **class Box** is executed. Recall that, if a subclass overrides a method of the superclass, the redefinition applies only to the objects of the subclass. Thus, the output of the statement in Line 3 is:

```
Length = 5.0; Width = 3.0
```

The output of the statement in Line 5 is:

```
Length = 6.0; Width = 5.0; Height = 4.0
```

The program in Example 2-2 shows how the objects of a superclass and a subclass behave.

Example 2-2

Consider the following Java application program:

```
public class SubClassSuperClassMethods
{
    public static void main(String[] args)
    {
        Rectangle myRectangle1 = new Rectangle();          //Line 1
        Rectangle myRectangle2 = new Rectangle(8, 6);      //Line 2

        Box myBox1 = new Box();                            //Line 3
        Box myBox2 = new Box(10, 7, 3);                    //Line 4

        System.out.print("Line 5: myRectangle1: ");        //Line 5
        myRectangle1.print();                              //Line 6
        System.out.println();                              //Line 7
        System.out.println("Line 8: Area of myRectangle1: "
                          + myRectangle1.area());          //Line 8
        System.out.print("Line 9: myRectangle2: ");        //Line 9
        myRectangle2.print();                              //Line 10
        System.out.println();                              //Line 11
        System.out.println("Line 12: Area of myRectangle2: "
                          + myRectangle2.area());          //Line 12

        System.out.print("Line 13: myBox1: ");             //Line 13
        myBox1.print();                                    //Line 14
        System.out.println();                              //Line 15
        System.out.println("Line 16: Surface Area of myBox1: "
                          + myBox1.area());                //Line 16
        System.out.println("Line 17: Volume of myBox1: "
                          + myBox1.volume());              //Line 17

        System.out.print("Line 18: myBox2: ");             //Line 18
        myBox2.print();                                    //Line 19
        System.out.println();                              //Line 20
        System.out.println("Line 21: Surface Area of myBox2: "
                          + myBox2.area());                //Line 21
        System.out.println("Line 22: Volume of myBox2: "
                          + myBox2.volume());              //Line 22
    }
}
```

Output

```
Line 5: myRectangle1: Length = 0.0; Width = 0.0
Line 8: Area of myRectangle1: 0.0
Line 9: myRectangle2: Length = 8.0; Width = 6.0
Line 12: Area of myRectangle2: 48.0
Line 13: myBox1: Length = 0.0; Width = 0.0; Height = 0.0
```

```
Line 16: Surface Area of myBox1: 0.0
Line 17: Volume of myBox1: 0.0
Line 18: myBox2: Length = 10.0; Width = 7.0; Height = 3.0
Line 21: Surface Area of myBox2: 242.0
Line 22: Volume of myBox2: 210.0
```

The preceding program works as follows: The statement in Line 1 creates the **Rectangle** object **myRectangle1** and initializes its instance variables to 0. The statement in Line 2 creates the **Rectangle** object **myRectangle2** and initializes its instance variables **length** and **width** to **8.0** and **6.0**, respectively.

The statement in Line 3 creates the **Box** object **myBox1** and initializes its instance variables to 0. The statement in Line 4 creates the **Box** object **myBox2** and initializes its instance variables **length**, **width**, and **height** to **10.0**, **7.0**, and **3.0**, respectively.

The statements in Lines 5 through 8 output the length, width, and area of **myRectangle1**. Because the default constructor initializes the instance variables of **myRectangle1** to 0, the area of the rectangle is 0 square units. See the output of the line marked Line 8 in the output.

The statements in Lines 9 through 12 output the length, width, and area of **myRectangle2**. Because the instance variables **length** and **width** of **myRectangle2** are initialized to **8.0** and **6.0**, respectively, by the constructor with parameters, the area of this rectangle is **48.0** square units. See the output of the line marked Line 12 in the output.

The statements in Lines 13 through 17 output the length, width, height, surface area, and **volume** of **myBox1**. Because the default constructor initializes the instance variables of **myBox1** to 0, the surface area of this box is **0.0** square units, and the volume is **0.0** cubic units. See the output of the lines marked Lines 16 and 17 in the output.

The statements in Lines 18 through 22 output the length, width, height, surface area, and **volume** of **myBox2**. Because the instance variables **length**, **width**, and **height** of **myBox2** are initialized to **10.0**, **7.0**, and **3.0**, respectively, by the constructor with parameters, the surface area of this box is **242.0** square units, and the volume is **210.0** cubic units. See the output of the lines marked Line 21 and 22 in the output.

From the output of this program it follows that the redefinition of the methods **print** and **area** in the **class Box** applies to only the object of the type **Box**.

Example 2-3

Suppose that you want to define a class to group the attributes of an employee. There are both full-time employees and part-time employees. Part-time employees are paid based on the number of hours worked and an hourly rate. Suppose that you want to define a class to keep track of a part-time employee's information such as name, pay rate, and hours worked. You can then print the employee's name together with his or her wages. Because every employee is a person, and Example 1-5 (Chapter 1) defined the **class Person** to store the first name and the last name together with the necessary operations on name, we can define the class PartTimeEmployee derived from the class Person. (See Figure 2-5.) You can also override the method print of the class Person to print the appropriate information.

The members of the class PartTimeEmployee are as follows:

Instance Variables:

```
private double payRate;      //store the pay rate
private double hoursWorked; //store the hours worked
```

Instance Methods:

```
public String toString()
    //Method to return the string consisting of the
    //first name, last name, and the wages in the form:
    //firstName lastName wages are $$$$.$$

public void setNameRateHours(String first, String last,
                               double rate, double hours)
    //Method to set the first name, last name, payRate,
    //and hoursWorked according to the parameters.
    //The parameters first and last are passed to the superclass.
    //Postcondition: firstName = first; lastName = last;
    //               payRate = rate; hoursWorked = hours;

public double getPayRate()
    //Method to return the pay rate.
    //Postcondition: The value of payRate is returned

public double getHoursWorked()
    //Method to return the number of hours worked.
    //Postcondition: The value of hoursWorked is returned

public double calculatePay()
    //Method to calculate and return the wages.
    //Postcondition: The wages are calculated and returned.

public PartTimeEmployee(String first, String last,
                          double rate, double hours)
    //Constructor with parameters
    //Set the first name, last name, payRate, and
    //hoursWorked according to the parameters.
    //Parameters first and last are passed to the superclass.
    //Postcondition: firstName = first; lastName = last;
    //               payRate = rate; hoursWorked = hours;

public PartTimeEmployee()
    //Default constructor
    //Set the first name, last name, payRate, and
    //hoursWorked to the default values.
    //The first name and last name are initialized to an empty
```

```
//string by the default constructor of the superclass.
//Postcondition: firstName = ""; lastName = "";
//                payRate = 0; hoursWorked = 0;
```

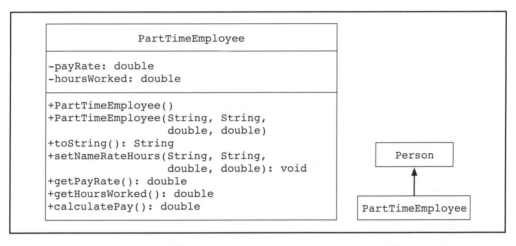

Figure 2-5 UML diagram of the class `PartTimeEmployee` and the inheritance hierarchy

The definitions of the methods of the **class PartTimeEmployee** are as follows:

```
public String toString()
{
    return (super.toString() + " wages are: " + calculatePay());
}

public double getPayRate()
{
    return payRate;
}

public double getHoursWorked()
{
    return hoursWorked;
}

public double calculatePay()
{
    return (payRate * hoursWorked);
}
```

```
public void setNameRateHours(String first, String last,
                             double rate, double hours)
{
    setName(first,last);
    payRate = rate;
    hoursWorked = hours;
}
```

The definition of the constructor with parameters is as follows (notice that the body contains a call to the superclass's constructor with parameters):

```
public PartTimeEmployee(String first, String last,
                        double rate, double hours)
{
    super(first, last);
    payRate = rate;
    hoursWorked = hours;
}
```

The definition of the default constructor is:

```
public PartTimeEmployee()
{
    super();
    payRate = 0;
    hoursWorked = 0;
}
```

The definition of the **class PartTimeEmployee** is:

```
public class PartTimeEmployee extends Person
{
    private double payRate;     //store the pay rate
    private double hoursWorked; //store the hours worked

        //Default constructor
        //Set the first name, last name, payRate, and
        //hoursWorked to the default values.
        //The first name and last name are initialized to an
        //empty string by the default constructor of the super-
        //class.
        //Postcondition: firstName = ""; lastName = "";
        //                 payRate = 0; hoursWorked = 0;
    public PartTimeEmployee()
    {
        super();
        payRate = 0;
        hoursWorked = 0;
    }
```

```
    //Constructor with parameters
    //Set the first name, last name, payRate, and
    //hoursWorked according to the parameters.
    //Parameters first and last are passed to the
    //superclass.
    //Postcondition: firstName = first; lastName = last;
    //                payRate = rate; hoursWorked = hours;
public PartTimeEmployee(String first, String last,
                        double rate, double hours)
{
    super(first, last);
    payRate = rate;
    hoursWorked = hours;
}


    //Method to return the string consisting of the
    //first name, last name, and the wages in the form:
    //firstName lastName wages are $$$$.$$
public String toString()
{
    return (super.toString() + " wages are: " + calculatePay());
}


    //Method to calculate and return the wages
public double calculatePay()
{
    return (payRate * hoursWorked);
}


    //Method to set the first name, last name, payRate,
    //and hoursWorked according to the parameters.
    //The parameters first and last are passed to the
    //superclass.
    //Postcondition: firstName = first; lastName = last;
    //                payRate = rate; hoursWorked = hours;
public void setNameRateHours(String first, String last,
                             double rate, double hours)

{
    setName(first,last);
    payRate = rate;
    hoursWorked = hours;
}


    //Method to return the pay rate
    //Postcondition: The value of payRate is returned
public double getPayRate()
{
    return payRate;
}
```

```
        //Method to return the number of hours worked
        //Postcondition: The value of hoursWorked is returned
    public double getHoursWorked()
    {
        return hoursWorked;
    }
}
```

 The definition of the subclass is typically placed in a separate file. As usual, the name of the file must be the same as the name of the class and the file extension must be `java`.

Protected Members of a Class

The `private` members of a class are `private` to the class and cannot be directly accessed outside the class. Only methods of that class can access the `private` members. As discussed previously, the subclass cannot directly access `private` members of the superclass. However, it is sometimes necessary for a subclass to access a `private` member of a superclass. If you make a `private` member `public`, then anyone can access that member. Recall that the members of a class are classified into three categories: `public`, `private`, and `protected`. So, for a superclass to give access to a member to its subclass and still prevent its direct access outside the class, you must declare that member using the modifier `protected`. Thus, the accessibility of a `protected` member of a class is in between `public` and `private`. A subclass can directly access the `protected` member of a superclass.

To summarize, if a member of a superclass needs to be accessed by a subclass, that member is declared by using the modifier `protected`.

Example 2-4 illustrates how the methods of the subclass can directly access a `protected` member of the superclass.

Example 2-4

Consider the following definition of the classes `BClass` and `DClass` (see Figures 2-6 and 2-7):

```
public class BClass
{
    protected char bCh;
    private double bX;

        //default constructor
    public BClass()
    {
        bCh = '*';
        bX = 0.0;
    }
```

```
        //constructor with parameters
    public BClass(char ch, double u)
    {
        bCh = ch;
        bX = u;
    }

    public void setData(double u)
    {
        bX = u;
    }

    public void setData(char ch, double u)
    {
        bCh = ch;
        bX = u;
    }

    public String toString()
    {
        return("Superclass: bCh = " + bCh + ", bX = " + bX + '\n');
    }
}
```

```
                        BClass

    #bCh: char
    -bX: double

    +BClass()
    +BClass(char, double)
    +setData(double): void
    +setData(char, double): void
    +toString(): String
```

Figure 2-6 UML diagram of the class BClass

The definition of the class BClass contains the protected data member bCh of the type char, and the private data member bX of the type double. It also contains an overloaded method setData, one version of which is used to set both the data members, and the other version is used to set only the private data member. The class BClass also has a constructor with default parameters.

Next, we derive the **class DClass** from the **class BClass**. The **class DClass** contains a **private** data member **dA** of the type **int**. It also contains a method **setData**, with three parameters, and the method **toString**.

```
public class DClass extends BClass
{
    private int dA;

    public DClass()
    {
        //The definition as shown below
    }

    public void DClass(char ch, double v, int a)
    {
        //The definition as shown below
    }

    public void setData(char ch, double v, int a)
    {
        //The definition as shown below
    }

    public string toString()
    {
        //The definition as shown below
    }
}
```

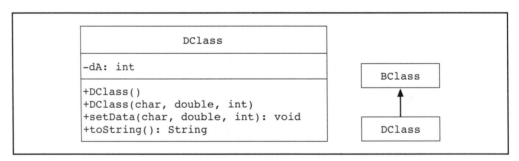

Figure 2-7   UML diagram of the **class DClass** and inheritance hierarchy

Let us now write the definition of the method **setData** of the **class DClass**. Because bCh is a **protected** data member of the **class BClass**, it can be directly accessed in the definition of the method **setData**. However, because **bX** is a **private** data member of the **class BClass**, the method **setData** of the **class DClass** cannot directly access it.

Thus, the method `setData` of the `class DClass` must set `bX` by using the method `setData` of the `class BClass`. The definition of the method `setData` of the `class DClass` can be written as follows:

```
public void setData(char ch, double v, int a)
{
    super.setData(v);

    bCh = ch;        //initialize bCh using the assignment
                     //statement
    dA = a;
}
```

Note that the definition of the method `setData` contains the statement

```
super.setData(v);
```

to call the method `setData` with one parameter (of the superclass) to set the data member `bX` and then directly set the value of `bCh`.

Next, let us write the definition of the method `toString` (of the `class DClass`).

```
public String toString()
{
    return (super.toString() + "Subclass dA = " + dA + '\n');
}
```

The definitions of the constructors are:

```
public DClass()
{
    super();
    dA = 0;
}

public void DClass(char ch, double v, int a)
{
    super(ch, v);
    dA = a;
}
```

The following program illustrates how the objects of `BClass` and `DClass` work.

```
public class ProtectedMemberProg
{
    public static void main(String[] args)
    {
        BClass bObject = new BClass();              //Line 1

        DClass dObject = new DClass();              //Line 2

        System.out.println("Line 3: " + bObject);   //Line 3
```

```
          System.out.println("Line 4: ***   "
                        + "Subclass object ***");    //Line 4

          dObject.setData('&', 2.5, 7);              //Line 5

          System.out.println("Line 6: " + dObject);  //Line 6
      }
  }
```

Output

```
Line 3: Superclass: bCh = *, bX = 0.0

Line 4: *** Subclass object ***
Line 6: Superclass: bCh = &, bX = 2.5
Subclass dA = 7
```

When you write the definitions of the methods of the **class DClass**, the **protected** data member **bCh** can be accessed directly. However, **DClass** objects cannot directly access **bCh**. That is, the following statement is illegal (it is, in fact, a syntax error):

```
dObject.bCh = '&';        //Illegal
```

The class Object

In Chapter 1, we defined the **class Clock** and later included the method **toString** (see "The Method **toString**," Chapter 1) to return the time as a string. When we included the method **toString**, we said that every Java class (built-in or user-defined) is automatically provided the method **toString**. If a user-defined class doesn't provide its own definition of the method **toString**, then the default definition of the method **toString** is invoked. The methods **print** and **println** use the method **toString** to determine what to print. As shown in Chapter 1, the default definition of the method **toString** outputs the class name followed by the hash code of the object. The obvious question is, where, in fact, is the method **toString** defined?

The method **toString** comes from the Java **class Object**, and it is a **public** member of this class. In Java, if you define a class and do not use the reserved word **extends** to derive the new class from an existing class, then the class you define is automatically considered to be derived from the **class Object**. Therefore, the **class Object** directly or indirectly becomes the superclass of every class in Java. From this, it follows that the following definition of the **class Clock** (given in Chapter 1):

```
public class Clock
{
    //Declare instance variables as given in Chapter 1
    //Definition of instance methods as given in Chapter 1
    //...
}
```

is, in fact, equivalent to the following:

```
public class Clock extends Object
{
    //Declare instance variables as given in Chapter 1
    //Definition of instance methods as given in Chapter 1
    //...
}
```

Using the mechanism of inheritance, every **public** member of the **class Object** can be overriden and/or invoked by every object of any class type. Table 2-1 describes some of the constructors and methods of the **class Object**.

Table 2-1 Some Constructors and Methods of the **class Object**

```
public Object()
//Constructor
```

```
public String toString()
//Method to return a string to describe the object
```

```
public boolean equals(Object obj)
//Method to determine if two objects are same
//Returns true if the object invoking the method and the object
//specified by the parameter obj refer to the same memory space;
//otherwise it returns false.
```

```
protected Object clone()
//Method to return a reference to a copy of the object invoking
//this method
```

```
protected void finalize()
//The body of this method is invoked when the object goes out
//of scope
```

Because every Java class is directly or indirectly derived from the **class Object**, from Table 2-1, it follows that the method **toString** becomes a **public** member of every Java class. Therefore, if a class does not override this method, whenever this method is invoked the default definition of this method executes. As indicated previously, the default definition outputs the class name followed by the hash code of the object. Usually, every Java class overrides the method **toString**. The **class String** overrides it so that the string stored in the object is returned. The **class Clock** overrides it so that the string containing the time in the form **hh:mm:ss** is returned. Similarly, the **class Person** also overrides it.

The method **equals** is also a very useful method of the **class Object**. The definition of this method as given in the **class Object** determines if the object invoking this method and the object that is passed as a parameter refer to the same memory space; that is, they point to the data in the same memory space. In other words, the method `equals` determines if the two objects are aliases. As in the case of the method `toString`, every user-defined `class` also usually overrides it to implement its own needs. For example, for the `class Clock`, this method was overridden to determine if the instance variables (`hr`, `min`, and `sec`) of two `Clock` objects contain the same value.

As usual, the default constructor is used to initialize an object. The method `clone` makes a copy of the object invoking this method and returns a reference of the copy. However, the method `clone` only makes a memberwise, that is, field by field, copy of the object.

Objects of Superclasses and Subclasses

Java allows us to treat an object of a subclass as an object of its superclass. In other words, a reference variable of a superclass type can point to an object of its subclass; that is, an object of a subclass is also an object of its superclass. There are situations when this feature of Java can be used to develop a generic code for a variety of applications. On the other hand, you *cannot* automatically consider a superclass object to be an object of a subclass. In other words you *cannot* automatically make a reference variable of a subclass type point to an object of its superclass.

Suppose that `supRef` is a reference variable of a superclass type. Moreover, suppose that `supRef` points to an object of a subclass. You can use an appropriate cast operator on `supRef` and make a reference variable of its subclass point to the object. On the other hand, if `supRef` does not point to a subclass object and you use a cast operator on `supRef` to make a reference variable of the subclass point to the object, Java throws a `ClassCastException`—indicating that the class cast is not allowed. Below we illustrate these concepts with the help of examples.

Consider the following statements (the `class`es `Person` and `PartTimeEmployee` are as defined before):

```
Person name, nameRef;                                //Line 1
PartTimeEmployee employee, employeeRef;              //Line 2

name = new Person("John", "Blair");                  //Line 3
employee = new PartTimeEmployee("Susan", "Johnson",
                           12.50, 45);               //Line 4
```

The statement in Line 1 declares `name` and `nameRef` to be reference variables of the type `Person`. Similarly, the statement in Line 2 declares `employee` and `employeeRef` to be reference variables of the type `PartTimeEmployee`. The statement in Line 3 instantiates the object `name`, and the statement in Line 4 instantiates the object `employee`.

Now consider the following statements:

```
nameRef = employee;                                  //Line 5
System.out.println("nameRef: " + nameRef);           //Line 6
```

The statement in Line 5 makes **nameRef** point to the object **employee**. After the execution of the statement in Line 5, the object **nameRef** (which, in fact, is the object **employee**) is treated as an object of the **class Person**. The statement in Line 6 outputs the value of the object **nameRef**. The output of the statement in Line 6 is:

```
nameRef: Susan Johnson wages are: 562.5
```

Notice that even though **nameRef** is declared as a reference variable of the type **Person**, when the program executes, the statement in Line 6 outputs the first name, the last name, and the wages. This is because when the statement in Line 6 executes to output **nameRef**, the method **toString** of the **class PartTimeEmployee** executes, not the method **toString** of the **class Person**. This is called **dynamic binding** (also called **run-time binding**), that is, which method gets executed is determined at the execution time, not at the compile time.

Now consider the following statement:

```
employeeRef = (PartTimeEmployee) name;  //Illegal
```

This statement throws a **ClassCastException** because **name** points to an object of the **class Person**, it does not refer to an object of the **class PartTimeEmployee**. However, the following statement is legal:

```
employeeRef = (PartTimeEmployee) nameRef;
```

Because **nameRef** refers to the object **employee** (as set by the statement in Line 5), and **employee** is a reference variable of the type **PartTimeEmployee**, this statement would make **employeeRef** point to the object **employee**. Therefore, the output of the statement:

```
System.out.println(employeeRef);
```

is

```
Susan Johnson wages are: 562.5
```

The Operator instanceof

As described in the previous section, an object of a subclass type can be considered as an object of the superclass type. Moreover, by using the appropriate cast operator, you can treat an object of a superclass type as an object of a subclass type. To determine whether a reference variable that points to an object is of a particular class type, Java provides the operator **instanceof**. Consider the following expression (suppose that **p** is an object of a class type):

```
p instanceof PartTimeEmployee
```

This expression evaluates to **true** if **p** refers to an object of the **class PartTimeEmployee**; otherwise, it evaluates to **false**.

Example 2-5, among others, further illustrates how the operator `instanceof` works.

Example 2-5

Consider the following classes. (The classes `RectangleShape` and `BoxShape` are the same as the classes `Rectangle` and `Box` given earlier in this chapter. The only difference is that the instance variables of the classes `Rectangle` and `Box` are `private` while those of the classes `RectangleShape` and `BoxShape` are `protected`. Because the instance variables of the class `RectangleShape` are `protected`, they can be directly accessed in the class `BoxShape`. Therefore, the definitions of the methods `area` and `volume` of the class `BoxShape` directly access the instance variables `length` and `width` of the class `RectangleShape`.)

```
public class RectangleShape
{
    protected double length;
    protected double width;

    public RectangleShape()
    {
        length = 0;
        width = 0;
    }

    public RectangleShape(double l, double w)
    {
        setDimension(l, w);
    }

    public void setDimension(double l, double w)
    {
        if(l >= 0)
            length = l;
        else
            length = 0;

        if(w >= 0)
            width = w;
        else
            width = 0;
    }

    public double getLength()
    {
        return length;
    }
```

```java
    public double getWidth()
    {
        return width;
    }

    public double area()
    {
        return length * width;
    }

    public double perimeter()
    {
        return 2 * (length + width);
    }

    public String toString()
    {
        return("Length = "  + length
             + ", Width = " + width
             + ", Perimeter = " + perimeter()
             + ", Area = " + area());
    }
}
```

The class BoxShape, given next, is derived from the class RectangleShape.

```java
public class BoxShape extends RectangleShape
{
    protected double height;

    public BoxShape()
    {
        super();
        height = 0;
    }

    public BoxShape(double l, double w, double h)
    {
        super(l, w);
        height = h;
    }

    public void setDimension(double l, double w, double h)
    {
        super.setDimension(l, w);

        if(h >= 0)
            height = h;
        else
            height = 0;
    }
```

```
    public double getHeight()
    {
        return height;
    }

    public double area()
    {
        return  2 * (length * width + length * height
                    + width * height);
    }

    public double volume()
    {
        return length * width * height;
    }

    public String toString()
    {
        return("Length = "  + length
            + ", Width = " + width
            + ", Height = " + height
            + ", Surface Area = " + area()
            + ", Volume = " + volume());
    }
}
```

Next consider the following application program:

```
public class SuperSubClassObjects
{

    public static void main(String[] args)
    {
        RectangleShape   rectangle, rectRef;            //Line 1
        BoxShape box, boxRef;                           //Line 2

        rectangle = new RectangleShape(12, 4);          //Line 3
        System.out.println("Line 4: Rectangle \n"
                        + rectangle + "\n");            //Line 4
        box = new BoxShape(13, 7, 4);                   //Line 5
        System.out.println("Line 6: Box\n"
                        + box + "\n");                  //Line 6
        rectRef = box;                                  //Line 7
        System.out.println("Line 8: Box via rectRef\n"
                        + rectRef + "\n");              //Line 8

        boxRef = (BoxShape) rectRef;                    //Line 9
        System.out.println("Line 10: Box via boxRef\n"
                        + boxRef + "\n");               //Line 10
```

```
        if(rectRef instanceof BoxShape)                    //Line 11
            System.out.println("Line 12: rectRef is "
                          + "an instance of BoxShape");  //Line 12
        else                                               //Line 13
            System.out.println("Line 14: rectRef is not "
                          + "an instance of BoxShape");  //Line 14

        if(rectangle instanceof BoxShape)                  //Line 15
            System.out.println("Line 16: rectangle is "
                          + "an instance of BoxShape");  //Line 16
        else                                               //Line 17
            System.out.println("Line 18: rectangle is not "
                          + "an instance of BoxShape");  //Line 18
    }
}
```

Output

```
Line 4: Rectangle
Length = 12.0, Width = 4.0, Perimeter = 32.0, Area = 48.0

Line 6: Box
Length = 13.0, Width = 7.0, Height = 4.0, Surface Area = 342.0,
Volume = 364.0

Line 8: Box via rectRef
Length = 13.0, Width = 7.0, Height = 4.0, Surface Area = 342.0,
Volume = 364.0

Line 10: Box via boxRef
Length = 13.0, Width = 7.0, Height = 4.0, Surface Area = 342.0,
Volume = 364.0

Line 12: rectRef is an instance of BoxShape
Line 18: rectangle is not an instance of BoxShape
```

The preceding program works as follows: The statement in Line 1 declares `rectangle` and `rectRef` to be reference variables of the `RectangleShape` type. Similarly, the statement in Line 2 declares `box` and `boxRef` to be reference variables of the `BoxShape` type.

The statement in Line 3 instantiates the object `rectangle` and initializes the instance variables `length` and `width` to `12.0` and `4.0`, respectively. The statement in Line 4 outputs the length, width, perimeter, and area of `rectangle`.

The statement in Line 5 instantiates the object `box` and initializes the instance variables `length`, `width`, and `height` to `13.0`, `7.0`, and `4.0`, respectively. The statement in Line 6 outputs the length, width, height, surface area, and volume of `box`.

The statement in Line 7 copies the value of `box` into `rectRef`. After this statement executes, `rectRef` points to the object `box`. Notice that `rectRef` is a reference variable of the

RectangleShape (the superclass) type and box is a reference variable of the BoxShape (the subclass of RectangleShape) type.

The statement in Line 8 outputs the length, width, height, surface area, and volume of box via the reference variable rectRef. Notice that rectRef is a reference variable of the RectangleShape type. However, when the statement in Line 8 executes, to output rectRef the method toString of the class BoxShape executes, not of the class RectangleShape.

Because the reference variable rectRef points to an object of the BoxShape type, the statement in Line 9 uses the cast operator and copies the value of rectRef into boxRef. (If the reference variable rectRef doesn't point to an object of the type BoxShape, then the statement in Line 9 results in error.) The statement in Line 10 outputs the length, width, height, surface area, and volume of the object pointed to by boxRef.

The statements in Lines 11 through 14 determine whether rectRef is an instance of BoxShape, that is, if rectRef points to an object of the BoxShape type. Similarly, the statements in Lines 15 through 18 determine whether the reference variable rectangle is an instance of BoxShape.

ABSTRACT METHODS AND CLASSES

An **abstract method** is a method that only has a heading. Moreover, the heading of an abstract method contains the reserved word **abstract** and ends with a semicolon. The following are examples of abstract methods:

```
public abstract void print();
public abstract Object larger(Object, Object);
abstract void insert(int insertItem);
```

An **abstract class** is a class that is declared with the reserved word **abstract** in its heading. The following are some facts about abstract classes:

- An abstract class can contain instance variables, constructors, a finalizer, and non-abstract methods.

- An abstract class can contain abstract method(s).

- If a class contains an abstract method, then the class must be declared abstract.

- You cannot instantiate an object of an abstract class type. You can only declare a reference variable of an abstract class type.

- You can instantiate an object of a subclass of an abstract class only if the subclass gives the definitions of *all* the abstract methods of the superclass.

The following is an example of an abstract class:

```
public abstract class AbstractClassExample
{
    protected int x;

    public AbstractClassExample()
    {
        x = 0;
    }

    public abstract void print();

    public void setX(int a)
    {
        x = a;
    }
}
```

Abstract classes are used as superclasses from which other subclasses within the same context can be derived. They can be used to force subclasses to provide certain methods. Chapter 3 illustrates the use of abstract classes.

COMPOSITION

Composition is another way to relate two classes. In composition, one or more members of a class are objects of another class type. Composition is a "has-a" relation; for example, "every person has a date of birth."

Example 1-5, in Chapter 1, defined the **class Person**. The **class Person** stores a person's first name and last name. Suppose we want to keep track of additional information for a person, such as a personal ID and a date of birth. Because every person has a personal ID and a date of birth, we can define a new class, called **PersonalInfo**, in which one of the members is an object of the type **Person**. We can declare additional members to store the personal ID and date of birth for the **class PersonalInfo**.

First we define another class, **Date**, to store only a person's date of birth, and then construct the **class PersonalInfo** from the **class**es **Person** and **Date**. This way, we can demonstrate how to define a new class using two classes.

To define the **class Date**, we need three variables to store the month, day number, and year. Some of the operations that need to be performed on a date are to set the date and to print the date. The following statements define the **class Date** (see Figure 2-8):

```
public class Date
{
    private int dMonth;    //variable to store the month
    private int dDay;      //variable to store the day
    private int dYear;     //variable to store the year
```

```java
    //Default constructor
    //Instance variables dMonth, dDay, and dYear are set
    //to the default values
    //Postcondition: dMonth = 1; dDay = 1; dYear = 1900;
public Date()
{
    dMonth = 1;
    dDay = 1;
    dYear = 1900;
}


    //Constructor to set the date
    //Instance variables dMonth, dDay, and dYear are set
    //according to the parameters
    //Postcondition: dMonth = month; dDay = day;
    //                dYear = year;
public Date(int month, int day, int year)
{
    dMonth = month;
    dDay = day;
    dYear = year;
}


    //Method to set the date
    //Instance variables dMonth, dDay, and dYear are set
    //according to the parameters
    //Postcondition: dMonth = month; dDay = day;
    //                dYear = year;
public void setDate(int month, int day, int year)
{
    dMonth = month;
    dDay = day;
    dYear = year;
}

    //Method to return the month
    //Postcondition: The value of dMonth is returned
public int getMonth()
{
    return dMonth;
}

    //Method to return the day
    //Postcondition: The value of dDay is returned
public int getDay()
{
    return dDay;
}
```

```
     //Method to return the year
     //Postcondition: The value of dYear is returned
  public int getYear()
  {
      return dYear;
  }

     //Method to return the date in the form mm-dd-yyyy
  public String toString()
  {
      return (dMonth + "-" + dDay + "-" + dYear);
  }
}
```

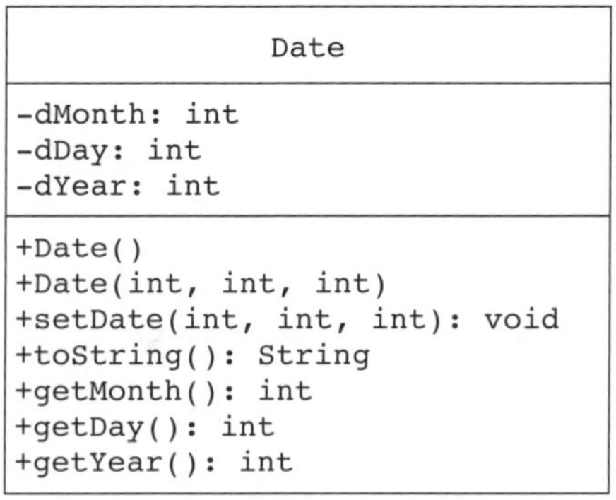

```
                        ┌─────────────────────────────┐
                        │             Date            │
                        ├─────────────────────────────┤
                        │ -dMonth: int                │
                        │ -dDay: int                  │
                        │ -dYear: int                 │
                        ├─────────────────────────────┤
                        │ +Date()                     │
                        │ +Date(int, int, int)        │
                        │ +setDate(int, int, int): void│
                        │ +toString(): String         │
                        │ +getMonth(): int            │
                        │ +getDay(): int              │
                        │ +getYear(): int             │
                        └─────────────────────────────┘
```

Figure 2-8   UML diagram of the class Date

The definition of the method **setDate**, before storing the date into the instance variables, does not check whether the date is valid. That is, it does not confirm whether **month** is between 1 and 12, **year** is greater than 0, and **day** is valid (for example, for January, **day** should be between 1 and 31). In Programming Exercise 2 at the end of this chapter, you are asked to rewrite the definition of the method **setDate** so that the date is validated before storing it in the instance variables. Similarly, in Programming Exercise 2, you are asked to rewrite the definition of the constructor with parameters so that it checks for valid values of **month**, **day**, and **year** before storing the date into data members.

Next, we specify the members of the **class PersonalInfo** (see Figure 2-9):

Instance Variables:

```
private Person name;
private Date bDay;
private int personID;
```

Instance Methods:

```
public void setPersonalInfo(String first, String last, int month,
                            int day, int year, int ID)
   //Method to set the personal information
   //Instance variables are set according to the parameters
   //Postcondition: firstName = first; lastName = last;
   //               dMonth = month; dDay = day; dYear = year;
   //               personID = ID;

public String toString()
   //Method to return the string containing personal information

public PersonalInfo()
   //Default constructor
   //Instance variables are set to the default values
   //Postcondition: firstName = ""; lastName = "";
   //               dMonth = 1; dDay = 1; dYear = 1900;
   //               personID = 0;

public PersonalInfo(String first, String last, int month,
                    int day, int year, int ID)
   //Constructor with parameters
   //Instance variables are set according to the parameters
   //Postcondition: firstName = first; lastName = last;
   //               dMonth = month; dDay = day; dYear = year;
   //               personID = ID;
```

```
              ┌─────────────────────────────────┐
              │           PersonalInfo           │
              ├─────────────────────────────────┤
              │ -name: Person                    │
              │ -bDay: Date                      │
              │ -personID: int                   │
              ├─────────────────────────────────┤
              │ +PersonalInfo()                  │
              │ +PersonalInfo(String, String, int,│
              │              int, int, int)      │
              │ +setPersonalInfo(String, String, int,│
              │                 int, int, int): void│
              │ +toString(): String              │
              └─────────────────────────────────┘
```

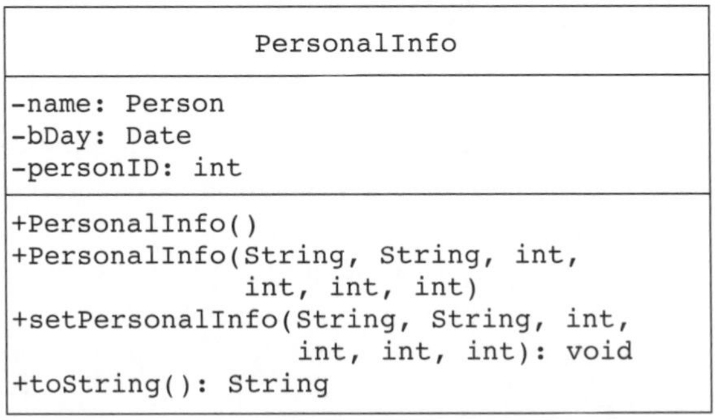

Figure 2-9   UML diagram of the class `PersonalInfo`

The definitions of the methods of the **class personalInfo** follow:

```
public void setPersonalInfo(String first, String last, int month,
                            int day, int year, int ID);
{
    name.setName(first, last);
    bDay.setDate(month, day, year);
    personID = ID;
}

public String toString()
{
    return ("Name: " + name.toString() + "\n"
        + "Date of birth: " + bDay.toString() + "\n"
        + "Personal ID: " + personID);
}

public PersonalInfo(String first, String last, int month,
                    int day, int year, int ID)
{
    name = new Person(first, last);   //instantiate and initialize
                                      //the object name
    bDay = new Date(month, day, year); //instantiate and
                                       //initialize the object bDay
    personID = ID;
}

public PersonalInfo()
{
    name = new Person();     //instantiate and initialize
                             //the object name
    bDay = new Date();       //instantiate and initialize
                             //the object bDay
    personID = 0;
}
```

Next, we give the definition of the **class PersonalInfo**.

```
public class PersonalInfo
{
    private Person name;
    private Date bDay;
    private int personID;

        //Default constructor
        //Instance variables are set to the default values
        //Postcondition: firstName = ""; lastName = "";
        //               dMonth = 1; dDay = 1; dYear = 1900;
        //               personID = 0;
```

```java
    public PersonalInfo()
    {
        name = new Person();
        bDay = new Date();
        personID = 0;
    }


    //Constructor with parameters
    //Instance variables are set according to the parameters
    //Postcondition: firstName = first; lastName = last;
    //               dMonth = month; dDay = day; dYear = year;
    //               personID = ID;
    public PersonalInfo(String first, String last, int month,
                        int day, int year, int ID)
    {
        name = new Person(first, last);
        bDay = new Date(month, day, year);
        personID = ID;
    }


    //Method to set the personal information
    //Instance variables are set according to the parameters
    //Postcondition: firstName = first; lastName = last;
    //               dMonth = month; dDay = day; dYear = year;
    //               personID = ID;
    public void setPersonalInfo(String first, String last,
                                int month, int day, int year,
                                int ID);
    {
        name.setName(first, last);
        bDay.setDate(month, day, year);
        personID = ID;
    }
    //Method to return the string containing personal information
    public String toString()
    {
        return ("Name: " + name.toString() + "\n"
             + "Date of birth: " + bDay.toString() + "\n"
             + "Personal ID: " + personID);
    }
}
```

EXCEPTION HANDLING

When you execute a Java program, several things can happen; for example, an inadvertent attempt to divide by 0, trying to tokenize a string that does not exist, or an array index going out of bound. These types of errors are called **exceptions** in Java. If your program does not include the necessary code to deal with exceptions, then the program abnormally terminates with an appropriate error message. However, there are situations when an exception occurs and the program cannot simply ignore the exception and terminate. For example, a program that monitors stock performance should not automatically sell if the account balance goes below a certain level. It should inform the stockholder and request an appropriate action.

Chapter 1 discussed how to create your own classes. Every class you design can possibly create its own exceptions. Java provides extensive support for exception handling by providing a number of exception classes. Java also allows the user to create and implement their own exception classes to handle the exceptions not covered by Java's exception classes and to handle their own exceptions.

The code to handle exceptions depends on the type of application you develop. One of the common ways to provide the exception-handling code is to provide it at the point where an error can occur. This technique allows the programmer reading the code to see the exception-handling code together with the actual code and determine if the error-checking code is properly implemented. The disadvantage of this approach is that the actual program can become polluted with the exception-handling code and can distract the programmer from making sure that the program is functioning correctly. Moreover, it can also make understanding and maintaining the program difficult.

Java Exception Hierarchy

The Java system provides a set of predefined classes to deal with errors and exceptions. The **class Throwable**, which is derived from the **class Object**, is the superclass of the classes designed to handle exceptions, as shown in Figure 2-10.

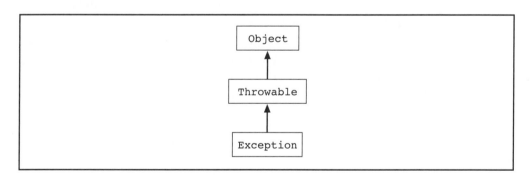

Figure 2-10 Java exception hierarchy

The **class Throwable** contains various constructors and methods, some which are described in Table 2-2.

Table 2-2 Some Constructors and Methods of the `class Throwable`

```
public Throwable()
//Default constructor
//Creates an instance of Throwable with an empty message string

public Throwable(String strMessage)
//Constructor with parameters
//Creates an instance of Throwable with message string specified
//by the parameter strMessage

public String getMessage()
//Returns the detailed message stored in the object

public void printStackTrace()
//Method to print the stack trace showing the sequence of
//method calls when an exception occurs

public void printStackTrace(PrintStream stream)
//Method to print the stack trace showing the sequence of
//method calls when an exception occurs
//Output is sent to the stream specified by the parameter stream

public void printStackTrace(PrintWriter stream)
//Method to print the stack trace showing the sequence of
//method calls when an exception occurs
//Output is sent to the stream specified by the parameter stream

public String toString()
//Returns a string representation of the Throwable object
```

The methods `getMessage`, `printStackTrace`, and `toString` are `public` and so they are inherited by the subclasses of the `class Throwable`.

The `class Exception` and its subclasses, some of which are shown in Figures 2-11 through 2-13, are designed to catch exceptions that should be caught and processed during program execution to make a program more robust. Next, we discuss how to use the `class Exception` and its subclasses to handle various types of exceptions as well as how to create your own exception classes.

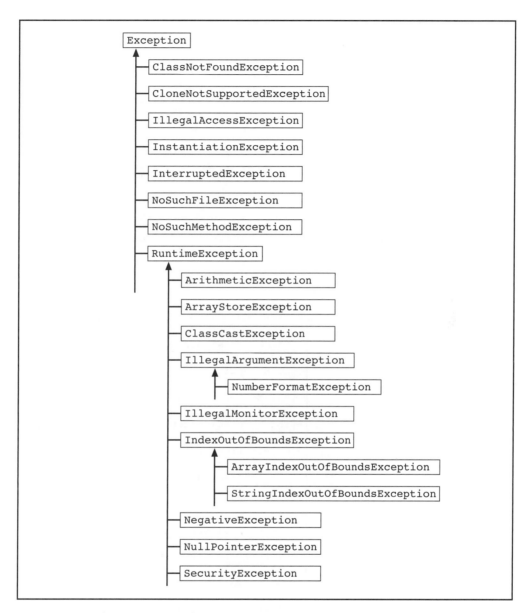

Figure 2-11   The class Exception and some of its subclasses from the package
java.lang

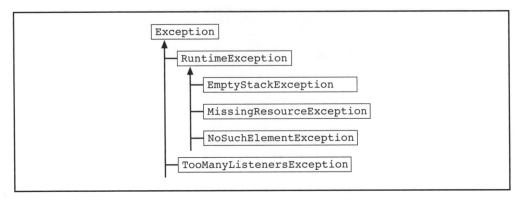

Figure 2-12   The class Exception and some of its subclasses from the package java.util (notice that the class RuntimeException is in the package java.lang)

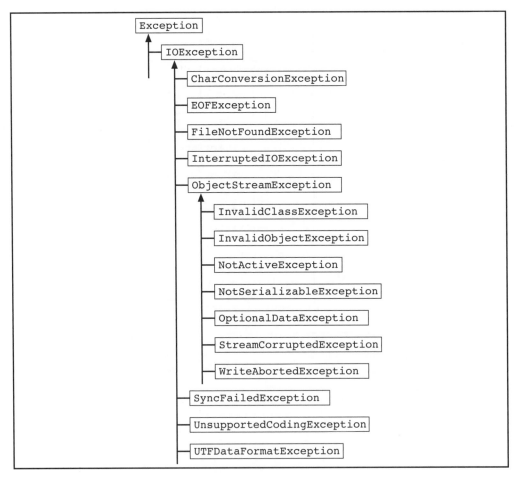

Figure 2-13   The class IOException and its subclasses from the package java.io

The Exception Hierarchy

The **class Exception** is the superclass of the classes designed to handle exceptions. There are various types of exceptions, such as I/O exceptions, number format exceptions, file not found exceptions, array index out of bound exceptions, and so on. Java categorizes these exceptions into separate classes. Moreover, these predefined exception classes are contained in various packages. The **class Exception** is contained in the package **java.lang**. The classes to deal with I/O exceptions, such as the file not found exception, are contained in the package **java.io**. Similarly, the classes to deal with number format exceptions and arithmetic exceptions, such as division by zero, are contained in the package **java.lang**. Generally, exception classes are placed in the package that contains the methods that throw these exceptions.

The **class Exception** is very simple. It only contains two constructors, as shown by Table 2-3.

Table 2-3 The **class Exception** and its Constructors

```
public Exception()
//Default constructor
//Creates a new instance of the class Exception
```

```
public Exception(String str)
//Constructor with parameters
//Creates a new instance of the class Exception. The parameter str
//specifies the message string
```

Because the **class Exception** is a subclass of the **class Throwable**, the **class Exception** and its subclass inherit the methods **getMessage**, **printStackTrace**, and **toString**. The method **getMessage** returns the string containing the detailed message stored in the exception object. The method **toString** returns the detailed message stored in the exception object as well as the name of the exception class.

The **class RuntimeException** is the superclass of the classes designed to deal with exceptions such as division by zero, array index out of bounds, and number format (see Figure 2-11).

Table 2-4 lists some of the exception classes and the type of exceptions they throw.

Table 2-4 Some of Java's Exception Classes

Exception class	Description
ArithmeticException	An arithmetic error such as division by zero
ArrayIndexOutOfBoundsException	Array index is either less than 0 or greater than or equal to the length of the array

Table 2-4 Some of Java's Exception Classes (continued)

Exception class	Description
FileNotFoundException	Reference to a file that cannot be found
IllegalArgumentException	Calling a method with illegal arguments
IndexOutOfBoundsException	An array index is out of bound
NullPointerException	Reference to an object that has not been instantiated
NumberFormatException	Use of an illegal number format
StringIndexOutOfBoundsException	A string index is either less than 0 or greater than or equal to the length of the string

As inputs, a Java program excepts only strings. Numbers, integer or decimal, are entered as strings. We then use the method `parseInt` of the `class Integer` to convert an integer string into the equivalent integer. If the string containing the integer contains only digits, the method `parseInt` returns the integer. However, if the string contains a letter or any other nondigit character, the method `parseInt` throws a `NumberFormatException` exception. Similarly, the method `parseDouble` also throws this exception if the string does not contain a valid number. Until now the programs that we wrote ignored these exceptions. Later in this chapter you learn how to handle these and other exceptions.

Tables 2-5, 2-6, and 2-7 list some of the exceptions thrown by the methods of the `class`es `Integer`, `Double`, and `String`.

Table 2-5 Exceptions Thrown by the Methods of the `class Integer`

Method	Exception thrown	Description
parseInt(String str)	NumberFormatException	The string str does not contain an int value
valueOf(String str)	NumberFormatException	The string str does not contain an int value

Table 2-6 Exceptions Thrown by the Methods of the `class Double`

Method	Exception thrown	Description
parseDouble(String str)	NumberFormatException	The string str does not contain a double value
valueOf(String str)	NumberFormatException	The string str does not contain a double value

Table 2-7 Exceptions Thrown by the Methods of the `class String`

Method	Exception thrown	Description
`String(String str)`	`NullPointerException`	str is null
`charAt(int a)`	`StringIndexOutOfBoundsException`	The value of a is not a valid index
`indexOf(String str)`	`NullPointerException`	str is null
`lastIndexOf(String str)`	`NullPointerException`	str is null
`substring(int a)`	`StringIndexOutOfBoundsException`	The value of a is not a valid index
`substring(int a, int b)`	`StringIndexOutOfBoundsException`	The value of a and/or b is not a valid index

2

Checked and Unchecked Exceptions

In the preceding chapters, whenever we used the method `readLine` or `read` in the method `main`, we included the `throws` clause `throws IOException`. If we did not include this `throws` clause in the heading of the method `main`, then the compiler would generate a syntax error. However, we did not worry about situations such as division by zero or even array index out of bounds. If during program execution an attempt to divide a number by 0 occurs, the program terminates with an error message indicating division by zero. Similarly, if a program attempts to access an array component that does not exist, that is, the index is out of bounds, then the program also terminates in an error. However, for these types of exceptions we did not need to include any `throws` clause in the heading of any method. So the obvious question is, when do we use the `throws` clause in a method heading?

Java's predefined exceptions are divided into two categories—checked exceptions and unchecked exceptions. Any exception that can be analyzed by the compiler is called a **checked exception**. For example `IOException`s are checked exceptions. Because the methods `read` and `readLine` throw `IOException`, these methods throw checked exceptions. When the compiler encounters these method calls, it checks whether the program handles `IOException`s or declares them by throwing them. Enabling the compiler to check for these types of exceptions reduces the number of exceptions not properly handled by the program. Because our programs so far were not required to handle `IOException`s or other types of predefined exceptions, the programs declared the checked exceptions by throwing them. Later in this chapter we will show, using an example, how to handle `IOException`s.

When the program is being compiled, it is quite difficult for the compiler to determine if exceptions such as division by zero or index out of bounds will occur. Therefore, these types of exceptions, called **unchecked exceptions**, are not checked by the compiler. Thus, to significantly improve the correctness of the programs, programmers must check for these types of exceptions.

Because the compiler does not check for unchecked exceptions, the program does not need to declare them using a `throws` clause or to provide the code within the program to deal with them. The exceptions belonging to a subclass of the **class RuntimeException** are unchecked exceptions. By default, unchecked exceptions are handled by Java's default exception handler.

In the method heading, the `throws` clause lists the exceptions thrown by the method. The syntax of the throws clause is

```
throws ExceptionType1, ExceptionType2, ...
```

where `ExceptionType1`, `ExceptionType2`, and so on, are the names of the exception classes.

For example, consider the following method:

```
public static void exceptionMethod()
                   throws NumberFormatException, IOException
{
    //statements
}
```

The method `exceptionMethod` throws exceptions of the type `NumberFormatException` and `IOException`.

Handling Exceptions within a Program

This section describes how to include the necessary code to handle exceptions within a program.

try/catch/finally Block

Statements that might generate an exception are placed in a `try` block. The `try` block also contains statements that should not be executed if an exception occurs. The `try` block is followed by zero or more `catch` blocks. A `catch` block specifies the type of exception it can catch and contains an exception handler. The last `catch` block may or may not be followed by a `finally` block. Any code contained in a `finally` block always executes, regardless of whether an exception occurs. If a `try` block has no `catch` block, then it *must* have the `finally` block.

Before giving the general syntax of the `try/catch/finally` block, let's observe the following: When an exception occurs, the Java system creates an object of a specific exception class. For example, if a division by zero exception occurs, then Java creates an object of the `ArithmeticException class`.

The general syntax of the `try/catch/finally` block is:

```
try
{
     //statements
}
catch(ExceptionClassName1 objRef1)
{
     //exception handler code
}
catch(ExceptionClassName2 objRef2)
{
     //exception handler code
}
.
.
.
catch(ExceptionClassNameN objRefN)
{
     //exception handler code
}
finally
{
     //statements
}
```

Note the following about `try/catch/finally` blocks:

- If no exception is thrown in a `try` block, all `catch` blocks associated with the `try` block are ignored and program execution resumes after the last `catch` block.

- If an exception is thrown in a `try` block, the remaining statements in the `try` block are ignored. The program searches the `catch` blocks in the order in which they appear after the `try` block and looks for an appropriate exception handler. If the type of the thrown exception matches the parameter type in one of the `catch` blocks, the code of that `catch` block executes and the remaining `catch` blocks after this `catch` block are ignored.

- If there is a `finally` block after the last `catch` block, the `finally` block executes regardless of whether an exception occurred.

As noted, when an exception occurs, an object of a particular exception class type is created. The type of exception handled by a `catch` block is declared in the `catch` block heading, which is the statement between the parentheses after the keyword `catch`.

Consider the following `catch` block:

```
catch(ArithmeticException aeRef)
{
     //exception handler code
}
```

This `catch` block catches an exception of the type `ArithmeticException`. The identifier `aeRef` is a reference variable of the `ArithmeticException` type. If an exception of the `ArithmeticException` type is thrown by the `try` block associated with this `catch` block and control reaches this `catch` block, then the reference parameter `aeRef` contains the address of the exception object thrown by the `try` block. Because `aeRef` contains the address of the exception object, you can access the exception object through the variable `aeRef`. The object `aeRef` stores a detailed description of the thrown exception. You can use the method `getMessage` or the method `toString` to retrieve and print that message containing the description of the thrown exception. We will illustrate this with an example later in the chapter.

Order of `catch` blocks

A `catch` block can catch all exceptions of a specific type or all types of exceptions. The heading of a `catch` block specifies the type of exception it handles. As discussed earlier in this chapter (section "Objects of Superclasses and Subclasses"), a reference variable of a superclass type can point to an object of a subclass type. Therefore, if in the heading of a `catch` block you declare an exception using the **class Exception**, then that `catch` block can catch all types of exceptions because the **class Exception** is the superclass of all exception classes.

Suppose that an exception occurs in a `try` block and that exception is caught by a `catch` block. Then the remaining `catch` blocks associated with that `try` block are ignored. Therefore, you should be careful about the order in which you list `catch` blocks following a `try` block. For example, consider the following sequence of `try/catch` blocks:

```
try                                   //Line 1
{
     //statements
}
catch(Exception eRef)                 //Line 2
{
     //statements
}
catch(ArithmeticException aeRef)      //Line 3
{
     //statements
}
```

Suppose that an exception is thrown in the `try` block. Because the `catch` block at Line 2 can catch exceptions of all types, the `catch` block at Line 3 cannot be reached. This sequence of `try/catch` blocks would, in fact, result in a compile-time error. In a sequence of `catch` blocks following a `try` block, `catch` blocks declaring exceptions of a subclass type should be placed before `catch` blocks declaring exceptions of a superclass type. Often it is useful to make sure that all exceptions thrown by a `try` block are caught. In that case, you should make the `catch` block that declares an exception of the **class Exception** type the last `catch` block.

Using `try`/`catch` Blocks in a Program

Next, we give some examples illustrating how `try`/`catch` blocks might appear in a program.

One of the common errors that might occur while inputting numeric data is typing a nonnumeric character such as a letter. Because Java only accepts strings as input, inputting data into a string variable won't cause any problem. However, when we use the methods `parseInt`, `parseFloat`, or `parseDouble` to convert the numeric string into its respective numeric form, the program may terminate with a number format error. This is because each of the methods `parseInt`, `parseFloat`, and `parseDouble` throw a number format exception if the numeric string does not contain a number. For example, if the numeric string does not contain an `int` value, then when the method `parseInt` tries to determine the numeric form of the integer string, it throws the `NumberFormatException`.

Another error that might occur when performing numeric calculation is division by zero with integer values. During program execution, if division by zero occurs with integer values and it is not addressed by the program, then the program terminates with an error message indicating an attempt to divide by zero. In this case, the program throws an exception of the `class ArithmeticException`.

Example 2-6

This example illustrates how to catch and handle number format and division by zero exceptions. The program in this example also illustrates how a `try`/`catch` block might appear in a program.

```
import java.io.*;

public class ExceptionExample1
{
   static BufferedReader keyboard = new
            BufferedReader(new InputStreamReader(System.in));

   public static void main (String[] args)
                    throws IOException                //Line 1
   {
      int dividend, divisor, quotient;                //Line 2

      try                                             //Line 3
      {
         System.out.print("Line 4: Enter dividend: "); //Line 4
         System.out.flush();                          //Line 5
         dividend =
               Integer.parseInt(keyboard.readLine()); //Line 6
         System.out.println();                        //Line 7
```

```
        System.out.print("Line 8: Enter divisor: ");    //Line 8
        System.out.flush();                             //Line 9
        divisor =
            Integer.parseInt(keyboard.readLine());      //Line 10
        System.out.println();                           //Line 11

        quotient = dividend / divisor;                  //Line 12
        System.out.println("Line 13: quotient = "
                          + quotient);                  //Line 13
    }
    catch(ArithmeticException aeRef)                    //Line 14
    {
        System.out.println("Line 15: Exception "
                          + aeRef.toString());          //Line 15
    }
    catch(NumberFormatException nfeRef)                 //Line 16
    {
        System.out.println("Line 17: Exception "
                          + nfeRef.toString());         //Line 17
    }
  }
}
```

Sample Run 1: In this sample run, the user input is shaded.

```
Line 4: Enter dividend: 45

Line 8: Enter divisor: 2

Line 13: quotient = 22
```

Sample Run 2: In this sample run the user input is shaded.

```
Line 4: Enter dividend: 18

Line 8: Enter divisor: 0

Linev15: Exception java.lang.ArithmeticException: / by zero
```

Sample Run 3: In this sample run the user input is shaded.

```
Line 4: Enter dividend: 75

Line 8: Enter divisor: f5

Line 17: Exception java.lang.NumberFormatException: f5
```

The program works as follows. The method **main** starts at Line 1, which throws the **IOException**. The statement in Line 2 declares the **int** variables **dividend**, **divisor**, and **quotient**. The **try** block starts at Line 3. The statement in Line 4 prompts the user to enter the value of the dividend. The statement in Line 6 stores the number in the variable **dividend**. The statement in Line 8 prompts the user to enter the value of the divisor, and the statement in Line 10 stores the number in the variable `divisor`. The statement in Line 12 divides the value of `dividend` by the value of `divisor` and stores the result in `quotient`. The statement in Line 13 outputs the value of `quotient`.

The first `catch` block starts at Line 14 and the second `catch` block starts at Line 16. The `catch` block at Line 14 catches an exception of the `class ArithmeticException`, and the `catch` block at Line 16 catches an exception of the `class NumberFormatException`.

In Sample Run 1, the program did not throw any exceptions.

In Sample Run 2, the entered value of `divisor` is 0. Therefore, when `dividend` is divided by `divisor`, the statement in Line 12 throws the `ArithmeticException`, which is caught by the `catch` block starting at Line 14. The statement in Line 15 outputs the appropriate message.

In Sample Run 3, the value entered at Line 10 for the variable `divisor` contains the letter `f`, a nondigit character. Because this value cannot be converted to an integer, the statement in Line 10 throws the `NumberFormatException`. Notice that the `NumberFormatException` is thrown by the method `parseInt` of the `class Integer`. The `catch` block starting at Line 16 catches this exception, and the statement in Line 17 outputs the appropriate message.

Notice that in Example 2-6 the method `main` still throws the `IOException` (see Line 1). This is because we did not include the code to handle this exception. Let us redo the program in Example 2-6 and include a `catch` block for the `IOException`.

Example 2-7

Consider the following code:

```
import java.io.*;

public class ExceptionExample2
{
    static BufferedReader keyboard = new
            BufferedReader(new InputStreamReader(System.in));

    public static void main(String[] args)                 //Line 1
    {
        int dividend, divisor, quotient;                   //Line 2

        try                                                //Line 3
        {
            System.out.print("Line 4: Enter dividend: ");  //Line 4
            System.out.flush();                            //Line 5
            dividend
                = Integer.parseInt(keyboard.readLine());   //Line 6
            System.out.println();                          //Line 7
```

```
        System.out.print("Line 8: Enter divisor: ");   //Line 8
        System.out.flush();                             //Line 9
        divisor
            = Integer.parseInt(keyboard.readLine());    //Line 10
        System.out.println();                           //Line 11

        quotient = dividend / divisor;                  //Line 12
        System.out.println("Line 13: quotient = "
                            + quotient);                //Line 13
    }
    catch(ArithmeticException aeRef)                    //Line 14
    {
        System.out.println("Line 15: Exception "
                            + aeRef.toString());        //Line 15
    }
    catch(NumberFormatException nfeRef)                 //Line 16
    {
        System.out.println("Line 17: Exception "
                            + nfeRef.toString());       //Line 17
    }
    catch(IOException ioeRef)                           //Line 18
    {
        System.out.println("Line 19: Exception "
                            + ioeRef.toString());       //Line 19
    }
  }
}
```

This program works the same way as the program in Example 2-6. Here the IOException is also handled by the program; see the statements in Lines 18 and 19.

Rethrowing and Throwing an Exception

When an exception occurs in a **try** block, the control immediately passes to one of the **catch** blocks. Typically, a **catch** block does the following:

- Completely handles the exception.

- Partially processes the exception. In this case the **catch** block either rethrows the same exception or throws another exception for the calling environment to handle the exception.

- Rethrows the same exception for the calling environment to handle the exception.

The **catch** block in Examples 2-6 and 2-7 handled the exception. The mechanism of rethrowing or throwing an exception is quite useful in cases when a **catch** block catches the exception but the **catch** block cannot handle the exception, or when the **catch** block decides that the exception should be handled by the calling block or environment. This allows the programmer to provide the exception-handling code in one place.

Rethrowing an exception or throwing an exception is accomplished by the **throw** statement. Moreover, a **throw** statement can throw either a checked or an unchecked exception.

Now, exceptions are objects of a specific class type. Therefore, if you have a reference to an exception object, you can use the reference to throw the exception. In this case, the general syntax to rethrow an exception caught by a **catch** block is:

```
throw exceptionReference;
```

Example 2-8 shows how to rethrow the same exception caught by a **catch** block.

Example 2-8

Consider the following Java code:

```
//RethrowExceptionExmp1

import java.io.*;

public class RethrowExceptionExmp1
{
   static BufferedReader keyboard = new
           BufferedReader(new InputStreamReader(System.in));

   public static void main(String[] args)                    //Line 1
   {
      int number;                                            //Line 2

      try                                                    //Line 3
      {
         number = getNumber();                               //Line 4
         System.out.println("Line 5: number = "
                        + number);                           //Line 5
      }
      catch(NumberFormatException nfeRef)                    //Line 6
      {
         System.out.println("Line 7: Exception "
                        + nfeRef.toString());                //Line 7
      }
      catch(IOException ioeRef)                              //Line 8
      {
         System.out.println("Line 9: Exception "
                        + ioeRef.toString());                //Line 9
      }
   }

   public static int getNumber()
           throws NumberFormatException, IOException         //Line 10
```

```
{
    int num;                                         //Line 11

    try                                              //Line 12
    {
        System.out.print("Line 13: Enter an integer: "); //Line 13
        System.out.flush();                          //Line 14
        num = Integer.parseInt(keyboard.readLine()); //Line 15

        return num;                                  //Line 16
    }
    catch(NumberFormatException nfeRef)              //Line 17
    {
        throw nfeRef;                                //Line 18
    }
}
}
```

Sample Run 1: In this sample run, the user input is shaded.

```
Line 13: Enter an integer: 12
Line 5: number = 12
```

Sample Run 2: In this sample run, the user input is shaded.

```
Line 13: Enter an integer: 56t7
Line 7: Exception java.lang.NumberFormatException: 56t7
```

The preceding program contains the method getNumber, which reads an integer and returns it to the method main. If the number entered by the user contains a nondigit character, the method getNumber throws the NumberFormatException. This exception is caught by the catch block at Line 17. Rather than handle this exception, the method getNumber rethrows this exception (see the statement in Line 18).

The catch block at Line 6 of the method main also catches the NumberFormatException.

In Sample Run 1, the method getNumber successfully reads the number and returns the number to the method main. In Sample Run 2, the user enters an illegal number. The statement in Line 15 throws the NumberFormatException, which is caught and rethrown by the catch block at Line 17. After the statement in Line 18 executes, the control goes back to the method main at Line 4, which throws the NumberFormatException thrown by the method getNumber. The catch block at Line 6 catches this exception and the statement in Line 7 outputs the appropriate message.

Notice that the method getNumber also throws an IOException, because this method contains an input statement that could throw an IOException. Because an IOException is a checked exception, the method getNumber should handle this exception or this exception will be implicitly thrown by the system. Therefore, the method getNumber throws the exception using the throw statement in its heading. This exception is handled in the method main.

Example 2-8 illustrates how to rethrow an exception caught by a **catch** block. When an exception occurs, an object of a specific exception **class** is created by the system. In fact, you can create your own exception objects and throw them using the **throw** statement. In this case, the general syntax used for the **throw** statement is:

```
throw new ExceptionClassName(messageString);
```

Of course, you could have first created the object and then used the reference of the object in the **throw** statement.

Example 2-9 illustrates how to throw an exception object.

Example 2-9

```
//RethrowExceptionExmp2

import java.io.*;

public class RethrowExceptionExmp2
{
    static BufferedReader keyboard = new
            BufferedReader(new InputStreamReader(System.in));

    public static void main (String[] args)               //Line 1
    {
        int number;                                       //Line 2

        try                                               //Line 3
        {
            number = getNumber();                         //Line 4
            System.out.println("Line 5: number = "
                            + number);                    //Line 5
        }
        catch(NumberFormatException nfeRef)               //Line 6
        {
            System.out.println("Line 7: Exception "
                            + nfeRef.toString());         //Line 7
        }
        catch(IOException ioeRef)                         //Line 8
        {
            System.out.println("Line 9: Exception "
                            + ioeRef.toString());         //Line 9
        }
    }

    public static int getNumber()
                throws NumberFormatException, IOException  //Line 10
```

```
{
    int num;                                              //Line 11

    try                                                   //Line 12
    {
        System.out.print("Line 13: Enter an integer: "); //Line 13
        System.out.flush();                               //Line 14
        num = Integer.parseInt(keyboard.readLine());      //Line 15

        return num;                                        //Line 16
    }
    catch(NumberFormatException nfeRef)                    //Line 17
    {
        System.out.println("Line 18: Exception "
                            + nfeRef.toString());          //Line 18
        throw new NumberFormatException("getNumber");      //Line 19
    }
  }
}
```

Sample Run: In this sample run, the user input is shaded.

```
Line 13: Enter an integer: 563r9
Line 18: Exception java.lang.NumberFormatException: 563r9
Line 7: Exception java.lang.NumberFormatException: getNumber
```

The preceding program works in a manner similar to the program in Example 2–8. The difference is in the `catch` block at Line 17, in the method `getNumber`. The `catch` block at Line 17 catches a `NumberFormatException`, outputs an appropriate message at Line 18, and then at Line 19 creates a `NumberFormatException` object with the message string `"getNumber"` and throws the object. The thrown object is caught by the `catch` block at Line 6 in the method `main`. The statement in Line 7 outputs the appropriate message. Notice that the output of the statement in Line 18, the second line of the sample run, outputs the number entered by the user, while the statement in Line 7, the third line of the sample run, outputs the string `getNumber`. This is because the statement in Line 19 creates and throws an object that is different from the `NumberFormatException` object thrown by the statement in Line 15. The object thrown by the statement in Line 19 contains the message string `"getNumber"`.

The programs in Examples 2–8 and 2–9 illustrate how a method can rethrow the same exception object or create an exception object and throw it for the calling method to handle. This mechanism is quite useful; it allows a program to handle exceptions in one location rather than spread the exception-handling code throughout the program.

Exception Handling: Techniques

When an exception occurs in a program, usually the program has three choices—terminate the program, include code in the program to recover from the exception, or log the error and continue. Next, each of these situations is discussed.

Terminating the Program

In some cases, it is best to let the program terminate when an exception occurs. Suppose you have written a program that inputs data from a file. If the input file does not exist when the program executes, then there is no point in continuing with the program. In this case, the program can output an appropriate error message and terminate.

Fix the Error and Continue

In other cases, you want to handle the exception and let the program continue. Suppose you have a program that takes a number as input. If a user inputs a character in place of a digit, the program throws a `NumberFormatException`. This is a situation where you can include the necessary code to keep prompting the user to input a number until the number is valid. For example, you could include the following code in the program (assume that all variables are properly declared):

```
done = false;

do
{
    try
    {
        System.out.print("Enter an integer: ");
        System.out.flush();
        number = Integer.parseInt(keyboard.readLine());
        System.out.println();
        done = true;
    }
    catch(NumberFormatException nfeRef)
    {
        System.out.println("\nException " + nfeRef.toString());
    }
}while(!done);
```

The `do...while` loop continues to prompt the user until the user inputs a valid integer.

Log the Error and Continue

A program that terminates when an exception occurs usually assumes that termination is reasonably safe. On the other hand, consider a program that is designed to run a nuclear reactor or a program that monitors a satellite. Such a program cannot be terminated if an exception occurs. These programs should report the exception, but the program must continue to run.

For example, consider a program that analyzes airline ticketing transactions for the day. Because a large number of ticketing transactions take place each day, to validate the transactions for the day a program is run. These types of programs usually take a good amount of time to process the transactions. Therefore, when an exception occurs, the program should write the exception into a file and continue to analyze the transactions.

Creating Your Own Exception Classes

When you create your own classes or write programs, exceptions are likely to occur. As you have seen, Java provides a substantial number of exception classes to deal with these. However, Java does not provide all the exception classes you will ever need. Therefore, Java enables programmers to create their own exception classes to handle the exceptions not covered by Java's exception classes or to handle your own exceptions. This section describes how to create your own exception classes.

Java's mechanism to process the exceptions you define is the same as that for built-in exceptions. However, you must throw your own exceptions using the **throw** statement.

The exception **class** that you define extends either the **class Exception** or one of its subclasses. Moreover, the subclass of the **class Exception** is either a predefined class or a user-defined class. In other words, if you have created an exception **class**, you can define other exception classes extending the definition of the exception **class** you created.

Typically, constructors are the only methods that you include when you define your own exception class. Because the exception class you define is a subclass of an existing exception class, either built-in or user-defined, the exception class that you define inherits the members of the superclass. Therefore, objects of exception classes can use the public members of the superclasses.

Because the **class Exception** is derived from the **class Throwable**, it inherits the methods **getMessage** and **toString** of the **class Throwable**. Moreover, because these methods are **public**, they can be inherited by the **class Exception** and any of its subclasses.

Example 2-10 shows how to create your own division by zero exception class.

Example 2-10

```
package dsuj.ch2.myExceptionClasses;

public class myDivisionByZeroException extends Exception
{
    public myDivisionByZeroException()
    {
        super("Cannot divide by zero");
    }
```

```
    public myDivisionByZeroException(String strMessage)
    {
        super(strMessage);
    }
}
```

The program in Example 2-11 uses the **class myDivisionByZeroException** designed in Example 2-10.

Example 2-11

```
import java.io.*;

import dsuj.ch2.myExceptionClasses.myDivisionByZeroException;

public class myDivisionByZeroExceptionTestProg
{
   static BufferedReader keyboard
         = new BufferedReader(new InputStreamReader(System.in));

   public static void main(String[] args)
   {
      double numerator;                                    //Line 1
      double denominator;                                  //Line 2

      try                                                  //Line 3
      {
         System.out.print("Line 4: Enter numerator: ");    //Line 4
         System.out.flush();                               //Line 5
         numerator
             = Double.parseDouble(keyboard.readLine());    //Line 6
         System.out.println();                             //Line 7

         System.out.print("Line 8: Enter denominator: ");  //Line 8
         System.out.flush();                               //Line 9
         denominator
             = Double.parseDouble(keyboard.readLine());    //Line 10
         System.out.println();                             //Line 11

         if(denominator == 0.0)                            //Line 12
            throw new myDivisionByZeroException();         //Line 13

         System.out.println("Line 14: Quotient = "
                      + (numerator / denominator));        //Line 14
      }
```

```
        catch(myDivisionByZeroException mdbzeRef)              //Line 15
        {
            System.out.println("Line 16: "
                            + mdbzeRef.toString());            //Line 16
        }
        catch(Exception eRef)                                  //Line 17
        {
            System.out.println("Line 18: "
                            + eRef.toString());                //Line 18
        }
    }
}
```

Sample Run 1: In this sample run, the user input is shaded.

```
Line 4: Enter numerator: 25

Line 8: Enter denominator: 4

Line 14: Quotient = 6.25
```

Sample Run 2: In this sample run, the user input is shaded.

```
Line 4: Enter numerator: 20

Line 8: Enter denominator: 0

Line 16: dsuj.ch2.myExceptionClasses.myDivisionByZeroException:
Cannot divide by zero
```

 The class `myDivisionByZeroException` is placed in the package `dsuj.ch2.myExceptionClasses`, and the program in Example 2-11 imports this class from this package. However, if the `class myDivisionByZeroException` and the program in Example 2-11 reside in the same subdirectory, then it is not necessary to first create the package and then import the class. For more information, see Appendix D.

 If the exception class you create is a direct subclass of the `Exception class` or a direct subclass of an exception class whose exceptions are checked exceptions, then the exceptions of the class you created are checked exceptions.

Programming Example: Grade Report

This programming example further illustrates the concepts of inheritance, composition, and exception handling.

The midsemester point at your local university is approaching. The registrar's office wants to prepare the grade reports as soon as the students' grades are recorded. Some of the students enrolled have not yet paid their tuition, however.

If a student has paid the tuition, the grades are shown on the grade report together with the grade-point average (GPA).

If a student has not paid the tuition, the grades are not printed. For these students, the grade report contains a message indicating that the grades have been held for nonpayment of the tuition. The grade report also shows the billing amount.

The registrar's office and the business office want your help in writing a program that can analyze the students' data and print the appropriate grade reports. The data is stored in a file in the following form:

```
numberOfStudents quotientRate
studentName studentID isTuitionPaid numberOfCourses
courseName courseNumber creditHours grade
courseName courseNumber creditHours grade
 .
 .
 .

studentName studentID isTuitionPaid numberOfCourses
courseName courseNumber creditHours grade
courseName courseNumber creditHours grade
 .
 .
 .
```

The first line indicates the number of students enrolled and the tuition rate per credit hour. The students' data is given thereafter.

A sample input file follows:

```
3 345
Lisa Miller 890238 Y 4
Mathematics MTH345 4 A
Physics PHY357 3 B
ComputerSci CSC478 3 B
History HIS356 3 A
```

The first line indicates that 3 students are enrolled and the tuition rate is $345 per credit hour. Next, the course data for student **Lisa Miller** is given: Lisa Miller's ID is **890238**, she has paid the tuition, and is taking 4 courses. The course number for the mathematics class she is taking is MTH345, the course has 4 credit hours, her midsemester grade is A, and so on.

The desired output for each student is in following form:

```
Student Name: Lisa Miller
Student ID: 890238
Number of courses enrolled: 4
Course No Course Name      Credits    Grade
MTH345    Mathematics         4         A
PHY357    Physics             3         B
CSC478    ComputerSci         3         B
HIS356    History             3         A

Total number of credit hours: 13.00
Midsemester GPA: 3.54
-*-*-*-*-*-*-*-*-*-*-*-*-*-*-*-*-*-*-*-*-*-
```

To calculate the GPA, we assume that the grade A is equivalent to 4 points, B is equivalent to 3 points, C is equivalent to 2 points, D is equivalent to 1 point, and F is equivalent to 0 points.

Input   A file containing the data in the form given previously. For easy reference in the rest of the discussion, let us assume that the name of the input file is stData.txt and this file is on floppy disk A:.

Output   A file containing the output of the form given previously.

Problem Analysis and Algorithm Design

We must first identify the main components of the program. The university has students, and every student takes courses. Thus, the two main components are the student and the course.

Let us first describe the course component.

Course

The main characteristics of a course are the course name, course number, and number of credit hours. Although the grade a student receives is not really a characteristic of a course, to simplify the program, this component also includes the student's grade.

Some of the basic operations that need to be performed on an object of the course type follow:

1. Set the course information.
2. Print the course information.
3. Show the credit hours.
4. Show the course number.
5. Show the grade.

The following defines the members of the **class Course** (see Figure 2-14):

```
class Course:
```

Instance Variables:

```
private String courseName;    //object to store the course name
private String courseNo;      //object to store the course number
private char courseGrade;     //variable to store the grade
private int courseCredits;    //variable to store the
                              //course credits
```

Instance Methods:

```
public void setCourseInfo(String cName, String cNo,
                          char grade, int credits)
   //Method to set the course information
   //The course information is set according to the
   //incoming parameters.
   //Postcondition: courseName = cName; courseNo = cNo;
   //               courseGrade = grade; courseCredits = credits;

public void setCourseName(String cName)
   //Method to set the course Name
   //Postcondition: courseName = cName;

public void setCourseNumber(String cNo)
   //Method to set the course Number
   //Postcondition: courseNo = cNo;

public void setCourseGrade(char grade)
   //Method to set the course Grade
   //Postcondition: courseGrade = grade;

public void setCourseCredits(int credits)
   //Method to set the course credits
   //Postcondition: courseCredits = credits;

public void print(boolean isGrade)
   //Method to print the course information
   //Postcondition: This method prints the course information
   //on the screen. Furthermore, if the boolean parameter
   //isGrade is true, the grade is shown, otherwise three stars
   //are printed.
```

```
public void print(PrintWriter outp, boolean isGrade)
   //Method to print the course information
   //Postcondition: This method sends the course information
   //to a file. Furthermore, if the boolean parameter isGrade
   //is true, the grade is shown, otherwise three stars are
   //shown.

public int getCredits()
   //Method to return the credit hours
   //Postcondition: The value of the instance variable
   //               courseCredits is returned.

public String getCourseNumber()
   //Method to return the course number
   //Postcondition:  The value of the instance variable
   //                courseNo is returned;

public char getGrade()
   //Method to return the grade for the course
   //Postcondition: The value of the instance variable
   //               courseGrade is returned.

public String getCourseInfo(boolean isGrade)
   //Method to return the course information as a string
   //Postcondition: The course no, course name,
   //               course credits, and grade are returned
   //               as a string

public Course(String cName, String cNo,
                char grade, int credits)
   //Constructor
   //The object is initialized according to the parameters.
   //Postcondition: courseName = cName; courseNo = cNo;
   //               courseGrade = grade; courseCredits = credits;

public Course()
   //Default Constructor
   //The object is initialized to the default values.
   //Postcondition: courseName = ""; courseNo = "";
   //               courseGrade = '*'; courseCredits = 0;

public void copyCourseInfo(Course otherCourse)
   //otherCourse is copied into this course
   //Postcondition: courseName = otherCourse.courseName;
   //               courseNo = otherCourse.courseNo;
   //               courseGrade = otherCourse.courseGrade;
   //               courseCredits = otherCourse.courseCredits;
```

```
                          Course
  -courseName: String
  -courseNo: String
  -courseGrade: char
  -courseCredits: int

  +Course()
  +Course(String, String, char, int)
  +setCourseInfo(String, String,
                       char, int): void
  +setCourseName(String): void
  +setCourseNumber(String): void
  +setCourseGrade(char): void
  +setCourseCredits(int): void
  +print(boolean): void
  +print(PrintWriter, boolean): void
  +getCredits(): int
  +getCourseNumber(): String
  +getGrade(): char
  +getCourseInfo(boolean): String
  +copyCourseInfo(Course): void
```

Figure 2-14   UML diagram of the class Course

Next, we discuss the definition of the methods to implement the operations of the class Course.

The method setCourseInfo sets the values of the instance variables according to the values of the parameters. Its definition is:

```
public void setCourseInfo(String cName, String cNo,
                          char grade, int credits)
{
    courseName = cName;
    courseNo = cNo;
    courseGrade = grade;
    courseCredits = credits;
}
```

The definitions of the methods setCourseName, setCourseNumber, setCourseGrade, and setCourseCredits are similar to the method setCourseInfo. Their definitons are:

```
public void setCourseName(String cName)
{
    courseName = cName;
}
```

```
public void setCourseNumber(String cNo)
{
    courseNo = cNo;
}

public void setCourseGrade(char grade)
{
    courseGrade = grade;
}

public void setCourseCredits(int credits)
{
    courseCredits = credits;
}
```

The method `print` with one parameter prints the course information on the screen. If the `bool` parameter `isGrade` is `true`, the grade is printed on the screen; otherwise, three stars are shown in place of the grade. The following steps describe this method:

1. Print the course number, the course name, and the credit hours.

2. if `isGrade` is `true`
      Output the grade
   else
      Output three stars.

The definition of the method `print` is:

```
public void print(boolean isGrade)
{
    System.out.print(courseNo + "\t   "
                + courseName + "\t\t"
                + courseCredits + "\t");     //Step 1

    if(isGrade)                              //Step 2
       System.out.println(courseGrade);
    else
       System.out.println("***");
}
```

The method `print`, which has two parameters, sends the course information to a file. Other than sending the output to a file, which is passed as a parameter, this method has exactly the same definition as the definition of the previous `print` method. The definition of this method is:

```
public void print(PrintWriter outp, boolean isGrade)
{
    outp.print(courseNo + "\t   "
            + courseName + "\t\t"
            + courseCredits + "\t");
```

```
     if(isGrade)
        outp.println(courseGrade);
     else
        outp.println("***");
}
```

The constructor with parameters uses the values specified by the formal parameters to initialize the instance variables. The default constructor uses the default values to initialize the instance variables. Their definitions are as follows:

```
public Course(String cName, String cNo,
              char grade, int credits)
{
    courseName = cName;
    courseNo = cNo;
    courseGrade = grade;
    courseCredits = credits;
}

public Course()
{
    courseName = "";
    courseNo = "";
    courseGrade = '*';
    courseCredits = 0;
}
```

The definitions of the remaining methods are straightforward.

```
public int getCredits()
{
    return courseCredits;
}

public String getCourseNumber()
{
    return courseNo;
}

public char getGrade()
{
    return courseGrade;
}

public String getCourseInfo(boolean isGrade)
{
    String str;
```

```
        str = courseNo + "\t   "
            + courseName + "\t\t"
            + courseCredits + "\t";

    if(isGrade)
        str = str + courseGrade;
    else
        str = str + "***";

    return str;
}

public void copyCourseInfo(Course otherCourse)
{
    courseName = otherCourse.courseName;
    courseNo = otherCourse.courseNo;
    courseGrade = otherCourse.courseGrade;
    courseCredits = otherCourse.courseCredits;
}
```

The definition of the **class Course** looks like:

```
public class Course
{
    private String courseName;   //object to store the course name
    private String courseNo;          //object to store the course
                                      //           number
    private char courseGrade;         //variable to store the grade
    private int courseCredits;   //variable to store the
                                 //course credits


    //Place the definitions of the constructors and instance
    //methods as discussed here.
    //...
}
```

(The complete definition of this class is left as an exercise for you.)

The next section discusses the student component.

Student

The main characteristics of a student are the student name, student ID, number of courses in which enrolled, courses in which enrolled, and grade for each course. Because every student has to pay tuition, we also include a member to indicate whether the student has paid the tuition.

Every student is a person, and every student takes courses. We have already designed a **class Person** to process a person's first name and last name. We have also designed a class to process the information of a course. Thus, we see that we can derive the **class**

`Student` to keep track of a student's information from the **class Person**, and one member of this class is object of the **class Course**. We can add more members as needed. The basic operations to be performed on an object of the type **Student** are as follows:

1. Set the student information.
2. Print the student information.
3. Calculate the number of credit hours taken.
4. Calculate the GPA.
5. Calculate the billing amount.

The following defines the members of the **class Student** (see Figure 2-15):

`class Student:`

Instance Variables:

```
private int sId;                //variable to store the student ID
private int numberOfCourses;    //variable to store the number
                                //of courses
private boolean isTuitionPaid;    //variable to indicate if
                                  //the tuition is paid
private Course[] coursesEnrolled; //array to store
                                  //the courses
```

Instance Methods:

```
public void setInfo(String fname, String lName, int ID,
                    int nOfCourses, boolean isTPaid,
                    Course[] courses)
   //Method to set a student's information
   //Postcondition: The instance variables are set according
   //               to the parameters

public void setStudentId(int ID)
   //Method to set a student ID
   //Postcondition: sId = ID;

public void setIsTuitionPaid(boolean isTPaid)
   //Method to set whether on not tuition paid
   //Postcondition: isTuitionPaid = isTPaid;

public void setNumberOfCourses(int nOfCourses)
   //Method to set number of courses taken
   //Postcondition: numberOfCourses = nOfCourses;

public void setCoursesEnrolled(Course[] courses)
   //Method to set courses enrolled
   //Postcondition: array courses is copied into the array
   //         coursesEnrolled
```

```
public void print(double tuitionRate)
   //Method to print a student's grade report

public void print(PrintWriter outp, double tuitionRate)
   //Method to print a student's grade report
   //The output is stored in a file specified by the
   //parameter out

public Student()
   //Default constructor
   //Postcondition: Instance variables are initialized

public String getName()
   //Method to return a String with value
   //firstName + " " + lastname
   //Postcondition: returns firstName concatenated
   //        with a space and last name

public int getStudentId()
   //Method to get a student ID
   //Postcondition: The value of sId is returned

public boolean getIsTuitionPaid()
   //Method to determine if tuition is paid
   //Postcondition: The value of isTuitionPaid is returned

public int getNumberOfCourses()
   //Method to get the number of courses taken
   //Postcondition: The value of numberOfCourses is returned

public Course getCourse(int i)
   //Method to get a copy of a course taken
   //Postcondition: A copy of coursesEnrolled[i] is returned

public int getHoursEnrolled()
   //Method to return the credit hours in which a
   //student is enrolled
   //Postcondition: Total credits are calculated and returned

public double getGpa()
   //Method to return the grade point average
   //Postcondition: GPA is calculated and returned

public double billingAmount(double tuitionRate)
   //Method to return the tuition fees
   //Postcondition: Billing amount is calculated and returned
```

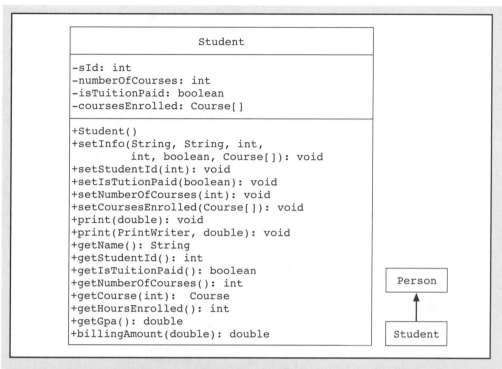

Figure 2-15   UML diagram of the `class` `Student`

Next, we discuss the definitions of the methods to implement the operations of the `class Student`.

The method `setInfo` initializes the **private** data members according to the incoming parameters. The **class Student** is derived from the **class Person**, and the variables to store the first name and last name are **private** members of that class. Therefore, we call the method `setName` of the **class Person**, and we pass the appropriate variables to set the first and last names. The definition of the method `setInfo` is as follows:

```
public void setInfo(String fname, String lName, int ID,
                    int nOfCourses, boolean isTPaid,
                    Course[] courses)
{
    int i;

    super.setName(fName,lName);        //set the name
```

```
        sId = ID;                          //set the student ID
        isTuitionPaid = isTPaid;           //set isTuitionPaid
        numberOfCourses = nOfCourses ;     //set the number of courses

    for(i = 0; i < numberOfCourses; i++) //set the array
        coursesEnrolled[i].copyCourseInfo(courses[i]);
}
```

The definitions of the methods setStudentId, setIsTuitionPaid, setNumberOfCourses, and setCoursesEnrolled are similar to the definition of the method setInfo and are given next.

```
public void setStudentId(int ID)
{
    sId = ID;
}

public void setIsTuitionPaid(boolean isTPaid)
{
    isTuitionPaid = isTPaid;
}

public void setNumberOfCourses(int nOfCourses)
{
    numberOfCourses = nOfCourses;
}

public void setCoursesEnrolled(Course[] courses)
{
    for(int i = 0; i < numberOfCourses; i++)
        coursesEnrolled[i].copyCourseInfo(courses[i]);
}
```

The default constructor initializes the instance variables to the default values. Note that because the private data member coursesEnrolled is of the type Course and is an array, the default constructor of the class Course executes automatically and the entire array is initialized.

```
public Student()
{
    super();
    numberOfCourses = 0;
    sId = 0;
    isTuitionPaid = false;
    coursesEnrolled = new Course[6];
    for(int i = 0; i < 6;  i++)
        coursesEnrolled[i] = new Course();
}
```

The method `print`, which has one parameter, prints the grade report on the screen. If the student has paid his or her tuition, the grades and the GPA are shown. Otherwise, three stars are printed in place of each grade, the GPA is not shown, a message indicates that the grades are being held for nonpayment of the tuition, and the amount due is shown. This method has the following steps:

1. To output the GPA and billing amount in a fixed decimal format, declare and instantiate a `DecimalFormat` object.
2. Output the student's name.
3. Output the student's ID.
4. Output the number of courses in which enrolled.
5. Output heading: CourseNo CourseName Credits   Grade
6. Print each course's information.
7. Print the total credit hours.
8. If `isTuitionPaid` is `true`
       Output the GPA
   else
       Output the billing amount and a message about withholding the grades.

```
public void print(double tuitionRate)
{
    int i;

    DecimalFormat twoDecimal =
              new DecimalFormat("0.00");              //Step 1

    System.out.println("Student Name: "
                    + super.toString());              //Step 2

    System.out.println("Student ID: " + sId);         //Step 3
    System.out.println("Number of courses enrolled: "
                    + numberOfCourses);               //Step 4
    System.out.println("Course No Course Name"
              + "\t    Credits"
              + "   Grade");                          //Step 5

    for(i = 0; i < numberOfCourses; i++)              //Step 6
        coursesEnrolled[i].print(isTuitionPaid);

    System.out.println();

    System.out.println("Total number of credit hours: "
         + twoDecimal.format(getHoursEnrolled()));  //Step 7
```

```
    if(isTuitionPaid)                                    //Step 8
       System.out.println("Midsemester GPA: "
                          + twoDecimal.format(getGpa()));
    else
    {
       System.out.println("*** Grades are being held for "
                          + "not paying the tuition. ***");
       System.out.println("Amount Due: $"
               + twoDecimal.format(billingAmount(tuitionRate)));
    }

    System.out.println("-*-*-*-*-*-*-*-*-*-*-*-*-*-"
                       + "*-*-*-*-*-*-*-*-*-*-\n");
}
```

The method `print`, which has two parameters, sends the output to a file. Its definition is:

```
public void print(PrintWriter outp, double tuitionRate)
{
    int i;

    DecimalFormat twoDecimal =
                new DecimalFormat("0.00");

    outp.println("Student Name: "
                 + super.toString());

    outp.println("Student ID: " + sId);

    outp.println("Number of courses enrolled: "
                 + numberOfCourses);
    outp.println("Course No Course Name"
                 + "\t    Credits"
                 + "   Grade");
    for(i = 0; i < numberOfCourses; i++)
       coursesEnrolled[i].print(outp, isTuitionPaid);

    outp.println();

    outp.println("Total number of credit hours: "
                 + twoDecimal.format(getHoursEnrolled()));

    if(isTuitionPaid)
       outp.println("Midsemester GPA: "
                    + twoDecimal.format(getGpa()));
    else
    {
       outp.println("*** Grades are being held for "
                    + "not paying the tuition. ***");
```

```
            outp.println("Amount Due: $"
                + twoDecimal.format(billingAmount(tuitionRate)));
        }
        outp.println("-*-*-*-*-*-*-*-*-*-*-*-*-*-*-"
                + "*-*-*-*-*-*-*-*-*-*-*-\n");
}
```

The definitions of the methods getName, getStudentId, getIsTuitionPaid, getNumberOfCourses, and getCourse are quite straightforward and are given next.

```
public String getName()
{
    return(super.getFirstName() + " " + super.getLastName());
}

public int getStudentId()
{
    return sId;
}

public boolean getIsTuitionPaid()
{
    return isTuitionPaid;
}

public int getNumberOfCourses()
{
    return numberOfCourses;
}

public Course getCourse(int i)
{
    Course temp = new Course();
    temp.copyCourseInfo(coursesEnrolled[i]);
    return temp;
}
```

The method getHoursEnrolled calculates and returns the total credit hours that a student is taking. These credit hours are needed to calculate both the GPA and the billing amount. The total credit hours are calculated by adding the credit hours of each course in which the student is enrolled. Because the credit hours for a course are in the private data member of an object of type Course, we use the method getCredits of the class Course to retrieve the credit hours. The definition of this method is:

```
public int getHoursEnrolled()
{
    int totalCredits = 0;
    int i;
```

```
    for(i = 0; i < numberOfCourses; i++)
        totalCredits += coursesEnrolled[i].getCredits();

    return totalCredits;
}
```

The method **billingAmount** calculates and returns the amount due, based on the number of credit hours enrolled. The definition of this method is:

```
public double billingAmount(double tuitionRate)
{
    return tuitionRate * getHoursEnrolled();
}
```

We now discuss the method **getGpa**. This method calculates a student's GPA. To find the GPA, we find the equivalent points for each grade, add the points, and then divide the sum by the total credit hours the student is taking. The definition of this method is:

```
public double getGpa()
{
    int i;
    double sum = 0.0;

    for(i = 0; i < numberOfCourses; i++)
    {
        switch(coursesEnrolled[i].getGrade())
        {
        case 'A': sum += coursesEnrolled[i].getCredits() * 4;
                break;
        case 'B': sum += coursesEnrolled[i].getCredits() * 3;
                break;
        case 'C': sum += coursesEnrolled[i].getCredits() * 2;
                break;
        case 'D': sum += coursesEnrolled[i].getCredits() * 1;
                break;
        case 'F': sum += coursesEnrolled[i].getCredits() * 0;
                break;
        default: System.out.println("Invalid Course Grade");
        }
    }

    return sum / getHoursEnrolled();
}
```

The definition of the **class Student** looks like:

```
public class Student extends Person
{
    private int sId;            //variable to store the student ID
    private int numberOfCourses;   //variable to store the
                                   //number of courses
```

```
    private boolean isTuitionPaid; //variable to indicate if
                                   //the tuition is paid
    private Course [] coursesEnrolled; //array to store
                                       //the courses

       //Place the definitions of the instance methods
       //as discussed here.
       //...
}
```

The complete definition of this class is left as an exercise for you.

Main Program

Now that we have designed the **classes Course** and **Student**, we will use these classes to complete the program.

We will restrict our program to process a maximum of 10 students. Note that this program can easily be enhanced to process any number of students.

Because the **print** method of the class does the necessary computations to print the final grade report, the main program has very little work to do. In fact, all that is left for the main program is to create the objects to hold the students' data, load the data into these objects, and then print the grade reports. Because the input is in a file and the output will be sent to a file, we declare stream variables to access the input and output files. Essentially, the main algorithm for the program is:

1. Declare the variables.
2. Open the input file.
3. If the input file does not exist, exit the program.
4. Open the output file.
5. Get the number of students registered and the tuition rate.
6. Load the students' data.
7. Print the grade reports.

Variables

This program processes a maximum of 10 students. Therefore, we must declare an array of 10 components of the type **Student** to hold the students' data. We also need to store the number of students registered and the tuition rate. Because the data will be read from a file, and because the output is sent to a file, we need two stream variables to access the input and output files. Thus, we need the following variables:

```
Student[] studentList = new Student[maxNumberOfStudents];

int noOfStudents;
double tuitionRate;
```

```
BufferedReader infile = new
        BufferedReader(new FileReader("a:\\stData.txt"));
PrintWriter outfile = new
        PrintWriter(new FileWriter("a:\\sDataOut.out"));
```

To simplify the complexity of the method **main**, we write a method, **getStudentData**, to load the students' data.

Method getStudentData   This method has three parameters: a parameter to access the input file, a parameter to access the array **studentList**, and a parameter to know the number of students registered. In pseudocode, the definition of this method is as follows:

For each student in the university,

   1. Get the first name, last name, student ID, and **isPaid**
   2. **if isPaid is 'Y'**
           set **isTuitionPaid** to **true**
      else
           set **isTuitionPaid** to **false**
   3. Get the number of courses the student is taking
   4. For each course
      a. Get the course name, course number, credit hours, and grade
      b. Load the course information into a **Course** object
   5. Load the data into a **Student** object

We need to declare several local variables to read and store the data. The definition of the method **getStudentData** is:

```
public static void getStudentData(BufferedReader infile,
                                  Student[] sList,
                                  int numberOfStudents)
                                    throws IOException
{
        //Local variable
    String fName;       //variable to store the first name
    String lName;       //variable to store the last name
    int ID;             //variable to store the student ID
    int noOfCourses;    //variable to store the number of courses
    char isPaid;        //variable to store Y/N; that is,
                        //is tuition paid?
    boolean isTuitionPaid;  //variable to store true/false

    String cName;  //variable to store the course name
    String cNo;    //variable to store the course number
    int credits;   //variable to store the course credit hours
    char grade;    //variable to store the course grade

    int count;     //loop control variable
    int i;         //loop control variable
```

```
Course[] courses = new Course[6]; //array of objects to
                                  //store course information
StringTokenizer tokenizer;

for(i = 0; i < 6; i++)
    courses[i] = new Course();

for(count = 0; count < numberOfStudents; count++)
{
              //Step 1
   tokenizer = new StringTokenizer(infile.readLine());
   fName = tokenizer.nextToken();
   lName = tokenizer.nextToken();
   ID = Integer.parseInt(tokenizer.nextToken());
   isPaid = tokenizer.nextToken().charAt(0);

   if(isPaid == 'Y')                                    //Step 2
      isTuitionPaid = true;
   else
      isTuitionPaid = false;

   noOfCourses =
       Integer.parseInt(tokenizer.nextToken());   //Step 3
   for(i = 0; i < noOfCourses; i++)                     //Step 4
   {
       tokenizer = new StringTokenizer(infile.readLine());
       cName = tokenizer.nextToken();
       cNo = tokenizer.nextToken();
       credits =
           Integer.parseInt(tokenizer.nextToken());
       grade = tokenizer.nextToken().charAt(0);   //Step 4.a
       courses[i].setCourseInfo(cName, cNo,
                           grade, credits);       //Step 4.b
   }

   sList[count].setInfo(fName, lName, ID, noOfCourses,
                      isTuitionPaid, courses); //Step 5
   }//end for
}
```

Method printGradeReports   This method prints the grade reports. For each student, it calls the method print of the class Student to print the grade report. The definition of the method printGradeReports is:

```
public static void printGradeReports(PrintWriter outfile,
                                     Student[] sList,
                                     int numberOfStudents,
                                     double tuitionRate)
```

```
{
    int count;

    for(count = 0; count < numberOfStudents; count++)
        sList[count].print(outfile,tuitionRate);
}
```

Program Listing

```java
import java.io.*;
import java.util.*;

public class GradeReportProgram
{
    static final int maxNumberOfStudents = 10;

    public static void main(String[] args)
    {
        Student[] studentList = new Student[maxNumberOfStudents];

        int noOfStudents;
        double tuitionRate;
        StringTokenizer tokenizer;

        try
        {
            BufferedReader infile = new
                BufferedReader(new FileReader("a:\\stData.txt"));
            PrintWriter outfile =
                new PrintWriter(new FileWriter("a:\\sDataOut.out"));

            for(int i = 0; i < maxNumberOfStudents; i++)
                studentList[i] = new Student();


            tokenizer = new StringTokenizer(infile.readLine());
            noOfStudents =
                Integer.parseInt(tokenizer.nextToken());  //get the
                                                //number of students
            tuitionRate =
                Double.parseDouble(tokenizer.nextToken()); //get the
                                                //tuition rate

            getStudentData(infile, studentList, noOfStudents);
            printGradeReports(outfile, studentList,
                            noOfStudents, tuitionRate);

            outfile.close();
        }
```

```
    catch(FileNotFoundException fnfe)
    {
         System.out.println(fnfe.toString());
    }
    catch(Exception e)
    {
         System.out.println(e.toString());
    }
 }


    //Place the definition of the method getStudentData as
    //described above


    //Place the definition of the method printGradeReports as
    //described above
}
```

Sample Output

```
Student Name: Lisa Miller
Student ID: 890238
Number of courses enrolled: 4
Course No Course Name        Credits     Grade
MTH345     Mathematics          4          A
PHY357     Physics              3          B
CSC478     ComputerSci          3          B
HIS356     History              3          A

Total number of credit hours: 13.00
Midsemester GPA: 3.54
-*-*-*-*-*-*-*-*-*-*-*-*-*-*-*-*-*-*-*-*-*-*-*-

Student Name: Bill Wilton
Student ID: 798324
Number of courses enrolled: 5
Course No Course Name        Credits     Grade
ENG378     English              3         ***
PHL534     Philosophy           3         ***
CHM256     Chemistry            4         ***
BIO234     Biology              4         ***
MTH346     Mathematics          3         ***

Total number of credit hours: 17.00
*** Grades are being held for not paying the tuition. ***
Amount Due: $5865.00
-*-*-*-*-*-*-*-*-*-*-*-*-*-*-*-*-*-*-*-*-*-*-*-
```

```
Student Name: Dandy Goat
Student ID: 746333
Number of courses enrolled: 6
Course No Course Name       Credits    Grade
HIS101     History             3          A
ENG328     English             3          B
MTH137     Mathematics         3          A
CHM348     Chemistry           4          B
CSC201     ComputerSci         3          B
BUS128     Business            3          C

Total number of credit hours: 19.00
Midsemester GPA: 3.16
_*_*_*_*_*_*_*_*_*_*_*_*_*_*_*_*_*_*_*_*_*_*_
```

Input File

```
3 345
Lisa Miller 890238 Y 4
Mathematics MTH345 4 A
Physics PHY357 3 B
ComputerSci CSC478 3 B
History HIS356 3 A
Bill Wilton 798324 N 5
English ENG378 3 B
Philosophy PHL534 3 A
Chemistry CHM256 4 C
Biology BIO234 4 A
Mathematics MTH346 3 C
Dandy Goat 746333 Y 6
History HIS101 3 A
English ENG328 3 B
Mathematics MTH137 3 A
Chemistry CHM348 4 B
ComputerSci CSC201 3 B
Business BUS128 3 C
```

QUICK REVIEW

1. Inheritance and composition are meaningful ways to relate two or more classes.

2. Inheritance is an "is–a" relation.

3. Composition is a "has–a" relation.

4. In single inheritance, the subclass is derived only from one existing class, called the superclass.

5. In multiple inheritance, a subclass is derived from more than one superclass.

6. The `private` members of a superclass are `private` to the superclass. The subclass cannot directly access them.

7. A subclass can override, that is, redefine the method of a superclass, but this redefinition applies only to the objects of the subclass.

8. In general, while writing the definition of the methods of a subclass to specify a call to a `public` method of a superclass we do the following:

   - If the subclass overrides a `public` method of the superclass, then the subclass specifies a call to that `public` method of the superclass by using the reserved word `super` followed by the dot operator followed by the method name with an appropriate parameter list.

   - If the subclass does not override a `public` method of the superclass, the the superclass can call that `public` method of the superclass by using the name of the method and an appropriate parameter list.

9. While writing the definition of the constructor of a subclass, a call to a constructor of the superclass is specified using the reserved word `super` with an appropriate parameter list. Moreover, the call to a constructor of the superclass must be the first statement.

10. For a superclass to give access to a member to its subclass and still prevent its direct access outside the class, you must declare that member using the modifier `protected`.

11. If you define a class and do not use the reserved word `extends` to derive it from an existing class, then the class you define is automatically considered to be derived from the `class Object`.

12. The `class Object` directly or indirectly becomes the superclass of every class in Java.

13. Java allows you to treat an object of its subclass as an object of a superclass; that is, a reference variable of a superclass type can point to an object of its subclass.

14. You *cannot* automatically consider a superclass object to be an object of a subclass. In other words, you *cannot* automatically make a reference variable of a subclass type point to an object of its superclass.

15. Suppose that `supRef` is a reference variable of a superclass type. Moreover, suppose that `supRef` points to an object of a subclass. You can use an appropriate cast operator on `supRef` and make a reference variable of the subclass point to the object. On the other hand, if `supRef` does not point to a subclass object and you use a cast operator on

supRef to make a reference variable of the subclass point to the object, Java will throw a ClassCastException—indicating that the class cast is not allowed.

16. An abstract method is a method that only has a heading. Moreover, the heading of an abstract method contains the reserved word **abstract** and ends with a semicolon.

17. An abstract class is a class that is declared with the reserved word **abstract** in its heading. The following are some facts about abstract classes:

   - An **abstract** class can contain instance variables, constructors, a finalizer, and non-**abstract** methods.

   - An **abstract** class can contain **abstract** method(s).

   - If a **class** contains an abstract method, it must be declared **abstract**.

   - You cannot instantiate an object of an **abstract class** type. You can only declare a reference variable of an **abstract** class type.

   - You can instantiate an object of a subclass of an **abstract class** only if the subclass gives the definitions of *all* the **abstract** methods of the superclass.

18. The **class Throwable**, which is derived from the **class Object**, is the superclass of the **class Exception**.

19. The methods **getMessage**, **printStackTrace**, and **toString** of the **class Throwable** are **public** and therefore are inherited by the subclasses of the **class Throwable**.

20. The method **getMessage** returns the string containing the detailed message stored in the exception object.

21. The method **toString** returns the detailed message stored in the exception object as well as the name of the exception class.

22. The **class Exception** and its subclasses are designed to catch exceptions that should be caught and processed during program execution to make a program more robust.

23. The **class Exception** is the superclass of the classes designed to handle exceptions.

24. The **class Exception** is contained in the package **java.lang**.

25. The classes to deal with I/O exceptions, such as the file not found exception, are contained in the package **java.io**.

26. The classes to deal with number format exceptions and arithmetic exceptions, such as division by zero, are contained in the package **java.lang**.

27. Generally, exception classes are placed in the package that contains the methods that throws these exceptions.

28. Java's predefined exceptions are divided into two categories—checked exceptions and unchecked exceptions.

29. Any exception that can be analyzed by the compiler is called a checked exception. For example, **IOExceptions** are checked exceptions.

30. Unchecked exceptions are exceptions that are not checked by the compiler.

31. The `try/catch/finally` block is used to handle exceptions within a program.

32. Statements that may generate an exception are placed in a `try` block. The `try` block also contains statements that should not be executed if an exception occurs.

33. The `try` block is followed by zero or more `catch` blocks.

34. A `catch` block specifies the type of exception it can catch and contains an exception handler.

35. The last `catch` block may or may not be followed by a `finally` block.

36. The code contained in the `finally` block always executes, regardless of whether an exception occurs.

37. If a `try` block has no catch block, then it *must* have the `finally` block.

38. When an exception occurs, an object of a specific exception class is created.

39. A `catch` block can catch all exceptions of a specific type, or all types of exceptions.

40. The heading of a `catch` block specifies the type of exception it handles.

41. When an exception occurs in a `try` block, the control immediately passes to one of the `catch` blocks. Typically, a `catch` block does the following:

- Completely handles the exception.

- Partially processes the exception. In this case, the `catch` block either rethrows the same exception or throws another exception for the calling environment to handle the exception.

- Rethrows the same exception for the calling environment to handle the exception.

42. The general syntax to rethrow an exception caught by a `catch` block is:

```
throw exceptionReference;
```

43. The general syntax to throw your own exception object is:

```
throw new ExceptionClassName(messageString);
```

44. The exception `class` that you define extends either the `class Exception` or one of its subclasses.

EXERCISES

1. Mark the following statements as true or false.

a. The constructor of a subclass specifies a call to the constructor of the superclass in the heading of the method definition.

b. The constructor of a subclass specifies a call to the constructor of the superclass using the name of the class.

c. Suppose that `x` and `y` are classes. One of the data members of `x` is an object of type `y`, and both classes have constructors. The constructor of `x` specifies a call to the constructor of `y` by using the object name of the type `y`.

    d. A subclass must have a constructor.

    e. The block `finally` is always executed.

    f. Division by zero is a checked exception.

    g. File not found is an unchecked exception

    h. Exceptions are thrown in a `try` block in a method or from a method called directly or indirectly from a `try` block.

    i. The order in which `catch` blocks are listed is not important.

    j. An exception can be caught either in the method it occurred or in any one of the methods that led to the invocation of this method.

    k. One way to handle an exception is to print an error message and exit the program.

    l. All exceptions need to be reported to avoid compilation errors.

2. Draw a class hierarchy in which several classes are subclasses from a single superclass.

3. Suppose that a `class Employee` is derived from the `class Person` (see Example 1-5, in Chapter 1). Give examples of data and method members that can be added to the `class Employee`.

4. Explain the difference between the `private` and `protected` members of a class.

5. What is the difference between overloading a method name and overriding a method name?

6. Name two situations where you would use the reserved word `super`.

7. Consider the following class definition:

```
public class AClass
{
      private int u;
      private int v;

      public void print()
      {
      }

      public void set(int x, int y)
      {
      }

      public AClass()
      {
      }

      public AClass(int x, int y)
      {
      }
}
```

2

What is wrong with the following class definition?

```
class BClass AClass
{
    private int w;

    public void print()
    {
        System.out.println("u + v + w = " + (u + v + w);
    }

    public BClass()
    {
        super();
        w = 0;
    }

    public BClass(int x, int y, int z)
    {
        super(x, y);
        w = z;
    }

}
```

8. Consider the following statements:

```
public class YClass
{
    private int a;
    private int b;

    public void one()
    {
    }

    public void two(int x, int y)
    {
    }

    public YClass()
    {
    }
}
```

```
class XClass extends YClass
{
    private int z;

    public void one()
    {
    }

    public XClass()
    {
    }
}
```

```
YClass yObject;
XClass xObject;
```

a. The **private** members of **YClass** are **public** members of **XClass**. True or False?

b. Mark the following as valid or invalid. If invalid, explain why.

i. In the following, one is a method of the **class YClass**.

```
public void one()
{
    System.out.println(a + b);
}
```

ii.

```
yObject.a = 15;
xObject.b = 30;
```

iii. In the following, one is a method of the **class XClass**.

```
public  void one()
{
    a = 10;
    b = 15;
    z = 30;
    System.out.println(a + b + z);
}
```

iv.

```
System.out.println(yObject.a + " " + yObject.b + " "
                        + xObject.z);
```

9. Assume the declaration of Exercise 8.

   a. Write the definition of the default constructor of YClass so that the instance variables of YClass are initialized to 0.

   b. Write the definition of the default constructor of XClass so that the instance variables of XClass are initialized to 0.

   c. Write the definition of the method two of YClass so that the instance variable a is initialized to the value of the first parameter of two, and the instance variable b is initialized to the value of the second parameter of two.

10. Suppose that you have the following class:

```
public class classA
{
    private int x;                       //Line 1
    protected void setX(int a)           //Line 2
    {                                    //Line 3
        x = a;                           //Line 4
    }
}
```

What is wrong with the following code?

```
public class Exercise10                  //Line 5
{
    public static void main(String[] args) //Line 6
    {
        classA aObject;                  //Line 7

        aObject.setX(4);                 //Line 8
    }
}
```

11. Suppose that you have the following class definition:

```
public class One
{
    private int x;
    private int y;

    public void print()
    {
        System.out.println(x + " " + y);
    }

    protected void setData(int u, int v)
    {
        x = u;
        y = v;
    }
}
```

Consider the following class definition:

```
public class Two extends One
{
    private int z;

    public void setData(int a, int b, int c)
    {
        //Postcondition: x = a; y = b; z = c;
    }

    public void print()
    {
        //Output the values of x, y, and z
    }
}
```

a. Write the definition of the method **setData** of the **class Two** as described in the class definition.

b. Write the definition of the method **print** of the **class Two** as described in the class definition.

12. Suppose that you have the following class definitions:

```
public class SuperClass
{
    protected int x;

    private String str;

    public void print()
    {
        System.out.println(x + " " + str);
    }

    public SuperClass()
    {
        str = "";
        x = 0;
    }

    public SuperClass(string s, int a)
    {
        str = s;
        x = a;
    }
}
```

2

```java
public class SubClass extends SuperClass
{
    private int y;

    public void print()
    {
        System.out.println("SubClass: " + y);
        Super.print();
    }

    public SubClass()
    {
        super();
        y = 0;
    }

    public SubClass(string s, int a, int b)
    {
        super("Hello Super", a + b);
        y = b;
    }
}
```

What is the output of the following Java code?

```java
SuperClass superObject = new SuperClass("This is superclass", 2);
SubClass subObject = new SubClass("DDDDDD", 3, 7);

superObject.print();
subObject.print();
```

13. What does the operator `instanceof` do?

14. What is an abstract method?

15. Consider the following Java code:

```java
int lowerLimit;

...

try
{
    System.out.println("Entering the try block.");
    if(lowerLimit < 100)
        throws new Exception("Lower limit violation.");
    System.out.println("Exiting the try block.");
}
catch(Exception e)
{
    System.out.println("Exception: " + e.getMessage());
}
System.out.println("After the catch block");
```

What is the output if:

a. The value of `lowerLimit` is 50?

b. The value of `lowerLimit` is 150?

16. Consider the following Java code:

```java
int lowerLimit;
int divisor;
int result;

try
{
    System.out.println("Entering the try block.");
    result = lowerLimit / divisor;
    if(lowerLimit < 100)
        throw new Exception("Lower limit violation.");
    System.out.println("Exiting the try block.");
}
catch(DivideByZeroException e)
{
    System.out.println("Exception: " + e.getMessage());
    result = 110;
}
catch(Exception e)
{
    System.out.println("Exception: " + e.getMessage());
}
System.out.println("After the catch block");
```

What is the output if:

a. The value of `lowerLimit` is 50, and the value of `divisor` is 10.

b. The value of `lowerLimit` is 50, and the value of `divisor` is 0.

c. The value of `lowerLimit` is 150, and the value of `divisor` is 10.

d. The value of `lowerLimit` is 150, and the value of `divisor` is 0.

17. Rewrite the Java code given in Exercise 16 such that the new equivalent code has exactly one `catch` block.

18. Define the exception `class` called `TornadoException`. The class should have two constructors including one default constructor. If the exception is thrown with the default constructor, the method `getMessage` should return

"Tornado: Take cover immediately!"

The other constructor has a single parameter, m, of `int` type. If the exception is thrown with this constructor, the `getMessage` should return

"Tornado: m miles away; and approaching!"

19. Write a Java program to test the `class TornadoException` specified in Exercise 18.

20. Suppose the exception **class MyException** is defined as follows:

```
public class MyException extends Exception
{
    public MyException()
    {
        super("MyException thrown!");
        System.out.println("Immediate attention required!");
    }
    public MyException(String msg)
    {
        super(msg);
        System.out.println("Attention required!");
    }
}
```

What output is produced if the exception is thrown with the default constructor? What output is produced if the exception is thrown with the nondefault constructor with actual parameter **"May Day, May Day"**?

PROGRAMMING EXERCISES

1. In Chapter 1, the **class Clock** was designed to implement the time of day in a program. Certain applications, in addition to hours, minutes, and seconds, might require you to store the time zone. Derive the **class ExtClock** from the **class Clock** by adding a data member to store the time zone. Add the necessary methods and constructors to make the class functional. Also, write the definitions of the member methods and the constructors. Finally, write a test program to test your class.

2. In this chapter, the **class Date** was designed to implement the date in a program, but the member method **setDate** and the constructor with parameters do not check whether the date is valid before storing the date in the data members. Rewrite the definitions of the method **setDate** and the constructor with parameters so that the values for the month, day, and year are checked before storing the date into the data members. Add a method member, **isLeapYear**, to check whether a year is a leap year. Moreover, write a test program to test your class.

3. A point in the x-y plane is represented by its x-coordinate and y-coordinate. Design the **class Point** that can store and process a point in the x-y plane. You should then perform operations on a point, such as showing the point, setting the coordinates of the point, printing the coordinates of the point, returning the x-coordinate, and returning the y-coordinate. Also, write a test program to test the various operations on a point.

4. Every circle has a center and a radius. Given the radius, you can determine the circle's area and circumference. Given the center, you can determine its position in the *x-y* plane. The center of a circle is a point in the *x-y* plane. Design the **class Circle** that can store the radius and center of the circle. Because the center is a point in the *x-y* plane and you designed the class to capture the properties of a point in Programming Exercise 3, you must derive the **class Circle** from the **class Point**. You should be able to perform the usual operations on a circle, such as setting the radius, printing the radius, calculating and printing the area and circumference, and carrying out the usual operations on the center.

5. Every cylinder has a base and height, where the base is a circle. Design the **class Cylinder** that can capture the properties of a cylinder and perform the usual operations on a cylinder. Derive this class from the **class Circle** designed in Programming Exercise 4. Some the operations that can be performed on a cylinder are as follows: calculate and print the volume, calculate and print the surface area, set the height, set the radius of the base, and set the center of the base.

6. Using classes, design an online address book to keep track of the names, addresses, phone numbers, and dates of birth of family members, close friends, and certain business associates. Your program should be able to handle a maximum of 500 entries.

   a. Define the **class Address** that can store a street address, city, state, and zip code. Use the appropriate methods to print and store the address. Also, use constructors to automatically initialize the data members.

   b. Define the **class ExtPerson** using the **class Person** (as defined in Example 1-5, Chapter 1), the **class Date** (as designed in this chapter's Programming Exercise 2), and the **class Address**. Add a data member to this class to classify the person as a family member, friend, or business associate. Also, add a data member to store the phone number. Add (or override) the methods to print and store the appropriate information. Use constructors to automatically initialize the data members.

   c. Define the **class AddressBook** using previously defined classes. An object of the type **AddressBook** should be able to process at least 500 entries.

   The program should perform the following operations:

   i. Load the data into the address book from a disk.

   ii. Search for a person by last name.

   iii. Print the address, phone number, and date of birth (if it exists) of a given person.

   iv. Print the names of the people whose birthdays are in a given month or between two given dates.

   v. Print the names of all the people between two last names.

   vi. For special occasions, such as birthdays, print three different messages: one for family members, one for friends, and one for business associates. Your program should be able to print the names of all family members, friends, or business associates.

7. In Programming Exercise 2, the **class Date** was designed and implemented to keep track of a date, but it has very limited operations. Redefine the **class Date** so that it can perform the following operations on a date in addition to the operations already defined:

   a. Set the month.

   b. Set the day.

   c. Set the year.

   d. Return the month.

   e. Return the day.

   f. Return the year.

   g. Test whether the year is a leap year.

   h. Return the number of days in the month. For example, if the date is 3-12-2003, the number of days to be returned is 31 because there are 31 days in March.

   i. Return the number of days passed in the year. For example, if the date is 3-18-2003, the number of days passed in the year is 77. Note that the number of days returned also includes the current day.

   j. Return the number of days remaining in the year. For example, if the date is 3-18-2003, the number of days remaining in the year is 288.

   k. Calculate the new date by adding a fixed number of days in the date. For example, if the date is 3-18-2003 and the days to be added are 25, the new date is 4-12-2003.

   l. Return a reference to the object containing a copy of the date.

   m. Make a copy of another date. Given a reference to an object containing a date, copy the data members of the object into the corresponding data members of this object.

   n. Write the definitions of the methods to implement the operations defined for the **class Date**.

8. The **class Date** defined in Programming Exercise 7 prints the date in numerical form. Some applications might require the date to be printed in another form, such as March 24, 2003. Derive the **class ExtDate** so that the date can be printed in either form.

Add a data member to the **class ExtDate** so that the month can also be stored in string form. Add a method member to output the month in the string format followed by the year—for example, in the form March 2003.

Write the definitions of the method to implement the operations for the **class ExtDate**.

9. Using the **classes ExtDate** (Programming Exercise 8) and **Day** (Chapter 1, Programming Exercise 2), design the **class Calendar** so that, given the month and the year, you can print the calendar for that month. To print a monthly calendar, you must know the first day of the month and the number of days in that month. Thus, you must store the first day of the month, which is of the form **Day**, and the month and the year of the calendar. Clearly, the month and the year can be stored in an object of the form **ExtDate** by setting the day component of the date to **1**, and the month and year as specified by the user. Thus, the class calendar has two data members: an object of the type **Day**, and an object of the type **ExtDate**.

   Design the **class Calendar** so that the program can print a calendar for any month starting January 1, 1500. Note that the day for January 1 of the year 1500 is a Monday. To calculate the first day of a month, you can add the appropriate days to Monday of January 1, 1500.

   For the **class Calendar**, include the following operations:

   a. Determine the first day of the month for which the calendar will be printed. Call this operation **firstDayOfMonth**.

   b. Set the month.

   c. Set the year.

   d. Return the month.

   e. Return the year.

   f. Print the calendar for the particular month.

   g. Add the appropriate constructors to initialize the data members.

10. a. Write the definitions of the methods of the **class Calendar** (designed in Programming Exercise 9) to implement the operations of the **class Calendar**.

    b. Write a test program to print the calendar for either a particular month or a particular year. For example, the calendar for September 2003 is:

```
                  September 2003
  Sun    Mon    Tue    Wed    Thu    Fri    Sat
          1      2      3      4      5      6
   7      8      9     10     11     12     13
  14     15     16     17     18     19     20
  21     22     23     24     25     26     27
  28     29     30
```

3

ARRAY-BASED LISTS

In this chapter, you will:

♦ Learn about lists

♦ Explore how various operations, such as search, insert, and remove, on lists are implemented

♦ Learn how to design and implement a generic class to process various types of lists

♦ Become aware of the class Vector

A local hardware store is about to open and needs to maintain a list of the items it sells. For each item sold, the list contains the name of the item, an identification number, the price of the item, the number of pieces of the item currently in stock, and so on. Like the list of items sold by the hardware store, we come across various types of lists. For example, we might have a list consisting of employee data, a list of student data, a list of sales data, or a list of rental properties. One thing common to all lists is that all the elements of a list are of the same type. More formally, we can define a list as follows:

List: A collection of elements of the same type. The **length** of a list is the number of elements in the list.

Let us further consider the list of items sold by the hardware store. If a particular item is discontinued or the store does not sell the item, it is removed from the list; if a new item is available for sale, it is added to the list. Any time an item is sold, the remaining number of pieces in stock must be updated. If an item goes on sale, its sale price must be updated. All these operations require you to access the elements of the list. As you can see, there are various types of operations performed on a list.

Typically, the operations performed on a list are as follows:

1. Create the list. The list is initialized to an empty state.

2. Determine whether the list is empty.

3. Determine whether the list is full.

4. Find the size of the list.

5. Clear the list.

6. Determine whether an item is the same as a given list element.

7. Insert an item in the list at the specified location.

8. Remove an item from the list at the specified location.

9. Replace an item at the specified location with another item.

10. Retrieve an item from the list from the specified location.

11. Search the list for a given item.

Before discussing how to implement these operations, we must first decide how to store the list in the computer's memory. Because all the elements of a list are of the same type, an effective, convenient, and common way to process a list is to store it in an array. Initially, the size of the array holding the list elements is usually larger than the number of elements in the list so that, at a later stage, the list can grow to a specific size. Thus, we must know how full the array is; that is, we must keep track of the number of list elements stored in the array. Java allows the programmer to create dynamic arrays. Therefore, we leave it for the user to specify the size of the array. The size of the array can be specified when a list object is declared. It follows that, in order to maintain and process the list in an array, we need the following three variables:

- the array, `list`, holding the list elements

- a variable, `length`, to store the length of the list (that is, the number of list elements currently in the array)

- a variable, `maxSize`, to store the size of the array (that is, the maximum number of elements that can be stored in the array)

We will design the **class ArrayListClass** to implement a list in a program. This class will have at least three instance variables, `list`, `length`, and `maxSize` as described in the preceding list.

TYPE OF LIST ELEMENTS

The variables `length` (indicating the number of elements in the list) and `maxSize` (indicating the maximum number of elements that can be stored in the list) as defined in the preceding section are nonnegative integers, and therefore we can declare them to be of the type `int`. What about the type of the array, that is, the data type of the array elements? If we have a list of numbers, then the array elements could be of the type `int` or `double`. If we have a list of names, then the array elements are of the type `String`. Similarly, if we have a list of students, then the array elements are of the type `Student` (the data type we defined in the Programming Example of Chapter 2). We, therefore, see that there are various types of lists.

A list, such as of sales data or student data, is empty if its length is zero. To insert an item at the end of a list of any type requires us to add the element after the current last element and then increment the length by one. Similarly, it can be seen that for the most part the algorithms to implement operations on a list of names, or a list of sales data, or a list of student data, are the same. We do not wish to spend time and effort to develop separate code for each type of list we encounter. Instead, we want to develop a generic code that can be used to implement any type of list in a program. In other words, while designing the algorithms, we do not want to be concerned whether we are processing a list of numbers, a list of names, or a list of student data. However, while illustrating a particular operation, we will consider a specific type of list.

To develop generic algorithms to implement list operations, we use the following facts (see Chapter 2). In Java:

- A subclass object can be regarded as a superclass object.

- The binding of methods takes place at execution time, that is, binding of methods is dynamic.

As stated in Chapter 2, the `class Object` directly or indirectly becomes a superclass of every Java class, whether user-defined or built-in. Therefore, a reference variable of `Object` type can refer to any object of any class. While writing the algorithms to implement list operations, we could think of list elements as objects of the type `Object`. In order to use the list to store and manipulate data, the user can organize the data in the form of a Java class and, among other things, provide the basic operations on the data such as comparing two data elements, copying data of one object into another object, and so on.

The `class Object` contains the method `equals`, to compare two objects for equality, and the method `clone`, which returns a reference of a copy of an object. However, the `class Object` does not contain any method to compare two objects for a less-than or greater-than relationship. Certain list operations, such as searching an ordered list for a specific item, require the less-than or greater-than comparison. In order to force the class (organizing specific data) to provide at least the following operations (on the data):

1. Compare two objects for equality

2. Compare two objects for a less-than or greater-than relationship

3. Make a copy of another object's data

4. Return a reference to a copy of an object's data

We create an **abstract class**, **DataElement**, as described below. (Items 3 and 4 ensure that the shallow copying of data is avoided.) Recall that objects of an **abstract** class cannot be instantiated.

While writing the algorithms to implement list operations, we assume that every list element is an object of the type **DataElement**. To organize specific data, the user can extend the definition of the **class DataElement**. In other words, the **class DataElement** becomes the superclass of every class specifying the data type of the list elements.

The following statements define **DataElement** to be an **abstract** class with operations described previously (see also Figure 3-1):

```
public abstract class DataElement
{
    public abstract boolean equals(DataElement otherElement);
        //Method to determine whether two objects contain the same data.
        //Postcondition: Returns true if this object contains the
        //               same data as the object otherElement;
        //               otherwise, it returns false.

    public abstract int compareTo(DataElement otherElement);
        //Method to compare two objects.
        //Postcondition: Returns a value < 0 if this object is
        //                   less than the object otherElement.
        //               Returns 0 if this object is the same as
        //                   the object otherElement.
        //               Returns a value > 0 if this object is
        //                   greater than the object otherElement.

    public abstract void makeCopy(DataElement otherElement);
        //Method to copy otherElement into this object.
        //Postcondition: The data of otherElement is copied into
        //               this object.

    public abstract DataElement getCopy();
        //Method to return a copy of this object.
        //Postcondition: A copy of this object is created and
        //               a reference of the copy is returned.
}
```

DataElement
+equals(DataElement): boolean +compareTo(DataElement): int +makeCopy(DataElement otherElement): void +getCopy(): DataElement

Figure 3-1   UML diagram of the class DataElement

 To see how the methods makeCopy and getCopy work, see Chapter 1.

class IntElement

Suppose that you need to implement a list of integers in a program. The following class defines the data element to be of the type int (see also Figure 3-2):

```
public class IntElement extends DataElement
{
    protected int num;

      //default constructor
    public IntElement()
    {
        num = 0;
    }

      //constructor with parameters
    public IntElement(int x)
    {
        num = x;
    }

      //copy constructor
    public IntElement(IntElement otherElement)
    {
        num = otherElement.num;
    }
```

```java
    //Method to set the value of the instance variable num.
    //Postcondition: num = x;
public void setNum(int x)
{
    num = x;
}

    //Method to return the value of the instance variable num.
    //Postcondition: The value of num is returned.
public int getNum()
{
    return num;
}

public boolean equals(DataElement otherElement)
{
    IntElement temp = (IntElement) otherElement;

    return (num == temp.num);
}

public int compareTo(DataElement otherElement)
{
    IntElement temp = (IntElement) otherElement;

    return (num - temp.num);
}

public void makeCopy(DataElement otherElement)
{
    IntElement temp = (IntElement) otherElement;

    num = temp.num;
}

public DataElement getCopy()
{
    IntElement temp = new IntElement(num);
    return temp;
}

public String toString()
{
    return String.valueOf(num);
}
}
```

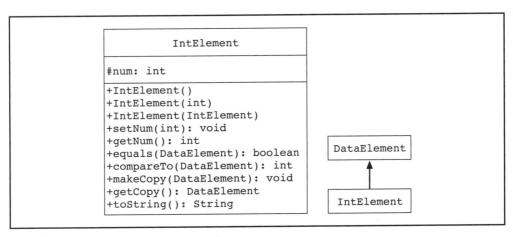

Figure 3-2   UML diagram of the `class IntElement` and the inheritance hierarchy

Similarly, you can create the **class DoubleElement** to implement a list of decimal numbers, such as sales data.

class StringElement

If you need to implement a list of names in a program you can create the **class StringElement** as follows (see also Figure 3-3):

```
public class StringElement extends DataElement
{
    protected String str;

      //default constructor
    public StringElement()
    {
        str = null;
    }

      //constructor with parameters
    public StringElement(String s)
    {
        str = s;
    }

      //copy constructor
    public StringElement(StringElement otherString)
    {
        str = otherString.str;
    }
```

```java
    //Method to set the value of the instance variable str.
    //Postcondition: str = x;
public void setString(String x)
{
    str = x;
}
public boolean equals(DataElement otherElement)
{
    StringElement temp = (StringElement) otherElement;

    return (str.compareTo(temp.str) == 0);
}

public int compareTo(DataElement otherElement)
{
    StringElement temp = (StringElement) otherElement;

    return (str.compareTo(temp.str));
}

public void makeCopy(DataElement otherElement)
{
    StringElement temp = (StringElement) otherElement;

    str = new String(temp.str);
}

public DataElement getCopy()
{
    StringElement temp = new StringElement(str);

    return temp;
}

public String toString()
{
    return str;
}
}
```

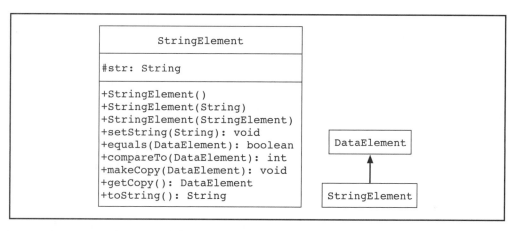

Figure 3-3 UML diagram of the class StringElement and the inheritance hierarchy

class ArrayListClass

Now that we know the basic operations on a list and how to create a specific list element, we can describe the class implementing a list as an array and the algorithms to implement the list operations.

The following statements define the class ArrayListClass as an abstract data type (ADT), as shown in Figure 3-4:

Abstract Class: ArrayListClass

Instance Variables:

```
protected int length;    //to store the length of the list
protected int maxSize;   //to store the maximum size of the list
protected DataElement[] list; //array of reference variables
```

Instance Methods:

```
public ArrayListClass()
    //default constructor
    //Creates an array of size 100.
    //Postcondition: list points to the array, length = 0,
    //                and maxSize = 100

public ArrayListClass(int size)
    //constructor with parameter
    //Creates an array of size specified by the parameter
    //size.
    //Postcondition: list points to the array, length = 0,
    //                and maxSize = size
```

```
public ArrayListClass(ArrayListClass otherList)
   //copy constructor

public boolean isEmpty()
   //Method to determine whether the list is empty.
   //Postcondition: Returns true if the list is empty;
   //               otherwise, returns false.

public boolean isFull()
   //Method to determine whether the list is full.
   //Postcondition: Returns true if the list is full;
   //               otherwise, returns false.

public int listSize()
   //Method to return the number of elements in the list.
   //Postcondition: Returns the value of length.

public int maxListSize()
   //Method to return the maximum size of the list.
   //Postcondition: Returns the value of maxSize.

public void print()
   //Method to output the elements of the list.
   //Postcondition: Elements of the list are output on the
   //standard output device.

public boolean isItemAtEqual(int location, DataElement item)
   //Method to determine whether item is the same as the item in
   //the list at the position specified by location.
   //Postcondition: Returns true if list[location] is
   //               same as item; otherwise, returns false.

public void insertAt(int location, DataElement insertItem)
   //Method to insert insertItem in the list at the position
   //specified by location.
   //Postcondition: Starting at location, the elements of the list
   //               are shifted to make room for the new item,
   //               list[location] = insertItem;, and
   //               length++;
   //     If the list is full or location is out of range,
   //     an appropriate message is displayed.

public void insertEnd(DataElement insertItem)
   //Method to insert insertItem at the end of the list.
   //Postcondition: list[length] = insertItem; and length++;
   //               If the list is full, an appropriate
   //               message is displayed.
```

```
public void removeAt(int location)
    //Method to remove the item from the list at the position
    //specified by location.
    //Postcondition: The list element at list[location] is removed
    //      and length is decremented by 1.
    //      If location is out of range, an appropriate message
    //      is printed.

public DataElement retrieveAt(int location)
    //Method to retrieve the element from the list at the
    //position specified by location.
    //Postcondition: A copy of the element at the position
    //      specified by location is returned. If location
    //      is out of range, an appropriate message is
    //      printed and null is returned.

public void replaceAt(int location, DataElement repItem)
    //Method to replace the element in the list at
    //the position specified by location with repItem.
    //Postcondition: list[location] = repItem
    //      If location is out of range, an appropriate
    //      message is printed.

public void clearList()
    //Method to remove all the elements from the list.
    //Postcondition: length = 0

public abstract int seqSearch(DataElement searchItem);
    //Method to determine whether searchItem is in the list.
    //Postcondition: If searchItem is found, returns the location
    //              in the array where the searchItem is found;
    //              otherwise, returns -1.

public abstract void insert(DataElement insertItem);
    //Method to insert insertItem in the list.
    //However, first the list is searched to
    //see whether the item to be inserted is already in the list.
    //Postcondition: insertItem is inserted and length++
    //      If insertItem is already in the list or list
    //      is full, an appropriate message is output.

public abstract void remove(DataElement removeItem);
    //Method to remove an item from the list.
    //The parameter removeItem specifies the item to
    //be removed.
    //Postcondition: If removeItem is found in the list, it is
    //              removed from the list and length is
    //              decremented by one.
```

```
public void copyList(ArrayListClass otherList)
   //Method to make a copy of the other list.
   //Postcondition: This list is destroyed and a copy of
   //                otherList is assigned to this list.
```

```
                        ArrayListClass

          #length: int
          #maxSize: int
          #list: DataElement[]

          +ArrayListClass()
          +ArrayListClass(int)
          +ArrayListClass(ArrayListClass)
          +isEmpty(): boolean
          +isFull(): boolean
          +listSize(): int
          +maxListSize(): int
          +print(): void
          +isItemAtEqual(int, DataElement): boolean
          +insertAt(int, DataElement): void
          +insertEnd(DataElement): void
          +removeAt(int): void
          +retrieveAt(int): DataElement
          +replaceAt(int, DataElement): void
          +clearList(): void
          +seqSearch(DataElement): int
          +insert(DataElement): void
          +remove(DataElement): void
          +copyList(ArrayListClass): void
```

Figure 3-4 UML diagram of the `class ArrayListClass`

Notice that the instance variables of the `class ArrayListClass` are declared as `protected`. Moreover, notice that the methods `seqSearch`, `insert`, and `remove` are declared as abstract. This is because of the following reasons.

In general, we deal with two types of lists: lists whose elements are arranged according to some criteria, such as sorted lists, and lists whose elements are in no particular order, as in unsorted lists. The algorithms to implement the operations of search, insert, and remove differ slightly for sorted and unsorted lists. Therefore, we define the `class ArrayListClass` as an abstract class. By using the principle of inheritance, from the `class ArrayListClass`, we, in fact, derive two `class`es, `UnorderedArrayList` and `OrderedArrayList`.

Objects of the `class UnorderedArrayList` arrange list elements in no particular order; that is, these lists are unsorted. On the other hand, objects of the `class OrderedArrayList` arrange elements according to some comparison criteria, usually greater than or equal to. That is, these lists are in ascending order. Moreover, after inserting an element into—or removing an element from—an ordered list, the resulting list is ordered. We, therefore, separately describe the algorithm to implement the operations search, insert, and remove for unsorted and sorted lists. The next section describes these operations for unsorted lists. Chapters 8 and 9 deal with sorted lists. Because each of the classes **UnorderedArrayList** and **OrderedArrayList** provide separate definitions of the methods **seqsearch**, **insert**, and **remove**, and because these methods access the instance variables, to provide direct access to the instance variables, the instance variables are declared as **protected**.

Next, we write the definitions of the nonabstract methods of the **class ArrayListClass**.

The list is empty if **length** is **zero**; it is full if **length** is equal to **maxSize**. Therefore, the definitions of the methods **isEmpty** and **isFull** are:

```
public boolean isEmpty()
{
    return (length == 0);
}

public boolean isFull()
{
    return (length == maxSize);
}
```

The data member **length** of the class stores the number of elements currently in the list. Similarly, because the size of the array holding the list elements is stored in the data member **maxSize**, **maxSize** specifies the maximum size of the list. Therefore, the definitions of the methods **listSize** and **maxListSize** are:

```
public int listSize()
{
    return length;
}

public int maxListSize()
{
    return maxSize;
}
```

Each of the methods **isEmpty**, **isFull**, **listSize**, and **maxListSize** contain only one statement, which is either a comparison statement or a statement returning a value. It follows that each of these methods is of $O(1)$.

The member method **print** outputs the elements of the list. We assume that the output is sent to the standard output device.

```
public void print()
{
    for(int i = 0; i < length; i++)
        System.out.print(list[i] + " ");
    System.out.println();
}
```

The method **print** uses a loop to output the elements of the list. The number of times the **for** loop executes depends on the number of elements in the list. If the list has 100 elements, the **for** loop executes 100 times. In general, suppose that the number of elements in the list is n. Then the method **print** is of $O(n)$.

Following is the definition of the method **isItemAtEqual**:

```
public boolean isItemAtEqual(int location, DataElement item)
{
    return (list[location].equals(item));
}
```

There is only one statement in the body of method **isItemAtEqual**, a comparison statement. It is easy to see that the method is of $O(1)$.

The method **insertAt** inserts an item at a specific location in the list. The item to be inserted, and the insert location in the array, are passed as parameters to this method. In order to insert the item somewhere in the middle of the list, we must first make room for the new item. That is, we need to move certain elements one array slot to the right. Consider the list of Figure 3-5.

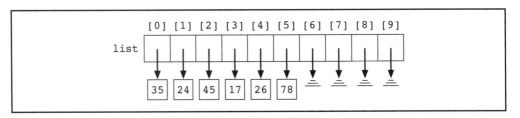

Figure 3-5   Array **list**

The number of elements currently in the list is **6** and so **length** is **6**. Thus, after inserting a new element, the **length** of the list is **7**. If the item is to be inserted at, say, location **6**, we can easily accomplish this by copying the item in **list[6]**. On the other hand, if the item is to be inserted at, say location **3**, we first need to move elements **list[3]**, **list[4]**, and **list[5]** one array slot to the right to make room for the new item. Thus, we must first copy **list[5]** into **list[6]**, **list[4]** into **list[5]**, and **list[3]** into **list[4]**, in this order. Then we can copy the new item into **list[3]**.

Of course, special cases, such as trying to insert in a full list, must be handled separately. Some of these cases can be accomplished by other member methods.

The definition of the method `insertAt` is as follows:

```
public void insertAt(int location, DataElement insertItem)
{
    if(location < 0 || location >= maxSize)
        System.err.println("The position of the item to "
                            + "be inserted is out of range");
    else
        if(length >= maxSize)  //list is full
            System.err.println("Cannot insert in a full list.");
        else
        {
            for(int i = length; i > location; i--)
                list[i] = list[i - 1];   //move the elements down

            list[location] = insertItem.getCopy();  //insert the
                                    //item at the specified position

            length++;       //increment the length
        }
}//end insertAt
```

The method `insertAt` uses a **for** loop to shift the elements of the list. The number of times the **for** loop executes depends on where in the list the item is inserted. If the item is to be inserted at the first position, then all the elements of the list are to be shifted. It can be easily shown that this method is of $O(n)$.

The method `insertEnd` can be implemented by using the method `insertAt`. However, the method `insertEnd` does not require the shifting of elements. Therefore, we give its definition directly, as follows:

```
public void insertEnd(DataElement insertItem)
{
    if(length >= maxSize)  //the list is full
        System.err.println("Cannot insert in a full list.");
    else
    {
        list[length] = insertItem.getCopy();   //insert the item
                                            //at the end
        length++;           //increment the length
    }
}//end insertEnd
```

The number of statements, and hence the number of operations, executed in the body of the method `insertEnd`, are fixed. Therefore, this method is of $O(1)$.

The method `removeAt` is the opposite of the method `insertAt`. The method `removeAt` removes an item from a specific location in the list. The location of the item to be removed is passed as a parameter to this method. After removing the item from the list, the length of the list is reduced by 1. If the item to be removed is somewhere in the middle of the list, after removing the item we must move certain elements one array slot to the left because we cannot leave holes in the portion of the array containing the list. Consider the list of Figure 3-6.

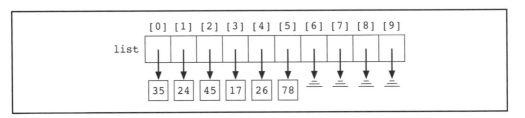

Figure 3-6 Array list

The number of elements currently in the list is 6, and so length is 6. Thus, after removing an element, the length of the list is 5. Suppose that the item to be removed is at, say, location 3. Clearly, we must move list[4] into list[3] and list[5] into list[4], in this order.

The definition of the method removeAt is:

```
public void removeAt(int location)
{
    if(location < 0 || location >= length)
        System.err.println("The location of the item to "
                          + "be removed is out of range.");
    else
    {
        for(int i = location; i < length - 1; i++)
            list[i] = list[i + 1];

        list[length - 1] = null;

        length--;
    }
}//end removeAt
```

Similar to the method insertAt, it can be seen that the method removeAt is of order $O(n)$.

The definition of the method retrieveAt is given next. The index of the item to be retrieved is passed as a parameter to this method. The definition of this method is as follows:

```
public DataElement retrieveAt(int location)
{
    if(location < 0 || location >= length)
    {
        System.err.println("The location of the item to be "
                          + "retrieved is out of range.");
```

```
          return null;
      }
      else
          return list[location].getCopy();
}//end retrieveAt
```

The definition of the method **replaceAt** is as follows:

```
public void replaceAt(int location, DataElement repItem)
{
    if(location < 0 || location >= length)
        System.err.println("The location of the item to "
                            + "be replaced is out of range.");
    else
        list[location].makeCopy(repItem);
}//end replaceAt
```

The method **clearList** removes the elements from the list, leaving it empty. Because the data member **length** indicates the number of elements in the list, after setting the references of **list**, in the range 0... **length** − 1 to **null**, we set **length** to 0. Therefore, the definition of this method is:

```
public void clearList()
{
    for(int i = 0; i < length; i++)
        list[i] = null;

    length = 0;

    System.gc();
}//end clearList
```

As before, it is easy to see that each of the methods **retrieveAt** and **replaceAt** are of $O(1)$ and the method **clearList** is of $O(n)$.

We now discuss the definition of the constructors. The constructor with parameters creates an array of the size specified by the user, and initializes the **length** of the list to 0 and the **maxSize** to the size of the array specified by the user. The size of the array is passed as a parameter to the constructor. The default array size is **100**. The definitions of the constructors are as follows:

```
public ArrayListClass()
{
    maxSize = 100;
    length = 0;
    list = new DataElement[maxSize];
}
```

```
public ArrayListClass(int size)
{
    if(size <= 0)
    {
        System.err.println("The array size must be positive. "
                         + "Creating an array of size 100. ");
        maxSize = 100;
    }
    else
        maxSize = size;

    length = 0;
    list = new DataElement[maxSize];
}
```

As before, it is easy to see that each of the constructors is of O(1).

Copy Constructor

Recall that the copy constructor is called when an object is declared and initialized using the value of another object of the same type. It copies the data members of the actual object into the corresponding data members of the object being created. Its definition is:

```
public ArrayListClass(ArrayListClass otherList)
{
    maxSize = otherList.maxSize;
    length = otherList.length;
    list = new DataElement[maxSize];    //create the array

    for(int j = 0; j < length; j++)     //copy otherList
        list[j] = otherList.list[j].getCopy();
}//end copy constructor
```

Method copyList

The method **copyList** makes a copy of a list into this list. The reference, say **otherList**, of the list to be copied is passed as a parameter to this method. If the list making a copy of **otherList** is nonempty, then first it is destroyed.

```
public void copyList(ArrayListClass otherList)
{
    if(this != otherList)        //avoid self-copying
    {
        for(int j = 0; j < length; j++) //destroy this list
            list[j] = null;
        System.gc();

        maxSize = otherList.maxSize;
        length = otherList.length;
        list = new DataElement[maxSize];    //create the array
```

```
        for(int j = 0; j < length; j++)  //copy otherList
            list[j] = otherList.list[j].getCopy();
    }
}
```

Similar to the method print, it can be seen that the copy constructor is of $O(n)$.

You can write the definition of ArrayListClass as follows:

```
public abstract class ArrayListClass
{
    protected int length;      //to store the length of the list
    protected int maxSize;     //to store the maximum size
                               //of the list
    protected DataElement[] list;  //array to hold the
                                   //list elements

        //Place the definitions of the instance methods and
        //abstract methods here.

}
```

UNORDERED LIST

As described in the preceding section, we derive the **class UnorderedArrayList** from the **abstract class ArrayListClass** and implement the operations **search**, **insert**, and **remove** (see Figure 3-7).

Class: UnorderedArrayList

public class UnorderedArrayList extends ArrayListClass

Instance Variables:

Same as the instance variables of the **class ArrayListClass**.

Constructors and Instance Methods:

```
public UnorderedArrayList()
   //default constructor

public UnorderedArrayList(int size)
   //constructor with parameter

public UnorderedArrayList(UnorderedArrayList otherList)
   //Copy constructor

public int seqSearch(DataElement searchItem)
   //Method to determine whether searchItem is in the list.
   //Postcondition: If searchItem is found, returns the location
   //               in the array where searchItem is found;
   //               otherwise, returns -1.
```

```
public void insert(DataElement insertItem)
    //Method to insert insertItem at the end
    //of the list. However, first the list is searched to
    //see whether the item to be inserted is already in the list.
    //Postcondition: list[length] = insertItem and length++
    //               If insertItem is already in the list or the list
    //               is full, an appropriate message is output.

public void remove(DataElement removeItem)
    //Method to remove an item from the list.
    //The parameter removeItem specifies the item to
    //be removed.
    //Postcondition: If removeItem is found in the list, it is
    //               removed from the list and length is
    //               decremented by one.
```

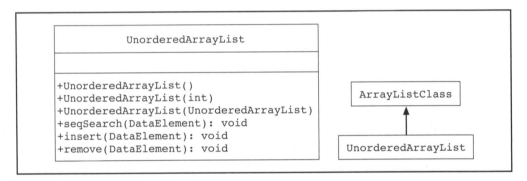

Figure 3-7   UML diagram of the `class` `UnorderedArrayList` and the inheritance hierarchy

Search

The search algorithm described next is called a **sequential**, or **linear**, search. Consider the list of seven elements shown in Figure 3-8.

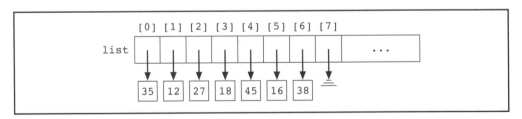

Figure 3-8   List of seven elements

Suppose that you want to determine whether 27 is in the list. The sequential search works as follows: First, you compare 27 with the element at list[0]—that is, compare 27 with 35. Because the element at list[0] is not equal to 27, you then compare 27 with the element at list[1]—that is, with 12, the second item in the list. Because the element at list[1] is not equal to 27, you compare 27 with the next element in the list—that is, compare 27 with the element at list[2]. Because the element at list[2] is equal to 27, the search stops. This is a successful search.

Let us now search for 10. As before, the search starts with the first element in the list—that is, at list[0]. This time the search item, which is 10, is compared with every item in the list. Eventually, no more data is left in the list to compare with the search item. This is an unsuccessful search.

It now follows that, as soon as you find an element in the list that is equal to the search item, you must stop the search and report "success." (In this case, you usually also tell the location in the list where the search item was found.) Otherwise, after the search item is compared with every element in the list, you must stop the search and report "failure."

Suppose that the name of the array containing the list elements is list. The previous discussion translates into the following algorithm for the sequential search:

```
found is set to false;

for(loc = 0; loc < length; loc++)
    if(element at list[loc] is equal to searchItem)
    {
        found is set to true
        exit loop
    }

if(found)
    return loc;
else
    return -1;
```

The following method performs a sequential search on a list:

```java
public int seqSearch(DataElement searchItem)
{
    int loc;
    boolean found = false;

    for(loc = 0; loc < length; loc++)
        if(list[loc].equals(searchItem))
        {
            found = true;
            break;
        }
```

3

```
        if(found)
            return loc;
        else
            return -1;
}//end seqSearch
```

Now that you know how to implement the (sequential) search algorithm, we can give the definitions of the methods **insert** and **remove**. Recall that the method **insert** inserts a new item at the end of the list if this item does not exist in the list and the list is not full. The method **remove** removes an item from the list if the list is not empty.

Chapter 8 explicitly shows that the method **seqSearch** is of $O(n)$.

Insert

The method **insert** inserts a new item in the list. Because duplicates are not allowed, this method first searches the list to determine whether the item to be inserted is already in the list. To determine whether or not the item to be inserted is already in the list, this method calls the member method **seqSearch**, described previously. If the item to be inserted is not in the list, the new item is inserted at the end of the list and the **length** of the list is increased by 1. Also, the item to be inserted is passed as a parameter to this method. The definition of this method is:

```
public void insert(DataElement insertItem)
{
    int loc;

    if(length == 0)                   //list is empty
        list[length++] = insertItem;  //insert the item and
                                      //increment the length
    else
        if(length == maxSize)
            System.err.println("Cannot insert in a full list.");
        else
        {
            loc = seqSearch(insertItem);

            if(loc == -1)        //the item to be inserted
                                 //does not exist in the list
                list[length++] = insertItem.getCopy();
            else
                System.err.println("The item to be inserted is "
                            + "already in the list. No "
                            + "duplicates are allowed.");

        }
}//end insert
```

The method **insert** uses the method **seqSearch** to determine whether **insertItem** is already in the list. Now, because the method **seqSearch** is of $O(n)$, it follows that the method **insert** is of $O(n)$.

Remove

The method **remove** deletes an item from the list. The item to be deleted is passed as a parameter to this method. In order to delete the item, that method calls the method **seqSearch** to determine whether or not the item to be deleted is in the list. If the item to be deleted is found in the list, the item is removed from the list and the length of the list is decremented by 1. Moreover, the method **seqSearch** returns the **index** of the item in the list to be deleted. We can now use the **index** returned by the method **seqSearch**, and use the method **removeAt** to remove the item from the list. If the item to be deleted is not in the list, this method outputs an appropriate message. The definition of the method **remove** is:

```
public void remove(DataElement removeItem)
{
    int loc;

    if(length == 0)
        System.err.println("Cannot delete from an empty list.");
    else
    {
        loc = seqSearch(removeItem);

        if(loc != -1)
            removeAt(loc);
        else
            System.out.println("The item to be deleted is "
                             + "not in the list.");
    }
}//end remove
```

The method **remove** uses the methods **seqSearch** and **removeAt** to remove an item from the list. Because each of these methods is of $O(n)$ and are called in sequence, it follows that the method **remove** is of $O(n)$.

The definitions of the constructors are left as an exercise for you.

You can write the definition of the **class UnorderedArrayList** as follows:

```
public class UnorderedArrayList extends ArrayListClass
{
    //Place the definitions of the methods as described above
    //and the definitions of the constructors here.
}
```

Time-Complexity of List Operations

Table 3-1 summarizes the time-complexity of the methods of the **class ArrayListClass**.

Table 3-1 Time-Complexity of the Methods of the `class ArrayListClass`

Method	Time-Complexity
isEmpty	$O(1)$
isFull	$O(1)$
listSize	$O(1)$
maxListSize	$O(1)$
print	$O(n)$
isItemAtEqual	$O(1)$
insertAt	$O(n)$
insertEnd	$O(1)$
removeAt	$O(n)$
retrieveAt	$O(1)$
replaceAt	$O(1)$
clearList	$O(n)$
constructors	$O(1)$
copy constructor	$O(n)$
copyList	$O(n)$
seqSearch	$O(n)$
insert	$O(n)$
remove	$O(n)$

Example 3-1

The following program tests various operations on an integer list.

```
//Test Program Integer Array List

import java.io.*;
import java.util.*;

public class Example3_1
{
    static BufferedReader keyboard = new
            BufferedReader(new InputStreamReader(System.in));

    public static void main(String[] args) throws IOException
    {
        UnorderedArrayList intList =
                    new UnorderedArrayList(50);        //Line 1
        UnorderedArrayList temp =
                    new UnorderedArrayList();          //Line 2
```

```
IntElement num = new IntElement();                      //Line 3

int counter;                                            //Line 4
int position;                                           //Line 5

StringTokenizer tokenizer;                              //Line 6

System.out.println("Line 7: Processing the "
                   + "integer list");                   //Line 7
System.out.print("Line 8: Enter 8 integers on the "
                 + "same line: ");                      //Line 8
System.out.flush();                                     //Line 9

tokenizer = new
        StringTokenizer(keyboard.readLine());           //Line 10

for(counter = 0; counter < 8; counter++)                //Line 11
{
   num.setNum(
      Integer.parseInt(tokenizer.nextToken()));         //Line 12
   intList.insert(num);                                 //Line 13
}

temp.copyList(intList);                                 //Line 14

System.out.println();                                   //Line 15
System.out.print("Line 16: The list you "
                 + "entered is: ");                     //Line 16
intList.print();                                        //Line 17
System.out.println();                                   //Line 18

System.out.print("Line 19: Enter the num to "
                 + "be deleted: ");                      //Line 19
System.out.flush();                                     //Line 20
num.setNum(Integer.parseInt(keyboard.readLine()));      //Line 21
System.out.println();                                   //Line 22

intList.remove(num);                                    //Line 23
System.out.println("Line 24: After removing "
                   + num
                   + " the list is:");                  //Line 24
intList.print();                                        //Line 25
System.out.println();                                   //Line 26

System.out.print("Line 27: Enter the position of "
                 + "the num to be deleted: ");           //Line 27
System.out.flush();                                     //Line 28
position = Integer.parseInt(keyboard.readLine());       //Line 29
System.out.println();                                   //Line 30
```

```
        intList.removeAt(position);                        //Line 31
        System.out.println("Line 32: After removing the "
                       + "element at position "
                       + position
                       + ", intList:");                     //Line 32

        intList.print();                                    //Line 33
        System.out.println();                               //Line 34

        System.out.print("Line 35: Enter the search "
                       + "item: ");                          //Line 35
        System.out.flush();                                 //Line 36

        num.setNum(Integer.parseInt(keyboard.readLine())); //Line 37
        System.out.println();                               //Line 38

        if(intList.seqSearch(num) != -1)                    //Line 39
           System.out.println("Line 40: Item found in "
                         + "the list");                      //Line 40
        else                                                //Line 41
           System.out.println("Line 42: Item not found");  //Line 42

        System.out.print("List 43: The list temp: ");      //Line 43
        temp.print();                                       //Line 44
        System.out.println();                               //Line 45
    }
}
```

Sample Run: In this sample run, the user input is shaded.

```
Line 7: Processing the integer list
Line 8: Enter 8 integers on the same line: 23 54 32 78 27 87 45 66

Line 16: The list you entered is: 23 54 32 78 27 87 45 66

Line 19: Enter the num to be deleted: 32

Line 24: After removing 32 the list is:
23 54 78 27 87 45 66

Line 27: Enter the position of the num to be deleted: 2

Line 32: After removing the element at position 2, intList:
23 54 27 87 45 66

Line 35: Enter the search item: 23

Line 40: Item found in the list
List 43: The list temp: 23 54 32 78 27 87 45 66
```

The preceding program works as follows. The statement in Line 1 declares `intList` to be an object of the type `UnorderedArrayList`. The data member `list` of `intList` is an array of 50 components. The statement in Line 2 declares `temp` to be an object of the type `UnorderedArrayList`. The statement in Line 3 declares and instantiates the object `num` of the type `IntElement`. The statements in Lines 4 and 5 declare the `int` variables `counter` and `position`. The statement in Line 6 declares `tokenizer` to be a reference variable of the type `StringTokenizer`. The statement in Line 8 prompts the user to enter 8 integers in the same line. The statement in Line 10 reads the line containing the 8 integers and tokenizes it by creating the object `tokenizer`. The statement in Lines 11 through 13 retrieves the numbers from the `tokenizer` (one at a time), stores them in the object `num` (Line 12), and inserts a copy of the object into `intList` (Line 13).

The statement in Line 14 copies `intList` into `temp`. The statement in Line 17 uses the method `print` of `intList` to output the elements of `intList` (see the Sample Run, Line marked 16). The statement in Line 19 prompts the user to enter the number to be deleted from `intList`; the statement in Line 21 reads and stores the number into the object `num`. The statement in Line 23 uses the member method `remove` of `intList` to remove the number from `intList`.

The statements in Lines 24–26 output the number that was deleted and `intList` after deleting this number.

The statement in Line 27 prompts the user to enter the position, in `intList`, of the item to be deleted. The statement in Line 29 stores the position of the item to be deleted into the variable `position`. The statement in Line 31 removes the desired item from `intList`. The statements in Lines 32 and 33 output the position of the item that was deleted and `intList` after deleting the item. The statements in Lines 35–42 prompt the user to enter the item to be searched and then output the results of the search. The statement in Line 44 outputs the list `temp`. Notice that the list `temp` is created by making a copy of `intList` at Line 14. Because no changes were made to `temp`, the elements in `temp` are the same as the elements in the original `intList` (see the output of the statements of Lines 16 and 43).

Notice that the method `main` in Example 3-1 throws the `IOException`. This is because the method `main` uses the method `readLine` to input data, the method `readLine` throws the `IOException` (which is a checked exception), and the method `main` does not provide the code to handle this exception.

Example 3-2

The program in this example is similar to the program in Example 3-1; here, we work with a string list.

```
//Test Program String Array List

import java.io.*;
import java.util.*;

public class Example3_2
{
    static BufferedReader keyboard = new
            BufferedReader(new InputStreamReader(System.in));

    public static void main(String[] args) throws IOException
    {
        UnorderedArrayList stringList =
                            new UnorderedArrayList(50); //Line 1
        UnorderedArrayList tempList =
                            new UnorderedArrayList();   //Line 2

        StringElement strObject = new StringElement();  //Line 3
        int counter;                                    //Line 4
        int position;                                   //Line 5

        StringTokenizer tokenizer;                      //Line 6

        System.out.println("Line 7: Processing the "
                        + "string list");               //Line 7
        System.out.print("Line 8: Enter 5 strings on "
                        + "the same line: ");           //Line 8
        System.out.flush();                             //Line 9

        tokenizer = new
                StringTokenizer(keyboard.readLine());   //Line 10

        for(counter = 0; counter < 5; counter++)        //Line 11
        {
            strObject.setString(tokenizer.nextToken()); //Line 12
            stringList.insert(strObject);               //Line 13
        }

        tempList.copyList(stringList);                  //Line 14

        System.out.println();                           //Line 15
        System.out.print("Line 16: The list you "
                        + "entered is: ");              //Line 16
        stringList.print();                             //Line 17
        System.out.println();                           //Line 18
```

```
        System.out.print("Line 19: Enter the item to "
                    + "be deleted: ");              //Line 19
        System.out.flush();                          //Line 20
        strObject.setString(keyboard.readLine());    //Line 21
        System.out.println();                        //Line 22

        stringList.remove(strObject);                //Line 23
        System.out.println("Line 24: After removing "
                    + strObject
                    + " the list is:");              //Line 24

        stringList.print();                          //Line 25
        System.out.println();                        //Line 26

        System.out.print("Line 27: Enter the position of "
                    + "the string to be deleted: ");  //Line 27
        System.out.flush();                          //Line 28
        position = Integer.parseInt(keyboard.readLine()); //Line 29
        System.out.println();                        //Line 30

        stringList.removeAt(position);               //Line 31
        System.out.println("Line 32: After removing the "
                    + "element at position "
                    + position
                    + ", stringList:");              //Line 32

        stringList.print();                          //Line 33
        System.out.println();                        //Line 34

        System.out.print("Line 35: Enter the search "
                    + "item: ");                     //Line 35
        System.out.flush();                          //Line 36

        strObject.setString(keyboard.readLine());    //Line 37
        System.out.println();                        //Line 38

        if(stringList.seqSearch(strObject) != -1)    //Line 39
            System.out.println("Line 40: Item found in "
                        + "the list");               //Line 40
        else                                         //Line 41
            System.out.println("Line 42: Item not found"); //Line 42

        System.out.print("List 43: tempList: ");     //Line 43
        tempList.print();                            //Line 44
        System.out.println();                        //Line 45
    }
}
```

Sample Run:

```
Line 7: Processing the string list
```

Line 8: Enter 5 strings on the same line: Hello Winter Spring Summer Fall

Line 16: The list you entered is: Hello Winter Spring Summer Fall

Line 19: Enter the item to be deleted: Hello

Line 24: After removing Hello the list is:
Winter Spring Summer Fall

Line 27: Enter the position of the string to be deleted: 3

Line 32: After removing the element at position 3, stringList:
Winter Spring Summer

Line 35: Enter the search item: Spring

Line 40: Item found in the list
List 43: tempList: Hello Winter Spring Summer Fall

The preceding program works the same way as the program in Example 3-1. The details are left as an exercise for you.

class Vector

In the preceding sections, we designed and implemented the classes `ArrayListClass` and `UnorderedArrayList` to manipulate data in an array. One of the limitations of these classes is that once you create, say, an `ArrayListClass` object, the size of the array used to manage objects remains fixed. Therefore, only a fixed number of objects can be maintained in an `ArrayListClass` object and in an `UnorderedArrayList` object. Java also provides the class `Vector`. Unlike an array, the size of a `Vector` object can grow and shrink during program execution. Therefore, you do not need to be concerned with the number of data elements. Before describing how a `Vector` object is used to manage a list, Table 3-2 describes some the members of the class `Vector`.

Table 3-2 Various Members of the class `Vector`

Instance Variables
`protected int elementCount;` `protected Object[] elementData; //array of references`
Constructors
`public Vector()` `//Creates an empty vector of the default length 10.`
`public Vector(int size)` `//Creates an empty vector of the length specified by size.`

Table 3-2 Various Members of the `class Vector` (continued)

Methods
`public void addElement(Object insertObj)` `//Add the object insertObj at the end.`

`public void insertElementAt(Object insertObj, int index)`
`//Insert the object insertObj at the position specified by index.`
`//If index is out of range, this method throws`
`//ArrayIndexOutOfBoundsException.`

`public Object clone()` `//Returns a copy of the vector.`

`public boolean contains(Object obj)`
`//Returns true if the Vector object contains the object specified`
`//by obj; otherwise, it returns false.`

`public void copyInto(Object[] dest)` `//Copies the elements of this vector into the array dest.`

`public Object elementAt(int index)`
`//Returns the element of the vector at the location specified by`
`//index.`

`public Object firstElement()`
`//Returns the first element of the vector.`
`//If the vector is empty, the method throws NoSuchElementException.`

`public Object lastElement()`
`//Returns the last element of the vector.`
`//If the vector is empty, the method throws NoSuchElementException.`

`public int indexOf(Object obj)`
`//Returns the position of the first occurrence of the element`
`//specified by obj in the vector.`
`//If obj is not in the vector, the method returns -1.`

`public int indexOf(Object obj, int index)`
`//Starting at index, the method returns the position of the`
`//first occurrence of the element specified by obj in the vector.`
`//If obj is not in the vector, the method returns -1.`

`public boolean isEmpty()` `//Returns true if the vector is empty; otherwise, it returns false`

`public int lastIndexOf(Object obj)`
`//Starting at the last element, using a backward search, this`
`//method returns the position of the first occurrence from the`
`//end, which is the last element of the list, of the element`
`//specified by obj in the vector.`
`//If obj is not in the vector, the method returns -1.`

3

Table 3-2 Various Members of the `class Vector` (continued)

Methods

`public int lastIndexOf(Object item, int index)`
`//Starting at the position specified by index and using a`
`//backward search, this method returns the position of`
`//the first occurrence from the end, which is the last element`
`//of the list, of the element specified obj in the vector.`
`//If item is not in the vector, the method returns -1.`

`public void removeAllElements()` `//Remove all the elements of the vector.`

`public boolean removeElement(Object obj)`
`//If an element specified by obj exists in the vector, the element`
`//is removed and the value true is returned; otherwise the value`
`//false is returned.`

`public void removeElementAt(int index)`
`//If an element at the position specified by index exists, it is`
`//removed from the vector.`
`//If index is out of range, this method throws`
`//ArrayIndexOutOfBoundsException.`

`public void setElementAt(Object obj, int index)`
`//The element specified by obj is stored at the position specified by`
`//index.`
`//If index is out of range, this method throws`
`//ArrayIndexOutOfBoundsException.`

`public int size()` `//Returns the number of elements in the vector.`
`public String toString()` `//Returns a string representation of this vector.`

From Table 3-2, it follows that every element of a `Vector` object is a reference variable of the type `Object`. Because the `class Object`, directly or indirectly, is a superclass of every Java class, a reference variable of the `Object` type can store the address of any object. Because every component of a `Vector` object is a reference, to add an element into a `Vector` object, you first must create the appropriate object and store the data into that object. You can then store the address of the object holding the data into a `Vector` object element. Because every string in Java is considered a `String` object, we illustrate some of the operations on a `Vector` object using string data.

Consider the following statement:

```
Vector stringList = new Vector();    //Line 1
```

This statement declares `stringList` to be a reference variable of the `Vector` type, instantiates an empty `Vector` object, and stores the address of the object into `stringList`. Next, consider the following statements:

```
stringList.addElement("Spring");
```

```
stringList.addElement("Summer");
stringList.addElement("Fall");
stringList.addElement("Winter");
```

After these statements execute, **stringList** is as shown in Figure 3-9.

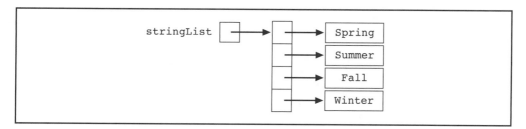

Figure 3-9   **stringList** after adding four strings

The statement:

```
System.out.println(stringList);
```

outputs the elements of **stringList** in the following form:

```
[Spring, Summer, Fall, Winter]
```

Now consider the following statement:

```
stringList.addElement("Cool", 1);
```

This statement adds the string **"Cool"**, at position 1, as shown in Figure 3-10.

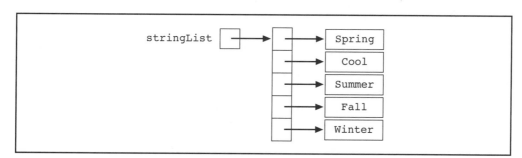

Figure 3-10   **stringList** after adding a string at position 1

The output of the statement:

```
System.out.println(stringList);
```

is:

```
[Spring, Cool, Summer, Fall, Winter]
```

The **class Vector** is contained in the package **java.util.** Therefore, to use the **class Vector,** your program must include either the statement:

```
import java.util.*;
```

or the statement:

```
import java.util.Vector;
```

The program in Example 3-3 further illustrates how a **Vector** object works.

Example 3-3

```
//StringVectorExample

import java.io.*;
import java.util.Vector;

public class StringVectorExample
{
    public static void main(String[] args)
    {
        Vector stringList = new Vector();                      //Line 1

        System.out.println("Line 2: Empty stringList?: "
                    + stringList.isEmpty());                   //Line 2
        System.out.println("Line 3: Size of stringList?: "
                    + stringList.size());                      //Line 3
        System.out.println();                                  //Line 4

        stringList.addElement("Spring");                       //Line 5
        stringList.addElement("Summer");                       //Line 6
        stringList.addElement("Fall");                         //Line 7
        stringList.addElement("Winter");                       //Line 8
        stringList.addElement("Sunny");                        //Line 9

        System.out.println("Line 10: **** After adding "
                    + "elements to stringList ****");  //Line 10
        System.out.println("Line 11: Empty stringList?: "
                    + stringList.isEmpty());                   //Line 11
        System.out.println("Line 12: Size of stringList?: "
                    + stringList.size());                      //Line 12
        System.out.println("Line 13: stringList: "
                    + stringList);                             //Line 13

        System.out.println("Line 14: stringList contains Fall?: "
                    + stringList.contains("Fall"));    //Line 14
        System.out.println();                                  //Line 15
```

```
        stringList.insertElementAt("Cool", 1);               //Line 16
        System.out.println("Line 17: **** After adding an "
                        + "element at position 1 ****");   //Line 17
        System.out.println("Line 18: stringList: "
                        + stringList);                     //Line 18

        System.out.println();                              //Line 19

        stringList.removeElement("Fall");                  //Line 20
        stringList.removeElementAt(2);                     //Line 21
        System.out.println("Line 22: **** After the remove "
                        + "operations ****");              //Line 22
        System.out.println("Line 23: stringList: "
                        + stringList);                     //Line 23
        System.out.println("Line 24: Size of stringList?: "
                        + stringList.size());              //Line 24
        System.out.println("Line 25: indexOf(\"Sunny\"): "
                        + stringList.indexOf("Sunny"));    //Line 25
    }
}
```

Sample Run:

```
Line 2: Empty stringList?: true
Line 3: Size of stringList?: 0

Line 10: **** After adding elements to stringList ****
Line 11: Empty stringList?: false
Line 12: Size of stringList?: 5
Line 13: stringList: [Spring, Summer, Fall, Winter, Sunny]
Line 14: stringList contains Fall?: true

Line 17: **** After adding an element at position 1 ****
Line 18: stringList: [Spring, Cool, Summer, Fall, Winter, Sunny]

Line 22: **** After the remove operations ****
Line 23: stringList: [Spring, Cool, Winter, Sunny]
Line 24: Size of stringList?: 4
Line 25: indexOf("Sunny"): 3
```

In this example, we restrict a **Vector** object to manage elements of the same type. In the program in Example 3-3, the object **stringList** manages strings. As stated earlier, every element of a **Vector** object is a reference that can point to any object, and the same **Vector** object can be used to manage various types of objects. For example, see Exercise 5 at the end of this chapter.

Primitive Data Types and the `class Vector`

As described in the preceding section, every component of a **Vector** object is a reference. Therefore, values of primitive data types cannot be directly assigned to a **Vector** element. You must first wrap the primitive data type element into an appropriate wrapper class such as the **class Integer** for **int** values. You can also use the **class IntElement** to wrap **int** values.

Suppose that you have the declaration

```
Vector list = new Vector();
```

The following statements create **Integer** objects with **int** values of **13** and **25**, and the **Integer** objects are assigned to **list**:

```
list.addElement(new Integer(13));
list.addElement(new Integer(25));
```

PROGRAMMING EXAMPLE: POLYNOMIAL OPERATIONS

You learned in a college algebra or a calculus course that a polynomial $p(x)$, in one variable, x, is an expression of the form:

$$p(x) = a_0 + a_1x + \ldots + a_{n-1}x^{n-1} + a_nx^n,$$

where a_i are real (or complex) numbers and n is a nonnegative integer. If $p(x) = a_0$, then $p(x)$ is called a **constant** polynomial. If $p(x)$ is a nonzero constant polynomial, then the degree of $p(x)$ is defined to be 0. Even though in mathematics the degree of the zero polynomial is undefined, for the purpose of this program, we consider the degree of such polynomials to be zero. If $p(x)$ is not constant and $a_n \neq 0$, then n is called the degree of $p(x)$; that is, the degree of a nonconstant polynomial is defined to be the exponent of the highest power of x.

Some of the operations performed on polynomials are add, subtract, and multiply polynomials, and evaluate a polynomial at a given point. For example, suppose that:

$$p(x) = 1 + 2x + 3x^2$$

and:

$$q(x) = 4 + x$$

The degree of $p(x)$ is 2 and the degree of $q(x)$ is 1. Moreover,

$$p(2) = 1 + 2 \cdot 2 + 3 \cdot 2^2 = 17$$

$$p(x) + q(x) = 5 + 3x + 3x^2$$

$$p(x) - q(x) = -3 + x + 3x^2$$

$$p(x) * q(x) = 4 + 9x + 14x^2 + 3x^3$$

The purpose of this programming example is to design and implement the **class Polynomial** to perform various polynomial operations in a program.

To be specific, in this program, we implement the following operations on polynomials:

1. Evaluate a polynomial at a given value.
2. Add polynomials.
3. Subtract polynomials.
4. Multiply polynomials.

Moreover, we assume that the coefficients of polynomials are real numbers. You will be asked in Programming Exercise 7b to generalize it so that coefficients can also be complex numbers.

To store a polynomial, we use a dynamic array of objects as follows. Suppose $p(x)$ is a polynomial of degree $n \geq 0$. Let **list** be an array of objects of size $n + 1$. Then **list[i]** refers to the coefficient a_i of x^i. See Figure 3-11.

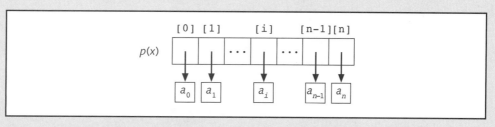

Figure 3-11   Polynomial $p(x)$

From Figure 3-11 it is clear that if $p(x)$ is a polynomial of degree n, then we need an array of size $n + 1$ to store the coefficients of $p(x)$. Suppose that:

$$p(x) = 1 + 8x - 3x^2 + 5x^4 + 7x^8$$

Then the array storing the coefficient of $p(x)$ is given in Figure 3-12.

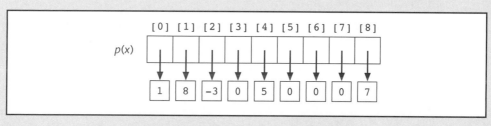

Figure 3-12   Polynomial $p(x)$ of degree 8 and its coefficients

Similarly, if:

$$q(x) = -5x^2 + 16x^5$$

then the array storing the coefficient of $q(x)$ is given in Figure 3-13.

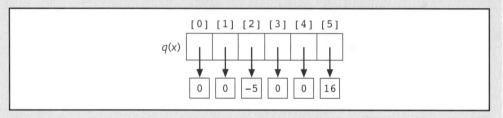

Figure 3-13 Polynomial $q(x)$ of degree 5 and its coefficients

Next, we define the operations $+$, $-$, and $*$. Suppose that:

$$p(x) = a_0 + a_1x + \ldots + a_{n-1}x^{n-1} + a_nx^n$$

and

$$q(x) = b_0 + b_1x + \ldots + b_{m-1}x^{m-1} + a_mx^m$$

Let $t = max(n, m)$. Then

$$p(x) + q(x) = c_0 + c_1x + \ldots + c_{t-1}x^{t-1} + c_tx^t$$

where for $i = 0, 1, 2, \ldots, t$

$$c_i = \begin{cases} a_i + b_i & \text{if } i \le min(n,m) \\ a_i & \text{if } i > m \\ b_i & \text{if } i > n \end{cases}$$

The difference, $p(x) - q(x)$, of $p(x)$ and $q(x)$ can be defined similarly. It follows that the degrees of the polynomials $p(x) + q(x)$ and $p(x) - q(x)$ are less than or equal to $min(n,m)$.

The product, $p(x) * q(x)$, of $p(x)$ and $q(x)$ is defined as follows:

$$p(x) * q(x) = d_0 + d_1x + \ldots + d_{n+m}x^{n+m}$$

The coefficient d_k, for $k = 0, 1, 2, \ldots, n+m$, is given by the formula:

$$d_k = a_0 * b_k + a_1 * b_{k-1} + \ldots + a_k * b_0$$

where if either a_i or b_i does not exist, it is assumed to be zero. For example:

$$d_0 = a_0b_0$$
$$d_1 = a_0b_1 + a_1b_0$$

$$\ldots$$

$$d_{n+m} = a_nb_m$$

Because the coefficients of a polynomial are managed by an array of objects, we use the class `UnorderedArrayList` to store and manipulate the coefficients of a polynomial. We, in fact, derive the class `Polynomial` to implement polynomial operations from the class `UnorderedArrayList`, which requires us to implement only the operations needed to manipulate polynomials.

The following defines polynomials as an ADT:

```
public class Polynomial extends UnorderedArrayList
```

Instance Methods and Constructors:

```
public Polynomial()
   //default constructor
   //Postcondition: An array of the size 100, and
   //               length and maxSize are set to 100

public Polynomial(int size)
   //constructor with parameter
   //Postcondition: An array of the size specified by
   //     the parameter size is created, length and maxSize
   //     are initialized to size.

public Polynomial(Polynomial right)
   //copy constructor

public void copy(Polynomial right)
   //Method to copy the coefficients of the polynomial
   //specified by the parameter right.
   //Postcondition: The coefficients of the polynomial
   //               specified by right are copied.

public double evaluate(double x)
   //Method to evaluate a polynomial at a given value.
   //Postcondition: The polynomial is evaluated at x and
   //               the value is returned.

public Polynomial add(Polynomial right)
   //Method to add two polynomials.
   //Postcondition: This polynomial is added to the polynomial
   //               specified by the parameter right. A reference
   //               of the result is returned.

public Polynomial subtract(Polynomial right)
   //Method to subtract two polynomials.
   //Postcondition: The polynomial specified by the
   //               parameter right is subtracted from this
   //               polynomial. A reference of the result is
   //               returned.
```

```
public Polynomial multiply(Polynomial right)
   //Method to multiply two polynomials.
   //Postcondition: This polynomial is multiplied with the
   //               polynomial specified by the parameter right. A
   //               reference of the result is returned.

public int min(int x, int y)
   //Method to determine the smaller of x and y.
   //Postcondition: The smaller of x and y is returned.

public int max(int x, int y)
   //Method to determine the larger of x and y.
   //Postcondition: The larger of x and y is returned.

public void read() throws IOException
   //Method to read the coefficients of a polynomial.

public String toString()
   //Method to return the string containing the polynomial.
```

In Exercise 10 (at the end of the chapter), you are asked to draw the UML diagram of the **class Polynomial**.

If $p(x)$ is a polynomial of degree 3, we create an object, say p, of the type **Polynomial** and set the size of the array **list** to be 4. The following statement declares such an object p:

```
Polynomial p = new Polynomial(4);
```

The degree of the polynomial is stored in the data member **length**, which is inherited from the **class ArrayListClass**.

Next, we discuss the definitions of the methods.

The definitions of the default constructor, constructor with parameter, and the copy constructor are straightforward and are given next.

```
    //default constructor
public Polynomial()
{
    super();
    length = 100;
}


    //constructor with parameter
public Polynomial(int size)
{
    super(size);
    length = size;
}
```

```
    //copy constructor
public Polynomial(Polynomial right)
{
    super(right);
}
```

Next, we consider the definition of the method **evaluate**. Suppose that you have the polynomial *p* as shown in Figure 3-14.

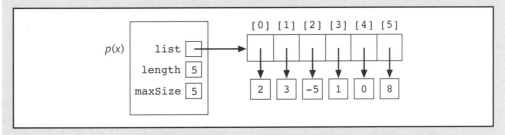

Figure 3-14   Polynomial *p*(*x*)

Suppose that we want to evaluate *p*(4). Clearly:

$$p(4) = 2 + 3 * 4 - 5 * 4^2 + 1 * 4^3 + 0 * 4^4 + 8 * 4^5$$

Clearly, we must retrieve the coefficients of the polynomial, multiply each coefficient with an appropriate power of 4, and add the numbers. Now each element **list[i]** is a reference to the object containing a coefficient. Moreover, **list[i]** is an object of the type **DataElement**, the object containing the coefficient is of the type **DoubleElement**, and the **class DoubleElement** is a subclass of the **class DataElement**. Suppose that we want to retrieve the coefficient of *x*. To retrieve the coefficient of *x* we use **list[1]**. In order to retrieve this coefficient, we declare the object **coeff** of the type **DoubleElement**, make a copy of the object **list[1]** into **coeff**, and then use the method **getNum** of the **class DoubleElement** to retrieve the coefficient. The following statements illustrate this:

```
DoubleElement coeff = new DoubleElement();

coeff.makeCopy((DoubleElement) list[1]); //get a copy of list[1]

coeff.getNum() //this expression returns the coefficient
```

The last two statements are repeated for each list element. You can write the definitions of the method **evaluate** as follows:

```
public double evaluate(double x)
{
    double value = 0.0;
```

```
DoubleElement coeff = new DoubleElement();

for(int i = 0; i < length; i++)
{
    coeff.makeCopy((DoubleElement) list[i]);

    if(coeff.getNum() != 0.0)
        value = value + coeff.getNum() * Math.pow(x,i);
}

    return value;
}
```

Suppose $p(x)$ is a polynomial of degree n and $q(x)$ is a polynomial of degree m. If $n = m$, then the method **add** adds the corresponding coefficients of $p(x)$ and $q(x)$. If $n > m$, then the first m coefficients of $p(x)$ are added to the corresponding coefficients of $q(x)$. The remaining coefficients of $p(x)$ are copied into the polynomial containing the sum of $p(x)$ and $q(x)$. Similarly, if $n < m$, the first n coefficients of $q(x)$ are added to the corresponding coefficients of $p(x)$. The remaining coefficients of $q(x)$ are copied into the polynomial containing the sum. Consider the polynomials $p(x)$ and $q(x)$ as given in Figures 3-15 and 3-16.

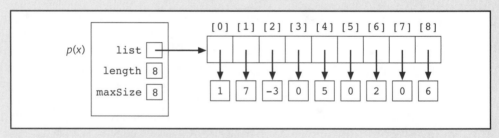

Figure 3-15   Polynomial $p(x)$

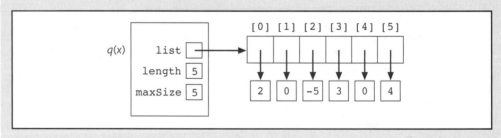

Figure 3-16   Polynomial $q(x)$

Suppose that the coefficients of $p(x) + q(x)$ will be stored in the polynomial *temp*. Then:

$deg(temp) = max(deg(p(x)), deg(q(x)))$

To add the corresponding coefficients of $p(x)$ and $q(x)$, we simultaneously retrieve the corresponding coefficients of $p(x)$ and $q(x)$ using techniques similar to those used in evaluating a polynomial. We declare two objects `coeffP` and `coeffQ` of the type `DoubleElement`. Suppose that we want to retrieve the coefficients of x^2. Consider the following statements:

```
DoubleElement coeffP = new DoubleElement();     //Line 1
DoubleElement coeffQ = new DoubleElement();     //Line 2
DoubleElement z;                                //Line 3

coeffP.makeCopy((DoubleElement) p.list[2]);     //Line 4
coeffQ.makeCopy((DoubleElement) q.list[2]);     //Line 5

sumCoeff = coeffP.getNum() + coeffQ.getNum();   //Line 6
z = new DoubleElement(sumCoeff);                //Line 7
temp.list[2] = z;                               //Line 8
```

The statements in Lines 1 and 2 create the `DoubleElement` objects `coeffP` and `coeffQ`. The statement in Line 3 declares `z` to be a reference variable of the type `DoubleElement`. The statement in Line 4 copies the coefficient of x^2 of $p(x)$ into the object `coeffP`. Similarly, the statement in Line 5 copies the coefficient of x^2 of $q(x)$ into the object `coeffQ`. The statement in Line 6 retrieves and then adds the coefficients of x^2, and stores the sum into `sumCoeff`. The statement in Line 7 instantiates the object z and stores the sum of the coefficient into z. The statement in Line 8 inserts the object z into the polynomial `temp`. We repeat this process for each corresponding coefficient of $p(x)$ and $q(x)$.

We can now write the definition of the method **add** as follows:

```
public Polynomial add(Polynomial right)
{
    int size = max(length, right.length);
    int i;
    double sumCoeff;

    DoubleElement coeffP = new DoubleElement();
    DoubleElement coeffQ = new DoubleElement();

    DoubleElement z;

    Polynomial temp = new Polynomial(size);

    for(i = 0; i < min(length, right.length); i++)
    {
        coeffP.makeCopy((DoubleElement) list[i]);
        coeffQ.makeCopy((DoubleElement) right.list[i]);
```

```
            sumCoeff = coeffP.getNum() + coeffQ.getNum();
            z = new DoubleElement(sumCoeff);
            temp.list[i] = z;
        }

        if(size == length)
            for(i = min(length, right.length); i < length; i++)
                temp.list[i] = list[i].getCopy();
        else
            for(i = min(length, right.length); i < right.length; i++)
                temp.list[i] = right.list[i].getCopy();

        return temp;
    }
```

The definition of the method **subtract** is similar to the definition of the method **add** and is given next.

```
public Polynomial subtract(Polynomial right)
{
    int size = max(length, right.length);
    int i;
    double diffCoeff;
    double coeff;

    DoubleElement coeffP = new DoubleElement();
    DoubleElement coeffQ = new DoubleElement();

    DoubleElement z;

    Polynomial temp = new Polynomial(size);

    for(i = 0; i < min(length, right.length); i++)
    {
        coeffP.makeCopy((DoubleElement) list[i]);
        coeffQ.makeCopy((DoubleElement) right.list[i]);

        diffCoeff = coeffP.getNum() - coeffQ.getNum();
        z = new DoubleElement(diffCoeff);
        temp.list[i] = z;
    }

    if(size == length)
        for(i = min(length, right.length); i < length; i++)
            temp.list[i] = list[i].getCopy();
    else
        for(i = min(length, right.length); i < right.length; i++)
        {
            z = new DoubleElement();
```

```
            z.makeCopy((DoubleElement) right.list[i]);
            coeff = z.getNum();
            z.setNum(-coeff);
            temp.list[i] = z;
        }

    return temp;
}
```

The definition of the method `multiply` to multiply two polynomials is left as an exercise for you. See Programming Exercise 5 at the end of this chapter. The definitions of the remaining methods of the `class Polynomial` are:

```
public int min(int x, int y)
{
    if(x <= y)
        return x;
    else
        return y;
}

public int max(int x, int y)
{
    if(x >= y)
        return x;
    else
        return y;
}

public void read() throws IOException
{
    BufferedReader keyboard = new
        BufferedReader(new InputStreamReader(System.in));

    DoubleElement x = new DoubleElement();

    System.out.println("The degree of this polynomial is: "
                    + (length - 1));
    for(int i = 0; i < length; i++)
    {
        System.out.print("Enter the coefficient of x^"
                        + i + ": ");
        System.out.flush();

        x.setNum(Double.parseDouble(keyboard.readLine()));

        list[i] = x.getCopy();
    }
}
```

```java
public String toString()
{
    int i;
    int firstNonzeroCoeff = 0;
    DoubleElement x = new DoubleElement();
    String str = "";

    for(i = 0; i < length; i++)
    {
        x.makeCopy((DoubleElement) list[i]);

        if(x.getNum() != 0.0)
        {
            firstNonzeroCoeff = i;
            break;
        }
    }

    if(firstNonzeroCoeff < length)
    {
        if(firstNonzeroCoeff == 0)
            str = list[firstNonzeroCoeff] + " ";
        else
            str = list[firstNonzeroCoeff] + "x^"
                    + firstNonzeroCoeff + " ";

        for(i = firstNonzeroCoeff + 1; i < length; i++)
        {
            x.makeCopy((DoubleElement) list[i]);

            if(x.getNum() != 0.0)
                if(x.getNum() > 0.0)
                    str += "+ " + x.getNum() + "x^" + i + " ";
                else
                    str += "- " + -x.getNum() + "x^" + i + " ";
        }
    }

    return str;
}
```

You can write the definition of the **class Polynomial** as follows:

```java
import java.io.*;

public class Polynomial extends UnorderedArrayList
{
    //Place the definitions of the instance methods here.
}
```

The following program tests various polynomial operations:

```java
//Test program: Polynomial Operations

import java.io.*;

public class ProgPolynomial
{
    public static void main(String[] args) throws IOException
    {
        Polynomial p = new Polynomial(4);                      //Line 1
        Polynomial q = new Polynomial(8);                      //Line 2

        p.read();                                              //Line 3
        System.out.println();                                  //Line 4
        System.out.println("Line 5: p(x): " + p);              //Line 5
        System.out.println("Line 6: p.evaluate(2): "
                        + p.evaluate(2));                      //Line 6
        System.out.println();                                  //Line 7

        q.read();                                              //Line 8
        System.out.println("Line 9: q(x): " + q);              //Line 9

        System.out.println("Line 10: p(x) + q(x): "
                        + p.add(q));                           //Line 10

        System.out.println("Line 11: p(x) - q(x): "
                        + p.subtract(q));                      //Line 11
    }
}
```

Sample Run: In this sample run, the user input is shaded.

```
The degree of this polynomial is: 3
Enter the coefficient of x^0: 1
Enter the coefficient of x^1: 2
Enter the coefficient of x^2: 0
Enter the coefficient of x^3: 3

Line 5: p(x): 1.0 + 2.0x^1 + 3.0x^3
Line 6: p.evaluate(2): 29.0

The degree of this polynomial is: 7
Enter the coefficient of x^0: 0
Enter the coefficient of x^1: 1
Enter the coefficient of x^2: 4
Enter the coefficient of x^3: 0
Enter the coefficient of x^4: 0
Enter the coefficient of x^5: 0
```

```
Enter the coefficient of x^6: 0
Enter the coefficient of x^7: 6
Line 9: q(x): 1.0x^1 + 4.0x^2 + 6.0x^7
Line 10: p(x) + q(x): 1.0 + 3.0x^1 + 4.0x^2 + 3.0x^3 + 6.0x^7
Line 11: p(x) - q(x): 1.0 + 1.0x^1 - 4.0x^2 + 3.0x^3 - 6.0x^7
```

QUICK REVIEW

1. A list is a collection of elements of the same type.

2. The commonly performed operations on a list are create the list, determine whether the list is empty, determine whether the list is full, find the size of the list, destroy or clear the list, determine whether an item is the same as a given list element, insert an item in the list at the specified location, remove an item from the list at the specified location, replace an item at the specified location with another item, retrieve an item from the list from the specified location, and search the list for a given item.

3. The **class Object** directly or indirectly becomes a superclass of every Java class, user defined or built in.

4. A reference variable of **Object** type can refer to any object of any class.

5. The **class DataElement**, designed in this chapter, is the superclass of every class specifying the data type of the list elements.

6. The **class DataElement** contains only four abstract methods—**equals**, **compareTo**, **makeCopy**, and **getCopy**.

7. The **class IntElement** is used when a list of integers is manipulated.

8. The **class DoubleElement** is used when a list of decimal numbers is manipulated.

9. The **class StringElement**, designed in this chapter, is used when a list of strings is manipulated.

10. The **class ArrayListClass** is an **abstract** class. It is the superclass of the classes that implement a list.

11. The three instance variables of the **class ArrayListClass** are **length**, **maxSize**, and **list**. The instance variable **length** specifies the number of elements currently in the list. The instance variable **maxSize** specifies the maximum number of elements that can be processed by the list. The instance variable **list** is an array of reference variables.

12. Review Table 3-1 for the time-complexity of the methods of the **class ArrayListClass**.

13. The **class UnorderedArrayList** is a subclass of the **class ArrayListClass**. The elements of an object of the **class UnorderedArrayList** are not necessarily sorted.

14. In addition to arrays, Java provides the **class Vector** to implement a list.

15. Unlike an array, the size of a **Vector** object can grow and shrink during program execution.

16. Review Table 3-2 for various methods provided by the **class Vector**.

EXERCISES

1. What is the effect of the following statements?

   a. `UnorderedArrayList intList(100);`

   b. `UnorderedArrayList stringList(1000);`

   c. `UnorderedArrayList salesList(-10);`

2. What is the effect of the following statement?

   ```
   Vector list = new Vector();
   ```

3. Suppose that you have the following **Vector** object list:

   ```
   list = ["One", "Two", "Three", "Four"];
   ```

   What are the elements of `list` after the following statements execute?

   ```
   list.addElement("Five");
   list.insertElementAt("Six", 1);
   ```

4. Suppose that you have the following **Vector** object names:

   ```
   names = ["Goofy", "Duckey", "Mickey", "Pluto", "Balto"];
   ```

   What are the elements of `list` after the following statements execute?

   ```
   list.removeElementAt(1);
   list.removeElementAt("Pluto");
   ```

5. What is the output of the following program?

   ```java
   import java.util.Vector;

   public class Exercise5
   {
       public static void main(String[] arg)
       {
           Vector list = new Vector();

           list.addElement("Hello");
           list.addElement(new Integer(10));
           list.addElement("Happy");
           list.addElement(new Integer(20));
           list.addElement("Sunny");
           list.addElement(new Integer(30));

           System.out.println(list);
   ```

```
            list.insertElementAt("Joy", 2);

            list.removeElement(new Integer(20));
            System.out.println(list);
        }
    }
```

6. Suppose that you have the following **Vector** objects:

   ```
   studentLastName = ["Smith", "Shue", "Cox", "Jordan"]
   studentFirstName = ["James", "Sherly", "Chris", "Eliot"]
   ```

   a. Write a Java statement that outputs the first name of the third student.

   b. Write a Java statement that outputs the last name of the second student.

   c. Write a Java statement that outputs the first name followed by the last name separated by a single blank space of the first student.

   d. Write the necessary Java statements so that the first name and last name of **Eliot Jordan** are interchanged.

7. Assume that you have the **Vector** objects of Exercise 6. Write a Java statement that changes the names **James Smith** and **Sherly Shue** to **Sherly Smith** and **James Shue**:

   a. by changing the **Vector** object **studentLastName**

   b. by changing the **Vector** object **studentFirstName**

8. Assume the **Vector** objects of Exercise 6. Write a **for** loop that prints all the students' names.

9. Draw the UML diagram of the **class Polynomial**. Also show the inheritance hierarchy.

PROGRAMMING EXERCISES

1. The method **removeAt** of the **class ArrayListClass** removes an element from the list by shifting the elements of the list. However, if the element to be removed is at the beginning of the list and the list is fairly large, it could take a lot of computer time. Because the list elements are in no particular order, you could simply remove the element by swapping the last element of the list with the item to be removed and reducing the length of the list. Rewrite the definition of the method **removeAt** using this technique. Also, write a program to test the method **removeAt**.

2. The method **remove** of the **class ArrayListClass** removes only the first occurrence of an element. Add the method **removeAll** as an abstract method to the **class ArrayListClass** that would remove all occurrences of a given element. Also, write the definition of the method **removeAll** for the **class UnorderedArrayList** and a program to test this method.

3. Add the method `min` to the **class `ArrayListClass`** to return the smallest element of the list. Also, write the definition of the method `min` and a program to test this method.

4. Add the method `max` to the **class `ArrayListClass`** to return the largest element of the list. Also, write the definition of the method `max` and a program to test this method.

5. Write the definition of the method `multiply` to overload the **class `Polynomial`** to multiply two polynomials. Also, write a test program to test the method `multiply`.

3

6. Let polynomial $p(x) = a_0 + a_1x + ... + a_{n-1}x^{n-1} + a_nx^n$ be a polynomial of degree n, where a_i are real (or complex) numbers and n is a nonnegative integer. The derivative of $p(x)$, written $p'(x)$, is defined to be $p'(x) = a_1 + 2a_2x + na_nx^{n-1}$. If $p(x)$ is constant, then $p'(x) = 0$. Write the definition of the method `derivative` for the **class `Polynomial`** to determine and return the derivative of a polynomial.

7. a. A number of the form $a + ib$, where $i^2 = -1$, and a and b are real numbers, is called a complex number. We call a the real part and b the imaginary part of $a + ib$. Complex numbers can also be represented as ordered pairs (a, b). The addition, subtraction, multiplication, and division of complex numbers is defined by the following rules:

$(a + ib) + (c + id) = (a + c) + i(b + d)$

$(a + ib) - (c + id) = (a - c) + i(b - d)$

$(a + ib) * (c + id) = (ac - bd) + i(ad + bc)$

$(a + ib) / (c + id) = ((ac + bd) / (c^2 + d^2)) + i (-ad + bc) / (c^2 + d^2))$, where $c + id \neq 0$.

Using the ordered pair notation, these rules are written as:

$(a, b) + (c, d) = ((a + c), (b + d))$

$(a, b) - (c, d) = ((a - c), (b - d))$

$(a, b) * (c, d) = ((ac - bd), (ad + bc))$

$(a, b) / (c, d) = ((ac + bd) / (c^2 + d^2), (-ad + bc) / (c^2 + d^2))$, where $(c, d) \neq (0, 0)$.

Design and implement the **class `ComplexElement`** that can be used to manipulate complex numbers. Use two instance variables of the type **double** to store the real and imaginary part of the complex number.

b. The **class `Polynomial`** as given in the Programming Example: Polynomial Operations processes polynomials with coefficients that are real numbers. Redesign this class so that this class can be used to process polynomials with coefficients that are complex numbers.

8. Redo Programming Exercise 6 of Chapter 2 so that the address book is kept in a **Vector** object. Your program should be able to process any number of entries.

9. Design a class to perform the various matrix operations. A matrix is a set of numbers arranged in rows and columns. Therefore, every element of a matrix has a row position and a column position. If A is a matrix of 5 rows and 6 columns, we say that the matrix A is of the size 5×6 and sometimes denote it as $A_{5\times6}$. Clearly, a convenient place to store a matrix is in a two-dimensional array. Two matrices can be added and subtracted if they have the same size. Suppose $A = [a_{ij}]$ and $B = [b_{ij}]$ are two matrices of the size $m \times n$, where a_{ij} denotes the element of A in the ith row and the jth column, and so on. The sum and difference of A and B given by:

$$A + B = [a_{ij} + b_{ij}]$$
$$A - B = [a_{ij} - b_{ij}]$$

The multiplication of A and B, $A * B$, is defined only if the number of columns of A is the same as the number of rows of B. If A is of the size $m \times n$ and B is of the size $n \times t$, then $A * B = [c_{ik}]$ is of the size $m \times t$ and the element c_{ik} is given by the formula:

$$c_{ik} = a_{i1}b_{1k} + a_{i2}b_{2k} + \ldots + a_{in}b_{nk}$$

Design and implement a **class Matrix** that can store a matrix of any size. Among others, provide the methods to perform the addition, subtraction, and multiplication operations, and a method to output a matrix. Also, write a test program to test the various operations on matrices.

4

LINKED LISTS

In this chapter, you will:

♦ Learn about linked lists
♦ Become aware of the basic properties of linked lists
♦ Explore the insertion and deletion operations on linked lists
♦ Discover how to build and manipulate a linked list
♦ Learn how to construct a doubly linked list
♦ Learn about linked lists with header and trailer nodes
♦ Become aware of circular linked lists

You have already seen how data can be organized and processed sequentially using an array, called a *sequential list*. You have performed several operations on sequential lists, such as sorting, inserting, deleting, and searching. You also found that if data is not sorted, then searching for an item in the list can be very time consuming, especially with large lists. Once the data is sorted, you can use another search algorithm, called the binary search (discussed in Chapter 8), and improve the search algorithm. However, if the list is sorted, insertion and deletion become time consuming, especially with large lists, because these operations require data movement since the resulting list must also be sorted. Moreover, because the array size must be fixed during execution, new items can be added only if there is room. Thus, there are limitations when you organize data in an array.

This chapter helps you to overcome some of these problems. Chapter 3 showed how memory can be dynamically allocated and deallocated using reference variables. This chapter uses reference variables to organize and process data in lists, called **linked lists**. Recall that when data is stored in an array, memory for the components of the array is contiguous—that is, blocks are allocated one after the other. On the other hand, as you will see, the dynamically allocated components of a linked list are not necessarily contiguous.

LINKED LISTS

A linked list is a collection of components, called **nodes**. Every node (except the last node) contains the address of the next node. Thus, every node in a linked list has two fields: one to store the relevant information (for example, the data); and one to store the address, called the **link**, of the next node in the list. The address of the first node in the list is stored in a separate location, called the **head** or **first**. Figure 4-1 is a pictorial representation of a node.

Figure 4-1   Structure of a node

In Java, there are two types of variables—variables of the primitive data type and reference variables. Therefore, in Figure 4-1, the `info` of the node can be either a value of a primitive type or a reference to an object.

Linked list: A list of items, called **nodes**, in which the order of the nodes is determined by the address, called the **link**, stored in each node.

The list in Figure 4-2 is an example of a linked list.

Figure 4-2   Linked list

The down arrow in the last node indicates that this link field is `null`. The arrow in each node indicates that the address of the node to which it is pointing is stored in that node. For a better understanding of this notation, suppose that the first node is at memory location `1200`, and the second node is at memory location `1575`. We thus have Figure 4-3.

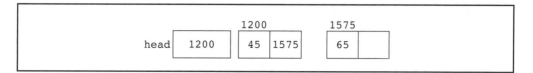

Figure 4-3   Linked list and the values of the links

4

The value of the head is 1200, the data part of the first node is 45, and the link field of the first node contains 1575, the address of the second node. We will use the arrow notation whenever we draw the figure of a linked list.

 In Figures 4-2 and 4-3, for illustration purposes, we assume that the data type of the variable info is int. However, as remarked previously, info can be either a variable of a primitive data type or a reference variable. In fact, after describing in the next few sections the basic properties of linked lists and how to build a linked list, we develop a generic code to process linked lists that can be used in a variety of applications. Moreover, for simplicity and ease of understanding and clarity, Figures 4-3, 4-4, 4-5, and 4-6 use integers as the values of memory addresses. However, in computer memory, the memory addresses are in binary.

Because each node of a linked list has two fields, we need to create a **class**, say, LinkedListNode. The data type of each node depends on the specific application—that is, what kind of data is being processed; however, the link field of each node is a reference variable. In fact, link is a reference variable of the **LinkedListNode** type. For the previous linked list, the definition of the node is as follows (suppose that **info** is of the type **int**):

```
public class LinkedListNode
{
    public int info;
    public LinkedListNode link;
}
```

 Notice that the class LinkedListNode to implement the nodes of a linked list is declared as public. Moreover, notice that instance variables of the class LinkedListNode are declared as public. The instance variables are declared as public for the simple reason that in the next few sections our focus is on the basic properties—such as traversing a linked list, item insertion, and item deletion—of a linked list. To directly access these instance variables, we have declared them public. If we declare them private or protected, then we have to provide methods such as set and get to manipulate the data stored in the node. However, when we study linked lists as abstract data types (ADTs) we will declare the class LinkedListNode as protected. We will also make it an inner class of the class that implements linked lists as an ADT so that the user does not have direct access to the instance variables of the class LinkedListNode. Furthermore, as remarked earlier, for illustration purposes the data type of the instance variable info is int.

The following statement declares `head` to be a reference variable of the `LinkedListNode` type:

```
LinkedListNode head;
```

Some Properties of Linked Lists

To help you better understand the concept of a linked list and a node, some important properties of linked lists are described next.

Consider the linked list in Figure 4-4.

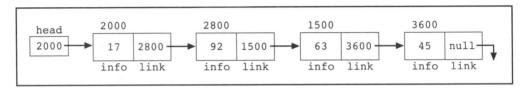

Figure 4-4   Linked list with four nodes

This linked list has four nodes. The address of the first node is stored in `head`. Each node has two fields: `info`, to store the info; and `link`, to store the address of the next node.

Suppose that the first node is at location 2000, the second node is at location 2800, the third node is at location 1500, and the fourth node is at location 3600. Therefore, the value of `head` is 2000, the value of the `link` field of the first node is 2800, the value of the `link` field of the second node is 1500, and so on. Also, `null` in the `link` field of the last node means that the link field of this node does not point to anything, which we indicate by drawing a down arrow. The number at the top of each node is the address of the node.

Table 4-1 shows the values of `head` and some of the nodes of the linked list in Figure 4-4.

Table 4-1   Values of head and Some of the Nodes of the Linked List in Figure 4-4.

	Value	
head	2000	
head.info	17	Because head is 2000 and the info of the node at location 2000 is 17
head.link 2800		
head.link.info	92	Because head.link is 2800 and the info of the node at location 2800 is 92

Suppose that **current** is a reference variable of the same type as **head**. Then the statement

`current = head;`

copies the value of **head** into **current**. See Figure 4-5.

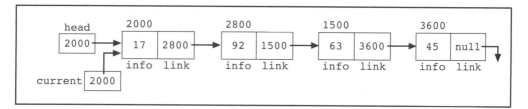

Figure 4-5 Linked list after the statement **current = head;** executes

Table 4-2 shows the values of **current** and some of the nodes of the linked list in Figure 4-5.

Table 4-2 Values of current and Some of the Nodes of the Linked List in Figure 4-5.

	Value
current	2000
current.info	17
current.link	2800
current.link.info	92

Now consider the statement:

`current = current.link;`

This statement copies the value of **current.link**, which is 2800, into **current**. Therefore, after this statement executes, **current** points to the second node in the list. (When working with linked lists, such as when we traverse a linked list, we typically use these types of statements to advance a reference variable to point to the next node in the list.) See Figure 4-6.

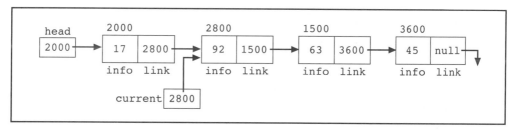

Figure 4-6 Linked list after the statement **current = current.link;** executes

Table 4-3 shows the values of `current` and some of the nodes of the linked list after advancing `current` to the next node.

Table 4-3 Values of current and Some of the Nodes of the Linked List in Figure 4-6.

	Value
`current`	2800
`current.info`	92
`current.link`	1500
`current.link.info`	63

Finally, Table 4-4 shows the values of some other reference variables and nodes of the linked list in Figure 4-6.

Table 4-4 Values of Various Reference Variables and Nodes of the Linked List in Figure 4-6.

	Value
`head.link.link`	1500
`head.link.link.info`	63
`head.link.link.link`	3600
`head.link.link.link.info`	45
`current.link.link`	3600
`current.link.link.info`	45
`current.link.link.link`	null
`current.link.link.link.info`	Does not exist

From now on, when we draw the figure of a linked list, we use only the arrow notation.

Traversing a Linked List

The basic operations of a linked list are:

- Search the list to determine whether a particular item is in the list.

- Insert an item in the list.

- Delete an item from the list.

These operations require the list to be traversed. That is, we must step through the nodes of the list.

Suppose that head points to the first node in the list, and the link of the last node is null. We cannot use the variable head to traverse the list because if we use head to traverse the list we would lose the nodes of the list. This problem occurs because the links go in only one direction. The reference variable head contains the address of the first node, the first node contains the address of the second node, the second node contains the address of the third node, and so on. If we move head to the second node, the first node is lost (unless we save the address of this node). If we keep advancing head to the next node, we will lose all the nodes of the list (unless we save the address of each node before advancing head, which is impractical because it would require additional computer time and memory space to maintain the list).

Therefore, we always want head to point to the first node. It now follows that we must traverse the list using another reference variable of the same type as head. Suppose that current is a reference variable of the same type as head. The following code traverses the list:

```
current = head;
while(current != null)
{
      //Process current
    current = current.link;
}
```

For example, suppose that head points to a linked list of numbers. The following code outputs the data stored in each node:

```
current = head;
while(current != null)
{
    System.out.println(current.info + " ");
    current = current.link;
}
```

ITEM INSERTION AND DELETION

This section discusses how to insert an item in, and delete an item from, a linked list. Consider the following definition of a node. (As before, for simplicity, we assume that the info type is int. The section "Linked List as an ADT" located later in this chapter, which discusses linked lists as an ADT, uses the generic definition of a node.)

```
public class LinkedListNode
{
    public int info;
    public LinkedListNode link;
}
```

We will use the following variable declaration, in which head, p, q, and newNode are reference variables of the LinkedListNode type:

```
LinkedListNode head, p, q, newNode;
```

Insertion

Consider the linked list shown in Figure 4-7.

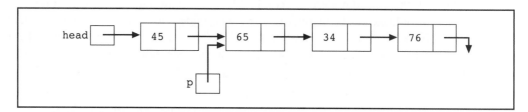

Figure 4-7   Linked list before item insertion

Suppose that **p** points to the node with **info 65**, and a new node with **info 50** is to be created and inserted after **p**. The following statements create and store 50 in the **info** field of a new node:

```
newNode = new LinkedListNode();    //create the object newNode
newNode.info = 50;        //store 50 in the object newNode
```

The first statement (that is, **newNode = new LinkedListNode();**) creates a node somewhere in memory and stores the address of the newly created node in **newNode**. The second statement (that is, **newNode.info = 50;**) stores 50 in the **info** field of the new node. See Figure 4-8.

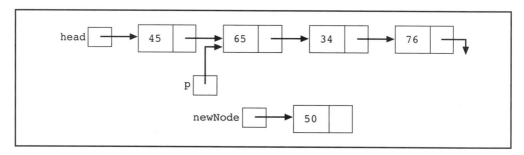

Figure 4-8   Create **newNode** and store 50 in it

The following statements insert the node in the linked list at the required place:

```
newNode.link = p.link;
p.link = newNode;
```

After the first statement (that is, `newNode.link = p.link;`) executes, the resulting list is as shown in Figure 4-9.

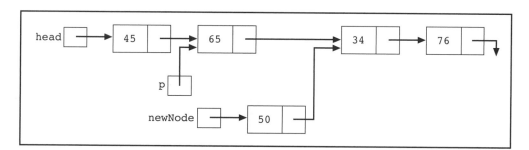

Figure 4-9   List after the statement `newNode.link = p.link;` executes

After the second statement (that is, `p.link = newNode;`) executes, the resulting list is as shown in Figure 4-10.

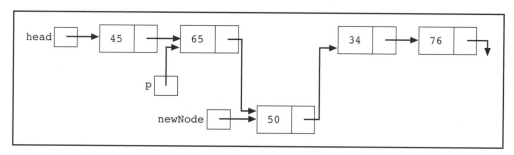

Figure 4-10   List after the statement `p.link = newNode;` executes

Note that the sequence of statements to insert the node is very important because to insert **newNode** in the list we used only one reference variable, **p**, to adjust the links of the node of the linked list. If we reverse the sequence of the statements, we do not get the desired result. For example, suppose that we execute the statements in the following order:

```
p.link = newNode;
newNode.link = p.link;
```

Figure 4-11 shows the resulting list after these statements execute.

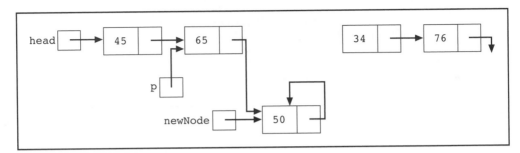

Figure 4-11 List after the execution of the statement p.link = newNode; followed by the execution of newNode.link = p.link;

From Figure 4-11, it is clear that **newNode** points back to itself and the remainder of the list is lost.

Using two reference variables, we can simplify the insertion code somewhat. Suppose **q** points to the node with **info 34**. See Figure 4-12.

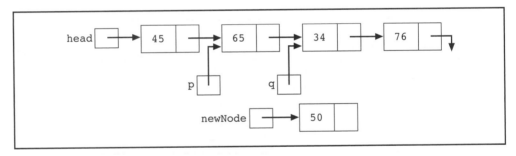

Figure 4-12 List with reference variables p and q

The following statements insert **newNode** between **p** and **q**:

```
newNode.link = q;
p.link = newNode;
```

The order in which these statements execute does not matter. To illustrate this, suppose that we execute the statements in the following order:

```
p.link = newNode;
newNode.link = q;
```

After the statement **p.link = newNode;** executes, the resulting list is as shown in Figure 4-13.

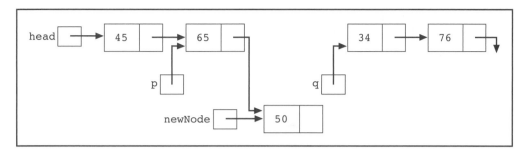

Figure 4-13   List after the statement `p.link = newNode;` executes

The remaining list is not lost. After the statement `newNode.link = q;` executes, the list is as shown in Figure 4-14.

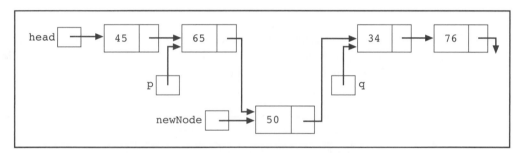

Figure 4-14   List after the statement `newNode.link = q;` executes

Deletion

Consider the linked list shown in Figure 4-15.

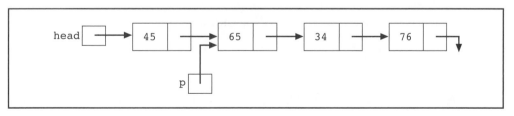

Figure 4-15   Node to be deleted is with `info 34`

Suppose that the node with `info` 34 is to be deleted from the list. The following statement removes the node from the list:

```
p.link = p.link.link;
```

Figure 4-16 shows the resulting list after the preceding statement executes.

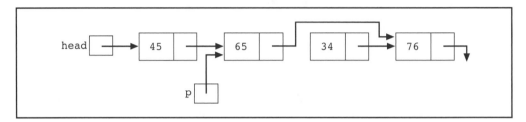

Figure 4-16 List after the statement `p.link = p.link.link;` executes

From Figure 4-16, it is clear that the node with `info` 34 is removed from the list. The Java system eventually reclaims the memory occupied by this node. Therefore, after deleting the node with `info` 34, the linked list is as shown in Figure 4-17.

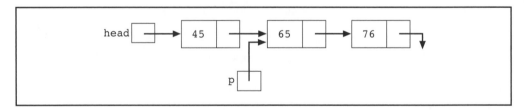

Figure 4-17 List after deleting the node with `info` 34

With two reference variables, you can somewhat simplify the deletion code as follows (suppose that **q** is a reference variable of the same type as **p**):

```
q = p.link;
p.link = q.link;
q = null;
```

After the statement `q = p.link;` executes, the resulting list is as shown in Figure 4-18.

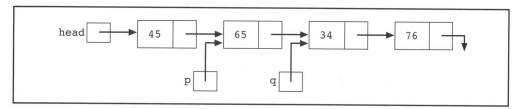

Figure 4-18   List after the statement q = p.link; executes

After the statement **p.link** = **q.link;** executes, the resulting list is as shown in Figure 4-19.

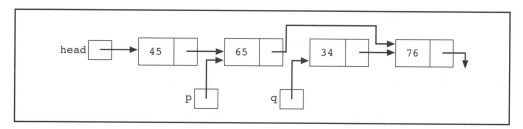

Figure 4-19   List after the statement p.link = q.link; executes

After the statement **q** = **null;** executes, the resulting list is as shown in Figure 4-20, which is the same as the list in Figure 4-17.

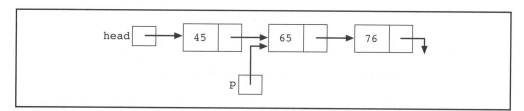

Figure 4-20 List after the statement q = null; executes

Suppose that the reference variable q points to a node and no other reference variable points to that node. If you set q to null, or if the reference variable q no longer exists, then the memory spaces occupied by the object will be reclaimed by Java's system garbage collector when it executes. Similarly, suppose that the reference variable head points to a linked list, such as in Figure 4-19. If you set head to null or the reference variable head no longer exists, the memory space occupied by the linked list will eventually be reclaimed by the system garbage collector. The system garbage collector executes periodically, and if it finds an object to which no reference variable points, the garbage collector reclaims, or frees up, the memory space occupied by the object. If you want, you can use the statement System.gc(); to execute the garbage collector. However, when the program is running out of memory space, the garbage collector executes automatically.

BUILDING A LINKED LIST

Now that you know how to insert a node in a linked list, next you learn how to build a linked list. First, we consider a linked list in general. If the data we read is not in order, that is, unsorted, then the linked list need not be in order, that is, sorted. Such a list can be built in two ways: in the forward manner and in the backward manner. In the forward manner, a new node is always inserted at the end of the linked list; in the backward manner, a new node is always inserted at the beginning of the linked list. We consider both cases.

Building a Linked List Forward

Suppose that the nodes are in the usual info-link form and info is of the type int. Let us assume that we process the following data:

```
2 15 8 24 34
```

We need three reference variables to build the list: one to point to the first node in the list, which cannot be moved; one to point to the last node in the list; and one to create the new node. Consider the following variable declaration:

```
LinkedListNode  first, last, newNode;
int num;
```

Suppose that first points to the first node in the list. Initially, the list is empty, so both first and last are null. Thus, we must have the statements:

```
first = null;
last = null;
```

to initialize first and last to null.

Next, consider the following statements:

```
1   num = Integer.parseInt(keyboard.readLine());   //read and
                                        //store a number in num
2   newNode = new LinkedListNode();  //create the object newNode
3   newNode.info = num;           //copy the value of num
                                  //into the info field
                                  //of newNode
4   newNode.link = null;          //initialize the link
                                  //field of newNode to
                                  //null
5   if(first == null)             //if first is null, the
                                  //list is empty; make
                                  //first and last point to
                                  //newNode
    {
5a      first = newNode;
5b      last = newNode;
    }
6   else                          //the list is not empty
    {
6a      last.link = newNode;      //insert newNode at the
                                  //end of the list
6b      last = newNode;           //set last so that it
                                  //points to the actual
                                  //last node in the list
    }
```

Let us now execute these statements. Initially, both `first` and `last` are `null`. Therefore, we have the list as shown in Figure 4-21.

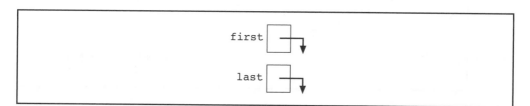

Figure 4-21   Empty list

After statement 1 executes, `num` is 2. Statement 2 creates a node and stores the address of that node in `newNode`. Statement 3 stores 2 in the `info` field of `newNode`; statement 4 stores `null` in the link field of `newNode`. See Figure 4-22.

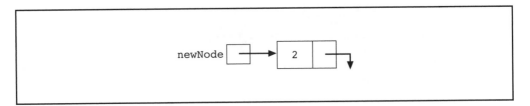

Figure 4-22   newNode with `info 2`

Because `first` is `null`, we execute statements 5a and 5b. Figure 4-23 shows the resulting list.

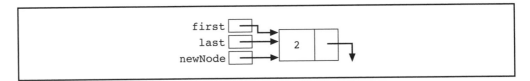

Figure 4-23   List after inserting newNode in it

We now repeat statements 1 through 6b. After statement 1 executes, **num** is **15**. Statement 2 creates a node and stores the address of the node in **newNode**. Statement 3 stores **15** in the `info` field of **newNode**; statement 4 stores `null` in the link field of **newNode**. See Figure 4-24.

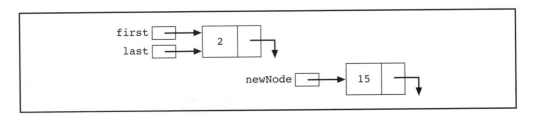

Figure 4-24   List and newNode with `info 15`

Because `first` is not `null`, we execute statements 6a and 6b. Figure 4-25 shows the resulting list.

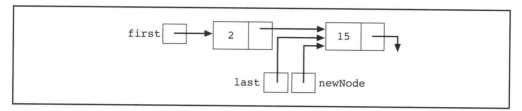

Figure 4-25   List after inserting `newNode` at the end

We now repeat statements 1 through 6b three more times. Figure 4–26 shows the resulting list.

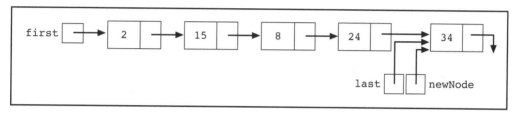

Figure 4-26   List after inserting 8, 24, and 34

We can put the previous statements in a loop and execute the loop until certain conditions are met to build the linked list. We can, in fact, write a method to build a linked list.

Suppose that we read a list of integers ending with **-999**. The following method, **buildListForward**, builds a linked list (in a forward manner) and returns the reference, that is, the address of the first node of the built list:

```
public LinkedListNode buildListForward()
{
    LinkedListNode  first, newNode, last;
    int num;
    String inputLine;
    StringTokenizer tokenizer;

    System.out.println("Enter integers ending with -999 "
                    + "in one line.");
    inputLine = keyboard.readLine();
    tokenizer = new StringTokenizer(inputLine);
    num = Integer.parseInt(tokenizer.nextToken());

    first = null;
```

```
      while(num != -999)
      {
          newNode = new LinkedListNode();

          newNode.info = num;
          newNode.link = null;

          if(first == null)
          {
              first = newNode;
              last = newNode;
          }
          else
          {
              last.link = newNode;
              last = newNode;
          }

          num = Integer.parseInt(tokenizer.nextToken());
      }//end while

      return first;
}//end buildListForward
```

Building a Linked List Backwards

We now consider the case of building a linked list backwards. For the previously given data—2, 15, 8, 24, and 34—the linked list is as shown in Figure 4-27.

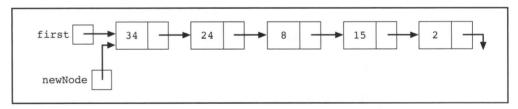

Figure 4-27   List after building it backward

Because the new node is always inserted at the beginning of the list, we do not need to know the end of the list, so the reference variable **last** is not needed. Also, after inserting the new node at the beginning, the new node becomes the first node in the list. Thus, we need to update the value of **first** to correctly point to the first node in the list. We see, then, that we need only two reference variables to build the linked list: one to point to the list, and one to create the new node. Because initially the list is empty, `first` must be initialized to `null`. In pseudocode, the algorithm is:

1. Initialize `first` to `null`.

2. For each item in the list:

   a. Create the object `newNode`.

   b. Store the item in `newNode`.

   c. Insert `newNode` before `first`.

   d. Update the value of `first`.

The following Java method builds the linked list backwards and returns the reference of the first node of the built list:

```java
public LinkedListNode buildListBackward()
{
    LinkedListNode  first, newNode;
    int num;
    String inputLine;
    StringTokenizer tokenizer;

    System.out.println("Enter integers ending with -999 "
                    + "in one line.");
    inputLine = keyboard.readLine();
    tokenizer = new StringTokenizer(inputLine);
    num = Integer.parseInt(tokenizer.nextToken());

    first = null;

    while(num != -999)
    {
        newNode = new LinkedListNode();  //create the object newNode
        newNode.info = num;              //store the data in
                                         //newNode
        newNode.link = first;            //put newNode at the
                                         //beginning of the list
        first = newNode;                 //update the value of first

        num = Integer.parseInt(tokenizer.nextToken()); //get the
                                                       //next number
    }

    return first;
}//end buildListBackward
```

LINKED LIST AS AN ADT

The previous sections taught you the basic properties of linked lists and how to construct and manipulate linked lists. Because a linked list is a very important data structure, rather than discuss specific lists such as a list of integers or a list of strings, this section discusses linked lists as an ADT. The programming example at the end of this chapter also uses this generic definition of linked lists.

The basic operations on linked lists are:

1. Initialize the list.

2. Determine whether the list is empty.

3. Output the list.

4. Find the length of the list.

5. Retrieve the `info` contained in the first node.

6. Retrieve the `info` contained in the last node.

7. Search the list for a given item.

8. Insert an item in the list.

9. Delete an item from the list.

10. Make a copy of the linked list.

As in the case of array-based lists, there are two types of linked lists—lists whose elements are arranged according to some criteria, such as sorted lists, and lists whose elements are in no particular order, called unsorted lists. The algorithms to implement the operations of search, insert, and remove differ slightly for sorted and unsorted lists. Therefore, we define the **class LinkedListClass** to implement the basic operations on a linked list as an **abstract class**. By using the principle of inheritance, from the **class LinkedListClass** we, in fact, derive the two **classes, UnorderedLinkedList** and **OrderedLinkedList**.

Objects of the **class UnorderedLinkedList** would arrange the list elements in no particular order; that is, these lists might not be sorted. On the other hand, objects of the **class OrderedLinkedList** would arrange the elements according to some comparison criteria, usually less than or equal to. These lists are in ascending order. Moreover, after inserting an element into, or removing an element from, an ordered list, the resulting list will be ordered.

If a linked list is arbitrary, we can insert a new item at either the end or the beginning. Furthermore, such a list may initially be built in either a forward manner or a backward manner. The method **buildListForward** requires the new item to be inserted at the end, whereas the method **buildListBackward** requires the new item to be inserted at the beginning. To accommodate both operations, we write two methods: **insertFirst**, to insert the new item at the beginning of the list; and `insertLast`, to insert the new item at the end of the list. Also, to make the algorithms somewhat efficient, we use two reference variables to maintain the list: `first`, which points to the first node in the list; and `last`, which points to the last node in the list.

Now that we want to study linked lists as an ADT, while implementing the basic operations of a linked list we do not want to be concerned with what type of data a linked list is processing. In Chapter 3, we designed the **abstract class DataElement** to study array-based lists as ADTs. We do the same thing here. We make the **info** of the node a reference variable, which can contain the address of the object containing the data. When we use a linked list to process data, first we design a class that extends the definition of the **abstract class DataElement** to store the data. Because the **class DataElement** is the superclass of the classes whose objects store the actual data, a reference variable of the **DataElement** type can point to an object of those classes. (For information on the **class DataElement**, see Chapter 3.)

The following statements define the members of the **class LinkedListClass**, which will be implemented as ADT:

Class: `LinkedListClass`

```
      //Definition of the node
protected class LinkedListNode
{
    DataElement info;
    LinkedListNode link;
}
```

Instance Variables:

```
protected LinkedListNode first; //variable to point to
                                //the first node
protected LinkedListNode last;  //variable to point to the
                                //last node
protected int count;  //variable to store the number of nodes
                      //in the list
```

Constructors and Instance Methods:

```
public LinkedListClass()
   //default constructor
   //Initializes the list to an empty state.
   //Postcondition: first = null, last = null,
   //               count = 0

public LinkedListClass(LinkedListClass otherList)
   //copy constructor
```

```
public void initializeList()
    //Method to initialize the list to an empty state.
    //Postcondition: first = null, last = null,
    //               count = 0

public boolean isEmptyList()
    //Method to determine whether the list is empty.
    //Postcondition: Returns true if the list is empty,
    //               false otherwise.

public void print()
    //Method to output the data contained in each node.

public int length()
    //Method to return the number of nodes in the list.
    //Postcondition: The value of count is returned.

public DataElement front()
    //Method to return the reference of the object containing
    //the data of the first node of the list.
    //Precondition: The list must exist and must not be empty.
    //Postcondition: The reference to the object that
    //               contains the info of the first node
    //               is returned.

public DataElement back()
    //Method to return the reference of the object containing
    //the data of the last node of the list.
    //Precondition: The list must exist and must not be empty.
    //Postcondition: The reference to the object that
    //               contains the info of the last node
    //               is returned.

public abstract boolean search(DataElement searchItem);
    //Method to determine whether searchItem is in the list.
    //Postcondition: Returns true if searchItem is found
    //               in the list; false otherwise.

public void insertFirst(DataElement newItem)
    //Method to insert newItem in the list.
    //Postcondition: first points to the new list
    //               and newItem is inserted at the
    //               beginning of the list. Also,
    //               last points to the last node and
    //               count is incremented by 1.
```

```
public void insertLast(DataElement newItem)
   //Method to insert newItem at the end of the list.
   //Postcondition: first points to the new list and
   //               newItem is inserted at the end
   //               of the list. Also, last points to
   //               the last node and
   //               count is incremented by 1.

public abstract void deleteNode(DataElement deleteItem);
   //Method to delete deleteItem from the list.
   //Postcondition: If found, the node containing
   //               deleteItem is deleted from the
   //               list. Also, first points to the first
   //               node, last points to the last
   //               node of the updated list, and count
   //               is decremented by 1.

private void copy(LinkedListClass otherList)
   //Method to return the reference of the copy of otherList.

public void copyList(LinkedListClass otherList)
   //Method to return the reference of the copy of otherList.
```

Notice that the method **copy** is declared as **private**. This is because we use this method only to implement the copy constructor and the method **copyList**.

To insert an item in the linked list, the methods **insertFirst** and **insertLast** are declared as nonabstract methods. This is because both of these methods can be implemented the same way for ordered or unordered lists. In fact, objects of the **class UnorderedLinkedList** can use the methods **insertFirst** or **insertLast** to insert an element in the list. For the objects of the **class OrderedLinkedList**, we include the method **insertNode**, as described in the upcoming section "Ordered Linked List," to insert an element in the list at the proper place.

Moreover, notice that the instance variables of the **class LinkedListClass** are **protected**, not **private**, because as noted previously we will derive the **classes UnorderedLinkedList** and **OrderedLinkedList**. Each of the classes **UnorderedLinkedList** and **OrderedLinkedList** will provide separate definitions of the methods **search** and **deleteNode**, and these methods will access the instance variables. Therefore, to provide direct access to the instance variables, the instance variables are declared as **protected**.

Next, we write the definitions of the nonabstract methods of the **class LinkedListClass**.

isEmptyList

The list is empty if `first` is `null`. Therefore, the definition of the method `isEmptyList` is:

```
public boolean isEmptyList()
{
    return (first == null);
}
```

Default Constructor

The default constructor initializes the list to an empty state. Recall that when an object of the type `LinkedListClass` is declared and no value is passed, the default constructor executes automatically. Its definition is:

```
public LinkedListClass()
{
    first = null;
    last = null;
    count = 0;
}
```

From the definitions of the method `isEmptyList` and the default constructor, it follows that each of these methods is of $O(1)$.

Initialize List

The method `initializeList` initializes the list to an empty state. Note that the default constructor or the copy constructor has already initialized the list when the list object was created. This operation, in fact, reinitializes the list to an empty state. This can be accomplished simply by setting the reference variables `first` and `last` to `null`, and `count` to 0. (The system's garbage collector eventually reclaims the memory space occupied by the list and the objects of the list.)

```
public void initializeList()
{
    first = null;
    last = null;
    count = 0;
}
```

It can be shown that the method `initializeList` is of $O(1)$.

Print List

The method `print` outputs the data stored in the nodes of a linked list. To output the data contained in each node, we must traverse the list starting at the first node. Because `first` always points to the first node in the list, we need another reference variable to traverse the list. (If we use `first` to traverse the list, then the entire list is lost.) The definition of the method `print` is:

```
public void print()
{
    LinkedListNode current; //variable to traverse the list

    current = first;   //set current so that it points to
                       //the first node
    while(current != null) //while more data to print
    {
        System.out.print(current.info + " ");
        current = current.link;
    }
}//end print
```

The method `print` assumes that the method `toString` is defined for the class that defines the type of `info`. For example, to process integers, the `class IntElement`, discussed in Chapter 3, defines the method `toString` to return the number as a string stored in an object of the `class IntElement`. Also, note that the method `print` is of $O(n)$.

Length of the List

The length of the linked list (that is, how many nodes are in the list) is stored in the variable `count`. Therefore, this method returns the value of this variable. Its definition is:

```
public int length()
{
    return count;
}//end length
```

Retrieve Data from the First and the Last Nodes

The method `front` returns the data stored in the object that the instance variable `info` of the first node points to. To do so, first we create an object and copy the data of the object to which `info` points and then return the reference, that is, the address of the object. To create an object and copy the data, we use the method `getCopy` of the `class DataElement`. (See Chapters 1 and 3 to review how the method `getCopy` works.) Similarly, the method `back` returns the address of the object containing a copy of the data to which the instance variable `info` of the last node points. The definitions of these methods are:

```
public DataElement front()
{
    DataElement temp = first.info.getCopy();
    return temp;
}//end front
```

```
public DataElement back()
{
    DataElement temp = last.info.getCopy();
    return temp;
}//end back
```

Notice that if the list is empty, `first` and `last` are `null`. In this case, `first.info` and `last.info` do not exist. Therefore, if the list is empty, both the methods `front` and `back` terminate the program with an error message, `NullPointerException`. Therefore, before calling these methods, check to see whether the list is nonempty.

From the definitions of the methods `length`, `front`, and `back`, it follows that each of these methods is of O(1).

Insert First Node

The method `insertFirst` inserts the new item at the beginning of the list—that is, before the node pointed to by `first`. The following steps are needed to implement this method:

1. Create a new node.

2. Store the new item in the new node.

3. Insert the node before `first`.

4. Increment `count`.

To create a node, we use the operator `new`. Let us elaborate on Step 2 a bit more. Notice that the parameter `newItem` of the method `insertFirst` is a reference variable of the `DataElement` type; in other words, `newItem` points to the object that contains the data. To insert the object in the list and to avoid the shallow copying of data, we use the method `getCopy` to create a copy of the object to which `newItem` points, and then store the address of the created object into the field `info` of the node that was created in Step 1. Step 3 is implemented by changing the value of `first` and the link field of the node created in Step 1. The definition of the method `insertFirst` is:

```
public void insertFirst(DataElement newItem)
{
    LinkedListNode newNode;        //variable to create the
                                   //new node

    newNode = new LinkedListNode();    //create the new node
    newNode.info = newItem.getCopy(); //assign a copy of
                                       //newItem to the node
    newNode.link = first;      //insert newNode before first
    first = newNode;           //make first point to the
                               //actual first node
```

```
    if(last == null)        //if the list was empty, newNode is
                            //also the last node in the list
        last = newNode;

    count++;
}//end insertFirst
```

Insert Last Node

The definition of the method `insertLast` is similar to the definition of the method `insertFirst`. Here we insert the new node after `last`. Essentially, the definition of the method `insertLast` is:

```
public void insertLast(DataElement newItem)
{
    LinkedListNode newNode; //variable to create the new node

    newNode = new LinkedListNode();    //create the new node
    newNode.info = newItem.getCopy(); //assign a copy of
                                      //newItem to the node
    newNode.link = null;            //set the link field of
                                    //newNode to null

    if(first == null)   //if the list is empty, newNode is
                        //both the first and last node
    {
        first = newNode;
        last = newNode;
    }
    else     //if the list is not empty, insert newNode after last
    {
        last.link = newNode; //insert newNode after last
        last = newNode; //set last to point to the actual last node
    }

    count++;
}//end insertLast
```

From the definitions of the methods `insertFirst` and `insertLast`, it follows that each of these methods is of $O(1)$.

Copy

The method **copy** is declared as a **private** member of the **class LinkedListClass**. This is because, for the most part, the algorithm to implement the method **copyList** and the copy constructor is the same. Therefore, rather than repeat the same code, and to make debugging easier, we include the method **copy**, which contains the code that is common to the method **copyList** and the copy constructor. We use the method **copy** to implement only the method **copyList** and the copy constructor.

The method **copy** makes an identical copy of a linked list. Therefore, we traverse the list to be copied starting at the first node. Corresponding to each node in the original list, we:

1. Create a node, and call it **newNode**.

2. Assign a copy of the object pointed to by **info** (of the node of the original list) to **newNode**.

3. Insert **newNode** at the end of the list being created.

The definition of the method **copy** is:

```
private void copy(LinkedListClass otherList)
{
    LinkedListNode newNode; //variable to create a node
    LinkedListNode current; //variable to traverse the list

    first = null;  //make this list empty

    if(otherList.first == null) //otherList is empty
    {
        first = null;
        last = null;
        count = 0;
    }
    else
    {
        count = otherList.count;
        current = otherList.first;  //current points to the
                                    //list to be copied

            //copy the first element
        first = new LinkedListNode();         //create the node
        first.info = current.info.getCopy();  //copy the info
        first.link = null;    //set the link field of
                              //the node to null
        last = first;         //make last point to the first node
        current = current.link; //make current point to the next
                                //node of the list being copied

            //copy the remaining list
        while(current != null)
        {
            newNode = new LinkedListNode();
            newNode.info = current.info.getCopy();
            newNode.link = null;
            last.link = newNode;
            last = newNode;
            current = current.link;
        }//end while
    }//end else
}//end copy
```

The method `copy` contains a `while` loop. The number of times the `while` loop executes depends on the number of items in the list. If the list contains n items, the `while` loop executes n times. From this, it can be shown that the method `copy` is of $O(n)$.

Copy Constructor

Recall that the copy constructor executes when an object is declared and initialized using another object. The copy constructor makes an identical copy of the linked list. This can be done by calling the method `copy`. The definition of the copy constructor is:

```
public LinkedListClass(LinkedListClass otherList)
{
    copy(otherList);
}//end copy constructor
```

Copy List

The method `copyList` is declared `public` so that the user can use it to make a copy of a linked list. To make a copy of a linked list, the method `copyList` uses the method `copy`. The definition of the method `copyList` is:

```
public void copyList(LinkedListClass otherList)
{
    if(this != otherList)   //avoid self-copy
        copy(otherList);
}
```

The copy constructor and the method `copyList` use the method `copy`, which is of $O(n)$. Therefore, the copy constructor and the method `copyList` are of $O(n)$.

Definition of the `class LinkedListClass`

In the preceding sections, we discussed how to implement the operations of the `class LinkedListClass`. We now describe how to write the definition of the `class LinkedListClass`.

Earlier we gave the definition of the `class LinkedListNode` to implement the node of the linked list. Now we want the `class LinkedListNode` to be used only by the `class LinkedListClass` and its subclasses. Therefore, we declare the `class LinkedListNode` as an inner class of the `class LinkedListClass`. You can write the definition of the `class LinkedListClass` as:

```
public abstract class LinkedListClass
{
    protected class LinkedListNode
    {
        DataElement info;
        LinkedListNode link;
    }
```

```
        protected LinkedListNode first;  //variable to store the
                                         //address of the first
                                         //node of the list
        protected LinkedListNode last;   //variable to store the
                                         //address of the last
                                         //node of the list

        protected int count;

        //Place the definitions of the nonabstract methods and the
        //abstract methods here.
}
```

UNORDERED LINKED LISTS

As described in the preceding section, we derive the **class UnorderedLinkedList** from the **abstract class LinkedListClass** and implement the operations **search** and **deleteNode**.

Class: UnorderedLinkedList

```
public class UnorderedLinkedList extends LinkedListClass
```

Instance Variables:

Same as the instance variables of the **class LinkedListClass**

Constructors and Instance Methods:

```
public UnorderedLinkedList()
    //default constructor

public UnorderedLinkedList(UnorderedLinkedList otherList)
    //copy constructor

public boolean search(DataElement searchItem)
    //Method to determine whether searchItem is in the list.
    //Postcondition: Returns true if searchItem is found
    //               in the list; false otherwise.

public void deleteNode(DataElement deleteItem)
    //Method to delete deleteItem from the list.
    //Postcondition: If found, the node containing
    //               deleteItem is deleted from the
    //               list. Also, first points to the first
    //               node, last points to the last
    //               node of the updated list, and count
    //               is decremented by 1.
```

We leave the UML diagram of the **class UnorderedLinkedList** and of the inheritance hierarchy as an exercise for you.

Search List

The method **search** searches the list for a given item. If the item is found, it returns **true**; otherwise, it returns **false**. Because a linked list is not a random access data structure, we must sequentially search the list starting from the first node.

The following steps describe this method:

1. Compare the search item with the current node in the list. If the object that the **info** of the current node points to contains the same data as the object pointed to by the parameter **searchItem**, stop the search; otherwise, make the next node the current node. To compare the objects, we use the method **equals** of the **class DataElement**.

2. Repeat Step 1 until the item is found or no more data is left in the list to compare with the search item.

The definition of the method **search** is:

```
public boolean search(DataElement searchItem)
{
    LinkedListNode current; //variable to traverse the list
    boolean found;

    current = first;   //set current to point to the first
                       //node in the list

    found = false;     //set found to false

    while(current != null && !found) //search the list
        if(current.info.equals(searchItem))  //item is found
            found = true;
        else
            current = current.link; //make current point to
                                    //the next node
    return found;
}
```

The number of times the **while** loop executes, in the method **search**, depends on where in the list the search item is located. Suppose the list has n items. If the search item is not in the list, the **while** loop executes n times. On the other hand, if the search item is the first item, the **while** loop executes 1 time. Similarly, if the search item is the ith item in the list, the while loop executes i times. From these observations, we can show that the method **search** is of $O(n)$. We will explicitly analyze a sequential search algorithm in Chapter 8.

Delete Node

Next, we discuss the implementation of the method `deleteNode`. The reference of the object specifying the node to be deleted is passed as a parameter to this method. We need to consider the followings cases:

Case 1: The list is empty.

Case 2: The first node is the node to be deleted. In this case, we need to adjust the value of `first`.

Case 3: The node to be deleted is somewhere in the list. If the node to be deleted is the last node, we must adjust the value of `last`.

Case 4: The list does not contain the node to be deleted.

If the list is empty, we can simply print a message indicating that the list is empty. If the list is not empty, we search the list for the node with the given `info` and, if such a node is found, delete this node. After deleting the node, `count` is decremented by `1`. In pseudocode, the algorithm is:

```
if the list is empty
    Output(cannot delete from an empty list);
else
{
    if the first node is the node to be deleted,
        adjust the value of first, last (if necessary),
        and count;
    else
    {
        search the list for the node to be deleted
        if such a node is found, delete it, and adjust
            the values of last (if necessary) and count;
    }
}
```

Case 1: The list is empty. If the list is empty, output an error message as shown in the pseudocode.

Case 2: The list is not empty. The node to be deleted is the first node.

This case has two scenarios: `list` has only one node, and `list` has more than one node. Consider the list of one node as shown in Figure 4-28.

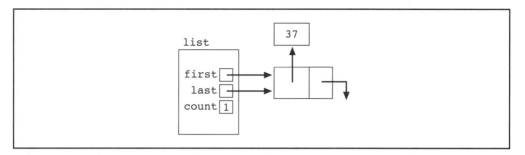

Figure 4-28   `list` with one node

Suppose that we want to delete 37. After deletion, the list becomes empty. Therefore, after deletion, both `first` and `last` are set to `null` and `count` is set to 0.

Now consider the list of more than one node, as shown in Figure 4-29.

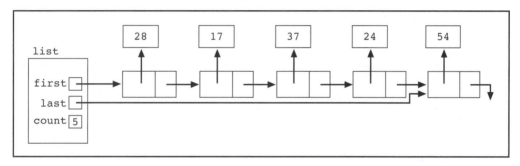

Figure 4-29   `list` with more than one node

Suppose that the node to be deleted is the node with data 28. After deleting this node, the second node becomes the first node. Therefore, after deleting this node the value of `first` changes; that is, after deletion, `first` contains the address of the node with `info` 17. Also, `count` is decremented by 1. Figure 4-30 shows the list after deleting 28.

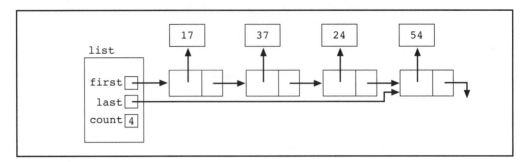

Figure 4-30 `list` after deleting the node with data `28`

Case 3: The node to be deleted is not the first node, but is somewhere in this list.

This case has two subcases: (a) the node to be deleted is not the last node, and (b) the node to be deleted is the last node. Let us illustrate both cases.

Case 3a: The node to be deleted is not the last node.

Consider the list shown in Figure 4-31.

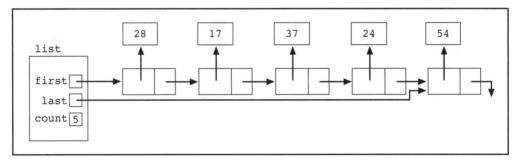

Figure 4-31 `list` before deleting `37`

Suppose that the node to be deleted is the node with data `37`. After deleting this node, the resulting list is as shown in Figure 4-32. (Notice that the deletion of the node with data `37` does not require us to change the values of **first** and **last**. The link field of the previous node—that is, the node with data `17`—changes. After deletion, the node with data `17` contains the address of the node with data `24`. Also, **count** is decremented by `1`.)

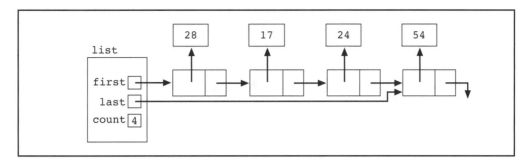

Figure 4-32   list after deleting 37

Case 3b: The node to be deleted is the last node.

Consider the list shown in Figure 4-33. Suppose that the node to be deleted is the node with data 54.

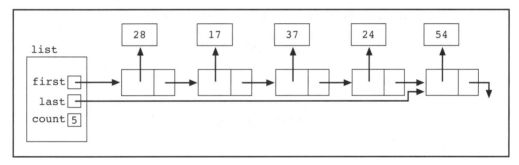

Figure 4-33   list before deleting 54

After deleting the node with data 54, the node with data 24 becomes the last node. Therefore, the deletion of 54 requires us to change the value of last. After deleting 54, last contains the address of the node with data 24. Also, count is decremented by 1. Figure 4-34 shows the resulting list.

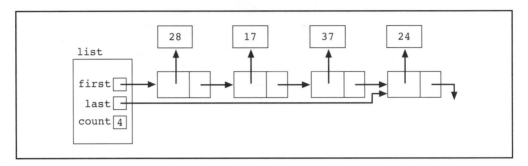

Figure 4-34 `list` after deleting 5 4

Case 4: The node to be deleted is not in the list. In this case, the list requires no adjustment. We simply output an error message, indicating that the item to be deleted is not in the list.

From Cases 2, 3, and 4, it follows that the deletion of a node requires us to traverse the list. Because a linked list is not a random access data structure, we must sequentially search the list. (We handle Case 1 separately, because it does not require us to traverse the list.) We sequentially search the list starting at the second node. If the node to be deleted is not the first node of the list, we need to adjust the link field of the node just before the node to be deleted. Thus, we need a reference variable to the previous node. When we search the list for the given data, we use two reference variables: one to check the data of the current node, and one to keep track of the node just before the current node. If the node to be deleted is the last node, we must change the value of **last**.

The definition of the method **deleteNode** is:

```
public void deleteNode(DataElement deleteItem)
{
    LinkedListNode current; //variable to traverse the list
    LinkedListNode trailCurrent; //variable just before current
    boolean found;

    if(first == null)     //Case 1; the list is empty
        System.err.println("Cannot delete from an empty list.");
    else
    {
        if(first.info.equals(deleteItem)) //Case 2
        {
            first = first.link;

            if(first == null)     //the list had only one node
                last = null;
            count--;
        }
```

```
        else  //search the list for the node with the given info
        {
            found = false;
            trailCurrent = first;    //set trailCurrent to point to
                                     //the first node
            current = first.link;    //set current to point to the
                                     //second node

            while(current != null && !found)
            {
                if(current.info.equals(deleteItem))
                    found = true;
                else
                {
                    trailCurrent = current;
                    current = current.link;
                }
            }//end while

            if(found) //Case 3; if found, delete the node
            {
                count--;
                trailCurrent.link = current.link;

                if(last == current)     //node to be deleted was
                                        //the last node
                    last = trailCurrent;  //update the value of last
            }
            else
                System.out.println("Item to be deleted is "
                                + "not in the list.");
        }//end else
    }//end else
}//end deleteNode
```

 Suppose that the reference variable q points to a node and no other reference variable points to that node. If you set q to null, then the memory spaces occupied by the object are reclaimed by Java's system garbage collector when it executes. Here, because q.info is also a reference variable, it may also be pointing to an object. If no other reference variable points to that object, when the system reclaims the memory space occupied by the node, it eventually reclaims the memory space occupied by the object.

From the definition of the method deleteNode, it can be shown that this method is of $O(n)$.

You can write the definition of the `class UnorderedLinkedList` as follows:

```
public class UnorderedLinkedList extends LinkedListClass
{
        //default constructor
    public UnorderedLinkedList()
    {
       super();
    }

      //copy constructor
    public UnorderedLinkedList(UnorderedLinkedList otherList)
    {
       super(otherList);
    }

    //Place the definition of the methods search and
    //deleteNode here.
}
```

Table 4-5 summarizes the time-complexity of the operations of the `classes LinkedListClass` and `UnorderedLinkedList`.

Table 4-5 Time-Complexity of the Operations of the `classes LinkedListClass` and `UnorderedLinkedList`

Method	Time-Complexity
`isEmptyList`	$O(1)$
default constructor	$O(1)$
`initializeList`	$O(1)$
`print`	$O(n)$
`length`	$O(1)$
`front`	$O(1)$
`back`	$O(1)$
`search`	$O(n)$
`insertFirst`	$O(1)$
`insertLast`	$O(1)$
`deleteNode`	$O(n)$
`copy`	$O(n)$
copy constructor	$O(n)$
`copyList`	$O(n)$

ORDERED LINKED LISTS

The preceding section described the operations on an arbitrary linked list. This section deals with ordered linked lists. As noted earlier, we derive the `class OrderedLinkedList` from the `class LinkedListClass`, and provide the definitions of the methods `search` and `deleteNode` to take advantage of the fact that the elements of an ordered linked list are arranged using some ordering criteria. For simplicity, we assume that the elements of an ordered linked list are arranged in ascending order.

Because the elements of an ordered linked list are in order, we include the method `insertNode` to insert an element in an ordered list at the proper place.

The following statements define an ordered linked list as an ADT:

Class: `OrderedLinkedList`

`public class OrderedLinkedList extends LinkedListClass`

Instance Variables: Same as the instance variables of the `class LinkedListClass`

Instance Methods:

```
public OrderedLinkedList()
   //default constructor

public OrderedLinkedList(OrderedLinkedList otherList)
   //copy constructor

public boolean search(DataElement searchItem)
   //Method to determine whether searchItem is in
   //the list.
   //Postcondition: Returns true if searchItem is found
   //               in the list; false otherwise.

public void insertNode(DataElement insertItem)
   //Method to insert insertItem in the list.
   //Postcondition: first points to the new list,
   //        insertItem is inserted at the proper place
   //        in the list, and count is incremented by 1.

public void deleteNode(DataElement deleteItem)
   //Method to delete deleteItem from the list.
   //Postcondition: If found, the node containing
   //               deleteItem is deleted from the
   //               list. Also, first points to the first
   //               node, last points to the last
   //               node of the updated list, and count
   //               is decremented by 1.
```

4

The class `OrderedLinkedList` is derived from the class `LinkedListClass`. The class `LinkedListClass` provides the method `insertFirst` to insert an element at the beginning of the list, and the method `insertLast` to insert an element at the end of the list. However, we are now discussing ordered linked lists, in which the elements are ordered according to some criteria. If an element is to be inserted in an ordered list, it must be inserted at the proper place. Even though you can use the methods `insertFirst` and `insertLast` to insert an item at the beginning or the end, there is no guarantee that the resulting list would be ordered. Therefore, we shall not use these methods with ordered linked lists. Moreover, because the elements are to be inserted at the proper place, as described in the section "Insert Node," `last` plays no role in constructing ordered lists. Therefore, we ignore `last`, which is set to `null`, and use only `first`. Also, the method `back` of the class `LinkedListClass` uses `last` to return the last element of the list. Because `last` is not used for ordered linked lists, we do not use the method `back` to return the last element of an ordered linked list (unless you override the definition of this method for the `class OrderedLinkedList`; see Programming Exercise 6).

 Recall that the elements of an ordered list are arranged according to some criteria. Suppose that the elements of a linked list are in ascending order. Another common operation on ordered linked lists is to output the data in reverse order. This requires us to traverse the linked list backwards starting from the last node. However, because the links go in only one direction, from what we have learned so far, we cannot easily traverse the linked list backwards. In Chapter 5, we show how to use recursion to traverse a linked list backwards.

Next, we discuss how to implement the methods `search`, `insertNode`, and `deleteNode` of the `class OrderedLinkedList`.

Search List

First, we discuss the search operation. The algorithm to implement the search operation is similar to the search algorithm for general lists discussed in the section "Unordered Linked Lists" located earlier in this chapter. Here, because the list is sorted, we can improve the search algorithm somewhat. As before, we start the search at the first node in the list. We stop the search as soon as we either find a node in the list with the `info` greater than or equal to the search item, or we have searched the entire list. The parameter `searchItem` points to the object that contains the data to be compared with the data stored in the list.

This algorithm has the following steps:

1. Compare the search item with the current node in the list. If the data in the object that the `info` of the current node points to is greater than or equal to the data of the object `searchItem` points to, stop the search; otherwise, make the next node the current node. To compare the data stored in the objects, we use the method `compareTo` of the `class DataElement`. Chapter 3 explains how the method `compareTo` works.

2. Repeat Step 1 until either an item in the list that is greater than or equal to the search item is found, or no more data is left in the list to compare with the search item.

Note that the loop does not explicitly check whether the search item is equal to an item in the list. Thus, after the loop executes, we must check whether the search item is equal to the item in the list.

```java
public boolean search(DataElement searchItem)
{
    LinkedListNode current; //variable to traverse the list
    boolean found;

    current = first;   //set current to point to the first
                       //node in the list

    found = false;     //set found to false

    while(current != null && !found ) //search the list
        if(current.info.compareTo(searchItem) >= 0)
            found = true;
        else
            current = current.link; //make current point to
                                    //the next node

    if(found)
        found = current.info.equals(searchItem);

    return found;
}
```

Insert Node

To insert an item in an ordered linked list, we first find the place where the new item is supposed to go, and then insert it in the list. To find the place for the new item in the list, as before, we search the list. Here we use two reference variables, `current` and `trailCurrent`, to search the list. The variable `current` points to the node whose `info` is being compared with the item to be inserted, and `trailCurrent` points to the node just before `current`. Because the list is in order, the search algorithm is the same as in the preceding section. The following cases arise:

Case 1: The list is initially empty. The node containing the new item is the only node and thus the first node in the list.

Case 2: The list is not empty and the new item is smaller than the smallest item in the list. The new item goes at the beginning of the list. In this case, we need to adjust `first`.

Case 3: The list is not empty, and the item to be inserted is larger than the first item in the list. The item is to be inserted somewhere in the list.

Case 3a: The new item is larger than all the items in the list. In this case, the new item is inserted at the end of the list. Thus, the value of **current** is **null** and the new item is inserted after **trailCurrent**.

Case 3b: The new item is to be inserted somewhere in the middle of the list. In this case, the new item is inserted between **trailCurrent** and **current**.

The following statements can accomplish both Cases 3a and 3b (assume **newNode** points to the new node):

```
trailCurrent.link = newNode;
newNode.link = current;
```

Let us next illustrate these cases.

Case 1: The list is empty.

Consider the list shown in Figure 4–35.

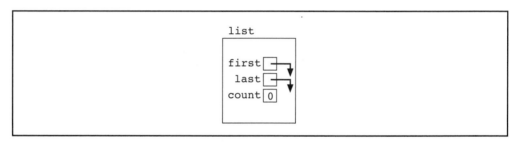

Figure 4-35   Empty `list`

Suppose that we want to insert **27** in the list. To accomplish this task, we create a node, make **info** point to an object with value **27**, set the link of the node to **null**, and have **first** point to the node. Also, **count** is incremented by 1. Figure 4-36 shows the resulting list.

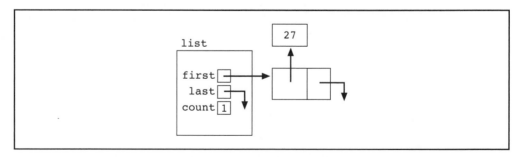

Figure 4-36   `list` after inserting 27

Notice that, after inserting 27, the values of **first** and **count** change.

Case 2: The list is not empty, and the item to be inserted is smaller than the smallest item in the list. Consider the list shown in Figure 4-37.

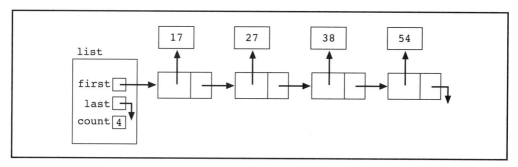

Figure 4-37   Nonempty **list** before inserting 10

Suppose that 10 is to be inserted. After inserting 10 in the list, the node with data 10 becomes the first node of **list**. This requires us to change the values of **first** and **count**. Figure 4-38 shows the resulting list.

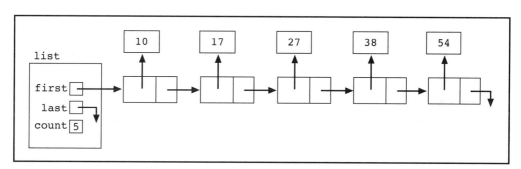

Figure 4-38   **list** after inserting 10

Case 3: The list is not empty, and the item to be inserted is larger than the first item in the list. As indicated previously, this case has two scenarios.

Case 3a: The item to be inserted is larger than the largest item in the list; that is, it goes at the end of the list. Consider the list shown in Figure 4-39.

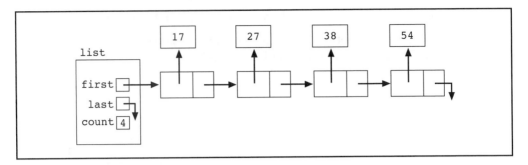

Figure 4-39 `list` before inserting 65

Suppose that we want to insert **65** in the list. After inserting **65**, the resulting list is as shown in Figure 4-40.

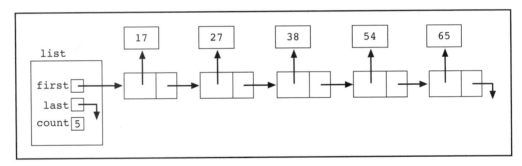

Figure 4-40 `list` after inserting 65

Case 3b: The item to be inserted goes somewhere in the middle of the list. Consider the list shown in Figure 4-41.

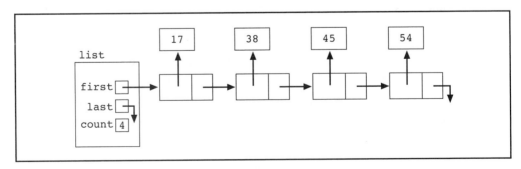

Figure 4-41 `list` before inserting 27

Suppose that we want to insert 27 in this list. Clearly, 27 goes between 17 and 38, which would require the link of the node with data 17 to be changed. Also, count is incremented by 1. After inserting 27, the resulting list is as shown in Figure 4-42.

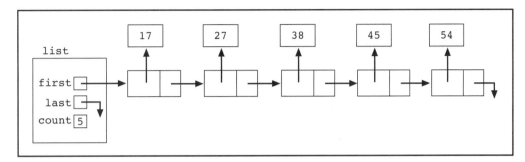

Figure 4-42 list after inserting 27

From Case 3, it follows that we must first traverse the list to find the place where the new item is to be inserted. As indicated previously, we must traverse the list with two reference variables—say, current and trailCurrent. The variable current traverses the list and compares the data of the node in the list with the item to be inserted. The reference variable trailCurrent points to the node just before current. For example, in Case 3b, when the search stops, trailCurrent points to node 17 and current points to node 38. The item is inserted after trailCurrent. In Case 3a, after searching the list to find the place for 65, trailCurrent points to node with data 54 and current is null.

Essentially, the method insertNode is:

```java
public void insertNode(DataElement insertItem)
{
    LinkedListNode current;          //variable to traverse the list
    LinkedListNode trailCurrent;     //variable just before current
    LinkedListNode newNode;          //variable to create a node

    boolean  found;

    newNode = new LinkedListNode(); //create the node
    newNode.info = insertItem.getCopy(); //store newItem
                                //in the node
    newNode.link = null;     //set the link field of the node
                             //to null

    if(first == null)  //Case 1
    {
        first = newNode;
        count++;
    }
```

```
          else
          {
             trailCurrent = first;
             current = first;
             found = false;

             while(current != null && !found) //search the list
                 if(current.info.compareTo(insertItem) >= 0)
                     found = true;
                 else
                 {
                     trailCurrent = current;
                     current = current.link;
                 }

             if(current == first)    //Case 2
             {
                 newNode.link = first;
                 first = newNode;
                 count++;
             }
             else            //Case 3
             {
                 trailCurrent.link = newNode;
                 newNode.link = current;
                 count++;
             }
          }//end else
}//end insertNode
```

Notice that the method `insertNode` does not check whether the item to be inserted is already in the list, that is, it does not check for duplicates. Programming Exercise 8, at the end of this chapter, asks you to revise the definition of the method `insertNode`, so that before inserting the item, the method checks to see whether it is already in the list. If the item to be inserted is already in the list, the method outputs an appropriate error message. In other words, duplicates are not allowed.

Delete Node

To delete a given item from an ordered linked list, first we search the list to see whether the item to be deleted is in the list. The method to implement this operation is the same as the delete operation on general linked lists. Here, because the list is sorted, we can somewhat improve the algorithm for ordered linked lists.

As in the case of the method `insertNode`, we search the list with two reference variables, `current` and `trailCurrent`. Similar to the operation `insertNode`, several cases arise:

Case 1: The list is initially empty. We have an error. We cannot delete from an empty list.

Case 2: The item to be deleted is contained in the first node of the list. We must adjust the value of `first`.

Case 3: The item to be deleted is somewhere in the list. In this case, `current` points to the node containing the item to be deleted, and `trailCurrent` points to the node just before the node pointed to by `current`.

Case 4: The list is not empty, but the item to be deleted is not in the list.

The definition of the method `deleteNode` is:

```
public void deleteNode(DataElement deleteItem)
{
    LinkedListNode current;       //variable to traverse the list
    LinkedListNode trailCurrent;  //variable just before current
    boolean found;

    if(first == null)     //Case 1; list is empty.
        System.err.println("Cannot delete from an "
                        + "empty list.");
    else
    {
        if(first.info.equals(deleteItem)) //Case 2
        {
            first = first.link;
            count--;
        }
        else   //search the list for the node with the given info
        {
            found = false;
            trailCurrent = first;   //set trailCurrent to point to
                                    //the first node
            current = first.link;   //set current to point to the
                                    //second node

            while(current != null && !found)
            {
                if(current.info.compareTo(deleteItem) >= 0)
                    found = true;
                else
                {
                    trailCurrent = current;
                    current = current.link;
                }
            }//end while
```

```
            if(current == null)    //Case 4
                System.out.println("Item to be deleted is "
                                   + "not in the list.");
            else
                if(current.info.equals(deleteItem)) //item to be
                                               //deleted is in the list
                {
                    if(first == current)                //Case 2
                    {
                        first = first.link;
                        count--;
                    }
                    else                                //Case 3
                    {
                        trailCurrent.link = current.link;
                        count--;
                    }
                }
                else                                    //Case 4
                    System.out.println("Item to be deleted is "
                                       + " not in the list.");
        }
    }//end else
}//end deleteNode
```

You can write the definition of the **class OrderedLinkedList** as follows:

```
public class OrderedLinkedList extends LinkedListClass
{
        //default constructor
    public OrderedLinkedList()
    {
        super();
    }

        //copy constructor
    public OrderedLinkedList(OrderedLinkedList otherList)
    {
        super(otherList);
    }

    //Place the definitions of the methods search,
    //insert, and deleteNode here.
}
```

The following program tests various operations on an ordered linked list:

```
//Program to test various operations on an ordered linked list

import java.io.*;
import java.util.*;

public class TestProgOrderedLinkedList
{
    static BufferedReader keyboard = new
            BufferedReader(new InputStreamReader(System.in));

    public static void main(String[] args) throws IOException
    {
        OrderedLinkedList list1
                    = new OrderedLinkedList();              //Line 1
        OrderedLinkedList list2
                    = new OrderedLinkedList();              //Line 2
        IntElement num = new IntElement();                  //Line 3
        StringTokenizer tokenizer;                          //Line 4

        System.out.println("Line 5: Enter integers ending "
                      + "with -999 in one line");           //Line 5
        tokenizer =
            new StringTokenizer(keyboard.readLine());       //Line 6
        num.setNum(
              Integer.parseInt(tokenizer.nextToken()));     //Line 7

        while(num.getNum() != -999)                         //Line 8
        {
           list1.insertNode(num);                           //Line 9
           num.setNum(
               Integer.parseInt(tokenizer.nextToken()));    //Line 10
        }

        System.out.println();                               //Line 11

        System.out.println("Line 12: list1: ");             //Line 12
        list1.print();                                      //Line 13
        System.out.println();                               //Line 14
        System.out.println("Line 15: Length of list1: "
                      + list1.length());                    //Line 15

        list2.copyList(list1);                              //Line 16

        System.out.println("Line 17: list2: ");             //Line 17
        list2.print();                                      //Line 18
        System.out.println();                               //Line 19
        System.out.println("Line 20: Length of list2: "
                      + list2.length());                    //Line 20
```

4

```
        System.out.print("Line 21: Enter the number "
                       + "to be deleted: ");              //Line 21
        System.out.flush();
        num.setNum(Integer.parseInt(keyboard.readLine())); //Line 22
        System.out.println();                             //Line 23

        list2.deleteNode(num);                            //Line 24

        System.out.println("Line 25: After deleting "
                       + "the node, list2: ");            //Line 25
        list2.print();                                    //Line 26
        System.out.println();                             //Line 27

        System.out.println("Line 28: Length of list2: "
                       + list2.length());                 //Line 28

        System.out.println();                             //Line 29
        System.out.println("Line 30: list1: ");           //Line 30
        list1.print();                                    //Line 31
        System.out.println();                             //Line 32
        System.out.println("Line 33: Length of list1: "
                       + list1.length());                 //Line 33
    }
}
```

Sample Run: In this sample run, the user input is shaded.

```
Line 5: Enter integers ending with -999 in one line
26 53 78 29 66 19 45 -999

Line 12: list1:
19 26 29 45 53 66 78
Line 15: Length of list1: 7
Line 17: list2:
19 26 29 45 53 66 78
Line 20: Length of list2: 7
Line 21: Enter the number to be deleted: 29

Line 25: After deleting the node, list2:
19 26 45 53 66 78
Line 28: Length of list2: 6

Line 30: list1:
19 26 29 45 53 66 78
Line 33: Length of list1: 7
```

The details of the preceding program output are left as an exercise for you.

DOUBLY LINKED LISTS

A doubly linked list is a linked list in which every node has a reference of the next node and a reference of the previous node. In other words, every node (except the last node) contains the address of the next node and every node (except the first node) contains the address of the previous node. See Figure 4-43.

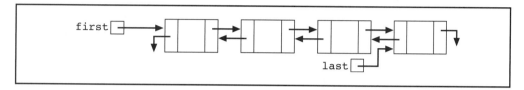

Figure 4-43   Doubly linked list

A doubly linked list can be traversed in either direction. That is, we can traverse the list starting at the first node or, if a reference variable to the last node is given, we can traverse the list starting at the last node.

As before, the usual operations on a doubly linked list are:

1. Initialize the list.

2. Determine whether the list is empty.

3. Find the length of the list.

4. Output the list.

5. Search the list for a given item.

6. Retrieve the first element of the list.

7. Retrieve the last element of the list.

8. Insert an item in the list.

9. Delete an item from the list.

10. Make a copy of the list.

The following statements define a doubly linked list as an ADT:

Class: `DoublyLinkedList`

Definition of the Node:

```
protected class DoublyLinkedListNode
{
    DataElement info;
    DoublyLinkedListNode next;
    DoublyLinkedListNode back;
}
```

Instance Variables:

```
protected int count;
protected DoublyLinkedListNode first; //variable to store the
                                      //number of nodes
                                      //reference variable to
                                      //point to the first node
protected DoublyLinkedListNode last;  //reference variable to
                                      //point to the last node
```

Constructors and Instance Methods:

```
public DoublyLinkedList()
    //default constructor
    //Initializes the list to an empty state.
    //Postcondition: first = null; last = null; count = 0

public DoublyLinkedList(DoublyLinkedList otherList)
    //copy constructor

public boolean isEmptyList()
    //Method to determine whether the list is empty.
    //Postcondition: Returns true if the list is empty,
    //               false otherwise.

public void initializeList()
    //Method to initialize the list to an empty state.
    //Postcondition: first = null; last = null; count = 0

public int length()
    //Method to return the number of nodes in the list.
    //Postcondition: The value of count is returned.

public void print()
    //Method to output the info contained in each node.

public void reversePrint()
    //Method to output the info contained in each node
    //in the reverse order.
```

```
public boolean search(DataElement searchItem)
    //Method to determine whether searchItem is in the list.
    //Postcondition: Returns true if searchItem is found
    //               in the list, false otherwise.

public DataElement front()
    //Method to return the first element of the list.
    //Precondition: The list must exist and must not be
    //              empty.
    //Postcondition: If the list is empty, the program
    //               terminates; otherwise, the first
    //               element of the list is returned.

public DataElement back()
    //Method to return the last element of the list.
    //Precondition: The list must exist and must not
    //              be empty.
    //Postcondition: If the list is empty, the
    //               program terminates; otherwise,
    //               the last element of the list is
    //               returned.

public void insertNode(DataElement insertItem)
    //Method to insert insertItem in the list.
    //Precondition: If the list is nonempty, it must
    //              be in order.
    //Postcondition: insertItem is inserted at the
    //        proper place in the list. Also, first points
    //        to the first node, last points to the
    //        last node of the new list, and count
    //        is incremented by 1.

public void deleteNode(DataElement deleteItem)
    //Method to delete deleteItem from the list.
    //Postcondition: If found, the node containing
    //        deleteItem is deleted from the list. Also,
    //        first points to the first node of the new
    //        list, last points to the last node of the new
    //        list, and count is decremented by 1.
    //        Otherwise, an appropriate message
    //        is printed.

private void copy(DoublyLinkedList otherList)
    //Method to make a copy of otherList.
    //Postcondition: A copy of otherList is created
    //               and assigned to this list.

public void copyList(DoublyLinkedList otherList)
    //Method to make a copy of otherList.
    //Postcondition: A copy of otherList is created
    //               and assigned to this list.
```

4

The methods to implement the operations of a doubly linked list are similar to the ones discussed in the previous two sections. Here, because every node has two links, **back** and **next**, some of the operations require the adjustment of two links in each node. We give the definition of each method here, with three exceptions. Definitions of the methods **copy**, **copyList**, and the copy constructor are left as exercises for you (see Programming Exercise 10 at the end of this chapter).

Default Constructor

The default constructor initializes the doubly linked list to an empty state. It sets **first** and **last** to **null**, and **count to 0**. Its definition is:

```
public DoublyLinkedList()
{
    first= null;
    last = null;
    count = 0;
}
```

isEmptyList

This operation returns **true** if the list is empty; otherwise, it returns **false**. The list is empty if **first** is **null**. Its definition is:

```
public boolean isEmptyList()
{
    return (first == null);
}
```

Initialize List

This operation reinitializes the doubly linked list to an empty state. The definition of the method **initializeList** is:

```
public void initializeList()
{
    first = null;
    last = null;
    count = 0;
}
```

Length of the List

The length of a list is the number of nodes in the list. This operation returns the value of **count**. Its definition is:

```
public int length()
{
    return count;
}
```

Print

The method `print` outputs the data stored in the nodes of a doubly linked list. To output the data contained in each node, we must traverse the list starting at the first node. Because `first` always points to the first node in the list, we use another variable to traverse the list. The definition of the method `print` is:

```
public void print()
{
    DoublyLinkedListNode current; //variable to traverse the list

    current = first;  //set current to point to the first node

    while(current != null)
    {
        System.out.print(current.info + "  ");
        current = current.next;
    }//end while
}
```

Reverse Print List

This method outputs the data contained in each node in reverse order. We traverse the list in reverse order starting at the last node. Its definition is:

```
public void reversePrint()
{
    DoublyLinkedListNode current; //variable to traverse the list

    current = last;  //set current to point to the last node

    while(current != null)
    {
        System.out.print(current.info + "  ");
        current = current.back;
    }//end while
}//end reversePrint
```

Search List

The method `search` returns `true` if the search item is in the list; otherwise, it returns `false`. This search algorithm is exactly the same as the search algorithm for an ordered linked list. Its definition is:

```
public boolean search(DataElement searchItem)
{
    boolean found;
    DoublyLinkedListNode current; //variable to traverse the list
```

```
        found = false;
        current = first;

        while(current != null && !found)
            if(current.info.compareTo(searchItem) >= 0)
                found = true;
            else
                current = current.next;

        if(found)
            found = current.info.equals(searchItem); //test for equality

        return found;
}//end search
```

First and the Last Element

The method **front** returns the first element of the list; the method **back** returns the last element. The definitions of these methods are similar to the definitions of the corresponding methods of the **class LinkedListClass**. Their definitions are:

```
public DataElement front()
{
    DataElement temp = first.info.getCopy();
    return temp;
}

public DataElement back()
{
    DataElement temp = last.info.getCopy();
    return temp;
}
```

If the list is empty, both the methods **front** and **back** terminate the program.

Insert Node

Because we are inserting an item in a doubly linked list, the insertion of a node in the list requires the adjustment of two links in certain nodes. As before, we find the place where the new item is supposed to be inserted, create the node, store the new item, and adjust the link fields of the new node and other specific nodes in the list. There are four cases:

Case 1: Insertion in an empty list.

Case 2: Insertion at the beginning of a nonempty list.

Case 3: Insertion at the end of a nonempty list.

Case 4: Insertion somewhere in a nonempty list.

Case 1 requires us to change the values of **first** and **last**. Case 2 requires us to change the value of **first**. Cases 3 and 4 are similar. Next, we show Case 4.

Consider the doubly linked list shown in Figure 4-44.

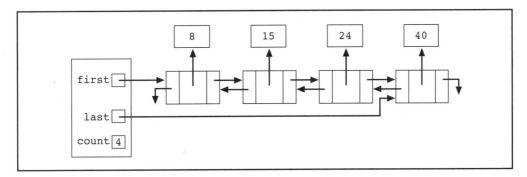

Figure 4-44   Doubly linked list before inserting 20

Suppose that 20 is to be inserted in the list. After inserting 20, Figure 4-45 shows the resulting list.

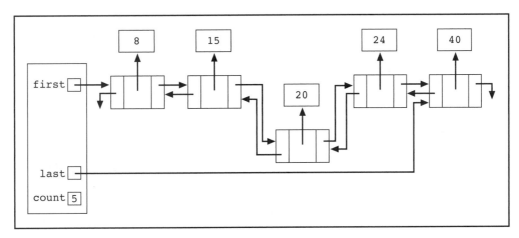

Figure 4-45   Doubly linked list after inserting 20

From Figure 4-45, it follows that the link **next** of the node with data 15, the link **back** of the node with data 24, and both the links **next** and **back** of the node with data 20 need to be adjusted. Also, **count** is incremented by 1. The definition of the method **insertNode** is:

```
public void insertNode(DataElement insertItem)
{
    DoublyLinkedListNode current; //variable to traverse the list
    DoublyLinkedListNode trailCurrent = null; //variable just
                                              //before current
    DoublyLinkedListNode newNode;  //variable to create a node
    boolean found;

    newNode = new DoublyLinkedListNode(); //create the node

    newNode.info = insertItem.getCopy(); //store new item in the
                                          //node
    newNode.next = null;
    newNode.back = null;

    if(first == null) //if the list is empty, newNode is the
                      //only node
    {
        first = newNode;
        last = newNode;
        count++;
    }
    else
    {
        found = false;
        current = first;

        while(current != null && !found) //search the list
            if(current.info.compareTo(insertItem) >= 0)
                found = true;
            else
            {
                trailCurrent = current;
                current = current.next;
            }

        if(current == first) //insert new node before first
        {
            first.back = newNode;
            newNode.next = first;
            first = newNode;
            count++;
        }
        else
        {
                //insert newNode between trailCurrent and current
            if(current != null)
            {
                trailCurrent.next = newNode;
                newNode.back = trailCurrent;
```

```
         newNode.next = current;
         current.back = newNode;
      }
      else
      {
         trailCurrent.next = newNode;
         newNode.back = trailCurrent;
         last = newNode;
      }
      count++;
   }//end else
  }//end else
}//end insertNode
```

Delete Node

This operation deletes a given item (if found) from a doubly linked list. As before, we first search the list to see whether the item to be deleted is in the list. The search algorithm is the same as before. Similar to the `insertNode` operation, this operation (if the item to be deleted is in the list) requires the adjustment of two links in certain nodes. The delete operation has several cases:

Case 1: The list is empty.

Case 2: The item to be deleted is in the first node of the list, which would require us to change the value of `first`.

Case 3: The item to be deleted is somewhere in the list.

Case 4: The item to be deleted is not in the list.

Let us demonstrate Case 3. Consider the list shown in Figure 4-46.

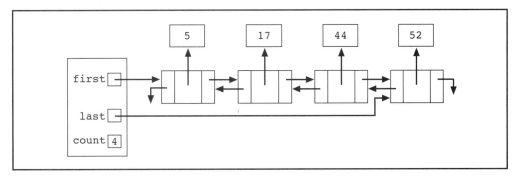

Figure 4-46   Doubly linked list before deleting 17

Suppose that the item to be deleted is 17. We search the list, find the node with `info` 17, and then adjust the link fields of the affected nodes. See Figure 4-47.

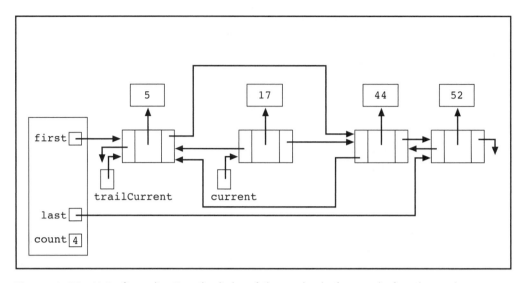

Figure 4-47 List after adjusting the links of the nodes before and after the node with data 17

Next, we decrement **count** by 1. See Figure 4-48.

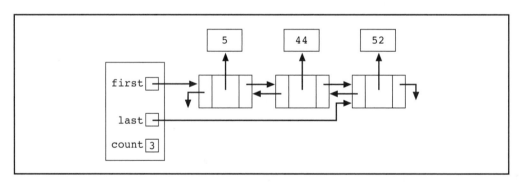

Figure 4-48 List after deleting the node with data 17

The definition of the method **deleteNode** is:

```
public void deleteNode(DataElement deleteItem)
{
    DoublyLinkedListNode current; //variable to traverse the list
    DoublyLinkedListNode trailCurrent; //variable just
                                       //before current

    boolean found;
```

```
    if(first == null)
        System.err.println("Cannot delete from an empty list.");
    else
        if(first.info.equals(deleteItem)) //node to be deleted is
                                          //the first node
        {
            current = first;
            first = first.next;

            if(first != null)
                first.back = null;
            else
                last = null;

            count--;
        }
        else
        {
            found = false;
            current = first;

            while(current != null && !found)  //search the list
                    if(current.info.compareTo(deleteItem) >= 0)
                        found = true;
                    else
                        current = current.next;

            if(current == null)
                System.out.println("The item to be deleted "
                                    + "is not in the list.");
            else
                if(current.info.equals(deleteItem))//check for equality
                {
                    trailCurrent = current.back;
                    trailCurrent.next = current.next;

                    if(current.next != null)
                        current.next.back = trailCurrent;

                    if(current == last)
                        last = trailCurrent;

                    count--;
                }
                else
                    System.out.println("The item to be deleted "
                                        + "is not in list.");
        }//end else
}//end deleteNode
```

4

The analyses of the methods of the `class DoublyLinkedList` are similar to that of the `class LinkedListClass` and, therefore, are left as exercises for you.

LINKED LISTS WITH HEADER AND TRAILER NODES

When inserting items into and deleting items from a linked list (especially an ordered list), we saw that there are special cases, such as inserting (or deleting) at the beginning (the first node) of the list or in an empty list. These cases need to be handled separately. As a result, the insertion and deletion algorithms are not as simple and straightforward as we might like. One way to simplify these algorithms is to never insert an item before the first or after the last item and to never delete the first node. Next, we discuss how to do this.

Suppose the nodes of a list are in order; that is, they are arranged with respect to a given key. Further suppose that it is possible for us to determine what the smallest and largest keys are in the given data set. In this case we can set up a node, called the **header**, at the beginning of the list containing a value smaller than the smallest value in the data set. Similarly, we can set up a node, called the **trailer**, at the end of the list containing a value larger than the largest value in the data set. These two nodes, header and trailer, serve merely to simplify the insertion and deletion algorithms and are not part of the actual list. The actual list is between these two nodes.

For example, suppose the data is ordered according to the last name. Further assume that the last name is a string of at most **8** characters. The smallest last name is larger than the string `"A"` and the largest last name is smaller than the string `"zzzzzzzz"`. We can set up the header node with the value `"A"` and the trailer node with the value `"zzzzzzzz"`. The list in Figure 4-49 illustrates this concept.

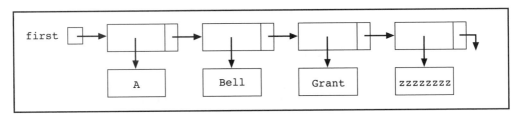

Figure 4-49 Nonempty linked list with header and trailer nodes

An empty linked list with header and trailer nodes has only two nodes, header and trailer. Figure 4-50 shows an empty linked list with header and trailer nodes.

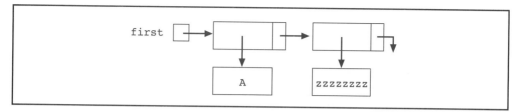

Figure 4-50   Empty linked list with header and trailer nodes

As before, the usual operations on lists with header and trailer nodes are:

1. Initialize the list (to an empty state).
2. Determine whether the list is empty.
3. Output the list.
4. Find the length of the list.
5. Search the list for a given item.
6. Retrieve the `info` contained in the first node.
7. Retrieve the `info` contained in the last node.
8. Insert an item in the list.
9. Delete an item from the list.
10. Copy the list.

We leave it as an exercise for you to design a class to implement a linked list with header and trailer nodes (see Programming Exercise 12 at the end of this chapter).

CIRCULAR LINKED LISTS

A linked list in which the last node points to the first node is called a **circular linked list**. Figures 4-51 through 4-53 show various circular linked lists.

Figure 4-51   Empty circular linked list

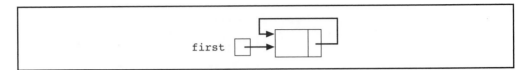

Figure 4-52 Circular linked list with one node

In a circular linked list with more than one node, it is convenient to make the reference variable `first` point to the last node of the list. Then, by using `first` you can access both the first and the last node of the list. For example, `first` points to the last node and `first.link` points to the first node. Figure 4-53 shows a circular linked list with more than one node.

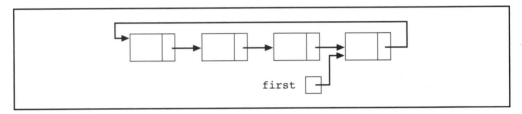

Figure 4-53 Circular linked list with more than one node

As before, the usual operations on circular linked lists are:

1. Initialize the list (to an empty state).

2. Determine whether the list is empty.

3. Print the list.

4. Find the length of the list.

5. Search the list for a given item.

6. Retrieve the `info` contained in the first node.

7. Retrieve the `info` contained in the last node.

8. Insert an item in the list.

9. Delete an item from the list.

10. Copy the list.

We leave it as an exercise for you design a class to implement a sorted circular linked list (see Programming Exercise 13 at the end of this chapter).

PROGRAMMING EXAMPLE: VIDEO STORE

For a family or an individual, a favorite place to go on weekends or holidays is to a video store to rent movies. A new video store in your neighborhood is about to open. However, it does not have a program to keep track of its videos and customers. The store managers want someone to write a program for their system so that the video store can function. The program should be able to perform the following operations:

1. Rent a video; that is, check out a video.
2. Return, or check in, a video.
3. Create a list of videos owned by the store.
4. Show the details of a particular video.
5. Print a list of all the videos in the store.
6. Check whether a particular video is in the store.
7. Maintain a customer database.
8. Print a list of all the videos rented by each customer.

Let us write a program for the video store. This example further illustrates the object-oriented design methodology and, in particular, inheritance and polymorphism.

The programming requirement tells us that the video store has two major components: videos and customers. We will describe these two components in detail. We also need to maintain the following lists:

- A list of all the videos in the store
- A list of all the store's customers
- Lists of the videos currently rented by the customers

We will develop the program in two parts. In Part 1, we design, implement, and test the video component. In Part 2, we design and implement the customer component, which we then add to the video component developed in Part 1. After completing Parts 1 and 2, we can perform all the operations previously listed.

To maintain the list of videos owned by the store, the list of customers, and the lists of videos rented by the customers, we use the **class UnorderedLinkedList**. The instance variable **info** is a reference variable of the **class DataElement**, and is used to point to the object containing the relevant data. Therefore, the classes to implement the video objects and customers objects are derived from the **class DataElement**. For example, suppose that the **class Video** (described in the next section) is designed to implement the video objects. Then the **class DataElement** is the superclass of the **class Video**.

Part 1: The Video Component

The Video Object

This is the first stage, wherein we discuss the components of a video object. The common characteristics of a video are the:

- Name of the movie
- Names of the stars
- Name of the producer
- Name of the director
- Name of the production company
- Number of copies in the store

From this list, we see that some of the operations to be performed on the video object are:

1. Set the video information—that is, the title, stars, production company, and so on.
2. Show the details of a particular video.
3. Check the number of copies in the store.
4. Check out (that is, rent) the video. In other words, if the number of copies is greater than zero, decrement the number of copies by one.
5. Check in (that is, return) the video. To check in a video, first we must check whether the store owns such a video and, if it does, increment the number of copies by one.
6. Check whether a particular video is available—that is, the number of copies currently in the store is greater than zero.

To delete a video from the video list, the video list must be searched for the video. Thus, we need to check the title of a video to find out which video is to be deleted. Two videos are the same if they have the same title.

The following statements define the video object as an ADT:

Class: `VideoElement`

```
public class VideoElement extends DataElement
```

Instance Variables:

```
private String videoTitle;      //variable to store the name
                                //of the movie
private String movieStar1;      //variable to store the name
                                //of the star
private String movieStar2;      //variable to store the name
                                //of the star
private String movieProducer;   //variable to store the name
                                //of the producer
private String movieDirector;   //variable to store the name
                                //of the director
```

```
private String movieProductionCo;    //variable to store the name
                                     //of the production company
private int copiesInStock;    //variable to store the number of
                              //copies in stock
```

Constructors and Instance Methods:

```
public VideoElement()
   //default constructor
   //Instance variables are initialized to their default values.
   //Postcondition: videoTitle = ""; movieStar1 = "";
   //          movieStar2 = ""; movieProducer = "";
   //          movieDirector = "";
   //          movieProductionCo = "";
   //          copiesInStock = 0;


public VideoElement(String title, String star1,
                    String star2, String producer,
                    String director, String productionCo,
                    int setInStock)
   //constructor with parameters
   //Instance variables are set according to the parameters.
   //Postcondition: videoTitle = title; movieStar1 = star1;
   //          movieStar2 = star2; movieProducer = producer;
   //          movieDirector = director;
   //          movieProductionCo = productionCo;
   //          copiesInStock = setInStock;

public void setVideoInfo(String title, String star1,
                         String star2, String producer,
                         String director, String productionCo,
                         int setInStock)
   //Method to set the details of a video.
   //Instance variables are set according to the parameters.
   //Postcondition: videoTitle = title; movieStar1 = star1;
   //             movieStar2 = star2; movieProducer = producer;
   //             movieDirector = director;
   //             movieProductionCo = productionCo;
   //             copiesInStock = setInStock;

public int getNoOfCopiesInStock()
   //Method to check the number of copies in stock.
   //Postcondition:  The value of the instance variable
   //             copiesInStock is returned.

public void checkIn()
   //Method to check in a video.
   //Postcondition: The number of copies in stock is incremented
   //             by one.
```

```
public void checkOut()
   //Method to rent a video.
   //Postcondition: If there is a video in stock, its number of
   //               copies in stock is decremented by one;
   //               otherwise, an appropriate message is printed.

public void printTitle()
   //Method to print the title of a movie.

public void printInfo()
   //Method to print the details of a video.

public boolean checkTitle(String title)
   //Method to determine whether title is the same as the
   //title of the video.
   //Postcondition: Returns the value true if the title is the
   //               same as the title of the video,
   //               false otherwise.

public void updateInStock(int num)
   //Method to increment the number of copies in stock by
   //adding the value of the parameter num.
   //Postcondition: copiesInStock = copiesInStock  + num;

public void setCopiesInStock(int num)
   //Method to set the number of copies in stock.
   //Postcondition: copiesInStock = num;

public String getTitle()
   //Returns the title of the video.
   //Postcondition: The value of the instance variable
   //               videoTitle is returned.

      //abstract methods of the class DataElement
public boolean equals(DataElement otherElement)
public int compareTo(DataElement otherElement)
public void makeCopy(DataElement otherElement)
public DataElement getCopy()
```

We leave the UML diagram of the **class VideoElement** as an exercise for you.

Next, we write the definitions of each method in the **class VideoElement**. The definitions of these methods are given next and are easy to follow.

```
public void setVideoInfo(String title, String star1,
                         String star2, String producer,
                         String director, String productionCo,
                         int setInStock)
```

```java
{
    videoTitle = title;
    movieStar1 = star1;
    movieStar2 = star2;
    movieProducer = producer;
    movieDirector = director;
    movieProductionCo = productionCo;
    copiesInStock = setInStock;
}

public int getNoOfCopiesInStock()
{
    return copiesInStock;
}

public void checkIn()
{
    copiesInStock++;
}

public void checkOut()
{
    if(getNoOfCopiesInStock() > 0)
        copiesInStock--;
    else
        System.out.println("Currently out of stock.");
}

public void printTitle()
{
    System.out.println("Video Title: " + videoTitle);
}

public void printInfo()
{
    System.out.println("Video Title: " + videoTitle);
    System.out.println("Stars: " + movieStar1 + " and "
                     + movieStar2);
    System.out.println("Producer: " + movieProducer);
    System.out.println("Director: " + movieDirector);
    System.out.println("Production Company: "
                     + movieProductionCo);
    System.out.println("Copies in stock: " + copiesInStock);
    System.out.println();
}
```

```java
public boolean checkTitle(String title)
{
    return (videoTitle.compareTo(title) == 0);
}

public void updateInStock(int num)
{
    copiesInStock += num;
}

public void setCopiesInStock(int num)
{
    copiesInStock = num;
}

public String getTitle()
{
    return videoTitle;
}

public VideoElement(String title, String star1,
                    String star2, String producer,
                    String director, String productionCo,
                    int setInStock)
{
    videoTitle = title;
    movieStar1 = star1;
    movieStar2 = star2;
    movieProducer = producer;
    movieDirector = director;
    movieProductionCo = productionCo;
    copiesInStock = setInStock;
}

public VideoElement()
{
    videoTitle = "";
    movieStar1 = "";
    movieStar2 = "";
    movieProducer = "";
    movieDirector = "";
    movieProductionCo = "";
    copiesInStock = 0;
}
```

```java
public boolean equals(DataElement otherElement)
{
    VideoElement temp = (VideoElement) otherElement;

    return (videoTitle.compareTo(temp.videoTitle) == 0);
}

public int compareTo(DataElement otherElement)
{
    VideoElement temp = (VideoElement) otherElement;

    return (videoTitle.compareTo(temp.videoTitle));
}

public void makeCopy(DataElement otherElement)
{
    VideoElement temp = (VideoElement) otherElement;

    videoTitle = temp.videoTitle;
    movieStar1 = temp.movieStar1;
    movieStar2 = temp.movieStar2;
    movieProducer = temp.movieProducer;
    movieDirector = temp.movieDirector;
    movieProductionCo = temp.movieProductionCo;
    copiesInStock = temp.copiesInStock;
}

public DataElement getCopy()
{
    VideoElement temp = new VideoElement(videoTitle, movieStar1,
                            movieStar2, movieProducer,
                            movieDirector,
                            movieProductionCo, copiesInStock);
    return temp;
}
```

You can write the definition of the class VideoElement as follows:

```java
public class VideoElement extends DataElement
{
      //Place the instance variables here.
      //Place the definitions of the constructors and
      //instance methods here.
}
```

Video List

This program requires us to maintain a list of all the videos in the store, and we should be able to add a new video to our list. Typically, we do not know how many videos are in the store, and adding or deleting a video changes the number of videos in the store. Therefore, as remarked previously, we use a linked list to create a list of videos. See Figure 4-54. (Notice that, for simplicity, the figure does not show the instance variable count.)

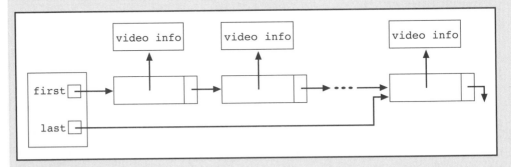

Figure 4-54 videoList

Earlier in this chapter, we defined the class UnorderedLinkedList to create a linked list of objects. We also defined the basic operations such as insertion and deletion of a video in the list. However, some operations are very specific to a video list, such as check out a video, check in a video, set the number of copies of a video, and so on. These operations are not available in the class UnorderedLinkedList. Therefore, we derive the class videoList from the class UnorderedLinkedList and add these operations.

The following statements define the class VideoList as an ADT:

Class: VideoList

```
public class VideoList extends UnorderedLinkedList
```

Instance Variables:

Same as the instance variables of the class UnorderedLinkedList

Constructors and Instance Methods:

```
public VideoList()
    //default constructor

public VideoList(VideoList otherList)
    //copy constructor
```

```
private LinkedListNode searchVideoList(String title)
   //Method to search the video list for a particular
   //video, specified by the parameter title.
   //Postcondition: If the video is found, a reference to
   //               the node containing the video is returned;
   //               otherwise, the null reference is returned.

public boolean videoSearch(String title)
   //Method to search the list to see whether a particular
   //title, specified by the parameter title, is in the store.
   //Postcondition: Returns true if the title is found,
   //               false otherwise.

public boolean isVideoAvailable(String title)
   //Method to determine whether the video specified by the
   //parameter title is available.
   //Postcondition: Returns true if at least one copy of the
   //               video is available, false otherwise.

public void videoCheckIn(String title)
   //Method to check in a video returned by a customer.
   //Postcondition: If the video returned is from the
   //               store, its copiesInstock is incremented
   //               by one; otherwise, an appropriate message
   //               is printed.

public void videoCheckOut(String title)
   //Method to check out a video, that is, rent a video.
   //Postcondition: If a video is available, its copiesInStock
   //               is decremented by one; otherwise, an
   //               appropriate message is printed.

public boolean videoCheckTitle(String title)
   //Method to determine whether the video specified by the
   //parameter title is in the store.
   //Postcondition: Returns true if the video is
   //               in the store, false otherwise.

public void videoUpdateInStock(String title, int num)
   //Method to update the number of copies of a video
   //by adding the value of the parameter num. The
   //parameter title specifies the name of the video
   //for which the number of copies is to be updated.
   //Postcondition: If video is found; then
   //               copiesInStock = copiesInStock + num;
   //               otherwise, an appropriate message is
   //               printed.
```

```
public void videoSetCopiesInStock(String title, int num)
   //Method to reset the number of copies of a video.
   //The parameter title specifies the name of the video
   //for which the number of copies is to be reset, and the
   //parameter num specifies the number of copies.
   //Postcondition: If video is found, then
   //                 copiesInStock = num;
   //                 otherwise, an appropriate message
   //                 is printed.

public void videoPrintTitle()
   //Method to print the titles of all the videos in the store.

public void print()
   //Method to print the info of all the videos in the store.
```

 We derive the class VideoList from the class UnorderedLinkedList so that the items can be inserted quickly at the beginning (using the method insertFirst) or at the end of the list (using the method insertLast). However, you can also derive the class VideoList from the class OrderedLinkedList, in which case the video list would be in order. We leave it as an exercise for you to derive the class VideoList from the class OrderedLinkedList.

The definitions of the methods to implement the operations of the **class VideoList** are given next.

The primary operations on the video list are to check in a video and to check out a video. Both operations require the list to be searched, and the location of the video being checked in or checked out to be found in the video list. Other operations such as checking whether a particular video is in the store, updating the number of copies, and so on also require the video list to be searched. To simplify the search process, we write a method that searches the video list for a particular video. If the video is found, it returns the reference of the node containing the search item; otherwise, it returns the value **null**; and other operations on the video object can be performed. Note that the method **searchVideoList** is a **private** data member of the **class VideoList** because it is used only for internal manipulation. First, we describe the search procedure.

Consider the node of the video list shown in Figure 4-55.

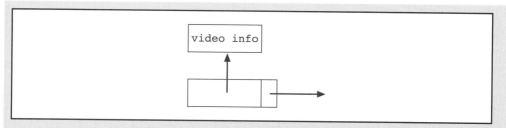

Figure 4-55 Node of a video list

The instance variable `info` points to an object of the **class VideoElement**, and the object contains the necessary information about a video. A `VideoElement` object has seven instance variables: `videoTitle`, `movieStar1`, `movieStar2`, `movieProducer`, `movieDirector`, `movieProductionCo`, and `copiesInStock` (see the definition of the **class VideoElement**). Therefore, the node of a video list has the form shown in Figure 4-56.

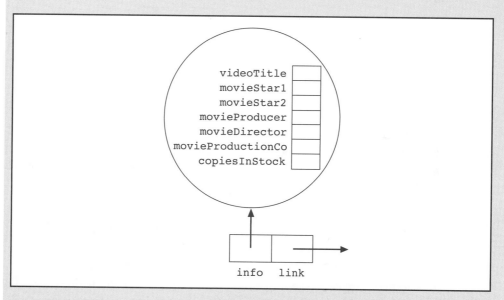

Figure 4-56   Video list node showing the object `info`

The instance variables of a `VideoElement` object are **private** and cannot be accessed directly. The methods of the **class VideoElement** help us to check and/or set the value of a particular instance variable.

Suppose `current` points to a node in the video list. See Figure 4-57.

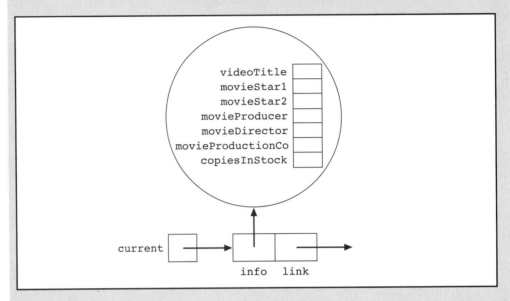

Figure 4-57 Variable `current` and a node of the video list

Now

`current.info`

refers to the `info` part of the node. Suppose that we want to know whether the title of the video stored in this node is the same as the title specified by the variable `title`. The expression:

`current.info.checkTitle(title)`

is `true` if the title of the video stored in this node is the same as the title specified by the parameter `title`, and `false` otherwise. (Note that the method `checkTitle` is a value-returning method. See its declaration in the **class VideoElement**.)

As another example, suppose that we want to set the value of the instance variable `copiesInStock` of this object to 10. Because `copiesInStock` is a `private` data member, it cannot be accessed directly. Therefore, the statement:

`current.info.copiesInStock = 10;  //illegal`

is incorrect and generates a compile-time error. We have to use the method `setCopiesInStock` as follows:

`current.info.setCopiesInStock(10);`

Now that we know how to access a data member of a video stored in a node, let us describe the algorithm to search the video list.

```
if the video list is empty
    Error
else
    while(not found)
        if the title of the current video is the same as the
            desired title, stop the search
        else
            check the next node
```

The following method performs the desired search:

```
private LinkedListNode searchVideoList(String title)
{
    boolean found = false;    //set found to false
    LinkedListNode current = null;
    VideoElement temp = new VideoElement();

    if(first == null)  //the list is empty
        System.out.println("Cannot search an empty list. ");
    else
    {
        current = first;   //set current to point to first node
                           //in the list
        found = false;     //set found to false

        while(current != null && !found)     //search the list
        {
            temp = (VideoElement) current.info;

            if(temp.checkTitle(title)) //item is found
                found = true;
            else
                current = current.link; //advance current to
                                        //the next node
        }
    }//end else

    return current;
}//end searchVideoList
```

If the search is successful, the reference of the node containing the search item is returned; otherwise, null is returned.

The definitions of the other methods of the class VideoList are:

```
public boolean videoSearch(String title)
{
    LinkedListNode location;

    location = searchVideoList(title);
    return (location != null);
}

public boolean isVideoAvailable(String title)
{
    LinkedListNode location;
    VideoElement temp;

    location = searchVideoList(title);

    if(location != null)
    {
        temp = (VideoElement) location.info;
        return (temp.getNoOfCopiesInStock() > 0);
    }
    else
        return false;
}
```

Consider the statement

```
temp = (VideoElement) location.info;
```

in the definition of the method isVideoAvailable. Notice that temp is a reference variable of the VideoElement type, and location.info is a reference variable of the DataElement type. Now location.info points to the object containing such information as the number of copies of the video currently in the store. Because DataElement is the superclass of the class VideoElement, we use the cast operator and make temp point to the object containing the video data. The variable temp then uses the method getNoOfCopiesInStock to see whether there is a copy of this video available in the store. Notice that the definitions of the methods given next use a similar statement to access the data stored in a VideoElement object.

```
public void videoCheckIn(String title)
{
    LinkedListNode location;
    VideoElement temp;

    location = searchVideoList(title);   //search the list
```

```
        if(location != null)
        {
           temp = (VideoElement) location.info;
           temp.checkIn();
        }
        else
           System.out.println("The store does not carry "
                             + "this video.");
    }

    public void videoCheckOut(String title)
    {
        LinkedListNode location;
        VideoElement temp;

        location = searchVideoList(title);   //search the list

        if(location != null)
        {
           temp = (VideoElement) location.info;
           temp.checkOut();
        }
        else
           System.out.println("The store does not carry "
                             + "this video.");
    }

    public boolean videoCheckTitle(String title)
    {
        LinkedListNode location;

        location = searchVideoList(title); //search the list

        return (location != null);
    }

    public void videoUpdateInStock(String title, int num)
    {
        LinkedListNode location;
        VideoElement temp;

        location = searchVideoList(title); //search the list

        if(location != null)
        {
           temp = (VideoElement) location.info;
           temp.updateInStock(num);
        }
```

```
        else
            System.out.println("The store does not carry "
                                + "this video.");
}

public void videoSetCopiesInStock(String title, int num)
{
    LinkedListNode location;
    VideoElement temp;

    location = searchVideoList(title);

    if(location != null)
    {
        temp = (VideoElement) location.info;
        temp.setCopiesInStock(num);
    }
    else
        System.out.println("The store does not carry "
                            + "this video.");
}

public void videoPrintTitle()
{
    LinkedListNode current;
    VideoElement temp;

    current = first;
    while(current != null)
    {
        temp = (VideoElement) current.info;
        temp.printTitle();
        current = current.link;
    }
}

public void print()
{
    LinkedListNode current; //variable to traverse the list
    VideoElement temp;

    current = first;       //set current so that it points to
                            //the first node
```

```
        while(current != null) //while more data to print
        {
            temp = (VideoElement) current.info;
            temp.printInfo();
            current = current.link;
        }
}
    //default constructor
public VideoList()
{
    super();
}

    //copy constructor
public VideoList(VideoList otherList)
{
    super(otherList);
}
```

You can write the definition of the **class VideoList** as follows:

```
public class VideoList extends UnorderedLinkedList
{
        //Place the instance variables here.
        //Place the definitions of the constructors and
        //the instance methods here.
}
```

Part 2: The Customer Component

The **Customer** Object

The primary characteristics of a customer are:

- First name
- Last name
- Account number
- The list of rented videos

Suppose that we want to know only the number of videos rented by a customer. Instead of searching the list of rented videos (which could take a long time if the list has many entries), we add a fourth member to our **Customer** object, the number of rentals.

Every customer is a person. We have already designed the **class Person** in Example 1-6 (Chapter 1) and described the necessary operations on the name of a person. Therefore, we can derive the **class Customer** from the **class Person** and add the additional members that we need.

The basic operations on a **Customer** object are:

1. Print the name, account number, and number of rentals.
2. Set the name, account number, and number of rentals.
3. Rent a video, i.e., add the video to the list of rented videos.
4. Return a video, i.e., delete the video from the list of rented videos.
5. Show the account number.

The details of implementing the customer component are left as an exercise for you (see Programming Exercise 14 at the end of this chapter).

Main Program

We now write the main program to test the video object. We assume that the necessary data for the videos are stored in a file. We open the file and create the list of videos owned by the video store. The data in the input file is in the following form:

```
video title (the name of the movie)
movie star1
movie star2
movie producer
movie director
movie production company
number of copies
```

We write a method, createVideoList, to read data from the input file and create the list of videos. We also write a method, displayMenu, to show the different choices—such as check in a movie or check out a movie—that the user can make. The algorithm of the method main is:

1. Open the input file.
2. if the input file does not exist, exit the program.
3. Create the list of videos (createVideoList).
4. Show the menu (displayMenu).
5. while not done

    Perform the various operations.

Opening the input file is straightforward. Let us describe Steps 3 and 4, which are done by writing two separate methods: createVideoList and displayMenu.

createVideoList

This method reads the data from the input file and creates a linked list of videos. Because the data is read from a file and the input file was opened in the method main, we pass the appropriate input stream object to this method. We also pass the reference variable used to create the video list, declared in the method main, to this method. Next, we read the data for each video and then insert the video in the list. The general algorithm is:

    a. Read the data and store it in a video object.

    b. Insert the video in the list.

    c. Repeat Steps a and b for each video's data in the file.

`displayMenu`

This method informs the user what to do. It contains the following output statements:

```
Select one of the following:
1: To check whether a particular video is in the store
2: To check out a video
3: To check in afvideo
4: To check whether a particular title is in stock
5: To print the titles of all the videos
6: To print a list of all the videos
9: To exit
```

In pseudocode, Step 4 is:

```
get choice
while(choice != 9)
{
    switch(choice)
    {
    case 1:   a. get the movie name
              b. search the video list
              c. if found, report "success"
                 else report "failure"
    case 2:   a. get the movie name
              b. search the video list
              c. if found, check out the video
                 else report "failure"
    case 3:   a. get the movie name
              b. search the video list
              c. if found, check in the video
                 else report "failure"
    case 4:   a. get the movie name
              b. search the video list
              c. if found
                      if number of copies > 0
                          report "success"
                      else
                          report "currently out of stock"
                 else report "failure"
    case 5: print the titles of the videos
    case 6: print all the videos in the store
    default: bad selection
    }//end switch
```

```
    displayMenu();
    get choice;
}//end while
```

Main Program Listing

```java
import java.io.*;

public class mainProgVideoStore
{
    static BufferedReader keyboard = new
            BufferedReader(new InputStreamReader(System.in));

    public static void main(String[] args)
    {
        VideoList  videoList = new VideoList();
        int choice;
        String title;

        try
        {
            BufferedReader infile = new
                BufferedReader(new FileReader("a:\\videoDat.txt"));

            createVideoList(infile, videoList);

            displayMenu();
            System.out.print("Enter your choice: ");
            choice = Integer.parseInt(keyboard.readLine());
            System.out.println();

            while(choice != 9)
            {
                switch(choice)
                {
                case 1: System.out.print("Enter the title: ");
                        title = keyboard.readLine();
                        System.out.println();

                        if(videoList.videoSearch(title))
                            System.out.println("Title found.");
                        else
                            System.out.println("Video not in store.");
                        break;
                case 2: System.out.print("Enter the title: ");
                        title = keyboard.readLine();
                        System.out.println();
```

```
                  if(videoList.videoSearch(title))
                  {
                     if(videoList.isVideoAvailable(title))
                     {
                        videoList.videoCheckOut(title);
                        System.out.println("Enjoy your movie: "
                                          + title);
                     }
                     else
                        System.out.println("Currently " + title
                                          + " is out of stock.");
                  }
                  else
                     System.out.println("The store does not "
                                       + "carry" + title);
                  break;
         case 3: System.out.print("Enter the title: ");
                 title = keyboard.readLine();
                 System.out.println();

                 if(videoList.videoSearch(title))
                 {
                    videoList.videoCheckIn(title);
                    System.out.println("Thanks for returning "
                                      + title);
                 }
                 else
                    System.out.println("This video is not "
                                      + "from our store.");
                 break;
         case 4: System.out.print("Enter the title: ");
                 title = keyboard.readLine();
                 System.out.println();

                 if(videoList.videoSearch(title))
                 {
                    if(videoList.isVideoAvailable(title))
                       System.out.println(title
                                 + " is currently in stock.");
                    else
                       System.out.println(title +
                                 " is not in the store.");
                 }
                 else
                    System.out.println(title + " is not "
                                      + "from this store.");
                 break;
```

```
            case 5: videoList.videoPrintTitle();
                    break;
            case 6: videoList.print();
                    break;
            default: System.out.println("Invalid selection");
            }//end switch

            displayMenu();
            System.out.print("Enter your choice: ");
            choice = Integer.parseInt(keyboard.readLine());
            System.out.println();
        }//end while
    catch(FileNotFoundException fnfe)
    {
        System.out.println(fnfe.toString());
    }
    catch(IOException ioe)
    {
        System.out.println(ioe.toString());
    }
}

public static void createVideoList(BufferedReader infile,
                                   VideoList videoList)
                                   throws IOException
{
    String Title;
    String Star1;
    String Star2;
    String Producer;
    String Director;
    String ProductionCo;
    int InStock;

    VideoElement newVideo = new VideoElement();

    Title = infile.readLine();

    while(Title != null)
    {
        Star1 = infile.readLine();
        Star2 = infile.readLine();
        Producer = infile.readLine();
        Director = infile.readLine();
        ProductionCo = infile.readLine();
        InStock = Integer.parseInt(infile.readLine());
```

```
              newVideo.setVideoInfo(Title,Star1,Star2,Producer,
                               Director,ProductionCo,InStock);
              videoList.insertFirst(newVideo);

              Title = infile.readLine();
        }//end while
    }//end createVideoList

    public static void displayMenu()
    {
        System.out.println("Select one of the following: ");
        System.out.println("1: To check if a particular video "
                            + "is in the store");
        System.out.println("2: To check out a video");
        System.out.println("3: To check in a video");
        System.out.println("4: To see if a particular video "
                            + "is in the store");
        System.out.println("5: To print the titles of all videos");
        System.out.println("6: To print a list of all the videos");
        System.out.println("9: To exit");
    }
}
```

QUICK REVIEW

1. A linked list is a list of items, called nodes, in which the order of the nodes is determined by the address, called a link, stored in each node.

2. The address of the first node of a linked list is stored in a separate location, called the head or first.

3. A linked list is a dynamic data structure.

4. The length of a linked list is the number of nodes in the list.

5. Item insertion and deletion from a linked list does not require data movement; only the links are adjusted.

6. A (single) linked list is traversed in only one direction.

7. A search on a linked list is sequential.

8. The variable first (or head) pointing to a linked list is always fixed, pointing to the first node in the list.

9. To traverse a linked list, the program must use a reference variable different from the reference variable that is pointing to the first node of the linked list.

10. In a doubly linked list, every node has two links: one points to the next node, and one points to the previous node.

11. A doubly linked list can be traversed in either direction.

12. In a doubly linked list, item insertion and deletion requires the adjustment of two links in a node.

13. A linked list with header and trailer nodes simplifies the insertion and deletion operations.

14. The header and trailer nodes are not part of the actual list. The actual list elements are between the header and trailer nodes.

15. A linked list with header and trailer nodes is empty if the only nodes in the list are the header and the trailer.

16. A circular linked list is a list in which, if the list is nonempty, the last node points to the first node.

EXERCISES

1. Mark the following statements as true or false.

   a. In a linked list, the order of the elements is determined by the order in which the nodes were created to store the elements.

   b. In a linked list, memory allocated for the nodes is sequential.

   c. A single linked list can be traversed in either direction.

   d. In a linked list, the nodes are always inserted either in the beginning or at the end because a linked list is not a random access data structure.

   e. Item insertion (and deletion) in a linked list with header and trailer nodes is simpler than in an ordinary linked list because the former list has no special cases.

   Consider the linked list shown in Figure 4-58. Assume that the nodes are in the usual `info-link` form with the `info` of the type `int`. Use this list to answer Exercises 2 through 7. If necessary, declare additional variables. (Assume that `list`, `p`, `s`, `A`, and `B` are reference variables of the `LinkedListNode` type.)

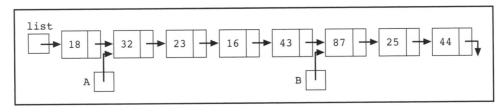

Figure 4-58 Linked list for Exercises 2 through 7

2. What is the output of the following Java statements?

   a. `System.out.println(list.info);`

   b. `System.out.println(A.info);`

   c. `System.out.println(B.link.info);`

   d. `System.out.println(list.link.link.info);`

3. What is the value of each of the following relational expressions?

   a. `list.info >= 18`

   b. `list.link == A`

   c. `A.link.info == 16`

   d. `B.link == null`

   e. `list.info == 18`

4. Mark each of the following statements as valid or invalid. If a statement is invalid, explain why.

   a. `A = B;`

   b. `list.link = A.link;`

   c. `list.link.info = 45;`

   d. `list = B;`

   e. `B = A.link.info;`

   f. `A.info = B.info;`

   g. `list = B.link.link;`

   h. `B = B.link.link.link;`

5. Write Java statements to do the following:

   a. Make `A` point to the node containing `info 23`.

   b. Make `list` point to the node containing `info 16`.

   c. Make `B` point to the last node in the list.

   d. Make `list` point to an empty list.

   e. Set the value of the node containing `25` to `35`.

   f. Create and insert the node with `info 10` after the node pointed to by `A`.

   g. Delete the node with `info 23`. Also, deallocate the memory occupied by this node.

6. What is the output of the following Java code?

```
p = List;
while(p != null)
    System.out.print(p.info + " ");
    p = p.link;
System.out.println();
```

7. If the following Java code is valid, show the output. If it is invalid, explain why.

a.

```
s = A;
p = B;
s.info = B;
p = p.link;
System.out.println(s.info + " " + p.info);
```

b.

```
p = A;
p = p.link;
s = p;
p.link = null;
s = s.link;
System.out.println(p.info + " " + s.info);
```

8. Show what is produced by the following Java code. Assume the node is in the usual info-link form with the info of the type int. (list and ptr are reference variables of the type LinkedListNode.)

```
list = new LinkedListNode();
list.info = 10;
ptr = new LinkedListNode();
ptr.info = 13;
ptr.link = null;
list.link = ptr;
ptr = new LinkedListNode();
ptr.info = 18;
ptr.link = list.link;
list.link = ptr;
System.out.print(list.info + "   " + ptr.info + " ");
ptr = ptr.link;
System.out.println(ptr.info);
```

9. Show what is produced by the following Java code. Assume the node is in the usual info-link form with the info of the type int. (list and ptr are reference variables of the LinkedListNode type.)

```
list = new LinkedListNode();
list.info = 20;
ptr = new LinkedListNode();
ptr.info = 28;
ptr.link = null;
list.link = ptr;
ptr = new LinkedListNode();
ptr.info = 30;
ptr.link = list;
```

```
        list = ptr;
        ptr = new LinkedListNode();
        ptr.info = 42;
        ptr.link = list.link;
        list.link = ptr;
        ptr = list;
        while(ptr != null)
        {
            System.out.println(ptr.info);
            ptr = ptr.link;
        }
```

4

10. Consider the following Java statements. (The **class UnorderedLinkedList** is as defined in this chapter.)

```
UnorderedLinkedList list = new UnorderedLinkedList();
IntElement num = new IntElement();

num.setNum(15);
list.insertFirst(num);
num.setNum(28);
list.insertLast(num);
num.setNum(30);
list.insertFirst(num);
num.setNum(2);
list.insertFirst(num);
num.setNum(45);
list.insertLast(num);
num.setNum(38);
list.insertFirst(num);
num.setNum(25);
list.insertLast(num);
num.setNum(30);
list.deleteNode(num);
num.setNum(18);
list.insertFirst(num);
num.setNum(28);
list.deleteNode(num);
num.setNum(12);
list.deleteNode(num);
list.print();
System.out.println();
```

What is the output of this program segment?

11. Suppose the input is:

```
18 30 4 32 45 36 78 19 48 75
```

What is the output of the following Java code? (The **class UnorderedLinkedList** is as defined in this chapter.)

```
BufferedReader keyboard = new
            BufferedReader(new InputStreamReader(System.in));

UnorderedLinkedList list = new UnorderedLinkedList();
UnorderedLinkedList tempList = new UnorderedLinkedList();
IntElement num = new IntElement();
StringTokenizer tokenizer;

tokenizer = new StringTokenizer(keyboard.readLine());

while(tokenizer.hasMoreTokens())
{
    num.setNum(Integer.parseInt(tokenizer.nextToken()));
    if(num.getNum() % 5 == 0 || num.getNum() % 5 == 3)
       list.insertFirst(num);
    else
       list.insertLast(num);
}

System.out.print("List: ");
list.print() ;
System.out.println();

tempList.copyList(list);

num.setNum(78);
tempList.deleteNode(num);

num.setNum(66);
tempList.deleteNode(num);

System.out.print("tempList: ");
tempList.print();
System.out.println();
```

12. Draw the UML diagram of the **class VideoElement** of the Programming Example in this chapter.

13. Draw the UML diagram of the **class VideoList** of the Programming Example in this chapter.

PROGRAMMING EXERCISES

1. **(Online Address Book Revisited)** Programming Exercise 8 in Chapter 3 could handle a maximum of only 500 entries. Using linked lists, redo the program to handle as many entries as required. Add the following operations to your program:

   a. Add or delete a new entry to the address book.

   b. When the program terminates, write the data in the address book to a disk.

2. Write a program to test the insertion, deletion, search, `copyList`, and the copy constructor operations for an object in the `class UnorderedLinkedList`. You may assume that you are manipulating a list of positive integers. Print the length of the list after each operation.

3. Extend the `class LinkedListClass` by adding the following operations:

   a. Find and delete the node with the smallest `info` in the list. (Delete only the first occurrence. Traverse the list only once.) Call the method implementing this operation `deleteSmallest` and include it as an `abstract` method in the `class LinkedListClass`. Write the definition of this method for the `class UnorderedLinkedList`. Also, write a program to test your method.

   b. Find and delete all the occurrences of a given `info` from the list. (Traverse the list only once.) Call the method implementing this operation `deleteAll` and include it as an `abstract` method in the `class LinkedListClass`. Write the definition of this method for the `class UnorderedLinkedList`. Also, write a program to test your method.

4. Extend the `class LinkedListClass` by adding the following operations:

   a. Write the method `getKThElement` that returns the info of the *k*th element of the linked list. If no such element exists, terminate the program. Also, write a program to test your method for an object of the `class UnorderedLinkedList`.

   b. Write the method `deleteKthElement` that deletes the *k*th element of the linked list. If no such element exists, output an appropriate message. Also, write a program to test your method for an object of the `class UnorderedLinkedList`.

5. Add the method `splitMid` to split a linked list into two sublists of (almost) equal size as described here. For example, suppose the given list is 13 72 89 65 34. Then the two sublists are 13 72 89 and 65 34. Similarly, if the original list is 12 67 34 65, the two sublists are 12 67 and 34 65.

   a. Add the operation `splitMid` to the `class LinkedListClass` as follows:

```
public void splitMid(LinkedListClass sublist)
   //This operation splits the given list into two
   //sublists of (almost) equal size.
   //Precondition: The list must exist.
   //Postcondition: first points to the first node,
   //                and last points to the last
   //                node of the first sublist.
```

4

```
//    sublist.first points to the first node,
//    and sublist.last points to the last node
//    of the second sublist.
```

Consider the following statements:

```
UnorderedLinkedList myList;
UnorderedLinkedList subList;
```

Suppose `myList` points to the list with elements 34 65 27 89 12 (in this order). The statement

```
myList.splitMid(subList);
```

splits `myList` into two sublists: `myList` points to the list with elements 34 65 27, and `subList` points to the sublist with elements 89 12.

b. Write the definition of the method to implement the operation `splitMid`. Also, write a program to test the definition of your method.

6. Add the method `splitAt` to split a linked list at a node whose info is given.

Suppose `oldList` points to a list with the elements:

10 18 34 6 28 92 56 48

and the list is to be split at the node whose `info` is 6. The two sublists are then:

10 18 34 and 6 28 92 56 48

a. Add the following method to the **class LinkedListClass**:

```
public void splitAt(LinkedListClass secondList, DataElement item)
   //Split the list at the node with the info item
   //into two sublists.
   //Precondition: The list must exist.
   //Postcondition: first and last point to the
   //                    first and last nodes of the
   //                    first sublist.
   //    secondList.first and secondList.last
   //    point to the first and last nodes of
   //    the second sublist.
```

Consider the following statements:

```
UnorderedLinkedList myList;
UnorderedLinkedList otherList;
```

Suppose `myList` points to the linked list with the elements 34 65 18 39 27 89 12 (in this order). The statement:

```
myList.splitAt(otherList, 18);
```

splits `myList` into two sublists: `myList` points to the list with elements 34 65, and `otherList` points to the sublist with elements 18 39 27 89 12.

b. Write the definition of the method to implement the operation `splitAt`. Also, write a program to test the definition of your method.

7. a. Add the following operation to the `class OrderedLinkedList`:

```
public void mergeLists(OrderedLinkedList list1,
                       OrderedLinkedList list2)
   //This operation creates a new list by merging the
   //elements of list1 and list2.
   //Precondition: Both lists, list1 and list2, are
   //              ordered.
   //Postcondition: first points to the merged list,
   //              and list1 and list2 are empty.
```

For example, consider the following statements:

```
OrderedLinkedList newList;
OrderedLinkedList list1;
OrderedLinkedList list2;
```

Suppose `list1` points to the list with elements `2 6 7`, and `list2` points to the list with elements `3 5 8`. The statement:

```
newList.mergeLists(list1,list2);
```

creates a new linked list with the elements in the order `2 3 5 6 7 8`, and the object `newList` points to this list. Also, after the preceding statement executes, `list1` and `list2` are empty.

b. Write the definition of the method `mergeLists` to implement the operation `mergeLists`.

8. The method `insertNode` of the `class OrderedLinkedList` does not check whether the item to be inserted is already in the list, that is, it does not check for duplicates. Rewrite the definition of `insertNode` so that before it inserts the item it checks whether the item to be inserted is already in the list. If the item to be inserted is already in the list, the method outputs an appropriate error message.

9. Write the definition of the method `back` to return the last element of an ordered linked list. If the list is empty, print an appropriate error message. Moreover, add this operation to the `class OrderedLinkedList`. Also, write a program to test the definition of your method.

10. Write the definitions of the methods `copy`, `copyList`, and the copy constructor for the `class DoublyLinkedList`.

11. Write a program to test various operations such as insert, delete, search, and `copyList` of the `class DoublyLinkedList`.

12. (Linked List with Header and Trailer Nodes) This chapter defined and identified various operations on a linked list with header and trailer nodes.

a. Write the definition of the class that defines a linked list with header and trailer nodes as an ADT.

b. Write the definitions of the member methods of the class defined in (a). (You may assume that the elements of the linked list with header and trailer nodes are in ascending order.)

c. Write a program to test various operations of the class defined in (a).

13. **(Circular Linked Lists)** This chapter defined and identified various operations on a circular linked list.

   a. Write the definition of the class that defines a sorted circular linked list as an ADT.

   b. Write the definitions of the member methods of the class defined in (a). (You may assume that the elements of the circular linked list are in ascending order.)

   c. Write a program to test various operations of the class defined in (a).

14. **(Programming Example: Video Store)**

   a. Complete the design and implementation of the `class Customer` defined in the Programming Example: Video Store.

   b. Design and implement the `class CustomerList` to create and maintain a list of customers for the video store.

   c. Write a program to test the definitions of your classes.

15. **(Programming Example: Video Store)** Complete the design and implementation of the video store program.

CHAPTER

5

RECURSION

In this chapter, you will:

♦ Learn about recursive definitions

♦ Explore the base case and the general case of a recursive definition

♦ Discover what a recursive algorithm is

♦ Learn about recursive methods

♦ Explore how to use recursive methods to implement recursive algorithms

♦ Learn how recursion implements backtracking

In previous chapters, to devise problem solutions we used the most common technique, called iteration. For certain problems, however, using the iterative technique to obtain the solution is quite complicated. This chapter introduces another problem-solving technique, called recursion, and provides several examples demonstrating how recursion works.

RECURSIVE DEFINITIONS

The process of solving a problem by reducing it to smaller versions of itself is called **recursion**. Recursion is a very powerful way to solve certain problems for which the solution would otherwise be very complicated. Let us consider a problem that is familiar to most everyone.

In mathematics, the factorial of an integer is defined as follows:

$$0! = 1 \qquad\qquad (5\text{-}1)$$

$$n! = n \times (n - 1)! \quad \text{if} \quad n > 0 \qquad (5\text{-}2)$$

In this definition, $0!$ is defined to be 1, and if n is an integer greater than 0, first we find $(n - 1)!$ and then multiply it by n. To find $(n - 1)!$, we apply the definition again. If $(n - 1) > 0$, then we use Equation 5-2; otherwise, we use Equation 5-1. Thus, for an integer n greater than 0, $n!$ is obtained by first finding $(n - 1)!$ (that is, $n!$ is reduced to a smaller version of itself), and then multiplying $(n - 1)!$ by n.

Let us apply this definition to find $3!$. Here $n = 3$. Because $n > 0$, we use Equation 5-2 to obtain

$$3! = 3 \times 2!$$

Next, we find $2!$ Here $n = 2$. Because $n > 0$, we use Equation 5-2 to obtain

$$2! = 2 \times 1!$$

Now to find $1!$, we again use Equation 5-2 because $n = 1 > 0$. Thus

$$1! = 1 \times 0!$$

Finally, we use Equation 5-1 to find $0!$, which is 1. Substituting $0!$ into $1!$ gives $1! = 1$. This gives $2! = 2 \times 1! = 2 \times 1 = 2$, which in turn gives $3! = 3 \times 2! = 3 \times 2 = 6$.

The solution in Equation 5-1 is direct—that is, the right side of the equation contains no factorial notation. Note that the solution in Equation 5-2 is given in terms of a smaller version of itself. The definition of the factorial as given in Equations 5-1 and 5-2 is called a **recursive definition**. Equation 5-1 is called the **base case** (that is, the case for which the solution is obtained directly); Equation 5-2 is called the **general case** or **recursive case**.

Recursive definition: A definition in which something is defined in terms of a smaller version of itself.

From the previous example, it is clear that:

1. Every recursive definition must have one (or more) base cases.

2. The general case must eventually be reduced to a base case.

3. The base case stops the recursion.

The concept of recursion in computer science works similarly. Here we talk about recursive algorithms and recursive methods. An algorithm that finds the solution to a given problem by reducing the problem to smaller versions of itself is called a **recursive algorithm**. The recursive algorithm must have one or more base cases, and the general solution must eventually be reduced to a base case.

A method that calls itself is called a **recursive method**. That is, the body of the recursive method contains a statement that causes the same method to execute before completing the current call. Recursive algorithms are implemented using recursive methods.

Next, let us write the recursive method that implements the factorial method.

```
public static int fact(int num)
{
    if(num == 0)
        return 1;
    else
        return num * fact(num - 1);
}
```

Figure 5-1 traces the execution of the following statement:

```
System.out.println(fact(4));
```

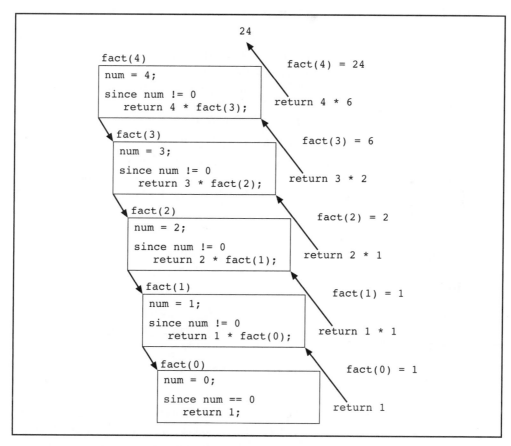

Figure 5-1   Execution of the expression `fact(4)`

The output of the preceding output statement is:

24

In Figure 5-1, the down arrows represent the successive calls to the method `fact`, and the upward arrows represent the values returned to the caller, that is, the calling method.

While tracing through the execution of the recursive method `fact`, note the following:

- Logically, you can think of a recursive method as having unlimited copies of itself.

- Every call to a recursive method—that is, every recursive call—has its own code and its own set of parameters and local variables.

- After completing a particular recursive call, the control goes back to the calling environment, which is the previous call. The current (recursive) call must execute completely before the control goes back to the previous call. The execution in the previous call begins from the point immediately following the recursive call.

Direct and Indirect Recursion

A method is called **directly recursive** if it calls itself. A method that calls another method and eventually results in the original method call is said to be **indirectly recursive**. For example, if method A calls method B and method B calls method A, then method A is indirectly recursive. Indirect recursion could be several layers deep. For example, suppose that method A calls method B, method B calls method C, method C calls method D, and method D calls method A. Then method A is indirectly recursive.

Indirect recursion requires the same careful analysis as direct recursion. The base cases must be identified and appropriate solutions to them must be provided. However, tracing through indirect recursion could be a tedious process. Therefore, extra care must be exercised when designing indirect recursive methods. For simplicity, this book only considers problems that involve direct recursion.

A recursive method in which the last statement executed is the recursive call is called a **tail recursive method**. The method `fact` is an example of a tail recursive method.

Infinite Recursion

Figure 5-1 shows that the sequence of recursive calls reached a call that did not make any further recursive calls. That is, the sequence of recursive calls eventually reached a base case. However, if every recursive call results in another recursive call, then the recursive method (algorithm) is said to have infinite recursion. In theory, infinite recursion executes forever. Now, every call to a recursive method requires the system to allocate memory for the local variables and formal parameters. In addition to this, the system also saves the information so that after completing a call, the control can be transferred back to the right caller. Therefore, because computer memory is finite, if you execute an infinite recursive method on a computer, the method will execute until the system runs out of memory and results in an abnormal termination of the program.

Recursive methods (algorithms) must be carefully designed and analyzed. You must make sure that every recursive call must eventually reduce to a base case. In what follows, we give various examples illustrating how to design and implement recursive algorithms.

To design a recursive method, you must do the following:

1. Understand the problem requirements.

2. Determine the limiting conditions. For example, for a list, the limiting condition is determined by the number of elements in the list.

3. Identify the base cases and provide a direct solution to each base case.

4. Identify the general cases and provide a solution to each general case in terms of a smaller version of itself.

PROBLEM SOLVING USING RECURSION

Examples 5-1 through 5-3 illustrate how recursive algorithms are developed and implemented in Java using recursive methods.

Example 5-1: Largest Element in the Array

In this example, we use a recursive algorithm to find the largest element in an array. Consider the list given in Figure 5-2.

Figure 5-2   List with six elements

The largest element in the list given in Figure 5-2 is 10.

Suppose `list` is the name of the array containing the list elements. Also, suppose that `list[a]...list[b]` stands for the array elements `list[a]`, `list[a + 1]`, `...`, `list[b]`. For example, `list[0]...list[5]` represents the array elements `list[0]`, `list[1]`, `list[2]`, `list[3]`, `list[4]`, and `list[5]`. Similarly, `list[1]...list[5]` represents the array elements `list[1]`, `list[2]`, `list[3]`, `list[4]`, and `list[5]`. To write a recursive algorithm to find the largest element in `list`, let us think in terms of recursion.

If `list` is of length 1, then `list` has only one element, which is the largest element. Suppose the length of `list` is greater than 1. To find the largest element in `list[a]...list[b]`, we first find the largest element in `list[a + 1]...list[b]` and then compare this largest element with `list[a]`. That is, the largest element in `list[a]...list[b]` is given by

```
maximum(list[a], largest(list[a + 1]...list[b]))
```

Let us apply this formula to find the largest element in the list shown in Figure 5-2. This list has six elements, given by `list[0]...list[5]`. Now the largest element in `list` is

```
maximum(list[0], largest(list[1]...list[5]))
```

That is, the largest element in `list` is the maximum of `list[0]` and the largest element in `list[1]...list[5]`. To find the largest element in `list[1]...list[5]`, we use the same formula again because the length of this list is greater than 1. The largest element in `list[1]...list[5]` is then

```
maximum(list[1], largest(list[2]...list[5]))
```

and so on. We see that every time we use the preceding formula to find the largest element in a sublist, the length of the sublist in the next call is reduced by one. Eventually, the sublist is of length 1, in which case the sublist contains only one element, which is the largest element in the sublist. From this point onward, we backtrack through the recursive calls. This discussion translates into the following recursive algorithm, which is presented in pseudocode:

```
if the size of the list is 1
   the only element in the list is the largest element
else
    to find the largest element in list[a]...list[b]
      a. find the largest element in list[a + 1]...list[b] and call
         it max
      b. compare the elements list[a] and max
         if(list[a] >= max)
            the largest element in list[a]...list[b] is list[a]
         else
            the largest element in list[a]...list[b] is max
```

This algorithm translates into the following Java method to find the largest element in an array:

```java
public static int largest(int[] list, int lowerIndex,
                                       int upperIndex)
{
    int max;

    if(lowerIndex == upperIndex)    //size of the sublist is 1
       return list[lowerIndex];
    else
    {
       max = largest(list, lowerIndex + 1, upperIndex);
       if(list[lowerIndex] >= max)
          return list[lowerIndex];
       else
          return max;
    }
}
```

Consider the list given in Figure 5-3.

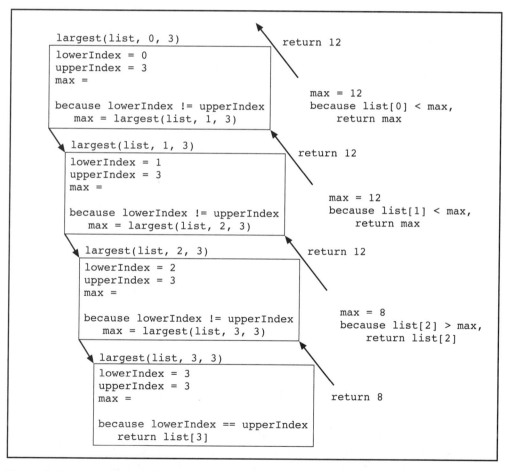

Figure 5-3 `list` with four elements

Let us trace the execution of the following statement:

`System.out.println(largest(list, 0, 3));`

Here `upperIndex` = 3 and the list has four elements. Figure 5-4 traces the execution of the expression `largest(list, 0, 3)`.

Figure 5-4 Execution of the expression `largest(list, 0, 3)`

The value returned by the expression `largest(list, 0, 3)` is 12, which is the largest element in `list`.

The following Java program uses the method `largest` to determine the largest element in the list:

```
//Recursion: Largest Element in an Array

import java.io.*;

public class  largestElementInAnArray
{
   public static void main(String[] args)
   {
      int[] intArray = {23, 43, 35, 38, 67, 12, 76, 10, 34, 8};

      System.out.println("The largest element in intArray: "
                  + largest(intArray, 0, intArray.length - 1));
   }

   public static int largest(int[] list, int lowerIndex,
                                         int upperIndex)
   {
      int max;

      if(lowerIndex == upperIndex)    //size of the sublist is 1
         return list[lowerIndex];
      else
      {
         max = largest(list, lowerIndex + 1, upperIndex);
         if(list[lowerIndex] >= max)
            return list[lowerIndex];
         else
            return max;
      }
   }
}
```

Sample Run:

```
The largest element in intArray: 76
```

Example 5-2: Print a Linked List in Reverse Order

The nodes of an ordered linked list (as constructed in Chapter 4) are in ascending order. Certain applications, however, might require the data to be printed in descending order, which means that we must print the list backwards. We now discuss the method `reversePrint`. Given a reference of the first node of a linked list, this method prints the elements of the list in reverse order.

Consider the linked list shown in Figure 5-5.

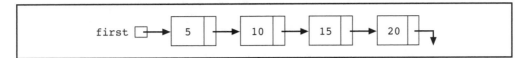

Figure 5-5 Linked list

For the list in Figure 5-5, the output should be in the following form:

```
20  15  10  5
```

Because the links are in only one direction, we cannot traverse the list backward starting from the last node. Let us see how we can effectively use recursion to print the list in reverse order.

Let us think in terms of recursion. We cannot print the **info** of the first node until we have printed the remainder of the list (that is, the tail of the first node). Similarly, we cannot print the **info** of the second node until we have printed the tail of the second node, and so on. Every time we consider the tail of a node, we reduce the size of the list by 1. Eventually the size of the list is reduced to zero, in which case the recursion stops.

Base Case: List is empty

               no action

General Case: List is nonempty

            a. Print the tail

            b. Print the element

Let us write this algorithm in pseudocode. (Suppose that **current** is a reference variable that points to a linked list.)

```
if(current != null)
{
    reversePrint(current.link);              //print the tail
    System.out.print(current.info + " ");    //print the element
}
```

Here, we do not see the base case; it is hidden. The list is printed only if **current** is not null. Also, inside the **if** statement the recursive call is on the tail of the list. Because eventually the tail of a list is empty, the **if** statement in the next call fails and the recursion stops. Also, note that the statement to print the **info** of a node appears after the recursive call; thus, when the transfer comes back to the calling method, we must execute this statement. Recall that the method exits only after the last statement executes. (By the "last statement" we do not mean the physical last statement, but rather the logical last statement.)

Let us write a method template to implement the preceding algorithm and then apply it to a list.

```
void reversePrint(LinkedListNode current)
{
    if(current != null)
    {
```

```
        reversePrint(current.link);              //print the tail
        System.out.print(current.info + " "); //print the element
    }
    System.out.println();
}
```

Consider the statement:

```
reversePrint(first);
```

where **first** is a reference variable of the **LinkedListNode** type.

Let us trace the execution of this statement, which is a method call, for the list shown in Figure 5-6.

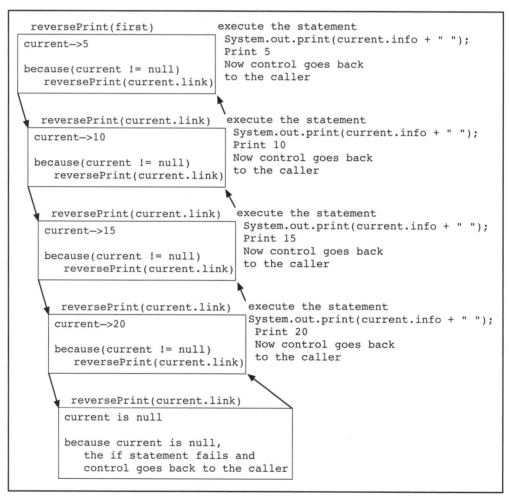

Figure 5-6   Execution of the statement `reversePrint(first);`

Method `printListReverse`

Now that we have written the method `reversePrint`, we can write the definition of the method `printListReverse`, which can be used to print an ordered linked list contained in an object of the type `OrderedLinkedList`. Its definition is:

```
public void printListReverse()
{
    reversePrint(first);
    System.out.println();
}
```

We can include the method `printListReverse` as a `public` member in the definition of the class and the method `reversePrint` as a `private` member. We include the method `reversePrint` as a `private` member because it is used only to implement the method `printListReverse`.

5

Example 5-3: Fibonacci Number

Consider the following sequence of numbers:

1, 1, 2, 3, 5, 8, 13, 21, 34, ...

Given the first two numbers of the sequence (say a_1 and a_2), the nth number a_n, $n >= 3$, of this sequence is given by

$$a_n = a_{n-1} + a_{n-2}$$

Thus

$$a_3 = a_2 + a_1$$
$$= 1 + 1$$
$$= 2,$$
$$a_4 = a_3 + a_2$$
$$= 2 + 1$$
$$= 3,$$

and so on.

Such a sequence is called a **Fibonacci sequence**. In the preceding sequence, $a_2 = 1$ and $a_1 = 1$. However, given any first two numbers, using this process, you can determine the nth number, a_n, $n >= 3$, of the sequence. The number determined this way is called the **nth Fibonacci number**. Suppose $a_2 = 6$ and $a_1 = 3$. Then

$$a_3 = a_2 + a_1 = 6 + 3 = 9$$
$$a_4 = a_3 + a_2 = 9 + 6 = 15$$

In this example, we write the recursive method `rFibNum` to determine the desired Fibonacci number. The method `rFibNum` takes as parameters three numbers representing the first two numbers of the Fibonacci sequence and a number n, the desired nth Fibonacci number. The method `rFibNum` returns the nth Fibonacci number in the sequence.

Recall that the third Fibonacci number is the sum of the first two Fibonacci numbers. The fourth Fibonacci number in a sequence is the sum of the second and third Fibonacci numbers. Therefore, to calculate the fourth Fibonacci number, we add the second Fibonacci number and the third Fibonacci number (which is itself the sum of the first two Fibonacci numbers). The following recursive algorithm calculates the nth Fibonacci number, where a denotes the first Fibonacci number, b the second Fibonacci number, and n the nth Fibonacci number:

$$rFibNum(a,b,n) = \begin{cases} a & \text{if } n = 1 \\ b & \text{if } n = 2 \qquad (5\text{-}3) \\ rFibNum(a,b,n-1) + rFibNum(a,b,n-2) & \text{if } n > 2 \end{cases}$$

Suppose that we want to determine:

1. $rFibNum(2,5,4)$

Here $a = 2$, $b = 5$, and $n = 4$. That is, we want to determine the fourth Fibonacci number of the sequence whose first number is 2 and whose second number is 5. Because n is $4 > 2$,

$rFibNum(2,5,4) = rFibNum(2,5,3) + rFibNum(2,5,2)$

Next, we determine $rFibNum(2,5,3)$ and $rFibNum(2,5,2)$. Let us first determine $rFibNum(2,5,3)$. Here, $a = 2$, $b = 5$, and n is 3. Because n is 3,

    1.a $rFibNum(2,5,3) = rFibNum(2,5,2) + rFibNum(2,5,1)$

        This statement requires us to determine $rFibNum(2,5,2)$ and $rFibNum(2,5,1)$. In $rFibNum(2,5,2)$, $a = 2$, $b = 5$, and $n = 2$. Therefore, from the definition given in Equation 5-3, it follows that

        1.a.1 $rFibNum(2,5,2) = 5$

            To find $rFibNum(2,5,1)$, note that $a = 2$, $b = 5$, and $n = 1$. Therefore, by the definition given in Equation 5-3,

        1.a.2 $rFibNum(2,5,1) = 2$

            We substitute the values of $rFibNum(2,5,2)$ and $rFibNum(2,5,1)$ into (1.a) to get

            $rFibNum(2,5,3) = 5 + 2 = 7$

Next, we determine $rFibNum(2,5,2)$. As in (1.a.1), $rFibNum(2,5,2) = 5$. We can substitute the values of $rFibNum(2,5,3)$ and $rFibNum(2,5,2)$ into (1) to get

$rFibNum(2,5,4) = 7 + 5 = 12$

The following recursive method implements this algorithm:

```java
public static int rFibNum(int a, int b, int n)
{
    if(n == 1)
        return a;
    else if(n == 2)
            return b;
```

```
    else
        return rFibNum(a, b, n - 1) + rFibNum(a, b, n - 2);
}
```

Let us trace the execution of the following statement:

```
System.out.println(rFibNum(2, 3, 5));
```

In this statement, the first number is 2, the second number is 3, and we want to determine the fifth Fibonacci number of the sequence. Figure 5-7 traces the execution of the expression `rFibNum(2,3,5)`. The value returned is 13, which is the fifth Fibonacci number of the sequence whose first number is 2 and whose second number is 3.

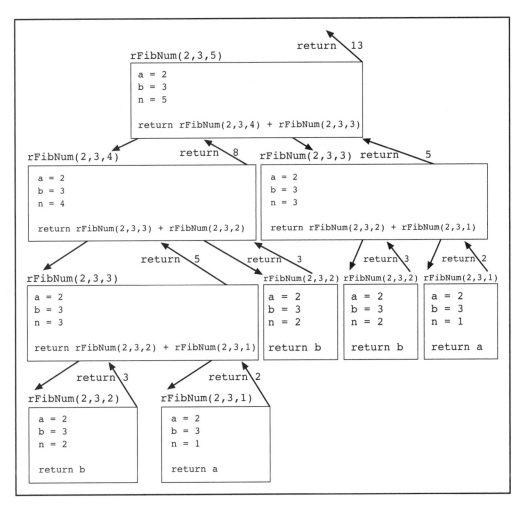

Figure 5-7 Execution of the expression `rFibNum(2,3,5)`

The following Java program uses the method rFibNum:

```
//Recursion: Fibonacci Number

import java.io.*;

public class FibonacciNumber
{
    static BufferedReader keyboard = new
            BufferedReader(new InputStreamReader(System.in));

    public static void main(String[] args) throws IOException
    {
        int firstFibNum;
        int secondFibNum;
        int nth;

        System.out.print("Enter the first Fibonacci number: ");
        firstFibNum = Integer.parseInt(keyboard.readLine());
        System.out.println();

        System.out.print("Enter the second Fibonacci number: ");
        secondFibNum = Integer.parseInt(keyboard.readLine());
        System.out.println();

        System.out.print("Enter the position of the desired "
                        + "Fibonacci number: ");
        nth = Integer.parseInt(keyboard.readLine());
        System.out.println();

        System.out.println("The Fibonacci number at position "
                        + nth + " is: "
                        + rFibNum(firstFibNum, secondFibNum, nth));
    }

    public static int rFibNum(int a, int b, int n)
    {
        if(n == 1)
           return a;
        else if(n == 2)
                return b;
        else
            return rFibNum(a, b, n - 1) + rFibNum(a, b, n - 2);
    }
}
```

Sample Runs: In these sample runs, the user input is shaded.

Sample Run 1:

```
Enter the first Fibonacci number: 2

Enter the second Fibonacci number: 5

Enter the position of the desired Fibonacci number: 6

The Fibonacci number at position 6 is: 31
```

Sample Run 2:

```
Enter the first Fibonacci number: 3

Enter the second Fibonacci number: 4

Enter the position of the desired Fibonacci number: 6

The Fibonacci number at position 6 is: 29
```

Sample Run 3:

```
Enter the first Fibonacci number: 12

Enter the second Fibonacci number: 18

Enter the position of the desired Fibonacci number: 15

The Fibonacci number at position 15 is: 9582
```

Example 5-4: Tower of Hanoi

In the nineteenth century, a game called the Tower of Hanoi became popular in Europe. This game represents work that is under way in the temple of Brahma. At the creation of the universe, priests in the temple of Brahma were supposedly given three diamond needles, with one needle containing 64 golden disks. Each golden disk is slightly smaller than the disk below it. The priests' task is to move all 64 disks from the first needle to the third needle. The rules for moving the disks are as follows:

1. Only one disk can be moved at a time.

2. The removed disk must be placed on one of the needles.

3. A larger disk cannot be placed on top of a smaller disk.

The priests were told that once they had moved all the disks from the first needle to third needle, the universe would come to an end.

Our objective is to write a program that prints the sequence of moves needed to transfer the disks from the first needle to the third needle. Figure 5-8 shows the Tower of Hanoi problem with three disks.

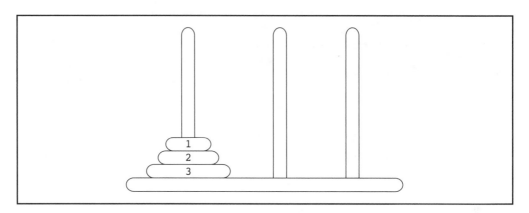

Figure 5-8 Tower of Hanoi problem with three disks

As before, we think in terms of recursion. Let us first consider the case when the first needle contains only one disk. In this case, the disk can be moved directly from needle 1 to needle 3. Now let us consider the case when the first needle contains only two disks. In this case, first we move the first disk from needle 1 to needle 2, and then we move the second disk from needle 1 to needle 3. Finally, we move the first disk from needle 2 to needle 3. Next, we consider the case when the first needle contains three disks, and then generalize this to the case of 64 disks (in fact, to an arbitrary number of disks).

Suppose that needle 1 contains three disks. To move disk number 3 to needle 3, the top two disks must first be moved to needle 2. Disk number 3 can then be moved from needle 1 to needle 3. To move the top two disks from needle 2 to needle 3, we use the same strategy as before. This time we use needle 1 as the intermediate needle. Figure 5-9 shows a solution to the Tower of Hanoi problem with three disks.

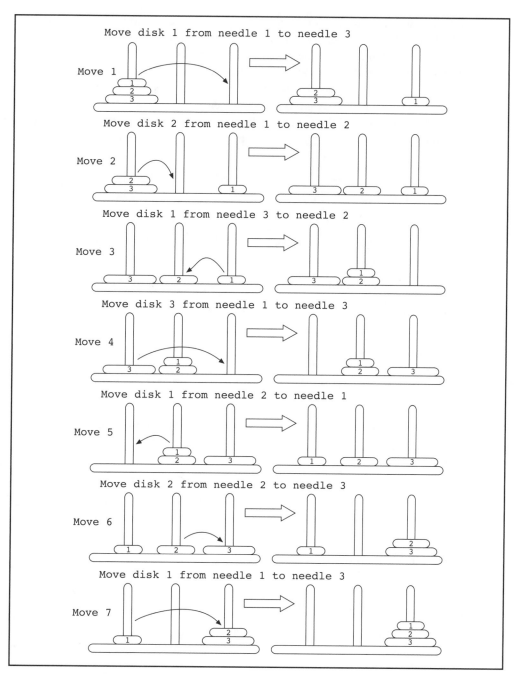

Figure 5-9   Solution to the Tower of Hanoi problem with three disks

Let us now generalize this problem to the case of 64 disks. To begin, the first needle contains all 64 disks. Disk number 64 cannot be moved from needle 1 to needle 3 unless the top 63 disks are on the second needle. So first we move the top 63 disks from needle 1 to needle 2, and then we move disk number 64 from needle 1 to needle 3. Now the top 63 disks are all on needle 2. To move disk number 63 from needle 2 to needle 3, we first move the top 62 disks from needle 2 to needle 1, and then we move disk number 63 from needle 2 to needle 3. To move the remaining 62 disks, we use a similar procedure. This discussion translates into the following recursive algorithm given in pseudocode: (suppose that needle 1 contains n disks, where $n \geq 1$).

1. Move the top $n-1$ disks from needle 1 to needle 2 using needle 3 as the intermediate needle.

2. Move disk number n from needle 1 to needle 3.

3. Move the top $n-1$ disks from needle 2 to needle 3 using needle 1 as the intermediate needle.

This recursive algorithm translates into the following Java method:

```
public static void moveDisks(int count, int needle1,
                             int needle3, int needle2)
{
    if(count > 0)
    {
        moveDisks(count - 1, needle1, needle2, needle3);
        System.out.println("Move disk " + count + " from "
                     + needle1 + " to " + needle3 + ".");
        moveDisks(count - 1, needle2, needle3, needle1);
    }
}
```

Next, let us determine how long it would take to move all the disks from needle 1 to needle 3.

If needle 1 contains three disks, then the number of moves required to move all three disks from needle 1 to needle 3 is $2^3 - 1 = 7$. Similarly, if needle 1 contains 64 disks, then the number of moves required to move all 64 disks from needle 1 to needle 3 is $2^{64} - 1$. Because

$$2^{10} = 1024 \approx 1000 = 10^3,$$

we have

$$2^{64} = 2^4 * 2^{60} \approx 2^4 * 10^{18} = 1.6 * 10^{19}.$$

(Here the symbol $\approx$ means approximately equal to.) The number of seconds in one year is approximately $3.2 * 10^7$. Suppose the priests move one disk per second and they do not rest. Now

$$1.6 * 10^{19} = 5 * 3.2 * 10^{18} = 5 * (3.2 * 10^7) * 10^{11} = (3.2 * 10^7) * (5 * 10^{11})$$

The time required to move all 64 disks from needle 1 to needle 3 is roughly $5 * 10^{11}$ years. It is estimated that our universe is about 15 billion $= 1.5 * 10^{10}$ years old. Also,

$$5 * 10^{11} = 50 * 10^{10} \approx 33 * (1.5 * 10^{10}).$$

This calculation shows that our universe would last about 33 times as long as it already has.

Assume that a computer can generate 1 billion ($= 10^9$) moves per second. Then the number of moves that the computer can generate in one year is

$(3.2 * 10^7) * 10^9 = 3.2 * 10^{16}$.

So the computer time required to generate 2^{64} moves is

$2^{64} \approx 1.6 * 10^{19} = 1.6 * 10^{16} * 10^3 = (3.2 * 10^{16}) * 500$.

Thus, it would take about 500 years for the computer to generate 2^{64} moves at the rate of 1 billion moves per second.

5

PROGRAMMING EXAMPLE: CONVERTING A NUMBER FROM DECIMAL TO BINARY

This programming example discusses and designs a program that uses recursion to convert a nonnegative integer in decimal format—that is, base 10—into the equivalent binary number—that is, base 2. First we define some terms.

Let x be a nonnegative integer. We call the remainder of x after division by 2 the **rightmost bit** of x.

Thus, the rightmost bit of 33 is 1 because 33 % 2 is 1, and the rightmost bit of 28 is 0 because 28 % 2 is 0.

We first illustrate the algorithm to convert an integer in base 10 to the equivalent number in binary format with the help of an example.

Suppose we want to find the binary representation of 35. First, we divide 35 by 2. The quotient is 17 and the remainder—that is, the rightmost bit of 35—is 1. Next, we divide 17 by 2. The quotient is 8 and the remainder—that is, the rightmost bit of 17—is 1. Next, we divide 8 by 2. The quotient is 4 and the remainder—that is, the rightmost bit of 8—is 0. We continue this process until the quotient becomes 0.

The rightmost bit of 35 cannot be printed until we have printed the rightmost bit of 17. The rightmost bit of 17 cannot be printed until we have printed the rightmost bit of 8, and so on. Thus, the binary representation of 35 is the binary representation of 17 (that is, the quotient of 35 after division by 2), followed by the rightmost bit of 35.

Thus, to convert a non-negative integer num in base 10 into the equivalent binary number, we first convert the quotient num/2 into an equivalent binary number, and then append the rightmost bit of num to the binary representation of num/2.

This discussion translates into the following recursive algorithm, where binary(num) denotes the binary representation of num:

1. binary(num) = num if num = 0.
2. binary(num) = binary(num/2) followed by num % 2 if num > 0.

The following recursive method implements this algorithm:

```java
public static void decToBin(int num, int base)
{
    if(num > 0)
    {
        decToBin(num/base, base);
        System.out.print(num % base);
    }
}
```

Figure 5-10 traces the execution of the following statement:

```
decToBin(13, 2);
```

where num is 13 and base is 2.

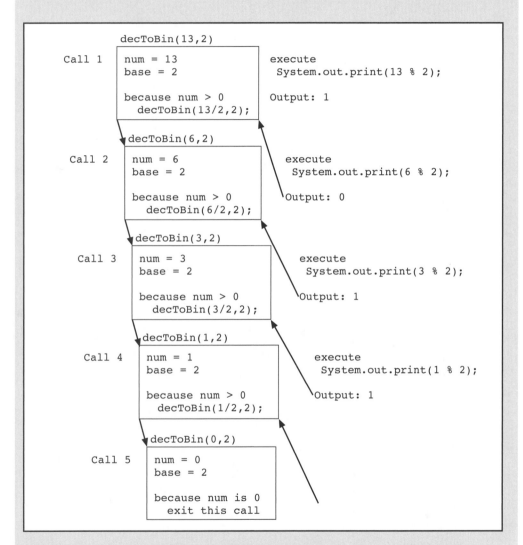

Figure 5-10   Execution of the statement decToBin(13, 2);

Because the if statement in call 5 fails, this call does not print anything. The first output is produced by call 4, which prints 1; the second output is produced by call 3, which prints 1; the third output is produced by call 2, which prints 0; and the fourth output is produced by call 1, which prints 1. Thus, the output of the statement

```
decToBin(13, 2);
```

is

```
1101
```

The following Java program tests the method `decToBin`:

```java
//Recursion: Program - Decimal to Binary

import java.io.*;

public class DecimalToBinary
{
    static BufferedReader keyboard = new
            BufferedReader(new InputStreamReader(System.in));

    public static void main(String[] args) throws IOException
    {
        int decimalNum;
        int base;

        base = 2;

        System.out.print("Enter number in decimal: ");
        decimalNum = Integer.parseInt(keyboard.readLine());
        System.out.println();
        System.out.print("Decimal " + decimalNum + " = ");
        decToBin(decimalNum, base);
        System.out.println(" binary");
    }

    public static void decToBin(int num, int base)
    {
        if(num > 0)
        {
            decToBin(num/base, base);
            System.out.print(num % base);
        }
    }
}
```

Sample Run: In this sample run, the user input is shaded.

```
Enter number in decimal: 57

Decimal 57 = 111001 binary
```

PROGRAMMING EXAMPLE: SIERPINSKI GASKET

To draw the shapes of natural scenes such as mountains, trees, and clouds, graphic programmers typically use special types of mathematical tools, called **fractals**, related to the area of fractal geometry. The area of fractal geometry is a major area of research in mathematics in its own right. The term fractal was introduced by the mathematician Benoit Mandelbrot in the late 1970s. Roughly speaking, a fractal is a geometric shape in which certain patterns repeat, perhaps at a different scale and orientation. Mandelbrot is credited to be the first person to demonstrate that fractals occur in various places in mathematics and nature.

Because in a fractal certain patterns occur at various places, a convenient and effective way to write programs to draw fractals is to use recursion. In this section, we describe a special type of fractal called a **Sierpinski gasket**.

Suppose that you have the triangle ABC given in Figure 5-11(a). Now determine the midpoints P, Q, and R of the sides AB, AC, and BC, respectively. Next, draw the lines PQ, QR, and PR. This creates three triangles APQ, BPR, and CRQ (see Figure 5-11(b)), of similar shape as the triangle ABC. The process of finding the midpoints of the sides and then drawing the lines through midpoints is now repeated on each of the triangles APQ, BPR, and CRQ, as shown in Figure 5-11(c). Figure 5-11(a) is called a Sierpinski gasket of order or level 0, Figure 5-11(b) is called a Sierpinski gasket of order or level 1, Figure 5-11(c) is called a Sierpinski gasket of order or level 2, and Figure 5-11(d) is called a Sierpinski gasket of order or level 3.

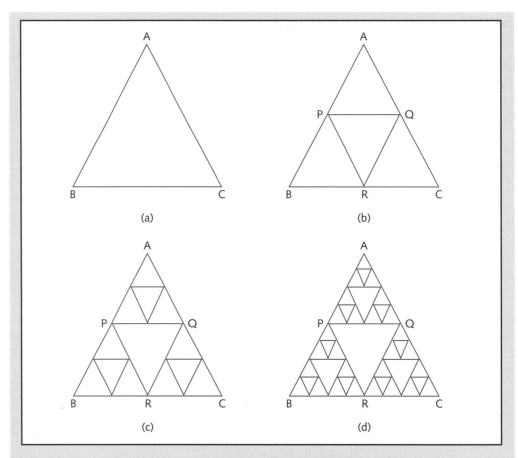

Figure 5-11   Sierpinski gaskets of various orders (levels)

Input   The input to the program is a nonnegative integer indicating the level of the Sierpinski gasket.

Output   The geometric shape displaying a Sierpinski gasket of the given order.

Problem Analysis and Algorithm Design

The problem is as described above. Initially, we specify the coordinates of the first triangle and then draw the triangle. We use the **class Point** to store the x-y coordinates of a point. We also use the method **drawLine** to draw a line between two points.

For each triangle, we need three objects of the **class Point** to store the vertices and three more objects to store the midpoints of a side. Because we frequently need to find the midpoints of a line, we write the method `midPoint` that returns the coordinates of the midpoint of a line. Its definition is:

```
private Point midPoint(Point pOne, Point pTwo)
{
    Point mid = new Point((pOne.x + pTwo.x) / 2,
                          (pOne.y + pTwo.y) / 2 );

    return mid;
}
```

The recursive algorithm to draw a Sierpinski gasket is as follows:

Base case: If the level is 0, draw the first triangle.

Recursive Case: If the level is greater than 0, for each triangle in the Sierpinski gasket, find the midpoints of the sides and draw lines through those points.

Suppose that `p1`, `p2`, and `p3` are the three vertices of a triangle and `lev` denotes the number of levels of the Sierpinski gasket to be drawn. The following method implements the recursive algorithm to draw a Sierpinski gasket:

```
private void drawSierpinski(Graphics g, int lev,
                            Point p1, Point p2, Point p3)
{
    Point midP1P2;
    Point midP2P3;
    Point midP3P1;

    if(lev > 0)
    {
        g.drawLine(p1.x, p1.y, p2.x, p2.y);
        g.drawLine(p2.x, p2.y, p3.x, p3.y);
        g.drawLine(p3.x, p3.y, p1.x, p1.y);

        midP1P2 = midPoint(p1, p2);
        midP2P3 = midPoint(p2, p3);
        midP3P1 = midPoint(p3, p1);

        drawSierpinski(g, lev - 1, p1, midP1P2, midP3P1);
        drawSierpinski(g, lev - 1, p2, midP2P3, midP1P2);
        drawSierpinski(g, lev - 1, p3, midP3P1, midP2P3);
    }
}
```

The complete algorithm to draw a Sierpinski gasket of a given order is as given next. Notice that the program uses an input dialog box to get the user's input.

Complete Program Listing

```java
//Java program to draw SierpinskiGasket

import java.awt.*;
import javax.swing.*;

public class SierpinskiGasket extends JApplet
{
    int level = 0;

    public void init()
    {
        String levelStr = JOptionPane.showInputDialog
                    ("Enter the depth of recursion: ");

        level = Integer.parseInt(levelStr);
    }

    public void paint(Graphics g)
    {
        Point pointOne = new Point(20, 280);
        Point pointTwo = new Point(280, 280);
        Point pointThree = new Point(150, 20);

        drawSierpinski(g, level, pointOne, pointTwo, pointThree);
    }

    private void drawSierpinski(Graphics g, int lev,
                                Point p1, Point p2, Point p3)
    {
        Point midP1P2;
        Point midP2P3;
        Point midP3P1;

        if(lev > 0)
        {
            g.drawLine(p1.x, p1.y, p2.x, p2.y);
            g.drawLine(p2.x, p2.y, p3.x, p3.y);
            g.drawLine(p3.x, p3.y, p1.x, p1.y);

            midP1P2 = midPoint(p1, p2);
            midP2P3 = midPoint(p2, p3);
            midP3P1 = midPoint(p3, p1);

            drawSierpinski(g, lev - 1, p1, midP1P2, midP3P1);
            drawSierpinski(g, lev - 1, p2, midP2P3, midP1P2);
            drawSierpinski(g, lev - 1, p3, midP3P1, midP2P3);
        }
    }
```

```
        private Point midPoint(Point pOne, Point pTwo)
        {
            Point mid = new Point((pOne.x + pTwo.x) / 2,
                                  (pOne.y + pTwo.y) / 2 );

            return mid;
        }
}
```

Sample Runs: In these sample runs, the user input is shown in input dialog boxes.

Sample Run 1: Figure 5-12 shows Sample Run 1.

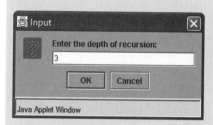

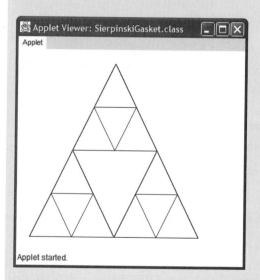

Figure 5-12   Sample Run 1: Sierpinski gasket

Notice that a recursion depth of 3 produces a Sierpinski gasket of order 2.

Sample Run 2: Figure 5-13 shows Sample Run 2.

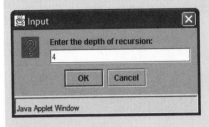

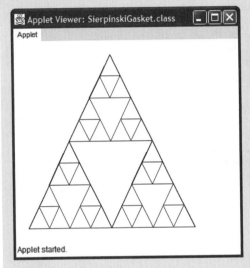

Figure 5-13   Sample Run 2: Sierpinski gasket

Notice that a recursion depth of 4 produces a Sierpinski gasket of order 3.

RECURSION OR ITERATION?

The programs in the preceding chapters used a loop to repeat a set of statements to perform certain calculations. In other words, the programs in the preceding chapters used an iterative control structure to repeat a set of statements. More formally, **iterative control structures** use a looping structure, such as `while`, `for`, or `do...while`, to repeat a set of statements. In Example 5-1, we designed a recursive method to calculate the factorial of a nonnegative integer. From Example 5-1, it follows that in recursion a set of statements is repeated by having the method call itself. Moreover, a selection control structure is used to control the repeated calls in recursion.

In this chapter, we also used recursion to determine the largest element in a list and to determine a Fibonacci number. Using an iterative control structure, we can also write an algorithm to find the largest number in an array. Similarly, an algorithm that uses an iterative control structure can be designed to find the factorial of a nonnegative integer. The only reason to give a recursive solution to these problems is to illustrate how recursion works.

We thus see that there are usually two ways to solve a particular problem—iteration and recursion. The obvious question is which method is better—iteration or recursion? There is no simple answer to this question. In addition to the nature of the problem, the other key factor in determining the best solution method is efficiency.

When a method is called, memory space for its formal parameters and local variables is allocated. When the method terminates, that memory space is then deallocated. This chapter, while tracing the execution of recursive methods, shows us that every (recursive) call has its own set of parameters and local variables. That is, every (recursive) call requires the system to allocate memory space for its formal parameters and local variables, and then deallocate the memory space when the method exits. Thus, there is overhead associated with executing a (recursive) method both in terms of memory space and computer time. Therefore, a recursive method executes more slowly than its iterative counterpart. On slower computers, especially those with limited memory space, the (slow) execution of a recursive method would be visible.

Today's computers, however, are fast and have inexpensive memory. Therefore, the execution of a recursive method is not noticeable. Keeping the power of today's computer in mind, the choice between the two alternatives—recursion or iteration—depends on the nature of the problem. Of course, for problems such as mission control systems, efficiency is absolutely critical and, therefore, the efficiency factor would dictate the solution method.

As a general rule, if you think that an iterative solution is more obvious and easier to understand than a recursive solution, use the iterative solution, which would be more efficient. On the other hand, problems exist for which the recursive solution is more obvious or easier to construct, such as the Tower of Hanoi problem. (In fact, it turns out that it is difficult to construct an iterative solution for the Tower of Hanoi puzzle.) Keeping the power of recursion in mind, if the definition of a problem is inherently recursive, then you should consider a recursive solution.

RECURSION AND BACKTRACKING: 8-QUEENS PUZZLE

In this section, we describe a problem-solving and algorithm design technique called backtracking. Let us consider the following 8-queens puzzle: place 8 queens on a chessboard (8 × 8 square board) so that no two queens can attack each other. For any two queens to be non-attacking, they cannot be in the same row, same column, or same diagonals. Figure 5-14 gives one possible solution to the 8-queens puzzle.

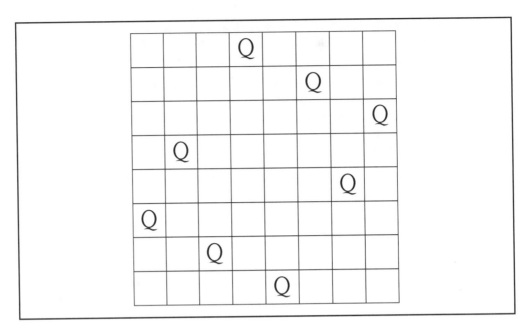

Figure 5-14   A solution to the 8-queens puzzle

In 1850, the 8-queens puzzle was considered by the great C. F. Gauss, who was unable to obtain a complete solution. The term backtrack was first coined by D. H. Lehmer in 1950. In 1960, R. J. Walker gave an algorithmic account of backtracking. A general description of backtracking with a variety of applications was presented by S. Golomb and L. Baumert.

Backtracking

The backtracking algorithm attempts to find solutions to a problem by constructing partial solutions and making sure that the partial solution does not violate problem requirements. The algorithm tries to extend a partial solution toward completion. However, if it is determined that the partial solution would not lead to a solution, that is, the partial solution would end in a dead end, then the algorithm backs up by removing the most recently added part and trying other possibilities.

n-Queens Puzzle

In backtracking, the solution of the *n*-queens puzzle, because each queen must be placed in a different row, can be represented as an *n*-tuple $(x_1, x_2, ..., x_n)$, where x_i is an integer such that $1 \leq x_i \leq n$. In this tuple, x_i specifies the column number where to place the *i*th queen in the *i*th row. Therefore, for the 8-queens puzzle the solution is an 8-tuple $(x_1, x_2, x_3, x_4, x_5, x_6, x_7, x_8)$, where x_i is the column where to place the *i*th queen in the *i*th row. For example, the solution to Figure 5-14 can be represented as the 8-tuple $(4, 6, 8, 2, 7, 1, 3, 5)$. That is, the first queen is placed in the first row and fourth column, the second queen is placed in the second row and sixth column, and so on. Clearly, each x_i is an integer such that $1 \le x_i \le 8$.

Let us again consider the 8-tuple $(x_1, x_2, x_3, x_4, x_5, x_6, x_7, x_8)$, where x_i is an integer such that $1 \le x_i \le 8$. Because each x_i has 8 choices, there are 8^8 such tuples, and so there are possibly 8^8 solutions. However, because no two queens can be placed in the same row, no two elements of the 8-tuple $(x_1, x_2, x_3, x_4, x_5, x_6, x_7, x_8)$ are the same. From this, it follows that the number of 8-tuples possibly representing solutions is 8!.

The solution that we will develop can, in fact, be applied to any number of queens. Therefore, to illustrate the backtracking technique, we consider the 4-queens puzzle. That is, you are given a 4 × 4 square board (see Figure 5-15) and you are to place four queens on the board so that no two queens attack each other.

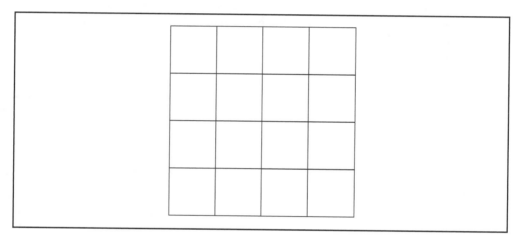

Figure 5-15   Square board for the 4-queens puzzle

We start by placing the first queen in the first row and first column as shown in Figure 5-16(a). (A cross in a box means that no other queen can be placed in that box.)

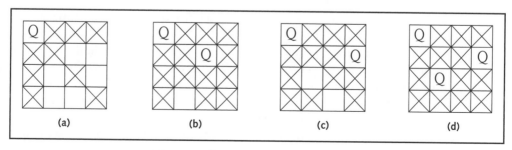

Figure 5-16   Finding a solution to the 4-queens puzzle

After placing the first queen, we try to place the second queen in the second row. Clearly, the first square in the second row where the second queen can be placed is the third column. So we place the second queen in that column, see Figure 5-16(b).

Next, we try to place the third queen in the third row. We find that the third queen cannot be placed in the third row and so we arrive at a dead end. At this point, we backtrack to the previous board configuration and place the second queen in the fourth column; see Figure 5-16(c). Next, we try to place the third queen in the third row. This time, we successfully place the third queen in the second column of the third row; see Figure 5-16(d). After placing the third queen in the third row, when we try to place the fourth queen, we discover that the fourth queen cannot be placed in the fourth row.

We backtrack to the third row and try placing the queen in any other column. Because no other column is available for queen three, we backtrack to row two and try placing the second queen in any other column, which cannot be done. We, therefore, backtrack to the first row and place the first queen in the next column. After placing the first queen in the second column, we place the remaining queens in the successive rows. This time we obtain the solution as shown by Figure 5-17.

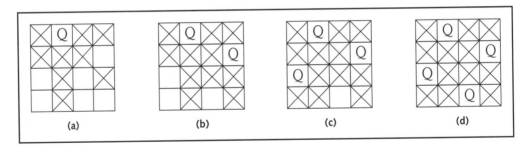

Figure 5-17   Solution to the 4-queens puzzle

Backtracking and 4-Queens Puzzle

Suppose that the rows of the square board of the 4-queens puzzle are numbered 0 through 3 and the columns are numbered 0 through 3. (Recall that, in Java, array index starts at 0.)

For the 4-queens puzzle, we start by placing the first queen in the first row and first column, thus generating the tuple (0). We then place the second queen in the third column of the second row and so generate the tuple (0, 2). When we try to place the third queen in the third row, we determine that the third queen cannot be placed in the third row. Therefore, we back up to the partial solution (0, 2), remove 2 from the tuple, and then generate the tuple (0, 3), that is, the second queen is placed in the fourth column of the second row. With the partial solution (0, 3), next we try to place the third queen in the third row and generate the tuple (0, 3, 1). Then with the partial solution (0, 3, 1), when we try to place the fourth queen in the fourth row, it is determined that it cannot be done and so the partial solution (0, 3, 1) ends up in a dead end.

From the partial solution $(0, 3, 1)$, the backtracking algorithm, in fact, backs up to placing the first queen and so removes all the elements of the tuple. The algorithm then places the first queen in the second column of the first row, and thus generates the partial solution (1). In this case, the sequence of partial solution generated is: (1), $(1, 3)$, $(1, 3, 0)$, and $(1, 3, 0, 2)$, which represents a solution to the 4-queens puzzle. The solutions generated by the backtracking algorithm can be represented by a tree, as shown in Figure 5-18.

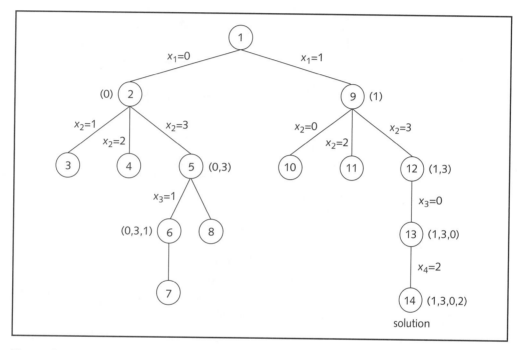

Figure 5-18   4-queens tree

8-Queens Puzzle

Let us now consider the 8-queens puzzle. Again, no two queens can be in the same row, same column, or same diagonal. Determining whether two queens are in the same row or same column is easy because we can check their row and column positions. Let us describe how to determine whether two queens are in the same diagonal or not.

Consider the 8×8 square board shown in Figure 5-19. The rows are numbered 0 through 7 and columns are numbered 0 through 7. (Recall that, in Java, the array index starts at 0.)

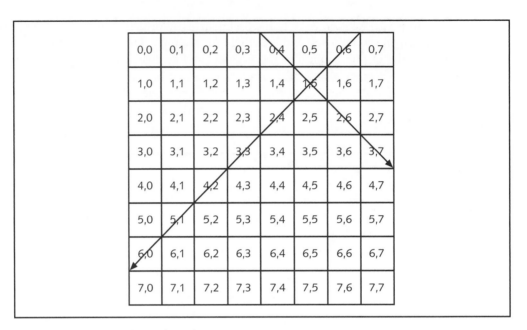

Figure 5-19 8 × 8 square board

Consider the diagonal from upper left to lower right, as indicated by the arrow. The positions of the squares on this diagonal are (0, 4), (1, 5), (2, 6), and (3, 7). Notice that for these entries `rowPosition – columnPosition` is -4. For example, $0 - 4 = 1 - 5 = 2 - 6 = 3 - 7 = -4$. It can be shown that for each square on a diagonal from upper left to lower right, `rowPosition – columnPosition` is the same.

Now consider the diagonal from upper right to lower left as indicated by the arrow. The positions of the squares on this diagonal are (0,6), (1,5), (2,4), (3,3), (4,2), (5,1), and (6,0). Here `rowPosition + columnPosition = 6`. It can be shown that for each square on a diagonal from upper right to lower left, `rowPosition + columnPosition` is the same.

We can use these results to determine whether two queens are on the same diagonal or not. Suppose that there is queen at position (i, j) (row i and column j), and another queen at position (k, l) (row k and column l). These queens are on the same diagonal if either $i + j = k + l$ or $i - j = k - l$. The first equation implies that $j - l = k - i$; the second equation implies that $j - l = i - k$. From this it follows that two queens are on the same diagonal if $|j - l| = |i - k|$, where $|j - l|$ is the absolute value of $j - l$ and so on.

Because a solution to the 8-queens puzzle is represented as an 8-tuple, we use the array `queensInRow` of size 8, where `queensInRow[k]` specifies the column position of the *k*th queen in row k. For example, `queensInRow[0]= 3` means that the first queen is placed in column 3 (which is the fourth column) of row 0 (which is the first row).

Suppose that we place the first $k-1$ queens in the first $k-1$ rows. Next, we try to place the kth queen in a column of the kth row. We write the method `canPlaceQueen(k,i)`, which returns `true` if the kth queen can be placed in the ith column of row k; otherwise, it returns `false`.

The first $k-1$ queens are in the first $k-1$ rows and we are trying to place the kth queen in the kth row. Therefore, before placing the kth queen in the kth row, the kth row must be empty. From this it follows that the kth queen can be placed in column i of row k, provided there is no other queen in column i and no queens on the diagonals on which square (k, i) lies. The general algorithm for the method `canPlaceQueen(k,i)` is:

```
for(int j = 0; j < k; j++)
    if((queensInRow[j] == i)   //there is already a queen in column i
       || (Math.abs(queensInRow[j] - i) == Math.abs(j-k))) //there is
                            //already a queen in one of the
                            //diagonals on which the square
                            //(k, i) lies
        return false;

return true;
```

The `for` loop checks whether there is already a queen in column i or if there is already a queen in one of the diagonals on which the square (k, i) lies. If it finds a queen at any such position, the `for` loop returns the value `false`. Otherwise, the value `true` is returned.

Class: NQueensPuzzle

Instance Variables:

```
private int noOfSolutions;
private int noOfQueens;
private int[] queensInRow;
```

Constructors and Instance Methods:

```
public NQueensPuzzle()
   //default constructor
   //Postcondition: noOfSolutions = 0; noOfQueens = 8;
   //               the array queensInRow is instantiated to
   //               store the 8-tuple

public NQueensPuzzle(int queens)
   //constructor
   //Postcondition: noOfSolutions = 0; noOfQueens = queens;
   //               the array queensInRow is instantiated to
   //               store the n-tuple

public boolean canPlaceQueen(int k, int i)
   //Method to determine whether a queen can be placed
   //in row k and column i.
```

```
    //Postcondition: Returns true if a queen can be placed in row
    //                k and column i, false otherwise.

public void queensConfiguration(int k)
    //Method to determine all solutions to the n-queens
    //puzzle using backtracking.
    //The method is called with the value 0.
    //Postcondition: All n-tuples representing solutions to the
    //               n-queens puzzle are generated and printed.

public void printConfiguration()
    //Method to output an n-tuple containing a solution
    //to the n-queens puzzle.

public int solutionsCount()
    //Method to return the total number of solutions.
    //Postcondition: The value of noOfSolutions is returned.
```

The definitions of the methods of the **class NQueensPuzzle** are given next.

```
public NQueensPuzzle()
{
    noOfQueens = 8;
    queensInRow = new int[8];
    noOfSolutions = 0;
}

public NQueensPuzzle(int queens)
{
    noOfQueens = queens;
    queensInRow = new int[noOfQueens];
    noOfSolutions = 0;
}

public boolean canPlaceQueen(int k, int i)
{
    for(int j = 0; j < k; j++)
        if((queensInRow[j] == i)
            || (Math.abs(queensInRow[j] - i) == Math.abs(j - k)))
            return false;
    return true;
}
```

Using recursion, the method **queensConfiguration** implements the backtracking technique to determine all the solutions to the *n*-queens problem. The parameter *k* specifies the
queen to be placed in the *k*th row. Its definition is straightforward and is given next.

```java
public void queensConfiguration(int k)
{
    for(int i = 0; i < noOfQueens; i++)
    {
        if(canPlaceQueen(k, i))
        {
            queensInRow[k] = i;  //place the kth queen in column i
            if(k == noOfQueens - 1)   //all queens are placed
                printConfiguration(); //print the n-tuple
            else
                queensConfiguration(k + 1);   //determine the place
                                              //for the (k+1)th queen
        }
    }
}

public void printConfiguration()
{
    noOfSolutions++;
    System.out.print("(");
    for(int i = 0; i < noOfQueens - 1; i++)
        System.out.print(queensInRow[i] + ", ");

    System.out.println(queensInRow[noOfQueens - 1] + ")");
}

public int solutionsCount()
{
    return noOfSolutions;
}
```

We leave it as an exercise for you to write a program to test the *n*-queens puzzle class for various board sizes.

QUICK REVIEW

1. The process of solving a problem by reducing it to smaller versions of itself is called recursion.
2. A recursive definition defines the problem in terms of smaller versions of itself.
3. Every recursive definition has one or more base cases.
4. A recursive algorithm solves a problem by reducing it to smaller versions of itself.
5. Every recursive algorithm has one or more base cases.
6. The solution to the problem in a base case is obtained directly.
7. A method is called recursive if it calls itself.
8. Recursive algorithms are implemented using recursive methods.
9. Every recursive method must have one or more base cases.
10. The general solution breaks the problem into smaller versions of itself.

11. The general case must eventually be reduced to a base case.

12. The base case stops the recursion.

13. While tracing a recursive method:

- Logically, you can think of a recursive method as having unlimited copies of itself.

- Every call to a recursive method—that is, every recursive call—has its own code and its own set of parameters and local variables.

- After completing a particular recursive call, the control goes back to the calling environment, which is the previous call. The current (recursive) call must execute completely before the control goes back to the previous call. The execution in the previous call begins from the point immediately following the recursive call.

14. A method is called directly recursive if it calls itself.

15. A method that calls another method and eventually results in the original method call is said to be indirectly recursive.

16. A recursive method in which the last statement executed is the recursive call is called a tail recursive method.

17. To design a recursive method, you must do the following:

a. Understand the problem requirements.

b. Determine the limiting conditions. For example, for a list the limiting condition is the number of elements in the list.

c. Identify the base cases and provide a direct solution to each base case.

d. Identify the general cases and provide a solution to each general case in terms of a smaller version of itself.

18. The backtracking algorithm attempts to find solutions to a problem by constructing partial solutions and making sure that the partial solution does not violate problem requirements. The algorithm tries to extend a partial solution towards completion. However, if it is determined that the partial solution would not lead to a solution, that is, the partial solution would end in a dead end, then the algorithm backs up by removing the most recently added part and trying other possibilities.

EXERCISES

1. Mark the following statements as true or false.

a. Every recursive definition must have one or more base cases.

b. Every recursive method must have one or more base cases.

c. The general case stops the recursion.

d. In the general case, the solution to the problem is obtained directly.

e. A recursive method always returns a value.

2. What is a base case?

3. What is a recursive case?

4. What is direct recursion?

5. What is indirect recursion?

6. What is tail recursion?

7. Consider the following recursive method:

```
public static int mystery(int number)             //Line 1
{
    if(number == 0)                               //Line 2
        return number;                            //Line 3
    else                                          //Line 4
        return(number + mystery(number - 1));     //Line 5
}
```

a. Identify the base case.

b. Identify the general case.

c. What valid values can be passed as parameters to the method `mystery`?

d. If `mystery(0)` is a valid call, what is its value? If not valid, explain why.

e. If `mystery(5)` is a valid call, what is its value? If not valid, explain why.

f. If `mystery(-3)` is a valid call, what is its value? If not valid, explain why.

8. Consider the following recursive method:

```
public static void funcRec(int u, char v)              //Line 1
{
    if(u == 0)                                         //Line 2
        System.out.print(v);                           //Line 3
    else if(u == 1)                                    //Line 4
            System.out.print((char)((int)(v) + 1));    //Line 5
    else                                               //Line 6
        funcRec(u - 1, v);                             //Line 7
}
```

a. Identify the base case.

b. Identify the general case.

c. What is the output of the following statement?

```
funcRec(5,'A');
```

9. Consider the following recursive method:

```java
void exercise(int x)
{
    if(x > 0 && x < 10)
    {
        System.out.print(x + " ");
        exercise(x + 1);
    }
}
```

What is the output of the following statements?

a. `exercise(0);`

b. `exercise(5);`

c. `exercise(10);`

d. `exercise(-5);`

10. Consider the following method:

```java
int test(int x, int y)
{
    if(x == y)
        return x;
    else if(x > y)
            return (x + y);
    else
        return test(x + 1, y - 1);
}
```

What is the output of the following statements?

a. `System.out.println(test(5,10));`

b. `System.out.println(test(3,9));`

11. Consider the following method:

```java
int Func(int x)
{
    if(x == 0)
        return 2;
    else if(x == 1)
            return 3;
    else
        return (Func(x - 1) + Func(x - 2));
}
```

What is the output of the following statements?

a. `System.out.println(Func(0));`

b. `System.out.println(Func(1));`

c. `System.out.println(Func(2));`

d. `System.out.println(Func(5));`

12. Suppose that `intArray` is an array of integers, and `length` specifies the number of elements in `intArray`. Also suppose that `low` and `high` are two integers such that `0 <= low < length, 0 <= high < length` and `low < high`. That is, `low` and `high` are two indices in `intArray`. Write a recursive definition that reverses the elements in `intArray` between `low` and `high`.

13. Write a recursive algorithm to multiply two positive integers *m* and *n* using repeated addition. Specify the base case and the recursive case.

14. Consider the following problem: how many ways can a committee of 4 people be selected from a group of 10 people? There are many other similar problems, where you are asked to find the number of ways to select a set of items from a given set of items. The general problem can be stated as follows: find the number of ways *r* different things can be chosen from a set of *n* items, where *r* and *n* are nonnegative integers and $r \le n$. Suppose $C(n, r)$ denotes the number of ways *r* different things can be chosen from a set of *n* items. Then $C(n, r)$ is given by the following formula:

$$C(n,r) = \frac{n!}{r! \ (n-r)!}$$

where the exclamation point denotes the factorial function. Moreover, $C(n, 0) = C(n, n) = 1$. It is also known that $C(n, r) = C(n - 1, \ r - 1) + C(n - 1, r)$.

a. Write a recursive algorithm to determine $C(n, r)$. Identify the base case(s) and the general case(s).

b. Using your recursive algorithm, determine $C(5, 3)$ and $C(9, 4)$.

PROGRAMMING EXERCISES

1. Write a recursive method that takes as a parameter a nonnegative integer and generates the following pattern of stars. If the nonnegative integer is 4, then the pattern generated is:

```
****
***
**
*
*
**
***
****
```

Also, write a program that prompts the user to enter the number of lines in the pattern and uses the recursive method to generate the pattern. For example, specifying 4 as the number of lines generates the above pattern.

2. Write a recursive method to generate a pattern of stars such as the following:

```
*
**
***
****
****
***
**
*
```

Also, write a program that prompts the user to enter the number of lines in the pattern and uses the recursive method to generate the pattern. For example, specifying 4 as the number of lines generates the above pattern.

3. Write a recursive method to generate the following pattern of stars:

```
    *
   * *
  * * *
 * * * *
  * * *
   * *
    *
```

Also, write a program that prompts the user to enter the number of lines in the pattern and uses the recursive method to generate the pattern. For example, specifying 4 as the number of lines generates the above pattern.

4. Write a recursive method, **vowels**, that returns the number of vowels in a string. Also, write a program to test your method.

5. Write a recursive method that finds and returns the sum of the elements of an **int** array. Also, write a program to test your method.

6. A palindrome is a string that reads the same both forwards and backwards. For example, the string "**madam**" is a palindrome. Write a program that uses a recursive method to check whether a string is a palindrome. Your program must contain a value-returning recursive method that returns **true** if the string is a palindrome, and **false** otherwise. Use the appropriate parameters.

7. Write a program that uses a recursive method to print a string backwards. Your program must contain a recursive method that prints the string backwards. Use the appropriate parameters.

8. Write a recursive method, **reverseDigits**, that takes an integer as a parameter and returns the number with the digits reversed. Also, write a program to test your method.

9. Write a recursive method, **power**, that takes as parameters two integers x and y such that x is nonzero and returns x^y. You can use the following recursive definition to calculate x^y. If $y \geq 0$,

$$power(x, y) = \begin{cases} 1 & \text{if } y = 0 \\ x & \text{if } y = 1 \\ x * power(x, y - 1) & \text{if } y > 1 \end{cases}$$

If $\gamma < 0$,

$$power(x, y) = \frac{1}{power(x, -y)}$$

Also, write a program to test your method.

10. **(Greatest Common Divisor)** Given two integers x and y, the following recursive definition determines the greatest common divisor of x and y, written gcd(x, y):

$$\gcd(x, y) = \begin{cases} x & \text{if } y = 0 \\ \gcd(y, x \% y) & \text{if } y \neq 0 \end{cases}$$

 Note: In this definition, % is the mod operator.

Write a recursive method, **gcd**, that takes as parameters two integers and returns the greatest common divisor of the numbers. Also, write a program to test your method.

11. Write a recursive method to implement the recursive algorithm of Exercise 12 (reversing the elements of an array between two indices). Moreover, write a program to test your method.

12. Write a recursive method to implement the recursive algorithm of Exercise 13 (multiplying two positive integers using repeated addition). Moreover, write a program to test your method.

13. Write a recursive method to implement the recursive algorithm of Exercise 14 (determining the number of ways to select a subset of things from a given set of things). Moreover, write a program to test your method.

14. In the Programming Example: Converting a Number from Decimal to Binary, given in this chapter, you learned how to convert a decimal number into its equivalent binary number. Two more number systems, octal (base 8) and hexadecimal (base 16), are of interest to computer scientists. In fact, in Java, you can instruct the computer to store a number in octal or hexadecimal.

The digits in the octal number system are 0, 1, 2, 3, 4, 5, 6, and 7. The digits in the hexadecimal number system are 0, 1, 2, 3, 4, 5, 6, 7, 8, 9, A, B, C, D, E, and F. So A in hexadecimal is 10 in decimal, B in hexadecimal is 11 in decimal, and so on.

The algorithm to convert a positive decimal number into an equivalent number in octal (or hexadecimal) is the same as discussed for binary numbers. Here we divide the decimal number by 8 (for octal) and by 16 (for hexadecimal). Suppose a_b represents the number a to the base b. For example, 75_{10} means 75 to the base 10 (that is, decimal), and 83_{16} means 83 to the base 16 (that is, hexadecimal). Then

$$753_{10} = 1361_8$$
$$753_{10} = 2F1_{16}$$

The method of converting a decimal number to base 2, or 8, or 16 can be extended to any arbitrary base. Suppose you want to convert a decimal number n into an equivalent number in base b, where b is between 2 and 36. You then divide the decimal number n by b as in the algorithm for converting decimal to binary.

Note that the digits in, say, base 20 are 0, 1, 2, 3, 4, 5, 6, 7, 8, 9, A, B, C, D, E, F, G, H, I, and J.

Write a program that uses a recursive method to convert a number in decimal to a given base b, where b is between 2 and 36. Your program should prompt the user to enter the number in decimal and in the desired base.

Test your program on the following data:

9098 and base 20

692 and base 2

753 and base 16

15. **(Converting a Number from Binary to Decimal)** The language of a computer, called machine language, is a sequence of 0s and 1s. When you press the key A on the keyboard, 01000001 is stored in the computer. Also, the collating sequence of A in the Unicode character set is 65. In fact, the binary representation of A is 01000001 and the decimal representation of A is 65.

The numbering system we use is called the decimal system, or base 10 system. The numbering system that the computer uses is called the binary system, or base 2 system. This chapter described how to convert a decimal number into an equivalent binary number. The purpose of this exercise is to write a program to convert a number from base 2 to base 10.

To convert a number from base 2 to base 10, we first find the weight of each bit in the binary number. The weight of each bit in the binary number is assigned from right to left. The weight of the rightmost bit is 0. The weight of the bit immediately to the left of the rightmost bit is 1, the weight of the bit immediately to the left of it is 2, and so on. Consider the binary number 1001101. The weight of each bit is as follows:

```
weight   6  5  4  3  2  1  0
         1  0  0  1  1  0  1
```

We use the weight of each bit to find the equivalent decimal number. For each bit, we multiply the bit by 2 to the power of its weight, and then we add all of the numbers. For the above binary number, the equivalent decimal number is

$$1 * 2^6 + 0 * 2^5 + 0 * 2^4 + 1 * 2^3 + 1 * 2^2 + 0 * 2^1 + 1 * 2^0$$
$$= 64 + 0 + 0 + 8 + 4 + 0 + 1$$
$$= 77$$

To write a program that converts a binary number into its equivalent decimal number, we note two things: (1) the weight of each bit in the binary number must be known, and (2) the weight is assigned from right to left. Because we do not know in advance how many bits are in the binary number, we must process the bits from right to left.

After processing a bit, we can add 1 to its weight, giving the weight of the bit immediately to the left to it. Also, each bit must be extracted from the binary number and multiplied by 2 to the power of its weight. To extract a bit, you can use the mod operator. Write a method that converts a binary number into an equivalent decimal number. Moreover, write a program and test your method for the following values: 11000101, 10101010, 11111111, 10000000, 1111100000.

16. Write a program that uses recursion to draw a Koch snowflake fractal of any given order. A Koch snowflake of order 0 is an equilateral triangle. To create the next higher order fractal, each line segment in the shape is modified by replacing its middle third with a sharp protrusion made of two line segments, each having the same length as the replaced one, as shown in Figure 5-20.

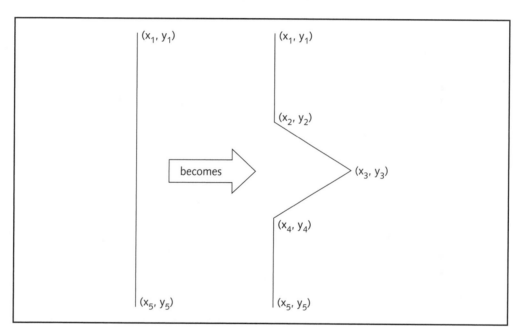

Figure 5-20   Line segments for Koch snowflakes

Here is the necessary information to compute the three new points (x_2, y_2), (x_3, y_3) and (x_4, y_4) in terms of (x_1, y_1) and (x_5, y_5).

Let

```
deltaX = x₅ - x₁
deltaY = y₅ - y₁
```

Then

$$x_2 = x_1 + \text{deltaX} / 3,$$
$$y_2 = y_1 + \text{deltaY} / 3,$$

$$x_3 = 0.5 * (x_1 + x_5) + \sqrt{3} * (y_1 - y_5) / 6,$$
$$y_3 = 0.5 * (y_1 + y_5) + \sqrt{3} * (x_5 - x_1) / 6,$$

$$x_4 = x_1 + 2 * \text{deltaX} / 3,$$
$$y_4 = y_1 + 2 * \text{deltaY} / 3,$$

The first three Koch snowflakes produced by the program may look like Figure 5-21:

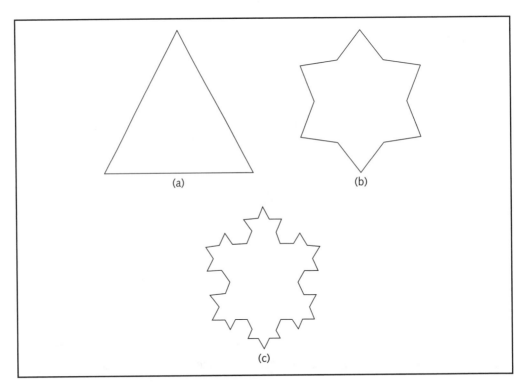

(a)   (b)

(c)

Figure 5-21   First three Koch snowflakes

17. Using Newton's method, you can write an algorithm to find the square root of a nonnegative real number within a given tolerance as follows: suppose x is a nonnegative real number, a is the approximate square root of x, and *epsilon* is the tolerance. Start with $a = x$;

   a. If $|a * a - x| \leq epsilon$, then a is the square root of x within the tolerance; otherwise,

b. Replace a with $(a*a+x)/(2*a)$ and repeat Step a where $|a*a-x|$ denotes the absolute value of $a*a-x$.

Write a recursive method to implement this algorithm to find the square root of a nonnegative real number. Also, write a program to test your method.

18. Write a program to find solutions to the n-queens puzzle for various values of n. To be specific, test your program for $n = 4$ and $n = 8$.

19. **(Knight's tour)** This chapter described the backtracking algorithm and how to use recursion to implement it. Another well-known chessboard problem that can be solved using the backtracking algorithm is a knight's tour. Given an initial board position, determine a sequence of moves by a knight that will visit every square of the chessboard exactly once. For example, for a 5×5 and 6×6 square board, the sequence of moves are shown in Figure 5-22.

1	16	7	26	11	14

1	6	15	10	21		34	25	12	15	6	27
14	9	20	5	16		17	2	33	8	13	10
19	2	7	22	11		32	35	24	21	28	5
8	13	24	17	4		23	18	3	30	9	20
25	18	3	12	23		36	31	22	19	4	29

Figure 5-22 Knight's tour

A knight moves by jumping two positions either vertically or horizontally and one position in the perpendicular direction. Write a recursive backtracking program that takes as input an initial board position and determines a sequence of moves by a knight that visits each square of the board exactly once.

6

STACKS

In this chapter, you will:

- ◆ Learn about stacks
- ◆ Examine various stack operations
- ◆ Learn how to implement a stack as an array
- ◆ Learn how to implement a stack as a linked list
- ◆ Discover stack applications
- ◆ Learn how to use a stack to remove recursion

This chapter discusses a very useful data structure called a stack. It has numerous applications in computer science.

STACKS

Suppose that you have a program with several methods. To be specific, suppose that your program has the methods A, B, C, and D. Now suppose that method A calls method B, method B calls method C, and method C calls method D. When method D terminates, control goes back to method C; when method C terminates, control goes back to method B; and when method B terminates, control goes back to method A. During program execution, how do you think the computer keeps track of the method calls? What about recursive methods? How does the computer keep track of recursive calls? In Chapter 5, we designed a recursive method to print a linked list backwards. What if you want to write a nonrecursive algorithm to print a linked list backwards?

This section discusses the data structure called a **stack**, which the computer uses to implement method calls. You can also use stacks to convert recursive algorithms into nonrecursive algorithms, especially recursive algorithms that are not tail recursive. Stacks have numerous other applications in computer science. After developing the tools necessary to implement a stack, we will examine some applications of stacks.

A stack is a list of homogeneous elements, wherein the addition and deletion of elements occurs only at one end, called the **top** of the stack. For example, in a cafeteria, the second tray in a stack of trays can be removed only if the first tray has been removed. For another example, to get to your favorite computer science book, which is underneath your math and history books, you must first remove the math and history books. After removing these books, the computer science book becomes the top book—that is, the top element of the stack. Figure 6-1 shows some examples of stacks.

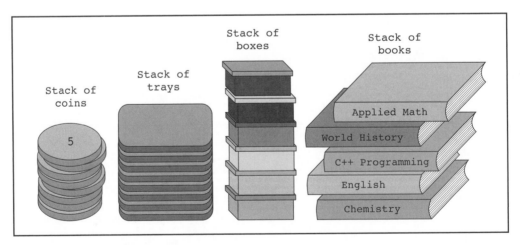

Figure 6-1   Various types of stacks

The elements at the bottom of the stack have been in the stack the longest. The top element of the stack is the last element added to the stack. Because elements are added and removed from one end (that is, the top), it follows that the item that is added last will be removed first. For this reason, a stack is also called a **Last In First Out (LIFO)** data structure.

Stack: A data structure in which the elements are added and removed from one end only, a Last In First Out (LIFO) data structure.

Now that you know what a stack is, let us see what kinds of operations can be performed on a stack. Because new items can be added to the stack, we can perform the add operation, called **push**, to add an element onto the stack. Similarly, because the top item can be retrieved and/or removed from the stack, we can perform the operation **top** to retrieve the top element of the stack and the operation **pop** to remove the top element from the stack. Figures 6-2 and 6-3 illustrate the **push**, **top**, and **pop** operations.

The **push**, **top**, and **pop** operations work as follows: suppose there are boxes lying on the floor that need to be stacked on a table. Initially, all of the boxes are on the floor and the stack is empty (see Figure 6-2).

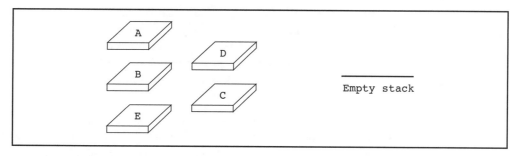

Figure 6-2 Empty stack

First we push box **A** onto the stack. After this **push** operation, the stack is as shown in Figure 6-3(a).

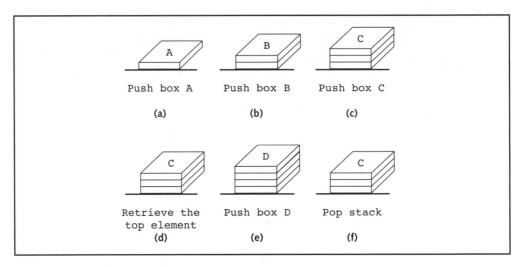

Figure 6-3 Stack operations

We then push box B onto the stack. After this **push** operation, the stack is as shown in Figure 6-3(b). Next, we push box C onto the stack. After this **push** operation, the stack is as shown in Figure 6-3(c). Next, we retrieve the top element of the stack. After this operation, the stack is unchanged and shown in Figure 6-3(d). We then push box D onto the stack. After this **push** operation, the stack is as shown in Figure 6-3(e). Next, we pop the stack. After the **pop** operation, the stack is as shown in Figure 6-3(f).

An element can be removed and/or retrieved from a stack only if there is something in the stack, and an element can be added to a stack only if there is room. The two operations that immediately follow from the **push**, **top**, and **pop** operations are **isFullStack** (determines whether the stack is full) and **isEmptyStack** (determines whether the stack is empty). Because a stack keeps changing as we add and remove elements, the stack must be empty before we first start using it. Thus, we need another operation, called **initializeStack**, which initializes the stack to an empty state. Therefore, to successfully implement a stack, we need at least six operations, which are described in the next section. We might also need other operations on a stack, depending on the specific implementation.

Stack Operations

The basic operations on a stack are:

- **initializeStack**: Initializes the stack to an empty state.

- **isEmptyStack**: Determines whether the stack is empty. If the stack is empty, it returns the value **true**; otherwise, it returns the value **false**.

- **isFullStack**: Determines whether the stack is full. If the stack is full, it returns the value **true**; otherwise, it returns the value **false**.

- **push:** Adds a new element to the top of the stack. The input to this operation consists of the stack and the new element. Prior to this operation, the stack must exist and must not be full.

- **top:** Returns the top element of the stack. Prior to this operation, the stack must exist and must not be empty.

- **pop:** Removes the top element of the stack. Prior to this operation, the stack must exist and must not be empty.

We now consider the implementation of stacks as an ADT. To develop generic algorithms, as we have done in Chapters 3 and 4, we treat stack elements as references to objects where actual data is stored.

A stack can be implemented either as an array or as a linked list. If we implement a stack as an array, then a stack is an array of reference variables. Similarly, if we implement a stack as a linked list, then the info of each node is a reference to the object storing the data. Both implementations are useful and are discussed in this chapter.

StackException Class

The preceding section describes the basic operations on a stack. The two main operations on a stack are the **push** and the **pop** operations. An element can be pushed onto the stack if the stack is not full. Similarly, an element can be removed from the stack only if the stack is non-empty. Adding an element to a full stack and removing an element from an empty stack generate errors or exceptions called stack overflow exception and stack underflow exception. To handle these exceptions, we design exception classes as follows:

```java
public class StackException extends RuntimeException
{
    public StackException()
    {
    }

    public StackException(String msg)
    {
        super(msg);
    }
}

public class StackOverflowException extends StackException
{
    public StackOverflowException()
    {
        super("Stack Overflow");
    }
```

```
    public StackOverflowException(String msg)
    {
        super(msg);
    }
}

public class StackUnderflowException extends StackException
{
    public StackUnderflowException()
    {
        super("Stack Underflow");
    }

    public StackUnderflowException(String msg)
    {
        super(msg);
    }
}
```

When we write the method to implement the **push** operation, if the stack is full, then this method would throw a **StackOverflowException**. Similarly, the method that implements the **pop** operation would throw a **StackUnderflowException** if we try to remove an item from an empty stack. Notice that the **class StackException** is derived from the **class RuntimeException**, and so the stack overflow and underflow exceptions as we have defined are unchecked exceptions. If you want to make these exceptions checked exceptions, then you should derive the **class StackException** from the **class Exception**. Suppose that you make these checked exceptions. Then if a program uses the **push** and **pop** operations, the program either provides the code to handle these exceptions or explicitly throws these exceptions. For simplicity, and to illustrate how to implement your own exception classes, we have made stack overflow and underflow as unchecked exceptions.

IMPLEMENTATION OF STACKS AS ARRAYS

This section describes how to implement a stack in an array. As remarked previously, because we will design a generic class to implement stacks, the array implementing a stack is an array of reference variables.

The first element of the stack can be referenced by the first array slot, the second element of the stack by the second array slot, and so on. The top of the stack is the index of the last element added to the stack.

In this implementation of a stack, the stack elements are managed by an array of reference variables, and an array is a random access data structure; that is, you can directly access any element of the array. However, by definition, a stack is a data structure in which the elements are accessed (popped or pushed) at only one end—that is, a Last In First Out data structure.

Thus, a stack element is accessed only through the top, not through the bottom or middle. This feature of a stack is extremely important and must be recognized in the beginning.

To keep track of the top position of the array, we can simply declare another variable, called **stackTop**.

The following statements define a stack as an ADT. Because we can specify the size of the array implementing the stack during program execution or at compile time, we leave it for the user to specify the size of the array (that is, the stack size). We assume that the default stack size is 100.

Class: StackClass

```
public class StackClass
```

Instance Variables:

```
private int maxStackSize;  //variable to store the maximum
                           //stack size
private int stackTop;      //variable to point to the top
                           //of the stack
private DataElement[] list;  //array of reference variables
```

Instance Methods and Constructors:

```
public void initializeStack()
   //Method to initialize the stack to an empty state.
   //Postcondition: stackTop = 0

public boolean isEmptyStack()
   //Method to determine whether the stack is empty.
   //Postcondition: Returns true if the stack is empty,
   //               false otherwise.
public boolean isFullStack()
   //Method to determine whether the stack is full.
   //Postcondition: Returns true if the stack is full,
   //               false otherwise.

public void push(DataElement newItem) throws StackOverflowException
   //Method to add newItem to the stack.
   //Precondition: The stack exists and is not full.
   //Postcondition: The stack is changed and newItem
   //               is added to the top of the stack.
   //               If the stack is full, the method throws
   //               StackOverflowException.
public DataElement top() throws StackUnderflowException
   //Method to return the top element of the stack.
   //Precondition: The stack exists and is not empty.
   //Postcondition: If the stack is empty, the method throws
   //               StackUnderflowException; otherwise, a
   //               reference to a copy of the top element
   //               of the stack is returned.
```

```
public void pop() throws StackUnderflowException
    //Method to remove the top element of the stack.
    //Precondition: The stack exists and is not empty.
    //Postcondition: The stack is changed and the top
    //               element is removed from the stack.
    //               If the stack is empty, the method throws
    //               StackUnderflowException.
public StackClass(int stackSize)
    //constructor with a parameter
    //Create an array of size stackSize to implement the stack.
    //Postcondition: The variable list contains the base
    //               address of the array, stackTop = 0, and
    //               maxStackSize = stackSize.
public StackClass()
    //default constructor
    //Create an array of size 100 to implement the stack.
    //Postcondition: The variable list contains the base
    //               address of the array, stackTop = 0, and
    //               maxStackSize = 100.

public void copyStack(StackClass otherStack)
    //Method to make a copy of otherStack.
    //Postcondition: A copy of otherStack is created and
    //               assigned to this stack.
public StackClass(StackClass otherStack)
    //copy constructor
private void copy(StackClass otherStack)
    //Method to make a copy of otherStack.
    //This method is used only to implement the method
    //copyStack and the copy constructor.
    //Postcondition: A copy of otherStack is created and
    //               assigned to this stack.
```

 Because Java arrays begin with the index 0, we need to distinguish between the value of stackTop and the array position indicated by stackTop. If stackTop is 0, the stack is empty; if stackTop is nonzero, then the stack is nonempty and the top element of the stack is given by stackTop − 1.

Notice that the method copy is included as a private member. This is because we want to use this method only to implement the method copyStack and the copy constructor.

Figure 6-4 shows this data structure, wherein stack is an object of the class Stack. Note that stackTop can range from 0 to maxStackSize. If stackTop is nonzero, then stackTop − 1 is the index of the top element of the stack. Suppose that maxStackSize = 100.

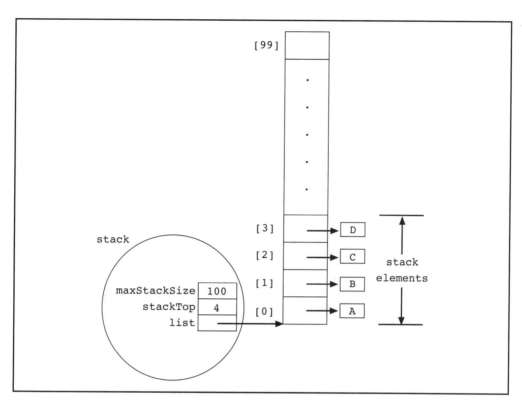

Figure 6-4   Example of a stack

Note that **list** contains the base address of the array (implementing the stack)—that is, the address of the first array component. The next ten sections of this chapter define the methods of the **class StackClass** that implement the stack operations.

Initialize Stack

Let us consider the **initializeStack** operation. The value of **stackTop** indicates whether the stack is empty. To initialize the stack to an empty state, we set the elements of the stack in the range 0 . . . **stackTop-1** to **null** and then set **stackTop** to 0 (see Figure 6-5).

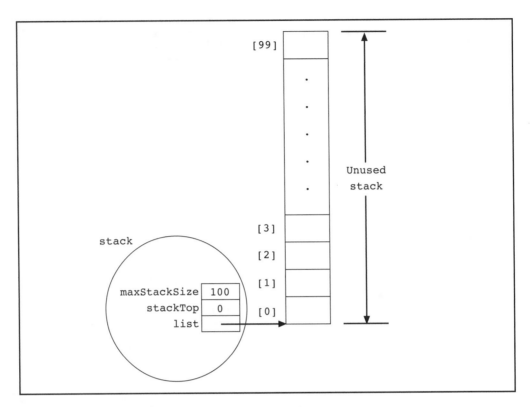

Figure 6-5 Empty stack

The definition of the method `initializeStack` is:

```
public void initializeStack()
{
    for(int i = 0; i < stackTop; i++)
        list[i] = null;
    stackTop = 0;
}//end initializeStack
```

Empty Stack

We have seen that the value of **stackTop** indicates whether a stack is empty. If **stackTop** is 0, the stack is empty; otherwise, the stack is not empty. The definition of the method **isEmptyStack** is:

```
public boolean isEmptyStack()
{
    return(stackTop == 0);
}//end isEmptyStack
```

Full Stack

Next, we consider the operation `isFullStack`. It follows that a stack is full if `stackTop` is equal to `maxStackSize`. The definition of the method `isFullStack` is:

```
public boolean isFullStack()
{
    return(stackTop == maxStackSize);
}//end isFullStack
```

Push

Adding, or pushing, an element onto the stack is a two-step process. Recall that the value of `stackTop` indicates the number of elements in a stack, and `stackTop - 1` gives the position of the top element of the stack. Therefore, the `push` operation is as follows:

    a. Assign `newItem` to the array component indicated by `stackTop`.

    b. Increment `stackTop`.

Figures 6-6 and 6-7 illustrate the `push` operation.

Suppose that before the `push` operation, the stack is as shown in Figure 6-6.

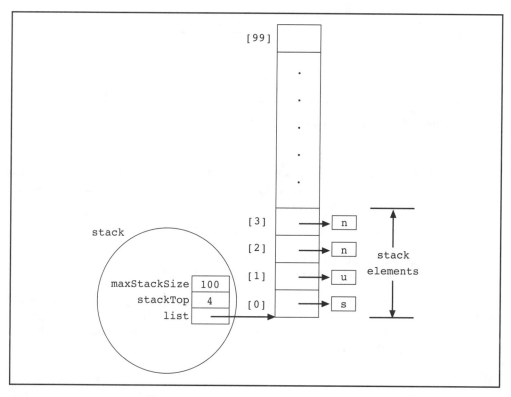

Figure 6-6　Stack before pushing `'y'`

Assume newItem is 'y'. After the push operation, the stack is as shown in Figure 6-7.

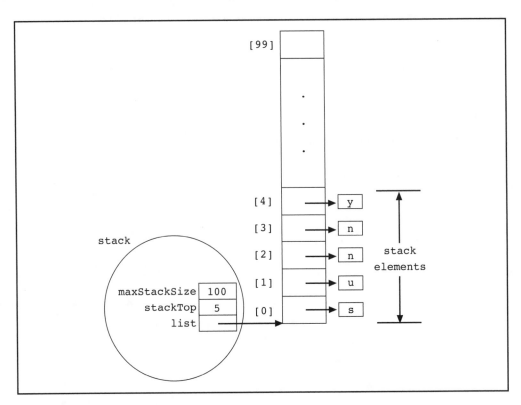

Figure 6-7 Stack after pushing 'y'

If the stack is full, of course, we cannot add any elements to the stack. Therefore, before adding an element to the stack, the method **push** checks whether the stack is full. The definition of the method **push** is:

```
public void push(DataElement newItem) throws StackOverflowException
{
    if(isFullStack())
        throw new StackOverflowException();

    list[stackTop] = newItem.getCopy(); //add newItem at the
                                        //top of the stack
    stackTop++;                         //increment stackTop
}//end push
```

Top Element

The operation **top** returns the top element of a stack. If the stack is empty, this method throws `StackUnderflowException`. Its definition is:

```
public DataElement top() throws StackUnderflowException
{
    if(isEmptyStack())
        throw new StackUnderflowException();

    DataElement temp = list[stackTop - 1].getCopy();

    return temp;
}//end top
```

Pop

To remove, or pop, an element from a stack, we decrement `stackTop` by 1 and set the array element indicated by `stackTop` to `null`.

Figures 6-8 and 6-9 illustrate the **pop** operation.

Suppose that before the **pop** operation, the stack is as shown in Figure 6-8.

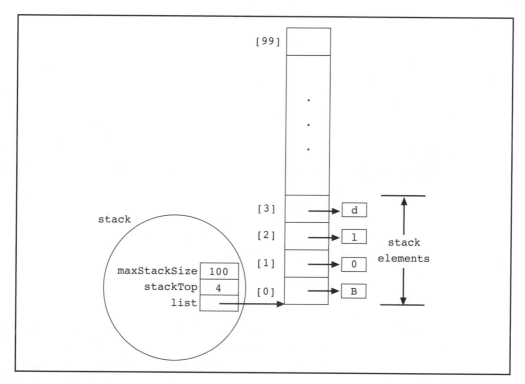

Figure 6-8   Stack before popping 'd'

After the pop operation, the stack is as shown in Figure 6-9.

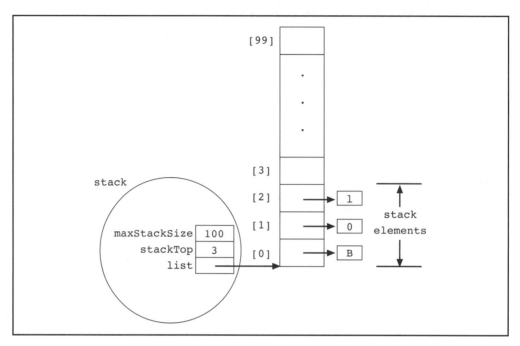

Figure 6-9   Stack after popping `'d'`

If the stack is empty, of course, we cannot remove any element from the stack. Therefore, before removing the top element from the stack, the method **pop** checks whether the stack is empty. The definition of the method **pop** is:

```
public void pop() throws StackUnderflowException
{
    if(isEmptyStack())
        throw new StackUnderflowException();

    stackTop--;          //decrement stackTop
    list[stackTop] = null;
}//end pop
```

Copy

The method **copy** makes a copy of a stack. The stack to be copied is passed as a parameter to the method **copyStack**. We, in fact, use this method to implement the copy constructor and overload the assignment operator. The definition of this method is:

```
private void copy(StackClass otherStack)
{
    list = null;
    System.gc();

    maxStackSize = otherStack.maxStackSize;
    stackTop = otherStack.stackTop;

    list = new DataElement[maxStackSize];

            //copy otherStack into this stack
    for(int i = 0; i < stackTop; i++)
        list[i] = otherStack.list[i].getCopy();
}//end copy
```

Constructors

The constructor with parameters sets the stack size to the size specified by the user, sets stackTop to 0, and creates an appropriate array of reference variables to implement the stack. The default constructor creates an array of size 100. The definitions of the constructors are:

```
    //constructor with a parameter
public StackClass(int stackSize)
{
    if(stackSize <= 0)
    {
        System.err.println("The size of the array to implement "
                        + "the stack must be positive.");
        System.err.println("Creating an array of size 100.");

        maxStackSize = 100;
    }
    else
        maxStackSize = stackSize;   //set the stack size to
                                    //the value specified by
                                    //the parameter stackSize

    stackTop = 0;                       //set stackTop to 0
    list = new DataElement[maxStackSize]; //create the array
}//end constructor

    //default constructor
public StackClass()
{
    maxStackSize = 100;
    stackTop = 0;              //set stackTop to 0
    list = new DataElement[maxStackSize]; //create the array
}//end default constructor
```

Copy Constructor

The copy constructor is called when a stack object is instantiated and initialized using another stack object, which is passed as a parameter.

```
public StackClass(StackClass otherStack)
{
      copy(otherStack);
}//end copy constructor
```

Copy Stack

The definition of the method `copyStack` is:

```
public void copyStack(StackClass otherStack)
{
      if(this != otherStack) //avoid self-copy
          copy(otherStack);
}//end copyStack
```

You can write the definition of the **class StackClass** as follows:

```
public class StackClass
{
      private int maxStackSize;    //variable to store the maximum
                                   //stack size
      private int stackTop;        //variable to point to the top
                                   //of the stack
      private DataElement[] list;  //array of reference variables

      //Place the definitions of the constructors and methods here.

}
```

The analysis of the stack operations is similar to the operations of the **class ArrayListClass** (Chapter 3). We, therefore, provide only a summary in Table 6-1.

Table 6-1 summarizes the time-complexity of the operations of the **class StackClass**.

Table 6-1 Time-Complexity of the Operations of the **class StackClass**

Method	Time-Complexity of Stack Operations
isEmptyStack	$O(1)$
isFullStack	$O(1)$
initializeStack	$O(n)$
constructors	$O(1)$
top	$O(1)$
push	$O(1)$
pop	$O(1)$
copy	$O(n)$
copyStack	$O(n)$
copy constructor	$O(n)$

The program in Example 6-1 tests various stack operations.

Example 6-1

```java
//Program to test various operations of a stack
public class StackProgram
{
    public static void main(String[] args)
    {
        StackClass intStack = new StackClass(50);
        StackClass tempStack = new StackClass();

        try
        {
           intStack.push(new IntElement(23));
           intStack.push(new IntElement(45));
           intStack.push(new IntElement(38));
        }
        catch(StackOverflowException sofe)
        {
           System.out.println(sofe.toString());
           System.exit(0);
        }

        tempStack.copyStack(intStack);   //copy intStack
                                         //into tempStack

        System.out.print("tempStack elements: ");

        while(!tempStack.isEmptyStack())  //print tempStack
        {
           System.out.print(tempStack.top() + " ");
           tempStack.pop();
        }

        System.out.println();

        System.out.println("The top element of intStack: "
                      + intStack.top());
    }
}
```

Output

```
tempStack elements: 38 45 23
The top element of intStack: 38
```

It is recommended that you do a walk-through of this program.

PROGRAMMING EXAMPLE: HIGHEST GPA

In this example, we write a Java program that reads a data file consisting of each student's GPA followed by the student's name. The program then prints the highest GPA and the names of all the students who received that GPA. The program scans the input file only once.

Input   The program reads an input file consisting of each student's GPA, followed by the student's name. Sample data is:

```
3.8 Lisa
3.6 John
3.9 Susan
3.7 Kathy
3.4 Jason
3.9 David
3.4 Jack
```

Output   The highest GPA and all the names associated with the highest GPA. For example, for the above data, the highest GPA is `3.9` and the students associated with that GPA are `Susan` and `David`.

Program Analysis and Algorithm Design

To store the highest GPA, we use the variable `highestGPA` of the type `double` initialized to `0`. For each line in the input file:

1. Get the input line and tokenize it.
2. Retrieve the GPA and the name of the student associated with this GPA.
3. Compare this GPA with `highestGPA`. Three cases arise:
    a. The new GPA is greater than the highest GPA so far. In this case, we:
        i.   Update the value of the highest GPA so far.
        ii. Initialize the stack—that is, remove the names of the students from the stack.
        iii. Save the name of the student having the highest GPA so far in the stack.
    b. The new GPA is equal to the highest GPA so far. In this case, we add the name of the new student to the stack.
    c. The new GPA is less than the highest GPA so far. In this case, we discard the name of the student having this grade.

From this discussion, it is clear that we need the following variables:

```
double GPA; //variable to hold the current GPA
double highestGPA = 0.0; //variable to hold the highest GPA

StringElement name = new StringElement(); //object to hold
                                          //name
String inputLine; //reference variable to read the input line
StringTokenizer tokenizer; //reference variable to tokenize
                           //the input line

StackClass nameStack = new StackClass(100); //stack to hold
                                            //names that have the
                                            //highest GPA

DecimalFormat twoDigits =
            new DecimalFormat("0.00"); //object to output
                                       //decimal numbers to two decimal
                                       //places
```

The preceding discussion translates into the following algorithm:

1. Declare and initialize the variables.

2. Create a `DecimalFormat` object to output a decimal number to two decimal places.

3. Open the input file.

4. If the input file does not exist, exit the program.

5. Read the next input line.

6. `while` (not end of file)
   {
   6.a. Tokenize the input line.

   6.b. Get the next `GPA`.

   6.c. Get the next name.

   6.d. `if (GPA > highestGPA)`
      {
      6.d.i.   `initialize stack`
      6.d.ii. `push(stack, student name);`
      6.d.iii. `highestGPA = GPA;`
      }

   6.e. `else`
         `if(GPA` is equal to `highestGPA)`
            `push(stack, student name);`

6.f. Read the next input line.

}

7. Output the highest GPA.

8. Output the names of the students having the highest GPA.

Complete Program Listing

```
//Program: Highest GPA

import java.io.*;
import java.text.*;
import java.util.*;

public class HighestGPA
{
    public static void main(String[] args)
    {
                //Step 1
        double GPA;
        double highestGPA = 0.0;

        StringElement name = new StringElement();
        String inputLine;
        StringTokenizer tokenizer;

        StackClass nameStack = new StackClass(100);
        DecimalFormat twoDigits =
                new DecimalFormat("0.00");           //Step 2

        try
        {
           BufferedReader infile = new BufferedReader  //Step 3
              (new FileReader("a:\\Ch6_HighestGPAData.txt"));

           inputLine = infile.readLine();              //Step 5

           while(inputLine != null)                    //Step 6
           {
               tokenizer =
                  new StringTokenizer(inputLine);      //Step 6.a
               GPA =                                   //Step 6.b
                 Double.parseDouble(tokenizer.nextToken());
               name.setString(tokenizer.nextToken());  //Step 6.c

               if(GPA > highestGPA)                     //Step 6.d
               {
                   nameStack.initializeStack();         //Step 6.d.i
```

```
            try
            {
               nameStack.push(name);         //Step 6.d.ii
            } //end try
            catch(StackOverflowException sofe)
            {
                System.out.println(sofe.toString());
                System.exit(0);
            }

            highestGPA = GPA;                 //Step 6.d.iii
         }
         else                                //Step 6.e
            if(GPA == highestGPA)
               try
               {
                  nameStack.push(name);
               } //end try
               catch(StackOverflowException sofe)
               {
                   System.out.println(sofe.toString());
                   System.exit(0);
               }

         inputLine = infile.readLine();       //Step 6.f
      }

      System.out.println("Highest GPA = "
               + twoDigits.format(highestGPA));//Step 7
      System.out.println("The students holding the "
                       + "highest GPA are:");

      while(!nameStack.isEmptyStack())         //Step 8
      {
          System.out.println(nameStack.top());
          nameStack.pop();
      }
      System.out.println();
}//end try
catch(FileNotFoundException fnfe)             //Step 4
{
    System.out.println(fnfe.toString());
}
catch(Exception e)
{
```

```
                System.out.println(e.toString());
        }
    }
}
```

Sample Run

Input File (Ch6_HighestGPAData.txt)

```
3.4  Holt
3.2  Bolt
2.5  Colt
3.4  Tom
3.8  Ron
3.8  Mickey
3.6  Pluto
3.5  Donald
3.8  Cindy
3.7  Dome
3.9  Andy
3.8  Fox
3.9  Minnie
2.7  Goofy
3.9  Doc
3.4  Danny
```

Output

```
Highest GPA = 3.90
The students holding the highest GPA are:
Doc
Minnie
Andy
```

LINKED IMPLEMENTATION OF STACKS

Because an array size is fixed, in the array (linear) representation of a stack, only a fixed number of elements can be pushed onto the stack. If in a program the number of elements to be pushed exceeds the size of the array, the program may terminate in an error. We must overcome these problems.

We have seen that by using reference variables we can dynamically allocate memory, and by using linked lists we can dynamically organize data (such as an ordered list). Next, we use these concepts to implement a stack dynamically.

Recall that in the linear representation of a stack, the value of `stackTop` indicates the number of elements in the stack, and the value of `stackTop - 1` indicates where the top item is in the stack. With the help of `stackTop`, we can do several things: find the top element, check whether the stack is empty, and so on.

Similar to the linear representation, in a linked representation, `stackTop` is used to locate the top element of the stack. However, there is a slight difference. In the former case, `stackTop` gives the index of the array; in the latter case, `stackTop` gives the reference of the node whose info contains the reference of the top element of the stack.

The following statements define a linked stack as an ADT:

Class: `LinkedStackClass`

```
public class LinkedStackClass

     //Definition of the node
protected class StackNode
{
    DataElement info;
    StackNode link;
}
```

Instance Variables:

```
private StackNode stackTop;   //reference variable to the
                              //top element of the stack
```

Instance Methods and Constructors:

```
public void initializeStack()
   //Method to initialize the stack to an empty state.
   //Postcondition: stackTop = null

public boolean isEmptyStack()
   //Method to determine whether the stack is empty.
   //Postcondition: Returns true if the stack is empty,
   //               false otherwise.
public boolean isFullStack()
   //Method to determine whether the stack is full.
   //Postcondition: Returns true if the stack is full,
   //               false otherwise.
```

```
public void push(DataElement newElement)
    //Method to add newElement to the stack.
    //Precondition: The stack exists.
    //Postcondition: The stack is changed and newElement
    //               is added to the top of the stack.

public DataElement top() throws StackUnderflowException
    //Method to return the top element of the stack.
    //Precondition: The stack exists and is not empty.
    //Postcondition: If the stack is empty, the method throws
    //               StackUnderflowException; otherwise, a
    //               reference to a copy of the top element
    //               of the stack is returned.
public void pop() throws StackUnderflowException
    //Method to remove the top element of the stack.
    //Precondition: The stack exists and is not empty.
    //Postcondition: The stack is changed and the top element
    //               is removed from the stack.
    //               If the stack is empty, the method throws
    //               StackUnderflowException.

public LinkedStackClass()
    //default constructor
    //Postcondition: stackTop = null
public void copyStack(LinkedStackClass otherStack)
    //Method to make a copy of otherStack.
    //Postcondition: A copy of otherStack is created and
    //               assigned to this stack.
public LinkedStackClass(LinkedStackClass otherStack)
    //copy constructor
private void copy(LinkedStackClass otherStack)
    //Method to make a copy of otherStack.
    //This method is used only to implement the method
    //copyStack and the copy constructor.
    //Postcondition: A copy of otherStack is created and
    //               assigned to this stack.
```

 In this linked implementation of stacks, the memory to store the stack elements is allocated dynamically. Therefore, logically the stack is never full. The stack is full only if we run out of memory space. Thus, it is not necessary to implement the operation isFullStack to determine whether the stack is full. However, the implementation of stacks as arrays does have the operation isFullStack to determine whether the stack is full. The user of a stack does not need to know the implementation details of the stack. Therefore, to be consistent, the implementation of stacks as linked lists also includes this operation.

The following example shows how both empty and nonempty linked stacks appear.

Example 6-2

Empty stack: Supose that a stack is a **LinkedStackClass** object. (See Figure 6-10.)

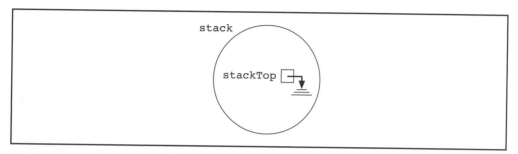

Figure 6-10   Empty linked stack

Nonempty stack: Figure 6-11 shows a nonempty stack.

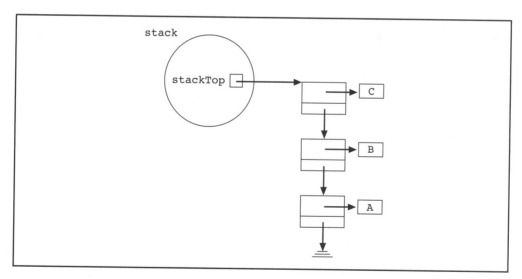

Figure 6-11   Nonempty linked stack

In Figure 6-11, the top element of the stack is C; that is, the last element pushed onto the stack is C.

Next, we discuss the definitions of the methods to implement the operations of a linked stack.

Default Constructor

The first operation that we consider is the default constructor. The default constructor initializes a stack to an empty state when a stack object is declared. Thus, this method sets `stackTop` to `null`. The definition of this method is:

```
public LinkedStackClass()
{
     stackTop = null;
}
```

Initialize Stack

The method `initializeStack` initializes a stack to an empty state. This is accomplished simply by setting `stackTop` to `null`. Once `stackTop` is set to `null`, there will not be any reference variable pointing to the first element of the stack. The system's garbage collector will eventually reclaim the memory occupied by the stack elements. The definition of this method is:

```
public void initializeStack()
{
     stackTop = null;
}//end initializeStack
```

The operations `isEmptyStack` and `isFullStack` are quite straightforward. The stack is empty if `stackTop` is `null`. Also, because the memory for a stack element is allocated and deallocated dynamically, the stack is never full. (The stack is full only if we run out of memory.) Thus, the method `isFullStack` always returns the value `false`. The definitions of the methods to implement these operations are:

```
public boolean isEmptyStack()
{
     return(stackTop == null);
}

public boolean isFullStack()
{
     return false;
}
```

Next, we consider the **push** and **pop** operations. From Figure 6-11, it is clear that `newElement` is added (in the case of **push**) at the beginning of the linked list pointed to by `stackTop`. In the case of **pop**, the node pointed to by `stackTop` is removed. In both cases, the value of `stackTop` is updated.

Push

Consider the stack shown in Figure 6-12.

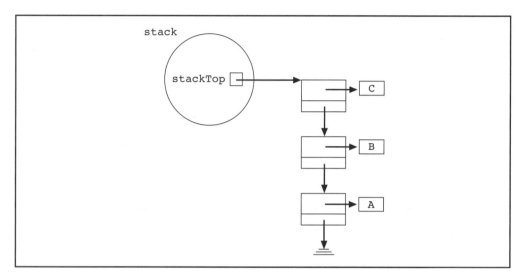

Figure 6-12   Stack before push operation

Assume that the new element to be pushed is D. First, we allocate memory for the new node. We then store D in the new node and insert the new node at the beginning of the list. Finally, we update the value of **stackTop**. The statements:

```
newNode = new StackNode(); //create the new node
newNode.info = newElement.getCopy();
```

create a node, store the address of the node in the variable **newNode**, and assign a copy of **newElement** to the **info** field of **newNode**. Thus, we have the situation shown in Figure 6-13.

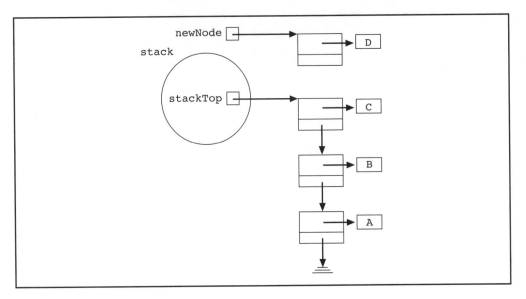

Figure 6-13   Stack and newNode

The statement:

```
newNode.link = stackTop;
```

inserts **newNode** at the top of the stack, as shown in Figure 6-14.

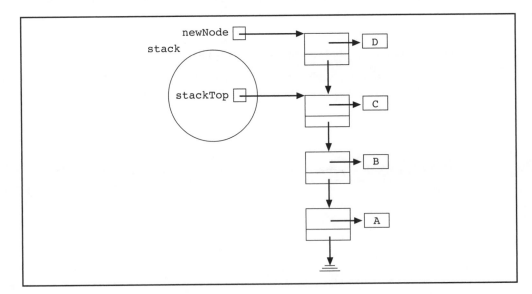

Figure 6-14   Stack after the statement newNode.link = stackTop; executes

Finally, the statement:

```
stackTop = newNode;
```

updates the value of **stackTop**, which results in Figure 6-15.

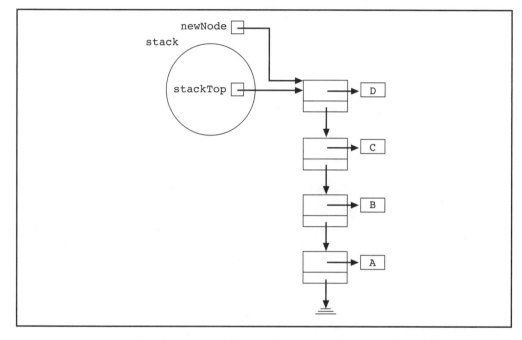

Figure 6-15   Stack after the statement `stackTop = newNode;` executes

The definition of the method **push** is:

```
public void push(DataElement newElement)
{
    StackNode newNode; //reference variable to create
                       //the new node

    newNode = new StackNode(); //create the new node
    newNode.info = newElement.getCopy();
    newNode.link = stackTop;      //insert newNode before
                                  //stackTop
    stackTop = newNode;           //set stackTop to point to
                                  //the top element
}//end push
```

We do not need to check whether the stack is full before we push an element onto the stack because in this implementation, logically, the stack is never full.

Return the Top Element

The method `top` returns the top element of the stack. However, if the stack is empty, it throws a `StackUnderflowException`. Its definition is:

```
public DataElement top() throws StackUnderflowException
{
    if(stackTop == null)
        throw new StackUnderflowException();

    return stackTop.info.getCopy();
}//end top
```

Pop

Now we consider the `pop` operation. Consider the stack shown in Figure 6-16.

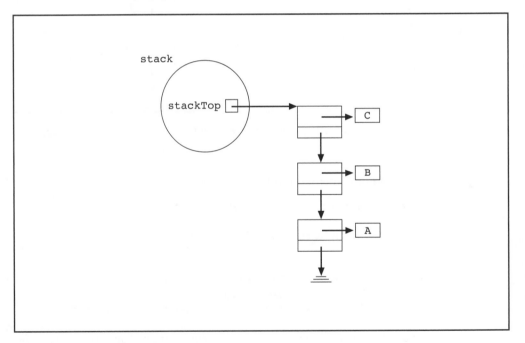

Figure 6-16   Stack before the `pop` operation

The statement:

```
stackTop = stackTop.link;
```

makes the second element of the stack become the top element of the stack. We then have the situation shown in Figure 6-17.

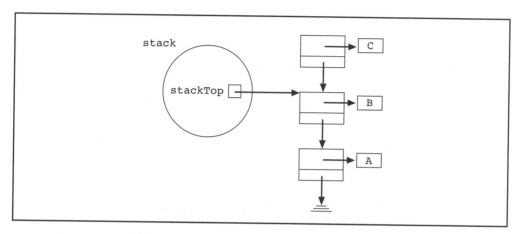

Figure 6-17   Stack after the statement `stackTop = stackTop.link;` executes

After making the second element the top element of the stack, there is no reference to the object containing C. Therefore, the memory space of this object is claimed by the garbage collector.

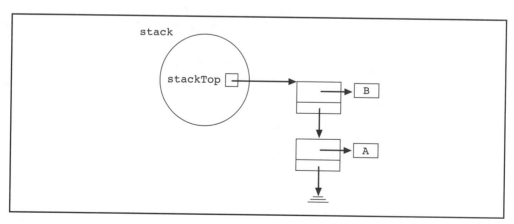

Figure 6-18   Stack after popping the top element

The definition of the method pop is:

```
public void pop() throws StackUnderflowException
{
    if(stackTop == null)
        throw new StackUnderflowException();

    stackTop = stackTop.link;    //advance stackTop to the
                                 //next node
}//end pop
```

We have already discussed the default constructor. To complete the implementation of the stack operations, we need to write the definitions of the methods copy, copyStack, and the copy constructor. These methods are similar to those discussed for linked lists in Chapter 4 and are, therefore, left as exercises for you.

We also leave it as an exercise for you to write the definition of the class LinkedStackClass.

STACK AS DERIVED FROM THE class LinkedListClass

If we compare the push method of a stack with the insertFirst method discussed for general linked lists in Chapter 4, we see that the algorithms to implement these operations are similar. A comparison of other methods, such as initializeStack and initializeList, isEmptyList and isEmptyStack, and so on, suggests that the class LinkedStackClass can be derived from the class LinkedListClass. Moreover, the methods isFullStack, top, and pop can be implemented as in the previous section.

Because the class LinkedListClass is an abstract class and we do not want to provide the definitions of the abstract methods of this class, we can derive the class LinkedStackClass from the class UnorderedLinkedList, which was designed in Chapter 4.

Next, we define the class LinkedStackClass that is derived from the class UnorderedLinkedList. The definitions of the methods to implement the stack operations are also given.

```
public class LinkedStackClass extends UnorderedLinkedList
{
    public LinkedStackClass()
    {
        super();
    }

        //copy constructor
    public LinkedStackClass(LinkedStackClass otherStack)
    {
        super(otherStack);
    }//end copy constructor
```

```java
public void initializeStack()
{
    initializeList();
}

public boolean isEmptyStack()
{
    return isEmptyList();
}

public boolean isFullStack()
{
    return false;
}

public void push(DataElement newElement)
{
    insertFirst(newElement);
}//end push

public DataElement top() throws StackUnderflowException
{
    if(first == null)
        throw new StackUnderflowException();

    return front();
}//end top

public void pop() throws StackUnderflowException
{
    if(first == null)
        throw new StackUnderflowException();

    first = first.link;

    count--;

    if(first == null)
        last = null;
}//end pop

public void copyStack(LinkedStackClass otherStack)
{
    copyList(otherStack);
}
}
```

6

APPLICATION OF STACKS: POSTFIX EXPRESSION CALCULATOR

The usual notation for writing arithmetic expressions (the notation we learned in elementary school) is called **infix** notation, in which the operator is written between the operands. For example, in the expression $a + b$, the operator + is between the operands a and b. In infix notation, the operators have precedence. That is, we evaluate expressions from left to right, and multiplication and division have higher precedence than addition and subtraction. If we want to evaluate an expression in a different order, we must include parentheses. For example, in the expression $a + b * c$, we first evaluate * using the operands b and c, and then we evaluate + using the operand a and the result of $b * c$.

In the early 1950s, the Polish mathematician Lukasiewicz discovered that if operators were written before the operands (**prefix** or **Polish** notation; for example, $+ a b$) or after the operands (**suffix**, **postfix**, or **reverse Polish** notation; for example, $a b +$), the parentheses can be omitted. For example, the expression:

$a + b * c$

in a postfix expression is:

$a b c * +$

The following example shows infix expressions and their equivalent postfix expressions.

Example 6-3

Table 6-2 shows various infix expressions and their equivalent postfix expressions.

Table 6-2 Infix Expressions and Their Equivalent Postfix Expressions

Infix Expression	Equivalent Postfix Expression
$a + b$	$a b +$
$a + b * c$	$a b c * +$
$a * b + c$	$a b * c +$
$(a + b) * c$	$a b + c *$
$(a - b) * (c + d)$	$a b - c d + *$
$(a + b) * (c - d / e) + f$	$a b + c d e / - * f +$

Shortly after Lukasiewicz's discovery, it was realized that postfix notation had important applications in computer science. In fact, many compilers now first translate arithmetic expressions into some form of postfix notation and then translate this postfix expression into machine code. Postfix expressions can be evaluated using the following algorithm:

Scan the expression from left to right. When an operator is found, back up to get the required number of operands, perform the operation, and continue.

Consider the following postfix expression:

6 3 + 2 * =

Let us evaluate this expression using a stack and the previous algorithm. (In the following discussion, we list the postfix expression after each step. The shading indicates the part of the expression that has been processed.)

6 3 + 2 * =

    1. Get the first symbol, **6**, which is a number. Push the number onto the stack (see Figure 6-19).

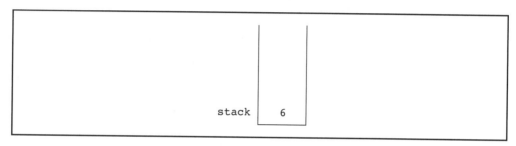

Figure 6-19   Stack after pushing 6

    6 3 + 2 * =

    2. Get the next symbol, **3**, which is a number. Push the number onto the stack (see Figure 6-20).

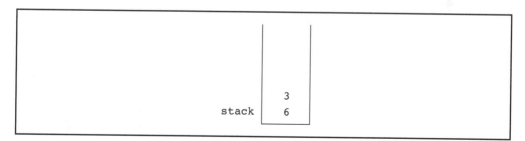

Figure 6-20   Stack after pushing 3

    6 3 + 2 * =

    3. Get the next symbol, **+**, which is an operator. Because an operator requires two operands to be evaluated, pop the stack twice. Perform the operation and put the result back onto the stack (see Figures 6-21 and 6-22).

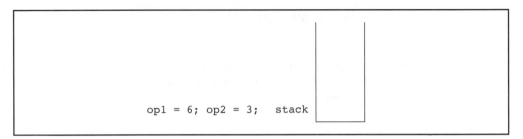

opl = 6; op2 = 3;   stack

Figure 6-21   Stack after popping twice

Perform the operation: op1 + op2 = 6 + 3 = 9.

Push the result onto the stack (see Figure 6-22).

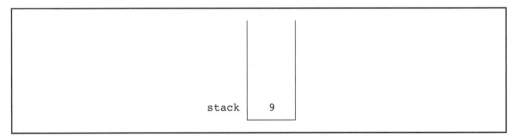

stack   9

Figure 6-22   Stack after pushing the result of op1 + op2, which is 9

6 3 + 2 * =

4. Get the next symbol, 2, which is a number. Push the number onto the stack (see Figure 6-23).

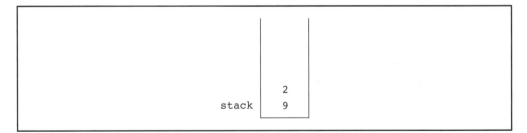

stack   2
          9

Figure 6-23   Stack after pushing 2

`6 3 + 2 * =`

5. Get the next symbol, *, which is an operator. Because an operator requires two operands to be evaluated, pop the stack twice. Perform the operation and put the result back onto the stack (see Figures 6-24 and 6-25).

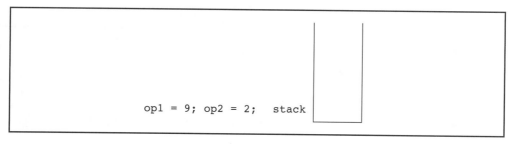

op1 = 9; op2 = 2;   stack

Figure 6-24   Stack after popping twice

Perform the operation: op1 * op2 = 9 * 2 = 18.

Push the result onto the stack (see Figure 6-25).

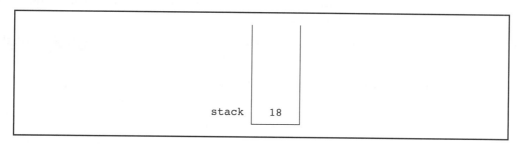

stack   18

Figure 6-25   Stack after pushing the result of op1 * op2, which is 18

`6 3 + 2 * =`

6. Scan the next symbol, =, which is the equal sign, indicating the end of the expression. Therefore, print the result. The result of the expression is in the stack, so pop and print are as shown in Figure 6-26.

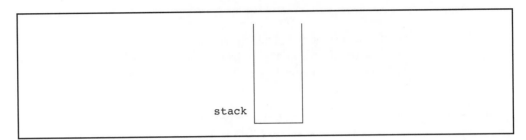

Figure 6-26 Stack after popping the element

The value of the expression 6 3 + 2 * = 18.

From this discussion, it is clear that when we read a symbol other than a number, the following cases arise:

1. The symbol we read is one of the following: +, −, *, /, or =.

   a. If the symbol is +, −, *, or /, the symbol is an operator and so we must evaluate it. Because an operator requires two operands, the stack must have at least two elements; otherwise, the expression has an error.

   b. If the symbol is = (an equal sign), the expression ends and we must print the answer. At this step, the stack must contain exactly one element; otherwise, the expression has an error.

2. The symbol we read is something other than +, −, *, /, or =. In this case, the expression contains an illegal operator.

It is also clear that when an operand (number) is encountered in an expression, it is pushed onto the stack because the operators come after the operands.

Consider the following expressions:

(i) 7 6 + 3 ; 6 − =

(ii) 14 + 2 3 * =

(iii) 14 2 3 + =

Expression (i) has an illegal operator, expression (ii) does not have enough operands for +, and expression (iii) has too many operands. In the case of expression (iii), when we encounter the equal sign (=), the stack has two elements and this error cannot be discovered until we are ready to print the value of the expression.

We assume that each expression contains only the +, −, *, and / operators.

This program outputs the entire postfix expression together with the answer. If the expression has an error, the expression is discarded. In this case, the program outputs the expression together with an appropriate error message. Because an expression may contain an error, we must clear the stack before processing the next expression. Also, the stack must be initialized; that is, the stack must be empty.

Main Algorithm

Pursuant to the previous discussion, the main algorithm in pseudocode is:

```
Get the next expression
while more data to process
{
    a. initialize the stack
    b. process the expression
    c. output the result
    d. get the next expression
}
```

To simplify the complexity of the method **main**, we write three methods— **evaluateExpression**, **evaluateOpr**, and **printResult**. The method **evaluateExpression**, if possible, evaluates the expression and leaves the result in the stack. If the postfix expression is error free, the method **printResult** outputs the result. To simplify the program, we use two instance variables: **strToken**—to store a token from the postfix expression; and **expressionOk**—to indicate whether the expression is error free. Next, we describe each of these methods.

 In the program that we write next, we ignore the stack overflow and underflow exceptions. In Programming Exercise 10, you are asked to rewrite this program so that the stack overflow and underflow exceptions are handled using the **try/catch** blocks.

Method evaluateExpression

The method **evaluateExpression** evaluates each postfix expression. Each expression ends with the symbol =. The general algorithm is:

```
tokenize the input line
get the next token

while(token != '=')
{
    if(token is a number)
    {
        output the number
        push number into stack
    }
    else
    {
        token is an operation
        call method evaluateOpr to evaluate the operation
    }
```

```
        if(no error in the expression)
           get next token
        else
           discard the expression
    }
```

From this algorithm it follows that this method has three parameters—a parameter to access the stack, a parameter to access the output file, and a parameter to access the input line. The definition of this method is:

```
public static void evaluateExpression(StackClass pStack,
                                      PrintWriter outp,
                                      String inpLine)
                                      throws IOException
{
    DoubleElement num = new DoubleElement();
    StringTokenizer tokenizer;

    tokenizer = new StringTokenizer(inpLine);
    strToken = tokenizer.nextToken();

    while(strToken.charAt(0) != '=')
    {
        if(Character.isDigit(strToken.charAt(0)))
        {
            num.setNum(Double.parseDouble(strToken));
            outp.print(num + " ");

            if(!pStack.isFullStack())
                pStack.push(num);
            else
            {
                System.out.print("Stack overflow. "
                           + "Program terminates!");
                System.exit(0);
            }
        }
        else
        {
            outp.print(strToken + " ");
            evaluateOpr(pStack, outp);
        }

        if(expressionOk) //if no error
            strToken = tokenizer.nextToken();
        else
        {
            while(tokenizer.hasMoreTokens())
                outp.print(tokenizer.nextToken() + " ");
```

```
                strToken = "=";
        }
    }//end while (!= '=')
}//end evaluateExpression
```

Method `evaluateOpr`

This method (if possible) evaluates an operation. Two operands are needed to evaluate an operation and operands are saved in the stack. Therefore, the stack must contain at least two numbers. If the stack contains fewer than two numbers, then the expression has an error. In this case, the entire expression is discarded and an appropriate message is printed. This method also checks for any illegal operations. In pseudocode, this method is:

```
if stack is empty
{
    error in the expression
    set expressionOk to false
}
else
{
    retrieve the top element of stack into op2
    pop stack
    if stack is empty
    {
        error in the expression
        set expressionOk to false
    }
    else
    {
        retrieve the top element of stack into op1
        pop stack

        //if the operation is legal, perform the
        //operation and push the result onto the stack
    switch(operator)
    {
    case '+': //perform the operation and push the result
              //onto the stack
              stack.push(op1 + op2);
              break;
        case '-': //perform the operation and push the result
              //onto the stack
              stack.push(op1 - op2);
              break;
        case '*': //perform the operation and push the result
              //onto the stack
              stack.push(op1 * op2);
              break;
        case '/': //if(op2 != 0), perform the operation and
              //push the result onto the stack
              stack.push(op1 / op2);
```

6

```
                        //otherwise, report error
                        //set expressionOk to false
                          break;
              otherwise operation is illegal
                 {
                     output an appropriate message;
                     set expressionOk to false
                 }
              }//end switch
}
```

To evaluate an operation, the method **evaluateOpr** must have access to the stack and the output file. If an error in the postfix expression is found, the instance variable **expressionOk** is set to **false**. This method has two parameters—a parameter to access the stack and another parameter to access the output file. The definition of this method is:

```
public static void evaluateOpr(StackClass pStack,
                               PrintWriter outp)
{
    DoubleElement op1 = new DoubleElement();
    DoubleElement op2 = new DoubleElement();
    DoubleElement answer = new DoubleElement();
    DoubleElement temp = new DoubleElement();

    if(pStack.isEmptyStack())
    {
       outp.print(" (Not enough operands) ");
       expressionOk = false;
    }
    else
    {
       op2 = (DoubleElement) pStack.top();
       pStack.pop();

       if(pStack.isEmptyStack())
       {
          outp.print(" (Not enough operands) ");
          expressionOk = false;
       }
       else
       {
          op1 = (DoubleElement) pStack.top();
          pStack.pop();

          switch(strToken.charAt(0))
          {
          case '+': answer.setNum(op1.getNum() + op2.getNum());
                    pStack.push(answer);
                    break;
```

```
        case '-': answer.setNum(op1.getNum() - op2.getNum());
                  pStack.push(answer);
                  break;
        case '*': answer.setNum(op1.getNum() * op2.getNum());
                  pStack.push(answer);
                  break;
        case '/': if(op2.getNum() != 0)
                  {
                      answer.setNum(op1.getNum() / op2.getNum());
                      pStack.push(answer);
                  }
                  else
                  {
                      outp.print(" Division by 0 ");
                      expressionOk = false;
                  }
                  break;
        default:  outp.print(" (Illegal operator) ");
                  expressionOk = false;
        }//end switch
    }//end else
    }//end else
}//end evaluateOpr
```

Method printResult

If the postfix expression contains no errors, the method printResult prints the result; otherwise, it outputs an appropriate message. The result of the expression is in the stack and the output is sent to a file. Therefore, this method must have access to the stack and the output file. Suppose that the method evaluateExpression did not encounter any errors. If the stack has only one element, then the expression is error free and the top element of the stack is printed. If either the stack is empty or it has more than one element, then there is an error in the postfix expression. In this case, this method outputs an appropriate error message. The definition of this method is:

```
public static void printResult(StackClass pStack, PrintWriter outp)
{
    DoubleElement result = new DoubleElement();
    DoubleElement temp = new DoubleElement();

    DecimalFormat twoDecimal = new DecimalFormat("0.00");

    if(expressionOk) //if no error, print the result
    {
        if(!pStack.isEmptyStack())
        {
            temp = (DoubleElement) pStack.top();
            result.setNum(temp.getNum());
            pStack.pop();
```

```
                if(pStack.isEmptyStack())
                    outp.println(strToken + " "
                                + twoDecimal.format(result.getNum()));
                else
                    outp.println(strToken
                                + " (Error: Too many operands)");
            }//end if
            else
                outp.println(" (Error in the expression)");
        }
        else
            outp.println(" (Error in the expression)");

        outp.println("_____");
}
```

Program Listing

```
//Postfix Calculator

import java.io.*;
import java.text.DecimalFormat;
import java.util.*;

public class PostfixCalculator
{
    static String strToken;
    static boolean expressionOk;

    public static void main(String[] args) throws
                                    FileNotFoundException,
                                    IOException
    {
        StackClass postfixStack = new StackClass(100);

        String inputLine;

        StringTokenizer tokenizer;

        BufferedReader inputStream = new BufferedReader(new
                        FileReader("a:\\Ch6_RpnData.txt"));
        PrintWriter outfile = new PrintWriter(new
                        FileWriter("a:\\Ch6_RpnOutput.out"));

        inputLine = inputStream.readLine();

        while(inputLine != null)
        {
            postfixStack.initializeStack();
            expressionOk = true;
```

```
        evaluateExpression(postfixStack, outfile,
                           inputLine);
        printResult(postfixStack, outfile);
        inputLine = inputStream.readLine(); //begin
                          //processing the next expression
    }//end while

    outfile.close();
}//end main

//Place the definitions of the methods evaluateExpression,
//evaluateOpr, and printResult as previously described here.
}
```

Sample Run

Input File

```
35 27 + 3 * =
26 28 + 32 2 ; - 5 / =
23 30 15 * / =
2 3 4 + =
23 0 / =
20 29 9 * ; =
25 23 - + =
34 24 12 7 / * + 23 - =
```

Output

```
35.0 27.0 + 3.0 * = 186.00
```

————————————

```
26.0 28.0 + 32.0 2.0 ;  (Illegal operator) - 5 / = (Error in the expression)
```

————————————

```
23.0 30.0 15.0 * / = 0.05
```

————————————

```
2.0 3.0 4.0 + = (Error: Too many operands)
```

————————————

```
23.0 0.0 /  Division by 0 =  (Error in the expression)
```

————————————

```
20.0 29.0 9.0 * ;  (Illegal operator) =  (Error in the expression)
```

————————————

```
25.0 23.0 - +  (Not enough operands) = (Error in the expression)
```

```
34.0 24.0 12.0 7.0 / * + 23.0 - = 52.14
```

Postfix Expression Calculator: Graphical User Interface (GUI)

 If the reader is not familiar with the GUI components of Java, then this section may be skipped without any discontinuation.

In the preceding section, we designed a Java application program to evaluate postfix expressions. In this section, we redo that program to create the graphical user interface (GUI) shown in Figure 6-27:

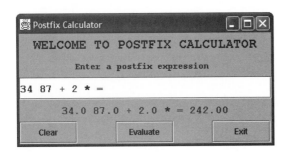

Figure 6-27   GUI for the postfix calculator

In this user interface, the user can enter the expression in the white area. After entering the expression, the user can either press the **Enter** key or the **Evaluate** button to evaluate the expression. The result is displayed below the white area. To evaluate the next expression, the user can click on the **Clear** button and type the new expression in the white area.

For the most part, the GUI version of the postfix calculator is the same as the non-GUI version. The methods **evaluateExpression**, **evaluateOpr**, and **printResult** need minor modification. Because the data is no longer coming from a file and the output is no longer stored in a file, we no longer need file stream objects. Moreover, to simplify the accessing of **postfixStack**, we declare it as the instance variable of the class containing the GUI program. To be specific, we use the following instance variables:

```
private String strToken;
private boolean expressionOk;
```

```
private String inputLine;
private String outputLine = "";

private StackClass postfixStack = new StackClass(100);
```

Before describing the GUI parts, let us first give the modified definitions of the methods `evaluateExpression`, `evaluateOpr`, and `printResult`. (Notice that because the stack object `postfixStack` is declared as the instance variable, it no longer needs to be passed as a parameter to these methods.)

```
public void evaluateExpression()
{
    postfixStack.initializeStack();
    expressionOk = true;
    DoubleElement num = new DoubleElement();
    StringTokenizer tokenizer;

    tokenizer = new StringTokenizer(inputLine);
    strToken = tokenizer.nextToken();

    while(strToken.charAt(0) != '=')
    {
        if(Character.isDigit(strToken.charAt(0)))
        {
            num.setNum(Double.parseDouble(strToken));
            outputLine += num + " ";

            if(!postfixStack.isFullStack())
                postfixStack.push(num);
            else
            {
                outputLine = "Stack overflow. "
                            + "Program terminates!";
                System.exit(0);
            }
        }
        else
        {
            outputLine += strToken + " ";
            evaluateOpr();
        }

        if(expressionOk) //if no error
            strToken = tokenizer.nextToken();
        else
        {
            while(tokenizer.hasMoreTokens())
                outputLine = outputLine + tokenizer.nextToken() + " ";
```

6

```
                strToken = "=";
            }
        }//end while (!= '=')
    }//end evaluateExpression

    public void evaluateOpr()
    {
        DoubleElement op1 = new DoubleElement();
        DoubleElement op2 = new DoubleElement();
        DoubleElement answer = new DoubleElement();
        DoubleElement temp = new DoubleElement();

        if(postfixStack.isEmptyStack())
        {
            outputLine = outputLine + " (Not enough operands) ";
            expressionOk = false;
        }
        else
        {
            op2 = (DoubleElement) postfixStack.top();
            postfixStack.pop();

            if(postfixStack.isEmptyStack())
            {
                outputLine = outputLine + " (Not enough operands) ";
                expressionOk = false;
            }
            else
            {
                op1 = (DoubleElement) postfixStack.top();
                postfixStack.pop();

                switch(strToken.charAt(0))
                {
                case '+': answer.setNum(op1.getNum() + op2.getNum());
                          postfixStack.push(answer);
                          break;
                case '-': answer.setNum(op1.getNum() - op2.getNum());
                          postfixStack.push(answer);
                          break;
                case '*': answer.setNum(op1.getNum() * op2.getNum());
                          postfixStack.push(answer);
                          break;
                case '/': if(op2.getNum() != 0)
                          {
                              answer.setNum(op1.getNum() / op2.getNum());
                              postfixStack.push(answer);
                          }
```

```
                  else
                  {
                      outputLine = outputLine + " Division by 0 ";
                      expressionOk = false;
                  }
                  break;
         default:  outputLine = outputLine + " (Illegal operator) ";
                   expressionOk = false;
         }//end switch
      }//end else
   }//end else
}//end evaluateOpr

public void printResult()
{
    DoubleElement result = new DoubleElement();
    DoubleElement temp = new DoubleElement();

    DecimalFormat twoDecimal = new DecimalFormat("0.00");

    if(expressionOk) //if no error, print the result
    {
       if(!postfixStack.isEmptyStack())
       {
          temp = (DoubleElement) postfixStack.top();
          result.setNum(temp.getNum());
          postfixStack.pop();

          if(postfixStack.isEmptyStack())
             outputLine += strToken + " "
                          + twoDecimal.format(result.getNum());
          else
             outputLine += strToken
                          + " (Error: Too many operands)";
       }//end if
       else
          outputLine += " (Error in the expression)";
    }
    else
       outputLine += " (Error in the expression)";
}//end printResult
```

Next, we discuss how to create the GUI. To create the GUI, we make the class containing the postfix calculator program extend the definition of the **class JFrame**. Suppose that the name of the class containing the application program to create the previous GUI is **PostfixCalculator**.

The GUI interface contains several labels, three buttons, and a text field. We, therefore, use the following reference variables to create these GUI components:

```
private JTextField inputTF;
private JLabel outputLabel;
private JButton clearB, evaluateB, exitB;
```

When the user clicks on a button, it generates an action event. We, therefore, need to write the definition of the method **actionPerformed**, and instantiate and register the listener object to these buttons. The definition of the method **actionPerformed** is as follows:

```
public void actionPerformed(ActionEvent e)
{
    if((e.getSource().equals(inputTF)) ||
        (e.getSource().equals(evaluateB)))
    {
        inputLine = inputTF.getText();

        if(inputLine != null)
        {
            evaluateExpression();

            printResult();
        }

        if(!expressionOk)
            outputLabel.setForeground(Color.red);
        else
            outputLabel.setForeground(Color.blue);

        outputLabel.setText(outputLine);
        outputLine = "";
        inputLine = "";
    }
    else
        if(e.getSource().equals(clearB))
        {
            inputTF.setText("");
            outputLabel.setText("");
            outputLine = "";
            inputLine="";
        }
        else
            if(e.getSource().equals(exitB))
                System.exit(0);
}
```

Next, we write the definition of the constructor **PostfixCalculator** to create the GUI components. The constructor gets access to the content pane; sets the title and the size of the window; instantiates the labels, text field, and buttons; and creates and registers the listener object to the labels. The definition of the constructor is:

```java
PostfixCalculator()
{
            //Setting up the GUI
        super("Postfix Calculator");
        setSize(400, 200);
        Container pane = getContentPane();
        pane.setLayout(new GridLayout(5, 1));

        JLabel welcomeLabel = new
                        JLabel("WELCOME TO POSTFIX CALCULATOR",
                                SwingConstants.CENTER);
        welcomeLabel.setForeground(Color.black);
        welcomeLabel.setFont(new Font("Courier", Font.BOLD, 20));

        JLabel inputLabel = new
                        JLabel("Enter a postfix expression ",
                                SwingConstants.CENTER);
        inputLabel.setForeground(Color.black);
        inputLabel.setFont(new Font("Courier", Font.BOLD, 14));

        inputTF = new JTextField(10);
        inputTF.setFont(new Font("Courier", Font.BOLD, 16));

        outputLabel = new JLabel("", SwingConstants.CENTER);
        outputLabel.setFont(new Font("Courier", Font.BOLD, 16));
        outputLabel.setForeground(Color.black);

        Panel buttonPanel = new Panel();
        clearB = new JButton("Clear");
        evaluateB = new JButton("Evaluate");
        exitB = new JButton("Exit");

        inputTF.addActionListener(this);
        clearB.addActionListener(this);
        evaluateB.addActionListener(this);
        exitB.addActionListener(this);

        pane.add(welcomeLabel);
        pane.add(inputLabel);
        pane.add(inputTF);
        pane.add(outputLabel);
        pane.add(buttonPanel);
        buttonPanel.setLayout(new GridLayout(1,3,60,10));
        buttonPanel.add(clearB);
        buttonPanel.add(evaluateB);
        buttonPanel.add(exitB);

        setVisible(true);
        setDefaultCloseOperation(EXIT_ON_CLOSE);
}
```

6

Next, we outline the definition of the **class PostfixCalculator** to create the complete program.

```java
import java.awt.*;
import java.awt.event.*;
import javax.swing.*;
import java.io.*;
import java.text.DecimalFormat;
import java.util.*;

public class PostfixCalculator extends JFrame
                                implements ActionListener
{
    private String strToken;
    private boolean expressionOk;

    private String inputLine;
    private String outputLine = "";

    private StackClass postfixStack = new StackClass(100);

    private JTextField inputTF;
    private JLabel outputLabel;
    private JButton clearB, evaluateB, exitB;

      //Place the definition of the constructor
      //PostfixCalculator here.

      //Place the definition of the method actionPerformed here.

      //Place the definition of the methods evaluateExpression,
      //evaluateOpr, and printExpression here.

    public static void main(String[] args)
    {
        PostfixCalculator pc = new PostfixCalculator();
    }
}//end PostfixCalculator
```

Sample Run1: Figure 6-28 shows a sample run of this program.

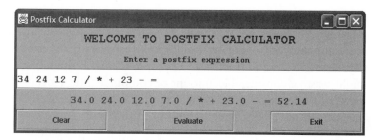

Figure 6-28   Sample run of the `PostfixCalculator` program

Sample Run2: Figure 6-29 shows a sample run of this program. The stack is never full. (The stack is full if we run out of memory.)

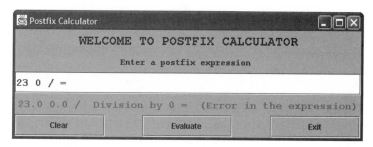

Figure 6-29   Sample run of the `PostfixCalculator` program

REMOVING RECURSION: NONRECURSIVE ALGORITHM TO PRINT A LINKED LIST BACKWARDS

 This section may be skipped without any discontinuation.

In Chapter 5, we used recursion to print a linked list backwards. In this section, you learn how a stack can be used to design a nonrecursive algorithm to print a linked list backwards.

Consider the linked list shown in Figure 6-30.

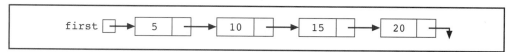

Figure 6-30   Linked list

To print the list backwards, first we need to get to the last node of the list, which we can do by traversing the linked list starting at the first node. However, once we are at the last node, how do we get back to the previous node, especially given that links go in only one direction? You can again traverse the linked list with the appropriate loop termination condition, but this approach might waste a considerable amount of computer time, especially if the list is very large. Moreover, if we do this for every node in the list, the program might execute very slowly. Let us see how to use a stack effectively to print the list backwards.

After printing the `info` of a particular node, we need to move to the node immediately behind this node. For example, after printing 20, we need to move to the node with `info 15`. Thus, while initially traversing the list to move to the last node, we must save references to each node. For example, for the list in Figure 6-30, we must save references to each of the nodes with `info 5, 10`, and `15`. After printing 20, we go back to the node with `info 15`; after printing 15, we go back to the node with `info 10`, and so on. From this, it follows that we must save references to each node in a stack, so as to implement the Last In First Out principle.

Because the number of nodes in a linked list is usually not known, we use the linked implementation of a stack. Suppose that `stack` is a `LinkedStackClass` object. Moreover, `current` is a reference variable of the same type as `first` and `first` points to the first node of the linked list. Consider the following statements:

```
current = first;                    //Line 1

while(current != null)              //Line 2
{
    stack.push(current);           //Line 3
    current = current.link;        //Line 4
}
```

After the statement in Line 1 executes, `current` points to the first node (see Figure 6-31).

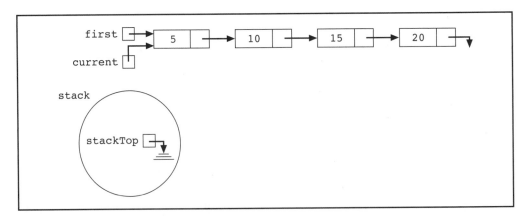

Figure 6-31 List after the statement `current = first;` executes

Because `current` is not `null`, the statements in Lines 3 and 4 execute (see Figure 6-32).

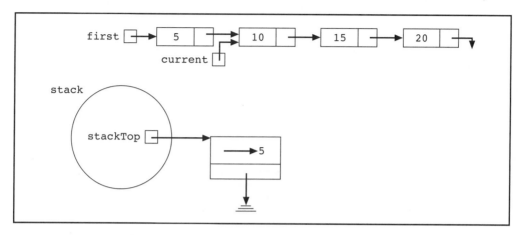

Figure 6-32   List and `stack` after the statements `stack.push(current);` and
`current = current.link;` execute

After the statement in Line 4 executes, the loop condition in Line 2 is evaluated. Because `current` is not `null`, the loop condition evaluates to **true**, and so the statements in Lines 3 and 4 execute (see Figure 6-33).

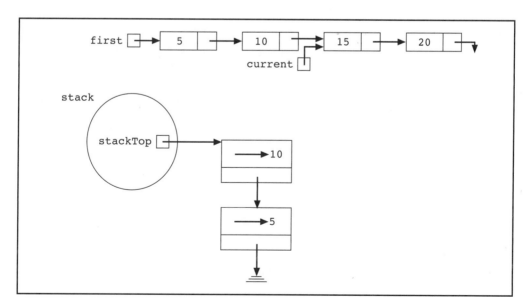

Figure 6-33   List and `stack` after the statements `stack.push(current);` and
`current = current.link;` execute

6

After the statement in Line 4 executes, the loop condition in Line 2 is evaluated again. Because **current** is not **null**, the loop condition evaluates to **true** and so the statements in Lines 3 and 4 execute (see Figure 6-34).

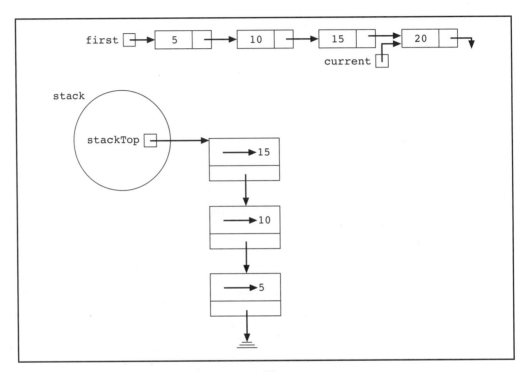

Figure 6-34 List and **stack** after the statements **stack.push(current);** and **current = current.link;** execute

After the statement in Line 4 executes, the loop condition in Line 2 is evaluated again. Because **current** is not **null**, the loop condition evaluates to **true**, and so the statements in Lines 3 and 4 execute (see Figure 6-35).

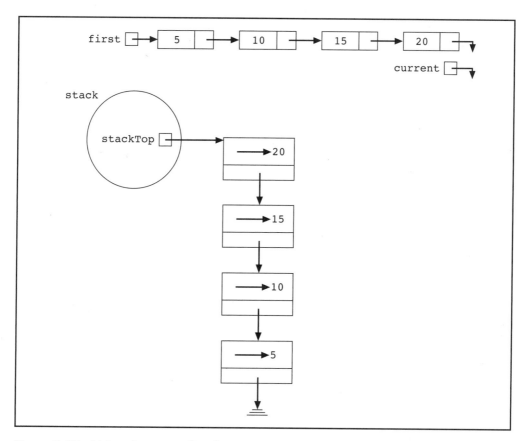

Figure 6-35 List and `stack` after the statements `stack.push(current);` and
`current = current.link;` execute

After the statement in Line 4 executes, the loop condition in Line 2 is evaluated again. Because **current** is **null**, the loop condition evaluates to **false**, and the **while** loop in Line 2 terminates. From Figure 6-35, it follows that a reference to each node in the linked list is saved in the stack. The top element of the stack contains a reference to the last node in the list, and so on. Let us now execute the following statements:

```
while(!stack.isEmptyStack())                    //Line 5
{
    current = stack.top();                      //Line 6
    stack.pop();                                //Line 7
    System.out.print(current.info + " ");       //Line 8
}
```

The loop condition in Line 5 evaluates to **true** because the stack is nonempty. Therefore, the statements in Lines 6, 7, and 8 execute. After the statement in Line 6 executes, **current** points to the last node, and after the statement in Line 7 executes, the top element of the stack is removed (see Figure 6-36).

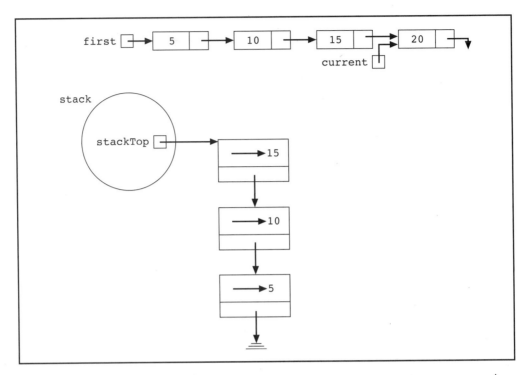

Figure 6-36 List and `stack` after the statements `current = stack.top();` and `stack.pop();` execute

The statement in Line 8 outputs `current.info`, which is `20`. Next, the loop condition in Line 5 is evaluated. Because the loop condition evaluates to `true`, the statements in Lines 6, 7, and 8 execute. After the statements in Lines 6 and 7 execute, Figure 6-37 results.

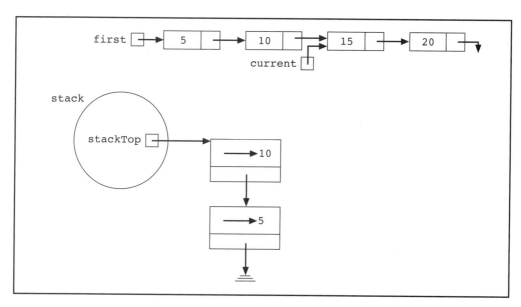

Figure 6-37   List and `stack` after the statements `current = stack.top();` and `stack.pop();` execute

The statement in Line 8 outputs `current.info`, which is **15**. Next, the loop condition in Line 5 is evaluated. Because the loop condition evaluates to **true**, the statements in Lines 6, 7, and 8 execute. After the statements in Lines 6 and 7 execute, Figure 6–38 results.

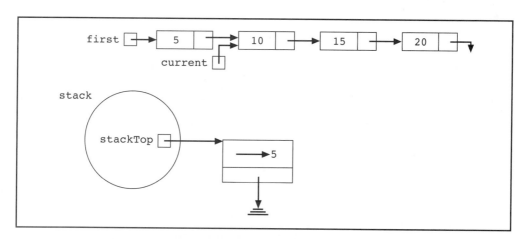

Figure 6-38   List and `stack` after the statements `current = stack.top();` and `stack.pop();` execute

The statement in Line 8 outputs `current.info`, which is `10`. Next, the loop condition in Line 5 is evaluated. Because the loop condition evaluates to `true`, the statements in Lines 6, 7, and 8 execute. After the statements in Lines 6 and 7 execute, Figure 6–39 results.

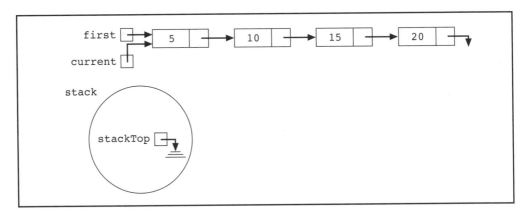

Figure 6-39 List and `stack` after the statements `current = stack.top();` and `stack.pop();` execute

The statement in Line 8 outputs `current.info`, which is `5`. Next, the loop condition in Line 5 is evaluated. Because the loop condition evaluates to `false`, the `while` loop terminates. The `while` loop in Line 5 produces the following output:
20 15 10 5

class Stack

The preceding sections discussed the data structure `stack` in detail. Because a stack is an important data structure, Java provides a class to implement a stack in a program. The name of the Java `class` defining a stack is `Stack`. Moreover, the `class Stack` is contained in the package `java.util`. Table 6-3 lists the members of the `class Stack`.

Table 6-3 Members of the `class Stack`

```
public Stack()
//Creates an empty Stack object.
```

```
public boolean empty()
//Returns true if the stack is empty,  false otherwise.
```

```
public Object peek() throws EmptyStackException
//Returns the top element of the stack. It does not remove the
//top element.
```

Table 6-3 Members of the `class Stack` (continued)

```
public Object pop() throws EmptyStackException
//Returns and removes the top element of the stack.
```

```
public Object push(Object obj)
//Pushes the item specified by obj onto the stack.
```

```
public int search(Object obj)
//Returns the relative position of the item specified by obj
//from top of the stack. If the item is not in the stack,
//it returns -1.
```

6

Notice that the formal parameter of the method **push** is a reference to an object. Therefore, to use a **Stack** object to manipulate values of primitive types they must be wrapped in an appropriate class. For example, to manipulate **int** values, use either the wrapper **class Integer**, provided by Java, or the **class IntElement**, designed in Chapter 3. Moreover, because elements in a **Stack** object are references of the type **Object**, you can push any type of element into a stack. That is, the elements that you store in a **Stack** object do not have to be of the same type.

The program in Example 6-4 illustrates how to use the **class Stack**. (In this example, we use the **class Integer** to wrap **int** values.)

Example 6-4

```java
//Program to illustrate how to use the class Stack.

import java.util.*;

public class Example_6_4
{
    public static void main(String[] args)
    {
        Stack myStack = new Stack();                     //Line 1

        myStack.push(new Integer(16));                   //Line 2
        myStack.push(new Integer(8));                    //Line 3
        myStack.push(new Integer(20));                   //Line 4
        myStack.push(new Integer(3));                    //Line 5

        System.out.println("Line 6: The top element of "
                    + "myStack: " + myStack.peek());      //Line 6

        myStack.pop();                                   //Line 7

        System.out.println("Line 8: After the pop operation, "
                    + "the top element of myStack: "
                    + myStack.peek());                    //Line 8
```

```
        System.out.print("Line 9: myStack elements: "); //Line 9

        while(!myStack.empty())                           //Line 10
        {
            System.out.print(myStack.peek() + " ");       //Line 11
            myStack.pop();                                //Line 12
        }

        System.out.println();                             //Line 13
    }
}
```

Output

```
Line 6: The top element of myStack: 3
Line 8: After the pop operation, the top element of myStack: 20
Line 9: myStack elements: 20 8 16
```

The preceding output is self-explanatory. The details are left as an exercise for you.

QUICK REVIEW

1. A stack is a data structure wherein the items are added and deleted from one end only.

2. A stack is a Last In First Out (LIFO) data structure.

3. The basic operations on a stack are: push an item onto the stack, pop an item from the stack, return the top element of the stack, initialize the stack, check whether the stack is empty, and check whether the stack is full.

4. A stack can be implemented either as an array or as a linked list.

5. The middle elements of a stack should not be accessed directly.

6. Stacks are restricted versions of arrays and linked lists.

7. The postfix notation does not require the use of parentheses to enforce operator precedence.

8. In postfix notation, the operators are written after the operands.

9. Postfix expressions are evaluated according to the following rules:

   a. Scan the expression from left to right.

   b. If an operator is found, back up to get the required number of operands, evaluate the operator, and continue.

EXERCISES

1. Consider the following statements:

```
StackClass stack = new StackClass();
IntElement x = new IntElement();
IntElement y = new IntElement();
```

Show what is output by the following segment of code.

```
x.setNum(4);
stack.push(new IntElement(7));
stack.push(x);
stack.push(new IntElement(x.getNum() + 5));
y = (IntElement) stack.top();
stack.pop();
stack.push(new IntElement(x.getNum() + y.getNum()));
stack.push(new IntElement(y.getNum() - 2));
stack.push(new IntElement(3));
x = (IntElement) stack.top();
stack.pop();
System.out.println("x = " + x);
System.out.println("y = " + y);

while(!stack.isEmptyStack())
{
    y = (IntElement) stack.top();
    System.out.println(y);
    stack.pop();
}
```

2. Consider the following statements.

```
StackClass stack = new StackClass();
IntElement x = new IntElement();
IntElement y = new IntElement();
```

Suppose that the input is:

```
14 45 34 23 10 5 -999
```

What is the output of the following segment of code? (Assume that the keyboard is a BufferedReader object initialized to the standard input device.)

```
StringTokenizer tokenizer =
                new StringTokenizer(keyboard.readLine());
stack.push(new IntElement(5));
x.setNum(Integer.parseInt(tokenizer.nextToken()));
while (x.getNum() != -999)
{
    if(x.getNum() % 2 == 0)
    {
        if(!stack.isFullStack())
            stack.push(x);
    }
```

```
        else
            System.out.println("x = " + x);
        x.setNum(Integer.parseInt(tokenizer.nextToken()));
    }

    System.out.print("Stack Elements: ");

    while(!stack.isEmptyStack())
    {
        y = (IntElement) stack.top();
        System.out.print(y + " ");
        stack.pop();
    }
    System.out.println()
```

3. Evaluate the following postfix expressions:

    a. 6 4 + 3 * 16 4 / - =

    b. 12 25 5 1 / / * 8 7 + - =

    c. 70 14 4 5 15 3 / * - - / 6 + =

    d. 3 5 6 * + 13 - 18 2 / + =

4. Convert the following infix expressions to postfix notations. (For an algorithm to convert an infix expression into an equivalent postfix expression, see Programming Exercise 11 of this chapter.)

    a. (A + B) * (C + D) — E

    b. A — (B + C) * D + E / F

    c. ((A + B) / (C — D) + E) * F — G

    d. A + B * (C + D) — E / F * G + H

5. Write the equivalent infix expressions for the following postfix expressions:

    a. a b * c +

    b. a b + c d - *

    c. a b — c — d *

6. What is the output of the following program?

```
public class Exercise6
{
    public static void main(String[] args)
    {
        StackClass s1 = new StackClass();
        StackClass s2 = new StackClass();

        String list[] = {"Winter", "Spring", "Summer", "Fall",
                        "Cold", "Warm", "Hot"};
```

```
        for(int i = 0; i < 7; i++)
            s1.push(new StringElement(list[i]));

        mystery(s1, s2);

        while(!s2.isEmptyStack())
        {
            System.out.print(s2.top() + " ");
            s2.pop();
        }
        System.out.println();
    }

    public static void mystery(StackClass s, StackClass t)
    {
        while(!s.isEmptyStack())
        {
            t.push(s.top());
            s.pop();
        }
    }
}
```

7. What is the output of the following program?

```
public class Exercise7
{
    public static void main(String[] args)
    {
        int list[] = {5, 10, 15, 20, 25};

        StackClass  s1 = new StackClass();
        StackClass  s2 = new StackClass();

        for(int i = 0; i < 5; i++)
        s1.push(new IntElement(list[i]));

        mystery(s1, s2);

        while(!s2.isEmptyStack())
        {
            System.out.print(s2.top() + " ");
            s2.pop();
        }
        System.out.println();
    }

    public static void mystery(StackClass s, StackClass t)
    {
        int num;
        IntElement temp;
```

```
            while(!s.isEmptyStack())
            {
                temp = (IntElement) s.top();
                num = temp.getNum();

                t.push(new IntElement(2 * num));

                s.pop();
            }
        }
    }
```

8. Write the definition of the method **second** that takes as a parameter a stack object and returns the second element of the stack. The original stack remains unchanged.

9. Write the definition of the method **clear** that takes as a parameter a stack object of the type **Stack** (the class provided by Java) and removes all the elements from the stack.

PROGRAMMING EXERCISES

1. Write the definitions of the methods **copy**, **copyStack**, and the copy constructor for the **class LinkedStackClass**. Also, write a program to test the definitions of these methods.

2. Two stacks are the same if they have the same size and their elements at the corresponding positions are the same. Add the method **equalStack** to the **class StackClass** that takes as a parameter a **StackClass** object, say, **otherStack**, and returns **true** if this stack is the same as **otherStack**. Furthermore, write the definition of the method **equalStack** and a program to test your method.

3. Repeat Programming Exercise 2 for the **class LinkedStackClass**.

4. a. Add the following operation to the **class StackClass**:

   ```
   void reverseStack(StackClass otherStack)
   ```

   This operation copies the elements of a stack in reverse order onto another stack.

   Consider the following statements:

   ```
   StackClass stack1;
   StackClass stack2;
   ```

   The statement:

   ```
   stack1.reverseStack(stack2);
   ```

   copies the elements of **stack1** onto **stack2** in reverse order. That is, the top element of **stack1** is the bottom element of **stack2**, and so on. The old contents of **stack2** are destroyed and **stack1** is unchanged.

   b. Write the definition of the method to implement the operation **reverseStack**. Also write a program to test the method **reverseStack**.

5. Repeat Exercises 4a. and 4b. for the `class LinkedStackClass`. Also, write a program to test your method.

6. Write a program that outputs an appropriate message for grouping symbols, such as parentheses and braces, if an arithmetic expression matches. For example, the expression `{25 + (3 − 6) * 8}` contains matching grouping symbols.

7. Write a program that uses a stack to print the prime factors of a positive integer in descending order.

8. Programming Exercise 15 in Chapter 5, Converting a Number from Binary to Decimal, uses recursion to convert a binary number into an equivalent decimal number. Write a program that uses a stack to convert a binary number into an equivalent decimal number.

9. Example 5-5 (in Chapter 5), Converting a Number from Decimal to Binary, contains a program that uses recursion to convert a decimal number into an equivalent binary number. Write a program that uses a stack to convert a decimal number into an equivalent binary number.

10. Redo the Postfix Expressions Calculator program so that the stack overflow and underflow exceptions are handled using the `try/catch` blocks.

11. **(Infix to Postfix)** Write a program that converts an infix expression into an equivalent postfix expression.

The rules to convert an infix expression into an equivalent postfix expression are as follows:

a. Scan the expression from left to right. One pass is sufficient.

b. If the next scanned symbol is an operand, append it to the postfix expression.

c. If the next scanned symbol is a left parenthesis, push it onto the stack.

d. If the next scanned symbol is a right parenthesis, pop and append all the symbols from the stack until the most recent left parenthesis. Pop and discard the left parenthesis.

e. If the next scanned symbol is an operator:

    i. Pop and append to the postfix expression every operator from the stack that is above the most recently scanned left parenthesis, and that has precedence greater than or equal to the new operator.

    ii. Push the new operator onto the stack.

f. After the infix string is completely processed, pop and append to the postfix string everything from the stack.

In this program, you are to consider the following (binary) arithmetic operators: `+`, `−`, `*`, and `/`. You may assume that the expressions you process are error free.

Design a class that stores the infix and postfix strings. The class must include the following operations:

`getInfix:` Stores the infix expression.

`showInfix:` Outputs the infix expression.

showPostfix: Outputs the postfix expression.

Some other operations that you might need are the following:

convertToPostfix: Converts the infix expression into a postfix expression.

precedence: Determines the precedence between two operators. If the first operator is of higher or equal precedence than the second operator, it returns the value **true**; otherwise, it returns the value **false**.

Include the constructors for automatic object initialization.

Test your program on the following expressions:

1. `A + B - C;`
2. `(A + B) * C;`
3. `(A + B) / (C - D);`
4. `A + ((B + C) * (E - F) - G) / (H - I);`
5. `A + B * (C + D) - E / F * G + H;`

For each expression, your answer should be in the following form:

```
Infix Expression: A + B - C;
Postfix Expression: AB+C-
```

12. Redo the program in the section, Application of Stacks: Postfix Expressions Calculator (the non-GUI version) of this chapter so that it uses the Java **class Stack** to evaluate the postfix expressions.

13. Redo Programming Exercise 11 so that it uses the Java **class Stack** to convert the infix expressions to postfix expressions.

14. Write the definition of the method **printListReverse** that uses a stack to print a linked list in reverse order. Include this method as a **public** member of the **class LinkedListClass** as designed in Chapter 4. Also, write a program to test the definition of the method **printListReverse**. (*Note:* In order to print the linked list backwards, we use a stack (as explained in this chapter) to save the reference, that is, the address of each node. We can, therefore, for example, use the **class LinkedStackClass** to implement this stack. A reference to a node is stored in a reference variable of the **LinkedListNode** type. Also, the **info** of a stack element, as given in this chapter, is a reference variable of the **DataElement** type. To use a **StackClass** object to save the reference of a node, we need to modify the definition of the **class LinkedListNode**, given in Chapter 4, as follows. Derive the **class LinkedListNode** from the **class DataElement** and provide the definitions of the **abstract** methods. For this exercise, you must at least provide the complete definition of the method **getCopy**. Alternatively, you can use the Java **class Stack** to implement a stack.)

QUEUES

In this chapter, you will:

- Learn about queues
- Examine various queue operations
- Learn how to implement a queue as an array
- Learn how to implement a queue as a linked list
- Discover priority queues
- Discover queue applications

This chapter discusses another important data structure: the **queue**. The notion of a queue in computer science is the same as the notion of the queues to which you are accustomed in everyday life. There are queues of customers in a bank or in a grocery store, and queues of cars waiting to pass through a tollbooth. Similarly, because a computer can send a print request faster than a printer can print, a queue of documents is often waiting to be printed at a printer. The general rule to process elements in a queue is that the customer at the front of the queue is served next and that when a new customer arrives, he or she stands at the end of the queue. That is, a queue is a First In First Out data structure.

Queues have numerous applications in computer science. Whenever a system is modeled on the First In First Out principle, queues are used. This chapter discusses one of the most widely used applications of queues, computer simulation. First, however, we need to develop the tools necessary to implement a queue. The next few sections discuss how to design classes to implement queues as an abstract data type (ADT).

QUEUES

A queue is a set of elements of the same type in which the elements are added at one end, called the **back** or **rear**, and deleted from the other end, called the **front** or **first**. For example, consider a line of customers in a bank, wherein customers are waiting to withdraw or deposit money or to conduct some other business. Each new customer gets in the line at the rear. Whenever a teller is ready for a new customer, the customer at the front of the line is served.

The rear of the queue is accessed whenever a new element is added to the queue; the front of the queue is accessed whenever an element is deleted from the queue. Like a stack, the middle elements of the queue are inaccessible, even if the queue is implemented as an array.

Queue: A data structure in which the elements are added at one end, called the **rear** or **back**, and deleted from the other end, called the **front** or **first**; a First In First Out (FIFO) data structure.

Queue Operations

From the definition of queues, we see that the two key operations are add and delete. We call the add operation **addQueue** and the delete operation **deleteQueue**. Because elements can be neither deleted from an empty queue nor added to a full queue, we need two more operations to successfully implement the **addQueue** and **deleteQueue** operations: **isEmptyQueue** (determines whether the queue is empty) and **isFullQueue** (determines whether the queue is full).

We also need an operation, **initializeQueue**, to initialize the queue to an empty state. Moreover, to retrieve the first and last elements of the queue, we include the operations **front** and **back** as described in the following list. Therefore, some of the queue operations are:

- **initializeQueue**: Initializes the queue to an empty state.
- **isEmptyQueue**: Determines whether the queue is empty. If the queue is empty, it returns the value **true**; otherwise, it returns the value **false**.
- **isFullQueue**: Determines whether the queue is full. If the queue is full, it returns the value **true**; otherwise, it returns the value **false**.
- **front**: Returns the front, that is, the first element of the queue. Input to this operation consists of the queue. Prior to this operation, the queue must exist.
- **back**: Returns the last element of the queue. Input to this operation consists of the queue. Prior to this operation, the queue must exist.
- **addQueue**: Adds a new element to the rear of the queue. Input to this operation consists of the queue and the new element. Prior to this operation, the queue must exist and must not be full.
- **deleteQueue**: Removes the front element from the queue. Input to this operation consists of the queue. Prior to this operation, the queue must exist and must not be empty.

As in the case of a stack, a queue can be implemented using an array or a linked list. We consider both implementations. Because the elements are added at one end and removed from the other end, we need two variables to keep track of the front and rear of the queue, called **queueFront** and **queueRear**.

QUEUE EXCEPTION CLASS

The preceding section describes the basic operations on a queue. As in the case of a stack, the two main operations on a queue are **addQueue** and **deleteQueue**. An element can be added to the queue only if the queue is not full. Similarly, an element can be removed from the queue only if the queue is nonempty. Adding an element to a full queue, and removing an element from an empty queue, generates errors or exceptions called queue overflow exception and queue underflow exception, respectively. As in the case of stacks, to handle these exceptions we design exception classes as follows.

```java
public class QueueException extends RuntimeException
{
    public QueueException()
    {
    }

    public QueueException(String msg)
    {
        super(msg);
    }
}

public class QueueOverflowException extends QueueException
{
    public QueueOverflowException()
    {
        super("Queue Overflow");
    }

    public QueueOverflowException(String msg)
    {
        super(msg);
    }
}

public class QueueUnderflowException extends QueueException
{
    public QueueUnderflowException()
    {
        super("Queue Underflow");
    }
```

7

```
public QueueUnderflowException(String msg)
{
    super(msg);
}
}
```

When we write the method to implement the `addQueue` operation, if the queue is full, then this method throws a `QueueOverflowException`. Similarly, the method that implements the `deleteQueue` operation throws a `QueueUnderflowException` if we try to remove an item from an empty queue. Also, the methods that implement the operations `front` and `back` throw a `QueueUnderflowException` if we try to retrieve an item from an empty queue. As in the case of stacks, notice that the `class QueueException` is derived from the `class RuntimeException`, and so the queue overflow and underflow exceptions as we have defined them are unchecked exceptions.

IMPLEMENTATION OF QUEUES AS ARRAYS

Before giving the definition of the class to implement a queue as an ADT, we need to decide how many data members are needed to implement the queue. Of course, we need an array to implement the queue, the variables `queueFront` and `queueRear` to keep track of the first and last elements of the queue, and the variable `maxQueueSize` to specify the maximum size of the queue. Thus, we need at least four data members.

Before writing the algorithms to implement the queue operations, we need to decide how to use `queueFront` and `queueRear` to access the queue elements. How do `queueFront` and `queueRear` indicate that the queue is empty or full? Suppose that `queueFront` gives the index of the first element of the queue, and `queueRear` gives the index of the last element of the queue. To add an element to the queue, we first advance `queueRear` to the next array position and then add the element at the position to which `queueRear` is pointing. To delete an element from the queue, we advance `queueFront` to the next element of the queue. (We add the operation `front` that returns the front element of the queue.) Thus, `queueRear` changes after each `addQueue` operation, and `queueFront` changes after each `deleteQueue` operation.

Let us see what happens when `queueFront` changes after a `deleteQueue` operation and `queueRear` changes after an `addQueue` operation. Assume that the array to hold the queue elements is of the size 100.

Initially, the queue is empty. Assume that `queueFront` and `queueRear` point directly to the first and last elements of the queue, respectively. After the operation:

```
addQueue('A');
```

the array is as shown in Figure 7-1.

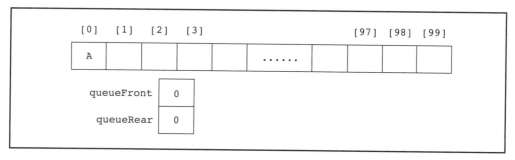

Figure 7-1   Queue after the first `addQueue` operation

After two more `addQueue` operations,

```
addQueue('B');
addQueue('C');
```

the array is as shown in Figure 7-2.

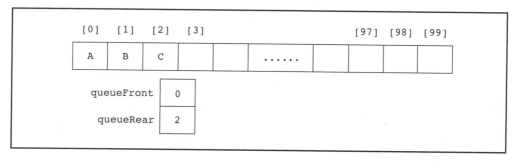

Figure 7-2   Queue after two more `addQueue` operations

Now consider the `deleteQueue` operation:

```
deleteQueue();
```

After this operation, the array containing the queue is as shown in Figure 7-3.

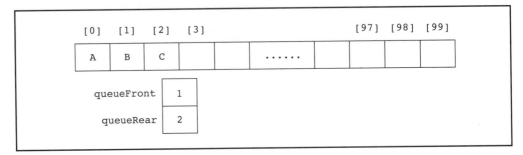

Figure 7-3   Queue after the `deleteQueue` operation

Will this queue design work? Suppose **A** stands for add (that is, `addQueue`) an element to the queue, and **D** stands for delete (that is, `deleteQueue`) an element from the queue. Consider the following sequence of operations:

AAADADADADADADADA...

This sequence of operations eventually sets the index `queueRear` to point to the last array position, giving the impression that the queue is full. However, the queue has only two or three elements and the front of the array is empty (see Figure 7-4).

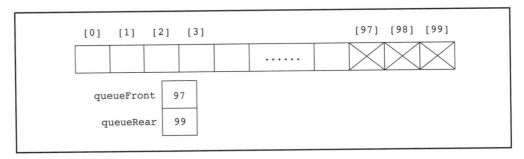

Figure 7-4   Queue after the sequence of operations AAADADADADADADADA...

One solution to this problem is that when the queue overflows to the rear (that is, `queueRear` points to the last array position), we can check the value of the index `queueFront`. If the value of `queueFront` indicates that there is room in the front of the array, then when `queueRear` gets to the last array position, we can slide all of the queue elements toward the first array position. This solution is good if the queue size is very small; otherwise, the program may execute slowly.

Another solution to this problem is to assume that the array is circular—that is, the first array position immediately follows the last array position (see Figure 7-5).

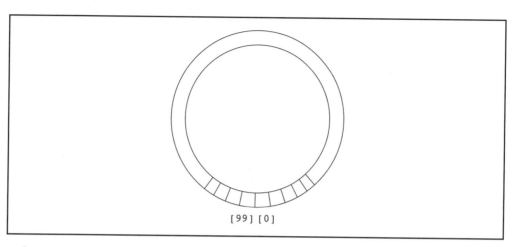

Figure 7-5   Circular queue

We consider the array containing the queue to be circular, although we draw the figures of the array holding the queue elements as before.

Suppose that we have the queue as shown in Figure 7-6.

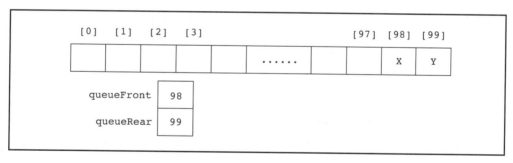

Figure 7-6   Queue with two elements at positions 98 and 99

After the operation

```
addQueue('Z');
```

the queue is as shown in Figure 7-7.

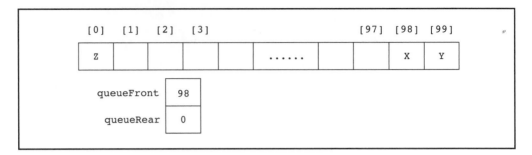

Figure 7-7   Queue after one more `addQueue` operation

Because the array containing the queue is circular, we can use the following statement to advance `queueRear` to the next array position:

```
queueRear = (queueRear + 1) % maxQueue;
```

If `queueRear < maxQueue - 1`, then `queueRear + 1 <= maxQueue - 1` and so `(queueRear + 1) % maxQueue = queueRear + 1`. If `queueRear == maxQueue - 1` (that is, `queueRear` points to the last array position), then `queueRear + 1 == maxQueue` and so `(queueRear + 1) % maxQueue == 0`. In this case, `queueRear` is set to 0, which is the first array position. We can use a statement similar to the previous statement to advance `queueFront` to the next array position.

This queue design seems to work well. Before we write the algorithms to implement the queue operations, consider the following two cases.

Case 1: Suppose that after certain operations, the array containing the queue is as shown in Figure 7-8.

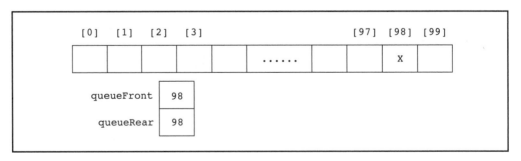

Figure 7-8   Queue with one element

After the operation

```
deleteQueue();
```

the resulting array is as shown in Figure 7-9.

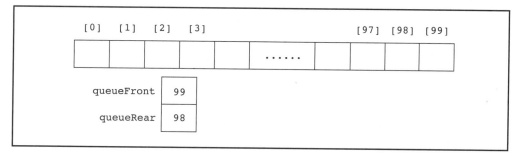

Figure 7-9   Queue after the `deleteQueue` operation

Case 2: Let us now consider the queue shown in Figure 7-10.

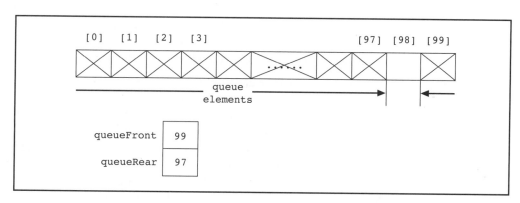

Figure 7-10   Queue with 99 elements

After the operation

```
addQueue('Z');
```

the resulting array is as shown in Figure 7-11.

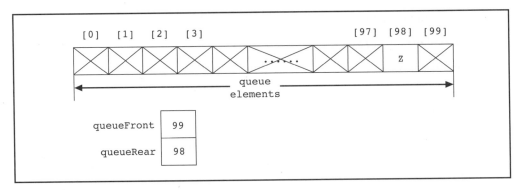

Figure 7-11   Queue after the addQueue operation; it is full

The arrays in Figures 7-9 and 7-11 have identical values for queueFront and queueRear. However, the resulting array in Figure 7-9 represents an empty queue, whereas the resulting array in Figure 7-11 represents a full queue. This latest queue design poses another problem: distinguishing between an empty and a full queue.

This problem has several possible solutions. One possible solution is to keep a count. In addition to queueFront and queueRear, we need another variable, count, to implement the queue. The value of count is incremented whenever a new element is added to the queue, and decremented whenever an element is removed from the queue. In this case, the method initializeQueue initializes count to 0. This solution is very useful if the user of the queue frequently needs to know the number of elements in the queue.

Another possible solution is to let queueFront indicate the index of the array position *preceding* the first element of the queue, rather than the index of the (actual) first element itself. In this case, assuming queueRear still indicates the index of the last element in the queue, the queue is empty if queueFront == queueRear. In this solution, the slot indicated by the index queueFront (that is, the slot preceding the first true element) is reserved. The queue is full if the next available space is this special reserved slot indicated by queueFront. Finally, because the array position indicated by queueFront is to be kept empty, if the array size is, say 100, then 99 elements can be stored in the queue (see Figure 7-12).

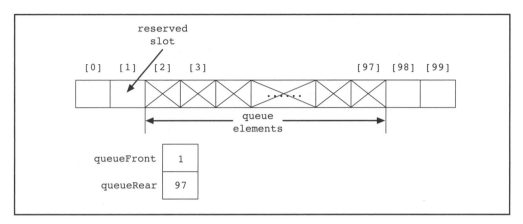

Figure 7-12   Array to store the queue elements with a reserved slot

7

Let us implement the queue using the first solution. That is, we use the variable `count` to indicate whether the queue is empty or full.

The following statements define a queue as an ADT (see also Figure 7-13). Because arrays can be allocated dynamically, we leave it for the user to specify the size of the array to implement the queue. The default size of the array is 100.

Class: `QueueClass`

Instance Variables:

```
private int maxQueueSize;
private int count;
private int queueFront;
private int queueRear;
private DataElement[] list;  //Array of references to the objects
                            //that store the queue elements.
```

Constructors and Instance Methods:

```
public void initializeQueue()
   //Method to initialize the queue to an empty state.
   //Postcondition: count = 0; queueFront = 0;
   //               queueRear = maxQueueSize - 1

public boolean isEmptyQueue()
   //Method to determine whether the queue is empty.
   //Postcondition: Returns true if the queue is empty,
   //               false otherwise.

public boolean isFullQueue()
   //Method to determine whether the queue is full.
   //Postcondition: Returns true if the queue is full,
   //               false otherwise.
```

```
public DataElement front() throws QueueUnderflowException
   //Method to return the first element of the queue.
   //Precondition: The queue exists and is not empty.
   //Postcondition: If the queue is empty, the method throws
   //               QueueUnderflowException; otherwise, a
   //               reference to a copy of the first element
   //               of the queue is returned.

public DataElement back() throws QueueUnderflowException
   //Method to return the last element of the queue.
   //Precondition: The queue exists and is not empty.
   //Postcondition: If the queue is empty, the method throws
   //               QueueUnderflowException; otherwise, a
   //               reference to a copy of the last element
   //               of the queue is returned.

public void addQueue(DataElement queueElement)
                       throws QueueOverflowException
   //Method to add queueElement to the queue.
   //Precondition: The queue exists and is not full.
   //Postcondition: The queue is changed and queueElement
   //               is added to the queue.

public void deleteQueue() throws QueueUnderflowException
   //Method to remove the first element of the queue.
   //Precondition: The queue exists and is not empty.
   //Postcondition: The queue is changed and the first
   //               element is removed from the queue.

public void copyQueue(QueueClass otherQueue)
   //Method to make a copy of otherQueue.
   //Postcondition: A copy of otherQueue is created and
   //               assigned to this queue.

public QueueClass()
   //default constructor
   //Postcondition: Creates an array of references to the
   //               objects that store queue elements.
   //               maxQueueSize = 100;
   //               count = 0; queueFront = 0;
   //               queueRear = maxQueueSize - 1;

public QueueClass (int queueSize)
   //constructor with a parameter
   //Postcondition: Creates an array of references to the
   //               objects that store queue elements.
   //               maxQueueSize = queueSize;
   //               count = 0; queueFront = 0;
   //               queueRear = maxQueueSize - 1;
   //               If queueSize <= 0, maxQueueSize = 100;
public QueueClass(QueueClass otherQueue)
   //copy constructor
```

```
                          QueueClass
 ┌────────────────────────────────────────────────────────────┐
 │ -maxQueueSize: int                                          │
 │ -count: int                                                 │
 │ -queueFront: int                                            │
 │ -queueRear: int                                             │
 │ -list: DataElement[]                                        │
 ├────────────────────────────────────────────────────────────┤
 │ +QueueClass()                                               │
 │ +QueueClass(int)                                            │
 │ +QueueClass(QueueClass)                                     │
 │ +initializeQueue(): void                                    │
 │ +isEmptyQueue(): boolean                                    │
 │ +isFullQueue(): boolean                                     │
 │ +front() throws QueueUnderflowException: DataElement        │
 │ +back() throws QueueUnderflowException: DataElement         │
 │ +addQueue(DataElement) throws QueueOverflowException: void  │
 │ +deleteQueue() throws QueueUnderflowException: void         │
 │ +copyQueue(QueueClass): void                                │
 └────────────────────────────────────────────────────────────┘
```

Figure 7-13   UML diagram of the `class QueueClass`

Next, we consider the implementation of the queue operations.

Initialize Queue

The first operation that we consider is `initializeQueue`. This operation initializes a queue to an empty state, and the first element is assigned to the first array position. Therefore, we initialize `queueFront` to 0, `queueRear` to `maxQueueSize – 1`, and `count` to 0. (See Figure 7-14.)

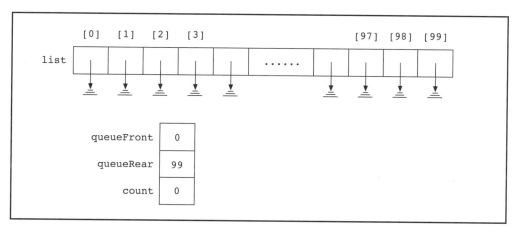

Figure 7-14   Empty queue

The definition of the method `initializeQueue` is:

```
public void initializeQueue()
{
    for(int i = queueFront; i < queueRear;
                            i = (i + 1) % maxQueueSize)
        list[i] = null;

    queueFront = 0;
    queueRear = maxQueueSize - 1;
    count = 0;
}
```

Empty Queue and Full Queue

As discussed earlier, the queue is empty if count is 0, and the queue is full if count is equal to maxQueueSize. So the methods to implement isEmptyQueue and isFullQueue are:

```
public boolean isEmptyQueue()
{
    return (count == 0);
}

public boolean isFullQueue()
{
    return (count == maxQueueSize);
}
```

front

This operation returns the first element of the queue. If the queue is nonempty, a reference of the copy of the first element of the queue is returned; otherwise, it throws a QueueUnderflowException.

```
public DataElement front() throws QueueUnderflowException
{
    if(isEmptyQueue())
        throw new QueueUnderflowException();

    DataElement temp = list[queueFront].getCopy();
    return temp;
}
```

back

This operation returns the last element of the queue. If the queue is nonempty, a reference of the copy of the last element of the queue is returned; otherwise, it throws a QueueUnderflowException.

```
public DataElement back() throws QueueUnderflowException
{
    if(isEmptyQueue())
        throw new QueueUnderflowException();

    DataElement temp = list[queueRear].getCopy();
    return temp;
}
```

Add Queue

Next, we implement the addQueue operation. Because queueRear points directly to the last element of the queue, to add a new element to the queue we first advance queueRear to the next array position and then add the new element to the array position to which queueRear is pointing. We also increment count by 1. If the queue is full, this method throws a QueueOverflowException. So the definition of the method addQueue is:

```
public void addQueue(DataElement queueElement)
                    throws QueueOverflowException
{
    if(isFullQueue())
        throw new QueueOverflowException();

    queueRear = (queueRear + 1) % maxQueueSize; //use the mod
                            //operator to advance queueRear
                            //because the array is circular
    count++;
    list[queueRear] = queueElement.getCopy();
}
```

Delete Queue

To implement the deleteQueue operation, we advance queueFront to the next queue element and decrement count by 1. If the queue is empty, this method throws a QueueUnderflowException. So the method deleteQueue is:

```
public void deleteQueue() throws QueueUnderflowException
{
    if(isEmptyQueue())
        throw new QueueUnderflowException();

    count--;
    list[queueFront] = null;
    queueFront = (queueFront + 1) % maxQueueSize; //use the mod
                            //operator to advance queueFront
                            //because the array is circular
}
```

Constructors

To complete the implementation of the queue operations, we next consider the implementation of the constructors. The default constructor creates an array of the size 100 and sets the variable maxQueueSize to the size of the array. The constructor with a parameter creates an array of the size specified by the user and sets the variable maxQueueSize to the size of the array. The constructors also initialize queueFront and queueRear to indicate that the queue is empty. The definitions of the constructors are:

```java
    //default constructor
public QueueClass()
{
    maxQueueSize = 100;

    queueFront = 0;                     //initialize queueFront
    queueRear = maxQueueSize - 1;    //initialize queueRear
    count = 0;
    list = new DataElement[maxQueueSize];    //create the array
                                //to implement the queue

}

    //constructor with a parameter
public QueueClass(int queueSize)
{
    if(queueSize <= 0)
    {
        System.err.println("The size of the array to implement "
                        + "the queue must be positive.");
        System.err.println("Creating an array of size 100.");

        maxQueueSize = 100;
    }
    else
        maxQueueSize = queueSize; //set maxQueueSize to queueSize

    queueFront = 0;                     //initialize queueFront
    queueRear = maxQueueSize - 1;    //initialize queueRear
    count = 0;
    list = new DataElement[maxQueueSize];    //create the array
                                //to implement the queue
}
```

The implementation of the copy constructor and the method copyQueue are left as exercises for you. (The definitions of these methods are similar to those discussed for linked lists and stacks.)

LINKED IMPLEMENTATION OF QUEUES

Because the size of the array to store the queue elements is fixed, only a finite number of queue elements can be stored in the array. Also, the array implementation of the queue requires the array to be treated in a special way together with the values of the indices `queueFront` and `queueRear`. The linked implementation of a queue simplifies many of the special cases of the array implementation and, because the memory to store a queue element is allocated dynamically, the queue is never full. This section discusses the linked implementation of a queue.

Because elements are added at one end, `queueRear`, and removed from the other end, `queueFront`, we need to know the front of the queue and the rear of the queue. Thus, we need two reference variables, **queueFront** and **queueRear**, to maintain the queue. The following statements define a linked queue as an ADT.

Class: `LinkedQueueClass`

```
public class LinkedQueueClass

        //Definition of the node
protected class QueueNode
{
    DataElement info;
    QueueNode link;
}
```

Instance Variables:

```
private QueueNode queueFront; //reference variable to the
                             //first element of the queue
private QueueNode queueRear;  //reference variable to the
                             //last element of the queue
```

Constructors and Instance Methods:

```
public void initializeQueue()
    //Method to initialize the queue to an empty state.
    //Postcondition: queueFront = null; queueRear = null

public boolean isEmptyQueue()
    //Method to determine whether the queue is empty.
    //Postcondition: Returns true if the queue is empty;
    //               otherwise, returns false.

public boolean isFullQueue()
    //Method to determine whether the queue is full.
    //Postcondition: Returns true if the queue is full;
    //               otherwise, returns false.
```

7

```
public DataElement front() throws QueueUnderflowException
    //Method to return the first element of the queue.
    //Precondition: The queue exists and is not empty.
    //Postcondition: If the queue is empty, the method throws
    //               QueueUnderflowException; otherwise, a
    //               reference to a copy of the first element
    //               of the queue is returned.

public DataElement back() throws QueueUnderflowException
    //Method to return the last element of the queue.
    //Precondition: The queue exists and is not empty.
    //Postcondition: If the queue is empty, the method throws
    //               QueueUnderflowException; otherwise, a
    //               reference to a copy of the last element
    //               of the queue is returned.

public void addQueue(DataElement queueElement)
    //Method to add queueElement to the queue.
    //Precondition: The queue exists.
    //Postcondition: The queue is changed and queueElement
    //               is added to the queue.

public void deleteQueue() throws QueueUnderflowException
    //Method to remove the first element of the queue.
    //Precondition: The queue exists and is not empty.
    //Postcondition: The queue is changed and the first
    //               element is removed from the queue.

public void copyQueue(Linked QueueClass otherQueue)
    //Method to make a copy of otherQueue.
    //Postcondition: A copy of otherQueue is created and
    //               assigned to this queue.

public LinkedQueueClass()
    //default constructor
public LinkedQueueClass(LinkedQueueClass otherQueue)
    //copy constructor
```

The UML diagram of the **class LinkedQueueClass** is left as an exercise for you.

Notice that the method **addQueue** does not throw **QueueOverflowException** because in the linked implementation of queues, logically, the queue is never full.

The definitions of the methods to implement the queue operations are given next.

The operation `initializeQueue` initializes the queue to an empty state. The queue is empty if there are no elements in the queue. This is easily accomplished by setting `queueFront` and `queueRear` to `null`. The definition of this method is:

```
public void initializeQueue()
{
    queueFront = null;
    queueRear = null;
}
```

The queue is empty if `queueFront` is `null`. Memory to store the queue elements is allocated dynamically. Therefore, the queue is never full and so the method to implement the `isFullQueue` operation returns the value `false`. (The queue is full only if we run out of memory.) The definitions of the methods to implement the operations `isEmptyQueue` and `isFullQueue` are:

```
public boolean isEmptyQueue()
{
    return (queueFront == null);
}

public boolean isFullQueue()
{
    return false;
}
```

7

addQueue, front, back, and deleteQueue Operations

The `addQueue` operation adds a new element at the end of the queue. To implement this operation, we use the instance variable `queueRear`.

If the queue is nonempty, the method `front` returns the first element of the queue, and so the element of the queue indicated by `queueFront` is returned. If the queue is empty, the method `front` throws a `QueueUnderflowException`.

If the queue is nonempty, the operation `back` returns the last element of the queue, and so the element of the queue indicated by `queueRear` is returned. If the queue is empty, the method `back` throws a `QueueUnderflowException`.

Similarly, if the queue is nonempty, the operation `deleteQueue` removes the first element of the queue, and so we use the instance variable `queueFront`. If the queue is empty, the method `deleteQueue` throws `QueueUnderflowException`.

The definitions of the methods to implement these operations are:

```
public void addQueue(DataElement queueElement)
{
    QueueNode newNode;

    newNode = new QueueNode();  //create the node
```

```
      newNode.info = queueElement.getCopy();   //store the info
      newNode.link = null;   //initialize the link field to null

      if(queueFront == null) //if initially the queue is empty
      {
         queueFront = newNode;
         queueRear = newNode;
      }
      else   //add newNode at the end
      {
         queueRear.link = newNode;
         queueRear = queueRear.link;
      }
}//end addQueue

public DataElement front() throws QueueUnderflowException
{
    if(isEmptyQueue())
       throw new QueueUnderflowException();

    DataElement temp = queueFront.info.getCopy();
    return temp;
}

public DataElement back() throws QueueUnderflowException
{
    if(isEmptyQueue())
       throw new QueueUnderflowException();

    DataElement temp = queueRear.info.getCopy();
    return temp;
}

public void deleteQueue() throws QueueUnderflowException
{
    if(isEmptyQueue())
       throw new QueueUnderflowException();

    queueFront = queueFront.link; //advance queueFront

    if(queueFront == null)  //if after deletion the queue is
       queueRear = null;    //empty, set queueRear to null
}//end deleteQueue
```

The definition of the method to implement the default constructor is similar to the definition of the method `initializeQueue`. Also, the methods to implement the copy constructor and `copyQueue` are similar to the corresponding methods for stacks. Implementing these operations is left as an exercise for you.

QUEUE DERIVED FROM THE class LinkedListClass

From the definitions of the methods to implement the queue operations, it is clear that the linked implementation of a queue is similar to the implementation of a linked list created in a forward manner (see Chapter 4). The addQueue operation is similar to the operation insertFirst. Likewise, the operations initializeQueue and initializeList, and isEmptyQueue and isEmptyList, are similar. The operations deleteQueue and isFullQueue can be implemented as in the previous section. The reference variable queueFront is the same as the reference variable first, and the reference variable queueRear is the same as the reference variable last. This correspondence suggests that we can derive the class to implement the queue from the class LinkedListClass (see Chapter 4).

Because the class LinkedListClass is an abstract class and we do not want to provide the definitions of the abstract methods of this class, we can derive the class LinkedQueueClass from the class UnorderedLinkedList, which was designed in Chapter 4.

Next, we define the class LinkedQueueClass that is derived from the class UnorderedLinkedList. The definitions of the methods to implement the queue operations are also given.

```
class LinkedQueueClass extends UnorderedLinkedList
{
        //default constructor
    public LinkedQueueClass()
    {
        super();
    }

        //copy constructor
    public LinkedQueueClass(LinkedQueueClass otherQueue)
    {
        super(otherQueue);
    }

    public void initializeQueue()
    {
        initializeList();
    }

    public boolean isEmptyQueue()
    {
        return isEmptyList();
    }
```

```java
    public boolean isFullQueue()
    {
        return false;
    }

    public void addQueue(DataElement newElement)
    {
        insertLast(newElement);
    }

    public DataElement front()
    {
        return super.front();
    }

    public DataElement back()
    {
        return super.back();
    }

    public void copyQueue(LinkedQueueClass otherQueue)
    {
        copyList(otherQueue);
    }

    public void deleteQueue() throws QueueUnderflowException
    {
        if(isEmptyQueue())
            throw new QueueUnderflowException();

        first = first.link; //advance first
        count--;

        if(first == null)   //if after deletion the queue is
            last = null;    //empty, set last to null
    }//end deleteQueue
}
```

The program in Example 7-1 tests various operations on a queue. It uses the linked version of the queue derived from the **class LinkedListClass**.

Example 7-1

```java
public class Example_7_1
{
    public static void main(String[] args)
    {
        LinkedQueueClass intQueue = new LinkedQueueClass();
```

```
        intQueue.addQueue(new IntElement(23));
        intQueue.addQueue(new IntElement(45));
        intQueue.addQueue(new IntElement(38));

        System.out.print("intQueue elements: ");

        while(!intQueue.isEmptyQueue())  //print intQueue
        {
            System.out.print(intQueue.front() + " ");
            intQueue.deleteQueue();
        }

        System.out.println();
    }
}
```

Sample Run

```
intQueue elements: 23 45 38
```

PRIORITY QUEUES

The preceding sections described how to implement a queue in a program. The use of a queue structure ensures that the items are processed in the order they are received. For example, in a banking environment, the customers who arrive first are served first. However, there are certain situations when this First In First Out rule needs to be relaxed somewhat. In a hospital environment, patients are, usually, seen in the order they arrive. Therefore, you could use a queue to ensure that the patients are seen in the order they arrive. However, a patient who arrives with severe or life-threatening symptoms is treated first. In other words, these patients take priority over the patients who can wait to be seen, such as those awaiting their routine annual checkup. For another example, in a shared environment, when print requests are sent to the printer, interactive programs take priority over batch-processing programs.

There are many other situations where some priority is assigned to the customers. To implement such a data structure in a program, we use special types of queues, called **priority queues**. In a priority queue, customers or jobs with higher priority are pushed to the front of the queue.

One way to implement a priority queue is to use an ordinary linked list, which keeps the items in order from the highest to lowest priority. However, an effective way to implement a priority queue is to use a treelike structure. In Chapter 9, we discuss a special type of sorting algorithm, called the **heap sort**, which uses a treelike structure to sort a list. After describing this algorithm, we then discuss how to implement a priority queue effectively.

APPLICATION OF QUEUES: SIMULATION

A technique in which one system models the behavior of another system is called **simulation**. For example, physical simulators include wind tunnels used to experiment with the design of car bodies and flight simulators used to train airline pilots. Simulation techniques are used when it is too expensive or dangerous to experiment with real systems. You can also design computer models to study the behavior of real systems. (We describe some real systems modeled by computers shortly.) Simulating the behavior of an expensive or dangerous experiment using a computer model is usually less expensive than using the real system, and a good way to gain insight without putting human life in danger. Moreover, computer simulations are particularly useful for complex systems where it is difficult to construct a mathematical model. For such systems, computer models can retain descriptive accuracy. In mathematical simulations, the steps of a program are used to model the behavior of a real system. Let us consider one such problem.

The manager of a local movie theater is hearing complaints from customers about the time they have to wait in line to buy tickets. The theater currently has only one cashier. Another theater is preparing to open in the neighborhood and the manager is afraid of losing customers. The manager wants to hire enough cashiers so that a customer does not have to wait too long to buy a ticket, but does not want to hire extra cashiers on a trial basis and potentially waste time and money. One thing that the manager would like to know is the average time a customer has to wait for service. The manager wants someone to write a program to simulate the behavior of the theater.

In computer simulation, the objects being studied are usually represented as data. For the theater problem, some of the objects are the customers and the cashier. The cashier serves the customers, and we want to determine a customer's average waiting time. Actions are implemented by writing algorithms, which in a programming language are implemented with the help of methods. Thus, methods are used to implement the actions of the objects.

In Java, we can combine the data, and the operations on that data, into a single unit with the help of classes. Thus, objects can be represented as classes. The data members of each class describe the properties of the object, and the method describes the actions on that data. The change in simulation results can occur if we change the values of the data or modify the definitions of the methods (that is, modify the algorithms implementing the actions). The main goal of a computer simulation is to either generate results showing the performance of an existing system or predict the performance of a proposed system.

In the theater problem, when the cashier is serving a customer, the other customers must wait. Because customers are served on a first come, first served basis and queues are an effective way to implement a First In First Out system, queues are important data structures for use in computer simulations. This section examines computer simulations in which queues are the basic data structure. These simulations model the behavior of systems, called **queuing systems**, in which queues of objects are waiting to be served by various servers. In other words, a queuing system consists of servers and queues of objects waiting to be served.

We deal with a variety of queuing systems on a daily basis. For example, a grocery store and a bank are both queuing systems. Furthermore, when you send a print request to a networked printer that is shared by many people, your print request goes in a queue. Print requests that arrive before your print request are usually completed before yours. Thus, the printer acts as the server when a queue of documents is waiting to be printed.

Designing a Queuing System

In this section, we describe a queuing system that can be used in a variety of applications, such as a grocery store, bank, movie theater, printer, or a mainframe environment in which several people are trying to use the same processors to execute their programs. To describe a queuing system, we use the term **server** for the object that provides the service. For example, in a bank, a teller is a server; in a grocery store or movie theater, a cashier is a server. We call the object receiving the service the **customer**, and the service time—the time it takes to serve a customer—the **transaction time**.

Because a queuing system consists of servers and a queue of waiting objects, we model a system that consists of a list of servers and a waiting queue holding the customers to be served. The customer at the front of the queue waits for the next available server. When a server becomes free, the customer at the front of the queue moves to the free server to be served.

When the first customer arrives, all servers are free and the customer moves to the first server. When the next customer arrives, if a server is available, the customer immediately moves to the available server; otherwise, the customer waits in the queue. To model a queuing system, we need to know the number of servers, the expected arrival time of a customer, the time between the arrivals of customers, and the number of events affecting the system.

Let us again consider the movie theater system. Suppose that the number of servers is 1, on average it takes 5 minutes to serve a customer, and on average a new customer arrives every 4 minutes. The performance of the system depends on how many servers are available, how long it takes to serve a customer, and how often a customer arrives. If it takes too long to serve a customer and customers arrive frequently, then more servers are needed. This system can be modeled as a time-driven simulation. In a **time-driven simulation**, the clock is implemented as a counter and the passage of, say, 1 minute can be implemented by incrementing the counter by 1. The simulation is run for a fixed amount of time. If the simulation needs to be run for 100 minutes, the counter starts at 1 and goes up to 100, which can be implemented by using a loop.

For the simulation described here, we want to determine the average wait time for a customer. To calculate the average wait time for a customer, we need to add the waiting time of each customer, and then divide the sum by the number of customers who have arrived. When a customer arrives, he or she goes to the end of the queue and the customer's waiting time starts. If the queue is empty and a server is free, the customer is served immediately and so this customer's waiting time is 0. On the other hand, if the customer arrives and either the queue is nonempty or all the servers are busy, the customer must wait for the next available server and, therefore, this customer's waiting time starts. We can keep track of the customer's waiting time by using a timer for each customer. When a customer arrives, the timer is set to 0, which is incremented after each clock unit.

Suppose that, on average, it takes 5 minutes for a server to serve a customer. When a server becomes free and the waiting customers' queue is nonempty, the customer at the front of the queue proceeds to begin the transaction. Thus, we must keep track of the time a customer is with a server. When the customer arrives at a server, the transaction time is set to 5 and is decremented after each clock unit. When the transaction time becomes 0, the server is marked as free. Hence, the two objects needed to implement a time-driven computer simulation of a queuing system are the customer and the server.

Next, before designing the main algorithm to implement this simulation, we design the classes to implement each of the two objects: customer and server.

Customer

Every customer has a customer number, arrival time, waiting time, transaction time, and departure time. If we know the arrival, waiting, and transaction times, we can determine the departure time by adding the arrival time, waiting time, and transaction time. Let us call the class to implement the customer object `Customer`. It follows that the `class Customer` has four data members: `customerNumber`, `arrivalTime`, `waitingTime`, and `transactionTime`, each of the data type `int`. The basic operations that must be performed on an object of the type `Customer` are as follows: set the customer's number, arrival time, and waiting time; increment the waiting time by one clock unit; return the waiting time; return the arrival time; return the transaction time; and return the customer number.

When a customer arrives, the customer is added to the queue. In this chapter, we designed the `class QueueClass` to implement a queue in a program. A queue element is a reference to an object of the `class DataElement`. Therefore, to create a queue of customers, we derive the `class Customer` from the `class DataElement`.

The following statements define `Customer` as an ADT (see also Figure 7-15):

Class: `Customer`

```
public class Customer extends DataElement
```

Instance Variables:

```
private int customerNumber;
private int arrivalTime;
private int waitingTime;
private int transactionTime;
```

Constructors and Instance Methods:

```
public void setCustomerInfo(int customerN, int arrvTime,
                            int wTime, int tTime)
   //Method to set the data members according to the
   //parameters.
   //Postcondition: customerNumber = customerN;
   //               arrivalTime = arrvTime;
   //               waitingTime = wTime;
   //               transactionTime = tTime
public int getWaitingTime()
   //Method to return the waiting time of a customer.
   //Postcondition: The value of waitingTime is returned.
public void setWaitingTime(int time)
   //Method to set the waiting time of a customer.
   //Postcondition: waitingTime = time
public void incrementWaitingTime()
   //Method to increment the waiting time.
   //Postcondition: waitingTime++
public int getArrivalTime()
   //Method to return the arrival time of a customer.
   //Postcondition: The value of arrivalTime is returned.
public int getTransactionTime()
   //Method to return the transaction time of a customer.
   //Postcondition: The value of transactionTime is returned.
public int getCustomerNumber()
   //Method to return the customer number.
   //Postcondition: The value of customerNumber is returned.
public Customer()
   //default constructor
   //Instance variables are initialized to the default values.
   //Postcondition: customerNumber = 0; arrivalTime = 0;
   //               waitingTime = 0; transactionTime = 0
public Customer(int customerN, int arrvTime, int wTime, int tTime)
   //constructor to initialize the data members according to
   //the parameters
   //Postcondition: customerNumber = customerN;
   //               arrivalTime = arrvTime; waitingTime = wTime;
   //               transactionTime = tTime


   // Methods of the class DataElement
public boolean equals(DataElement otherElement)
public int compareTo(DataElement otherElement)
public void makeCopy(DataElement otherElement)
public DataElement getCopy()
```

7

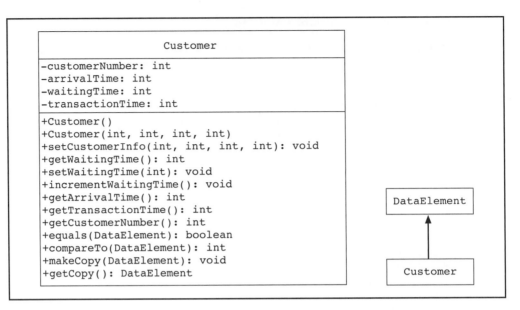

Figure 7-15   UML diagram of the **class Customer** and the inheritance hierarchy

Next, we give the definitions of the methods of the **class Customer**.

The method **setCustomerInfo** uses the values of the parameters to initialize **customerNumber**, **arrivalTime**, **waitingTime**, and **transactionTime**. Its definition is:

```
public void setCustomerInfo(int customerN, int arrvTime,
                            int wTime, int tTime)
{
    customerNumber = customerN;
    arrivalTime = arrvTime;
    waitingTime = wTime;
    transactionTime = tTime;
}
```

The definitions of the constructors are similar to the definition of the method **setCustomerInfo**. The default constructor initializes the instance variables to 0. The constructor with parameters uses the values of the parameters to initialize **customerNumber**, **arrivalTime**, **waitingTime**, and **transactionTime**. To make debugging easier, we use the method **setCustomerInfo** to write the definitions of the constructors, which are given next:

```
public Customer()
{
    setCustomerInfo(0, 0, 0, 0);
}
```

```
public Customer(int customerN, int arrvTime, int wTime, int tTime)
{
    setCustomerInfo(customerN, arrvTime, wTime, tTime);
}
```

The method getWaitingTime returns the current waiting time. Because the waiting time is stored in waitingTime, the method getWaitingTime returns the value of waitingTime. The definition of the method getWaitingTime is:

```
public int getWaitingTime()
{
    return waitingTime;
}
```

The method incrementWaitingTime increments the value of waitingTime. Its definition is:

```
public void incrementWaitingTime()
{
    waitingTime++;
}
```

The definitions of the methods setWaitingTime, getArrivalTime, getTransactionTime, getCustomerNumber, equals, compareTo, makeCopy, and getCopy are left as exercises for you.

Server

At any given time unit, the server is either busy serving a customer or is free. We use the String variable status to set the status of the server. Every server has a timer, and, because the program might need to know which server serves which customer, the server also stores the information of the customer being served. Thus, three data members are associated with a server: status of the type String, transactionTime of the type int, and currentCustomer of the type Customer. Some of the basic operations that must be performed on a server are as follows: check whether the server is free; set the server as free; set the server as busy; set the transaction time (that is, how long it takes to serve the customer); return the remaining transaction time (to determine whether the server should be set to free); if the server is busy after each time unit, decrement the transaction time by one time unit; and so on. The following statements define Server as an ADT (see also Figure 7-16):

Class: Server

Instance Variables:

```
private Customer currentCustomer;
private String status;
private int transactionTime;
```

Constructors and Instance Methods:

```
public boolean isFree()
   //Method to determine whether a server is free.
   //Postcondition: Returns true if the server is free,
   //               false otherwise.
public void setBusy()
   //Method to set the status of a server to "busy".
   //Postcondition: status = "busy"
public void setFree()
   //Method to set the status of a server to "free".
   //Postcondition: status = "free"
public void setTransactionTime(int t)
   //Method to set the transaction time according
   //to the parameter t.
   //Postcondition: transactionTime = t
public void setTransactionTime()
   //Method to set the transaction time according
   //to the transaction time of the current customer.
   //Postcondition: transactionTime = currentCustomer.transactionTime
public int getRemainingTransactionTime()
   //Method to return the remaining transaction time.
   //Postcondition: The value of the data member
   //               transactionTime is returned.
public void decreaseTransactionTime()
   //Method to decrease the transaction time by 1.
   //Postcondition: transactionTime--
public void setCurrentCustomer(Customer cCustomer)
   //Method to set the info of the current customer
   //according to the parameter cCustomer.
   //Postcondition: currentCustomer = cCustomer
public int getCurrentCustomerNumber()
   //Method to return the customer number of the
   //current customer.
   //Postcondition: The value of the data member
   //               customerNumber of the current customer
   //               is returned.
public int getCurrentCustomerArrivalTime()
   //Method to return the arrival time of the current customer.
   //Postcondition: The value of the data member arrivalTime
   //               of the current customer is returned.
public int getCurrentCustomerWaitingTime()
   //Method to return the current waiting time of the
   //current customer.
   //Postcondition: The value of the data member waitingTime
   //               of the current customer is returned.
```

```
public int getCurrentCustomerTransactionTime()
    //Method to return the transaction time of the
    //current customer.
    //Postcondition: The value of the data member transactionTime
    //               of the current customer is returned.
    //

public Server()
    //default constructor
    //Sets the values of the data members to their default
    //values.
    //Postcondition: currentCustomer is initialized by its
    //               default constructor; status = "free";
    //               the transaction time is initialized to 0.
```

```
                         Server

-currentCustomer: Customer
-status: String
-transactionTime: int

+Server()
+isFree(): boolean
+setBusy(): void
+setFree(): void
+setTransactionTime(): void
+setTransactionTime(int): void
+getRemainingTransactionTime(): int
+decreaseTransactionTime(): void
+setCurrentCustomer(Customer): void
+getCurrentCustomerNumber(): int
+getCurrentCustomerArrivalTime(): int
+getCurrentCustomerWaitingTime(): int
+getCurrentCustomerTransactionTime(): int
```

Figure 7-16   UML diagram of the `class Server`

The definitions of the member methods of the **class Server** are as follows:

```
public Server()
{
    status = "free";
    transactionTime = 0;
    currentCustomer = new Customer();
}
```

```
public boolean isFree()
{
    return (status.equals("free"));
}

public void setBusy()
{
    status = "busy";
}

public void setFree()
{
    status = "free";
}

public void setTransactionTime(int t)
{
    transactionTime = t;
}

public void setTransactionTime()
{
    int time;

    time = currentCustomer.getTransactionTime();

    transactionTime = time;
}

public void decreaseTransactionTime()
{
    transactionTime--;
}
```

We leave the definitions of the methods getRemainingTransactionTime, setCurrentCustomer, getCurrentCustomerNumber, getCurrentCustomerArrivalTime, getCurrentCustomerWaitingTime, and getCurrentCustomerTransactionTime as exercises for you.

Because we are designing a simulation program that can be used in a variety of applications, we need to design two more classes: a class to create and process a list of servers, and a class to create and process a queue of waiting customers. The next two sections describe each of these classes.

Server List

A server list is a set of servers, like a row of bank tellers. At any given time, a server is either free or busy. For the customer at the front of the queue, we need to find a server in the list that is free. If all the servers are busy, then the customer must wait until one of the servers becomes free. Thus, the class that implements a list of servers has two data members: one to store the number of servers, and one to maintain a list of servers. Depending on the number of servers specified by the user, a list of servers is created. Some of the operations that must be performed on a server list are as follows: return the server number of a free server; when a customer gets ready to conduct business and a server is available, set the server to "busy"; when the simulation ends, some of the servers might still be busy, so return the number of busy servers; after each time unit, reduce transactionTime of each busy server by one time unit; and if transactionTime of a server becomes 0, set the server to "free". The following statements define ServerList as an ADT (see also Figure 7-17):

Class: ServerList

Instance Variables:

```
private int numOfServers;
private Server[] servers;
```

Constructors and Instance Methods:

```
public int getFreeServerID()
   //Method to search the list of servers.
   //Postcondition: If a free server is found, return its ID;
   //     otherwise, return -1.
public int getNumberOfBusyServers()
   //Method to return the number of busy servers.
   //Postcondition: The number of busy servers is returned.
public void setServerBusy(int serverID, Customer cCustomer,
                          int tTime)
   //Method to set a server to "busy".
   //Postcondition: To serve the customer specified by
   //     cCustomer, the server specified by serverID is set
   //     to "busy", and the transaction time is set according
   //     to the parameter tTime.
public void setServerBusy(int serverID, Customer cCustomer)
   //Method to set a server to "busy".
   //Postcondition: To serve the customer specified by
   //     cCustomer, the server specified by serverID is set
   //     to "busy", and the transaction time is set according
   //     to the customer's transaction time.
```

```
public void updateServers()
   //Method to update the transaction time of each busy server.
   //Postcondition: The transaction time of each busy server
   //     is decremented by one time unit. If the transaction
   //     time of a busy server is reduced to zero, the
   //     server is set to "free" and a message indicating which
   //     customer was served, together with the customer's
   //     departing time, is printed on the screen.
public void updateServers(PrintWriter outF)
   //Method to update the transaction time of each busy server.
   //Postcondition: The transaction time of each busy server
   //     is decremented by one time unit. If the transaction
   //     time of a busy server is reduced to zero, the
   //     server is set to "free" and a message indicating which
   //     customer was served, together with the customer's
   //     departing time, is sent to the file specified by outF.

public ServerList()
   //default constructor to initialize a list of servers
   //Postcondition: numOfServers = 1
   //               A server is created.

public ServerList(int num)
   //constructor to initialize a list of servers
   //Postcondition: numOfServers = num
   //   A list of servers, specified by num, is created.
```

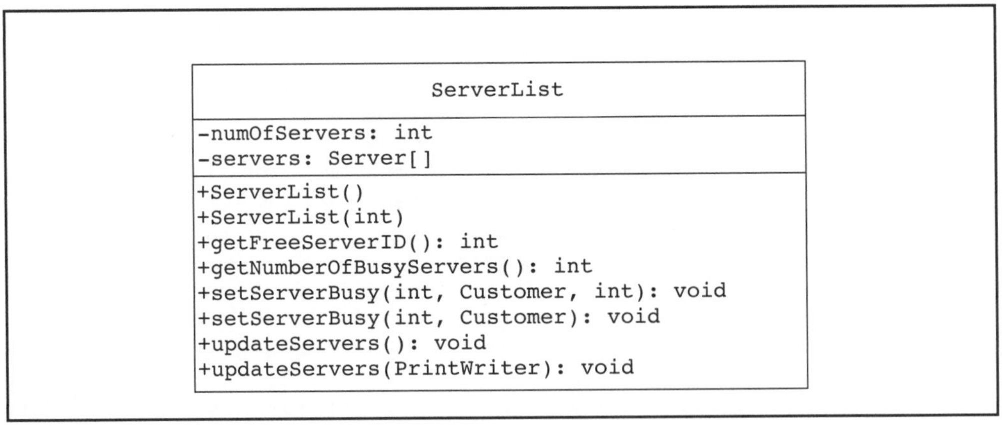

```
                    ServerList
  ─────────────────────────────────────────────
  -numOfServers: int
  -servers: Server[]
  ─────────────────────────────────────────────
  +ServerList()
  +ServerList(int)
  +getFreeServerID(): int
  +getNumberOfBusyServers(): int
  +setServerBusy(int, Customer, int): void
  +setServerBusy(int, Customer): void
  +updateServers(): void
  +updateServers(PrintWriter): void
```

Figure 7-17   UML diagram of the class ServerList

Following are the definitions of the methods of the **class ServerList**. The definitions of the constructors are as follows:

```java
public ServerList()
{
    numOfServers = 1;
    servers = new Server[1];
    servers[0] = new Server();
}

public ServerList(int num)
{
    numOfServers = num;
    servers = new Server[num];

    for(int i = 0; i < num; i++)
        servers[i] = new Server();
}
```

7

The method **getFreeServerID** searches the list of servers. If a free server is found, it returns the server's ID; otherwise, the value **-1** is returned, which indicates that all of the servers are busy. The definition of this method is:

```java
public int getFreeServerID()
{
    int serverID = -1;

    int i;

    for(i = 0; i < numOfServers; i++)
        if(servers[i].isFree())
        {
            serverID = i;
            break;
        }

    return serverID;
}
```

The method **getNumberOfBusyServers** searches the list of servers and determines the number of busy servers. The number of busy servers is returned. The definition of this method is:

```java
public int getNumberOfBusyServers()
{
    int busyServers = 0;

    int i;

    for(i = 0; i < numOfServers; i++)
        if(!servers[i].isFree())
            busyServers++;

    return busyServers;
}
```

The method `setServerBusy` sets a server to "busy"; this method is overloaded. The `serverID` of the server that is set to "busy" is passed as a parameter to this method. One method sets the server's transaction time according to the parameter `tTime`; the other method sets it by using the transaction time stored in the object `cCustomer`. The transaction time is later needed to determine the average wait time. The definitions of these methods are as follows:

```
public void setServerBusy(int serverID, Customer cCustomer,
                          int tTime)
{
    servers[serverID].setBusy();
    servers[serverID].setTransactionTime(tTime);
    servers[serverID].setCurrentCustomer(cCustomer);
}

public void setServerBusy(int serverID, Customer cCustomer)
{
    int time;

    time = cCustomer.getTransactionTime();

    servers[serverID].setBusy();
    servers[serverID].setTransactionTime(time);
    servers[serverID].setCurrentCustomer(cCustomer);
}
```

Next, we consider the definition of the method `updateServers`. Starting at the first server, it searches the list of servers for busy servers. When a busy server is found, its `transactionTime` is decremented by 1. If `transactionTime` reduces to 0, the server is set to "free". If `transactionTime` of a busy server reduces to 0, then the transaction of the customer being served by this server is completed. A message indicating the customer's server number, customer number, and departure time is then printed. The method `updateServers` is overloaded. One method sends the output to the screen; the other sends the output to a file. The definitions of these methods are as follows:

```
public void updateServers()
{
    int i;

    for(i = 0; i < numOfServers; i++)
        if(!servers[i].isFree())
        {
            servers[i].decreaseTransactionTime();
```

```
        if(servers[i].getRemainingTransactionTime() == 0)
        {
            System.out.println("Server No: " + (i+1) +
                        " Customer number "
                + servers[i].getCurrentCustomerNumber()
                + " departed at \n"
                + "              clock unit "
                + (servers[i].getCurrentCustomerArrivalTime()
                + servers[i].getCurrentCustomerWaitingTime()
                + servers[i].getCurrentCustomerTransactionTime()));
            servers[i].setFree();
        }
    }
}

public void updateServers(PrintWriter outF)
{
    int i;

    for(i = 0; i < numOfServers; i++)
        if(!servers[i].isFree())
        {
            servers[i].decreaseTransactionTime();

            if(servers[i].getRemainingTransactionTime() == 0)
            {
                outF.println("Server No: " + (i+1) +
                        " Customer number "
                    + servers[i].getCurrentCustomerNumber()
                    + " departed at \n"
                    + "              clock unit "
                    + (servers[i].getCurrentCustomerArrivalTime()
                    + servers[i].getCurrentCustomerWaitingTime()
                    + servers[i].getCurrentCustomerTransactionTime()));
                servers[i].setFree();
            }
        }
}
```

Waiting Customers' Queue

When a customer arrives, he or she goes to the end of the queue. When a server becomes available, the customer at the front of the queue leaves to conduct the transaction. After each time unit, the waiting time of each customer in the queue is incremented by 1. The ADT QueueClass designed in this chapter has all the operations needed to implement a queue, except the operation of incrementing the waiting time of each customer in the queue by one time unit. Thus, we derive the **class WaitingCustomerQueue** from the **class**

QueueClass and add the additional operations to implement the customers' queue. The definition of the class WaitingCustomerQueue is:

```
class WaitingCustomerQueue extends QueueClass
{
        //default constructor
    public WaitingCustomerQueue()
    {
        super();
    }

        //constructor with a parameter
    public WaitingCustomerQueue(int size)
    {
        super(size);
    }

        //copy constructor
    public WaitingCustomerQueue(WaitingCustomerQueue otherQ)
    {
        super(otherQ);
    }

        //Method to increment the waiting time of each
        //customer in the queue by one time unit.
        //Postcondition: The waiting time of each customer in
        //    the queue is incremented by one time unit.
    public void updateWaitingQueue()
    {
        //Definition as given below.
    }
}
```

Notice that the class WaitingCustomerQueue is derived from the class QueueClass, which implements the queue in an array. You can also derive the class WaitingCustomerQueue from the class LinkedQueueClass, which implements the queue in a linked list. We leave the details as an exercise for you.

The method updateWaitingQueue increments the waiting time of each customer in the queue by one time unit. The class WaitingCustomerQueue is derived from the class QueueClass. Because the data members of QueueClass are private, the method updateWaitingQueue cannot directly access the elements of the queue. The only way to access the elements of the queue is to use the front and deleteQueue operation. After incrementing the waiting time, the element can be put back into the queue by using the addQueue operation.

The addQueue operation inserts the element at the end of the queue. If we perform the front and deleteQueue operations followed by the addQueue operation for each element of the queue, then eventually the front element again becomes the front element. Given that each `front` and `deleteQueue` operation is followed by an `addQueue` operation, how do we determine that all the elements of the queue have been processed? We cannot use the `isEmptyQueue` or `isFullQueue` operations on the queue, because the queue is never empty or full.

One solution to this problem is to create a temporary queue. Every element of the original queue is removed, processed, and inserted into the temporary queue. When the original queue becomes empty, all of the elements in the queue are processed. We can then copy the elements from the temporary queue back into the original queue. However, this solution requires us to use extra memory space, which could be significant. Also, if the queue is large, extra computer time is needed to copy the elements from the temporary queue back into the original queue. Let us look into another solution.

Before starting to update the elements of the queue, we can insert a dummy customer with a waiting time of, say, –1. During the update process, when we arrive at the customer with the waiting time of –1, we can stop the update process without processing this customer. If we do not process the customer with the waiting time of –1, this customer is removed from the queue and, after processing all the elements of the queue, the queue contains no extra elements. This solution does not require us to create a temporary queue, so we do not need extra computer time to copy the elements back into the original queue. We will use this solution to update the queue. Therefore, the definition of the method `updateWaitingQueue` is:

```
public void updateWaitingQueue()
{
    Customer cust = new Customer();

    cust.setWaitingTime(-1);
    int wTime = 0;

    addQueue(cust);

    while(wTime != -1)
    {
        cust = (Customer) front();
        deleteQueue();
        wTime = cust.getWaitingTime();

        if(wTime == -1)
            break;

        cust.incrementWaitingTime();
        addQueue(cust);
    }
}
```

7

Main Program

To run the simulation, we first need to obtain the following information:

- The number of time units the simulation should run. Assume that each time unit is one minute.

- The number of servers.

- The amount of time it takes to serve a customer—that is, the transaction time.

- The approximate time between customer arrivals.

These pieces of information are called simulation parameters. By changing the values of these parameters, we can observe the changes in the performance of the system. The program that we write uses the following instance variables to store this information:

```
private static int simulationTime;
private static int numberOfServers;
private static int transactionTime;
private static int timeBetweenCustomerArrival;
```

We can write a method, `setSimulationParameters`, to prompt the user to specify these values. The definition of this method is:

```
public static void setSimulationParameters() throws IOException
{
    System.out.print("Enter the simulation time: ");
    System.out.flush();
    simulationTime = Integer.parseInt(keyboard.readLine());
    System.out.println();

    System.out.print("Enter the number of servers: ");
    System.out.flush();
    numberOfServers = Integer.parseInt(keyboard.readLine());
    System.out.println();

    System.out.print("Enter the transaction time: ");
    System.out.flush();
    transactionTime = Integer.parseInt(keyboard.readLine());
    System.out.println();

    System.out.print("Enter the time between customer arrivals: ");
    System.out.flush();
    timeBetweenCustomerArrival
                = Integer.parseInt(keyboard.readLine());
    System.out.println();
}
```

When a server becomes free and the customer queue is nonempty, we can move the customer at the front of the queue to the free server to be served. Moreover, when a customer starts the transaction, the waiting time ends. The waiting time of the customer is added to the total waiting time. The general algorithm to start the transaction (supposing that `serverID` denotes the ID of the free server) is:

1. Retrieve and remove the customer from the front of the queue.

   ```
   customer = customerQueue.front();
   customerQueue.deleteQueue();
   ```

2. Update the total waiting time by adding the current customer's waiting time to the previous total waiting time.

   ```
   totalWait = totalWait + customer.getWaitingTime();
   ```

3. Set the free server to begin the transaction.

   ```
   serverList.setServerBusy(serverID, customer, transTime);
   ```

To run the simulation, we need to know the number of customers arriving at a given time unit and how long it takes to serve each customer. We use the Poisson distribution from statistics, which says that the probability of y events occurring at a given time is given by the formula:

$$P(y) = \frac{\lambda^y e^{-\lambda}}{y!}, \quad y = 0, \ 1, \ 2, \ldots,$$

where λ is the expected value that y events occur at that time. Suppose that, on average, a customer arrives every 4 minutes. During this 4-minute period, the customer can arrive at any one of the 4 minutes. Assuming an equal likelihood of each of the 4 minutes, the expected value that a customer arrives in each of the 4 minutes is, therefore, $1 / 4 = .25$. Next, we need to determine whether or not the customer actually arrives at a given minute.

Now $P(0) = e^{-\lambda}$ is the probability that no event occurs at a given time. One of the basic assumptions of the Poisson distribution is that the probability of more than one outcome occurring in a short time interval is negligible. For simplicity, we assume that only one customer arrives at a given time unit. Thus, we use $e^{-\lambda}$ as the cutoff point to determine whether a customer arrives at a given time unit. Suppose that, on average, a customer arrives every 4 minutes. Then $\lambda = 0.25$. We can use an algorithm to generate a number between 0 and 1. If the value of the number generated is $> e^{-0.25}$, we can assume that the customer arrived at a particular time unit. For example, suppose that $rNum$ is a random number such that $0 \leq rNum \leq 1$. If $rNum > e^{-0.25}$, the customer arrived at the given time unit.

We now describe the method `runSimulation` to implement the simulation. Suppose that we run the simulation for 100 time units and customers arrive at time units 93, 96, and 100. The average transaction time is 5 minutes—that is, 5 time units. For simplicity, assume that we have only one server and the server becomes free at time unit 97, and that all customers arriving before time unit 93 have been served. When the server becomes free at time unit 97, the customer who arrived at time unit 93 starts the transaction. Because the transaction of the customer arriving at time unit 93 starts at time unit 97 and it takes 5 minutes to complete a transaction, when the simulation loop ends, this customer is still at the server. Moreover, customers who arrive at time units 96 and 100 are in the queue. For simplicity, we assume that when the simulation loop ends, the customers at the servers are considered served. The general algorithm for this method is:

1. Declare and initialize the variables, such as the simulation parameters, customer number, clock, total and average waiting times, number of customers arrived, number of customers served, number of customers left in the waiting queue, number of customers left with the servers, `WaitingCustomerQueue`, and a list of servers.

2. The main loop is:

```
for(clock = 1; clock <= simulationTime; clock++)
{
```

   a. Update the server list to decrement the transaction time of each busy server by one time unit.

   b. If the customers' queue is nonempty, increment the waiting time of each customer by one time unit.

   c. If a customer arrives, increment the number of customers by 1 and add the new customer to the queue.

   d. If a server is free and the customers' queue is nonempty, remove a customer from the front of the queue and send the customer to the free server.

```
}
```

3. Print the appropriate results. Your results must include the number of customers left in the queue, the number of customers still with servers, the number of customers arrived, and the number of customers who actually completed a transaction.

Once you have designed the method `runSimulation`, the definition of the method `main` is simple and straightforward because the method `main` calls only the methods `setSimulationParameters` and `runSimulation`.

When we tested our version of the simulation program, we generated the following results. We assumed that the average transaction time is 5 minutes and that, on average, a customer arrives every 4 minutes. We used a random number generator to generate a number between 0 and 1 to decide whether a customer arrived at a given time unit.

Sample Runs:

Sample Run 1:

```
Customer number 1 arrived at time unit 6
Customer number 2 arrived at time unit 7
Server No: 1 Customer number 1 departed at
           clock unit 11
Customer number 3 arrived at time unit 13
Customer number 4 arrived at time unit 15
Server No: 1 Customer number 2 departed at
           clock unit 16
```

Server No: 1 Customer number 3 departed at
            clock unit 21
Server No: 1 Customer number 4 departed at
            clock unit 26
Customer number 5 arrived at time unit 27
Customer number 6 arrived at time unit 29
Server No: 1 Customer number 5 departed at
            clock unit 32
Customer number 7 arrived at time unit 33
Server No: 1 Customer number 6 departed at
            clock unit 37
Server No: 1 Customer number 7 departed at
            clock unit 42
Customer number 8 arrived at time unit 46
Server No: 1 Customer number 8 departed at
            clock unit 51
Customer number 9 arrived at time unit 51
Server No: 1 Customer number 9 departed at
            clock unit 56
Customer number 10 arrived at time unit 59
Customer number 11 arrived at time unit 60
Customer number 12 arrived at time unit 61
Customer number 13 arrived at time unit 62
Customer number 14 arrived at time unit 63
Server No: 1 Customer number 10 departed at
            clock unit 64
Customer number 15 arrived at time unit 64
Server No: 1 Customer number 11 departed at
            clock unit 69
Server No: 1 Customer number 12 departed at
            clock unit 74
Customer number 16 arrived at time unit 77
Customer number 17 arrived at time unit 78
Server No: 1 Customer number 13 departed at
            clock unit 79
Customer number 18 arrived at time unit 79
Server No: 1 Customer number 14 departed at
            clock unit 84
Customer number 19 arrived at time unit 84
Customer number 20 arrived at time unit 86
Customer number 21 arrived at time unit 88
Server No: 1 Customer number 15 departed at
            clock unit 89
Server No: 1 Customer number 16 departed at
            clock unit 94
Customer number 22 arrived at time unit 96
Server No: 1 Customer number 17 departed at
            clock unit 99
Customer number 23 arrived at time unit 100

```
Simulation ran for 100 time units
Number of servers: 1
Average transaction time: 5
Average arrival time difference between customers: 4
Total wait time: 174
Number of customers who completed a transaction: 17
Number of customers left in the servers: 1
Number of customers left in the queue: 5
Average wait time: 7.57
************* END SIMULATION *************
```

Sample Run 2:

```
Customer number 1 arrived at time unit 4
Customer number 2 arrived at time unit 6
Server No: 1 Customer number 1 departed at
            clock unit 9
Customer number 3 arrived at time unit 10
Server No: 2 Customer number 2 departed at
            clock unit 11
Server No: 1 Customer number 3 departed at
            clock unit 15
Customer number 4 arrived at time unit 15
Customer number 5 arrived at time unit 17
Server No: 1 Customer number 4 departed at
            clock unit 20
Server No: 2 Customer number 5 departed at
            clock unit 22
Customer number 6 arrived at time unit 28
Customer number 7 arrived at time unit 31
Server No: 1 Customer number 6 departed at
            clock unit 33
Server No: 2 Customer number 7 departed at
            clock unit 36
Customer number 8 arrived at time unit 38
Customer number 9 arrived at time unit 39
Customer number 10 arrived at time unit 40
Customer number 11 arrived at time unit 42
Server No: 1 Customer number 8 departed at
            clock unit 43
Server No: 2 Customer number 9 departed at
            clock unit 44
Customer number 12 arrived at time unit 47
Server No: 1 Customer number 10 departed at
            clock unit 48
Server No: 2 Customer number 11 departed at
            clock unit 49
```

```
Server No: 1 Customer number 12 departed at
            clock unit 53
Customer number 13 arrived at time unit 54
Server No: 1 Customer number 13 departed at
            clock unit 59
Customer number 14 arrived at time unit 71
Customer number 15 arrived at time unit 72
Customer number 16 arrived at time unit 74
Server No: 1 Customer number 14 departed at
            clock unit 76
Server No: 2 Customer number 15 departed at
            clock unit 77
Customer number 17 arrived at time unit 78
Server No: 1 Customer number 16 departed at
            clock unit 81
Customer number 18 arrived at time unit 81
Server No: 2 Customer number 17 departed at
            clock unit 83
Customer number 19 arrived at time unit 84
Server No: 1 Customer number 18 departed at
            clock unit 86
Customer number 20 arrived at time unit 87
Server No: 2 Customer number 19 departed at
            clock unit 89
Server No: 1 Customer number 20 departed at
            clock unit 92
Customer number 21 arrived at time unit 92
Customer number 22 arrived at time unit 94
Customer number 23 arrived at time unit 95
Server No: 1 Customer number 21 departed at
            clock unit 97
Server No: 2 Customer number 22 departed at
            clock unit 99


Simulation ran for 100 time units
Number of servers: 2
Average transaction time: 5
Average arrival time difference between customers: 4
Total wait time: 10
Number of customers who completed a transaction: 22
Number of customers left in the servers: 1
Number of customers left in the queue: 0
Average wait time: 0.43
************* END SIMULATION *************
```

Sample Run 3:

In this output, to save space the details of the output of the customers' arrival and departure times are omitted.

```
Simulation ran for 1000 time units
Number of servers: 1
Average transaction time: 5
Average arrival time difference between customers: 4
Total wait time: 22313
Number of customers who completed a transaction: 197
Number of customers left in the servers: 1
Number of customers left in the queue: 30
Average wait time: 97.86
************* END SIMULATION *************
```

Sample Run 4:

In this output, to save space the details of the output of the customers' arrival and departure times are omitted.

```
Simulation ran for 1000 time units
Number of servers: 3
Average transaction time: 5
Average arrival time difference between customers: 4
Total wait time: 9
Number of customers who completed a transaction: 203
Number of customers left in the servers: 0
Number of customers left in the queue: 0
Average wait time: 0.04
************* END SIMULATION *************
```

QUICK REVIEW

1. A queue is a data structure wherein the items are added at one end and removed from the other end.

2. A queue is a First In First Out (FIFO) data structure.

3. The basic operations on a queue are: initialize the queue, determine whether the queue is empty, determine whether the queue is full, retrieve the first and last elements of the queue, add an item to the queue, and remove an item from the queue.

4. A queue can be implemented either as an array or as a linked list.

5. The middle elements of a queue should not be accessed directly.

6. If the queue is nonempty, the method **front** returns the front element of the queue, and the method **back** returns the last element of the queue.

7. Queues are restricted versions of arrays and linked lists.

EXERCISES

1. Suppose that queue is a QueueClass object and the size of the array implementing queue is 100. Also, suppose that the value of queueFront is 50 and the value of queueRear is 99.

   a. What are the values of queueFront and queueRear after adding an element to queue?

   b. What are the values of queueFront and queueRear after removing an element from queue?

2. Suppose that queue is a QueueClass object and the size of the array implementing queue is 100. Also, suppose that the value of queueFront is 99 and the value of queueRear is 25.

   a. What are the values of queueFront and queueRear after adding an element to queue?

   b. What are the values of queueFront and queueRear after removing an element from queue?

3. Suppose that queue is a QueueClass object and the size of the array implementing queue is 100. Also, suppose that the value of queueFront is 25 and the value of queueRear is 75.

   a. What are the values of queueFront and queueRear after adding an element to queue?

   b. What are the values of queueFront and queueRear after removing an element from queue?

4. Suppose that queue is a QueueClass object and the size of the array implementing queue is 100. Also, suppose that the value of queueFront is 99 and the value of queueRear is 99.

   a. What are the values of queueFront and queueRear after adding an element to queue?

   b. What are the values of queueFront and queueRear after removing an element from queue?

5. Suppose that queue is implemented as an array with the special reserved slot, as described in this chapter. Also, suppose that the size of the array implementing queue is 100. If the value of queueFront is 50, what is the position of the first queue element?

6. Suppose that queue is implemented as an array with the special reserved slot, as described in this chapter. Also, suppose that the value of queueFront is 74 and the value of queueRear is 99.

   a. What are the values of queueFront and queueRear after adding an element to queue?

   b. What are the values of queueFront and queueRear after removing an element from queue? Also, what is the position of the removed queue element?

7. Consider the following statements.

```
QueueClass queue = new QueueClass();
IntElement x = new IntElement();
IntElement y = new IntElement();
int num;
```

What is output by the following segment of code?

```
x.setNum(4);
y.setNum(5);
queue.addQueue(x);
queue.addQueue(y);
x = (IntElement) queue.front();
queue.deleteQueue();
num = x.getNum() + 5;
y.setNum(num);
queue.addQueue(y);
y.setNum(16);
queue.addQueue(y);
queue.addQueue(x);
num = y.getNum() - 3;
y.setNum(num);
queue.addQueue(y);

System.out.print("Queue Elements: ");

while(!queue.isEmptyQueue())
{
    System.out.print(" " + queue.front());
    queue.deleteQueue();
}

System.out.println();
```

8. Consider the following statements.

```
StackClass stack = new StackClass();
QueueClass queue = new QueueClass();
IntElement x = new IntElement(0);
int num;

StringTokenizer tokenizer;
```

Suppose the input is:

```
15 28 14 22 64 35 19 32 7 11 13 30 -999
```

Show what is output by the following segment of code. (Assume that **keyboard** is a **BufferedReader** object initialized to the standard input device.)

```
tokenizer = new StringTokenizer(keyboard.readLine());
stack.push(x);
queue.addQueue(x);
num = Integer.parseInt(tokenizer.nextToken());
```

```
while(num != -999)
{
    x.setNum(num);
    switch(num % 4)
    {
    case 0: stack.push(x);
            break;
    case 1: if(!stack.isEmptyStack())
            {
                System.out.println("Stack Element = "
                                    + stack.top());
                stack.pop();
            }
            else
                System.out.println("Sorry, the stack is empty.");
        break;
    case 2: queue.addQueue(x);
            break;
    case 3: if(!queue.isEmptyQueue())
            {
                System.out.println("Queue Element = "
                                    + queue.front());
                queue.deleteQueue();
            }
            else
                System.out.println("Sorry, the queue is empty.");
            break;
    }//end switch

    num = Integer.parseInt(tokenizer.nextToken());
}//end while

System.out.println("Stack Elements: ");
while(!stack.isEmptyStack())
 {
    System.out.print(stack.top() + " ");
    stack.pop();
}

System.out.println();
System.out.print("Queue Elements: ");
while(!queue.isEmptyQueue())
{
    System.out.print(queue.front() + " ");
    queue.deleteQueue();
}
System.out.println();
```

7

9. What does the following method do? (You may assume that the elements in q are references to the objects of the **class IntElement**.)

```
public static void mystery(QueueClass q)
{
    StackClass s = new StackClass();
    IntElement x = new IntElement();
    int num;

    while(!q.isEmptyQueue())
    {
        s.push(q.front());
        q.deleteQueue();
    }

    while(!s.isEmptyStack())
    {
        x = (IntElement) s.top();
        num = 2 * x.getNum();
        x.setNum(num);
        q.addQueue(x);
        s.pop();
    }
}
```

10. a. Add the operation **queueCount** to the **class QueueClass** (the array implementation of queues), which returns the number of elements in the queue. Write the definition of the method to implement this operation.

     b. Write the definition of the method **moveNthFront** that takes as a parameter a **QueueClass** object and a positive integer, *n*. The method moves the *n*th element of the queue to the front. The order of the remaining elements remains unchanged. For example, suppose:

         queue = {5, 11, 34, 67, 43, 55} and *n* = 3

         After a call to the method **moveNthFront**,

         queue = {34, 5, 11, 67, 43, 55}

11. Write a method, **reverseStack**, that takes as a parameter a stack object and a queue object whose elements are of the same type. The method **reverseStack** uses the queue to reverse the elements of the stack.

12. Write a method, **reverseQueue**, that takes as a parameter a stack object and a queue object whose elements are of the same type. The method **reverseQueue** uses the stack to reverse the elements of the queue.

PROGRAMMING EXERCISES

1. Write the definitions of the method `copyQueue` and the copy constructor for the `class QueueClass`. Also, write a program to test these operations.

2. Write the definitions of the method `copyQueue`, the default constructor, and the copy constructor for the `class LinkedQueueClass`. Also, write a program to test these operations.

3. This chapter explains how to implement a queue using a special array slot—a reserved slot—to distinguish between an empty queue and a full queue. Implement this queue design. Also, write a program to test various operations on the queue.

4. Write a program that reads a line of text, changes each lowercase letter to uppercase, and places each letter both in a queue and onto a stack. The program should then verify whether the line of text is a palindrome.

5. The implementation of a queue in an array, as given in this chapter, uses the variable `count` to determine whether the queue is empty or full. You can also use the variable `count` to return the number of elements in the `queue` (see Exercise 10.a of this chapter). On the other hand, the `class LinkedQueueClass` does not use such a variable to keep track of the number of elements in the queue. Redefine the `class LinkedQueueClass` by adding the instance variable `count` to keep track of the number of elements in the queue. Modify the definitions of the methods as necessary. Also, add the method `queueCount`, to return the number of elements in the queue. Moreover, write a program to test various operations of the class you defined.

6. a. Write the definitions of the methods `setWaitingTime`, `getArrivalTime`, `getTransactionTime`, `getCustomerNumber`, `equals`, `compareTo`, `makeCopy`, and `getCopy` of the `class Customer` as defined in the section "Application of Queues: Simulation."

   b. Write the definitions of the methods `getRemainingTransactionTime`, `setCurrentCustomer`, `getCurrentCustomerNumber`, `getCurrentCustomerArrivalTime`, `getCurrentCustomerWaitingTime`, and `getCurrentCustomerTransactionTime` of the `class Server` defined in the section "Application of Queues: Simulation."

   c. Write the definition of the method `runSimulation` to complete the design of the computer simulation program in the section "Application of Queues: Simulation." Test run your program for a variety of data. Moreover, use a random number generator to decide whether a customer arrived at a given time unit.

7

8

SEARCH ALGORITHMS

In this chapter, you will:

♦ Learn the various search algorithms

♦ Explore how to implement the sequential and binary search algorithms

♦ Discover how the sequential and binary search algorithms perform

♦ Become aware of the lower bound on comparison-based search algorithms

♦ Learn about hashing

Chapter 3 described how to organize data into computer memory using an array and how to perform basic operations on that data. Chapter 4 then described how to organize data using linked lists. The most important operation performed on a list is the search algorithm. Using the search algorithm, you can:

- Determine whether a particular item is in the list. If the data is specially organized (for example, sorted), find the location in the list where a new item can be inserted.

- Find the location of an item to be deleted.

The search algorithm's performance, therefore, is crucial. If the search is slow, it takes a large amount of computer time to accomplish your task; if the search is fast, you can accomplish your task quickly.

Search Algorithms

Chapters 3 and 5 described how to implement the sequential search algorithm. This chapter discusses other search algorithms and also analyzes the algorithms. Analysis of the algorithms enables programmers to decide which algorithm to use for a specific application. Before describing these algorithms, let us make the following observations.

Associated with each item in a data set is a special member that uniquely identifies the item in the data set. For example, if you have a data set consisting of student records, then the student ID uniquely identifies each student in a particular school. This unique member of the item is called the **key** of the item. The keys of the item in the data set are used in such operations as searching, sorting, insertion, and deletion. For instance, when we search the data set for a particular item, we compare the key of the item for which we are searching with the keys of the items in the data set.

As previously remarked, this chapter, in addition to describing the searching and sorting algorithms, analyzes these algorithms. In the analysis of an algorithm, the key comparisons refer to comparing the key of the search item with the key of an item in the list. Moreover, the number of key comparisons refers to the number of times the key of the item (in algorithms such as searching and sorting) is compared with the keys of the items in the list.

In Chapter 3, we designed and implemented the classes `ArrayListClass` and `UnorderedArrayList` to implement a list and the basic operations on an array. Because this chapter refers to these classes, for easy reference we give their descriptions without the documentation:

Abstract Class: `ArrayListClass`

Instance Variables:

```
protected int length;        //to store the length of the list
protected int maxSize;       //to store the maximum size of the list
protected DataElement[] list; //array of reference variables
```

Constructors and Instance Methods:

```
public ArrayListClass()
public ArrayListClass(int size)
public ArrayListClass(ArrayListClass otherList)
public boolean isEmpty()
public boolean isFull()
public int listSize()
public int maxListSize()
public void print()
public boolean isItemAtEqual(int location, DataElement item)
public void insertAt(int location, DataElement insertItem)
public void insertEnd(DataElement insertItem)
public void removeAt(int location)
public DataElement retrieveAt(int location)
public void replaceAt(int location, DataElement repItem)
public void clearList()
```

```
public abstract int seqSearch(DataElement searchItem);
public abstract void insert(DataElement insertItem);
public abstract void remove(DataElement removeItem);
public void copyList(ArrayListClass otherList)
```

Class: UnorderedArrayList

```
public class UnorderedArrayList extends ArrayListClass
```

Instance Variables:

Same as the instance variables of the **class ArrayListClass**.

Constructors and Instance Methods:

```
public UnorderedArrayList()
public UnorderedArrayList(int size)
public UnorderedArrayList(UnorderedArrayList otherList)
public int seqSearch(DataElement searchItem)
public void insert(DataElement insertItem)
public void remove(DataElement removeItem)
```

Sequential Search

The sequential search (also called the linear search) on array-based lists is described in Chapter 3, and the sequential search on linked lists is covered in Chapter 4. The sequential search works the same for both array-based and linked lists. The search always starts at the first element in the list and continues until either the item is found in the list or the entire list is searched.

Because we are interested in the performance of the sequential search (that is, the analysis of this type of search), for easy reference, next we give the sequential search algorithm for array-based lists (as described in Chapter 3). If the search item is found, its index (that is, its location in the array) is returned. If the search is unsuccessful, -1 is returned. (Note that the following sequential search does not require the list elements to be in any particular order.)

```
public int seqSearch(DataElement searchItem)
{
    int loc;
    boolean found = false;

    for(loc = 0; loc < length; loc++)
        if(list[loc].equals(searchItem))
        {
            found = true;
            break;
        }

    if(found)
        return loc;
    else
        return -1;
}//end seqSearch
```

> N O T E   The sequential search algorithm, as given here, uses an iterative control structure (the `for` loop) to compare the search item with the list elements. You can also write a recursive algorithm to implement the sequential search algorithm. (See Programming Exercise 1 at the end of this chapter.)

Sequential Search Analysis

This section analyzes the performance of the sequential search algorithm in both the worst case and the average case.

The statements before and after the loop are executed only once, and hence require very little computer time. The statements in the `for` loop are the ones that are repeated several times. For each iteration of the loop, the search item is compared with an element in the list, and a few other statements are executed, including some other comparisons. Clearly, the loop terminates as soon as the search item is found in the list. Therefore, the execution of the other statements in the loop is directly related to the outcome of the key comparison. Different programmers might implement the same algorithm differently, although the number of key comparisons would typically be the same. The speed of a computer can also easily affect the time an algorithm takes to perform, but not the number of key comparisons.

Therefore, when analyzing a search algorithm, we count the number of key comparisons because this number gives us the most useful information. Furthermore, the criteria for counting the number of key comparisons can be applied equally well to other search algorithms.

Suppose that the length of the list, say L, is n. We want to determine the number of key comparisons made by the sequential search when the list L is searched for a given item.

If the search item is not in the list, we then compare the search item with every element in the list, making n comparisons. This is an unsuccessful case.

Suppose that the search item is in the list. Then the number of key comparisons depends on where in the list the search item is located. If the search item is the first element of L, we make only one key comparison. This is the best case. On the other hand, if the search item is the last element in the list, the algorithm makes n comparisons. This is the worst case. The best and worst cases are not likely to occur every time we apply the sequential search on L, so it would be more helpful if we could determine the average behavior of the algorithm. That is, we need to determine the average number of key comparisons that the sequential search algorithm makes in the successful case.

To determine the average number of comparisons in the successful case of the sequential search algorithm:

    1. Consider all possible cases.

    2. Find the number of comparisons for each case.

    3. Add the number of comparisons and divide by the number of cases.

If the search item, called the **target**, is the first element in the list, one comparison is required. If the target is the second element in the list, two comparisons are required. Similarly, if the target is the kth element in the list, k comparisons are required. We assume that the target can be any element in the list; that is, all list elements are equally likely to be the target. Suppose that there are n elements in the list. The following expression gives the average number of comparisons:

$$\frac{1+2+\ldots+n}{n}$$

It is known that:

$$1+2+\ldots+n = \frac{n(n+1)}{2}$$

Therefore, the following expression gives the average number of comparisons made by the sequential search in the successful case:

$$\frac{1+2+\ldots+n}{n} = \frac{1}{n}\frac{n(n+1)}{2} = \frac{n+1}{2}$$

This expression shows that, on average, the sequential search searches half the list. It thus follows that if the list size is 1,000,000, on average, the sequential search makes 500,000 comparisons. As a result, the sequential search is not efficient for large lists.

Ordered Lists

A list is ordered if its elements are ordered according to some criteria. The elements of a list are usually in ascending order. Several operations that can be performed on an ordered list are similar to the operations performed on an arbitrary list. For example, determining whether the list is empty or full, determining the length of the list, printing the list, and clearing the list for an ordered list are the same operations as those on an unordered list. Therefore, to define an ordered list as an abstract data type (ADT), by using the mechanism of inheritance, we can derive the class to implement the ordered lists from the **class ArrayListClass** discussed in the previous section. Depending on a specific application, a list can be implemented either using an array or a linked list. We define two classes.

The following statements describe the **class OrderedArrayList** as an ADT:

Class: OrderedArrayList

```
public class OrderedArrayList extends ArrayListClass
```

Instance Variables:

Same as the instance variables of the **class ArrayListClass**.

Constructors and Instance Methods:

```
public OrderedArrayList()
   //default constructor
```

```
public OrderedArrayList(int size)
   //constructor with a parameter

public OrderedArrayList(OrderedArrayList otherList)
   //copy constructor

public int seqSearch(DataElement searchItem)
   //Method to determine whether searchItem is in the list.
   //Postcondition: If searchItem is found, returns the location
   //               in the array where searchItem is found;
   //               otherwise, returns -1.

public void insert(DataElement insertItem)
   //Method to insert insertItem in the list at the end
   //of the list. However, first the list is searched to
   //see whether the item to be inserted is already in the list.
   //Postcondition: insertItem is inserted and length++
   //               If insertItem is already in the list or the list
   //               is full, an appropriate message is output.

public void remove(DataElement removeItem)
   //Method to remove an item from the list.
   //The parameter removeItem specifies the item to
   //be removed.
   //Postcondition: If removeItem is found in the list, it is
   //               removed from the list and length is
   //               decremented by one.
```

The next sections describe the method **insert** and the searching algorithm, binary search, for sorted lists. We leave the definitions of the methods **seqSearch** and **remove** for ordered lists as exercises for you (see Programming Exercises 3 and 6).

Chapter 4 defined the following class to implement ordered linked lists, which we reproduce, for easy reference, without the documentation.

```
public class OrderedLinkedList extends LinkedListClass
```

Instance Variables: Same as the instance variables of the **class LinkedListClass**.

Constructors and Instance Methods:

```
public OrderedLinkedList()

public OrderedLinkedList(OrderedLinkedList otherList)

public boolean search(DataElement searchItem)

public void insertNode(DataElement insertItem)

public void deleteNode(DataElement deleteItem)
```

Binary Search

As you can see, the sequential search is not efficient for large lists because, on average, the sequential search searches half the list. We therefore describe another search algorithm, called the **binary search**, which is very fast. However, a binary search can be performed only on ordered lists. We therefore assume that the list is ordered.

The binary search algorithm uses the "divide and conquer" technique to search the list. First, the search item is compared with the middle element of the list. If the search item is less than the middle element of the list, we restrict the search to the first half of the list; otherwise, we search the second half of the list.

Consider the sorted list of `length = 12` in Figure 8-1.

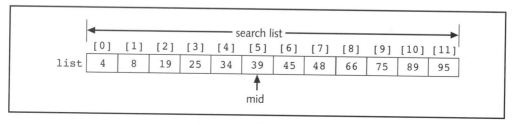

Figure 8-1 List of `length 12`

Suppose that we want to determine whether **75** is in the list. Initially, the entire list is the search list (see Figure 8-2).

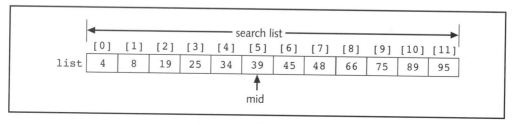

Figure 8-2 Search list, `list[0]...list[11]`

First, we compare 75 with the middle element in this list, `list[5]` (which is **39**). Because 75 ≠ `list[5]` and 75 > `list[5]`, we then restrict our search to the list `list[6]...list[11]`, as shown in Figure 8-3.

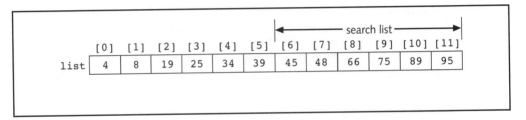

Figure 8-3 Search list, `list[6]...list[11]`

This process is now repeated on the list `list[6]...list[11]`, which is a list of `length = 6`.

Because we need frequently to determine the middle element of the list, the binary search algorithm is typically implemented for array-based lists. To determine the middle element of the list, we add the starting index, `first`, and the ending index, `last`, of the search list and then divide by 2 to calculate its index. That is,

$$mid = \frac{first+last}{2}$$

Initially, `first = 0` and (because an array index in Java starts at 0 and `length` denotes the number of elements in the list) `last = length − 1`.

The following Java method implements the binary search algorithm. If the item is found in the list, its location is returned; if the search item is not in the list, `−1` is returned.

```java
public int binarySearch(DataElement item)
{
    int first = 0;
    int last = length - 1;
    int mid = -1;

    boolean found = false;

    while(first <= last && !found)
    {
        mid = (first + last) / 2;

        if(list[mid].equals(item))
            found = true;
        else
            if(list[mid].compareTo(item) > 0)
                last = mid - 1;
            else
                first = mid + 1;
    }
```

```
    if(found)
        return mid;
    else
        return -1;
}//end binarySearch
```

In the binary search algorithm, each time through the loop we make two key comparisons. The only exception is in the successful case; the last time through the loop only one key (item) comparison is made.

 The binary search algorithm, as given previously, uses an iterative control structure (the `while` loop) to compare the search item with the list elements. You can also write a recursive algorithm to implement the binary search algorithm. (See Programming Exercise 2 at the end of this chapter.)

The following example further illustrates how the binary search algorithm works.

Example 8-1

Consider the list given in Figure 8-4.

	[0]	[1]	[2]	[3]	[4]	[5]	[6]	[7]	[8]	[9]	[10]	[11]
list	4	8	19	25	34	39	45	48	66	75	89	95

Figure 8-4   Sorted list for a binary search

The size of this list is `12`; that is, the length is `12`. Table 8-1 shows the values of `first`, `last`, and `middle` each time through the loop. It also shows the number of times the item is compared with an element in the list each time through the loop.

Suppose that we are searching for item `89`.

Table 8-1   Values of `first`, `last`, and `middle` and the Number of Comparisons for the Search Item `89`

Iteration	first	last	mid	list[mid]	Number of Comparisons
1	0	11	5	39	2
2	6	11	8	66	2
3	9	11	10	89	1 (found is true)

The item is found at `location 10`, and the total number of comparisons is 5.

Next, let us search the list for item 34. As in Table 8-1, Table 8-2 shows the values of `first`, `last`, and `middle` each time through the loop. It also shows the number of times the item is compared with an element in the list each time through the loop.

Table 8-2 Values of `first`, `last`, and `middle` and the Number of Comparisons for the Search Item 34

Iteration	first	last	mid	list[mid]	Number of Comparisons
1	0	11	5	39	2
2	0	4	2	19	2
3	3	4	3	25	2
4	4	4	4	34	1 (found is true)

The item is found at `location 4`, and the total number of comparisons is 7.

Let us now search for item 22, as shown in Table 8-3.

Table 8-3 Values of `first`, `last`, and `middle` and the Number of Comparisons for the Search Item 22

Iteration	first	last	mid	list[mid]	Number of Comparisons
1	0	11	5	39	2
2	0	4	2	19	2
3	3	4	3	25	2
4	3	2	the loop stops (because `first > last`)		

This is an unsuccessful search. The total number of comparisons is 6.

Performance of Binary Search

Suppose that `L` is a sorted list of 1000 elements, and you want to determine whether `x` is in `L`. Because `L` is sorted, you can apply the binary search algorithm to search for `x`. Suppose that `L` is as shown in Figure 8-5.

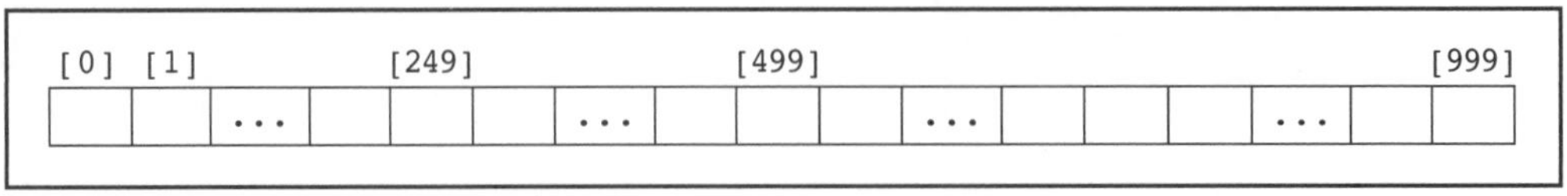

Figure 8-5 List `L`

The first iteration of the `while` loop searches for x in L[0]...L[999], which is a list of 1000 items. This iteration of the `while` loop compares x with L[499] (see Figure 8-6).

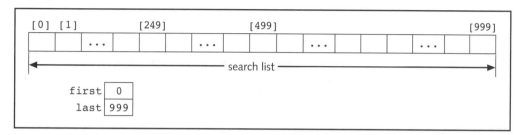

Figure 8-6   Search list

Suppose that x   L[499]. If x < L[499], then the next iteration of the `while` loop looks for x in L[0]...L[498]; otherwise, the `while` loop looks for x in L[500]...L[999]. Suppose that x < L[499]. Then the next iteration of the `while` loop looks for x in L[0]...L[498], which is a list of 499 items, as shown in Figure 8-7.

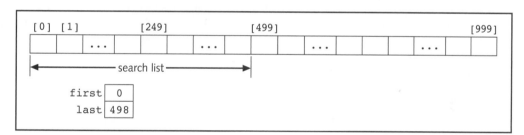

Figure 8-7   Search list after the first iteration

The second iteration of the `while` loop compares x with L[249]. Once again, suppose that x   L[249]. Further suppose that x > L[249]. The next iteration of the `while` loop searches for x in L[250]...L[498], which is a list of 249 items, as shown in Figure 8-8.

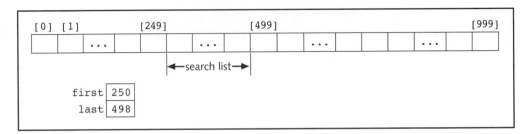

Figure 8-8 Search list after the second iteration

From these observations, it follows that every iteration of the `while` loop cuts the size of the search list in half. Because $1000 \approx 1024 = 2^{10}$, the `while` loop has at most 11 iterations to determine whether x is in L. (The symbol $\approx$ stands for "approximately equal to.") Because every iteration of the `while` loop makes 2 key comparisons—that is, x is compared twice with the elements of L—the binary search makes at most 22 comparisons to determine whether x is in L. By contrast, recall that the sequential search, on average, would make 500 comparisons to determine whether x is in L.

To have a better idea of how fast a binary search is as compared to a sequential search, suppose that L is of the size 1000000. Because $1000000 \approx 1048576 = 2^{20}$, it follows that the `while` loop in a binary search has at most 21 iterations to determine whether an element is in L. Every iteration of the `while` loop makes 2 item (that is, key) comparisons. Therefore, to determine whether an element is in L, a binary search makes at most 42 item comparisons. By contrast, on average, the sequential search makes 500,000 item (key) comparisons to determine whether an element is in L.

Note that

$$40 = 2 * 20 = 2 * \log_2 2^{20} = 2 * \log_2(1048576) \approx 2 * \log_2(1000000)$$

In general, if L is a sorted list of size n, to determine whether or not an element is in L, a binary search makes at most $2*\log_2 n + 2$ key comparisons.

Unsuccessful Search

In the case of an unsuccessful search, it can be shown that for a list of length n, a binary search makes approximately $2*\log_2(n+1)$ key comparisons.

Successful Search

In the case of a successful search, it can be shown that for a list of length n, on average, a binary search makes $2*\log_2 n - 4$ key comparisons.

Now that we know how to effectively search an ordered list stored in an array, let us discuss how to insert an item into an ordered list.

Insertion into an Ordered List

Suppose that you have an ordered list and want to insert an item in the list. After insertion, the resulting list must also be ordered. Chapter 4 describes how to insert an item into an ordered linked list. This section describes how to insert an item into an ordered list stored in an array.

To store the item in the ordered list, first we must find the place in the list where the item is to be inserted. Then we slide the list elements one array position down to make room for the item to be inserted, and then insert the item. Because the list is sorted and stored in an array, we can use an algorithm similar to the binary search algorithm to find the place in the list where the item is to be inserted. We can then use the method `insertAt` (of the `class ArrayListClass`) to insert the item. (Note that we cannot use the binary search algorithm as designed previously because it returns −1 if the item is not in the list. Of course, we can write another method using the binary search technique to find the position in the array where the item is to be inserted.) Therefore, the algorithm to insert the item is:

First, use an algorithm similar to the binary search algorithm to find the place where the item is to be inserted. (The special cases, such as inserting an item in an empty list or in a full list, are handled separately.)

```
if the item is already in this list
   output an appropriate message
else
     use the method insertAt to insert the item in the list.
```

The following method, `insertOrd`, implements this algorithm.

```
public void insert(DataElement insertItem)
{
   int first = 0;
   int last = length - 1;
   int mid = 0;

   boolean found = false;

   if(length == 0)   //list is empty
   {
      list[0] = insertItem.getCopy();
      length++;
   }
   else
      if(length == maxSize)
         System.err.println("Cannot insert into a full list.");
      else
      {
         while(first <= last && !found)
         {
             mid = (first + last) / 2;
```

8

```
                if(list[mid].equals(insertItem))
                    found = true;
                else
                    if(list[mid].compareTo(insertItem) > 0)
                        last = mid - 1;
                    else
                        first = mid + 1;
        }//end while

        if(found)
            System.err.println("The insert item is already "
                    + "in the list. Duplicates are not "
                    + "allowed.");
        else
        {
            if(list[mid].compareTo(insertItem) < 0)
                mid++;

            insertAt(mid, insertItem);
        }
    }
}//end insert
```

Similarly, you can write a method to remove an element from an ordered list; see Programming Exercise 6 at the end of this chapter.

If we add the binary search algorithm to the **class OrderedArrayList**, then the definition of this class is:

```
public class OrderedArrayList extends ArrayListClass
{
    public OrderedArrayList()
    {
        super();
    }

    public OrderedArrayList(int size)
    {
        super(size);
    }
    public OrderedArrayList(OrderedArrayList otherList)
    {
        super(otherList);
    }

    public int seqSearch(DataElement searchItem)
    {
        System.out.println("See Programming Exercise 3.");
        return -1;
    }
```

```
public int binarySearch(DataElement item)
{
    //Write the definition as given above.
}

public void insert(DataElement insertItem)
{
    //Write the definition as given above.
}
public void remove(DataElement removeItem)
{
    System.out.println("See Programming Exercise 6. ");
}
}
```

Table 8-4 summarizes the algorithm analysis of the search algorithms discussed earlier.

Table 8-4   Number of Comparisons for a List of Length n

Algorithm	Successful Search	Unsuccessful Search
Sequential search	$\dfrac{n+1}{2} = O(n)$	$n = O(n)$
Binary search	$2 * \log_2 n - 4 = O(\log_2 n)$	$2 * \log_2 (n+1) = O(\log_2 n)$

8

LOWER BOUND ON COMPARISON-BASED SEARCH ALGORITHMS

Sequential and binary search algorithms search the list by comparing the target element with the list elements. For this reason, these algorithms are called **comparison-based search algorithms**. Earlier sections of this chapter showed that a sequential search is of the order n, and a binary search is of the order $\log_2 n$, where n is the size of the list. The obvious question is: can we devise a search algorithm that has an order less than $\log_2 n$? Before we answer this question, first we obtain the lower bound on the number of comparisons for the comparison-based search algorithms.

Theorem: Let L be a list of size $n > 1$. Suppose that the elements of L are sorted. If SRH(n) denotes the minimum number of comparisons needed, in the worst case, by using a comparison-based algorithm to determine whether an element x is in L, then SRH(n) $\geq \log_2(n + 1)$.

Corollary: The binary search algorithm is the optimal worst-case algorithm for solving search problems by the comparison method.

From these results, it follows that if we want to design a search algorithm that is of an order less than $\log_2 n$, then it cannot be comparison based.

HASHING

Previous sections of this chapter discussed two search algorithms: binary and sequential. In a binary search, the data must be sorted; in a sequential search, the data does not need to be in any particular order. We also analyzed both these algorithms and showed that a sequential search is of the order n, and a binary search is of the order $\log_2 n$, where n is the length of the list. The obvious question is: can we construct a search algorithm that is of the order less than $\log_2 n$? Recall that both search algorithms, binary and sequential, are comparison-based algorithms. We obtained a lower bound on comparison-based search algorithms, which shows that comparison-based search algorithms are at least of the order $\log_2 n$. Therefore, if we want to construct a search algorithm that is of the order less than $\log_2 n$, it cannot be comparison based. This section describes an algorithm that, on average, is of the order 1.

The previous section showed that for comparison-based algorithms, a binary search achieves the lower bound. However, a binary search requires the data to be specially organized, that is, the data must be sorted. The search algorithm that we now describe, called **hashing**, also requires the data to be specially organized.

In hashing, the data is organized with the help of a table, called the **hash table**, denoted by HT, and the hash table is stored in an array. To determine whether a particular item with a key, say X, is in the table, we apply a function h, called the **hash function**, to the key X; that is, we compute $h(X)$, read as h of X. The function h is an arithmetic function, and $h(X)$ gives the address of the item in the hash table. Suppose that the size of the hash table, HT, is m. Then $0 \le h(X) < m$. Thus, to determine whether the item with key X is in the table, we look at the entry $HT[h(X)]$ in the hash table. Because the address of an item is computed with the help of a function, it follows that the items are stored in no particular order. Before continuing with this discussion, let us consider the following questions:

- How do we choose a hash function?

- How do we organize the data with the help of the hash table?

First, we discuss how to organize the data in the hash table.

There are two ways that data is organized with the help of the hash table. In the first approach, the data is stored within the hash table, that is, in an array. In the second approach, the data is stored in linked lists and the hash table is an array of reference variables to those linked lists. Each approach has its own advantages and disadvantages, and we discuss both approaches in detail. However, first we introduce some more terminology that is used in this section.

The hash table HT is usually divided into, say, b buckets $HT[0]$, $HT[1]$, ..., $HT[b-1]$. Each bucket is capable of holding, say, r items. It thus follows that $br = m$, where m is the size of HT. Generally, $r = 1$ and so each bucket can hold one item.

The hash function h maps the key X onto an integer t; that is, $h(X) = t$, such that $0 \le h(X) \le b-1$. Two keys, X_1 and X_2, such that $X_1 \ne X_2$, are called **synonyms** if $h(X_1) = h(X_2)$. Let X be a key and $h(X) = t$. If bucket t is full, we say that an **overflow** occurs. Let X_1 and X_2 be two nonidentical keys, that is, $X_1 \neq X_2$. If $h(X_1) = h(X_2)$, we say that a **collision** occurs. If $r = 1$, that is, the bucket size is 1, an overflow and a collision occur at the same time.

When choosing a hash function, the main objectives are to:

- Choose a hash function that is easy to compute
- Minimize the number of collisions

Next, we consider some examples of hash functions.

Suppose that *HTSize* denotes the size of the hash table, that is, the size of the array holding the hash table. We assume that the bucket size is 1. Thus, each bucket can hold one item and, therefore, overflow and collision occur simultaneously.

Hash Functions: Some Examples

Several hash functions are described in the literature. Here we describe some of the commonly used hash functions.

Mid-square: In this method, the hash function, h, is computed by squaring the identifier, and then using the appropriate number of bits from the middle of the square to obtain the bucket address. Because the middle bits of a square usually depend on all the characters, it is expected that different keys will yield different hash addresses with high probability, even if some of the characters are the same.

Folding: In folding, the key X is partitioned into parts such that all the parts, except possibly the last parts, are of equal length. The parts are then added, in some convenient way, to obtain the hash address.

Division (modular arithmetic): In this method, the key X is converted into an integer i_X. This integer is then divided by the size of the hash table to get the remainder, giving the address of X in *HT*. That is (in Java),

$h(X) = i_X \% HTSize;$

Suppose that each **key** is a string. The following Java method uses the division method to compute the address of the key.

```
int hashFunction(String insertKey)
{
   int sum = 0;

   for(int j = 0; j <= insertKey.length(); j++)
       sum = sum + (int)(insertKey.charAt(j));

   return (sum % HTSize);
}//end hashFunction
```

Collision Resolution

As noted previously, the hash function that we choose not only should be easy to compute, but it is most desirable that the number of collisions is minimized. However, in reality, collisions are unavoidable. Thus, in hashing, we must include algorithms to handle collisions. Collision resolution techniques are classified into two categories: **open addressing** (also called **closed hashing**), and **chaining** (also called **open hashing**). In open addressing, the data is stored within the hash table. In chaining, the data is organized in linked lists and the hash table is an array of references to the linked lists. First we discuss collision resolution by open addressing.

Collision Resolution: Open Addressing

As described previously, in open addressing, the data is stored within the hash table. Therefore, for each key X, $h(X)$ gives the index in the array where the item with key X is likely to be stored. Open addressing can be implemented in several ways. Next, we describe some of the common ways to implement open addressing.

Linear Probing

Suppose that an item with key X is to be inserted in HT. We use the hash function to compute the index $h(X)$ of this item in HT. Suppose that $h(X) = t$. Then $0 \leq h(X) \leq HTSize - 1$. If $HT[t]$ is empty, we store this item into this array slot. Suppose that $HT[t]$ is already occupied by another item; therefore, we have a collision. In linear probing, starting at location t, we search the array sequentially to find the next available array slot.

In linear probing, we assume that the array is circular so that if the lower portion of the array is full, we can continue the search in the top portion of the array. This can easily be accomplished by using the mod operator. That is, starting at t, we check the array locations t, $(t + 1)\%$ $HTSize$, $(t + 2)\%$ $HTSize$, ..., $(t + j)$ % $HTSize$. This is called the **probe sequence**.

The next array slot is given by:

$(h(X) + j)$ % $HTSize$

where j is the jth probe.

The following Java pseudocode implements linear probing:

```
hIndex = hashFunction(insertKey);
found = false;

while(HT[hIndex] != emptyKey && !found)
   if(HT[hIndex].key == insertKey)
      found = true;
   else
      hIndex = (hIndex + 1) % HTSize;

if(found)
   System.err.println("Duplicate items are not allowed.");
else
   HT[hIndex] = newItem;
```

From the definition of linear probing, we see that linear probing is easy to implement. However, linear probing causes **clustering**; that is, more and more new keys are likely to be hashed to the array slots that are already occupied. For example, consider the hash table of size 20, as shown in Figure 8-9.

Figure 8-9 Hash table of size 20

Initially, all the array positions are available. Because all the array positions are available, the probability of any position being probed is (1/20). Suppose that after storing some of the items, the hash table is as shown in Figure 8-10.

8

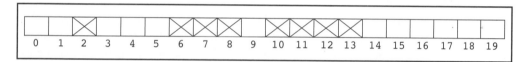

Figure 8-10 Hash table of size 20 with certain positions occupied

In this figure, a cross indicates that this array slot is occupied. Slot 9 will be occupied next if, for the next key, the hash address is 6, 7, 8 or 9. Thus, the probability that slot 9 will be occupied next is 4/20. Similarly, in this hash table, the probability that array position 14 will be occupied next is 5/20.

Now consider the hash table of Figure 8-11.

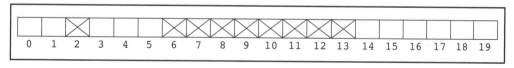

Figure 8-11 Hash table of size 20 with certain positions occupied

In this hash table, the probability that the array position 14 will be occupied next is 9/20, while the probability that the array positions, say, 15 or 16 or 17 will be occupied next is 1/20. We see that items tend to cluster, which would increase the search length. Linear probing, therefore, causes clustering. This clustering is called **primary clustering**.

One way to improve linear probing is to skip array positions by a fixed constant, say c, rather than 1. In this case, the hash address is:

$(h(X) + i * c)$ % $HTSize$

If $c = 2$ and $h(X) = 2k$, that is, $h(X)$ is even, only the even numbered array positions are visited. Similarly, if $c = 2$ and $h(X) = 2k + 1$, that is, $h(X)$ is odd, only the odd numbered array positions are visited. To visit all the array positions, the constant c must be relatively prime to $HTSize$.

Random Probing

This method uses a random number generator to find the next available slot. The ith slot in the probe sequence is

$(h(X) + r_i)$ % $HTSize$

where r_i is the ith value in a random permutation of the numbers 1 to $HTSize - 1$. All insertions and searches use the same sequence of random numbers.

Example 8-2 illustrates how to create the probe sequence using random probing.

Example 8-2

Suppose that the size of the hash table is 101, and for the keys X_1 and X_2, $h(X_1) = 26$, and $h(X_2) = 35$. Also suppose that $r_1 = 2, r_2 = 5$, and $r_3 = 8$. Then the probe sequence of X_1 has the elements 26, 28, 31, and 34. Similarly, the probe sequence of X_2 has the elements 35, 37, 40, and 43.

Rehashing

In this method, if a collision occurs with the hash function h, we use a series of hash functions, $h_1, h_2, ..., h_s$. That is, if the collision occurs at $h(X)$, the array slots $h_i(X), 1 \le h_i(X) \le s$ are examined.

Quadratic Probing

Suppose that an item with key X is hashed at t, that is, $h(X) = t$, and $0 \le t \le HTSize - 1$. Further suppose that position t is already occupied. In quadratic probing, starting at position t, we linearly search the array at locations $(t + 1^2)$ % $HTSize$, $(t + 2^2)$ % $HTSize = (t + 4)$ % $HTSize$, $(t + 3^2)$ % $HTSize = (t + 9)$ % $HTSize$, ..., $(t + i^2)$ % $HTSize$. That is, the probe sequence is: $t, (t + 1^2)$ % $HTSize, (t + 2^2)$ % $HTSize, (t + 3^2)$ % $HTSize, ..., (t + i^2)$ % $HTSize$.

Example 8-3 illustrates how to create the probe sequence using quadratic probing.

Example 8-3

Suppose that the size of the hash table is 101 and for the keys X_1, X_2, and X_3, $h(X_1) = 25$, $h(X_2) = 96$, and $h(X_3) = 34$. Then the probe sequence for X_1 is 25, 26, 29, 34, 41, and so on. The probe sequence for X_2 is 96, 97, 100, 4, 11, and so on. (Notice that $(96 + 3^2)$ % $101 = 105$ % $101 = 4$.)

The probe sequence for X_3 is 34, 35, 38, 43, 50, 59, and so on. Even though element 34 of the probe sequence of X_3 is the same as the fourth element of the probe sequence of X_1, both the probe sequences after 34 are different.

Although quadratic probing reduces primary clustering, we do not know if it probes all the positions in the table. In reality, it does not probe all the positions in the table. However, when *HTSize* is a prime, quadratic probing probes about half the table before repeating the probe sequence. Let us prove this observation.

Suppose that *HTSize* is a prime and for $0 \le i < j \le HTSize$,

$$(t + i^2) \text{ \% } HTSize = (t + j^2) \text{ \% } HTSize,$$

This implies that

$HTSize \mid (j^2 - i^2)$ or $HTSize \mid (j - i)(j + i)$

Here the symbol $\mid$ means divide. For example, $a \mid b$ means a divides b. Because *HTSize* is a prime, we get

$HTSize \mid (j - i)$ or $HTSize \mid (j + i)$

Now since $0 < j - i < HTSize$, it follows that *HTSize* does not divide $(j - i)$. Hence, $HTSize \mid (j + i)$. This implies that $j + i \ge HTSize$ and so

$$j \ge \frac{HTSize}{2}$$

Hence, quadratic probing probes half the table before repeating the probe sequence. It thus follows that if the size of *HTSize* is a prime and at least twice the number of items, we can resolve all the collisions.

Because probing half the table is already a considerable number of probes, after making this many probes we assume that the table is full and stop the insertion (and search). (This can occur when the table is actually half full; in practice, it seldom happens unless the table is nearly full.)

Next, we describe how to generate the probe sequence.

8

Note that

$$2^2 = 1 + (2 \cdot 2 - 1)$$
$$3^2 = 1 + 3 + (2 \cdot 3 - 1)$$
$$4^2 = 1 + 3 + 5 + (2 \cdot 4 - 1)$$
$$\vdots$$
$$i^2 = 1 + 3 + 5 + 7 + \ldots + (2 \cdot i - 1), \ i \geq 1$$

It thus follows that,

$$(t + i^2) \ \% \ HTSize = (t + 1 + 3 + 5 + 7 + \ldots + (2 \cdot i - 1)) \ \% \ HTSize$$

Consider the probe sequence:

$$t, (t + 1^2)\% \ HTSize, (t + 2^2)\% \ HTSize, (t + 3^2)\% \ HTSize, \ldots, (t + i^2) \ \% \ HTSize$$

The following Java code computes the ith probe, that is, $(t + i^2) \ \% \ HTSize$.

```java
int inc = 1;
int pCount = 0;

while(pCount < i)
{
    t = (t + inc) % HTSize;
    inc = inc + 2;
    pCount++;
}
```

The following pseudocode implements quadratic probing. (Assume that *HTSize* is a prime.)

```
int pCount;
int inc;
int hIndex;

hIndex = hashFunction(insertKey);

pCount = 0;
inc = 1;

while(HT[hIndex] is not empty
      && HT[hIndex] is not the same as the insert item
      && pCount < HTSize / 2)
{
    pCount++;
    hIndex = (hIndex + inc ) % HTSize;
    inc = inc + 2;
}

if(HT[hIndex] is empty)
    HT[hIndex] = newItem;
```

```
else
   if(HT[hIndex] is the same as the insert item)
      System.err.println("Error: No duplicates are allowed.");
   else
      System.err.println("Error: The table is full. "
                          + "Unable to resolve the collisions.");
```

Both random and quadratic probings eliminate primary clustering. However, if two nonidentical keys, say X_1 and X_2, are hashed to the same home position, that is, $h(X_1) = h(X_2)$, then the same probe sequence is followed for both keys. The same probe sequence is used for both keys because random probing and quadratic probing are functions of the home positions, not the original key. It follows that if the hash function causes a cluster at a particular home position, the cluster remains under these probings. This is called **secondary clustering**.

One way to solve secondary clustering is to use linear probing, with the increment value being a function of the key. This is called **double hashing**. In double hashing, if a collision occurs at $h(X)$, the probe sequence is generated by using the rule:

$$(h(X) + i * h'(X)) \% HTSize$$

where h' is the second hash function.

Example 8-4 illustrates how to create the probe sequence using double hashing.

Example 8-4

Suppose that the size of the hash table is 101 and for the keys X_1 and X_2, $h(X_1) = 35$ and $h(X_2) = 83$. Also suppose that $h'(X_1) = 3$ and $h'(X_2) = 6$. Then the probe sequence for X_1 is 35, 38, 41, 44, 47, and so on. The probe sequence for X_2 is 83, 89, 95, 0, 6, and so on. (Notice that $(83 + 3 * 6) \% 101 = 101 \% 101 = 0$.)

Deletion: Open Addressing

Suppose that an item, say R, is to be deleted from the hash table, HT. Clearly, we first must find the index of R in HT. To find the index of R, we apply the same criteria that was applied to R when R was inserted in HT. Let us further assume that after inserting R another item, R', was inserted in HT, and the home position of R and R' is the same. The probe sequence of R is contained in the probe sequence of R' because R' was inserted in the hash table after R. Suppose that we delete R simply by marking the array slot containing R as empty. If this array position stays empty, then while searching for R' and following its probe sequence, the search terminates at this empty array position. This gives the impression that R' is not in the table, which, of course, is incorrect. The item R cannot be deleted simply by marking its position as empty from the hash table.

One way to solve this problem is to create a special key to be stored in the keys of the items to be deleted. The special key in any slot indicates that this array slot is available for a new item to be inserted. However, during the search, the search should not terminate at this location. This, unfortunately, makes the deletion algorithm slow and complicated.

Another solution is to use another array, say `indexStatusList` of `int`, of the same size as the hash table as follows: initialize each position of `indexStatusList` to 0, indicating that the corresponding position in the hash table is empty. When an item is added to the hash table at position, say i, we set `indexStatusList[i]` to 1. When an item is deleted from the hash table at position, say k, we set `indexStatusList[k]` to –1. Therefore, each entry in the array `indexStatusList` is –1, 0, or 1.

For example, suppose that you have the hash table as shown in Figure 8-12.

	indexStatusList		HashTable
[0]	1	[0]	Mickey
[1]	1	[1]	Goofy
[2]	0	[2]	
[3]	1	[3]	Grumpy
[4]	0	[4]	
[5]	1	[5]	Balto
[6]	1	[6]	Duckey
[7]	0	[7]	
[8]	1	[8]	Minnie
[9]	0	[9]	

Figure 8-12 Hash table and `indexStatusList`

In Figure 8-12, the hash table positions 0, 1, 3, 5, 6, and 8 are occupied. Suppose that the entries at positions 3 and 6 are removed. To remove these entries from the hash table, we store –1 at positions 3 and 6 in the array `indexStatusList` (see Figure 8-13).

	indexStatusList		HashTable
[0]	1	[0]	Mickey
[1]	1	[1]	Goofy
[2]	0	[2]	
[3]	-1	[3]	Grumpy
[4]	0	[4]	
[5]	1	[5]	Balto
[6]	-1	[6]	Duckey
[7]	0	[7]	
[8]	1	[8]	Minnie
[9]	0	[9]	

Figure 8-13   Hash table and `indexStatusList` after removing the entries at positions 3 and 6

Hashing: Implementation Using Quadratic Probing

This section briefly describes how to design a class as an ADT to implement hashing using quadratic probing. To implement hashing, we use two arrays. One is used to store the data, and the other, `indexStatusList` as described in the previous section, is used to indicate whether a position in the hash table is free, occupied, or previously used. The following statements describe hashing as an ADT:

Class: HashTableClass

```
public class HashTableClass
```

Instance Variables:

```
private DataElement[] HTable;    //array of references to implement
                                 //the hash table
private int[] indexStatusList;   //array indicating the status of
                                 //a position in the hash table
private int length;     //number of items in the hash table
private int HTSize;     //maximum size of the hash table

public HashTableClass()
   //default constructor
   //Postcondition: Create the arrays HTable and
   //               indexStatusList of the sizes 101,
   //               length = 0, HTSize =  101.
```

```
public HashTableClass(int size)
   //constructor
   //Postcondition: Create the arrays HTable and
   //               indexStatusList of the sizes specified
   //               by the parameter size; length = 0;
   //               HTSize = size.

public void insert(int hashIndex, DataElement rec)
   //Method to insert an item in the hash table.
   //The first parameter specifies the initial hash index
   //of the item to be inserted.
   //The item to be inserted is specified by the parameter rec.
   //Postcondition: If an empty position is found in the
   //   hash table, rec is inserted and the length is
   //   incremented by one; otherwise, an appropriate error
   //   message is displayed.

public int search(int hashIndex, DataElement rec)
   //Method to determine whether the item specified by
   //the parameter rec is in the hash table.
   //The parameter hashIndex specifies the initial hash
   //index of rec.
   //Postcondition: If rec is found, returns the position
   //               where rec is found; otherwise, returns -1.

public boolean isItemAtEqual(int hashIndex, DataElement rec)
   //Method to determine whether the item specified by rec
   //is the same as the item in the hash table at position
   //hashIndex.
   //Postcondition: Returns true if HTable[hashIndex] == rec,
   //   false otherwise.

public DataElement retrieve(int hashIndex)
   //Method to retrieve the item at position hashIndex.
   //Postcondition: If the table has an item at position
   //   hashIndex, a reference of its copy is returned;
   //   otherwise, null is returned.

public void remove(int hashIndex, DataElement rec)
   //Method to remove an item from the hash table.
   //Postcondition: Given the initial hashIndex, if rec
   //   is found in the table it is removed; otherwise,
   //   an appropriate error message is displayed.

public void print()
   //Method to output the data.
```

We give the definition of only the method insert and leave the others as an exercise for you.

The definition of the method **insert** using quadratic probing is as follows:

```
public void insert(int hashIndex, DataElement rec)
{
    int pCount;
    int inc;

    pCount = 0;
    inc = 1;

    while(indexStatusList[hashIndex] == 1
          && (!HTable[hashIndex].equals(rec))
          && pCount < HTSize / 2)
    {
        pCount++;
        hashIndex = (hashIndex + inc ) % HTSize;
        inc = inc + 2;
    }

    if(indexStatusList[hashIndex] != 1)
    {
        HTable[hashIndex] = rec.getCopy();
        indexStatusList[hashIndex] = 1;
        length++;
    }
    else
        if(HTable[hashIndex].equals(rec))
            System.err.println("Error: No duplicates are allowed.");
        else
            System.err.println("Error: The table is full. "
                                + "Unable to resolve the collision.");
}
```

Collision Resolution: Chaining (Open Hashing)

In chaining, the hash table, *HT*, is an array of reference variables (see Figure 8-14). Therefore, for each *j*, where $0 \le j \le HTSize - 1$, $HT[j]$ is a reference to the first node of a linked list. The size of the hash table, *HTSize*, is less than or equal to the number of items.

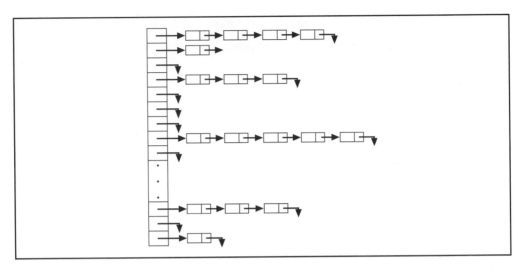

Figure 8-14 Linked hash table

Item Insertion and Collision

For each key X (in the item), we first find $h(X) = t$, where $0 \leq t \leq HTSize - 1$. The item with this key is then inserted in the linked list (which may be empty) pointed to by $HT[t]$. It then follows that for nonidentical keys X_1 and X_2, if $h(X_1) = h(X_2)$, the items with keys X_1 and X_2 are inserted in the same linked list and so collision is handled quickly and effectively. (A new item can be inserted at the beginning of the linked list because the data in a linked list is in no particular order.)

Search

Suppose that we want to determine whether an item R with key X is in the hash table. As usual, first we calculate $h(X)$. Suppose $h(X) = t$. Then the linked list pointed to by $HT[t]$ is searched sequentially.

Deletion

To delete an item, say R, from the hash table, first we search the hash table to find where in a linked list R exists. We then adjust the links at the appropriate locations and delete R.

Overflow

Because data is stored in linked lists, overflow is no longer a concern because memory space to store the data is allocated dynamically. Furthermore, the size of the hash table no longer needs to be greater than the number of items. If the size of the hash table is less than the number of items, some of the linked lists contain more than one item. However, with a good hash function, the average length of a linked list is still small and so the search is efficient.

Advantages of Chaining

From the construction of the hash table using chaining, we see that item insertion and deletion are straightforward. If the hash function is efficient, few keys are hashed to the same home position. Thus, on average, a linked list is short, which results in a shorter search length. If the item size is large, it saves a considerable amount of space. For example, suppose there are 1000 items and each item requires 10 words of storage. (Typically, 1 word is 4 bytes.) Further suppose that each reference, or address, requires one word of storage. We then need 1000 words for the hash table, 10000 words for the items, and 1000 words for the link in each node. Therefore, a total of 12000 words of storage space is required to implement chaining. On the other hand, if we use quadratic probing, if the hash table size is twice the number of items, we need 20000 words of storage.

Disadvantages of Chaining

If the item size is small, a considerable amount of space is wasted. For example, suppose there are 1000 items, each requiring 1 word of storage. Chaining then requires a total of 3000 words of storage. On the other hand, with quadratic probing, if the hash table size is twice the number of items, only 2000 words are required for the hash table. Also, if the table size is three times the number of items, then in quadratic probing, the keys are reasonably spread out. This results in fewer collisions and so the search is fast.

Hashing Analysis

Let

$$\alpha = \frac{\text{Number of records in the table}}{HTSize}$$

Then α is called the **load factor**.

The proofs of the following results about hashing analysis are left as exercises for you.

Linear Probing

The average number of comparisons for a successful search and an unsuccessful search are as follows:

1. Successful search

$$\frac{1}{2}\left\{1+\frac{1}{1-\alpha}\right\}$$

2. Unsuccessful search

$$\frac{1}{2}\left\{1+\frac{1}{(1-\alpha)^2}\right\}$$

Quadratic Probing

The average number of comparisons for a successful search and an unsuccessful search are as follows:

1. Successful search

$$\frac{-\log_2(1-\alpha)}{\alpha}$$

2. Unsuccessful search

$$\frac{1}{1-\alpha}$$

Chaining

The average number of comparisons for a successful search and an unsuccessful search are as follows:

1. Successful search

$$1+\frac{\alpha}{2}$$

2. Unsuccessful search

$$\alpha$$

QUICK REVIEW

1. A list is a set of elements of the same type.
2. The length of a list is the number of elements in the list.
3. A one-dimensional array is a convenient place to store and process lists.
4. The sequential search algorithm searches the list for a given item, starting with the first element in the list. It continues to compare the search item with the elements in the list until either the item is found or no more elements are left in the list with which it can be compared.
5. On average, the sequential search algorithm searches half the list.
6. For a list of length n, in a successful search, on average, a sequential search makes $\frac{n+1}{2} = O(n)$ comparisons.
7. A sequential search is not efficient for large lists.
8. A binary search is much faster than a sequential search.
9. A binary search requires the list elements to be in order—that is, sorted.
10. For a list of length 1024, to search for an item in the list, a binary search requires no more than 11 iterations of the loop, and so no more than 22 comparisons.

11. For a list of length n, in a successful search, on average, a binary search makes $2 * \log_2 n - 4 = O(\log_2 n)$ key comparisons.

12. Let L be a list of size $n > 1$. Suppose that the elements of L are sorted. If SRH(n) is the minimum number of comparisons needed, in the worst case, by using a comparison-based algorithm to determine whether an element x is in L, then SRH(n) $\geq \log_2(n + 1)$.

13. The binary search algorithm is the optimal worst-case algorithm for solving search problems by using the comparison method.

14. To construct a search algorithm of the order less than $\log_2 n$, it cannot be comparison based.

15. In hashing, the data is organized with the help of a table, called the hash table, denoted by HT. The hash table is stored in an array.

16. To determine whether a particular item with the key, say X, is in the hash table, we apply a function h, called the hash function, to the key X; that is, we compute $h(X)$, read as h of X. The function h is an arithmetic function, and $h(X)$ gives the address of the item in the hash table.

17. In hashing, because the address of an item is computed with the help of a function, it follows that the items are stored in no particular order.

18. Two keys X_1 and X_2, such that $X_1 \neq X_2$, are called synonyms if $h(X_1) = h(X_2)$.

19. Let X be a key and $h(X) = t$. If bucket t is full, we say that an overflow has occurred.

20. Let X_1 and X_2 be two nonidentical keys, that is, $X_1 \neq X_2$. If $h(X_1) = h(X_2)$, we say that a collision has occurred. If $r = 1$, that is, the bucket size is 1, an overflow and a collision occur at the same time.

21. Collision resolution techniques are classified into two categories: open addressing (also called closed hashing), and chaining (also called open hashing).

22. In open addressing, data is stored within the hash table.

23. In chaining, the data is organized in linked lists, and the hash table is an array of references to the first nodes of the linked lists.

24. In linear probing, if a collision occurs at location t, then, starting at location t, we search the array sequentially to find the next available array slot.

25. In linear probing, we assume that the array is circular so that if the lower portion of the array is full we can continue the search in the top portion of the array. If a collision occurs at location t, then starting at t, we check the array locations $t, (t + 1) \% HTSize$, $(t + 2) \% HTSize, ..., (t + j) \% HTSize$. This is called the probe sequence.

26. Linear probing causes clustering, called primary clustering.

27. In random probing, a random number generator is used to find the next available slot.

28. In rehashing, if a collision occurs with the hash function h, we use a series of hash functions.

29. In quadratic probing, if a collision occurs at position t, then starting at position t we linearly search the array at locations $(t + 1^2) \% HTSize, (t + 2^2) \% HTSize = (t + 4) \% HTSize, (t + 3^2) \% HTSize = (t + 9) \% HTSize, ..., (t + i^2) \% HTSize$. The probe sequence is: $t, (t + 1^2) \% HTSize, (t + 2^2) \% HTSize, (t + 3^2) \% HTSize, ..., (t + i^2) \% HTSize$.

30. Both random and quadratic probing eliminate primary clustering. However, if two nonidentical keys, say X_1 and X_2, are hashed to the same home position, that is, $h(X_1) = h(X_2)$, the same probe sequence is followed for both keys. This is because random probing and quadratic probing are functions of the home positions, not the original key. If the hash function causes a cluster at a particular home position, the cluster remains under these probings. This is called secondary clustering.

31. One way to solve secondary clustering is to use linear probing, wherein the increment value is a function of the key. This is called double hashing. In double hashing, if a collision occurs at $h(X)$, the probe sequence is generated by using the rule:

$$(h(X) + i * h'(X)) \% HTSize$$

where h' is the second hash function.

32. In open addressing, when an item is deleted, its position in the array cannot be marked as empty.

33. In chaining, for each key X (in the item), first we find $h(X) = t$, where $0 \leq t \leq HTSize - 1$. The item with this key is then inserted in the linked list (which may be empty) pointed to by $HT[t]$.

34. In chaining, for nonidentical keys X_1 and X_2, if $h(X_1) = h(X_2)$, the items with keys X_1 and X_2 are inserted in the same linked list.

35. In chaining, to delete an item, say R, from the hash table, first we search the hash table to find where in the linked list R exists. Then we adjust the links at the appropriate locations and delete R.

36. Let

$$\alpha = \frac{\text{Number of records in the table}}{HTSize}$$

Then α is called the **load factor**.

37. Linear probing: Average number of comparisons:

Successful search: $\frac{1}{2}\left\{1 + \frac{1}{1-\alpha}\right\}$

Unsuccessful search: $\frac{1}{2}\left\{1 + \frac{1}{(1-\alpha)^2}\right\}$

38. Quadratic probing: Average number of comparisons:

Successful search: $\frac{-\log_2(1-\alpha)}{\alpha}$

Unsuccessful search: $\frac{1}{1-\alpha}$

39. Chaining: Average number of comparisons:

Successful search: $1 + \dfrac{\alpha}{2}$

Unsuccessful search: α

EXERCISES

1. Mark the following statements as true or false.

a. A sequential search of a list assumes that the list is in ascending order.

b. A binary search of a list assumes that the list is sorted.

c. A binary search is faster on ordered lists and slower on unordered lists.

d. A binary search is faster on large lists, but a sequential search is faster on small lists.

2. Consider the following list:

```
63 45 32 98 46 57 28 100
```

Using the sequential search as described in this chapter, how many comparisons are required to find whether the following items are in the list? (Recall that by comparisons we mean item comparisons, not index comparisons.)

a. 90

b. 57

c. 63

d. 120

3. Consider the following list:

```
2 10 17 45 49 55 68 85 92 98 110
```

Using the binary search as described in this chapter, how many comparisons are required to find whether the following items are in the list? Show the values of `first`, `last`, and `middle` and the number of comparisons after each iteration of the loop.

a. 15

b. 49

c. 98

d. 99

4. Suppose that the size of the hash table is 150 and the bucket size is 5. How many buckets are in the hash table, and how many items can a bucket hold?

5. Explain how collision is resolved using linear probing.

6. Explain how collision is resolved using quadratic probing.

7. What is double hashing?

8

8. Suppose that the size of the hash table is 101 and items are inserted in the table using quadratic probing. Also, suppose that a new item is to be inserted in the table and its hash address is 30. If position 30 in the hash table is occupied and the next 4 positions given by the probe sequence are also occupied, determine where in the table the item will be inserted.

9. Suppose that the size of the hash table is 101. Further suppose that certain keys with the indices 15, 101, 116, 0, and 217 are to be inserted in this order into an initially empty hash table. Using modular arithmetic, find the indices in the hash table if:

a. Linear probing is used.

b. Quadratic probing is used.

10. Suppose that 50 keys are to be inserted into an initially empty hash table using quadratic probing. What should be the size of the hash table to guarantee that all the collisions are resolved?

11. Suppose that an item is to be removed from a hash table that was implemented using linear or quadratic probing. Why wouldn't you mark the position of the item to be deleted as empty?

12. What are the advantages of open hashing?

13. Give a numerical example to show that collision resolution by quadratic probing is better than chaining.

14. Give a numerical example to show that collision resolution by chaining is better that quadratic probing.

15. Suppose that the size of the hash table is 1001 and the table has 850 items. What is the load factor?

16. Suppose that the size of the hash table is 1001 and the table has 500 items. On average, in a successful search, how many comparisons are made to determine whether an item is in the list if:

a. Linear probing is used.

b. Quadratic probing is used.

c. Chaining is used.

17. Suppose that 550 items are to be stored in a hash table. If, on average, in a successful search, three key comparisons are needed to determine whether an item is in the table, what would be the size of the hash table if:

a. Linear probing is used.

b. Chaining is used.

PROGRAMMING EXERCISES

1. **(Recursive sequential search)** The sequential search algorithm given in this chapter is nonrecursive. Write and implement a recursive version of the sequential search algorithm. Moreover, write a program to test your algorithm.

2. **(Recursive binary search)** The binary search algorithm given in this chapter is nonrecursive. Write and implement a recursive version of the binary search algorithm. Also, write a version of the binary search algorithm that can be applied to sorted lists. Add this operation to the **class OrderedArrayList** for array-based lists. Moreover, write a program to test your algorithm.

3. Write the definition of the method **seqSearch** for the **class OrderedArrayList** to implement a version of the sequential search algorithm for ordered lists. Also, write a program to test it.

4. Write a program to find the number of comparisons using **binarySearch** and the sequential search algorithm as follows:

   Suppose **list** is an array of **1000** elements.

   a. Use a random number generator to fill **list**.

   b. Use any sorting algorithm to sort **list**. Alternatively, you can use the method **insert** to initially insert all the elements in the list.

   c. Search **list** for some items as follows:

   i. Use the binary search algorithm to search the list. (You may need to modify the algorithm given in this chapter to count the number of comparisons.)

   ii. Use the binary search algorithm to search the list, switching to a sequential search when the size of the search list reduces to less than 15. (Use the sequential search algorithm for a sorted list.)

   d. Print the number of comparisons for Steps c.i and c.ii. If the item is found in the list, then print its position.

5. Write a program to test the method **insert** that inserts an item into an array-based ordered list.

6. Write the definition of the method **remove**, of the **class OrderedArrayList**, to remove an item from an array-based ordered list. Also, write a program to test this method.

7. Write the definitions of the methods **search**, **isItemAtEqual**, **retrieve**, **remove**, and **print**, and the constructor for the **class HashTableClass**, as described in the section "Hashing: Implementation Using Quadratic Probing" of this chapter. Also, write a program to test various hashing operations.

8. a. Some of the attributes of a state in the United States are its name, capital, area, year of admission to the union, and the order of admission to the union. Design the **class StateData** to keep track of the information for a state. Your class must include appropriate methods to manipulate the state's data, such as the methods **setStateInfo**, **getStateName**, and so on.

b. Use the **class HashTableClass** as described in the section "Hashing: Implementation Using Quadratic Probing," which uses quadratic probing to resolve collision, to create a hash table to keep track of each state's information. Use the state's name as the key to determine the hash address. You may assume that a state's name is a string of no more than 15 characters.

Test your program by searching for and removing certain states from the hash table.

You may use the following method to determine the hash address of an item:

```
int hashFunc(String name)
{
    int i, k, sum;
    int len;

    i = 0;
    sum = 0;

    len = name.length();

    for(k = 0; k < 15 - len; k++)
        name = name + ' ';   //increase the length of the name
                             //to 15 characters

    for(k = 0; k < 5; k++)
    {
        sum = sum + (int)(name.charAt(i)) * 128 * 128
                  + (int)(name.charAt(i + 1)) * 128
                  + (int)(name.charAt(i + 2));
        i = i + 3;
    }

    return sum % HTSize;
}
```

SORTING ALGORITHMS

> **In this chapter, you will:**
> ♦ Learn the various sorting algorithms
> ♦ Explore how to implement the selection, insertion, quick, merge, and heap sorting algorithms
> ♦ Discover how the sorting algorithms discussed in this chapter perform
> ♦ Learn how priority queues are implemented

Chapter 8 discussed the search algorithms on lists. A sequential search does not assume that the data is in any particular order; however, as noted, this search does not work efficiently for large lists. By contrast, a binary search is very fast for array-based lists, but requires that the data be in order. Because a binary search requires the data to be in order and its performance is good for array-based lists, this chapter focuses on sorting algorithms.

SORTING ALGORITHMS

There are several sorting algorithms in the literature; in this chapter, we discuss some of the commonly used ones. To compare the performance of these algorithms, we also provide some analysis of these algorithms. These sorting algorithms can be applied to either array-based lists or linked lists. We will specify whether the algorithm being developed is for array-based lists or linked lists.

The methods implementing these sorting algorithms are included as `public` members of the related class. (For example, for an array-based list, these are the members of the `class OrderedArrayList`.) By doing so, the algorithms have direct access to the list elements.

Suppose that the sorting algorithm selection sort (described in the next section) is to be applied to array-based lists. The following statements show how to include a selection sort as a member of the `class OrderedArrayList`:

```
public class OrderedArrayList  extends ArrayListClass
{
    public void selectionSort()
    {
        //statements
    }
    ...
}
```

 For simplicity and ease of understanding, whenever we draw figures to illustrate a particular algorithm, for array-based lists we show that the data is stored in the array, and for linked lists the data is stored in the node. When we write a Java method to implement a particular algorithm, we use the fact that for array-based lists, an array component is a reference to the object storing the data. Similarly, for linked lists the info of a node is also a reference to the object storing the data.

SELECTION SORT: ARRAY-BASED LISTS

The selection sort algorithm sorts a list by selecting the smallest element in the (unsorted portion of the) list, and then moving this smallest element to the top of the (unsorted) list. The first time we locate the smallest item in the entire list, the second time we locate the smallest item in the list starting from the second element in the list, and so on. The selection sort algorithm described here is designed for array-based lists.

For example, suppose that you have the list as shown in Figure 9-1.

	[0]	[1]	[2]	[3]	[4]	[5]	[6]	[7]	[8]	[9]
list	16	30	24	7	25	62	45	5	65	50

Figure 9-1   List of 10 elements

Initially, the entire list is unsorted. So we find the smallest item in the list, which is at position 7, as shown in Figure 9-2.

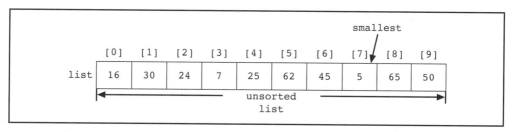

Figure 9-2   Smallest element of the unsorted list

Because this is the smallest item, it must be moved to position 0. We therefore swap 16 (that is, list[0]) with 5 (that is, list[7]), as shown in Figure 9-3.

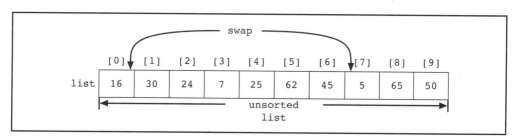

Figure 9-3   Swap elements list[0] and list[7]

After swapping these elements, Figure 9-4 shows the resulting list.

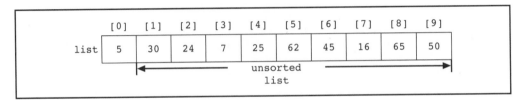

Figure 9-4 List after swapping `list[0]` and `list[7]`

Now the unsorted list is `list[1]...list[9]`. Next, we find the smallest element in the unsorted portion of the list. The smallest element is at position 3, as shown in Figure 9-5.

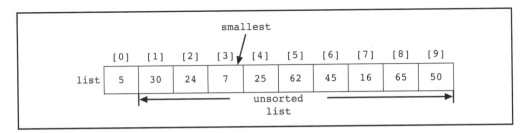

Figure 9-5 Smallest element in the unsorted portion of `list`

Because the smallest element in the unsorted list is at position 3, it must be moved to position 1. That is, we swap 7 (`list[3]`) with 30 (`list[1]`), as shown in Figure 9-6.

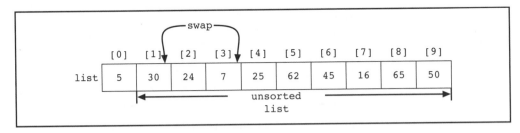

Figure 9-6 Swap `list[1]` with `list[3]`

After swapping `list[1]` with `list[3]`, Figure 9-7 shows the resulting list.

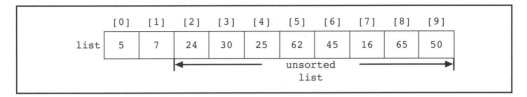

Figure 9-7   `list` after swapping `list[1]` with `list[3]`

Now the unsorted list is `list[2]...list[9]`. We repeat this process of finding the (position of the) smallest element in the unsorted portion of the list and moving it to the beginning of the unsorted portion of the list. The selection sort algorithm thus involves the following steps. In the unsorted portion of the list:

    a. Find the location of the smallest element.

    b. Move the smallest element to the beginning of the unsorted list.

Initially, the entire list, `list[0]...list[length - 1]`, is unsorted. After executing Steps a and b once, the unsorted list is `list[1]...list[length - 1]`. After executing Steps a and b a second time, the unsorted list is `list[2]...list[length - 1]`, and so on. We can keep track of the unsorted portion of the list and repeat Steps a and b with the help of a **for** loop as follows:

```
for(index = 0; index < length - 1; index++)
{
    a. Find the location, smallestIndex, of the smallest element in
       list[index]...list[length - 1].
    b. Swap the smallest element with list[index]. That is, swap
       list[smallestIndex] with list[index].
}
```

The first time through the loop, we locate the smallest element in `list[0]...list[length - 1]` and swap this smallest element with `list[0]`. The second time through the loop, we locate the smallest element in `list[1]...list[length - 1]` and swap this smallest element with `list[1]`, and so on. This process continues until the length of the unsorted list is 1. (Note that a list of length 1 is sorted.) It therefore follows that to implement the selection sort algorithm, we need to implement Steps a and b.

Given the starting index, **first**, and the ending index, **last**, of the list, the following Java method returns the index of the smallest element in `list[first]...list[last]`.

```
private int minLocation(int first, int last)
{
    int loc, minIndex;

    minIndex = first;
```

```
for(loc = first + 1; loc <= last; loc++)
    if(list[loc].compareTo(list[minIndex]) < 0)
        minIndex = loc;

    return minIndex;
}//end minLocation
```

Given the locations in the list of the elements to be swapped, the following Java method, **swap**, swaps those elements:

```
private void swap(int first, int second)
{
    DataElement temp;

    temp = list[first];
    list[first] = list[second];
    list[second] = temp;
}//end swap
```

We can now complete the definition of the method **selectionSort**.

```
public void selectionSort()
{
    int loc, minIndex;

    for(loc = 0; loc < length; loc++)
    {
        minIndex = minLocation(loc, length - 1);
        swap(loc, minIndex);
    }
}//end selectionSort
```

You can write the definition of the **class OrderedArrayList** to implement the selection sort algorithm as follows:

```
public class OrderedArrayList extends ArrayListClass
{
    //Place the definitions of the constructors here.

    //Place the definition of the method selectionSort as
    //described above.
    //Place the definition of the method swap as described
    //above.
    //Place the definition of the method minLocation as
    //described above.

    //Place the definitions of the methods seqSearch, insert,
    //binarySearch, and remove as described in Chapter 8
    //here.
}
```

Example 9-1

The following program tests the selection sort algorithm.

```java
import java.io.*;
import java.util.*;

public class SelectionSortProgram
{
    static BufferedReader keyboard =
            new BufferedReader(new InputStreamReader(System.in));

    public static void main(String[] args) throws IOException
    {
        OrderedArrayList list = new OrderedArrayList();   //Line 1
        IntElement num = new IntElement();                //Line 2

        StringTokenizer tokenizer;                        //Line 3

        System.out.println("Line 4: Enter integers, on "
            + "the same line, ending with -999");         //Line 4

        tokenizer =
            new StringTokenizer(keyboard.readLine());     //Line 5

        num.setNum
                (Integer.parseInt(tokenizer.nextToken())); //Line 6

        while(num.getNum() != -999)                       //Line 7
        {
            list.insertEnd(num);                          //Line 8
            num.setNum
                (Integer.parseInt(tokenizer.nextToken())); //Line 9
        }

        System.out.print("Line 10: The list before "
                        + "sorting: ");                   //Line 10
        list.print();                                     //Line 11
        System.out.println();                             //Line 12

        list.selectionSort();                             //Line 13

        System.out.print("Line 14: The list after "
                        + "sorting: ");                   //Line 14
        list.print();                                     //Line 15
        System.out.println();                             //Line 16
    }
}
```

Sample Run: In this sample run, the user input is shaded.

```
Line 4: Enter integers, on the same line, ending with -999
34 67 23 12 78 56 36 79 5 32 66 -999
Line 10: The list before sorting: 34 67 23 12 78 56 36 79 5 32 66

Line 14: The list after sorting: 5 12 23 32 34 36 56 66 67 78 79
```

For the most part, the preceding output is self-explanatory. Notice that the statement in Line 8 calls the method `insertEnd` of the `class ArrayListClass`, which is the superclass of the `class OrderedArrayList`. Similarly, the statements in Lines 11 and 15 call the method `print` of the `class ArrayListClass`. The statement in Line 13 calls the method `selectionSort` of the `class OrderedArrayList` to sort the list.

1. A selection sort can also be implemented by selecting the largest element in the (unsorted portion of the) list and moving it to the bottom of the list. You can easily implement this form of selection sort by altering the `if` statement in the method `minLocation`, and passing the appropriate parameters to the corresponding method and the method `swap`, when these methods are called in the method `selectionSort`.

2. A selection sort can also be applied to linked lists. The general algorithm is the same, and the details are left as an exercise for you. See Programming Exercise 1 at the end of this chapter.

Analysis: Selection Sort

In the case of search algorithms (Chapter 8), our only concern was with the number of key (item) comparisons. A sorting algorithm makes key comparisons and also moves the data. Therefore, in analyzing a sorting algorithm, we look at the number of key comparisons as well as the number of data movements. Let us look at the performance of a selection sort.

Suppose that the length of the list is n. The method `swap` does three item assignments and is executed $n - 1$ times. Hence, the number of item assignments is $3(n - 1)$.

The key comparisons are made by the method `minLocation`. For a list of length k, the method `minLocation` makes $k - 1$ key comparisons. Also, the method `minLocation` is executed $n - 1$ times (by the method `selectionSort`). The first time, the method `minLocation` finds the index of the smallest key item in the entire list and therefore makes $n - 1$ comparisons. The second time, the method `minLocation` finds the index of the smallest element in the sublist of length $n - 1$ and so makes $n - 2$ comparisons, and so on. Hence, the number of key comparisons is as follows:

$$
\begin{aligned}
(n-1)+(n-2)+\ldots+2+1 &= \frac{n(n-1)}{2} \\
&= \frac{1}{2}n^2 - \frac{1}{2}n \\
&= \frac{1}{2}n^2 + O(n) \\
&= O(n^2)
\end{aligned}
$$

It thus follows that if $n = 1000$, the number of key comparisons that the selection sort algorithm makes is $\frac{1}{2}(1000)^2 - \frac{1}{2}(1000) = 499500 \approx 500000$.

INSERTION SORT: ARRAY-BASED LISTS

The previous section described and analyzed the selection sort algorithm. It was shown that if $n = 1000$, the number of key comparisons is approximately 500,000, which is quite high. This section describes the sorting algorithm called the insertion sort, which tries to improve—that is, reduce—the number of key comparisons.

The insertion sort algorithm sorts the list by moving each element to its proper place. Consider the list given in Figure 9-8.

	[0]	[1]	[2]	[3]	[4]	[5]	[6]	[7]
list	10	18	25	30	23	17	45	35

Figure 9-8   `list`

The length of the list is 8. In this list, the elements `list[0]`, `list[1]`, `list[2]`, and `list[3]` are in order. That is, `list[0]...list[3]` is sorted (see Figure 9-9).

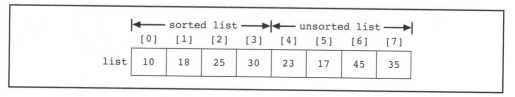

Figure 9-9   Sorted and unsorted portion of `list`

Next, we consider the element `list[4]`, the first element of the unsorted list. Because `list[4] < list[3]`, we need to move the element `list[4]` to its proper location. It thus follows that element `list[4]` should be moved to `list[2]` (see Figure 9-10).

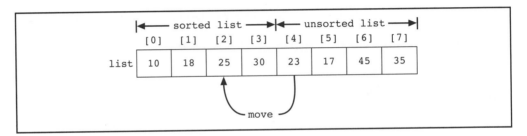

Figure 9-10 Move list[4] into list[2]

To move list[4] into list[2], first we copy list[4] into temp, a temporary memory space (see Figure 9-11).

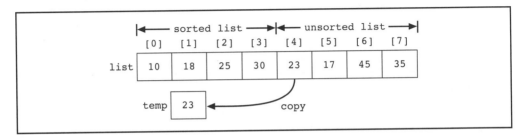

Figure 9-11 Copy list[4] into temp

Next, we copy list[3] into list[4], and then list[2] into list[3] (see Figure 9-12).

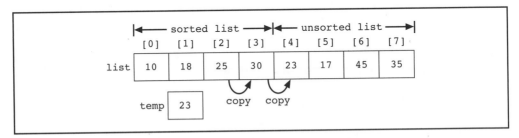

Figure 9-12 List before copying list[3] into list[4] and then list[2] into list[3]

After copying list[3] into list[4] and list[2] into list[3], the list is as shown in Figure 9-13.

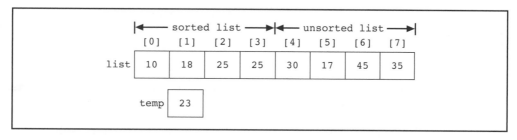

Figure 9-13   List after copying `list[3]` into `list[4]` and then `list[2]` into `list[3]`

We now copy `temp` into `list[2]`. Figure 9-14 shows the resulting list.

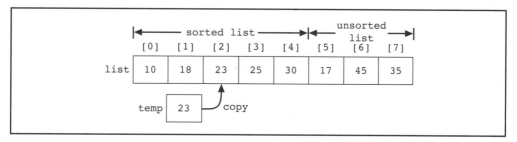

Figure 9-14   List after copying `temp` into `list[2]`

Now `list[0]...list[4]` is sorted and `list[5]...list[7]` is unsorted. We repeat this process on the resulting list by moving the first element of the unsorted list into the sorted list in the proper place.

From this discussion, we see that during the sorting phase the array containing the list is divided into two sublists, upper and lower. Elements in the upper sublist are sorted; elements in the lower sublist are to be moved to the upper sublist in their proper places one at a time. We use an index—say, `firstOutOfOrder`—to point to the first element in the lower sublist; that is, `firstOutOfOrder` gives the index of the first element in the unsorted portion of the array. Initially, `firstOutOfOrder` is initialized to `1`.

This discussion translates into the following pseudo algorithm:

```
for(firstOutOfOrder = 1; firstOutOfOrder < length;
                        firstOutOfOrder++)
  if(list[firstOutOfOrder] is less than list[firstOutOfOrder - 1])
  {
     copy list[firstOutOfOrder] into temp
```

```
initialize location to firstOutOfOrder

do
{
    a. move list[location - 1] one array slot down
    b. decrement location by 1 to consider the next element
       of the sorted portion of the array
}
while(location > 0 && the element in the upper sublist at
                     location - 1 is greater than temp)
}
copy temp into list[location]
```

Let us trace the execution of this algorithm on the list given in Figure 9-15.

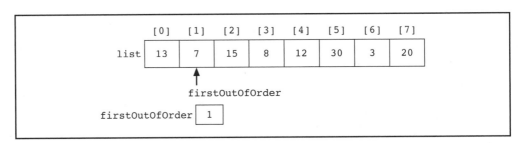

Figure 9-15   Unsorted list

The length of this list is 8; that is, `length = 8`. We initialize `firstOutOfOrder` to 1 (see Figure 9-16).

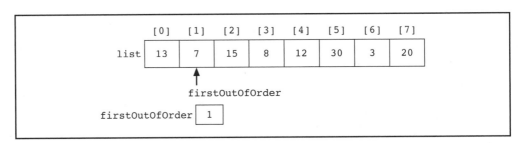

Figure 9-16   `firstOutOfOrder = 1`

Now `list[firstOutOfOrder] = 7`, `list[firstOutOfOrder - 1] = 13` and 7 < 13, and the expression in the `if` statement evaluates to `true`, so we execute the body of the `if` statement.

```
temp = list[firstOutOfOrder] = 7
location = firstOutOfOrder = 1
```

Next, we execute the **do...while** loop.

```
list[1] = list[0] = 13       (copy list[0] into list[1])
location = 0                 (decrement location)
```

The do...while loop terminates because `location = 0`. We copy `temp` into `list[location]`—that is, into `list[0]`.

Figure 9-17 shows the resulting list.

	[0]	[1]	[2]	[3]	[4]	[5]	[6]	[7]
list	7	13	15	8	12	30	3	20

Figure 9-17 List after the first iteration of the insertion sort algorithm

Now suppose that we have the list given in Figure 9-18.

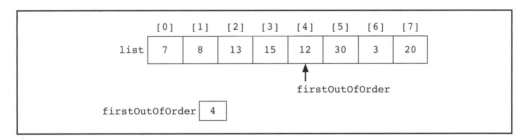

	[0]	[1]	[2]	[3]	[4]	[5]	[6]	[7]
list	7	8	13	15	12	30	3	20

firstOutOfOrder

firstOutOfOrder | 4

Figure 9-18 First out-of-order element is at position 4

Here `list[0]...list[3]`, or the elements `list[0]`, `list[1]`, `list[2]`, and `list[3]` are in order. Now `firstOutOfOrder = 4`. Because `list[4] < list[3]`, the element `list[4]`, which is 12, needs to be moved to its proper location.

As before,

```
temp = list[firstOutOfOrder] = 12
location = firstOutOfOrder   = 4
```

First, we copy `list[3]` into `list[4]` and decrement `location` by 1. Then we copy `list[2]` into `list[3]` and again decrement `location` by 1. Now the value of `location` is 2. At this point, the list is as shown in Figure 9-19.

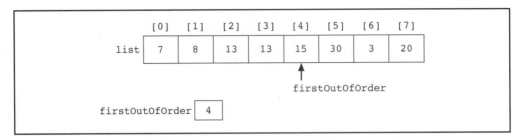

Figure 9-19 List after copying list[3] into list[4] and then list[2] into list[3]

Because list[1] < temp, the do...while loop terminates. Because at this point location is 2, we copy temp into list[2]. That is:

list[2] = temp = 12

Figure 9-20 shows the resulting list.

	[0]	[1]	[2]	[3]	[4]	[5]	[6]	[7]
list	7	8	12	13	15	30	3	20

Figure 9-20 List after copying temp into list[2]

We can repeat this process for the remaining elements of list to sort list.

The following Java method implements the previous algorithm:

```java
public void insertionSort()
{
  int unsortedIndex, location;
  DataElement temp;


  for(unsortedIndex = 1; unsortedIndex < length; unsortedIndex++)
    if(list[unsortedIndex].compareTo(list[unsortedIndex - 1]) < 0)
    {
      temp = list[unsortedIndex];
      location = unsortedIndex;

      do
      {
        list[location] = list[location - 1];
        location--;
```

```
        }while(location > 0 &&
              list[location - 1].compareTo(temp) > 0);

        list[location] = temp;
    }
}//end insertionSort
```

We leave it as an exercise for you to write a program to test the insertion sort algorithm. See Programming Exercise 2 at the end of this chapter.

INSERTION SORT: LINKED LIST-BASED LISTS

The insertion sort algorithm can also be applied to linked lists. Therefore, this section describes the insertion sort algorithm for linked lists. Consider the linked list shown in Figure 9-21.

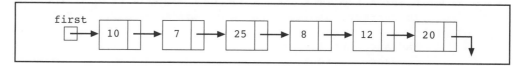

Figure 9-21 Linked list

In Figure 9-21, `first` points to the first node of the linked list.

If the list is stored in an array, we can traverse the list in either direction using an index variable. However, if the list is stored in a linked list, we can traverse the list in only one direction starting at the first node because the links are in only one direction, as shown in Figure 9-21. Therefore, in the case of a linked list, to find the location of the node to be inserted, we do the following. Suppose that `firstOutOfOrder` points to the node that is to be moved to its proper location, and `lastInOrder` points to the last node of the sorted portion of the list. For example, see the linked list in Figure 9-22.

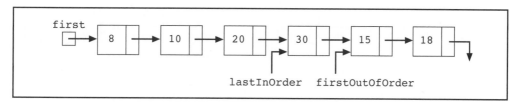

Figure 9-22 Linked list and reference variables `lastInOrder` and `firstOutOfOrder`

First, we compare the `info` of `firstOutOfOrder` with the `info` of the first node. If the `info` of `firstOutOfOrder` is smaller than the `info` of `first`, then the node `firstOutOfOrder` is to be moved before the first node of the list; otherwise, we search the list starting at the second node to find the location where to move `firstOutOfOrder`. As usual, we search the list using two reference variables, say `current` and `trailCurrent`. The reference variable `trailCurrent` points to the node just before `current`. In this case, the node `firstOutOfOrder` is to be moved between `trailCurrent` and `current`. Of course, we also handle any special cases such as an empty list, a list with only one node, or a list in which the node `firstOutOfOrder` is already in the proper place.

This discussion translates into the following algorithm:

```
if(firstOutOfOrder.info is less than first.info)
   move firstOutOfOrder before first
else
{
   set trailCurrent to first
   set current to the second node in the list

     //search the list
   while(current.info is less than firstOutOfOrder.info)
   {
       advance trailCurrent;
       advance current;
   }

   if(current is not equal to firstOutOfOrder)
   {    //insert firstOutOfOrder between current and trailCurrent
      lastInOrder.link = firstOutOfOrder.link;
      firstOutOfOrder.link = current;
      trailCurrent.link = firstOutOfOrder;
   }
   else          //firstOutOfOrder is already at the proper place
      lastInOrder = lastInOrder.link;
}
```

Let us illustrate this algorithm on the list shown in Figure 9-23. We consider several cases.

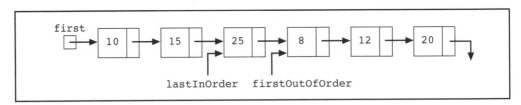

Figure 9-23 Linked list and reference variables `lastInOrder` and `firstOutOfOrder`

Case 1: Because `firstOutOfOrder.info` is less than `first.info`, the node `firstOutOfOrder` is to be moved before `first`. So we adjust the necessary links, and Figure 9-24 shows the resulting list.

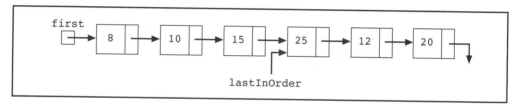

Figure 9-24   Linked list after moving the node with info 8 to the beginning

Case 2: Consider the list shown in Figure 9-25.

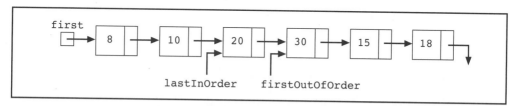

Figure 9-25   Linked list and reference variables lastInOrder and firstOutOfOrder

Because firstOutOfOrder.info is greater than first.info, we search the list to find the place where firstOutOfOrder is to be moved. As previously explained, we use trailCurrent and current to traverse the list. For this list, trailCurrent and current end up at the nodes as shown in Figure 9-26.

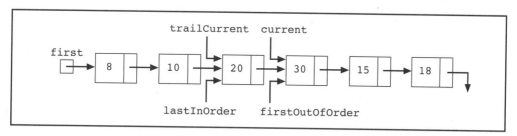

Figure 9-26   Linked list and reference variables trailCurrent and current

Because current is the same as firstOutOfOrder, the node firstOutOfOrder is in the right place. So no adjustment of the links is necessary.

Case 3: Consider the list in Figure 9-27.

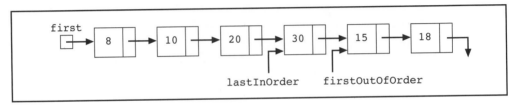

Figure 9-27 Linked list and reference variables `lastInOrder` and `firstOutOfOrder`

Because `firstOutOfOrder.info` is greater than `first.info`, we search the list to find the place where `firstOutOfOrder` is to be moved. As in Case 2, we use `trailCurrent` and `current` to traverse the list. For this list, `trailCurrent` and `current` end up at the nodes as shown in Figure 9-28.

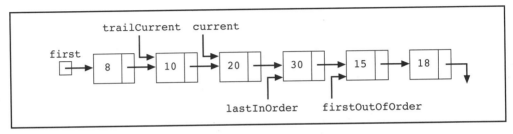

Figure 9-28 Linked list and reference variables `trailCurrent` and `current`

Now, `firstOutOfOrder` is to be moved between `trailCurrent` and `current`. So we adjust the necessary links and obtain the list as shown in Figure 9-29.

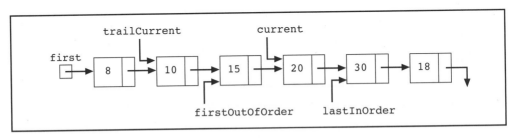

Figure 9-29 Linked list after moving `firstOutOfOrder` between `trailCurrent` and `current`

We now write the Java method, `linkedInsertionSort`, to implement the previous algorithm.

```java
public void linkedInsertionSort()
{
    LinkedListNode lastInOrder;
    LinkedListNode firstOutOfOrder;
    LinkedListNode current;
    LinkedListNode trailCurrent;

    lastInOrder = first;

    if(first == null)
        System.out.println("Cannot sort an empty list.");
    else
        if(first.link == null)
            System.out.println("The list is of length 1. "
                               + "Already in order.");
        else
            while(lastInOrder.link != null)
            {
                firstOutOfOrder = lastInOrder.link;

                if(firstOutOfOrder.info.compareTo(first.info) < 0)
                {
                    lastInOrder.link = firstOutOfOrder.link;
                    firstOutOfOrder.link = first;
                    first = firstOutOfOrder;
                }
                else
                {
                    trailCurrent = first;
                    current = first.link;
                    while(current.info.compareTo
                                      (firstOutOfOrder.info) < 0)
                    {
                        trailCurrent = current;
                        current = current.link;
                    }

                    if(current != firstOutOfOrder)
                    {
                        lastInOrder.link = firstOutOfOrder.link;
                        firstOutOfOrder.link = current;
                        trailCurrent.link = firstOutOfOrder;
                    }
                    else
                        lastInOrder = lastInOrder.link;
                }
            }
}//end linkedInsertionSort
```

9

We leave it as an exercise for you to write a program to test the insertion sort algorithm for linked lists. See Programming Exercise 3 at the end of this chapter.

Analysis: Insertion Sort

It can be shown that the average number of key comparisons and the average number of item assignments in an insertion sort algorithm are:

$$\frac{1}{4}n^2 + O(n) = O(n^2)$$

Table 9-1 summarizes the behavior of the selection and insertion sort algorithms.

Table 9-1   Average Case Behavior of the Selection and Insertion Sort Algorithms for a List of Length n

Algorithm	Number of Comparisons	Number of Swaps
Selection sort	$\dfrac{n(n-1)}{2} = O(n^2)$	$3(n-1) = O(n)$
Insertion sort	$\dfrac{1}{4}n^2 + O(n) = O(n^2)$	$\dfrac{1}{4}n^2 + O(n) = O(n^2)$

LOWER BOUND ON COMPARISON-BASED SORT ALGORITHMS

The previous sections discussed the selection and insertion sort algorithms, and noted that the average-case behavior of these algorithms is $O(n^2)$. Both of these algorithms are comparison-based algorithms; that is, the lists are sorted by comparing their respective keys. Before discussing any additional sorting algorithms, let us discuss the best-case scenario for the comparison-based sorting algorithms.

We can trace the execution of a comparison-based algorithm by using a graph called a **comparison tree**. Let L be a list of n distinct elements, where $n > 0$. For any j and k, where $1 \le j, k \le n$, either $L[j] < L[k]$ or $L[j] > L[k]$. Because each comparison of the keys has two outcomes, the comparison tree is a binary tree. While drawing this figure, we draw each comparison as a circle, called a **node**. The node is labeled as $j{:}k$, representing the comparison of $L[j]$ with $L[k]$. If $L[j] < L[k]$, follow the left branch; otherwise, follow the right branch. Figure 9-30 shows the comparison tree for a list of length 3. (In Figure 9-30, the rectangle, called a **leaf**, represents the final ordering of the nodes.)

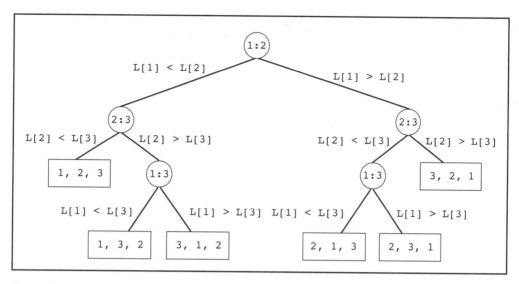

Figure 9-30 Comparison tree for sorting three items

We call the top node in the figure the **root** node. The straight line that connects two nodes is called a **branch**. A sequence of branches from a node, x, to another node, y, is called a **path** from x to y.

Associated with each path from the root to a leaf is a unique permutation of the elements of L. This uniqueness follows because the sort algorithm only moves the data and makes comparisons. Furthermore, the data movement on any path from the root to a leaf is the same regardless of the initial inputs. For a list of n elements, $n > 0$, there are $n!$ different permutations. Any one of these $n!$ permutations might be the correct ordering of L. Thus, the comparison tree must have at least $n!$ leaves.

Let us consider the worst case for all comparison-based sorting algorithms. We state the following result without proof.

Theorem: Let L be a list of n distinct elements. Any sorting algorithm that sorts L by comparison of the keys only, in its worst case, makes at least $O(n * \log_2 n)$ key comparisons.

As analyzed in the previous sections, both the selection and insertion sort algorithms are of the order $O(n^2)$. The remainder of this chapter discusses sorting algorithms that, on average, are of the order $O(n * \log_2 n)$.

QUICK SORT: ARRAY-BASED LISTS

The previous section noted that the lower bound on comparison-based algorithms is $O(n * \log_2 n)$. Both the selection sort and insertion sort algorithms discussed earlier in this chapter are $O(n^2)$. This and the next two sections discuss sorting algorithms that are of the order $O(n * \log_2 n)$. The first algorithm is the quick sort algorithm.

The quick sort algorithm uses the divide-and-conquer technique to sort a list. The list is partitioned into two sublists, and the two sublists are then sorted and combined into one list in such a way that the combined list is sorted. Thus, the general algorithm is:

```
if(the list size is greater than 1)
{
a.    Partition the list into two sublists, say lowerSublist and
      upperSublist.
b.    Quick sort lowerSublist.
c.    Quick sort upperSublist.
d.    Combine the sorted lowerSublist and sorted upperSublist.
}
```

After partitioning the list into two sublists—lowerSublist and upperSublist— these two sublists are sorted using the quick sort algorithm. In other words, we use *recursion* to implement the quick sort algorithm.

The quick sort algorithm described here is for array-based lists. The algorithm for linked lists can be developed in a similar manner and is left as an exercise for you.

In the quick sort algorithm, the list is partitioned in such way that combining the sorted lowerSublist and upperSublist is trivial. Therefore, in a quick sort, all the sorting work is done in partitioning the list. Because all the sorting work occurs during the partitioning of the list, we first describe the partition procedure in detail.

To partition the list into two sublists, first we choose an element of the list called **pivot**. The pivot is used to divide the list into two sublists: lowerSublist and upperSublist. The elements in lowerSublist are smaller than **pivot**; the elements in upperSublist are greater than **pivot**. For example, consider the list in Figure 9-31.

	[0]	[1]	[2]	[3]	[4]	[5]	[6]	[7]	[8]
list	45	82	25	94	50	60	78	32	92

Figure 9-31   list before the partition

There are several ways to determine **pivot**. However, **pivot** is chosen so that, it is hoped, lowerSublist and upperSublist are of nearly equal size. For illustration purposes, let us choose the middle element of the list as **pivot**. The partition procedure that we describe here partitions this list using **pivot** as the middle element, in our case 50, as shown in Figure 9-32.

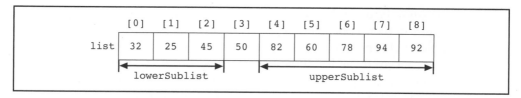

Figure 9-32 `list` after the partition

From Figure 9-32, it follows that after partitioning `list` into `lowerSublist` and `upperSublist`, `pivot` is in the right place. Thus, after sorting `lowerSublist` and `upperSublist`, combining the two sorted sublists is trivial.

The partition algorithm is as follows (we assume that `pivot` is chosen as the middle element of the list):

1. Determine `pivot`, and then swap `pivot` with the first element of the list.

   Suppose that the index `smallIndex` points to the last element that is less than `pivot`. The index `smallIndex` is initialized to the first element of the list.

2. For the remaining elements in the list (starting at the second element), if the current element is less than `pivot`:

   a. Increment `smallIndex`.

   b. Swap the current element with the array element pointed to by `smallIndex`.

3. Swap the first element, that is, `pivot`, with the array element pointed to by `smallIndex`.

Step 2 can be implemented using a `for` loop, with the loop starting at the second element of the list.

Step 1 determines `pivot` and moves it to the first array position. During the execution of Step 2, the list elements get arranged as shown in Figure 9-33. (Suppose the name of the array containing the list elements is `list`.)

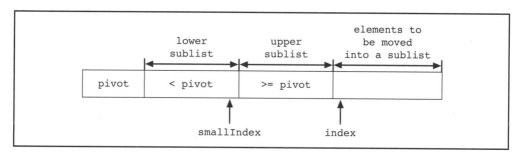

Figure 9-33   List during the execution of Step 2

As shown in Figure 9-33, `pivot` is in the first array position. Elements in the lower sublist are less than `pivot`; elements in the upper sublist are greater than or equal to `pivot`. The variable `smallIndex` contains the index of the last element of the lower sublist; the variable `index` contains the index of the next element that needs to be moved either to the lower sublist or into the upper sublist. As explained in Step 2, if the next element of the list (that is, `list[index]`) is less than `pivot`, we advance `smallIndex` to the next array position and swap `list[index]` with `list[smallIndex]`). Next, we illustrate Step 2.

Suppose that the list is as given in Figure 9-34.

[0]	[1]	[2]	[3]	[4]	[5]	[6]	[7]	[8]	[9]	[10]	[11]	[12]	[13]
32	55	87	13	78	96	52	48	22	11	58	66	88	45

Figure 9-34 List before sorting

For the list in Figure 9-34, `pivot` is at position **6**. After moving `pivot` to the first array position, the list is as shown in Figure 9-35. (Notice that in Figure 9-35, **52** is swapped with **32**.)

[0]	[1]	[2]	[3]	[4]	[5]	[6]	[7]	[8]	[9]	[10]	[11]	[12]	[13]
52	55	87	13	78	96	32	48	22	11	58	66	88	45

pivot

Figure 9-35 List after moving `pivot` to the first array position

Suppose that after executing Step 2 a few times, the list is as shown in Figure 9-36.

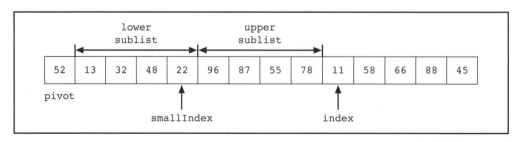

Figure 9-36 List after a few iterations of Step 2

As shown in Figure 9-36, the next element of the list that needs to be moved into a sublist is indicated by `index`. Because `list[index] < pivot`, we need to move the element `list[index]` into the lower sublist. To do so, we first advance `smallIndex` to the next array position and then swap `list[smallIndex]` with `list[index]`. The resulting list is as shown in Figure 9-37. (Notice that `11` is swapped with `96`.)

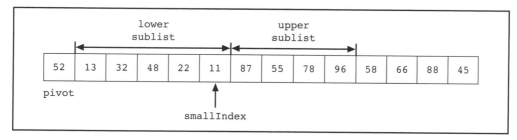

Figure 9-37   List after moving `11` into the lower sublist

Now consider the list in Figure 9-38.

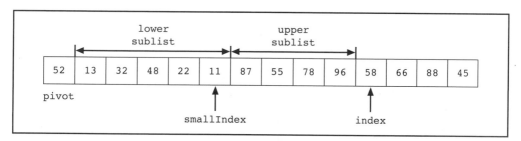

Figure 9-38   List before moving `58` into a sublist

For the list in Figure 9-38, `list[index]` is `58`, which is greater than `pivot`. Therefore, `list[index]` is to be moved into the upper sublist. This is accomplished by leaving `58` at its position and increasing the size of the upper sublist, by one, to the next array position. After moving `58` into the upper sublist, the list is shown in Figure 9-39.

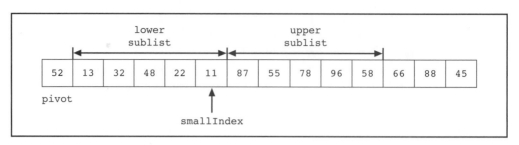

Figure 9-39 List after moving 58 into the upper sublist

After moving the elements that are less than `pivot` into the lower sublist and elements that are greater than `pivot` into the upper sublist (that is, after completely executing Step 2), Figure 9-40 shows the resulting list.

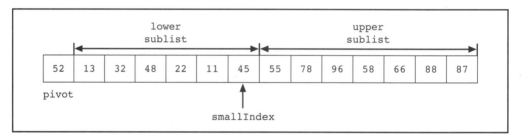

Figure 9-40 List elements after arranging into the lower sublist and upper sublist

Next, we execute Step 3 and move 52, `pivot`, to the proper position in the list. This is accomplished by swapping 52 with 45. The resulting list is as shown in Figure 9-41.

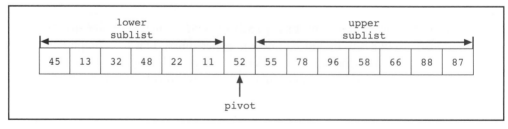

Figure 9-41 List after swapping 52 with 45

As shown in Figure 9-41, Steps 1, 2, and 3 in the preceding algorithm partition the list into two sublists. The elements less than `pivot` are in the lower sublist; the elements greater than or equal to `pivot` are in the upper sublist.

To partition the list into the lower and upper sublists, we need to keep track of only the last element of the lower sublist and the next element of the list that needs to be moved into either the lower sublist or the upper sublist. In fact, the upper sublist is between the indices `smallIndex` and `index`.

We now write the method, `partition`, to implement the preceding partition algorithm. After rearranging the elements of the list, the method returns the location of `pivot` so that we can determine the starting and ending locations of the sublists. Also, because the method `partition` is a member of the class, it has direct access to the array implementing the list. Thus, to partition a list, we need to pass only the starting and ending indices of the list:

```
private int partition(int first, int last)
{
    DataElement pivot;

    int index, smallIndex;

    swap(first, (first + last) / 2);

    pivot = list[first];
    smallIndex = first;

    for(index = first + 1; index <= last; index++)
        if(list[index].compareTo(pivot) < 0)
        {
            smallIndex++;
            swap(smallIndex, index);
        }

    swap(first, smallIndex);

    return smallIndex;
}//end partition
```

As you can see from the definition of the method `partition`, certain elements of the list need to be swapped. The following method, **swap**, accomplishes this task. (Notice that this swap method is the same as the one given earlier in this chapter for the selection sort algorithm.)

9

```
private void swap(int first, int second)
{
    DataElement temp;

    temp = list[first];
    list[first] = list[second];
    list[second] = temp;
}//end swap
```

Once the list is partitioned into `lowerSublist` and `upperSublist`, we again apply the quick sort method to sort the two sublists. Because both sublists are sorted using the same quick sort algorithm, the easiest way to implement this algorithm is to use recursion. Therefore, this section gives the recursive version of the quick sort algorithm. As explained previously, after rearranging the elements of the list, the method `partition` returns the index of `pivot` so that the starting and ending indices of the sublists can be determined.

Given the starting and ending indices of a list, the following method, `recQuickSort`, implements the recursive version of the quick sort algorithm:

```
private void recQuickSort(int first, int last)
{
    int pivotLocation;

    if(first < last)
    {
        pivotLocation = partition(first, last);
        recQuickSort(first, pivotLocation - 1);
        recQuickSort(pivotLocation + 1, last);
    }
}//end recQuickSort
```

Finally, we write the quick sort method, `quickSort`, that calls the method `recQuickSort` on the original list:

```
public void quickSort()
{
    recQuickSort(0, length - 1);
}//end quickSort
```

We leave it as an exercise for you to write a program to test the quick sort algorithm. See Programming Exercise 4 at the end of this chapter.

Analysis: Quick Sort

Table 9-2 summarizes the behavior of the quick sort algorithm for a list of length n. (The proofs of these results are beyond the scope of this book.)

Table 9-2 Analysis of the Quick Sort Algorithm for a List of Length n

	Number of Comparisons	Number of Swaps
Average case	$(1.39) * n * \log_2 n + O(n) = O(n * \log_2 n)$	$(0.69) * n * \log_2 n + O(n) = O(n * \log_2 n)$
Worst case	$\dfrac{n^2}{2} - \dfrac{n}{2} = O(n^2)$	$\dfrac{n^2}{2} + \dfrac{3n}{2} - 2 = O(n^2)$

MERGE SORT: LINKED LIST-BASED LISTS

The previous section described the quick sort algorithm and stated that the average-case behavior of a quick sort is $O(n * \log_2 n)$. However, the worst-case behavior of a quick sort is $O(n^2)$. This section describes the sorting algorithm whose behavior is always $O(n * \log_2 n)$.

Like the quick sort algorithm, the merge sort algorithm uses the divide–and–conquer technique to sort a list. A merge sort algorithm also partitions the list into two sublists, sorts the sublists, and then combines the sorted sublists into one sorted list. This section describes the merge sort algorithm for linked lists. We leave it for you to develop the merge sort algorithm for array-based lists, which can be done by using the techniques described for linked lists.

The merge sort and the quick sort algorithms differ in how they partition the list. As discussed earlier, a quick sort first selects an element in the list, called `pivot`, and then partitions the list so that the elements in one sublist are smaller than `pivot` and the elements in the other sublist are larger than `pivot`. By contrast, a merge sort chops the list into two sublists of nearly equal size. For example, consider the list whose elements are as follows:

```
list: 35   28   18   45   62   48   30   38
```

The merge sort algorithm partitions this list into two sublists as follows:

```
first sublist: 35   28   18   45
second sublist: 62   48   30   38
```

The two sublists are sorted using the same algorithm (that is, a merge sort) used on the original list. Suppose that we have sorted the sublists. That is, suppose that:

```
first sublist: 18   28   35   45
second sublist: 30   38   48   62
```

Next, the merge sort algorithm combines—that is, merges—the two sorted sublists into one sorted list.

Figure 9-42 further illustrates the merge sort process.

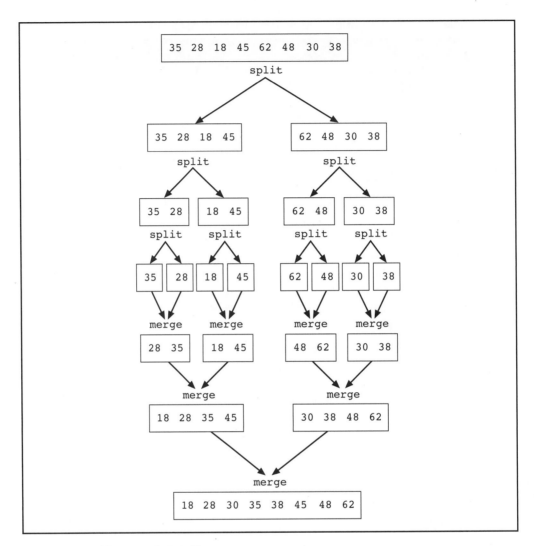

Figure 9-42 Merge sort algorithm

From Figure 9-42, it is clear that in the merge sort algorithm, most of the sorting work is done while merging the sorted sublists.

The general algorithm for the merge sort is as follows:

```
if the list is of a size greater than 1
{
    a. Divide the list into two sublists.
    b. Merge sort the first sublist.
    c. Merge sort the second sublist.
    d. Merge the first sublist and the second sublist.
}
```

As remarked previously, after dividing the list into two sublists—the first sublist and the second sublist—these two sublists are sorted using the merge sort algorithm. In other words, we use *recursion* to implement the merge sort algorithm.

We next describe the necessary algorithm to:

- Divide the list into two sublists of nearly equal size
- Merge sort both sublists
- Merge the sorted sublists

Divide

Because the data is stored in a linked list, we do not know the length of the list. Furthermore, a linked list is not a random access data structure. Therefore, to divide the list into two sublists, we need to find the middle node of the list.

Consider the list in Figure 9-43.

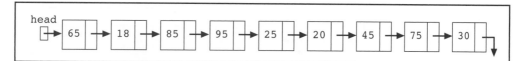

Figure 9-43 Unsorted linked list

To find the middle of the list, we traverse the list with two reference variables—say, `middle` and `current`. The reference variable `middle` is initialized to the first node of the list. Because this list has more than two nodes, we initialize `current` to the third node. (Recall that we sort the list only if it has more than one element because a list of size 1 is already sorted. Furthermore, if the list has only two nodes, we set `current` to `null`.) Consider the list shown in Figure 9-44.

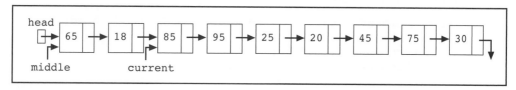

Figure 9-44 `middle` and `current` before traversing the list

Every time we advance `middle` by one node, we advance `current` by one node. After advancing `current` by one node, if `current` is not `null`, we again advance `current` by one node. That is, for the most part, every time `middle` advances by one node, `current` advances by two nodes. Eventually, `current` becomes `null` and `middle` points to the last

node of the first sublist. For example, for the list in Figure 9-44, when **current** becomes
null, **middle** points to the node with **info 25** (see Figure 9-45).

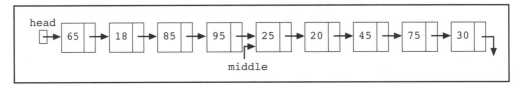

Figure 9-45   **middle** after traversing the list

It is now easy to divide the list into two sublists. First, using the link of **middle**, we assign a
reference variable to the node following **middle**. Then we set the link of **middle** to **null**.
Figure 9-46 shows the resulting sublists.

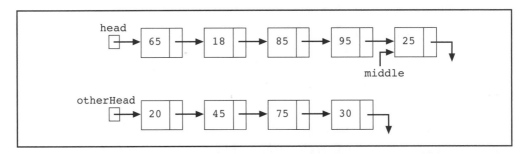

Figure 9-46   List after dividing it into two lists

This discussion translates into the following Java method, **divideList**. (Notice that the
method **divideList** divides the list that **head** points to and returns the reference of the
first node of the second sublist.)

```
private LinkedListNode divideList(LinkedListNode head)
{
    LinkedListNode middle;
    LinkedListNode current;

    LinkedListNode secondListHead;

    if(head == null)    //list is empty
        secondListHead = null;
    else
        if(head.link == null)    //list has only one node
            secondListHead = null;
        else
```

```
    {
        middle = head;
        current = head.link;

        if(current != null)  //list has more than two nodes
            current = current.link;

        while(current != null)
        {
            middle = middle.link;
            current = current.link;

            if(current != null)
                current = current.link;
        }//end while

        secondListHead = middle.link;   //secondListHead points
                                        //to the first node of the
                                        //second sublist
        middle.link = null;     //set the link of the last node
                                //of the first sublist to null
    }//end else

    return secondListHead;
}//end divideList
```

Now that we know how to divide a list into two sublists of nearly equal size, next we focus on merging the sorted sublists. Recall that, in a merge sort, most of the sorting work is done in merging the sorted sublists.

Merge

Once the sublists are sorted, the next step in the merge sort algorithm is to merge the sorted sublists. Sorted sublists are merged into a sorted list by comparing the elements of the sublists, and then adjusting the references of the nodes with the smaller **info**. Let us illustrate this procedure on the sublists shown in Figure 9-47. Suppose that **first1** points to the first node of the first sublist, and **first2** points to the first node of the second sublist.

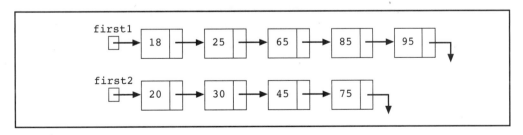

Figure 9-47   Sublists before merging

We first compare the `info` of the first node of each of the two sublists to determine the first node of the merged list. We set `newHead` to point to the first node of the merged list. We also use the reference variable, `lastSmall`, to keep track of the last node of the merged list. The reference variable of the first node of the sublist with the smaller node then advances to the next node of that sublist. Figure 9-48 shows the sublists of Figure 9-47 after setting `newHead` and `lastSmall`, and advancing `first1`.

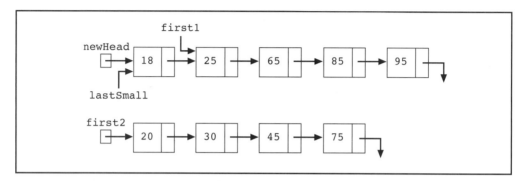

Figure 9-48   Sublists after setting `newHead` and `lastSmall` and advancing `first1`

In Figure 9-48, `first1` points to the first node of the first sublist that is yet to be merged with the second sublist. So we again compare the nodes pointed to by `first1` and `first2`, and adjust the link of the smaller node and the last node of the merged list so as to move the smaller node to the end of the merged list. For the sublists shown in Figure 9-48, after adjusting the necessary links, we have Figure 9-49.

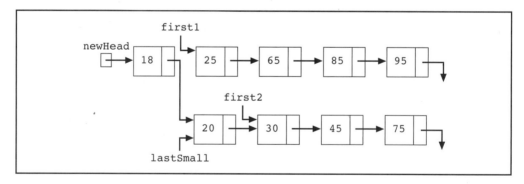

Figure 9-49   Merged list after putting the node with `info` 20 at the end of the merged list

We continue this process for the remaining elements of both sublists. Every time we move a node to the merged list, we advance either `first1` or `first2` to the next node. Eventually, either `first1` or `first2` becomes `null`. If `first1` becomes `null`, the first sublist is exhausted first, and so we attach the remaining nodes of the second sublist at the end of the partially merged list. If `first2` becomes `null`, the second sublist is exhausted first, and so we attach the remaining nodes of the first sublist at the end of the partially merged list.

Following this discussion, we can now write the Java method, `mergeList`, to merge the two sorted sublists. The references, that is, addresses, of the first nodes of the sublists are passed as parameters to the method `mergeList`.

```java
private LinkedListNode mergeList(LinkedListNode first1,
                                 LinkedListNode first2)
{
    LinkedListNode lastSmall;   //reference variable to the
                                //last node of the merged list
    LinkedListNode newHead;     //reference variable to the
                                //merged list

    if(first1 == null)          //the first sublist is empty
        return first2;
    else
        if(first2 == null)      //the second sublist is empty
            return first1;
        else
        {
            if(first1.info.compareTo(first2.info) < 0) //compare
                                                //the first nodes
            {
                newHead = first1;
                first1 = first1.link;
                lastSmall = newHead;
            }
            else
            {
                newHead = first2;
                first2 = first2.link;
                lastSmall = newHead;
            }

            while(first1 != null && first2 != null)
            {
                if(first1.info.compareTo(first2.info) < 0)
                {
                    lastSmall.link = first1;
                    lastSmall = lastSmall.link;
                    first1 = first1.link;
                }
```

9

```
            else
            {
                lastSmall.link = first2;
                lastSmall = lastSmall.link;
                first2 = first2.link;
            }
        }//end while

        if(first1 == null)  //first sublist is exhausted first
            lastSmall.link = first2;
        else                     //second sublist is exhausted first
            lastSmall.link = first1;

        return newHead;
    }
}//end mergeList
```

Finally, we write the recursive merge sort method, recMergeSort, which uses the divideList and mergeList methods to sort a list. The reference of the first node of the list to be sorted is passed as a parameter to the method recMergeSort:

```
private LinkedListNode recMergeSort(LinkedListNode head)
{
    LinkedListNode otherHead;

    if(head != null)  //if the list is not empty
        if(head.link != null)  //if the list has more
                               //than one node
        {
            otherHead = divideList(head);
            head = recMergeSort(head);
            otherHead = recMergeSort(otherHead);
            head = mergeList(head, otherHead);
        }

    return head;
}//end recMergeSort
```

We can now give the definition of the method mergeSort, which should be included as a public member of the class OrderedLinkedList. (Note that the methods divideList, mergeList, and recMergesort can be included as private members of the class OrderedLinkedList because these methods are used only to implement the method mergeSort.) The method mergeSort simply calls the method recMergeSort and passes first to this method. The definition of the method mergeSort is:

```
public void mergeSort()
{
    first = recMergeSort(first);
}//end mergeSort
```

We leave it as an exercise for you to write a program to test the merge sort algorithm. See Programming Exercise 7 at the end of this chapter.

Analysis: Merge Sort

Suppose that L is a list of n elements, where $n > 0$. Let $A(n)$ denote the number of key comparisons in the average case, and $W(n)$ denote the number of key comparisons in the worst case, to sort L. It can be shown that:

$$A(n) = n * \log_2 n - 1.26n = O(n * \log_2 n)$$

$$W(n) = n * \log_2 n - (n - 1) = O(n * \log_2 n)$$

HEAP SORT: ARRAY-BASED LISTS

In an earlier section, we described the quick sort algorithm for contiguous lists, that is, array-based lists. We remarked that, on average, the quick sort is of the order $O(n * \log_2 n)$. However, in the worst case, the quick sort is of the order $O(n^2)$. This section describes another algorithm, the **heap sort**, for array-based lists. This algorithm is of the order $O(n * \log_2 n)$ even in the worst case, therefore overcoming the worst case of the quick sort.

Definition: A **heap** is a list in which each element contains a key, such that the key in the element at position k in the list is at least as large as the key in the element at position $2k + 1$ (if it exists), and $2k + 2$ (if it exists).

Recall that in Java the array index starts at 0. Therefore, the element at position k is, in fact, the $k + 1$th element of the list.

Consider the list in Figure 9-50.

[0]	[1]	[2]	[3]	[4]	[5]	[6]	[7]	[8]	[9]	[10]	[11]	[12]
85	70	80	50	40	75	30	20	10	35	15	62	58

Figure 9-50   A list that is a heap

It can be checked that the list in Figure 9-50 is a heap.

Given a heap, we can construct a complete binary tree as follows: the root node of the tree is the first element of the list. The left child of the root is the second element of the list; the right child of the root node is the third element of the list. Thus, in general, for the node k, which is the $k + 1$th element of the list, its left child is the $2k$th (if it exists) element of the list, which is at position $2k + 1$ in the list, and the right child is the $2k + 1$st (if it exists) element of the list, which is at position $2k + 2$ in the list.

The diagram in Figure 9-51 represents the complete binary tree corresponding to the list in Figure 9-50.

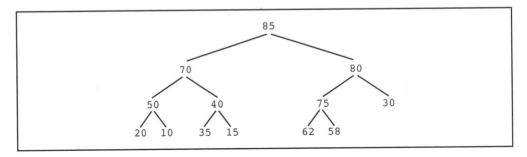

Figure 9-51 Complete binary tree corresponding to the list in Figure 9-50

Figure 9-51 shows that the list in Figure 9-50 is a heap. In fact, to demonstrate the heap sort algorithm, we will always draw the complete binary tree corresponding to a list.

We now describe the heap sort algorithm.

The first step in the heap sort algorithm is to convert the list into a heap, called `buildHeap`. After we convert the array into a heap, the sorting phase begins.

Build Heap

This section describes the build heap algorithm.

The general algorithm is as follows: suppose `length` denotes the length of the list. Let `index = length / 2 − 1`. Then `list[index]` is the last element in the list that is not a leaf; that is, this element has at least one child. Thus, the elements `list[index + 1]...list[length − 1]` are leaves.

First, we convert the subtree with the root node `list[index]` into a heap. Note that this subtree has at most three nodes. We then convert the subtree with the root node `list[index - 1]` into a heap, and so on.

To convert a subtree into a heap, we perform the following steps: suppose that `list[a]` is the root node of the subtree, and `list[b]` is the left child and `list[c]`, if it exists, is the right child of `list[a]`.

1. Compare `list[b]` with `list[c]` to determine the larger child. If `list[c]` does not exist, then `list[b]` is the larger child. Suppose that `largerIndex` indicates the larger child. (Notice that `largerIndex` is either **b** or **c**.)

2. Compare `list[a]` with `list[largerIndex]`. If `list[a] < list[largerIndex]`, then swap `list[a]` with `list[largerIndex]`; otherwise, the subtree with the root node `list[a]` is already in a heap.

3. Suppose that list[a] < list[largerIndex] and we swap the elements list[a] with list[largerIndex]. After making this swap, the subtree with the root node list[largerIndex] might not be in a heap. If this is the case, then we repeat Steps 1 and 2 at the subtree with the root node list[largerIndex], and continue this process until either the heaps in the subtrees are restored or we arrive at an empty subtree. This step is implemented using a loop, which is described when we write the algorithm.

Consider the list in Figure 9-52. Let us call this list.

	[0]	[1]	[2]	[3]	[4]	[5]	[6]	[7]	[8]	[9]	[10]
list	15	60	72	70	56	32	62	92	45	30	65

Figure 9-52   Array list

Figure 9-53 shows the complete binary tree corresponding to the list in Figure 9-52.

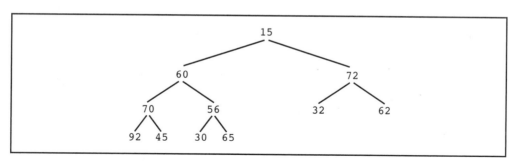

Figure 9-53   Complete binary tree corresponding to the list in Figure 9-52

To facilitate this discussion, when we say node 56 we mean the node with info 56.

This list has 11 elements and so the length of the list is 11. To convert the array into a heap, we start at the list element n/2 - 1 = 11/2 - 1 = 5 - 1 = 4, which is the fifth element of the list.

Now list[4] = 56. The children of list[4] are list[4 * 2 + 1] and list[4 * 2 + 2], that is, list[9] and list[10]. In the previous list, both list[9] and list[10] exist. To convert the tree with the root node list[4], we perform the following three steps:

1. Find the larger of list[9] and list[10], that is, the largest child of list[4]. In this case, list[10] is larger than list[9].

2. Compare the larger child with the parent node. If the larger child is larger than the parent, swap the larger child with the parent. Because `list[4]` < `list[10]`, we swap `list[4]` with `list[10]`.

3. Because `list[10]` does not have a subtree, Step 3 does not execute.

Figure 9-54 shows the resulting binary tree.

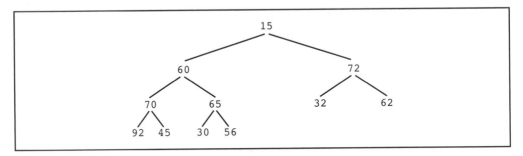

Figure 9-54 Binary tree after swapping `list[4]` with `list[10]`

Next, we consider the subtree with the root node `list[3]`, that is 70, and repeat the three steps given earlier to obtain the complete binary tree as given in Figure 9-55. (Notice that here, also, Step 3 does not execute.)

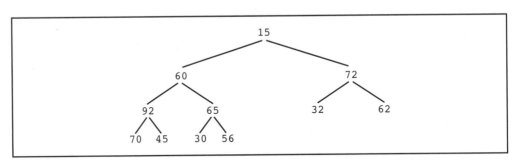

Figure 9-55 Binary tree after repeating Steps 1, 2, and 3 at the root node `list[3]`

Now we consider the subtree with the root node `list[2]`, that is, 72, and apply the three steps given earlier. Figure 9-56 shows the resulting binary tree. (Note that in this case, because the parent is larger than both children, this subtree is already in a heap.)

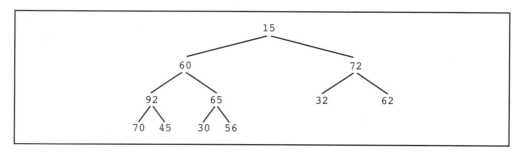

Figure 9-56   Binary tree after repeating Steps 1 and 2 at the root node list[2]

Next, we consider the subtree with the root node list[1], that is, 60. First we apply Steps 1 and 2. Because list[1] = 60 < list[3] = 92 (the larger child), we swap list[1] with list[3], to obtain the tree as given in Figure 9-57.

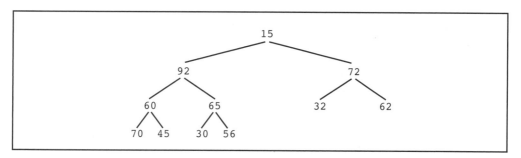

Figure 9-57   Binary tree after swapping list[1] with list[3]

However, after swapping list[1] with list[3], the subtree with the root node list[3], that is, 60, is no longer a heap. Thus, we must restore the heap in this subtree. To do this, we apply Step 3, find the larger child of 60, and swap it with 60. We then obtain the binary tree as given in Figure 9-58.

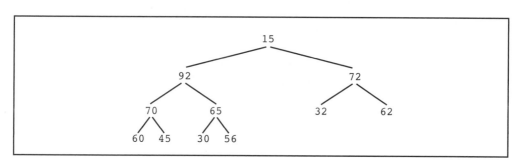

Figure 9-58   Binary tree after restoring the heap at list[3]

Once again, the subtree with the root node `list[1]`, that is, 92, is in a heap (see Figure 9-58).

Finally, we consider the tree with the root node `list[0]`, that is, 15. We repeat the previous three steps to obtain the binary tree as given in Figure 9-59.

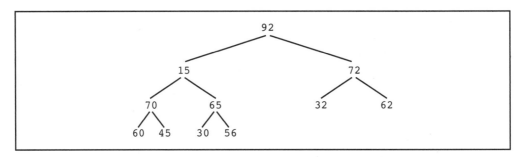

Figure 9-59   Binary tree after applying Steps 1 and 2 at `list[0]`

We see that the subtree with the root node `list[1]`, that is, 15, is no longer in a heap. So we must apply Step 3 to restore the heap in this subtree. (This requires us to repeat Steps 1 and 2 at the subtree with the root node `list[1]`.) We swap `list[1]` with the larger child, `list[3]` (that is, 70). We then get the binary tree of Figure 9-60.

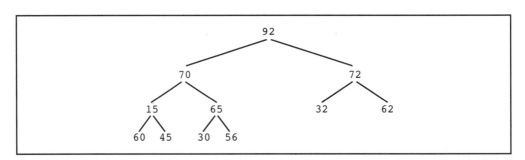

Figure 9-60   Binary tree after applying Steps 1 and 2 at `list[1]`

The subtree with the root node `list[3]` = 15 is not in a heap, and so we must restore the heap in this subtree. To do so, we apply Steps 1 and 2 at the subtree with the root node `list[3]`. We swap `list[3]` with the larger child, `list[7]` (that is, 60). Figure 9-61 shows the resulting binary tree.

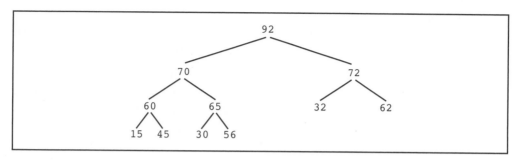

Figure 9-61   Binary tree after restoring the heap at `list[3]`

The resulting binary tree (in Figure 9-61) is in a heap, and so the list corresponding to this complete binary tree is in a heap.

Thus, in general starting at the lowest level from right to left, we look at a subtree and convert the subtree into a heap as follows: if the root node of the subtree is smaller than the larger child, we swap the root node with the larger child. After swapping the root node with the larger child, we must restore the heap in the subtree whose root node was swapped.

Suppose `low` contains the index of the root node of the subtree, and `high` contains the index of the last item in the list. The heap is to be restored in the subtree rooted at `list[low]`. The preceding discussion translates into the following Java algorithm:

```
int largeIndex = 2 * low + 1;    //the index of the left child

while(largeIndex <= high)
{
   if(largeIndex < high)
      if(list[largeIndex].compareTo(list[largeIndex + 1]) < 0)
         largeIndex = largeIndex + 1; //the index of the larger
                                      //child
   if(list[low] > list[largeIndex])   //the subtree is already in
                                      //a heap
      break;
   else
   {
      swap(list[low], list[largeIndex]);   //Line **
      low = largeIndex;   //go to the subtree to further
                          //restore the heap
      largeIndex = 2 * low + 1;
   }//end else
}//end while
```

The `swap` statement at the line marked **Line **** swaps the parent with the larger child. Because a `swap` statement makes three item assignments to swap the contents of two variables, each time through the loop three item assignments are made. The `while` loop moves the parent node to a place in the tree so that the resulting subtree with the root node `list[low]` is in a heap. We can easily reduce the number of assignments each time through the loop from three to one by first storing the root node in a temporary location, say `temp`. Then each time through the loop the larger child is compared with `temp`. If the larger child is larger than `temp`, we move the larger child to the root node of the subtree under consideration.

Next, we describe the method `heapify`, which restores the heap in a subtree by making one item assignment each time through the loop. The index of the root node of the list, and the index of the last element of the list, are passed as parameters to this method.

```
private void heapify(int low, int high)
{
    int largeIndex;

    DataElement temp = list[low]; //copy the root node of
                                  //the subtree

    largeIndex = 2 * low + 1;  //the index of the left child

    while(largeIndex <= high)
    {
        if(largeIndex < high)
            if(list[largeIndex].compareTo(list[largeIndex + 1]) < 0)
                largeIndex = largeIndex + 1; //the index of the
                                             //largest child

        if(temp.compareTo(list[largeIndex]) > 0) //the subtree is
                                                 //already in a heap
            break;
        else
        {
            list[low] = list[largeIndex]; //move the larger child
                                          //to the root
            low = largeIndex;     //go to the subtree to
                                  //restore the heap
            largeIndex = 2 * low + 1;
        }
    }//end while

    list[low] = temp; //insert temp into the tree, that is, list
}//end heapify
```

Next, we use the method `heapify` to implement the `buildHeap` method to convert the list into a heap:

```
private void buildHeap()
{
    int index;

    for(index = length / 2 - 1; index >= 0; index--)
        heapify(index, length - 1);
}//end buildHeap
```

We now describe the heap sort algorithm.

Suppose the list is in a heap. Consider the complete binary tree representing the list as given in Figure 9-62.

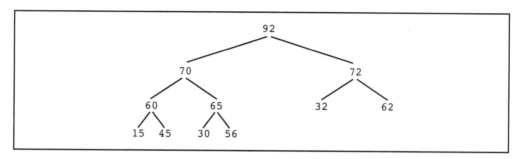

Figure 9-62 A heap

Because this is a heap, the root node is the largest element of the tree, that is, the largest element of the list. So it must be moved to the end of the list. We swap the root node of the tree, that is, the first element of the list, with the last node in the tree (which is the last element of the list). We then obtain the binary tree as shown in Figure 9-63.

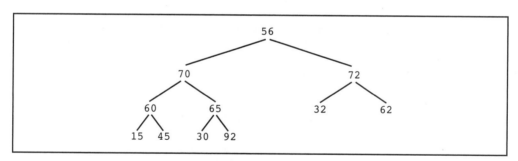

Figure 9-63 Binary tree after moving the root node to the end

Because the largest element is now in its proper place, we consider the remaining elements of the list, that is, elements `list[0]...list[9]`. The complete binary tree representing this list is no longer a heap, and so we must restore the heap in this portion of the complete binary tree. We use the method **heapify** to restore the heap. A call to this method is:

```
heapify(list, 0, 9);
```

We thus obtain the binary tree as shown in Figure 9-64.

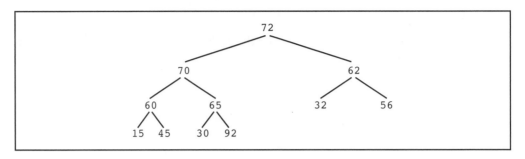

Figure 9-64 Binary tree after the statement `heapify (list, 0, 9);` executes

We repeat this process for the complete binary tree corresponding to the list elements `list[0]...list[9]`. We swap `list[0]` with `list[9]`, and then restore the heap in the complete binary tree corresponding to the list elements `list[0]...list[8]`. We continue this process.

The following Java method describes this algorithm:

```
public void heapSort()
{
    int lastOutOfOrder;
    DataElement temp;

    buildHeap();

    for(lastOutOfOrder = length - 1; lastOutOfOrder >= 0;
                                    lastOutOfOrder--)
    {
        temp = list[lastOutOfOrder];
        list[lastOutOfOrder] = list[0];
        list[0] = temp;
        heapify(0, lastOutOfOrder - 1);
    }//end for
}//end heapSort
```

We leave it as an exercise for you to write a program to test the heap sort algorithm. See Programming Exercise 8 at the end of this chapter.

Analysis: Heap Sort

Suppose that L is a list of n elements, where $n > 0$. In the worst case, the number of key comparisons in the heap sort algorithm to sort L (the number of comparisons in `heapSort` and the number of comparisons in `buildHeap`) is $2n * \log_2 n + O(n)$. Also, in the worst case, the number of item assignments in the heap sort algorithm to sort L is $n * \log_2 n + O(n)$. On average, the number of comparisons made by the heap sort algorithm to sort L is of $O(n * \log_2 n)$.

In the average case of the quick sort algorithm, the number of key comparisons is $1.39n * \log_2 n + O(n)$ and the number of swaps is $0.69 * \log_2 n + O(n)$. Because each swap is three assignments, the number of item assignments in the average case of the quick sort algorithm is at least $1.39n * \log_2 n + O(n)$. It now follows that for the key comparisons, the average case of the quick sort algorithm is somewhat better than the worst case of the heap sort algorithm. On the other hand, for the item assignments, the average case of the quick sort algorithm is somewhat poorer than the worst case of the heap sort algorithm. However, the worst case of the quick sort algorithm is $O(n^2)$. Empirical studies have shown that the heap sort algorithm usually takes twice as long as the quick sort algorithm, but avoids the slight possibility of poor performance.

Priority Queues (Revisited)

Chapter 8 introduced priority queues. Recall that in a priority queue, customers or jobs with higher priorities are pushed to the front of the queue. Chapter 8 stated that we would discuss the implementation of priority queues after describing the heap sort algorithm. For simplicity, we assume that the priority of the queue elements is assigned using the relational operators.

In a heap, the largest element of the list is always the first element of the list. After removing the largest element of the list, the method `heapify` restores the heap in the list. To ensure that the largest element of the priority queue is always the first element of the queue, we can implement priority queues as heaps. We can write algorithms similar to the ones used in the method `heapify` to insert (`addQueue` operation) an element in the priority queue, and remove (`deleteQueue` operation) an element from the queue. The next two sections describe these algorithms.

Insert an Element in the Priority Queue

Assuming the priority queue is implemented as a heap, we perform the following steps:

1. Insert the new element in the first available position in the list. (This ensures that the array holding the list is a complete binary tree.)
2. After inserting the new element in the heap, the list may no longer be a heap. So to restore the heap:

   `while` (the parent of the new entry is smaller than the new entry)
   swap the parent with the new entry.

Notice that restoring the heap might result in moving the new entry to the root node.

Remove an Element from the Priority Queue

Assuming the priority queue is implemented as a heap, to remove the first element of the priority queue, we perform the following steps:

1. Copy the last element of the list into the first array position.
2. Reduce the length of the list by 1.
3. Restore the heap in the list.

The other operations for priority queues can be implemented in the same way as implemented for queues. We leave the implementation of the priority queues as an exercise for you. See Programming Exercise 9 at the end of this chapter.

PROGRAMMING EXAMPLE: ELECTION RESULTS

The presidential election for the student council of your local university is about to be held. Due to confidentiality, the chair of the election committee wants to computerize the voting. The chair is looking for someone to write a program to analyze the data and report the winner. Let us write a program to help the election committee.

The university has four major divisions, and each division has several departments. For the election, the four divisions are labeled as region 1, region 2, region 3, and region 4. Each department in each division handles its own voting and directly reports the votes received by each candidate to the election committee. The voting is reported in the following form:

```
firstName lastName regionNumber numberOfVotes
```

The election committee wants the output in the following tabular form:

```
-------------------Election Results-------------------

                         Votes By Region
Candidate Name   Rgn#1    Rgn#2    Rgn#3    Rgn#4    Total
--------------   -----    -----    -----    -----    -----
Buddy Balto        0        0        0       272      272
Doctor Doc        25       71      156       97       349
Ducky Donald     110      158        0        0       268
  .
  .
  .

Winner: ???,  Votes Received: ???
Total votes polled: ???
```

The names of the candidates must be in alphabetical order in the output.

For this program, we assume that six candidates are seeking the student council's president post. This program can be enhanced to handle any number of candidates.

The data is provided in two files. One file, **candData.txt**, consists of the names of the candidates seeking the president's post. The names of the candidates in this file are in no particular order. In the second file, **voteData.txt**, each line consists of the voting results in the following form:

```
firstName lastName regionNumber numberOfVotes
```

That is, each line in the file **voteData.txt** consists of the candidate's name, the region number, and the number of votes received by the candidate in that region. There is one entry per line. For example, the input file containing the voting data looks like the following:

```
Ducky Donald 1 23
Peter Pluto 2 56
Doctor Doc 1 25
Peter Pluto 4 23
.
.
.
```

The first line indicates that **Ducky Donald** received **23** votes from region **1**.

Input   Two files: one containing the candidates' names, and the other containing the voting data as described previously

Output   The election results in a tabular form as described previously, and the winner

Problem Analysis and Algorithm Design

From the output, it is clear that the program must organize the voting data by region, and calculate the total votes both received by each candidate and polled for the election. Furthermore, the names of the candidates must appear in alphabetical order.

The main component of this program is a candidate. Therefore, first we design the **class Candidate** to implement a candidate object. Every candidate has a name and receives votes. Because there are four regions, we can use an array of four components. In Example 1-5 (Chapter 1), we designed the **class Person** to implement the name of a person. Recall that an object of the type **Person** can store the first name and the last name. Because every candidate is a person, we derive the **class Candidate** from the **class Person**.

In this program, we use an **OrderedArrayList** object to implement the list of candidates. A component of the array implementing the list is a reference variable of the **class DataElement** type. To make use of the **class OrderedArrayList** to implement the list of candidates, **class Person** must be derived from the **class DataElement**. Therefore, in the next section, we redefine the **class Person** by extending the **class DataElement**.

Person   As described in the previous section, we derive the **class Person** from the **class DataElement**. The **class Person** implements the first name and last name of a person. Therefore, the **class Person** has two data members: a data member, **firstName**, to store the first name; and a data member, **lastName**, to store the last name. We declare these as **protected** so that the definition of the **class Person** can be easily extended to accommodate the requirements of a specific application needed to implement a person's name.

Because the `class Person` is derived from the `class DataElement`, which is an abstract class, the `class Person` must provide the definitions of the abstract methods of the `class DataElement`.

The following statements define `class Person` as an ADT. (See also Figure 9-65).

Class: `Person`

```
public class Person extends DataElement
```

Instance Variables:

```
protected String firstName; //variable to store the first name
protected String lastName;  //variable to store the last name
```

Constructors and Instance Methods:

```
public Person()
   //default constructor
   //Initialize firstName and lastName to empty strings.
   //Postcondition: firstName = ""; lastName = ""

public Person(String first, String last)
   //constructor with parameters
   //Set firstName and lastName according to the parameters.
   //Postcondition: firstName = first; lastName = last

public String toString()
   //Method to return the first name and last name
   //as a string in the form firstName lastName.

public void setName(String first, String last)
   //Method to set firstName and lastName according to
   //the parameters.
   //Postcondition: firstName = first; lastName = last

public String getFirstName()
   //Method to return the first name.
   //Postcondition: The value of firstName is returned.

public String getLastName()
   //Method to return the last name.
   //Postcondition: The value of lastName is returned.

   //Methods of the class DataElement.
public boolean equals(DataElement otherElement)
public int compareTo(DataElement otherElement)
public void makeCopy(DataElement otherElement)
public DataElement getCopy()
```

Person
#firstName: String #lastName: String
+Person() +Person(String, String) +toString(): String +setName(String, String): void +getFirstName(): String +getLastName(): String +equals(DataElement): boolean +compareTo(DataElement): int +makeCopy(DataElement): void +getCopy(): DataElement

Figure 9-65   UML diagram of the `class Person`

The definitions of the constructors and the methods `toString`, `setName`, `getFirstName`, and `getLastName` are the same as given in Chapter 1. Next, we give the definition of the method `getCopy`:

```
public DataElement getCopy()
{
    Person temp = new Person();

    temp.firstName = firstName;
    temp.lastName = lastName;

    return temp;
}
```

The definitions of the methods `equals`, `compareTo`, and `makeCopy` are left as an exercise for you. See Programming Exercise 10 at the end of this chapter.

Candidate   The main component of this program is the candidate, which is described and implemented in this section. Every candidate has a first and a last name and receives votes. Because there are four regions, we declare an array of four components to keep track of the votes for each region. We also need a data member to store the total number of votes received by each candidate. Because every candidate is a person and we have designed a class to implement the first and last name, we derive the `class Candidate` from the `class Person`. Because the data members of the `class Person` are `protected`, these data members can be accessed directly in the `class Candidate`.

There are six candidates. Therefore, we declare a list of six candidates of the type
`Candidate`. This chapter defines and implements the `class OrderedArrayList` to
implement a sorted list; we use this class to maintain the list of candidates. This list of
candidates will be sorted and searched. Therefore, we must provide the definitions of the
methods `equals`, `compareTo`, `makeCopy`, and `getCopy` for the `class Candidate`
because some of these methods are used by the sorting and searching algorithms.

The following statements define `Candidate` as an ADT. (See also Figure 9-66).

Class: `Candidate`

```
public class Candidate extends Person
```

Instance Variables and Constants:

```
private final int noOfRegions = 4;

private int[] votesByRegion;
private int totalVotes;
```

Constructors and Instance Methods:

```
Candidate()
    //default constructor
    //Postcondition: Creates the array votesByRegion and
    //               sets totalVotes to zero.

public void setVotes(int region, int votes)
    //Method to set the votes of a candidate for a
    //particular region.
    //Postcondition: The votes specified by the parameter votes
    //               are assigned to the region specified by the
    //               parameter region.

public void updateVotesByRegion(int region, int votes)
    //Method to update the votes of a candidate for a
    //particular region.
    //Postcondition: The votes specified by the parameter votes
    //               are added to the region specified by the
    //               parameter region.

public void calculateTotalVotes()
    //Method to calculate the total votes received by a
    //candidate.
    //Postcondition: The votes received in each region are added.

public int getTotalVotes()
    //Method to return the total votes received by a
    //candidate.
```

```
//Postcondition: The total votes received by the candidate
//               are returned.

public void printData()
   //Method to output the candidate's name, the votes
   //received in each region, and the total votes received.

public boolean equals(DataElement otherElement)
public int compareTo(DataElement otherElement)
public void makeCopy(DataElement otherElement)
public DataElement getCopy()
```

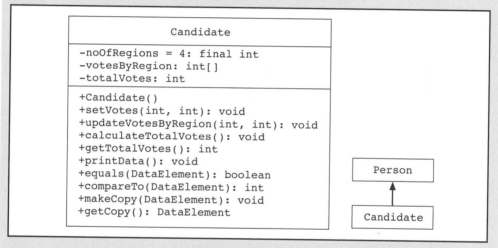

Figure 9-66 UML diagram of the class Candidate

The definitions of the methods of the class Candidate are given next.

To set the votes of a particular region, the region number and the number of votes are passed as parameters to the method setVotes. Because an array index starts at 0, region 1 corresponds to the array component at position 0, and so on. Therefore, to set the value of the correct array component, 1 is subtracted from the region. The definition of the method setVotes is:

```
public void setVotes(int region, int votes)
{
     votesByRegion[region - 1] = votes;
}
```

To update the votes for a particular region, the region number and the number of votes for that region are passed as parameters. The votes are then added to the region's previous value. The definition of the method updateVotesByRegion is:

```
public void updateVotesByRegion(int region, int votes)
{
    votesByRegion[region - 1] = votesByRegion[region - 1]
                                          + votes;
}
```

The definitions of the methods calculateTotalVotes, getTotalVotes, printData, and the default constructor are given next.

```
public void calculateTotalVotes()
{
    int i;

    totalVotes = 0;

    for(i = 0; i < noOfRegions; i++)
        totalVotes += votesByRegion[i];
}

public int getTotalVotes()
{
    return totalVotes;
}

public void printData()
{
    System.out.print(super.toString() + "\t  ");

    for(int i = 0; i < noOfRegions; i++)
        System.out.print(votesByRegion[i]+ "\t  ");
    System.out.println(totalVotes);
}

Candidate()
{
    super();
    totalVotes = 0;
    votesByRegion = new int[noOfRegions];
}
```

Next, we give the definition of the method equals and leave the others as an exercise for you (see Programming Exercise 10).

```
public boolean equals(DataElement otherElement)
{
    Candidate temp = (Candidate) otherElement;

    return(firstName.equals(temp.firstName)
        && lastName.equals(temp.lastName));
}
```

Main Program

Now that the **class Candidate** has been designed, we focus on designing the main program.

Because there are six candidates, we create a list, **candidateList**, containing six components of the type **Candidate**. The first thing that the program should do is read each candidate's name from the file **candData.txt** into the list **candidateList**. Next, we sort **candidateList**.

The next step is to process the voting data from the file **voteData.txt**, which holds the voting data. After processing the voting data, the program should calculate the total votes received by each candidate, and then print the data as shown previously. Thus, the general algorithm is:

1. Read each candidate's name into **candidateList**.
2. Sort **candidateList**.
3. Process the voting data.
4. Calculate the total votes received by each candidate.
5. Print the results.

The following statement creates the object **candidateList** of the type **OrderedArrayList**:

```
OrderedArrayList candidateList =
                new OrderedArrayList(noOfCandidates);
```

Figure 9-67 shows the object **candidateList**. Every component of the array list is an object of the **Candidate** type.

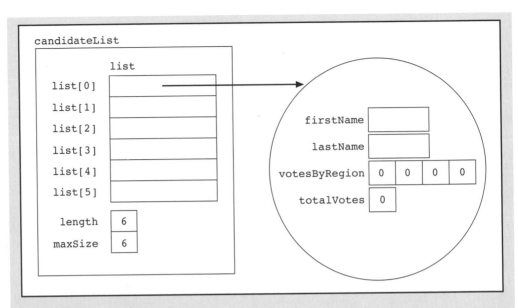

Figure 9-67 `candidateList`

In Figure 9-67, the array `votesByRegion` and the variable `totalVotes` are initialized to 0 by the default constructor of the `class Candidate`. To save space, whenever needed, we draw the object `candidateList` as shown in Figure 9-68.

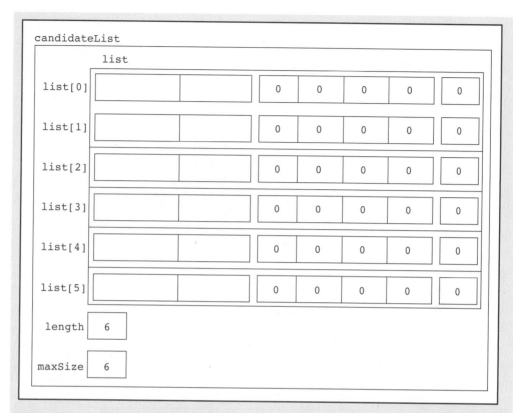

Figure 9-68 Object candidateList

fillNames The first thing that the program must do is to read the candidates' names into candidateList. Therefore, we write a method to accomplish this task. The file candData.txt is opened in the method main. The name of the input file and candidateList are therefore passed as parameters to the method fillNames. Because the data member list of the object candidateList is a protected data member, it cannot be accessed directly. We therefore create the Candidate object, temp, to store the candidates' names, and use the method insertAt (of the class ArrayListClass) to store each candidate's name in the object candidateList. The definition of the method fillNames is as follows:

```
public static void fillNames(BufferedReader inFile,
                   OrderedArrayList cList) throws IOException
{
    String firstN;
    String lastN;
    int i;
```

```
        StringTokenizer tokenizer;

        Candidate temp = new Candidate();

        for(i = 0; i < noOfCandidates; i++)
        {
            tokenizer = new StringTokenizer(inFile.readLine());
            firstN = tokenizer.nextToken();
            lastN = tokenizer.nextToken();
            temp.setName(firstN, lastN);
            cList.insertAt(i, temp);
        }
}
```

After a call to the method **fillNames**, Figure 9-69 shows the object **candidateList**.

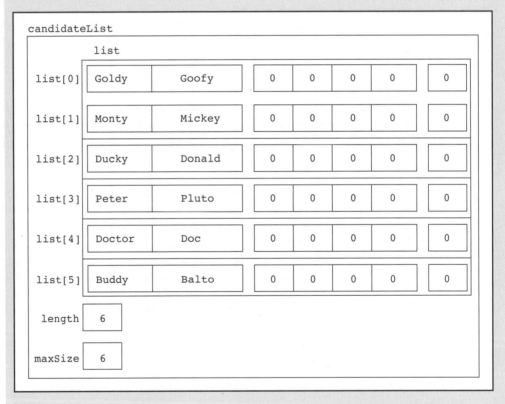

Figure 9-69   Object **candidateList** after a call to the function **fillNames**

Sort Names   After reading the candidates' names, next we sort the array `list` of the object `candidateList` using any of the (array-based) sorting algorithms discussed in this chapter. Because `candidateList` is an object of the type `OrderedArrayList`, all sorting algorithms discussed in this chapter are available to it. For illustration purposes, we use a selection sort. The following statement accomplishes this task:

`candidateList.selectionSort();`

After this statement executes, `candidateList` is as shown in Figure 9-70.

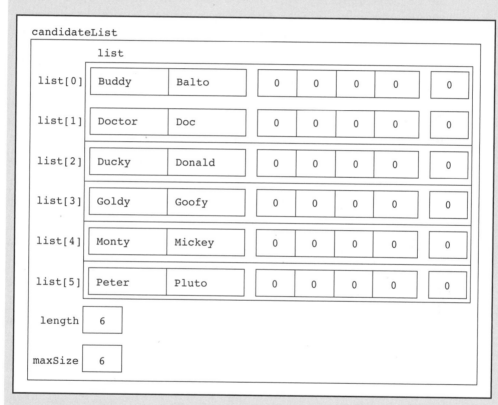

Figure 9-70   Object `candidateList` after the statement
`candidateList.selectionSort();` executes

Process Voting Data   We now discuss how to process the voting data. Each entry in the file `voteData.txt` is of the form:

`firstName lastName regionNumber numberOfVotes`

After reading an entry from the file **voteData.txt**, we locate the row in the array **list** (of the object **candidateList**) corresponding to the specific candidate, and update the entry specified by **regionNumber**.

The field **votesByRegion** is a **private** data member of each component of the array **list**. Moreover, **list** is a **private** data member of **candidateList**. The only way that we can update the votes of a candidate is to make a copy of that candidate's data into a temporary object, update the object, and then copy the temporary object back into **list** by replacing the old value with the new value of the temporary object. We use the method **retrieveAt** to make a copy of the candidate whose votes need to be updated. After updating the temporary object, we use the method **replaceAt** to copy the temporary object back into the list. Suppose the next entry read is:

```
Ducky Donald 2 35
```

This entry says that **Ducky Donald** received 35 votes from region 2. Suppose that before processing this entry, **candidateList** is as shown in Figure 9-71.

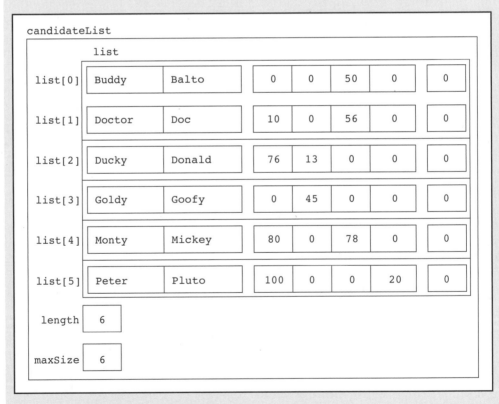

Figure 9-71   Object **candidateList** before processing the entry
              Ducky Donald 2 35

We make a copy of the row corresponding to `Ducky Donald` into `temp` (see Figure 9-72).

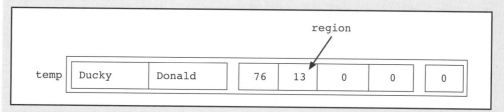

Figure 9-72   Object `temp`

Next, the following statement updates the voting data for region 2. (Here `region = 2` and `votes = 35`.)

`temp.updateVotesByRegion(region, votes);`

After this statement executes, the object `temp` is as shown in Figure 9-73.

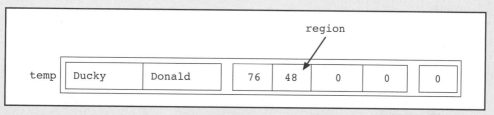

Figure 9-73   Object `temp` after the statement
`temp.updateVotesByRegion(region, votes);` executes

Now we copy the object `temp` into `list` (see Figure 9-74).

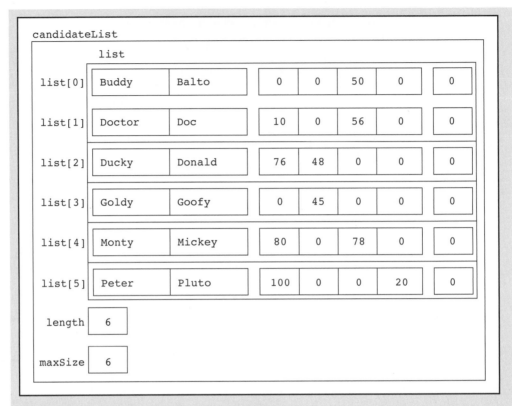

Figure 9-74 candidateList after copying temp

Because the data member list of candidateList is sorted, we can use the binary search algorithm to find the row position in list corresponding to the candidate whose votes need to be updated. Also, the method binarySearch is a member of the class OrderedArrayList, so we can use this method to search the array list. We leave the definition of the method processVotes to process the voting data as an exercise for you (see Programming Exercise 10 at the end of this chapter).

Add Votes After processing the voting data, the next step is to find the total votes received by each candidate. This is done by adding the votes received in each region. Now votesByRegion is a private data member of Candidate and list is a protected data member of candidateList. Therefore, to add the votes for each candidate, we use the retrieveAt method to make a temporary copy of each candidate's data, add the votes in the temporary object, and then copy the temporary object back into candidateList. The following method does this:

```
public static void addVotes(OrderedArrayList cList)
{
    int i;

    Candidate temp = new Candidate();

    for(i = 0; i < noOfCandidates; i++)
    {
        temp =(Candidate) cList.retrieveAt(i);
        temp.calculateTotalVotes();
        cList.replaceAt(i, temp);
    }
}
```

Figure 9-75 shows **candidateList** after adding the votes for each candidate—that is, after a call to the method **addVotes**.

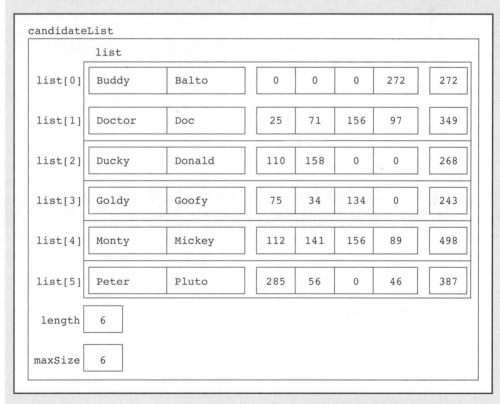

Figure 9-75 candidateList after a call to the function addVotes

Print Heading and Print Results To complete the program, we include a method to print the heading, which is the first four lines of the output. The following method accomplishes this task:

```
public static void printHeading()
{
    System.out.println("--------------------Election Results"
                    + "----------------\n");
    System.out.println("                             "
                    + "Votes By Region");
    System.out.println("Candidate Name  Rgn#1 \tRgn#2 \t"
                    + "Rgn#3 \tRgn#4 \tTotal");
    System.out.println("-------------  ----- \t----- "
                    + "\t----- \t----- \t-----");
}
```

We now describe the method `printResults`, which prints the results. Suppose that the variable `sumVotes` holds the total votes polled for the election, the variable `largestVotes` holds the largest number of votes received by a candidate, and the variable `winLoc` holds the index of the winning candidate in the array `list`. Further suppose that `temp` is a object `Candidate`. The algorithm for this method is:

1. Initialize `sumVotes`, `largestVotes`, and `winLoc` to 0.
2. For each candidate:
   a. Retrieve the candidate's data into `temp`.
   b. Print the candidate's name and relevant data.
   c. Retrieve the total votes received by the candidate and update `sumVotes`.

```
if(largestVotes < temp.getTotalVotes())
{
    largestVotes = temp.getTotalVotes();
    winLoc = i;
}
```

3. Output the final lines of the output.

We leave the definition of the method `printResults` to print the results as an exercise for you; see Programming Exercise 10 at the end of this chapter.

Program Listing (Main Program)

```
import java.io.*;

import java.util.*;

public class ElectionResult
{
    static final int noOfCandidates = 6;

    public static void main(String[] args)
```

```
    {
        OrderedArrayList candidateList =
                    new OrderedArrayList(noOfCandidates);

        Candidate temp;

        try
        {
            BufferedReader inFile =
                    new BufferedReader
                        (new FileReader("a:\\candData.txt"));

            fillNames(inFile, candidateList);

            candidateList.selectionSort();

            inFile = null;

            inFile = new BufferedReader
                    (new FileReader("a:\\voteData.txt"));

            processVotes(inFile, candidateList);

            addVotes(candidateList);

            printHeading();
            printResults(candidateList);
        }
        catch(FileNotFoundException fnfe)
        {
            System.out.println(fnfe.toString());
        }
        catch(IOException ioe)
        {
            System.out.println(ioe.toString());
        }
    }

    //Place the definitions of the methods fillNames,
    //addVotes, and printHeading here. Also, write and place
    //the definitions of the methods processVotes and
    //printResults here.
}
```

Sample Output   (After you have written the definitions of the methods of the classes Person and Candidate, and of the methods processVotes and printResults, and then run your program, it should produce the following output. See Programming Exercise 10.)

```
-------------------Election Results-----------------

                     Votes By Region
Candidate Name    Rgn#1    Rgn#2    Rgn#3    Rgn#4    Total
--------------    -----    -----    -----    -----    -----
Buddy Balto         0        0        0       272      272
Doctor Doc          25       71      156       97      349
Ducky Donald       110      158       0         0      268
Goldy Goofy         75       34      134        0      243
Monty Mickey       112      141      156       89      498
Peter Pluto        285       56       0        46      387

Winner: Monty Mickey,  Votes Received: 498

Total votes polled: 2017
```

Input Files:

candData.txt

```
Goldy Goofy
Monty Mickey
Ducky Donald
Peter Pluto
Doctor Doc
Buddy Balto
```

voteData.txt

```
Goldy Goofy 2 34
Monty Mickey 1 56
Ducky Donald 2 56
Peter Pluto 1 78
Doctor Doc 4 29
Buddy Balto 4 78
Monty Mickey 2 63
Ducky Donald 1 23
Peter Pluto 2 56
Doctor Doc 1 25
Peter Pluto 4 23
Doctor Doc 4 12
Goldy Goofy 3 134
Buddy Balto 4 82
Monty Mickey 3 67
Ducky Donald 2 67
Doctor Doc 3 67
Buddy Balto 4 23
Monty Mickey 1 56
Ducky Donald 2 35
```

```
Peter Pluto 1 27
Doctor Doc 2 34
Goldy Goofy 1 75
Peter Pluto 4 23
Monty Mickey 4 89
Peter Pluto 1 23
Doctor Doc 3 89
Monty Mickey 3 89
Peter Pluto 1 67
Doctor Doc 2 37
Buddy Balto 4 89
Monty Mickey 2 78
Ducky Donald 1 87
Peter Pluto 1 90
Doctor Doc 4 56
```

QUICK REVIEW

1. The selection sort algorithm sorts a list by finding the smallest (or equivalently largest) element in the list, and then moving it to the beginning (or end) of the list.

2. For a list of length n, where $n > 0$, the selection sort algorithm makes $\frac{1}{2}n^2 - \frac{1}{2}n$ key comparisons and $3(n-1)$ item assignments.

3. For a list of length n, where $n > 0$, on average, the insertion sort algorithm makes $\frac{1}{4}n^2 + O(n)$ key comparisons and $\frac{1}{4}n^2 + O(n)$ item assignments.

4. Let L be a list of n distinct elements. Any sorting algorithm that sorts L by comparison of the keys only, in its worst case, makes at least $O(n * \log_2 n)$ key comparisons.

5. Both the quick sort and merge sort algorithms sort a list by partitioning the list.

6. To partition a list, the quick sort algorithm first selects an item from the list, called `pivot`. The algorithm then rearranges the elements so that the elements in one of the sublists are less than `pivot`, and the elements in the other sublist are greater than or equal to `pivot`.

7. In a quick sort, the sorting work is done in partitioning the list.

8. On average, the number of key comparisons in a quick sort is $O(n * \log_2 n)$. In the worst case, the number of key comparisons in a quick sort is $O(n^2)$.

9. The merge sort algorithm partitions the list by dividing it in the middle.

10. In a merge sort, the sorting work is done in merging the lists.

11. The number of key comparisons in a merge sort is $O(n * \log_2 n)$.

12. A heap is a list in which each element contains a key, such that the key in the element at position k in the list is at least as large as the key in the element at position $2k + 1$ (if it exists), and $2k + 2$ (if it exists).

13. The first step in the heap sort algorithm is to convert the list into a heap, called `buildHeap`. After we convert the array into a heap, the sorting phase begins.

14. Suppose that L is a list of n elements, where $n > 0$. In the worst case, the number of key comparisons in the heap sort algorithm to sort L is $2n * \log_2 n + O(n)$. Also, in the worst case, the number of item assignments in the heap sort algorithm to sort L is $n * \log_2 n + O(n)$

EXERCISES

1. Assume the following list of keys:

5, 18, 21, 10, 55, 20

The first three keys are in order. To move 10 to its proper position using the insertion sort algorithm as described in this chapter, exactly how many key comparisons are executed?

2. Assume the following list of keys:

7, 28, 31, 40, 5, 20

The first four keys are in order. To move 5 to its proper position using the insertion sort algorithm as described in this chapter, exactly how many key comparisons are executed?

3. Assume the following list of keys:

28, 18, 21, 10, 25, 30, 12, 71, 32, 58, 15

This list is to be sorted using the insertion sort algorithm as described in this chapter for array-based lists. Show the resulting list after 6 passes of the sorting phase—that is, after 6 iterations of the `for` loop.

4. Recall the insertion sort algorithm (contiguous version) as discussed in this chapter. Assume the following list of keys:

18, 8, 11, 9, 15, 20, 32, 61, 22, 48, 75, 83, 35, 3

Exactly how many key comparisons are executed to sort this list using the insertion sort algorithm?

5. Both the merge sort and quick sort algorithms sort a list by partitioning the list. Explain how the merge sort algorithm differs from the quick sort algorithm in partitioning the list.

6. Assume the following list of keys:

16, 38, 54, 80, 22, 65, 55, 48, 64, 95, 5, 100, 58, 25, 36

This list is to be sorted using the quick sort algorithm as discussed in this chapter. Use `pivot` as the middle element of the list.

   a. Give the resulting list after one call to the `partition` procedure.

   b. Give the resulting list after two calls to the `partition` procedure.

7. Assume the following list of keys:

   18, 40, 16, 82, 64, 67, 57, 50, 37, 47, 72, 14, 17, 27, 35

   This list is to be sorted using the quick sort algorithm as discussed in this chapter. Use `pivot` as the median of the `first`, `last`, and `middle` elements of the list.

   a. What is the `pivot`?

   b. Give the resulting list after one call to the `partition` procedure.

8. Use the method `buildHeap` as given in this chapter to convert the following array into a heap. Show the final form of the array.

   47, 78, 81, 52, 50, 82, 58, 42, 65, 80, 92, 53, 63, 87, 95, 59, 34, 37, 7, 20

9. Suppose that the following list was created by the method `buildHeap` during the heap creation phase of the heap sort algorithm:

   100, 85, 94, 47, 72, 82, 76, 30, 20, 60, 65, 50, 45, 17, 35, 14, 28, 5

   Show the resulting array after two passes of the heap sort algorithm. (Use the `heapify` method as given in this chapter.) Exactly how many key comparisons are executed during the first pass?

PROGRAMMING EXERCISES

1. Write and test a version of the selection sort algorithm for linked lists.

2. Write a program to test the insertion sort algorithm for array-based lists as given in this chapter.

3. Write a program to test the insertion sort algorithm for linked lists as given in this chapter.

4. Write a program to test the quick sort algorithm for array-based lists as given in this chapter.

5. (C. A. R. Hoare) Let *L* be a list of size *n*. The quick sort algorithm can be used to find the *k*th smallest item in *L*, where $0 \leq k \leq n - 1$, without completely sorting *L*. Write and implement the Java method, `kThSmallestItem`, that uses a version of the quick sort algorithm to determine the *k*th smallest item in *L* without completely sorting *L*.

6. Sort an array of 10,000 elements using the quick sort algorithm as follows:

   a. Sort the array using `pivot` as the middle element of the array.

   b. Sort the array using `pivot` as the median of the first, last, and middle elements of the array.

c. Sort the array using `pivot` as the middle element of the array. However, when the size of any sublist reduces to less than 20, sort the sublist using an insertion sort.

d. Sort the array using `pivot` as the median of the first, last, and middle elements of the array. When the size of any sublist reduces to less than 20, sort the sublist using an insertion sort.

e. Calculate and print the CPU time for each of the preceding four steps.

(Note: Use the method `currentTimeMillis` of the `class System` to determine the current time in milliseconds. The method `currentTimeMillis` is a `static` value-returning method of the type `long`. If `x` is a variable of the type `long`, the statement:

```
x = System.currentTimeMillis();
```

stores the current time in `x`.)

7. Write a program to test the merge sort algorithm for linked lists as given in this chapter.

8. Write a program to test the heap sort algorithm as given in this chapter.

9. a. Write the definition of the class to define the priority queues, as discussed in this chapter, as an abstract data type (ADT).

b. Write the definitions of the methods to implement the operations of the priority queues as defined in (a).

c. Write a program to test various operations of the priority queues.

10. a. Write the definitions of the methods of the `class Person`, of the Programming Example: Election Results, not given in the programming example.

b. Write the definitions of the methods of the `class Candidate`, of the Programming Example: Election Results, not given in the programming example.

c. Write the definitions of the methods `processVotes` and `printResults` of the Programming Example: Election Results.

d. After completing (a), (b), and (c), write a program to produce the output shown in the Sample Run of the Programming Example Election Results.

11. In the Programming Example: Election Results, the `class Candidate` contains the method `calculateTotalVotes`. After processing the voting data, this method calculates the total number of votes received by a candidate. The method `updateVotesByRegion` (of the `class Candidate`) updates only the number of votes for a particular region. Modify the definition of this method so that it also updates the total number of votes received by the candidate. By doing so, the methods `addVotes` in the main program and `calculateTotalVotes` in the `class Candidate` are no longer needed. Modify and run your program with the modified definition of the method `updateVotesByRegion`.

12. In the Programming Example: Election Results, the object `candidateList` of the type `OrderedArrayList` is declared to process the voting data. The operations of inserting a candidate's data and updating and retrieving the votes were somewhat complicated. To update the candidate's votes, we copied that candidate's data from `candidateList` into a temporary object of the type `Candidate`, updated the

temporary object, and then replaced the candidate's data with the temporary object. This is because `list` is a `protected` member of `candidateList`, and each component of `list` is `private`. In this exercise, you are to modify the Programming Example: Election Results to simplify accessing a candidate's data as follows: derive the `class CandidateList` from the `class OrderedArrayList`.

```
public class CandidateList extends OrderedArrayList
{
    //constructors

        //Method to update the number of votes for a
        //particular candidate for a particular region.
        //Postcondition: The name of the candidate, the region
        //               number, and the number of votes are
        //               passed as parameters.
    public void processVotes(String fName, String lName,
                                int region, int votes)
    {
        //definition
    }

        //Method to find the total number of votes received
        //by each candidate.
    public void addVotes()
    {
        //definition
    }

        //Method to output the voting data.
    public void printResults()
    {
        //definition
    }

}
```

9

Because the `class CandidateList` is derived from the `class OrderedArrayList`, and `list` is a `protected` member of the `class OrderedArrayList` (inherited from the `class ArrayListClass`), `list` can be directly accessed by any member of the `class CandidateList`.

Write the definitions of the constructors and the methods of the `class CandidateList`. Rewrite and run your program using the `class CandidateList`.

BINARY TREES

When data is being organized, a programmer's highest priority is to organize it in such a way that item insertion, deletion, and lookups (searches) are fast. You have already seen how to store and process data in an array. Because an array is a random access data structure, if the data is properly organized (say, sorted), then we can use a search algorithm, such as a binary search, to effectively find and retrieve an item from the list. However, we know that storing data in an array has its limitations. For example, item insertion (especially if the array is sorted) and item deletion can be very time consuming, especially if the list size is very large, because each of these operations requires data movement. To speed up item insertion and deletion, we used linked lists. Item insertion and deletion in a linked list do not require any data movement; we simply adjust some of the links in the list. However, one of the drawbacks of linked lists is that they must be processed sequentially. That is, to insert or delete an item, or simply search the list for a particular item, we must begin our search at the first node in the list. As you know, a sequential search is good only for very small lists because the average search length of a sequential search is half the size of the list.

BINARY TREES

This chapter discusses how to dynamically organize data so that item insertion, deletion, and lookups are more efficient.

We first introduce some definitions to facilitate our discussion.

Definition: A **binary tree**, T, is either empty or such that:

      i. T has a special node called the **root** node;

      ii. T has two sets of nodes, L_T and R_T, called the left subtree and right subtree of T, respectively; and

      iii. L_T and R_T are binary trees.

A binary tree can be shown pictorially. Suppose that T is a binary tree with the root node A. Let L_A denote the left subtree of A and R_A denote the right subtree of A. Now L_A and R_A are binary trees. Suppose that B is the root node of L_A and C is the root node of R_A. B is called the **left child** of A; C is called the **right child** of A. Moreover, A is called the **parent** of B and C.

In the diagram of a binary tree, each node of the binary tree is represented as a circle and the circle is labeled by the node. The root node of the binary tree is drawn at the top. The left child of the root node (if any) is drawn below and to the left of the root node. Similarly, the right child of the root node (if any) is drawn below and to the right of the root node. Children are connected to the parent by an *arrow* from the parent to the child. An arrow is usually called a **directed edge** or a **directed branch** (or simply a **branch**). Because the root node, B, of L_A is already drawn, we apply the same procedure to draw the remaining parts of L_A. R_A is drawn similarly. If a node has no left child, for example, when we draw an arrow from the node to the left we end the arrow with three lines. That is, three lines at the end of an arrow indicate that the subtree is empty.

The diagram in Figure 10-1 is an example of a binary tree. The root node of this binary tree is A. The left subtree of the root node, which we denote by L_A, is the set $L_A = \{B, D, E, G\}$ and the right subtree of the root node, which we denote by R_A, is the set $R_A = \{C, F, H\}$. The root node of the left subtree of A—that is, the root node of L_A—is node B. The root node of R_A is C, and so on. Clearly, L_A and R_A are binary trees. Because three lines at the end of an arrow mean that the subtree is empty, it follows that the left subtree of D is empty.

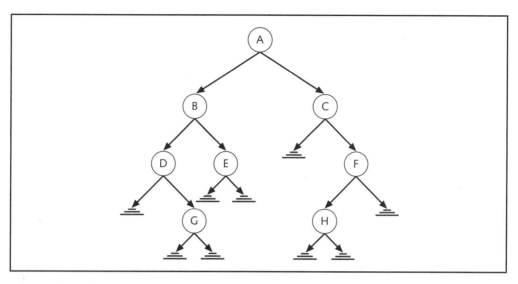

Figure 10-1 Binary tree

In Figure 10-1, the left child of **A** is **B** and the right child of **A** is **C**. Similarly, for node **F**, the left child is **H** and node **F** has no right child.

Examples 10-1 to 10-5 show nonempty binary trees.

Example 10-1

This example shows a binary tree with one node. See Figure 10-2.

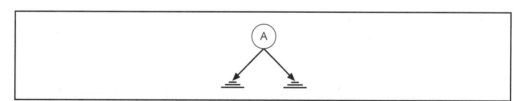

Figure 10-2 Binary tree with one node

In the binary tree of Figure 10-2:

The root node of the binary tree = **A**.

L_A = empty

R_A = empty

Example 10-2

This example shows a binary tree with two nodes. See Figure 10-3.

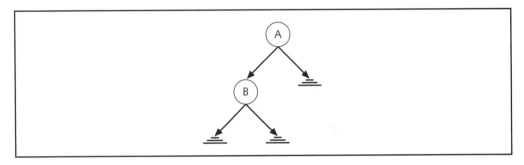

Figure 10-3 Binary tree with two nodes; the right subtree of the root node is empty

In the binary tree of Figure 10-3:

The root node of the binary tree = **A**.

$L_A = \{B\}$

R_A = empty

The root node of L_A = **B**.

L_B = empty

R_B = empty

Example 10-3

This example shows a binary tree with two nodes. See Figure 10-4.

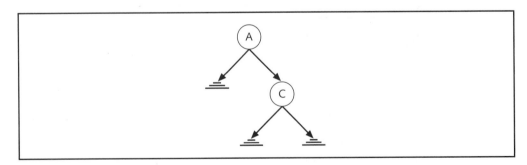

Figure 10-4 Binary tree with two nodes; the left subtree of the root node is empty

In the binary tree of Figure 10-4:

The root node of the binary tree = A.

L_A = empty

R_A = {C}

The root node of R_A = C.

L_C = empty

R_C = empty

Example 10-4

This example shows a binary tree with three nodes. See Figure 10-5.

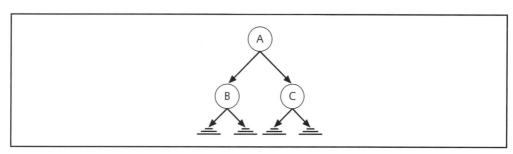

Figure 10-5 Binary tree with three nodes

In the binary tree of Figure 10-5:

The root node of the binary tree = A.

L_A = {B}

R_A = {C}

The root node of L_A = B.

L_B = empty

R_B = empty

The root node of R_A = C.

L_C = empty

R_C = empty

Example 10-5

This example shows other cases of nonempty binary trees with three nodes. See Figure 10-6.

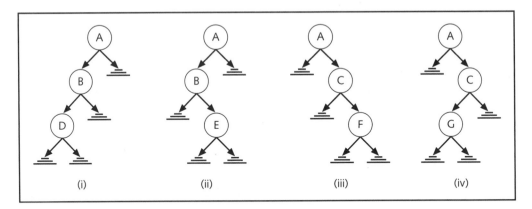

Figure 10-6 Various binary trees with three nodes

As you can see from the preceding examples, every node in a binary tree has at most two children. Thus, every node, other than storing its own information, must keep track of its left subtree and right subtree. This implies that every node has two links, say `llink` and `rlink`. The link `llink` points to the root node of the left subtree; the link `rlink` points to the root node of the right subtree.

The following class defines the node of a binary tree:

```
protected class BinaryTreeNode
{
    DataElement info;
    BinaryTreeNode llink;
    BinaryTreeNode rlink;
}
```

From the definition of the node it is clear that for each node:

- The field `info` points to the object where the data is stored.

- The reference of the left child is stored in `llink`.

- The reference of the right child is stored in `rlink`.

Furthermore, the reference of the root node of a binary tree is stored outside the binary tree in a reference variable, usually called the **root**, of the type `BinaryTreeNode`. Thus, in general, a binary tree looks like the diagram in Figure 10-7.

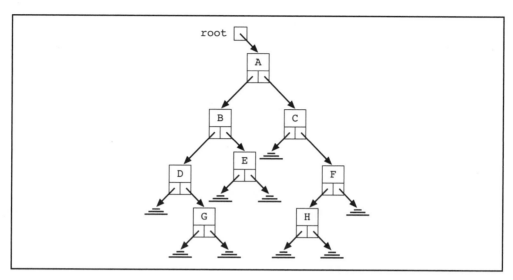

Figure 10-7   Binary tree

For simplicity, we will continue to draw binary trees as before. That is, we will use circles to represent nodes, and left and right arrows to represent links. As before, three lines at the end of an arrow mean that the subtree is empty.

Before we leave this section, let us define a few more terms.

A node in a binary tree is called a **leaf** if it has no left and right children. Let U and V be two nodes in the binary tree T. U is called the **parent** of V if there is a branch from U to V. A **path** from a node X to a node Y in a binary tree is a sequence of nodes $X_0, X_1, ..., X_n$ such that:

 i. $X = X_0, X_n = Y$

 ii. X_{i-1} is the parent of X_i for all $i = 1, 2, ..., n$. That is, there is a branch from X_0 to X_1, X_1 to $X_2, ..., X_{i-1}$ to $X_i, ..., X_{n-1}$ to X_n.

Because the branches go only from a parent to its children, from the previous discussion it is clear that in a binary tree, there is a unique path from the root to every node in the binary tree.

Definition: The **level of a node** in a binary tree is the number of branches on the path from the root to the node.

Clearly, the level of the root node of a binary tree is 0, and the level of the children of the root node is 1.

Definition: The **height of a binary tree** is the number of nodes on the longest path from the root to a leaf.

Suppose that a reference, **p**, of the root node of a binary tree is given. We next describe the Java method **height** to find the height of the binary tree. The reference of the root node is passed as a parameter to the method **height**.

If the binary tree is empty, then the `height` is 0. Suppose that the binary tree is nonempty. To find the height of the binary tree, we first find the height of the left subtree and the height of the right subtree. We then take the maximum of these two heights and add 1 to find the height of the binary tree. To find the height of the left (right) subtree, we apply the same procedure, because the left (right) subtree is a binary tree. Therefore, the general algorithm to find the height of a binary tree is as follows (suppose `height(p)` denotes the height of the binary tree with root p):

```
if(p is null)
    height(p) = 0
else
    height(p) = 1 + max(height(p.llink), height(p.rlink))
```

Clearly, this is a recursive algorithm. The following method implements this algorithm:

```
private int height(BinaryTreeNode p)
{
    if(p == null)
        return 0;
    else
        return 1 + max(height(p.llink), height(p.rlink));
}
```

The definition of the method **height** uses the method **max** to determine the larger of two integers. The method **max** can be easily implemented.

Similarly, we can implement algorithms to find the number of nodes and number of leaves in a binary tree.

Copy Tree

One useful operation on binary trees is to make an identical copy of a binary tree. A binary tree is a dynamic data structure; that is, memory for its nodes is allocated and deallocated during program execution. Therefore, if we use just the value of the reference variable of the root node to make a copy of a binary tree, we get a shallow copy of the data. To make an identical copy of a binary tree, we need to create as many nodes as there are in the binary tree to be copied. Moreover, in the copied tree, these nodes must appear in the same order as they are in the original binary tree.

Given the reference of the root node of a binary tree, we next describe the method **copy**, which makes a copy of a given binary tree and returns the reference of the root node of the copied tree. This method is also useful in implementing the copy constructor and the method **copyTree**, as described later in this chapter (see the section "Implementing Binary Trees").

```
BinaryTreeNode copy(BinaryTreeNode otherTreeRoot)
{
    BinaryTreeNode temp;

    if(otherTreeRoot == null)
        temp = null;
    else
    {
        temp = new BinaryTreeNode();
        temp.info = otherTreeRoot.info.getCopy();
        temp.llink = copy(otherTreeRoot.llink);
        temp.rlink = copy(otherTreeRoot.rlink);
    }

    return temp;
}//end copy
```

We use the method **copy** when we implement the copy constructor and the method **copyTree**.

BINARY TREE TRAVERSAL

The item insertion, deletion, and lookup operations require that the binary tree be traversed. Thus, the most common operation performed on a binary tree is to traverse the binary tree, or visit each node of the binary tree. As you can see from the diagram of a binary tree (for example, Figure 10-7), the traversal must start at the root node because we have the reference of the root node. For each node, we have two choices:

- Visit the node first.
- Visit the subtrees first.

These choices lead to three different traversals of a binary tree, as described in the ensuing three sections:

- Inorder traversal
- Preorder traversal
- Postorder traversal

Inorder Traversal

In an inorder traversal, the binary tree is traversed as follows:

1. Traverse the left subtree.
2. Visit the node.
3. Traverse the right subtree.

Preorder Traversal

In a preorder traversal, the binary tree is traversed as follows:

1. Visit the node.

2. Traverse the left subtree.

3. Traverse the right subtree.

Postorder Traversal

In a postorder traversal, the binary tree is traversed as follows:

1. Traverse the left subtree.

2. Traverse the right subtree.

3. Visit the node.

Clearly, each of these traversal algorithms is recursive.

The listing of the nodes produced by the inorder traversal of a binary tree is called the **inorder sequence**. The listing of the nodes produced by the preorder traversal of a binary tree is called the **preorder sequence**. The listing of the nodes produced by the postorder traversal of a binary tree is called the **postorder sequence**.

Before giving the Java code for each of these traversals, let us illustrate the inorder traversal of the binary tree in Figure 10-8. For simplicity, we assume that visiting a node means to output the data stored in the node.

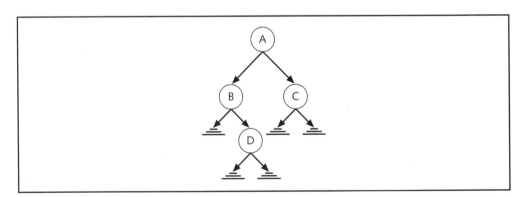

Figure 10-8 Binary tree for an inorder traversal

The reference of the root node of the binary tree in Figure 10-8 is stored in `root` (which points to the node with info A). Therefore, we start the traversal at A.

1. Traverse the left subtree of A; that is, traverse $L_A = \{B, D\}$.

2. Visit A.

3. Traverse the right subtree of A; that is, traverse $R_A = \{C\}$.

We cannot do Step 2 until we have finished Step 1.

1. Traverse the left subtree of A; that is, traverse $L_A = \{B, D\}$. Now L_A is a binary tree with the root node B. Because L_A is a binary tree, we apply the inorder traversal criteria to L_A.

   1.1. Traverse the left subtree of B; that is, traverse L_B = empty.

   1.2. Visit B.

   1.3. Traverse the right subtree of B; that is, traverse $R_B = \{D\}$.

As before, first we complete Step 1.1 before going to Step 1.2.

   1.1. Because the left subtree of B is empty, there is nothing to traverse. Step 1.1 is completed, so we proceed to Step 1.2.

   1.2. Visit B. That is, output B on an output device. Clearly, the first node printed is B. This completes Step 1.2, so we proceed to Step 1.3.

   1.3. Traverse the right subtree of B; that is, traverse $R_B = \{D\}$. Now R_B is a binary tree with the root node D. Because R_B is a binary tree, we apply the inorder traversal criteria to R_B.

      1.3.1. Traverse the left subtree of D; that is, traverse L_D = empty.

      1.3.2. Visit D.

      1.3.3. Traverse the right subtree of D; that is, traverse R_D = empty.

      1.3.1. Because the left subtree of D is empty, there is nothing to traverse. Step 1.3.1 is completed, so we proceed to Step 1.3.2.

      1.3.2. Visit D. That is, output D on an output device. This completes Step 1.3.2, so we proceed to Step 1.3.3.

      1.3.3. Because the right subtree of D is empty, there is nothing to traverse. Step 1.3.3 is completed.

This completes Step 1.3. Because Steps 1.1, 1.2, and 1.3 are completed, Step 1 is completed, and so we go to Step 2.

2. Visit A. That is, output A on an output device. This completes Step 2, so we proceed to Step 3.

10

3. Traverse the right subtree of A; that is, traverse $R_A = \{C\}$. Now R_A is a binary tree with the root node C. Because R_A is a binary tree, we apply the inorder traversal criteria to R_A.

   3.1. Traverse the left subtree of C; that is, traverse L_C = empty.

   3.2. Visit C.

   3.3. Traverse the right subtree of C; that is, traverse R_C = empty.

   3.1. Because the left subtree of C is empty, there is nothing to traverse. Step 3.1 is completed, so we proceed to Step 3.2.

   3.2. Visit C. That is, output C on an output device. This completes Step 3.2, so we proceed to Step 3.3.

   3.3. Because the right subtree of C is empty, there is nothing to traverse. Step 3.3 is completed.

This completes Step 3, which in turn completes the traversal of the binary tree.

Clearly, the inorder traversal of the previous binary tree outputs the nodes in the following order:

Inorder sequence: **B D A C**

Similarly, the preorder and postorder traversals output the nodes in the following order:

Preorder sequence: **A B D C**

Postorder sequence: **D B C A**

As you can see from the walk-through of the inorder traversal, after visiting the left subtree of a node we must come back to the node itself. The links are in only one direction; that is, the parent node points to the left and right children, but there is no link from each child to the parent. Therefore, before going to a child, we must somehow save the reference of the parent node. A convenient way to do this is to write a recursive inorder method; this is because in a recursive call, after completing a particular call, the control goes back to the caller. (Later we discuss how to write nonrecursive traversal methods.) The recursive definition of the method to implement the inorder traversal algorithm is:

```
private void inorder(BinaryTreeNode p)
{
    if(p != null)
    {
        inorder(p.llink);
        System.out.print(p.info + " ");
        inorder(p.rlink);
    }
}
```

To do the inorder traversal of a binary tree, the root node of the binary tree is passed as a parameter to the method `inorder`. For example, if the root points to the root node of the binary tree, a call to the method `inorder` is:

```
inorder(root);
```

Similarly, we can write the methods to implement the preorder and postorder traversals. The definitions of these methods are:

```
private void preorder(BinaryTreeNode p)
{
    if(p != null)
    {
        System.out.print(p.info + " ");
        preorder(p.llink);
        preorder(p.rlink);
    }
}

private void postorder(BinaryTreeNode p)
{
    if(p != null)
    {
        postorder(p.llink);
        postorder(p.rlink);
        System.out.print(p.info + " ");
    }
}
```

Implementing Binary Trees

The preceding sections described various operations that can be performed on a binary tree, as well as the methods to implement these operations. This section describes binary trees as an ADT. Before designing the class to implement a binary tree as an ADT, let us list various operations that are typically performed on a binary tree.

1. Determine whether the binary tree is empty.

2. Search the binary tree for a particular item.

3. Insert an item in the binary tree.

4. Delete an item from the binary tree.

5. Find the height of the binary tree.

6. Find the number of nodes in the binary tree.

7. Find the number of leaves in the binary tree.

8. Traverse the binary tree.

9. Copy the binary tree.

The item search, insertion, and deletion operations all require the binary tree to be traversed. However, because the nodes of a binary tree are in no particular order, these algorithms are not very efficient on arbitrary binary trees. That is, no criteria exist to guide the search on these binary trees, as we will see in the next section. Therefore, we will discuss these algorithms when we discuss special types of binary trees.

Other than the search, insertion, and deletion operations, the following class defines binary trees as an ADT. The definition of the node is the same as before. However, for the sake of completeness and easy reference, we give the definition of the node followed by the definition of the class.

Class: `BinaryTree`

```
public class BinaryTree

     //Definition of the node
protected class BinaryTreeNode
{
    DataElement info;
    BinaryTreeNode llink;
    BinaryTreeNode rlink;
}
```

Instance Variable:

```
protected BinaryTreeNode root;
```

Instance Methods and Constructors:

```
public BinaryTree()
   //default constructor
   //Postcondition: root = null;
public BinaryTree(BinaryTree otherTree)
   //copy constructor

public boolean isEmpty()
   //Method to determine whether the binary tree is empty.
   //Postcondition: Returns true if the binary tree is empty,
   //               false otherwise.
public void inorderTraversal()
   //Method to do an inorder traversal of the binary tree.
   //Postcondition: The nodes of the binary tree are output
   //               in the inorder sequence.
public void preorderTraversal()
   //Method to do a preorder traversal of the binary tree.
   //Postcondition: The nodes of the binary tree are output
   //               in the preorder sequence.
public void postorderTraversal()
   //Method to do a postorder traversal of the binary tree.
   //Postcondition: The nodes of the binary tree are output
   //               in the postorder sequence.

public int treeHeight()
   //Method to determine the height of the binary tree.
   //Postcondition: The height of the binary tree is returned.
public int treeNodeCount()
   //Method to determine the number of nodes in the
   //binary tree.
```

```
  //Postcondition: The number of nodes in the binary tree
  //              is returned.
public int treeLeavesCount()
  //Method to determine the number of leaves in the
  //binary tree.
  //Postcondition: The number of leaves in the binary tree
  //              is returned.
public void destroyTree()
  //Method to destroy the binary tree.
  //Postcondition: root = null

public void copyTree(BinaryTree otherTree)
  //Method to make a copy of the binary tree to which
  //otherTree points.
  //Postcondition: A copy of otherTree is assigned to
  //              this binary tree.

private BinaryTreeNode copy(BinaryTreeNode otherTreeRoot)
  //Method to make a copy of the binary tree to which
  //otherTreeRoot points.
  //Postcondition: A copy of the binary tree to which
  //              otherTreeRoot points is created and the reference
  //              of the root node of the copied binary tree
  //              is returned.

private void inorder(BinaryTreeNode p)
  //Method to do an inorder traversal of the binary
  //tree to which p points.
  //Postcondition: The nodes of the binary tree to which p
  //              points are output in the inorder sequence.
private void preorder(BinaryTreeNode p)
  //Method to do a preorder traversal of the binary
  //tree to which p points.
  //Postcondition: The nodes of the binary tree to which p
  //              points are output in the preorder sequence.
private void postorder(BinaryTreeNode p)
  //Method to do a postorder traversal of the binary
  //tree to which p points.
  //Postcondition: The nodes of the binary tree to which p
  //              points are output in the postorder sequence.

private int height(BinaryTreeNode p)
  //Method to determine the height of the binary tree
  //to which p points.
  //Postcondition: The height of the binary tree to which p
  //              points is returned.

private int max(int x, int y)
  //Method to determine the larger of x and y.
  //Postcondition: The larger of x and y is returned.
```

10

```
private int nodeCount(BinaryTreeNode p)
    //Method to determine the number of nodes in the binary
    //tree to which p points.
    //Postcondition: The number of nodes in the binary tree
    //                to which p points is returned.

private int leavesCount(BinaryTreeNode p)
    //Method to determine the number of leaves in the binary
    //tree to which p points.
    //Postcondition: The number of leaves in the binary tree
    //                to which p points is returned.
```

The definition of the **class BinaryTree** contains several methods that are **private** members of the class. These methods are used to implement the **public** methods of the class and the user need not know of their existence. For example, to do an inorder traversal, the method **inorderTraversal** calls the method **inorder** and passes **root** as a parameter to this method. Suppose that you have the following statement:

```
BinaryTree myTree;
```

Moreover, assume that the object **myTree** has been created. The following statement does an inorder traversal of **myTree**:

```
myTree.inorderTraversal();
```

Also, note that in the definition of the **class BinaryTree**, **root** is declared as a **protected** member so that we can later derive special binary trees.

Next, we give the definitions of the methods of the **class BinaryTree**.

The binary tree is empty if **root** is **null**. So the definition of the method **isEmpty** is:

```
public boolean isEmpty()
{
    return (root == null);
}
```

The default constructor initializes the binary tree to an empty state; that is, it sets **root** to **null**. Therefore, the definition of the default constructor is:

```
public BinaryTree()
{
    root = null;
}
```

The definitions of the other methods are:

```
public void inorderTraversal()
{
    inorder(root);
}
```

```java
public void preorderTraversal()
{
    preorder(root);
}

public void postorderTraversal()
{
    postorder(root);
}

public int treeHeight()
{
    return height(root);
}

public int treeNodeCount()
{
    return nodeCount(root);
}

public int treeLeavesCount()
{
    return leavesCount(root);
}

private void inorder(BinaryTreeNode p)
{
    if(p != null)
    {
        inorder(p.llink);
        System.out.print(p.info + " ");
        inorder(p.rlink);
    }
}

private void preorder(BinaryTreeNode p)
{
    if(p != null)
    {
        System.out.print(p.info + " ");
        preorder(p.llink);
        preorder(p.rlink);
    }
}

private void postorder(BinaryTreeNode p)
{
    if(p != null)
    {
        postorder(p.llink);
        postorder(p.rlink);
        System.out.print(p.info + " ");
    }
}
```

10

```
private int height(BinaryTreeNode p)
{
    if(p == null)
        return 0;
    else
        return 1 + max(height(p.llink), height(p.rlink));
}

private int max(int x, int y)
{
    if(x >= y)
        return x;
    else
        return y;
}
```

The definitions of the methods nodeCount and leavesCount are left as exercises for you. (See Programming Exercises 1 and 2 at the end of this chapter.)

Next, we give the definitions of the methods copy, copyTree, destroyTree, and the copy constructor.

The definition of the method copy is the same as before; here this method is a private member of the class BinaryTree.

```
private BinaryTreeNode copy(BinaryTreeNode otherTreeRoot)
{
    BinaryTreeNode temp;

    if(otherTreeRoot == null)
        temp = null;
    else
    {
        temp = new BinaryTreeNode();
        temp.info = otherTreeRoot.info.getCopy();
        temp.llink = copy(otherTreeRoot.llink);
        temp.rlink = copy(otherTreeRoot.rlink);
    }

    return temp;
}//end copy
```

The definition of the method copyTree is:

```
public void copyTree(BinaryTree otherTree)
{
    if(this != otherTree) //avoid self-copy
    {
        root = null;

        if(otherTree.root != null) //otherTree is nonempty
            root = copy(otherTree.root);
    }
}
```

To destroy a binary tree, we simply set `root` to `null`. The definition of the method `destroyTree` is:

```
public void destroyTree()
{
    root = null;
}
```

The definition of the copy constructor, given next, uses the method **copy** to make an identical copy of the binary tree.

```
        //copy constructor
public BinaryTree(BinaryTree otherTree)
{
    if(otherTree.root == null) //otherTree is empty
        root = null;
    else
        root = copy(otherTree.root);
}
```

BINARY SEARCH TREES

Now that you know the basic operations on a binary tree, this section discusses a special type of binary tree, called a binary search tree.

Consider the binary tree in Figure 10-9.

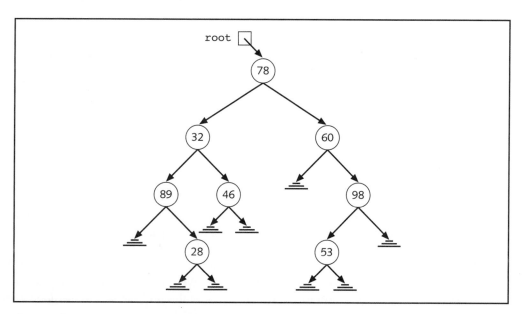

Figure 10-9 Arbitrary binary tree

Suppose that we want to determine whether 50 is in the binary tree. To do so, we can use any of the previous traversal algorithms to visit each node and compare the search item with the data stored in the node. However, this could require us to traverse a large part of the binary tree, so the search would be slow. We need to visit each node in the binary tree until either the item is found or we have traversed the entire binary tree because no criteria exist to guide our search. This case is like an arbitrary linked list where we must start our search at the first node, and continue looking at each node until either the item is found or the entire list is searched.

On the other hand, consider the binary tree in Figure 10-10.

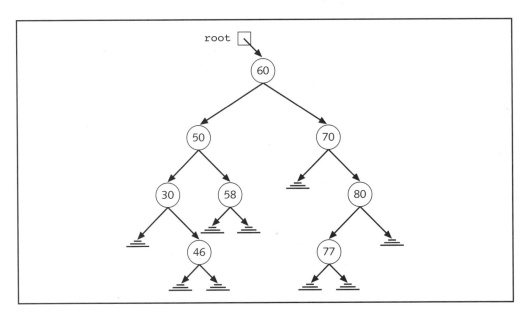

Figure 10-10 Binary search tree

In the binary tree in Figure 10-10, the data in each node is:

- Larger than the data in its left child
- Smaller than the data in its right child

The binary tree in Figure 10-10 has some structure. Suppose that we want to determine whether 58 is in this binary tree. As before, we must start our search at the root node. We compare 58 with the data in the root node; that is, we compare 58 with 60. Because 58   60 and 58 < 60, it is guaranteed that 58 is not in the right subtree of the root node. Therefore, if 58 is in the binary tree, then it must be in the left subtree of the root node. We follow the left link of the root node and go to the node with info 50. We now apply the same criteria at this node. Because 58 > 50, we must follow the right link of this node and go to the node with info 58. At this node we find item 58.

This example shows that every time we move down to a child, we eliminate one of the sub-trees of the node from our search. If the binary tree is nicely constructed, then the search is very similar to the binary search on arrays.

The binary tree given in Figure 10-10 is a special type of binary tree, called a binary search tree. (In the following definition, by the term *key* of a node we mean the key of the data item that uniquely identifies the item.)

Definition: A **binary search tree**, T, is either empty or:

     i. T has a special node called the **root** node;

    ii. T has two sets of nodes, L_T and R_T, called the left subtree and right subtree of T, respectively;

   iii. The key in the root node is larger than every key in the left subtree and smaller than every key in the right subtree; and

   iv. L_T and R_T are binary search trees.

 In this definition, because the left and right subtrees of the root node are again binary search trees, (iii) is equivalent to:

(iii)′. The key in the root node is larger than the key in its left child (if any) and smaller than the key in its right child (if any).

10

The following operations are typically performed on a binary search tree:

    1. Determine whether the binary search tree is empty.

    2. Search the binary search tree for a particular item.

    3. Insert an item in the binary search tree.

    4. Delete an item from the binary search tree.

    5. Find the height of the binary search tree.

    6. Find the number of nodes in the binary search tree.

    7. Find the number of leaves in the binary search tree.

    8. Traverse the binary search tree.

    9. Copy the binary search tree.

Clearly, every binary search tree is a binary tree. The height of a binary search tree is determined the same way as the height of a binary tree. Similarly, the operations to find the number of nodes, find the number of leaves, and to do inorder, preorder, and postorder traversals of a binary search tree are the same as those for a binary tree. Therefore, we can inherit all of these operations from the binary tree. That is, we can extend the definition of the binary tree by using the principle of inheritance, and hence define the binary search tree.

The following class defines a binary search tree as an ADT by extending the definition of the binary tree:

Class: `BinarySearchTree`

`public class BinarySearchTree extends BinaryTree`

Constructors and Instance Methods:

```
public BinarySearchTree()
   //default constructor
   //Postcondition: root = null;

public BinarySearchTree(BinarySearchTree otherTree)
   //copy constructor

public boolean search(DataElement searchItem)
   //Method to determine whether searchItem is in the binary
   //search tree.
   //Postcondition: Returns true if searchItem is found in the
   //               binary search tree, false otherwise.

public void insert(DataElement insertItem)
   //Method to insert insertItem in the binary search tree.
   //Postcondition: If no node in the binary search tree has
   //               the same info as insertItem, a node with
   //               the info insertItem is created and inserted
   //               in the binary search tree.

public void deleteNode(DataElement deleteItem)
   //Method to delete deleteItem from the binary search tree.
   //Postcondition: If a node with the same info as deleteItem
   //               is found, it is deleted from the binary
   //               search tree.

private BinaryTreeNode deleteFromTree(BinaryTreeNode p)
   //Method to delete the node to which p points from the
   //binary search tree.
   //Postcondition: The node to which p points is deleted
   //               from the binary search tree. The reference
   //               of the root node of the binary search tree
   //               after deletion is returned.
```

Next, we describe each of these operations.

Search

The method `search` searches the binary search tree for a given item. If the item is found in the binary search tree, it returns `true`; otherwise, it returns `false`. Because `root` points to the root node of the binary search tree, we must begin our search at the root node. Furthermore, because `root` must always point to the root node, we need a reference variable, say `current`, to traverse the binary search tree. The reference variable `current` is initialized to `root`.

If the binary search tree is nonempty, we first compare the search item with the info in the root node. If they are the same, we stop the search and return `true`. Otherwise, if the search item is smaller than the info in the node, we follow `llink` to go to the left subtree; otherwise, we follow `rlink` to go to the right subtree. We repeat this process for the next node. If the search item is in the binary search tree, our search ends at the node containing the search item; otherwise, the search ends at an empty subtree. Thus, the general algorithm is:

```
if root is null
   Cannot search an empty tree, returns false.
else
{
   current = root;
   while(current is not null and not found)
       if(current.info is the same as the search item)
           set found to true;
       else
           if(current.info is greater than the search item)
               follow the llink of current
           else
               follow the rlink of current
}
```

This pseudocode algorithm translates into the following Java method:

```java
public boolean search(DataElement searchItem)
{
    BinaryTreeNode current;
    boolean found = false;

    if(root == null)
       System.out.println("Cannot search an empty tree.");
    else
    {
       current = root;

       while(current != null && !found)
       {
           if(current.info.equals(searchItem))
              found = true;
           else
              if(current.info.compareTo(searchItem) > 0)
                 current = current.llink;
              else
                 current = current.rlink;
       }//end while
    }//end else

    return found;
}//end search
```

10

Insert

The method `insert` inserts a new item in the binary search tree. After inserting an item in a binary search tree, the resulting binary tree must also be a binary search tree. To insert a new item, first we search the binary search tree and find the place where the new item is to be inserted. The search algorithm is similar to the search algorithm of the method `search`. Here we traverse the binary search tree with two reference variables—say, `current`, to check the current node and, say, `trailCurrent`, pointing to the parent of `current`. Because duplicate items are not allowed, our search must end at an empty subtree. We can then use `trailCurrent` to insert the new item at the proper place. The item to be inserted, `insertItem`, is passed as a parameter to the method `insert`. The general algorithm is:

a. Create a new node and copy insertItem into the new node. Also, set llink and rlink of the new node to null.

b. if root is null,
       the tree is empty so make root point to the new node.

   else
   {
      current = root;

      while(current is not null)   //search the binary tree
      {
          trailCurrent = current;
          if(current.info is the same as insertItem)
             Error: Cannot insert duplicate items.
             exit
          else
             if(current.info is greater than insertItem)
                Follow llink of current
             else
                Follow rlink of current
      }
      //insert the new node in the binary tree

      if(trailCurrent.info is greater than insertItem)
         make the new node the left child of trailCurrent
      else
         make the new node the right child of trailCurrent

   }

This pseudocode algorithm translates into the following Java method:

```java
public void insert(DataElement insertItem)
{
    BinaryTreeNode current;          //reference variable to
                                     //traverse the tree
    BinaryTreeNode trailCurrent = null; //reference variable
                                        //behind current
    BinaryTreeNode newNode;          //reference variable to
                                     //create the node

    newNode = new BinaryTreeNode();

    newNode.info = insertItem.getCopy();
    newNode.llink = null;
    newNode.rlink = null;

    if(root == null)
        root = newNode;
    else
    {
        current = root;

        while(current != null)
        {
            trailCurrent = current;

            if(current.info.equals(insertItem))
            {
                System.err.print("The insert item is already in "
                            + "the list -- duplicates are "
                            + "not allowed.");
                return;
            }
            else
                if(current.info.compareTo(insertItem) > 0)
                    current = current.llink;
                else
                    current = current.rlink;
        }//end while

        if(trailCurrent.info.compareTo(insertItem) > 0)
            trailCurrent.llink = newNode;
        else
            trailCurrent.rlink = newNode;
    }
}//end insert
```

10

Delete

The method `deleteNode` deletes an item from the binary search tree. After deleting the item, the resulting binary tree must be a binary search tree. As before, first we search the binary search tree to find the node to be deleted. To help you better understand the delete operation, before describing the method to delete an item from the binary search tree, let us consider the binary search tree given in Figure 10-11.

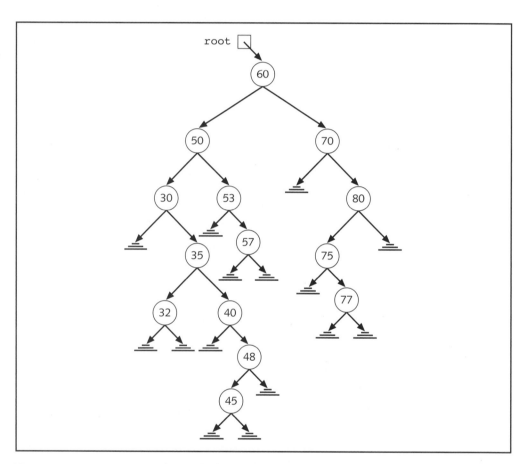

Figure 10-11   Binary search tree before deleting a node

After deleting the desired item (if it exists in the binary search tree), the resulting tree must be a binary search tree. The delete operation has four cases:

Case 1: The node to be deleted has no left and right subtrees; that is, the node to be deleted is a leaf. For example, the node with info **45** is a leaf.

Case 2: The node to be deleted has no left subtree; that is, the left subtree is empty, but it has a nonempty right subtree. For example, the left subtree of the node with info **40** is empty and its right subtree is nonempty.

Case 3: The node to be deleted has no right subtree; that is, the right subtree is empty, but it has a nonempty left subtree. For example, the right subtree of the node with info **80** is empty and its left subtree is nonempty.

Case 4: The node to be deleted has nonempty left and right subtrees. For example, the left and right subtrees of the node with info **50** are nonempty.

Case 1: Suppose that we want to delete **45** from the binary search tree in Figure 10-11. We search the binary search tree and arrive at the node containing **45**. Because this node is a leaf and is the left child of its parent, we can simply set the **llink** of the parent node of **45** to **null** and deallocate the memory occupied by this node. After deleting this node, Figure 10-12 shows the resulting binary search tree.

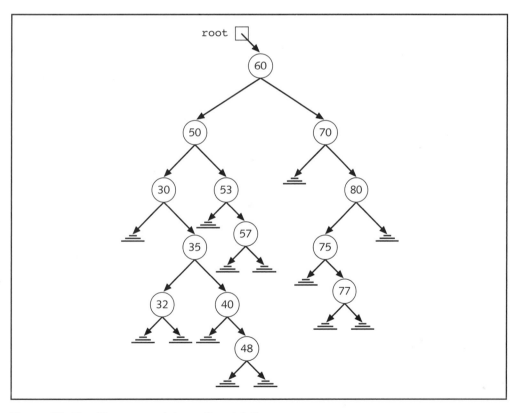

Figure 10-12   Binary search tree after deleting 45

Case 2: Suppose that we want to delete 30 from the binary search tree in Figure 10-11. In this case, the node to be deleted has no left subtree. Because 30 is the left child of its parent node, we make the llink of the parent node, of 30, point to the right child of 30—that is, 35—and then deallocate the memory occupied by 30. Figure 10-13 shows the resulting binary search tree.

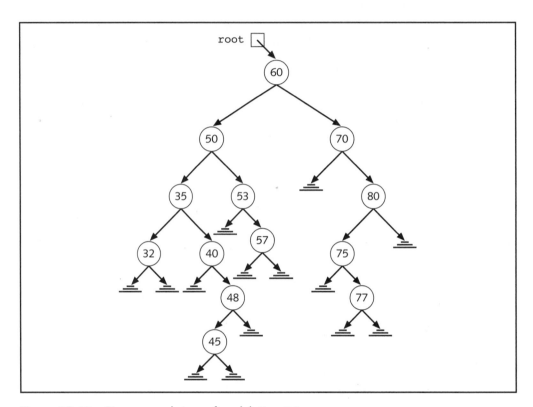

Figure 10-13 Binary search tree after deleting 30

Case 3: Suppose that we want to delete 80 from the binary search tree in Figure 10-11. The node containing 80 has no right child and is the right child of its parent. Thus, we make the rlink of the parent of 80—that is, 70—point to the left child of 80. Figure 10-14 shows the resulting binary search tree.

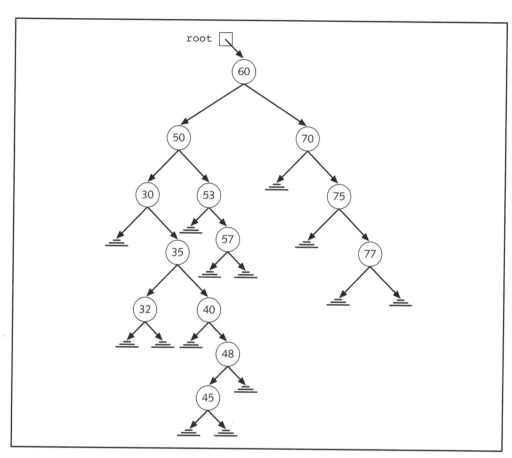

Figure 10-14   Binary search tree after deleting 80

Case 4: Suppose that we want to delete 50 from the binary search tree in Figure 10-11. The node with info 50 has a nonempty left subtree and a nonempty right subtree. Here, we first reduce this case to either case 2 or case 3 as follows. To be specific, suppose that we reduce it to case 3—that is, the node to be deleted has no right subtree. For this case, we find the immediate predecessor of 50 in this binary tree, which is 48. This is done by first going to the left child of 50 and then locating the rightmost node of the left subtree of 50. To do so, we follow the `rlink` of the nodes. Because the binary search tree is finite, we eventually arrive at a node that has no right subtree. Next, we swap the info of the node to be deleted with the info of its immediate predecessor. In this case, we swap 48 with 50. This reduces to the case wherein the node to be deleted has no right subtree. We now apply case 3 to delete the node. (Note that because we delete the immediate predecessor from the binary search tree, we, in fact, copy only the info of the immediate predecessor into the node to be deleted.) After deleting 50 from the binary search tree in Figure 10-11, the resulting binary tree is as shown in Figure 10-15.

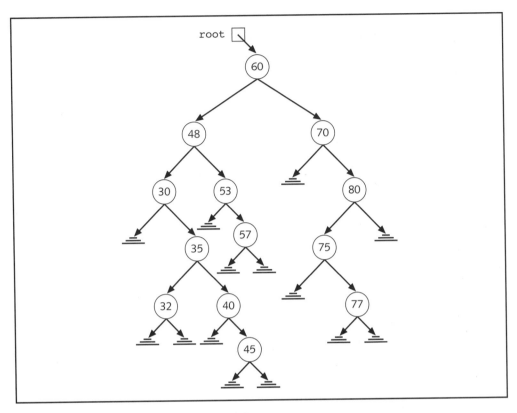

Figure 10-15   Binary search tree after deleting 50

In each case, we see that the resulting binary tree is again a binary search tree.

From this discussion, it follows that to delete an item from a binary search tree, we must do the following:

1. Find the node containing the item (if any) to be deleted.

2. Delete the node.

We accomplish the second step by a separate method, which we call `deleteFromTree`. Given a reference of the node to be deleted, this method deletes the node, by taking into account the previous four cases. Moreover, after deleting the node, it returns the reference of the root node of the binary search subtree.

These preceding examples show that whenever we delete a node from a binary search tree, we adjust one of the links of the parent node. Because the adjustment has to be made in the parent node, we must call the method `deleteFromTree` by using an appropriate link of the parent node. For example, suppose that the node to be deleted is **35**, which is the right child of its parent node. Further suppose that `trailCurrent` points to the node containing 30, the parent node of 35. A call to the method `deleteFromTree` is:

```
trailCurrent.rlink = deleteFromTree(trailCurrent.rlink);
```

Of course, if the node to be deleted is the root node, then the call to the method `deleteFromTree` is:

```
root = deleteFromTree(root);
```

We now define the Java method `deleteFromTree`:

```
private BinaryTreeNode deleteFromTree(BinaryTreeNode p)
{
    BinaryTreeNode current;         //reference variable to
                                    //traverse the tree
    BinaryTreeNode trailCurrent;    //reference variable
                                    //behind current

    if(p == null)
       System.err.println("Error: The node to be deleted "
                        + "is null.");
    else if(p.llink == null && p.rlink == null)
          p = null;
    else if(p.llink == null)
          p = p.rlink;
    else if(p.rlink == null)
          p = p.llink;
    else
    {
       current = p.llink;
       trailCurrent = null;

       while(current.rlink != null)
       {
           trailCurrent = current;
           current = current.rlink;
       }//end while

       p.info = current.info;

       if(trailCurrent == null) //current did not move;
                                //current == p.llink; adjust p
          p.llink = current.llink;
       else
          trailCurrent.rlink = current.llink;
    }//end else

    return p;
}//end deleteFromTree
```

Next, we describe the method `deleteNode`. The method `deleteNode` first searches the binary search tree to find the node containing the item to be deleted. The item to be deleted,

10

deleteItem, is passed as a parameter to the method. If the node containing deleteItem is found in the binary search tree, the method deleteNode calls the method deleteFromTree to delete the node. The definition of the method deleteNode is given next:

```
public void deleteNode(DataElement deleteItem)
{
    BinaryTreeNode current;   //reference variable to
                              //traverse the tree
    BinaryTreeNode trailCurrent; //reference variable
                                 //behind current
    boolean found = false;

    if(root == null)
       System.err.println("Cannot delete from an empty tree.");
    else
    {
       current = root;
       trailCurrent = root;

       while(current != null && !found)
       {
           if(current.info.equals(deleteItem))
              found = true;
           else
           {
              trailCurrent = current;

              if(current.info.compareTo(deleteItem) > 0)
                 current = current.llink;
              else
                 current = current.rlink;
           }
       }//end while

       if(current == null)
          System.out.println("The delete item is not in "
                             + "the list.");
       else
          if(found)
          {
             if(current == root)
                root = deleteFromTree(root);
             else
                if(trailCurrent.info.compareTo(deleteItem) > 0)
                    trailCurrent.llink =
                            deleteFromTree(trailCurrent.llink);
                else
                    trailCurrent.rlink =
                            deleteFromTree(trailCurrent.rlink);
          }//end if
    }
}//end deleteNode
```

BINARY SEARCH TREE: ANALYSIS

This section provides an analysis of the performance of binary search trees. Let T be a binary search tree with n nodes, where $n > 0$. Suppose that we want to determine whether an item, x, is in T. The performance of the search algorithm depends on the shape of T. Let us first consider the worst case. In the worst case, T is linear. That is, T is one of the forms shown in Figure 10-16.

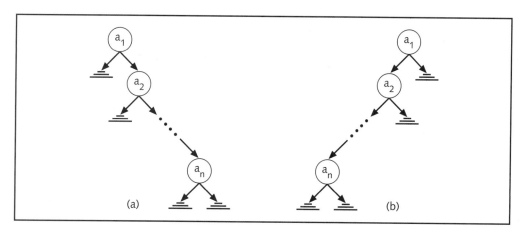

Figure 10-16   Linear binary search trees

Because T is linear, the performance of the search algorithm on T is the same as its performance on a linear list. Therefore, in the successful case, on average, the search algorithm makes $\dfrac{n+1}{2}$ key comparisons. In the unsuccessful case, it makes n comparisons.

Let us now consider the average-case behavior. In the successful case, the search would end at a node. Because there are n items, there are $n!$ possible orderings of the keys. We assume that all $n!$ orderings of the keys are possible. Let $S(n)$ denote the number of comparisons in the average successful case, and $U(n)$ denote the number of comparisons in the average unsuccessful case.

The number of comparisons required to determine whether x is in T is one more than the number of comparisons required to insert x in T. Furthermore, the number of comparisons required to insert x in T is the same as the number of comparisons made in the unsuccessful search, reflecting that x is not in T. From this, it follows that:

$$S(n) = 1 + \frac{U(0) + U(1) + \ldots + U(n-1)}{n} \qquad (10\text{-}1)$$

It is also known that:

$$S(n) = \left(1 + \frac{1}{n}\right) U(n) - 3 \qquad (10\text{-}2)$$

Solving Equations (10-1) and (10-2), it can be shown that:

$$U(n) \approx 2.77\log_2 n$$

and:

$$S(n) \approx 1.39\log_2 n$$

We can now formulate the following result.

Theorem: Let T be a binary search tree with n nodes, where $n > 0$. The average number of nodes visited in a search of T is approximately $1.39\log_2 n$.

NONRECURSIVE BINARY TREE TRAVERSAL ALGORITHMS

The previous sections described how to do the following:

- Traverse a binary tree using the inorder, preorder, and postorder methods.

- Construct a binary search tree.

- Insert an item in a binary search tree.

- Delete an item from a binary search tree.

The traversal algorithms—inorder, preorder, and postorder—discussed earlier are recursive. Because traversing a binary tree is a fundamental operation and recursive methods are somewhat less efficient then their iterative versions, this section discusses the nonrecursive inorder, preorder, and postorder traversal algorithms.

Nonrecursive Inorder Traversal

In an inorder traversal of a binary tree, for each node, the left subtree is visited first, then the node, and then the right subtree. It follows that in an inorder traversal, the first node visited is the leftmost node of the binary tree. For example, in the binary tree in Figure 10-17, the leftmost node is the node with info **28**.

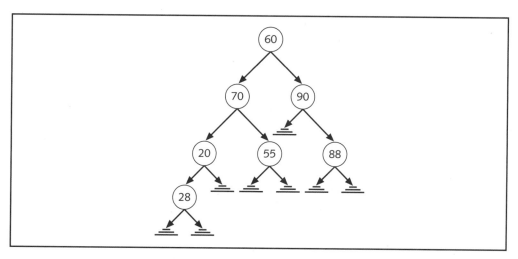

Figure 10-17 Binary tree; the leftmost node is 28

To get to the leftmost node of the binary tree, we start by traversing the binary tree at the root node and then follow the left link of each node until the left link of a node becomes null. We then back up to the parent node, visit the node, and then move to the right node. Because links go in only one direction, to get back to a node we must save the reference of the node before moving to the child node. Moreover, the nodes must be backtracked in the order they were traversed. It follows that while backtracking, the nodes must be visited in a Last In First Out manner. This can be done by using a stack. We, therefore, save the reference of a node in a stack. The general algorithm is as follows:

```
1. current = root;   //start traversing the binary tree at the
                      //root node
2. while(current is not null or stack is nonempty)
       if(current is not null)
       {
          push current onto stack;
          current = current.llink;
       }
       else
       {
          pop stack into current;
          visit current;       //visit the node
          current = current.rlink;  //move to the
                                    //right child
       }
```

The following Java method implements the preceding algorithm. (Note that the method nonRecursiveInTraversal uses the Java **class Stack**, described in Chapter 6, to implement a stack. You can also use the **class StackClass** as defined in Chapter 6, provided you modify the definition of the class `BinaryTreeNode` by deriving this class from the class `DataElement`.)

```java
public void nonRecursiveInTraversal()
{
    Stack stack = new Stack();
    BinaryTreeNode current;
    current = root;

    while((current != null) || (!stack.empty()))
        if(current != null)
        {
            stack.push(current);
            current = current.llink;
        }
        else
        {
            current = (BinaryTreeNode) stack.peek();
            stack.pop();
            System.out.print(current.info + " ");
            current = current.rlink;
        }

    System.out.println();
}
```

Nonrecursive Preorder Traversal

In a preorder traversal of a binary tree, for each node, first the node is visited, then the left subtree is visited, and then the right subtree is visited. As in the case of an inorder traversal, after visiting a node and before moving to the left subtree, we must save the reference of the node so that after visiting the left subtree, we can visit the right subtree. The general algorithm is as follows:

```
1.  current = root;   //start the traversal at the root node
2.  while(current is not null or stack is nonempty)
        if(current is not null)
        {
            visit current;
            push current onto stack;
            current = current.llink;
        }
        else
        {
            pop stack into current;
            current = current.rlink;   //prepare to visit the
                                       //right subtree

        }
```

We leave it as an exercise for you to write a Java method to implement the preceding algorithm (see Programming Exercise 6).

Nonrecursive Postorder Traversal

In a postorder traversal of a binary tree, for each node, first the left subtree is visited, then the right subtree is visited, and then the node is visited. As in the case of an inorder traversal, in a postorder traversal, the first node visited is the leftmost node of the binary tree. Because—for each node—the left and right subtrees are visited before visiting the node, we must indicate to the node whether the left and right subtrees have been visited. After visiting the left subtree of a node and before visiting the node, we must visit its right subtree. Therefore, after returning from a left subtree, we must tell the node that the right subtree needs to be visited, and after visiting the right subtree we must tell the node that it can now be visited. To do this, other than saving the reference of the node (to get back to the right subtree and to the node itself), we also save an integer value of 1 before moving to the left subtree and an integer value of 2 before moving to the right subtree. Whenever the stack is popped, the integer value associated with that reference is popped as well. This integer value tells whether the left and right subtrees of a node have been visited.

The general algorithm is:

```
1.  current = root;          //start the traversal at the root node
2.  v = 0;
3.  if(current is null)
        the binary tree is empty
4.  if(current is not null)
    a.  push current onto stack;
    b.  push 1 onto stack;
    c.  current = current.llink;
    d.  while(stack is not empty)
            if(current is not null and v is 0)
            {
                push current and 1 onto stack;
                current = current.llink;
            }
            else
            {
                pop stack into current and v;
                if(v == 1)
                {
                    push current and 2 onto stack;
                    current = current.rlink;
                    v = 0;
                }
                else
                    visit current;
            }
```

We use two (parallel) stacks: one to save the reference of a node, and another to save the integer value (1 or 2). We leave it as an exercise for you to write the definition of a Java method to implement the preceding postorder traversal algorithm (see Programming Exercise 6 at the end of this chapter).

AVL (Height-Balanced) Trees

In the previous sections, you learned how to build and manipulate a binary search tree. The performance of the search algorithm on a binary search tree depends on how the binary tree is built. The shape of the binary search tree depends on the data set. If the data set is sorted, then the binary search tree is linear and so the search algorithm would not be efficient. On the other hand, if the tree is nicely built, then the search would be fast. In fact, the smaller the height of the tree, the faster the search. Therefore, we want the height of the binary search tree to be as small as possible. This section describes a special type of binary search tree, called the **AVL tree** (also called the **height-balanced tree**), in which the resulting binary search tree is nearly balanced. AVL trees, were introduced by the mathematicians G. M. Adelson-Velskii and E. M. Landis in 1962 and are so named in their honor.

We begin by defining the following terms:

Definition: A **perfectly balanced** binary tree is a binary tree such that:

     i. The height of the left and right subtrees of the root are equal.

     ii. The left and right subtrees of the root are perfectly balanced binary trees.

Figure 10-18 shows a perfectly balanced binary tree.

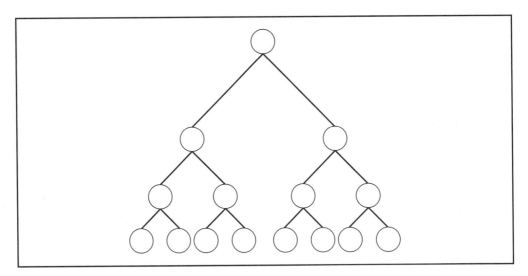

Figure 10-18   Perfectly balanced binary tree

Let T be a binary tree and x be a node in T. If T is perfectly balanced, then from the definition of the perfectly balanced tree it follows that the height of the left subtree of x is the same as the height of the right subtree of x.

It can be proved that if T is a perfectly balanced binary tree of height h, then the number of nodes in T is 2^{h-1}. From this, it follows that if the number of items in the data set is not a power of 2, then we cannot construct a perfectly balanced binary tree. Moreover, perfectly balanced binary trees are a too stringent refinement.

Definition: An **AVL tree** (or **height-balanced tree**) is a binary search tree such that:

    i. The height of the left and right subtrees of the root differ by at most 1.

    ii. The left and right subtrees of the root are AVL trees.

Figures 10-19 and 10-20 give examples of AVL and non-AVL trees.

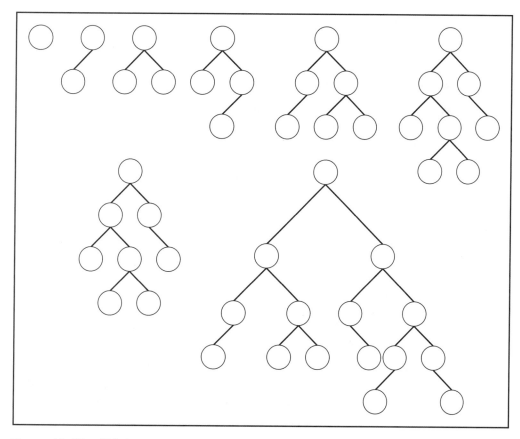

Figure 10-19 AVL trees

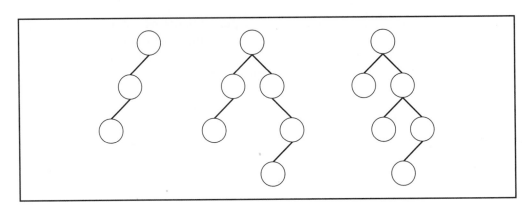

Figure 10-20 Non-AVL trees

Let x be a node in a binary tree. Let x_l denote the height of the left subtree of x, and x_r denote the height of the right subtree of x.

Proposition: Let T be an AVL tree and x be a node in T. Then $|x_r - x_l| \leq 1$, where $|x_r - x_l|$ denotes the absolute value of $x_r - x_l$.

Let x be a node in the AVL tree T.

    1. If $x_l > x_r$, we say that x is **left high**. In this case, $x_l = x_r + 1$.

    2. If $x_l = x_r$, we say that x is **equal high**.

    3. If $x_r > x_l$, we say that x is **right high**. In this case, $x_r = x_l + 1$.

Definition: The **balance factor** of x, written $bf(x)$, is defined as $bf(x) = x_r - x_l$.

Let x be a node in the AVL tree T. Then:

    1. If x is left high, then $bf(x) = -1$.

    2. If x is equal high, then $bf(x) = 0$.

    3. If x is right high, then $bf(x) = 1$.

Definition: Let x be a node in a binary tree. We say that the node x **violates the balance criteria** if $|x_r - x_l| > 1$, that is, the height of the left and right subtrees of x differ by more than 1.

From the previous discussion, it follows that in addition to the data and references of the left and right subtrees, one more thing associated with each node x in the AVL tree T is the balance factor of x. Thus, every node must keep track of its balance factor. To make the algorithms efficient, we store the balance factor of each node in the node itself. Hence, the definition of a node in an AVL tree is:

```
protected class AVLNode
{
    DataElement info;
    int bfactor;        //balance factor
    AVLNode llink;
    AVLNode rlink;
}
```

Because an AVL tree is a binary search tree, the search algorithm for an AVL tree is the same as the search algorithm for a binary search tree. Other operations, such as finding the height, determining the number of nodes, checking whether the tree is empty, tree traversal, and so on, on AVL trees can be implemented exactly the same way as they are implemented on binary trees. However, item insertion and deletion operations on AVL trees are somewhat different than the ones discussed for binary search trees. This is because after inserting (or deleting) a node from an AVL tree, the resulting binary tree must be an AVL tree. Next, we describe these operations.

Insertion into AVL Trees

To insert an item in an AVL tree, first we search the tree and find the place where the new item is to be inserted. Because an AVL tree is a binary search tree, to find the place for the new item we can search the AVL tree using a search algorithm similar to the search algorithm designed for binary search trees. If the item to be inserted is already in the tree, then the search ends at a nonempty subtree. Because duplicates are not allowed, in this case, we can output an appropriate error message. Suppose that the item to be inserted is not in the AVL tree. Then the search ends at an empty subtree and we insert the item in that subtree. After inserting the new item in the tree, the resulting tree might not be an AVL tree. Thus, we must restore the tree's balance criteria. This is accomplished by traveling the same path, back to the root node, which was followed when the new item was inserted in the AVL tree. The nodes on this path (back to the root node) are visited and either their balance factors are changed, or we might have to reconstruct part of the tree. We illustrate these cases with the help of the following examples.

 In Figures 10-21 through 10-32, for each node, we show only the data stored in the node. Moreover, an equal sign (=) on the top of a node indicates that the balance factor of this node is 0, the less than symbol (<) indicates that the balance factor of this node is −1, and the greater than symbol (>) indicates that the balance factor of this node is 1.

Consider the AVL tree of Figure 10-21.

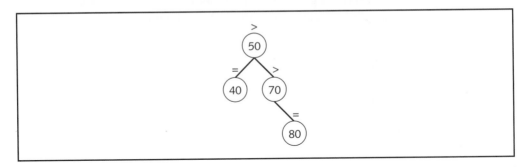

Figure 10-21   AVL tree before inserting 90

Let us insert 90 into this AVL tree. We search the tree starting at the root node to find the place for 90. The dotted arrow shows the path traversed. We insert the node with info 90 and obtain the binary search tree of Figure 10-22.

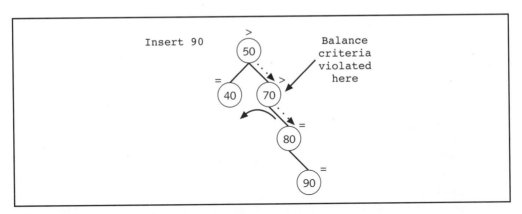

Figure 10-22   Binary tree of Figure 10-21 after inserting 90; nodes other than 90 show their balance factors before insertion

The binary search tree of Figure 10-22 is not an AVL tree. So we backtrack and go to node 80. Prior to insertion, bf(80) was 0. Because the new node was inserted into the (empty) right subtree of 80, we change its balance factor to 1 (not shown in the figure). Now we go back to node 70. Prior to insertion, bf(70) was 1. After insertion, the height of the right subtree of 70 is increased; thus, we see that the subtree with the root node 70 is not an AVL tree. In this case, we reconstruct this subtree (this is called rotating the tree at root node 70). We thus obtain the AVL tree as shown in Figure 10-23.

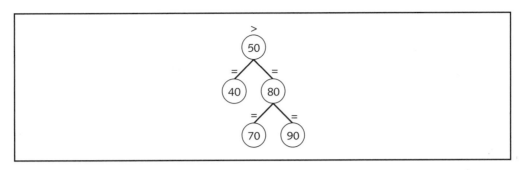

Figure 10-23   AVL tree of Figure 10-21 after inserting 90 and adjusting the balance factors

The binary search tree of Figure 10-23 is an AVL tree.

Now consider the AVL tree of Figure 10-24.

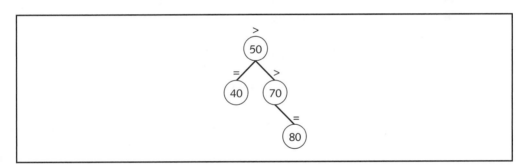

Figure 10-24   AVL tree before inserting 75

Let us insert 75 into the AVL tree of Figure 10-24.

As before, we search the tree starting at the root node. The dotted arrows show the path traversed. After inserting 75, the resulting binary search tree is as shown in Figure 10-25.

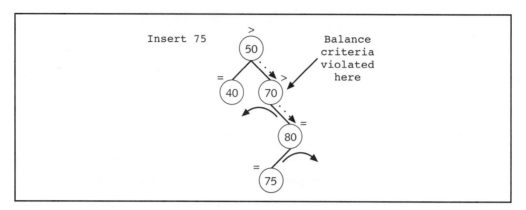

Figure 10-25 Binary tree of Figure 10-24 after inserting 75; nodes other than 75 show their balance factors before insertion

After inserting 75, we backtrack. First we go to node 80 and change its balance factor to -1. The subtree with the root node 80 is an AVL tree. Now we go back to 70. Clearly, the subtree with the root node 70 is not an AVL tree. So we reconstruct this subtree. In this case, we first reconstruct the subtree at root node 80, and then reconstruct the subtree at root node 70 to obtain the binary search tree as shown in Figure 10-26. (These constructions, that is, rotations, are explained in the next section, "AVL Tree Rotations.")

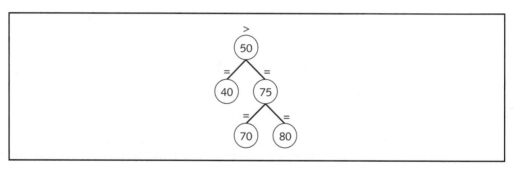

Figure 10-26 AVL tree of Figure 10-24 after inserting 75 and adjusting the balance factors

After reconstruction, the root of the constructed subtree is 75.

Notice that in Figures 10-23 and 10-26, after reconstructing the subtrees at the nodes, the subtrees no longer grew in height. At this point, we usually send the message, stating that overall the tree did not gain any height, to the remaining nodes on the path back to the root node of the tree. Thus, the remaining nodes on the path do not need to do anything.

Next, consider the AVL tree of Figure 10-27.

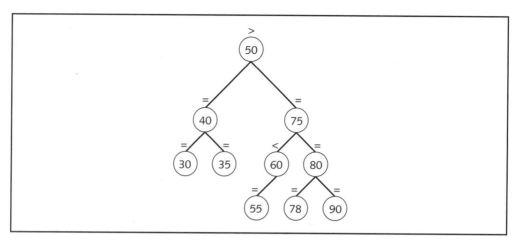

Figure 10-27   AVL tree before inserting 95

Let us insert 95 into this AVL tree. We search the tree and insert 95, as shown in Figure 10-28.

10

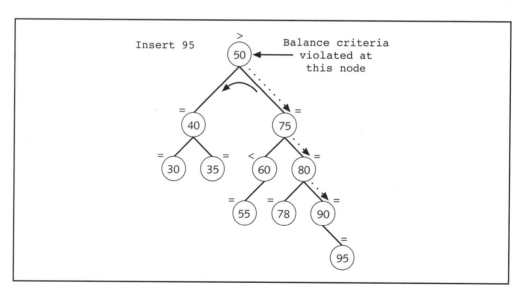

Figure 10-28   Binary tree of Figure 10-27 after inserting 95; nodes other than 95 show their balance factors before insertion

After inserting 95, we see that the subtrees with the root nodes 90, 80, and 75 are still AVL trees. When backtracking the path, we simply adjust the balance factors of these nodes (if needed). However, when we backtrack to the root node, we discover that the tree at this node is no longer an AVL tree. Prior to insertion, bf(50) was 1, that is, its right subtree was higher than its left subtree. After insertion, the right subtree grew in height, thus violating the balance criteria at **50**. So we reconstruct the binary search tree at node **50**. In this case, the tree is reconstructed as shown in Figure 10-29.

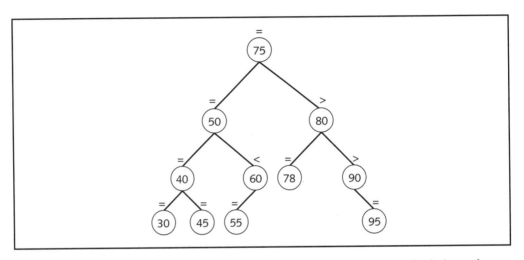

Figure 10-29 AVL tree of Figure 10-27 after inserting **95** and adjusting the balance factors

Before discussing the general algorithms for reconstructing (rotating) a subtree, let us consider one more case. Consider the AVL tree as shown in Figure 10-30.

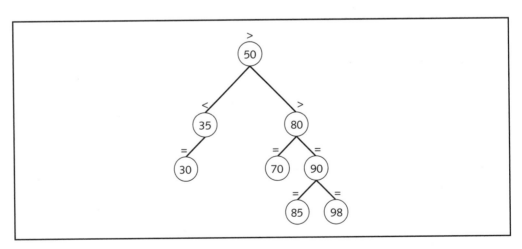

Figure 10-30 AVL tree before inserting **88**

Let us insert 88 into the tree of Figure 10-30. Following the insertion procedure as described previously, we obtain the binary search tree as shown in Figure 10-31.

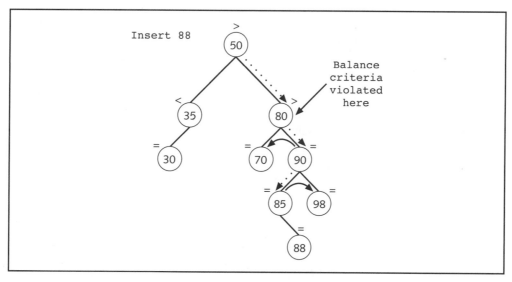

Figure 10-31 Binary tree of Figure 10-30 after inserting 88; nodes other than 88 show their balance factors before insertion

As before, we now backtrack to the root node. We adjust the balance factors of nodes 85 and 90. When we visit node 80, we discover that at this node we need to reconstruct the subtree. In this case, the subtree is reconstructed as shown in Figure 10-32.

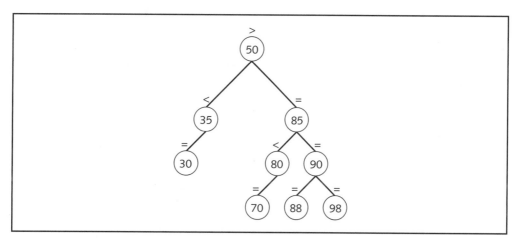

Figure 10-32 AVL tree of Figure 10-30 after inserting 88 and adjusting the balance factors

10

As before, after reconstructing the subtree, the entire tree is balanced. So for the remaining nodes on the path back to the root node, we do nothing.

The previous examples indicate that if part of the binary search tree requires reconstruction, then after reconstructing that part of the binary search tree, we can ignore the remaining nodes on the path back to the root node. (This is, indeed, the case.) Also, after inserting the node, the reconstruction can occur at any node on the path back to the root node.

AVL Tree Rotations

We now describe the reconstruction procedure, called **rotating** the tree. There are two types of rotations, **left rotation** and **right rotation**. Suppose that the rotation occurs at node x. If it is a left rotation, then certain nodes from the right subtree of x move to its left subtree; the root of the right subtree of x becomes the new root of the reconstructed subtree. Similarly, if it is a right rotation at x, certain nodes from the left subtree of x move to its right subtree; the root of the left subtree of x becomes the new root of the reconstructed subtree.

Case 1: Consider Figure 10-33.

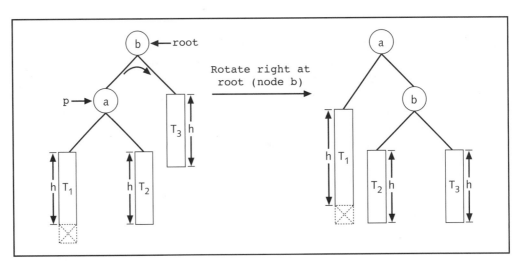

Figure 10-33   Right rotation at b

In Figure 10-33, subtrees T_1, T_2, and T_3 are of equal height, say h. The dotted rectangle shows an item insertion in T_1, causing the height of the subtree T_1 to increase by 1. The subtree at node a is still an AVL tree, but the balance criteria is violated at the root node. We note the following in this tree. Because the tree is a binary search tree:

- Every key in T_1 is smaller than the key in node a.
- Every key in T_2 is larger than the key in node a.
- Every key in T_2 is smaller than the key in node b.

Therefore:

1. We make T_2 (the right subtree of node a) the left subtree of node b.

2. We make node b the right child of node a.

3. Node a becomes the root node of the reconstructed tree, as shown in Figure 10-33.

Case 2: This case is a mirror image of Case 1. See Figure 10-34.

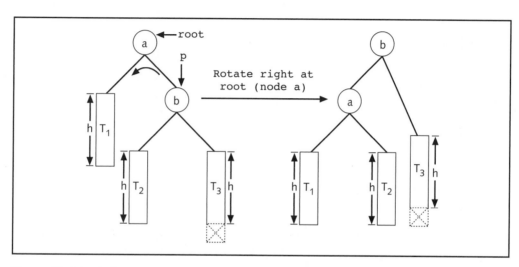

Figure 10-34   Left rotation at a

Case 3: Consider Figure 10-35.

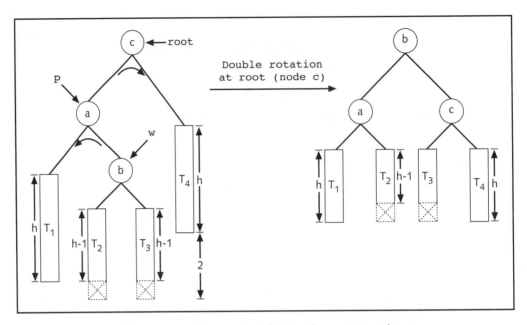

Figure 10-35 Double rotation: first rotate left at *a*, then rotate right at *c*

In Figure 10-35, the tree on the left is the tree prior to the reconstruction. The heights of the subtrees are shown in the figure. The dotted rectangle shows that a new item is inserted in the subtree, T_2 or T_3, causing the subtree to grow in height. We note the following (in the tree prior to reconstruction):

- All keys in T_3 are smaller than the key in node *c*.
- All keys in T_3 are larger than the key in node *b*.
- All keys in T_2 are smaller than the key in node *b*.
- All keys in T_2 are larger than the key in node *a*.
- After insertion, the subtrees with root nodes *a* and *b* are still AVL trees.
- The balance criteria is violated at the root node, *c*, of the tree.
- The balance factors of node *c*, $bf(c) = -1$, and node *a*, $bf(a) = 1$, are opposite.

This is an example of double rotation. One rotation is required at node *a*, and another rotation is required at node *c*. If the balance factor of the node where the tree is to be reconstructed and the balance factor of the higher subtree are opposite, that node requires a double rotation. First, we rotate the tree at node *a* and then at node *c*. The tree at node *a* is right high and so we make a left rotation at *a*. Next, because the tree at node *c* is left high, we make a right rotation at *c*. Figure 10-35 shows the resulting tree (which is to the right of the tree after insertion). Figure 10-36, however, shows both rotations in sequence.

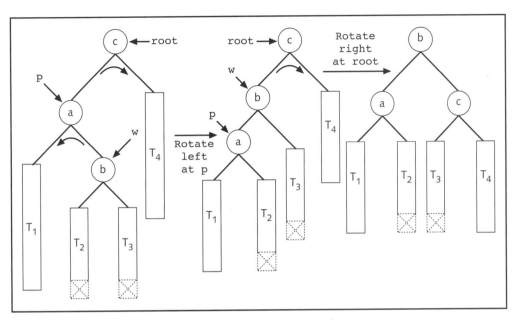

Figure 10-36   Left rotation at *a* followed by a right rotation at *c*

Case 4: This is a mirror image of Case 3. We illustrate this with the help of Figure 10-37.

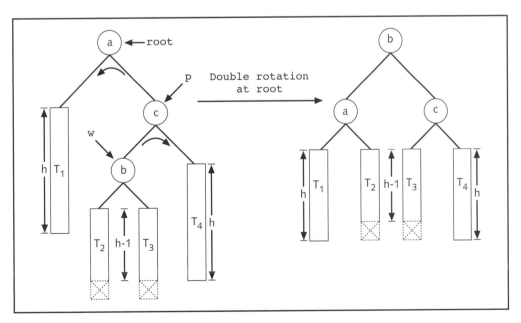

Figure 10-37   Double rotation: first rotate right at *c*, then rotate left at *a*

Using these four cases, we now describe what type of rotation might be required at a node.

Suppose that the tree is to be reconstructed, by rotation, at node x. The subtree with the root node x then requires either a single or a double rotation.

1. Suppose that the balance factor of the node x and the balance factor of the root node of the higher subtree of x have the same sign, that is, both positive or both negative.

   a. If these balance factors are positive, make a single *left* rotation at x. (Prior to insertion, the right subtree of x was higher than its left subtree. The new item was inserted in the right subtree of x, causing the height of the right subtree to increase in height, which in turn violated the balance criteria at x.)

   b. If these balance factors are negative, make a single *right* rotation at x. (Prior to insertion, the left subtree of x was higher than its right subtree. The new item was inserted in the left subtree of x, causing the height of the left subtree to increase in height, which in turn violated the balance criteria at x.)

2. Suppose that the balance factor of the node x and the balance factor of the higher subtree of x are opposite in sign. To be specific, suppose that the balance factor of node x prior to insertion was –1 and suppose that y is the root node of the left subtree of x. After insertion, the balance factor of node y is 1. That is, after insertion, the right subtree of node y grew in height. In this case, we require a *double* rotation at x. First we make a left rotation at y (because y is right high). Then we make a right rotation at x. The other case, which is a mirror image of this case, is handled similarly.

The following Java methods implement the left and right rotations of a node. The reference of the node requiring the rotation is passed as a parameter to the method.

```
private AVLNode rotateToLeft(AVLNode root)
{
    AVLNode p; //reference variable to the root of the
               //right subtree of root
    if(root == null)
        System.err.println("Error in the tree.");
    else
        if(root.rlink == null)
            System.err.println("Error in the tree: "
                            + "No right subtree to rotate.");
        else
        {
            p = root.rlink;
            root.rlink = p.llink; //the left subtree of p
                            //becomes the right subtree of root
            p.llink = root;
            root = p;      //make p the new root node
        }

    return root;
}//end rotateToLeft
```

```
private AVLNode rotateToRight(AVLNode root)
{
    AVLNode p;   //reference variable to the root of the
                 //left subtree of root

    if(root == null)
       System.err.println("Error in the tree.");
    else
       if(root.llink == null)
          System.err.println("Error in the tree: "
                             + "No left subtree to rotate.");
       else
       {
          p = root.llink;
          root.llink = p.rlink; //the right subtree of p
                                //becomes the left subtree of root
          p.rlink = root;
          root = p;    //make p the new root node
       }

    return root;
}//end rotateToRight
```

Now that we know how to implement both rotations, we next write the Java methods,
balanceFromLeft and balanceFromRight, which are used to reconstruct the tree at a
particular node. The reference of the node where the reconstruction occurs is passed as a parameter to this method. These methods use the methods rotateToLeft and rotateToRight
to reconstruct the tree, and also adjust the balance factors of the nodes affected by the reconstruction. The method balanceFromLeft is called when the subtree is left double high and
certain nodes need to be moved to the right subtree. The method balanceFromRight has
similar conventions.

```
private AVLNode balanceFromLeft(AVLNode root)
{
    AVLNode p;
    AVLNode w;

    p = root.llink;    //p points to the left subtree of root

    switch(p.bfactor)
    {
    case -1: root.bfactor = 0;
             p.bfactor = 0;
             root = rotateToRight(root);
             break;
    case 0:  System.err.println("Error: Cannot balance "
                               + "from the left.");
             break;
```

10

```
     case 1:  w = p.rlink;
              switch(w.bfactor)  //adjust the balance factors
              {
              case -1: root.bfactor = 1;
                       p.bfactor = 0;
                       break;
              case 0:  root.bfactor = 0;
                       p.bfactor = 0;
                       break;
              case 1:  root.bfactor = 0;
                       p.bfactor = -1;
              }//end switch

              w.bfactor = 0;
              p = rotateToLeft(p);
              root.llink = p;
              root = rotateToRight(root);
     }//end switch;

     return root;
}//end balanceFromLeft
```

For the sake of completeness, we also give the definition of the method `balanceFromRight`:

```
private AVLNode balanceFromRight(AVLNode root)
{
     AVLNode p;
     AVLNode w;

     p = root.rlink;   //p points to the right subtree of root

     switch(p.bfactor)
     {
     case -1: w = p.llink;
              switch(w.bfactor)  //adjust the balance factors
              {
              case -1: root.bfactor = 0;
                       p.bfactor = 1;
                       break;
              case 0:  root.bfactor = 0;
                       p.bfactor = 0;
                       break;
              case 1:  root.bfactor = -1;
                       p.bfactor = 0;
              }//end switch

              w.bfactor = 0;
              p = rotateToRight(p);
              root.rlink = p;
              root = rotateToLeft(root);
              break;
```

```
     case 0:  System.err.println("Error: Cannot balance "
                                   + "from the right.");
              break;
     case 1:  root.bfactor = 0;
              p.bfactor = 0;
              root = rotateToLeft(root);
     }//end switch;

     return root;
}//end balanceFromRight
```

We now focus our attention on the method `insertIntoAVL`. The method `insertIntoAVL` inserts a new item into an AVL tree. The item to be inserted, and the reference of the root node of the AVL tree, are passed as parameters to this method.

The following steps describe the method `insertIntoAVL`:

1. Create a node and copy the item to be inserted into the newly created node.

2. Search the tree and find the place for the new node in the tree.

3. Insert the new node in the tree.

4. Backtrack the path, which was constructed to find the place for the new node in the tree, to the root node. If necessary, adjust the balance factors of the nodes, or reconstruct the tree at a node on the path.

Because Step 4 requires us to backtrack the path to the root node, and in a binary tree we have links only from the parent to the children, the easiest way to implement the method `insertIntoAVL` is to use recursion. (Recursion automatically takes care of the backtracking.) This is exactly what we do. The method `insertIntoAVL` also uses a `boolean` instance variable, `isTaller`, to indicate to the parent whether the subtree grew in height or not.

```
private AVLNode insertIntoAVL(AVLNode root, AVLNode newNode)
{
    if(root == null)
    {
        root = newNode;
        isTaller = true;
    }
    else
        if(root.info.equals(newNode.info))
            System.err.println("No duplicates are allowed.");
        else
            if(root.info.compareTo(newNode.info) > 0) //newNode
                                          //goes in the left subtree
            {
                root.llink = insertIntoAVL(root.llink, newNode);

                if(isTaller)                //after insertion, the
                                            //subtree grew in height
```

10

```
            switch(root.bfactor)
            {
            case -1: root = balanceFromLeft(root);
                     isTaller = false;
                     break;
            case 0:  root.bfactor = -1;
                     isTaller = true;
                     break;
            case 1:  root.bfactor = 0;
                     isTaller = false;
            }//end switch
        }//end if
        else
        {
           root.rlink = insertIntoAVL(root.rlink, newNode);

           if(isTaller)                //after insertion, the
                                       //subtree grew in height
              switch(root.bfactor)
              {
              case -1: root.bfactor = 0;
                       isTaller = false;
                       break;
              case 0:  root.bfactor = 1;
                       isTaller = true;
                       break;
              case 1:  root = balanceFromRight(root);
                       isTaller = false;
              }//end switch
        }//end else

    return root;
}//end insertIntoAVL
```

Next, we illustrate how the method `insertIntoAVL` works and build an AVL tree from scratch. Initially the tree is empty. Each figure (Figures 10–37 through 10–45) shows the item to be inserted and the balance factor of each node. An equal sign (=) on the top of a node indicates that the balance factor of this node is 0; the less than symbol (<) indicates that the balance factor of this node is −1; and the greater than symbol (>) indicates that the balance factor of this node is 1.

Initially, the AVL tree is empty. Let us insert 40 into the empty AVL tree. See Figure 10–38.

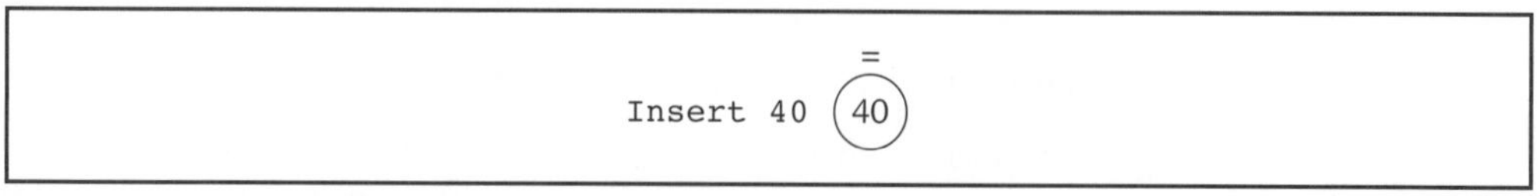

Figure 10-38 AVL tree after inserting 40

Next, we insert 30 into the AVL tree. See Figure 10-39.

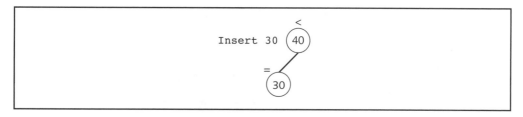

Figure 10-39   AVL tree after inserting 30

Item 30 is inserted into the left subtree of node 40, causing the left subtree of 40 to grow in height. After insertion, the balance factor of node 40 is -1.

Next, we insert 20 into the AVL tree. See Figure 10-40.

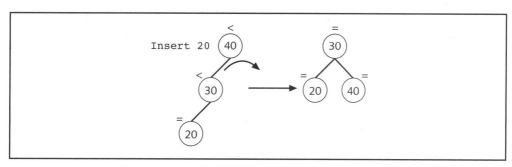

Figure 10-40   AVL tree after inserting 20

10

The insertion of 20 violates the balance criteria at node 40. The tree is reconstructed at node 40 by making a single right rotation.

Next, we insert 60 into the AVL tree. See Figure 10-41.

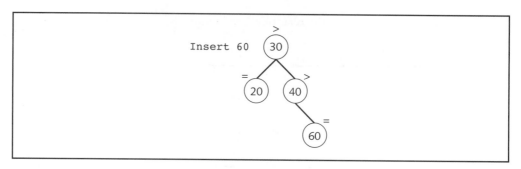

Figure 10-41 AVL tree after inserting 60

The insertion of 60 does not require reconstruction; only the balance factor is adjusted at nodes 40 and 30.

Next, we insert 50. See Figure 10-42.

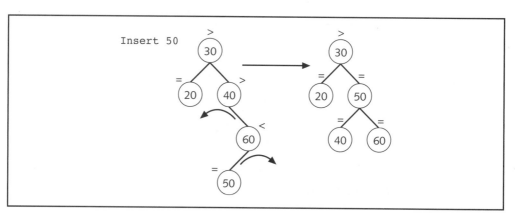

Figure 10-42 AVL tree after inserting 50

The insertion of 50 requires the tree to be reconstructed at 40. Notice that a double rotation is made at node 40.

Next, we insert 80. See Figure 10-43.

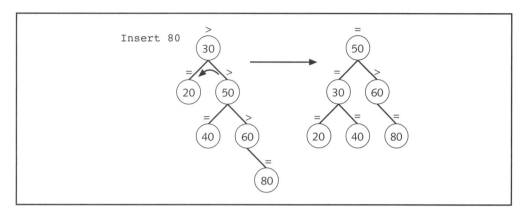

Figure 10-43   AVL tree after inserting 80

The insertion of 80 requires the tree to be reconstructed at node 30. Next, we insert 15. See Figure 10-44.

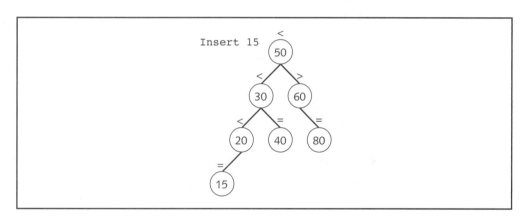

Figure 10-44   AVL tree after inserting 15

The insertion of node 15 does not require any part of the tree to be reconstructed. We need to only adjust the balance factors of nodes 20, 30, and 50.

Next, we insert 28. See Figure 10-45.

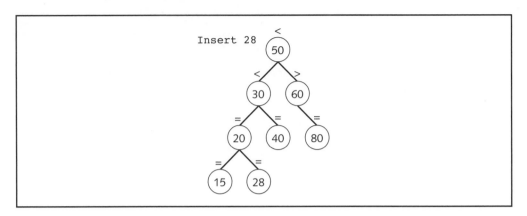

Figure 10-45 AVL tree after inserting 28

The insertion of node 28 also does not require any part of the tree to be reconstructed. We need only to adjust the balance factor of node 20.

Next, we insert 25. The insertion of 25 requires a double rotation at node 30. Figure 10-46 shows both rotations in sequence.

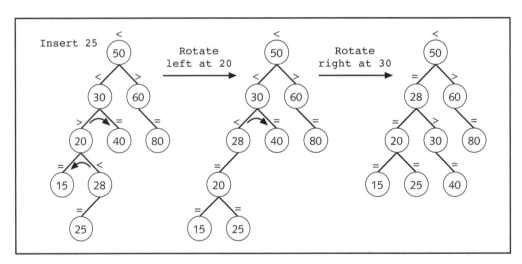

Figure 10-46 AVL tree after inserting 25

In Figure 10-46, the tree is first rotated left at node 20 and then right at node 30.

The following method creates a node, stores the info in the node, and calls the method `insertIntoAVL` to insert the new node into the AVL tree:

```
public void insert(DataElement newItem)
{
    isTaller = false;
    AVLNode newNode;

    newNode = new AVLNode();
    newNode.info = newItem.getCopy();
    newNode.bfactor = 0;
    newNode.llink = null;
    newNode.rlink = null;

    root = insertIntoAVL(root, newNode);
}
```

We leave it as an exercise for you to design the class to implement AVL trees as an ADT. See Programming Exercise 7 at the end of this chapter. (Notice that because the structure of the node of an AVL tree is different than the structure of the node of a binary tree discussed in the beginning of this chapter, you cannot use inheritance to derive the class to implement AVL trees from the **class BinaryTree**.)

Deletion from AVL Trees

To delete an item from an AVL tree, first we find the node containing the item to be deleted. The following four cases arise:

Case 1: The node to be deleted is a leaf.

Case 2: The node to be deleted has no right child, that is, its right subtree is empty.

Case 3: The node to be deleted has no left child, that is, its left subtree is empty.

Case 4: The node to be deleted has a left child and a right child.

Cases 1 through 3 are easier to handle than Case 4. Let us first discuss Case 4.

Suppose that the node to be deleted, say x, has a left and a right child. As in the case of deletion from a binary search tree, we reduce Case 4 to Case 2. That is, we find the immediate predecessor, say y of x. Then the data of y is copied into x and now the node to be deleted is y. Clearly, y has no right child.

To delete the node, we adjust one of the links of the parent node. After deleting the node, the resulting tree may no longer be an AVL tree. As in the case of insertion into an AVL tree, we traverse the path (from the parent node) back to the root node. For each node on this path, sometimes we need to change only the balance factor, while other times the tree at a particular node is reconstructed. The following steps describe what to do at a node on the path back to the root node. (As in the case of insertion, we use the **boolean** variable **shorter** to indicate whether the height of the subtree is reduced.) Let p be a node on the path back to the root node. We look at the current balance factor of p.

1. If the current balance factor of p is equal high, then the balance factor of p is changed according to whether the left subtree of p was shortened or the right subtree of p was shortened. The variable **shorter** is set to **false**.

2. Suppose that the balance factor of p is not equal high and the taller subtree of p is shortened. The balance factor of p is changed to equal high, and the variable `shorter` is left as `true`.

3. Suppose that the balance factor of p is not equal high and the shorter subtree of p is shortened. Further suppose that q points to the root of the taller subtree of p.

   a. If the balance factor of q is equal high, a single rotation is required at p and `shorter` is set to `false`.

   b. If the balance factor of q is the same as p, a single rotation is required at p and `shorter` is set to `true`.

   c. Suppose that the balance factors of p and q are opposite. A double rotation is required at p (a single rotation at q and then a single rotation at p). We adjust the balance factors and set `shorter` to `true`.

Analysis: AVL Trees

Consider all the possible AVL trees of height h. Let T_h be an AVL tree of height h such that T_h has the fewest number of nodes. Let T_{hl} denote the left subtree of T_h and T_{hr} denote the right subtree of T_h. Then,

$$|T_h| = |T_{hl}| + |T_{hr}| + 1$$

where $|T_h|$ denotes the number of nodes in T_h.

Because T_h is an AVL tree of height h such that T_h has the fewest number of nodes, it follows that one of the subtrees of T_h is of height $h - 1$ and the other is of height $h - 2$. To be specific, suppose that T_{hl} is of height $h - 1$ and T_{hr} is of height $h - 2$. From the definition of T_h, it follows that T_{hl} is an AVL tree of height $h - 1$ such that T_{hl} has the fewest number of nodes among all AVL trees of height $h - 1$. Similarly, T_{hr} is an AVL tree of height $h - 2$ that has the fewest number of nodes among all AVL trees of height $h - 2$. Thus, T_{hl} is of the form T_{h-1} and T_{hr} is of the form T_{h-2}. Hence,

$$|T_h| = |T_{h-1}| + |T_{h-2}| + 1$$

Clearly,

$$|T_0| = 1$$
$$|T_1| = 2$$

Let $F_{h+2} = |T_h| + 1$. Then,

$$F_{h+2} = F_{h+1} + F_h$$
$$F_2 = 2$$
$$F_3 = 3$$

This is called a Fibonacci sequence. The solution to F_h is given by

$$F_h \approx \frac{\phi^h}{\sqrt{5}}, \quad \text{where } \phi = \frac{1 + \sqrt{5}}{2}$$

Hence,

$$| T_h | \approx \frac{\phi^{h+2}}{\sqrt{5}} = \frac{1}{\sqrt{5}} \left[\frac{1+\sqrt{5}}{2} \right]^{h+2}$$

From this it can be concluded that,

$$h \approx (1.44)\log_2 | T_h |$$

This implies that, in the worst case, the height of an AVL tree with n nodes is approximately $1.44\log_2 n$. Because the height of a perfectly balanced binary tree with n nodes is $\log_2 n$, it follows that, in the worst case, the time to manipulate an AVL tree is no more than 44% of the optimum time. However, in general, AVL trees are not as sparse as in the worst case. It can be shown that the average search time of an AVL tree is about 4% more than the optimum.

PROGRAMMING EXAMPLE: VIDEO STORE (REVISITED)

In Chapter 4, we designed a program to help a video store automate its video rental process. That program used an (unordered) linked list to keep track of the video inventory in the store. Because the search algorithm on a linked list is sequential and the list is fairly large, the search could be time consuming. In this chapter, you learned how to organize data into a binary tree. If the binary tree is nicely constructed (that is, it is not linear), then the search algorithm can be improved considerably. Moreover, in general, item insertion and deletion in a binary search tree is faster than in a linked list. We will, therefore, redesign the video store program so that the video inventory can be maintained in a binary tree. As in Chapter 4, we leave the design of the customer list in a binary tree as an exercise for you.

Video Object

The `class VideoElement` is similar to the one given in Chapter 4. Here we add the method `toString` to return the video info, printed by the method `printInfo`, as a string. Next, we describe the members of the `class VideoElement`.

Class: `VideoElement`

```
public class VideoElement extends DataElement
```

Instance Variables:

Same as in Chapter 4.

Constructors and Instance Methods:

(In addition to the constructors and methods given in Chapter 4, we have the following method.)

```
public String toString()
    //Method to return the video info, as a string.
```

Video List

The video list is maintained in a binary search tree. Therefore, we derive the `class` `VideoBinaryTree` from the `class` `BinarySearchTree`.

Class: `VideoBinaryTree`

```
public class VideoBinaryTree extends BinarySearchTree
```

Constructors and Instance Methods:

```
public VideoBinaryTree()
   //default constructor
   //Postcondition: root = null;
public VideoBinaryTree(VideoBinaryTree otherList)
   //copy constructor

private BinaryTreeNode searchVideoList(String title)
   //Method to search the video list for a particular
   //video, specified by the parameter title.
   //Postcondition: If the video is found, a reference to
   //               the node containing the video is returned;
   //               otherwise, the value null is returned.

public boolean videoSearch(String title)
   //Method to search the list to see whether a particular
   //title, specified by the parameter title, is in the store.
   //Postcondition: Returns true if the title is found,
   //               false otherwise.

public boolean isVideoAvailable(String title)
   //Method to determine whether the video specified by the
   //parameter title is available.
   //Postcondition: Returns true if at least one copy of the
   //               video is available, false otherwise.

public void videoCheckIn(String title)
   //Method to check in a video returned by a customer.
   //The parameter title specifies the video to be checked in.
   //Postcondition: If the video returned is from the
   //               store, its copiesInstock is incremented
   //               by one; otherwise, an appropriate message
   //               is printed.

public void videoCheckOut(String title)
   //Method to check out a video, that is, rent a video.
   //The parameter title specifies the video to be checked out.
   //Postcondition: If a video is available, its copiesInStock
   //               is decremented by one; otherwise, an
   //               appropriate message is printed.

public boolean videoCheckTitle(String title)
   //Method to determine whether the video specified by the
   //parameter title is in the store.
   //Postcondition: Returns true if the video is in the
   //               store, false otherwise.
```

```
public void videoUpdateInStock(String title, int num)
    //Method to update the number of copies of a video
    //by adding the value of the parameter num. The
    //parameter title specifies the name of the video
    //for which the number of copies is to be updated.
    //Postcondition: If video is found, then
    //               copiesInStock = copiesInStock + num;
    //            otherwise, an appropriate message is
    //            printed.

public void videoSetCopiesInStock(String title, int num)
    //Method to reset the number of copies of a video.
    //The parameter title specifies the name of the video
    //for which the number of copies is to be reset; the
    //parameter num specifies the number of copies.
    //Postcondition: If video is found, then
    //               copiesInStock = num;
    //            otherwise, an appropriate message
    //            is printed.

public void videoPrintTitle()
    //Method to print the titles of all the videos in stock.

private void inorderTitle(BinaryTreeNode p)
    //Method to print the titles of all the videos in
    //the tree pointed to by p.
```

The definitions of the methods of the **class VideoBinaryTree** are similar to the ones given in Chapter 4. We give the definitions of only the methods **searchVideoList**, **videoCheckOut**, **inorderTitle**, and **videoPrintTitle**. (See Programming Exercise 8 at the end of the chapter.)

The method **searchVideoList** uses a search algorithm similar to the search algorithm for a binary search tree given earlier in this chapter. If the search item is found in the list, it returns the reference of the node containing the search item; otherwise, it returns the value **null**. Note that the method **searchVideoList** is a **private** member of the **class VideoBinaryTree**. So the user cannot directly use this method in a program. Therefore, even though this method returns a reference of a node in the tree, the user cannot directly access the node. The method **searchVideoList** is used only to implement the other methods of the **class VideoBinaryTree**. The definition of this method is as follows:

```
private BinaryTreeNode searchVideoList(String title)
{
    boolean found = false;    //set found to false
    BinaryTreeNode current = null;
    VideoElement temp = new VideoElement();

    temp.setVideoInfo(title, "", "", "", "", "", 0);
```

```
   if(root == null)   //the tree is empty
       System.out.println("Cannot search an empty list. ");
   else
   {
       current = root;    //set current to point to the root
                          //node of the binary tree
       found = false;     //set found to false

       while(current != null && !found) //search the tree
           if(current.info.equals(temp)) //the item is found
               found = true;
           else
               if(current.info.compareTo(temp) > 0)
                   current = current.llink;
               else
                   current = current.rlink;
   }//end else

   return current;
}//end searchVideoList
```

The definition of the method videoCheckOut is:

```
public void videoCheckOut(String title)
{
    BinaryTreeNode location;
    VideoElement temp;

    location = searchVideoList(title);   //search the list

    if(location != null)
    {
        temp = (VideoElement) location.info;
        temp.checkOut();
    }
    else
        System.out.println("The store does not carry "
                           + "this video");
}
```

Given a reference of the root node of the binary tree containing the videos, the method inorderTitle uses the inorder traversal algorithm to print the titles of the videos. Notice that this method outputs only the video titles. The definition of this method is as follows:

```
private void inorderTitle(BinaryTreeNode p)
{
    VideoElement temp;

    if(p != null)
    {
        inorderTitle(p.llink);
        temp = (VideoElement) p.info;
```

```
        temp.printTitle();
        inorderTitle(p.rlink);
    }
}
```

The method `videoPrintTitle` uses the method `inorderTitle` to print the titles of all the videos in the store. The definition of this method is:

```
public void videoPrintTitle()
{
    inorderTitle(root);
}
```

Main Program

For the most part, the main program is the same as before. Here, we give only the listing of this program.

```
import java.io.*;

public class MainProgVideoStore
{
    static BufferedReader keyboard = new
        BufferedReader(new InputStreamReader(System.in));

    public static void main(String[] args)
    {
        VideoBinaryTree  videoList = new VideoBinaryTree();
        int choice;
        String title;

        try
        {
          BufferedReader infile = new
             BufferedReader(new FileReader("a:\\videoDat.txt"));

          createVideoList(infile, videoList);

          displayMenu();
          System.out.print("Enter your choice: ");
          choice = Integer.parseInt(keyboard.readLine());
          System.out.println();

          while(choice != 9)
          {
            switch(choice)
            {
            case 1: System.out.print("Enter the title: ");
                    title = keyboard.readLine();
                    System.out.println();
                    if(videoList.videoSearch(title))
                        System.out.println("Title found.");
```

```
            else
                System.out.println("This video is not in "
                                    + "the store.");
            break;
case 2: System.out.print("Enter the title: ");
        title = keyboard.readLine();
        System.out.println();
        if(videoList.videoSearch(title))
        {
            if(videoList.isVideoAvailable(title))
            {
                videoList.videoCheckOut(title);
                System.out.println("Enjoy your movie: "
                                    + title);
            }
            else
                System.out.println("Currently " + title
                                    + " is out of stock.");
        }
        else
            System.out.println("The store does not "
                                + "carry " + title);
        break;
case 3: System.out.print("Enter the title: ");
        title = keyboard.readLine();
        System.out.println();
        if(videoList.videoSearch(title))
        {
            videoList.videoCheckIn(title);
            System.out.println("Thanks for returning "
                                + title);
        }
        else
            System.out.println("This video is not "
                                + "from our store.");
        break;
case 4: System.out.print("Enter the title: ");
        title = keyboard.readLine();
        System.out.println();
        if(videoList.videoSearch(title))
        {
            if(videoList.isVideoAvailable(title))
                System.out.println(title
                        + " is currently in stock.");
            else
                System.out.println(title +
                        " is not in the store.");
        }
        else
```

```
                        System.out.println(title + " is not "
                                         + "from this store.");
                   break;
          case 5: videoList.videoPrintTitle();
                   break;
          case 6: videoList.inorderTraversal();
                   break;
          default: System.out.println("Invalid selection");
          }//end switch

          displayMenu();
          System.out.print("Enter your choice: ");
          choice = Integer.parseInt(keyboard.readLine());
          System.out.println();
      }//end while
   }
   catch(FileNotFoundException fnfe)
   {
        System.out.println(fnfe.toString());
   }
   catch(IOException ioe)
   {
      System.out.println(ioe.toString());
   }
}
public static void createVideoList(BufferedReader infile,
                                VideoBinaryTree videoList)
                                throws IOException
{
    String  Title;
    String  Star1;
    String  Star2;
    String  Producer;
    String  Director;
    String  ProductionCo;
    int     InStock;

    VideoElement newVideo = new VideoElement();

    Title = infile.readLine();

    while(Title != null)
    {
        Star1 = infile.readLine();
        Star2 = infile.readLine();
        Producer = infile.readLine();
        Director = infile.readLine();
        ProductionCo = infile.readLine();
        InStock = Integer.parseInt(infile.readLine());
```

```
        newVideo.setVideoInfo(Title, Star1, Star2, Producer,
                     Director, ProductionCo, InStock);
        videoList.insert(newVideo);

        Title = infile.readLine();
    }//end while
}//end createVideoList

public static void displayMenu()
{
    System.out.println("Select one of the following: ");
    System.out.println("1: To check whether a particular "
                     + "video is in the store");
    System.out.println("2: To check out a video");
    System.out.println("3: To check in a video");
    System.out.println("4: To check whether a particular video "
                     + "is in stock");
    System.out.println("5: To print the titles of all "
                     + "the videos");
    System.out.println("6: To print a list of all "
                     + "the videos");
    System.out.println("9: To exit");
}

}
```

QUICK REVIEW

1. A binary tree is either empty or it has a special node called the root node. If the tree is nonempty, the root node has two sets of nodes, called the left and right subtrees, such that the left and right subtrees are also binary trees.

2. The node of a binary tree has two links in it.

3. A node in a binary tree is called a leaf if it has no left and right children.

4. A node U is called the parent of a node V if there is a branch from U to V.

5. A path from a node X to a node Y in a binary tree is a sequence of nodes $X_0, X_1, ..., X_n$ such that (a) $X = X_0$, $X_n = Y$, and (b) X_{i-1} is the parent of X_i for all $i = 1, 2, ..., n$. That is, there is a branch from X_0 to X_1, X_1 to X_2, ..., X_{i-1} to X_i, ..., X_{n-1} to X_n.

6. The level of a node in a binary tree is the number of branches on the path from the root to the node.

7. The level of the root node of a binary tree is 0; the level of the children of the root node is 1.

8. The height of a binary tree is the number of nodes on the longest path from the root to a leaf.

9. In an inorder traversal, the binary tree is traversed as follows:

   a. Traverse the left subtree.

   b. Visit the node.

   c. Traverse the right subtree.

10. In a preorder traversal, the binary tree is traversed as follows:

   a. Visit the node.

   b. Traverse the left subtree.

   c. Traverse the right subtree.

11. In a postorder traversal, the binary tree is traversed as follows:

   a. Traverse the left subtree.

   b. Traverse the right subtree.

   c. Visit the node.

12. A binary search tree T is either empty or:

   i. T has a special node called the root node;

   ii. T has two sets of nodes, L_T and R_T, called the left subtree and the right subtree of T, respectively;

   iii. The key in the root node is larger than every key in the left subtree and smaller than every key in the right subtree; and

   iv. L_T and R_T are binary search trees.

13. To delete a node from a binary search tree that has both left and right nonempty subtrees, first its immediate predecessor is located, then the predecessor's `info` is copied into the node, and finally the predecessor is deleted.

14. A perfectly balanced binary tree is a binary tree such that:

   (i) The height of the left and right subtrees of the root are equal.

   (ii) The left and right subtrees of the root are perfectly balanced binary trees.

15. An AVL (or height-balanced) tree is a binary search tree such that:

   (i) The height of the left and right subtrees of the root differ by at most 1.

   (ii) The left and right subtrees of the root are AVL trees.

16. Let x be a node in a binary tree. Then x_l denotes the height of the left subtree of x, and x_r denotes the height of the right subtree of x.

17. Let T be an AVL tree and x be a node in T. Then $|x_r - x_l| \le 1$, where $|x_r - x_l|$ denotes the absolute value of $x_r - x_l$.

18. Let x be a node in the AVL tree T.

   a. If $x_l > x_r$, we say that x is left high. In this case, $x_l = x_r + 1$.

   b. If $x_l = x_r$, we say that x is equal high.

   c. If $x_r > x_l$, we say that x is right high. In this case, $x_r = x_l + 1$.

10

19. The balance factor of x, written $bf(x)$, is defined as $bf(x) = x_r - x_l$.

20. Let x be a node in the AVL tree T. Then,

    a. If x is left high, then $bf(x) = -1$.

    b. If x is equal high, then $bf(x) = 0$.

    c. If x is right high, then $bf(x) = 1$.

21. Let x be a node in a binary tree. We say that node x violates the balance criteria if $|x_r - x_l| > 1$, that is, the height of the left and right subtrees of x differ by more than 1.

22. Every node x in the AVL tree T, in addition to the data and references of the left and right subtrees, must keep track of its balance factor.

23. In an AVL tree, there are two types of rotations, left rotation and right rotation. Suppose that the rotation occurs at node x. If it is a left rotation, then certain nodes from the right subtree of x move to its left subtree; the root of the right subtree of x becomes the new root of the reconstructed subtree. Similarly, if it is a right rotation at x, certain nodes from the left subtree of x move to its right subtree; the root of the left subtree of x becomes the new root of the reconstructed subtree.

EXERCISES

1. Mark the following statements as true or false.

   a. A binary tree must be nonempty.

   b. The level of the root node is 0.

   c. If a tree has only one node, the height of the tree is 0 because the number of levels is 0.

   d. The inorder traversal of a binary tree always outputs the data in ascending order.

2. There are 14 different binary trees with four nodes. Draw all of them.

The binary tree of Figure 10-47 is to be used for Exercises 3 through 8.

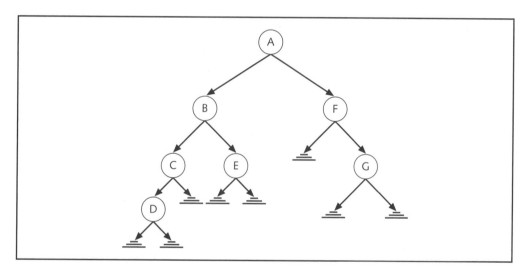

Figure 10-47   Figure for Exercises 3 through 8

3. Find L_A, the node in the left subtree of A.

4. Find R_A, the node in the right subtree of A.

5. Find R_B, the node in the right subtree of B.

6. List the nodes of this binary tree in an inorder sequence.

7. List the nodes of this binary tree in a preorder sequence.

8. List the nodes of this binary tree in a postorder sequence.

The binary tree of Figure 10-48 is to be used for Exercises 9 through 13.

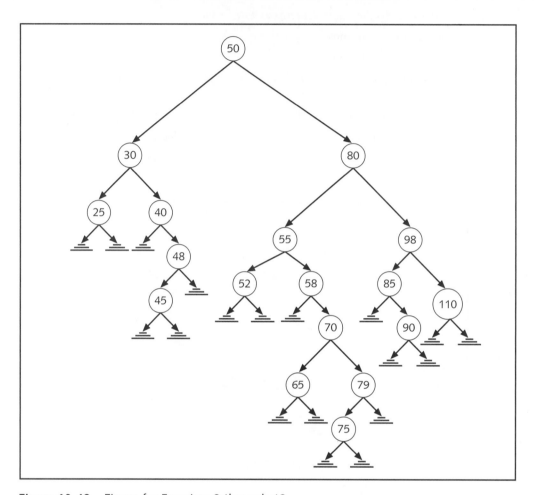

Figure 10-48 Figure for Exercises 9 through 13

9. List the path from the node with **info** 80 to the node with **info** 79.

10. A node with **info** 35 is to be inserted in the tree. List the nodes that are visited by the method **insert** to insert 35. Redraw the tree after inserting 35.

11. Delete node 52 and redraw the binary tree.

12. Delete node 40 and redraw the binary tree.

13. Delete nodes 80 and 58 in that order. Redraw the binary tree after each deletion.

14. Suppose that you are given two sequences of elements corresponding to the inorder sequence and the preorder sequence. Prove that it is possible to reconstruct a unique binary tree.

15. The following code lists the nodes in a binary tree in two different orders:

```
preorder:    ABCDEFGHIJKLM
inorder:     CEDFBAHJIKGML
```

Draw the binary tree.

16. Given the preorder sequence and the postorder sequence, show that it may not be possible to reconstruct the binary tree.

17. Insert 100 in the AVL tree of Figure 10-49. The resulting tree must be an AVL tree. What is the balance factor at the root node after the insertion?

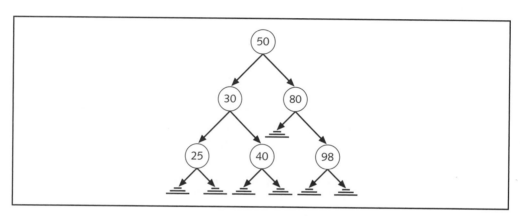

Figure 10-49   AVL tree for Exercise 17

18. Insert 45 in the AVL tree of Figure 10-50. The resulting tree must be an AVL tree. What is the balance factor at the root node after the insertion?

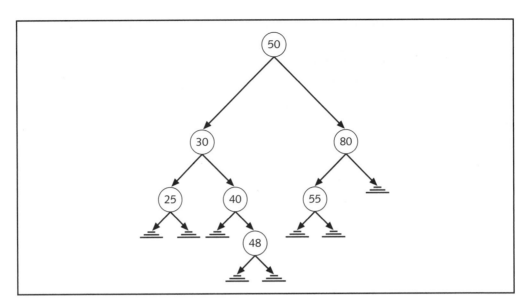

Figure 10-50 AVL tree for Exercise 18

19. Insert 42 in the AVL tree of Figure 10-51. The resulting tree must be an AVL tree. What is the balance factor at the root node after the insertion?

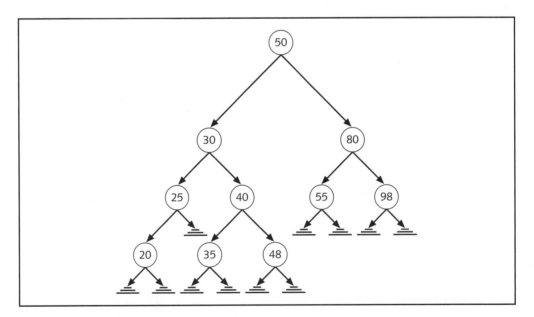

Figure 10-51 AVL tree for Exercise 19

20. The following keys are inserted (in the order given) into an initially empty AVL tree. Show the AVL tree after each insertion.

24, 39, 31, 46, 48, 34, 19, 5, 29

PROGRAMMING EXERCISES

1. Write the definition of the method `nodeCount` that returns the number of nodes in a binary tree. Add this method to the **class BinaryTree**, and create a program to test this method.

2. Write the definition of the method `leavesCount` that takes as a parameter a reference of the root node of a binary tree and returns the number of leaves in the binary tree. Add this method to the **class BinaryTree**, and create a program to test this method.

3. Write a method, `swapSubtrees`, that swaps all of the left and right subtrees of a binary tree. Add this method to the **class BinaryTree**, and create a program to test this method.

4. Write a method, `singleParent`, that returns the number of nodes in a binary tree that have only one child. Add this method to the **class BinaryTree**, and create a program to test this method. (Note: first create a binary search tree.)

5. Write a program to test various operations on a binary search tree.

6. a. Write the definition of the method to implement the nonrecursive preorder traversal algorithm.

b. Write the definition of the method to implement the nonrecursive postorder traversal algorithm.

c. Write a program to test the nonrecursive inorder, preorder, and postorder traversal algorithms. (Note: first create a binary search tree.)

7. a. Write the definition of the class that implements an AVL tree as an ADT. In addition to the methods to implement the operation to insert an item in an AVL tree, your class must, at least, contain the constructors, the methods `copy`, `copyTree`, and the traversal algorithms. (You do not need to implement the delete operation.)

b. Write the definitions of the constructors and the methods of the class that you defined in (a).

c. Write a program to test various operations of an AVL tree.

8. Write the definitions of the methods of the **class VideoBinaryTree** not given in the Programming Example: Video Store. Moreover, write a program to test the definition of your methods.

10

9. **(Video Store Program)**

   a. Redo Programming Exercise 14a in Chapter 4 so that the videos rented by a customer are maintained in a binary search tree.

   b. In Programming Exercise 14b in Chapter 4, you were asked to design and implement a class to maintain customer data in a linked list. Because the search on a linked list is sequential and therefore can be time consuming, design and implement the `class CustomerBinaryTree` so that the customer's data can be stored in a binary search tree. The `class CustomerBinaryTree` must be derived from the `class BinarySearchTree` as designed in this chapter.

   c. Write a program to test the customer component. Moreover, write the definition of the method `nodeCount` of the `class BinaryTree` before executing the program.

10. **(Video Store Program)** Using classes to implement the video data, video list data, customer data, and customer list data, as designed in this chapter and in Programming Exercises 8 and 9, design and complete the program to put the video store into operation. Write the definition of the method `nodeCount` of the `class BinaryTree` before executing the program.

GRAPHS

In this chapter, you will:

♦ Learn about graphs

♦ Become familiar with the basic terminology of graph theory

♦ Discover how to represent graphs in computer memory

♦ Explore graphs as ADTs

♦ Examine and implement various graph traversal algorithms

♦ Learn how to implement the shortest path algorithm

♦ Examine and implement the minimal spanning tree algorithm

♦ Explore the topological sort

In previous chapters, you learned various ways to represent and manipulate data. This chapter discusses how to implement and manipulate graphs, which have numerous applications in computer science.

INTRODUCTION

In 1736, the following problem was posed. In the town of Königsberg (now called Kaliningrad), the river Pregel (Pregolya) flows around the island Kneiphof and then divides into two. See Figure 11-1.

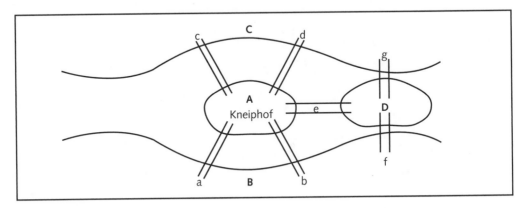

Figure 11-1   Königsberg bridge problem

The river has four land areas (A, B, C, D), as shown in the figure. These land areas are connected using seven bridges as shown in Figure 11-1. The bridges are labeled a, b, c, d, e, f, and g. The Königsberg bridge problem is as follows: starting at one land area, is it possible to walk across all the bridges exactly once and return to the starting land area? In 1736, Euler represented the Königsberg bridge problem as a graph, as shown in Figure 11-2, and answered the question in the negative. This marked (as recorded) the birth of graph theory.

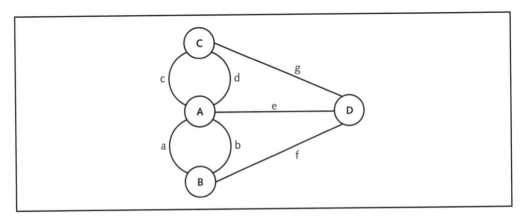

Figure 11-2   Graph representation of the Königsberg bridge problem

Over the past 200 years, graph theory has been applied to a variety of applications. Graphs are used to model electrical circuits, chemical compounds, highway maps, and so on. They are also used in the analysis of electrical circuits, finding the shortest route, project planning, linguistics, genetics, social science, and so forth. In this chapter, you learn about graphs and their applications in computer science.

GRAPH DEFINITIONS AND NOTATIONS

To facilitate and simplify our discussion, we borrow a few definitions and terminology from the set theory. Let X be a set. If a is an element of X, then we write $a \in X$. (The symbol "$\in$" means "belongs to.") A set Y is called a subset of X if every element of Y is also an element of X. If Y is a subset of X, we write $Y \subseteq X$. (The symbol "$\subseteq$" means "is a subset of.") The **intersection** of sets A and B, written $A \cap B$, is the set of all the elements that are in A and B; that is, $A \cap B = \{x \mid x \in A \text{ and } x \in B\}$. (The symbol "$\cap$" means "intersection.") The **union** of sets A and B, written $A \cup B$, is the set of all the elements that are in A or in B; that is, $A \cup B = \{x \mid x \in A \text{ or } x \in B\}$. (The symbol "$\cup$" means "union.") For sets A and B, the set $A \times B$ is the set of all the ordered pairs of elements of A and B; that is, $A \times B = \{(a, b) \mid a \in A, b \in B\}$.

A **graph** G is a pair, $G = (V, E)$, where V is a finite nonempty set, called the set of **vertices** of G, and $E \subseteq V \times V$. That is, the elements of E are the pair of elements of V. E is called the set of **edges**.

Let $V(G)$ denote the set of vertices, and $E(G)$ denote the set of edges of a graph G. If the elements of $E(G)$ are ordered pairs, G is called a **directed graph** or **digraph**; otherwise, G is called an **undirected graph**. In an undirected graph, the pairs (u, v) and (v, u) represent the same edge.

Let G be a graph. A graph H is called a **subgraph** of G if $V(H) \subseteq V(G)$ and $E(H) \subseteq E(G)$; that is, every vertex of H is a vertex of G, and every edge in H is an edge in G.

A graph can be shown pictorially. The vertices are drawn as circles, and a label inside the circle represents the vertex. In an undirected graph, the edges are drawn using lines. In a directed graph, the edges are drawn using arrows.

11

Example 11-1

Figure 11-3 shows some examples of undirected graphs.

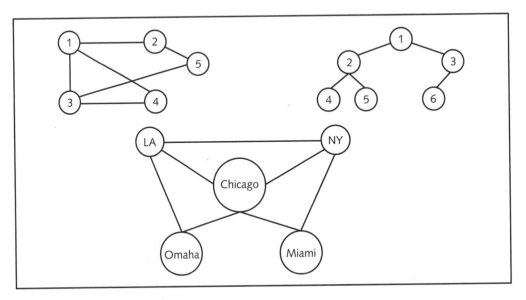

Figure 11-3   Various undirected graphs

Example 11-2

Figure 11-4 shows some examples of directed graphs.

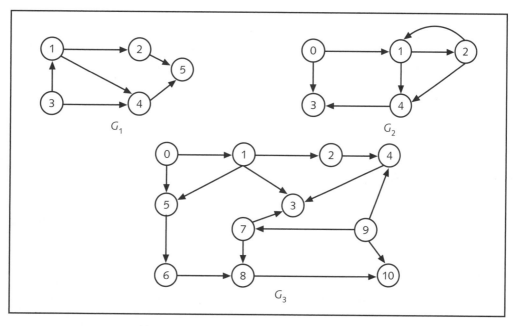

Figure 11-4 Various directed graphs

For the graphs of Figure 11-4, we have:

$V(G_1) = \{1, 2, 3, 4, 5\}$ $E(G_1) = \{(1, 2), (1, 4), (2, 5), (3, 1), (3, 4), (4, 5)\}$

$V(G_2) = \{0, 1, 2, 3, 4\}$ $E(G_2) = \{(0, 1), (0, 3), (1, 2), (1, 4), (2, 1), (2, 4), (4, 3)\}$

$V(G_3) = \{0, 1, 2, 3, 4, 5, 6, 7, 8, 9, 10\}$ $E(G_3) = \{(0, 1), (0, 5), (1, 2), (1, 3), (1, 5), (2, 4), (4, 3),$
$(5, 6), (6, 8), (7, 3), (7, 8), (8, 10), (9, 4),$
$(9, 7), (9, 10)\}$

Let G be an undirected graph. Let u and v be two vertices in G. Then u and v are called **adjacent** if there is an edge from one to the other; that is, $(u, v) \in E$. Let $e = (u, v)$ be an edge in G. We then say that edge e is **incident** on the vertices u and v. An edge incident on a single vertex is called a **loop**. If two edges, e_1 and e_2, are associated with the same pair of vertices, then e_1 and e_2 are called **parallel edges**. A graph is called a **simple graph** if it has no loops and no parallel edges. There is a **path** from u to v if there is a sequence of vertices $u_1, u_2, ..., u_n$ such that $u = u_1, u_n = v$, and (u_i, u_{i+1}) is an edge for all $i = 1, 2, ..., n - 1$. Vertices u and v are called **connected** if there is a path from u to v. A **simple path** is a path in which all the vertices, except possibly the first and last vertices, are distinct. A **cycle** in G is a simple path in which the first and last vertices are the same. G is called **connected** if there is a path from any vertex to any other vertex. A maximal subset of connected vertices is called a **component** of G.

11

Let G be a directed graph, and let u and v be two vertices in G. If there is an edge from u to v, that is, $(u, v) \in E$, then we say that u is **adjacent to** v and v is **adjacent from** u. The definitions of the paths and cycles in G are similar to those for undirected graphs. G is called **strongly connected** if any two vertices in G are connected.

Consider the directed graphs of Figure 11-4. In G_1, 1–4–5 is a path from vertex 1 to vertex 5. There are no cycles in G_1. In G_2, 1–2–1 is a cycle. In G_3, 0–1–2–4–3 is a path from vertex 0 to vertex 3; 1–5–6–8–10 is a path from vertex 1 to vertex 10. There are no cycles in G_3.

GRAPH REPRESENTATION

To write programs that process and manipulate graphs, the graphs must be stored—that is, represented—in computer memory. A graph can be represented (in computer memory) in several ways. We now discuss two commonly used ways: adjacency matrices and adjacency lists.

Adjacency Matrix

Let G be a graph with n vertices, where $n > 0$. Let $V(G) = \{v_1, v_2, ..., v_n\}$. The adjacency matrix A_G is a two-dimensional $n \times n$ matrix such that the (i, j)th entry of A_G is 1 if there is an edge from v_i to v_j; otherwise, the (i, j)th entry is zero. That is,

$$A_G(i, j) = \begin{cases} 1 & \text{if } (v_i, v_j) \in E(G) \\ 0 & \text{otherwise} \end{cases}$$

Example 11-3

Consider the directed graphs of Figure 11-4. The adjacency matrices of the directed graphs G_1, G_2, and G_3 are as follows:

$$A_{G_1} = \begin{bmatrix} 0 & 1 & 0 & 1 & 0 \\ 0 & 0 & 0 & 0 & 1 \\ 1 & 0 & 0 & 1 & 0 \\ 0 & 0 & 0 & 0 & 1 \\ 0 & 0 & 0 & 0 & 0 \end{bmatrix}$$

$$A_{G_2} = \begin{bmatrix} 0 & 1 & 0 & 1 & 0 \\ 0 & 0 & 1 & 0 & 1 \\ 0 & 1 & 0 & 0 & 1 \\ 0 & 0 & 0 & 0 & 0 \\ 0 & 0 & 0 & 1 & 0 \end{bmatrix}$$

$$A_{G_3} = \begin{matrix} 0 \\ 1 \\ 2 \\ 3 \\ 4 \\ 5 \\ 6 \\ 7 \\ 8 \\ 9 \\ 10 \end{matrix} \begin{bmatrix} 0 & 1 & 0 & 0 & 0 & 1 & 0 & 0 & 0 & 0 & 0 \\ 0 & 0 & 1 & 1 & 0 & 1 & 0 & 0 & 0 & 0 & 0 \\ 0 & 0 & 0 & 0 & 1 & 0 & 0 & 0 & 0 & 0 & 0 \\ 0 & 0 & 0 & 0 & 0 & 0 & 0 & 0 & 0 & 0 & 0 \\ 0 & 0 & 0 & 1 & 0 & 0 & 0 & 0 & 0 & 0 & 0 \\ 0 & 0 & 0 & 0 & 0 & 0 & 1 & 0 & 0 & 0 & 0 \\ 0 & 0 & 0 & 0 & 0 & 0 & 0 & 0 & 1 & 0 & 0 \\ 0 & 0 & 0 & 1 & 0 & 0 & 0 & 0 & 1 & 0 & 0 \\ 0 & 0 & 0 & 0 & 0 & 0 & 0 & 0 & 0 & 0 & 1 \\ 0 & 0 & 0 & 0 & 1 & 0 & 0 & 1 & 0 & 0 & 1 \\ 0 & 0 & 0 & 0 & 0 & 0 & 0 & 0 & 0 & 0 & 0 \end{bmatrix}$$

Adjacency Lists

Let G be a graph with n vertices, where $n > 0$. Let $V(G) = \{v_1, v_2, ..., v_n\}$. In the adjacency list representation, corresponding to each vertex, v, there is a linked list such that each node of the linked list contains the vertex, u, such that $(v, u) \in E(G)$. Because there are n nodes, we use an array, A, of size n, such that $A[i]$ is a reference variable pointing to the first node of the linked list containing the vertices to which v_i is adjacent. Clearly, each node has two components, say **vertex** and **link**. The component **vertex** contains the index of the vertex adjacent to vertex i.

Example 11-4

Consider the directed graphs of Figure 11-4. Figure 11-5 shows the adjacency list of the directed graph G_2.

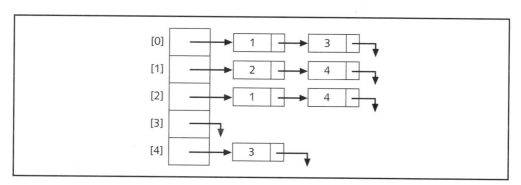

Figure 11-5   Adjacency list of graph G_2 of Figure 11-4

Figure 11-6 shows the adjacency list of the directed graph G_3.

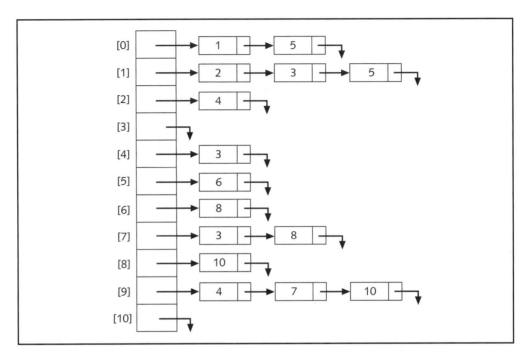

Figure 11-6 Adjacency list of graph G_3 of Figure 11-4

OPERATIONS ON GRAPHS

Now that you know how to represent graphs in computer memory, the next obvious step is to learn the basic operations on a graph. The operations commonly performed on a graph are as follows:

1. Create the graph; that is, store the graph in computer memory using a particular graph representation.

2. Clear the graph. This operation makes the graph empty.

3. Determine whether the graph is empty.

4. Traverse the graph.

5. Print the graph.

We will add more operations on a graph when we discuss a specific application or a particular graph later in this chapter.

How a graph is represented in computer memory depends on the specific application. For illustration purposes, we use the adjacency list (linked list) representation of graphs. Therefore, for each vertex, v, the vertices adjacent to v (in a directed graph, also called the **immediate successors**) are stored in the linked list associated with v.

To manage the data in a linked list, we use the **class UnorderedLinkedList**, discussed in Chapter 4. Graph traversal algorithms, and the algorithms that we will add and discuss in later sections, all require the linked list associated with each node to be traversed and to retrieve the vertex contained in each node. The **class UnorderedLinkedList** does not contain any method that can traverse the linked list and retrieve the data stored in each node one by one. (Note that the **print** method simply outputs the data to an output device.) Therefore, we first extend the definition of the **class UnorderedLinkedList** (using the inheritance mechanism) so that the vertices adjacent to a given vertex can be retrieved in an array. This simplifies the processing of vertices. Let us call this **class LinkedListGraph**. The definition of this class is:

```
public class LinkedListGraph extends UnorderedLinkedList
{
        //default constructor
    public LinkedListGraph()
    {
        super();
    }

        //copy constructor
    public LinkedListGraph(LinkedListGraph otherGraph)
    {
        super(otherGraph);
    }


        //Method to retrieve the vertices adjacent to a given
        //vertex.
        //Postcondition: The vertices adjacent to a given
        //               vertex from the linked list are retrieved
        //               in the array adjacencyList.
        //               The number of vertices are returned.

    public int getAdjacentVertices(DataElement[] adjacencyList)
    {
        LinkedListNode current;
        int length = 0;

        current = first;
```

```
        while(current != null)
        {
            adjacencyList[len++] = current.info.getCopy();
            current = current.link;
        }

        return length;
    }
}
```

GRAPHS AS ADTs

In this section, we describe the class to implement graphs as an ADT and provide the definitions of the methods to implement the operations on a graph.

The following statements define a graph as an ADT:

Class: Graph

Constants and Instance Variables:

```
protected final int infinity = 10000000;   //This will be used
                                    //in later parts of this chapter,
                                    //when we discuss weighted graphs.

protected int maxSize;              //maximum number of vertices
protected int gSize;                //current number of vertices
protected LinkedListGraph[] graph;  //array of reference variables
                                    //to create adjacency lists
```

Constructors and Instance Methods:

```
public Graph()
    //default constructor
    //Postcondition: The graph size is set to 0, that is,
    //               gSize = 0; maxSize = 100

public Graph(int size)
    //constructor
    //Postcondition: The graph size is set to 0, that is,
    //               gSize = 0; maxSize = size

public boolean isEmpty()
    //Method to determine whether the graph is empty.
    //Postcondition: Returns true if the graph is empty,
    //               false otherwise.

public void createGraph() throws IOException, FileNotFoundException
    //Method to create the graph.
    //Postcondition: The graph is created using the adjacency
    //               list representation.
```

```
public void clearGraph()
   //The memory occupied by each vertex is deallocated.

public void printGraph()
   //The graph is printed.
```

 In the rest of this chapter, whenever we write graph algorithms in Java, we assume that the *n* vertices of the graphs are numbered 0, 1, ..., *n* – 1. Therefore, the vertex type is an integer. Moreover, because the `info` of a node is a reference to the object holding the data, we use the `class IntElement`, designed in Chapter 3, to create the adjacency lists.

The definitions of the methods of the **class Graph** are discussed next.

A graph is empty if the number of vertices is zero—that is, if **gSize** is zero. Therefore, the definition of the method **isEmpty** is:

```
public boolean isEmpty()
{
    return (gSize == 0);
}
```

The definition of the method **createGraph** depends on how the data is input into the program. For illustration purposes, we assume that the data to the program is input from a file. The user is prompted for the input file. The data in the file appears in the following form:

```
5
0 2 4 ... −999
1 3 6 8 ... −999
...
```

The first line of input specifies the number of vertices in the graph. The first entry in the remaining lines specifies the vertex, and all of the remaining entries in the line (except the last) specify the vertices that are adjacent to the vertex. Each line ends with the number −999.

Using these conventions, the definition of the method **createGraph** is:

```
public void createGraph() throws IOException, FileNotFoundException
{
    BufferedReader keyboard = new
         BufferedReader(new InputStreamReader(System.in));

    String fileName;
    StringTokenizer tokenizer;

    int index;
    int vertex;
    int adjacentVertex;

    if(gSize != 0) //if the graph is not empty, make it empty
       clearGraph();
```

```
      System.out.print("Enter input file name: ");
      fileName = keyboard.readLine();
      System.out.println();

      BufferedReader infile =
            new BufferedReader(new FileReader(fileName));

      gSize = Integer.parseInt(infile.readLine()); //get the number
                                                   //of vertices
      for(index = 0; index < gSize; index++)
      {
         tokenizer = new StringTokenizer(infile.readLine());
         vertex = Integer.parseInt(tokenizer.nextToken());
         adjacentVertex = Integer.parseInt(tokenizer.nextToken());

         while(adjacentVertex != -999)
         {
            graph[vertex].insertLast(new IntElement(adjacentVertex));
            adjacentVertex = Integer.parseInt(tokenizer.nextToken());
         }//end while
      }// end for
}//end createGraph
```

The method **clearGraph** empties the graph by deallocating the storage occupied by each linked list and then setting the number of vertices to zero.

```
public void clearGraph()
{
    int index;

    for(index = 0; index < gSize; index++)
        graph[index] = null;

    gSize = 0;
}
```

The definition of the method **printGraph** is given next.

```
public void printGraph()
{
    int index;

    for(index = 0; index < gSize; index++)
    {
        System.out.print(index + " ");
        graph[index].print();
        System.out.println();
    }

    System.out.println();
}
```

The definitions of the constructors are given next.

```
public Graph()
{
    maxSize = 100;
    gSize = 0;
    graph = new LinkedListGraph[maxSize];

    for(int i = 0; i < maxSize; i++)
        graph[i] = new LinkedListGraph();
}

public Graph(int size)
{
    maxSize = size;
    gSize = 0;
    graph = new LinkedListGraph[maxSize];

    for(int i = 0; i < maxSize; i++)
        graph[i] = new LinkedListGraph();
}
```

GRAPH TRAVERSALS

Processing a graph requires the ability to traverse the graph. This section discusses the graph traversal algorithms.

Traversing a graph is similar to traversing a binary tree, except that traversing a graph is a bit more complicated. Recall that a binary tree has no cycles. Also, starting at the root node, we can traverse the entire tree. On the other hand, a graph might have cycles and we might not be able to traverse the entire graph from a single vertex (for example, if the graph is not connected). Therefore, we must keep track of the vertices that have been visited. We must also traverse the graph from each vertex (that has not been visited) of the graph. This ensures that the entire graph is traversed.

The two most common graph traversal algorithms are the depth first traversal and breadth first traversal, which are described next. For simplicity, we assume that when a vertex is visited, its index is output. Moreover, each vertex is visited only once. We use the **boolean** array **visited** to keep track of the visited vertices.

Depth First Traversal

The **depth first traversal** is similar to the preorder traversal of a binary tree. The general algorithm is:

```
for each vertex, v, in the graph
    if v is not visited
        start the depth first traversal at v
```

Consider the graph G_3 of Figure 11-4. It is shown here again as Figure 11-7 for easy reference.

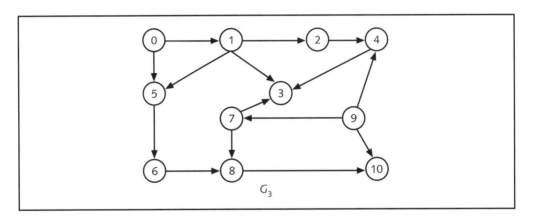

Figure 11-7 Directed graph G_3

The depth first ordering of the vertices of the graph G_3 in Figure 11-7 is:

```
0  1  2  4  3  5  6  8  10  7  9
```

The general algorithm to do a depth first traversal *at a given node, v,* is:

```
1. Mark node v as visited
2. Visit the node
3. for each vertex u adjacent to v
        if u is not visited
            start the depth first traversal at u
```

Clearly, this is a recursive algorithm. We use a recursive method, `dft`, to implement this algorithm. The vertex at which the depth first traversal is to be started, and the `boolean` array `visited`, are passed as parameters to this method.

```
private void dft(int v, boolean[] visited)
{
    int w;

    IntElement[] adjacencyList;    //array to retrieve
                                   //the adjacent vertices
```

```
adjacencyList = new IntElement[gSize];

int aLength; //the number of adjacent vertices

visited[v] = true;
System.out.print(" " + v + " ");   //visit the vertex

aLength = graph[v].getAdjacentVertices(adjacencyList);
        //retrieve the adjacent vertices into adjacencyList

for(int index = 0; index < aLength;
                    index++) //for each vertex
    {                                //adjacent to v
    w = adjacencyList[index].getNum();
    if(!visited[w])
        dft(w, visited);
    }//end while
}//end dft
```

Next, we give the definition of the method `depthFirstTraversal` to implement the depth first traversal of the graph.

```
public void depthFirstTraversal()
{
    boolean[] visited;   //array to keep track of the
                            //visited vertices

    visited = new boolean[gSize];

    int index;

    for(index = 0; index < gSize; index++)
        visited[index] = false;

    for(index = 0; index < gSize; index++) //for each vertex
        if(!visited[index])                 //that is not visited,
            dft(index, visited);            //do a depth first
                                            //traversal
}//end depthFirstTraversal
```

The method `depthFirstTraversal` performs a depth first traversal of the entire graph. The definition of the method `dftAtVertex`, which performs a depth first traversal at a given vertex, is as follows:

```
public void dftAtVertex(int vertex)
{
    boolean[] visited;

    visited = new boolean[gSize];
```

```
    for(int index = 0; index < gSize; index++)
        visited[index] = false;

    dft(vertex, visited);
}//end dftAtVertex
```

Breadth First Traversal

The **breadth first traversal** of a graph is similar to traversing a binary tree level by level (the nodes at each level are visited from left to right). All the nodes at any level, *i*, are visited before visiting the nodes at level $i + 1$.

The breadth first ordering of the vertices of the graph G_3 (Figure 11-7) is:

0   1   5   2   3   6   4   8   10   7   9

For the graph G_3, we start the breadth traversal at vertex 0. After visiting the vertex 0, next we visit the vertices that are directly connected to it and are not visited, which are 1 and 5. Next, we visit the vertices that are directly connected to 1 and are not visited, which are 2 and 3. After this, we visit the vertices that are directly connected to 5 and are not visited, which is 6. After this, we visit the vertices that are directly connected to 2 and are not visited, and so on.

As in the case of the depth first traversal, because it might not be possible to traverse the entire graph from a single vertex, the breadth first traversal also traverses the graph from each vertex that is not visited. Starting at the first vertex, the graph is traversed as much as possible; we then go to the next vertex that has not been visited. To implement the breadth first traversal algorithm, we use a queue. The general algorithm is:

```
a. for each vertex v in the graph
       if v is not visited
           add v to the queue   //start the breadth first search at v
b. Mark v as visited
c. while the queue is not empty
   c.1. Remove vertex u from the queue
   c.2. Retrieve the vertices adjacent to u
   c.3. for each vertex w that is adjacent to u
           if w is not visited
           c.3.1. Add w to the queue
           c.3.2. Mark w as visited
```

The following Java method, `breadthFirstTraversal`, implements this algorithm:

```
public void breadthFirstTraversal()
{
    LinkedQueueClass queue = new LinkedQueueClass();

    int u;

    IntElement temp = new IntElement();

    boolean[] visited;
    visited = new boolean[gSize];
```

```
    for(int ind = 0; ind < gSize; ind++)
        visited[ind] = false; //initialize the array
                                //visited to false

    IntElement[] adjacencyList;

    adjacencyList = new IntElement[gSize];

    int aLength;

    for(int index = 0; index < gSize; index++)
        if(!visited[index])
        {
            queue.addQueue(new IntElement(index));
            visited[index] = true;
            System.out.print(" " + index + " ");

            while(!queue.isEmptyQueue())
            {
                temp = (IntElement) queue.front();
                u = temp.getNum();
                queue.deleteQueue();
                aLength = graph[u].getAdjacentVertices
                                    (adjacencyList);

                for(int w = 0; w < aLength; w++)
                {
                    int w1 = adjacencyList[w].getNum();
                    if(!visited[w1])
                    {
                        queue.addQueue(new IntElement(w1));
                        visited[w1] = true;
                        System.out.print(" " + w1 + " ");
                    }
                }
            }//end while
        }//end if
}//end breadthFirstTraversal
```

After including the previous graph traversal algorithms, you can write the definition of the class Graph as follows:

```
import java.io.*;
import java.util.*;

public class Graph
{
    //Put constants and instance variables here.
    //Put the definitions of the constructors and the methods
    //described here.
}
```

As we continue to discuss graph algorithms, we will write Java methods to implement specific algorithms, and so derive (using inheritance) new classes from the **class Graph**.

SHORTEST PATH ALGORITHM

Graph theory has many applications. For example, we can use graphs to show how different chemicals are related or to show airline routes. They can also be used to show the highway structure of a city, state, or country. The edges connecting two vertices can be assigned a non-negative real number, called the **weight of the edge**. If the graph represents a highway structure, the weight can represent the distance between two places, or the travel time from one place to another. Such graphs are called **weighted graphs**.

Let G be a weighted graph. Let u and v be two vertices in G, and let P be a path in G from u to v. The **weight of the path** P is the sum of the weights of all the edges on the path P, which is also called the **weight** of v from u via P.

Let G be a weighted graph representing a highway structure. Suppose that the weight of an edge represents the travel time. For example, to plan monthly business trips, a salesperson wants to find the **shortest path** (that is, the path with the smallest weight) from her or his city to every other city in the graph. Many such problems exist in which we want to find the shortest path from a given vertex, called the **source**, to every other vertex in the graph.

This section describes the **shortest path algorithm**, also called the **greedy algorithm**, developed by Dijkstra.

Let G be a graph with n vertices, where $n > 0$. Let $V(G) = \{v_1, v_2, ..., v_n\}$. Let W be a two-dimensional $n \times n$ matrix such that

$$W(i,j) = \begin{cases} w_{ij} & \text{if } (v_i, v_j) \text{ is an edge in } G \text{ and } w_{ij} \text{ is the weight of the edge } (v_i, v_j) \\ \infty & \text{if there is no edge from } v_i \text{ to } v_j \end{cases}$$

The input to the program is the graph and the weight matrix associated with the graph. To make inputting the data easier, we extend the definition of the **class Graph** (using inheritance), and add the method **createWeightedGraph** to create the graph and the weight matrix associated with the graph. Let us call this **class WeightedGraph**. The methods to implement the shortest path algorithm are also added to this class.

Class: WeightedGraph extends Graph

```
public class WeightedGraph extends Graph
```

Instance Variables:

```
protected double[][] weights;          //weight matrix
protected double[] smallestWeight;     //smallest weight from
                                       //source to vertices
```

Constructors and Instance Methods:

```
public WeightedGraph()
   //default constructor

public WeightedGraph(int size)
   //constructor with a parameter

public void createWeightedGraph()
                  throws IOException, FileNotFoundException
   //Method to create the graph and the weight matrix.

public void shortestPath(int vertex)
   //Method to determine the smallest weight from
   //vertex, that is, the source to every other vertex
   //in the graph.

public void printShortestDistance(int vertex)
   //Method to print the smallest weight from the
   //source to the other vertices in the graph.
```

The definition of the method `createWeightedGraph` is left as an exercise for you. Next, we describe the shortest path algorithm.

Shortest Path

Given a vertex, say `vertex` (that is, a source), this section describes the shortest path algorithm.

The general algorithm is:

1. Initialize the array `smallestWeight` so that

   `smallestWeight[u] = weights[vertex, u]`.

2. Set `smallestWeight[vertex] = 0`.

3. Find the vertex, `v`, that is closest to `vertex` for which the shortest path has not been determined.

4. Mark `v` as the (next) vertex for which the smallest weight is found.

5. For each vertex `w` in `G`, such that the shortest path from `vertex` to `w` has not been determined and an edge `(v, w)` exists, if the weight of the path to `w` via `v` is smaller than its current weight, update the weight of `w` to the weight of `v` + the weight of the edge `(v, w)`.

Because there are `n` vertices, repeat Steps 3 through 5 $n - 1$ times.

Example 11-5 illustrates the shortest path algorithm. (We use the `boolean` array `weightFound` to keep track of the vertices for which the smallest weight from the source vertex has been found. If the smallest weight for a vertex, from the source, has been found, then this vertex's corresponding entry in the array `weightFound` is set to `true`; otherwise, the corresponding entry is `false`.)

11

Example 11-5

Let *G* be the graph shown in Figure 11-8.

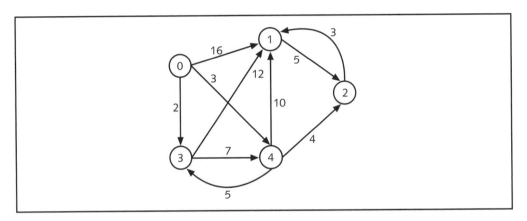

Figure 11-8 Weighted graph *G*

Suppose that the source vertex of *G* is 0. The graph shows the weight of each edge. After Steps 1 and 2 execute, the resulting graph is as shown in Figure 11-9. (In Figure 11-9, the symbol Θ means ∞.)

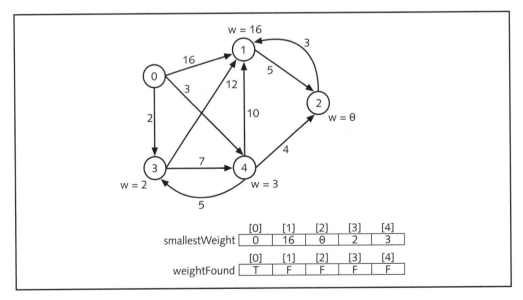

	[0]	[1]	[2]	[3]	[4]
smallestWeight	0	16	Θ	2	3

	[0]	[1]	[2]	[3]	[4]
weightFound	T	F	F	F	F

Figure 11-9 Graph after Steps 1 and 2 execute

First we select vertex 3 and mark `weightFound[3]` as `true`. Clearly, the weight of the path 0-3-1, which is 14, from 0 to 1 is less than the weight of the path 0-1. So we update `smallestWeight[1]` to 14. Figure 11-10 shows the resulting graph. (The dotted arrow shows the shortest path from the source—that is, from 0—to the vertex.)

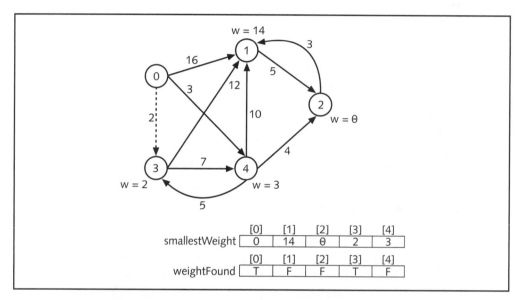

Figure 11-10   Graph after the first iteration of Steps 3, 4, and 5

Now we select vertex 4 because this is the vertex in the array `smallestWeight` that has the smallest weight and its corresponding entry in the array `weightFound` is `false`. Then we repeat the previous steps. We set `weightFound[4]` to `true`. Clearly, the weight of the path 0-4-1, which is 13, is smaller than the current weight of vertex 1, which is 14. So we update `smallestWeight[1]`. Similarly, we update `smallestWeight[2]`. Figure 11-11 shows the resulting graph.

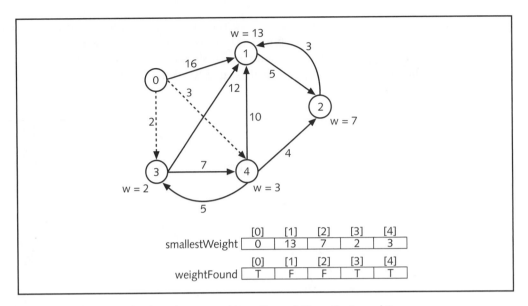

Figure 11-11   Graph after the second iteration of Steps 3, 4, and 5

The next vertex selected is 2. We set `weightFound[2]` to `true`. Clearly, the weight of the path 0-4-2-1, which is 10, from 0 to 1 is smaller than the current weight of vertex 1 (which is 13). So we update `smallestWeight[1]`. Figure 11-12 shows the resulting graph.

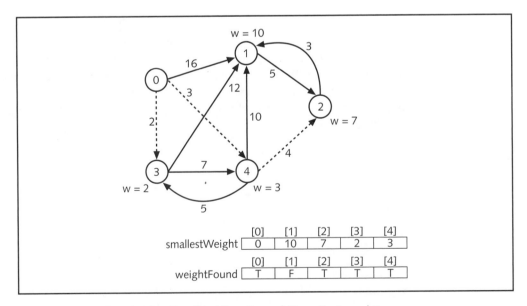

Figure 11-12   Graph after the third iteration of Steps 3, 4, and 5

Finally, vertex 1 is selected and the path is marked. Figure 11-13 shows the resulting graph.

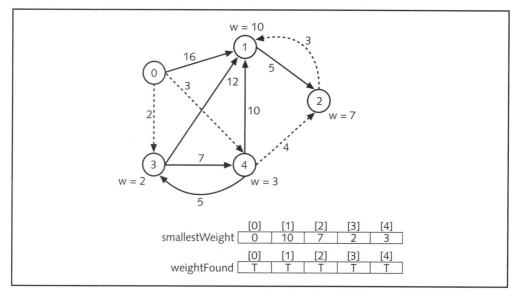

Figure 11-13   Graph after the fourth iteration of Steps 3, 4, and 5

The following Java method, `shortestPath`, implements the previous algorithm:

```
public void shortestPath(int vertex)
{
    int i, j;
    int v = 0;
    double minWeight;

    for(j = 0; j < gSize; j++)
        smallestWeight[j] = weights[vertex][j];

    boolean[] weightFound = new boolean[maxSize];

    for(j = 0; j < gSize; j++)
        weightFound[j] = false;

    weightFound[vertex] = true;
    smallestWeight[vertex] = 0;
```

```
    for(i = 0; i < gSize - 1; i++)
    {
        minWeight = infinity;

        for(j = 0; j < gSize; j++)
            if(!weightFound[j])
                if(smallestWeight[j] < minWeight)
                {
                    v = j;
                    minWeight = smallestWeight[v];
                }

        weightFound[v] = true;

        for(j = 0; j < gSize; j++)
            if(!weightFound[j])
                if(minWeight + weights[v][j] < smallestWeight[j])
                    smallestWeight[j] = minWeight + weights[v][j];
    }//end for
}//end shortestPath
```

Note that the method **shortestPath** records only the weight of the shortest path from the source to a vertex. We leave it for you to modify this method so that the shortest path from the source to a vertex is also recorded.

The definition of the method **printShortestDistance** is:

```
public void printShortestDistance(int vertex)
{
    DecimalFormat twoDigits = new DecimalFormat("0.00");

    System.out.println("Source Vertex: " + vertex);
    System.out.println("Shortest Distance from Source "
                    + "to each Vertex");
    System.out.println("Vertex  Shortest_Distance");

    for(int j = 0; j < gSize; j++)
        System.out.println("    " + j + " \t\t"
                            + twoDigits.format(smallestWeight[j]));
    System.out.println();
}
```

MINIMAL SPANNING TREE

Consider the graph of Figure 11-14, which represents the airline connections of a company between seven cities. The number on each edge represents some cost factor of maintaining the connection between the cities.

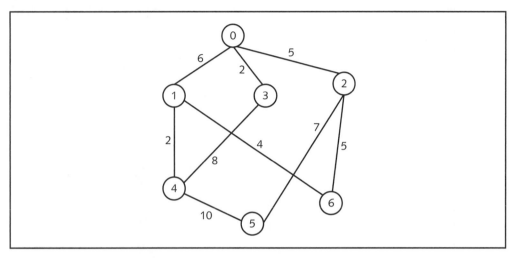

Figure 11-14   Airline connections between cities and the cost factor of maintaining the connections

Due to financial hardship, the company needs to shut down the maximum number of connections and still be able to fly from one city to another (may not be directly). The graphs of Figure 11-15(a), (b), and (c) show three different solutions.

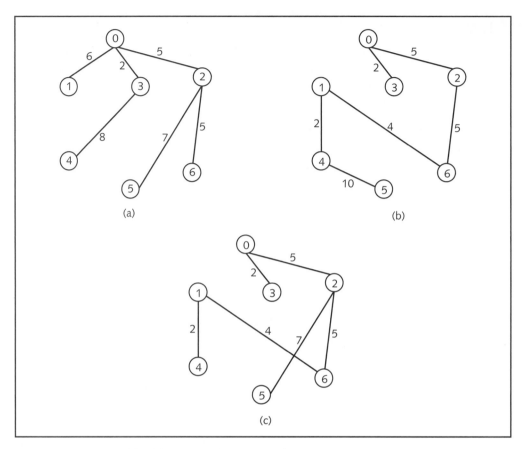

Figure 11-15 Possible solutions to the graph of Figure 11-14

The total cost factor of maintaining the remaining connections in Figure 11–15(a) is **33**, in Figure 11–15(b) it is **28**, and in Figure 11–15(c) it is **25**. Out of these three solutions, obviously, the desired solution is the one shown by the graph of Figure 11–15(c) because it gives the lowest cost factor. The graphs of Figure 11–15 are called spanning trees of the graph of Figure 11–14.

Let us note the following from the graphs of Figure 11–15. Each of the graphs of Figure 11–15 is a subgraph of the graph of Figure 11–14, and there is a unique path from a node to any other node. Such graphs are called trees. There are many other situations where, given a weighted graph, we need to determine a graph such as in Figure 11–15 with the smallest weight. In this section, we give an algorithm to determine such graphs. However, first we introduce some terminology.

A **(free) tree** T is a simple graph such that if u and v are two vertices in T, then there is a unique path from u to v. A tree in which a particular vertex is designated as a root is called a

rooted tree. If a weight is assigned to the edges in T, T is called a **weighted tree**. If T is a weighted tree, the **weight** of T, denoted by $W(T)$, is the sum of the weights of all the edges in T.

A tree T is called a **spanning tree** of graph G if T is a subgraph of G such that $V(T) = V(G)$, that is, all the vertices of G are in T.

Suppose G denotes the graph of Figure 11-14. Then the graphs of Figure 11-15 show three spanning trees of G. Let us note the following theorem.

Theorem: A graph G has a spanning tree if and only if G is connected.

From this theorem, it follows that in order to determine a spanning tree of a graph, the graph must be connected.

Let G be a weighted graph. A **minimal spanning tree** of G is a spanning tree with the minimum weight.

There are two well-known algorithms, Prim's algorithm and Kruskal's algorithm, to find the minimal spanning tree of a graph. This section discusses Prim's algorithm to find a minimal spanning tree.

Prim's algorithm builds the tree iteratively by adding edges until a minimal spanning tree is obtained. We start with a designated vertex, which we call the source vertex. At each iteration, a new edge that does not complete a cycle is added to the tree.

Let G be a weighted graph such that $V(G) = \{v_0, v_1,..., v_{n-1}\}$, where n, the number of vertices, is positive. Let v_0 be the source vertex. Let T be the partially built tree. Initially, $V(T)$ contains the source vertex and $E(T)$ is empty. At the next iteration, a new vertex that is not in $V(T)$ is added to $V(T)$, such that an edge exists from a vertex in T to the new vertex so that the corresponding edge has the smallest weight. The corresponding edge is added to $E(T)$.

The general form of Prim's algorithm is as follows (let n be the number of vertices in G):

```
1. Set V(T) = {source}
2. Set E(T) = empty
3. for i = 1 to n
      3.1 minWeight = infinity;
      3.2 for j = 1 to n
          if v_j is in V(T)
             for k = 1 to n
                if v_k is not in T and weight[v_j][v_k] < minWeight
                {
                    endVertex = v_k;
                    edge = (v_j, v_k);
                    minWeight = weight[v_j][v_k];
                }
      3.3 V(T) = V(T) ∪ {endVertex};
      3.4 E(T) = E(T) ∪ {edge};
```

Let us illustrate Prim's algorithm using the graph G of Figure 11-16 (which is the same as the graph of Figure 11-14).

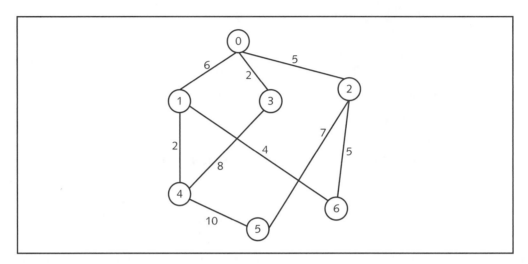

Figure 11-16 Weighted graph G

Let N denote the set of vertices of G that are not in T. Suppose that the source vertex is 0. After Steps 1 and 2 execute, $V(T)$, $E(T)$, and N are as shown in Figure 11-17.

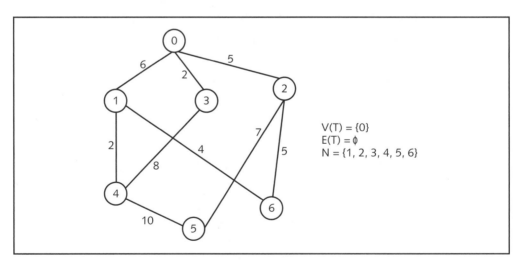

Figure 11-17 Graph G, $V(T)$, $E(T)$, and N after Steps 1 and 2 execute

Step 3.2 checks the following edges:

Edge	Weight of the Edge
(0,1)	6
(0,2)	5
(0,3)	2

Clearly, the edge (0,3) has the smallest weight. Therefore, vertex 3 is added to $V(T)$ and the edge (0,3) is added to $E(T)$. Figure 11-18 shows the resulting graph, $V(T)$, $E(T)$, and N. (The dotted line shows the edge in T.)

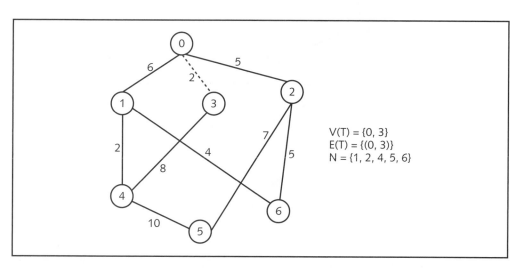

Figure 11-18   Graph G, $V(T)$, $E(T)$, and N after the first iteration of Step 3

Next, Step 3.2 checks the following edges:

Edge	Weight of the Edge
(0,1)	6
(0,2)	5
(3,4)	8

Clearly, the edge (0,2) has the smallest weight. Therefore, vertex 2 is added to $V(T)$ and the edge (0,2) is added to $E(T)$. Figure 11-19 shows the resulting graph, $V(T)$, $E(T)$, and N.

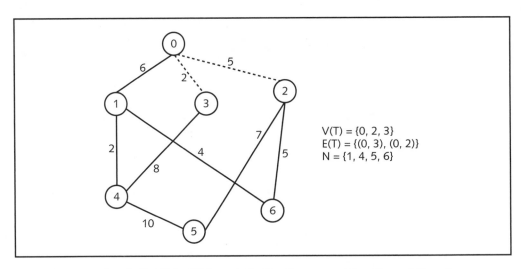

V(T) = {0, 2, 3}
E(T) = {(0, 3), (0, 2)}
N = {1, 4, 5, 6}

Figure 11-19 Graph G, $V(T)$, $E(T)$, and N after the second iteration of Step 3

At the next iteration, Step 3.2 checks the following edges:

Edge	Weight of the Edge
(0,1)	6
(2,5)	7
(2,6)	5
(3,4)	8

Clearly, the edge (2,6) has the smallest weight. Therefore, vertex 6 is added to $V(T)$ and the edge (2,6) is added to $E(T)$. Figure 11-20 shows the resulting graph, $V(T)$, $E(T)$, and N. (The dotted lines show the edges in T.)

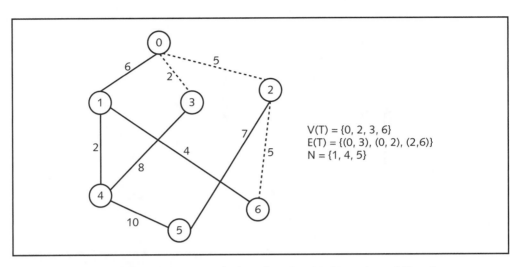

V(T) = {0, 2, 3, 6}
E(T) = {(0, 3), (0, 2), (2,6)}
N = {1, 4, 5}

Figure 11-20   Graph G, V(T), E(T), and N after the third iteration of Step 3

At the next iteration, Step 3.2 checks the following edges:

Edge	Weight of the Edge
(0,1)	6
(2,5)	7
(3,4)	8
(6,1)	4

Clearly, the edge (6,1) has the smallest weight. Therefore, vertex 1 is added to $V(T)$ and the edge (6,1) is added to $E(T)$. Figure 11-21 shows the resulting graph, $V(T)$, $E(T)$, and N. (The dotted lines show the edges in T.)

11

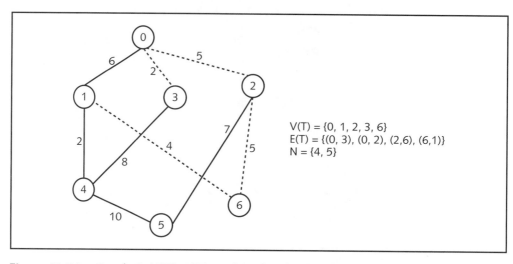

Figure 11-21 Graph G, V(T), E(T), and N after the fourth iteration of Step 3

At the next iteration, Step 3.2 checks the following edges:

Edge	Weight of the Edge
(1,4)	2
(2,5)	7
(3,4)	8

Clearly, the edge (1,4) has the smallest weight. Therefore, vertex 4 is added to $V(T)$ and the edge (1,4) is added to $E(T)$. Figure 11-22 shows the resulting graph, $V(T)$, $E(T)$, and N. (The dotted lines show the edges in T.)

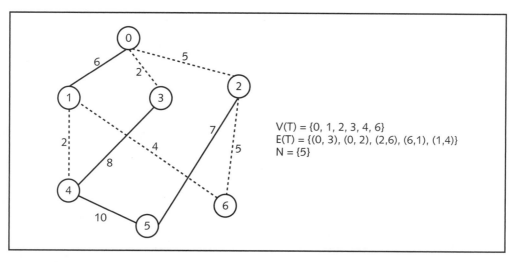

Figure 11-22   Graph *G*, *V*(*T*), *E*(*T*), and *N* after the fifth iteration of Step 3

At the next iteration, Step 3.2 checks the following edges:

Edge   **Weight of the Edge**
(2,5)   7
(4,5)   10

Clearly, the edge (2,5) has the smallest weight. Therefore, vertex 5 is added to *V*(*T*) and the edge (2,5) is added to *E*(*T*). Figure 11-23 shows the resulting graph, *V*(*T*), *E*(*T*), and *N*. (The dotted lines show the edges in *T*.)

11

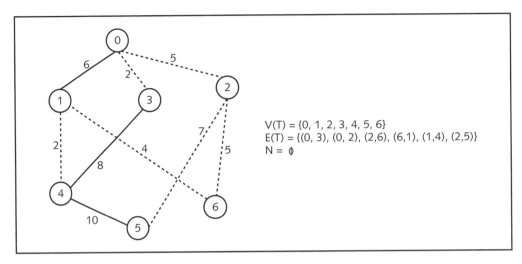

Figure 11-23 Graph *G*, *V*(*T*), *E*(*T*), and *N* after the sixth iteration of Step 3

The dotted lines show a minimal spanning tree of G of weight 25.

Before we give the definition of the method to implement Prim's algorithm, let us first define the spanning tree as an ADT.

Let `msvt` be the `boolean` array such that `msvt[i]` is `true` if the vertex v_i is in T, and `false` otherwise. Let `edges` be an array such that `edges[j]` = k, if there is an edge connecting vertices v_j and v_k. Suppose that the edge (v_i, v_j) is in the minimal spanning tree. Let `edgeWeights` be an array such that `edgeWeights[j]` is the weight of the edge (v_i, v_j).

Using these conventions, the following class defines a spanning tree as an ADT:

Class: `MSTree`
```
public MSTree extends Graph
```

Instance Variables:

```
protected int source;
protected double[][] weights;
protected int[] edges;
protected double[] edgeWeights;
```

Constructors and Instance Methods:

```
public MSTree()
   //default constructor

public MSTree(int size)
   //constructor with a parameter
```

```
public void createSpanningGraph()
                throws IOException, FileNotFoundException
   //Method to create the graph and the weight matrix.

public void minimalSpanning(int sVertex)
   //Method to create the edges of the minimal
   //spanning tree. The weight of the edges is also
   //saved in the array edgeWeights.

public void printTreeAndWeight()
   //Method to output the edges of the minimal
   //spanning tree and the weight of the minimal
   //spanning tree.
```

The definition of the method `createSpanningGraph` is left as an exercise for you. This method creates the graph and the weight matrix associated with the graph.

The following Java method, `minimalSpanning`, implements Prim's algorithm, as described previously:

```
public void minimalSpanning(int sVertex)
{
    int i, j, k;
    int startVertex = 0, endVertex = 0;
    double minWeight;

    source = sVertex;

    boolean[] mstv = new boolean[maxSize];

    for(j = 0; j < gSize; j++)
    {
        mstv[j] = false;
        edges[j] = source;
        edgeWeights[j] = weights[source][j];
    }

    mstv[source] = true;
    edgeWeights[source] = 0;

    for(i = 0; i < gSize - 1; i++)
    {
        minWeight = infinity;
```

```
            for(j = 0; j < gSize; j++)
                if(mstv[j])
                    for(k = 0; k < gSize; k++)
                        if(!mstv[k] && weights[j][k] < minWeight)
                        {
                            endVertex = k;
                            startVertex = j;
                            minWeight = weights[j][k];
                        }
            mstv[endVertex] = true;
            edges[endVertex] = startVertex;
            edgeWeights[endVertex] = minWeight;
        }//end for
}//end minimalSpanning
```

The definition of the method `minimalSpanning` contains three nested `for` loops. Therefore, in the worst case, Prim's algorithm given in this section is of the order $O(n^3)$. It is possible to design Prim's algorithm so that it is of the order $O(n^2)$; Programming Exercise 5 at the
end of this chapter asks you to do so.

The definition of the method `printTreeAndWeight` is given next.

```
public void printTreeAndWeight()
{
    double treeWeight = 0;
    DecimalFormat twoDigits = new DecimalFormat("0.00");

    System.out.println("Source Vertex: " + source);
    System.out.println("Edges    Weight");

    for(int j = 0; j < gSize; j++)
    {
        if(edges[j] != j)
        {
            treeWeight = treeWeight + edgeWeights[j];
            System.out.println("(" + edges[j] + ", " + j + ")      "
                            + twoDigits.format(edgeWeights[j]));
        }
    }

    System.out.println();
    System.out.println("Minimal Spanning Tree Weight: "
                        + twoDigits.format(treeWeight));
}//end printTreeAndWeight
```

The definitions of the constructors are as follows:

```
        //constructor with a parameter
public MSTree(int size)
{
    super(size);
```

```
    weights = new double[maxSize][maxSize];
    edges = new int[maxSize];
    edgeWeights = new double[maxSize];
}

    //default constructor
public MSTree()
{
    super();
    weights = new double[maxSize][maxSize];
    edges = new int[maxSize];
    edgeWeights = new double[maxSize];
}
```

TOPOLOGICAL ORDER

In college, before taking a particular course, students usually must take all its prerequisite courses, if any. For example, before taking the Programming II course, students must take the Programming I course. However, certain courses can be taken independently of each other. The courses within a department can be represented as a directed graph. A directed edge from, say, vertex u to vertex v, means that the course represented by the vertex u is a prerequisite of the course represented by the vertex v. It would be helpful for students to know, before starting a major, the sequence in which they can take the courses so that before taking a course they take all its prerequisite courses and fulfill the graduation requirements on time. This section describes an algorithm that can be used to output the vertices of a directed graph in such a sequence. Let us first introduce some terminology.

Let G be a directed graph and $V(G) = \{v_1, v_2, ..., v_n\}$, where $n > 0$. A **topological ordering** of $V(G)$ is a linear ordering $v_{i1}, v_{i2}, ..., v_{in}$ of the vertices such that if v_{ij} is a predecessor of v_{ik}, $j \neq k$, $1 \leq j \leq n$, and $1 \leq k \leq n$, then v_{ij} precedes v_{ik}, that is, $j < k$ in this linear ordering.

This section describes an algorithm that outputs the vertices of a directed graph in topological order. We assume that the graph has no cycles. We leave it for the reader, as an exercise, to modify the algorithm for the graphs that have cycles.

Because the graph has no cycles:

- There exists a vertex u in G such that u has no predecessor.

- There exists a vertex v in G such that v has no successor.

Suppose that the array `topologicalOrder` (of size n, the number of vertices) is used to store the vertices of G in topological order. Thus, if a vertex, say, u, is a successor of the vertex v and `topologicalOrder[j]` = v and `topologicalOrder[k]` = u, then j < k.

The topological sort algorithm can be implemented using either the depth first traversal or the breadth first traversal. This section discusses how to implement topological ordering using the breadth first traversal. Programming Exercise 7 at the end of this chapter describes how to implement the topological sort using the depth first traversal.

We extend the definition of the **class Graph** (using inheritance) to implement the breadth first topological ordering algorithm. Let us call this **class TopologicalOrder**. The following statements define this class as an ADT:

Class: TopologicalOrder

class TopologicalOrder extends Graph

Constructors and Instance Methods:

public void bfTopOrder()
    //output the vertices in breadth first topological order

public TopologicalOrder(int size)
    //constructor with a parameter

public TopologicalOrder()
    //default constructor

Next, we discuss how to implement the method **bfTopOrder**.

Breadth First Topological Ordering

Recall that the breadth first traversal algorithm is similar to traversing a binary tree level by level, and so the root node (which has no predecessor) is visited first. Therefore, in the breadth first topological ordering we first find a vertex that has no predecessor vertex and place it first in the topological ordering. We next find the vertex, say **v**, all of whose predecessors have been placed in the topological ordering and place **v** next in the topological ordering. To keep track of the number of vertices of a vertex we use the array **predCount**. Initially, **predCount[j]** is the number of predecessors of the vertex v_j. The queue used to guide the breadth first traversal is initialized to those vertices v_k such that **predCount[k]** is zero. In essence, the general algorithm is:

1. Create the array **predCount**, and initialize it so that **predCount[i]** is the number of predecessors of the vertex v_i.

2. Initialize the queue, say **queue**, to all those vertices v_k so that **predCount[k]** is zero. (Clearly, **queue** is not empty because the graph has no cycles.)

3. **while** the queue is not empty:

   3.1 Remove the front element, **u**, of the queue.

   3.2 Put **u** in the next available position, say **topologicalOrder[topIndex]**, and increment **topIndex**.

   3.3 For all the immediate successors **w** of **u**:

      3.3.1 Decrement the predecessor count of **w** by **1**.

      3.3.2 **if** the predecessor count of **w** is zero, add **w** to **queue**.

The graph G_3 of Figure 11-7 has no cycles. The vertices of G_3 in breadth first topological ordering are:

`Breadth First Topological order: 0 9 1 7 2 5 4 6 3 8 10`

Next, we illustrate the breadth first topological ordering of the graph G_3.

After Steps 1 and 2 execute, the arrays `predCount`, `topologicalOrder`, and `queue` are as shown in Figure 11-24. (Notice that for simplicity, we show only the elements of the queue.)

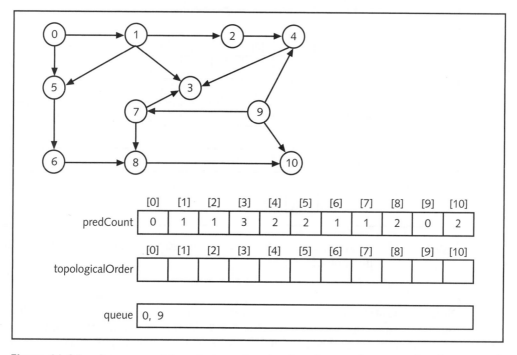

	[0]	[1]	[2]	[3]	[4]	[5]	[6]	[7]	[8]	[9]	[10]
predCount	0	1	1	3	2	2	1	1	2	0	2

	[0]	[1]	[2]	[3]	[4]	[5]	[6]	[7]	[8]	[9]	[10]
topologicalOrder											

queue	0, 9

Figure 11-24   Arrays `predCount`, `topologicalOrder`, and `queue` after Steps 1 and 2 execute

Step 3 executes as long as the queue is nonempty.

Step 3: Iteration 1: After Step 3.1 executes, the value of u is 0. Step 3.2 stores the value of u, which is 0, in the next available position in the array `topologicalOrder`. Notice that 0 is stored at position 0 in this array. Step 3.3 reduces the predecessor count of all the successors of 0 by 1, and if the predecessor count of any successor node of the node 0 reduces to 0, that node is added to `queue`. The successor nodes of the node 0 are the nodes 1 and 5. The predecessor count of the node 1 reduces to 0, and the predecessor count of the node 5 reduces to 1. The node 1 is added to `queue`. After the first iteration of Step 3, the arrays `predCount`, `topologicalOrder`, and `queue` are as shown in Figure 11-25.

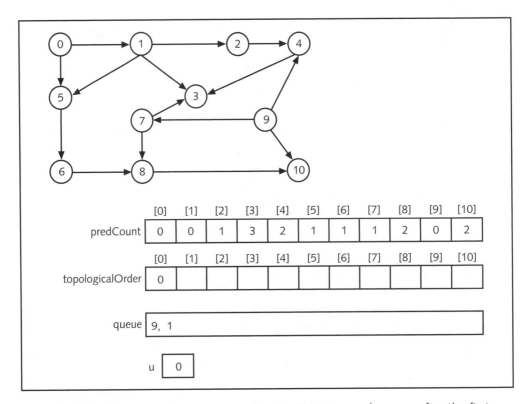

Figure 11-25 Arrays `predCount`, `topologicalOrder`, and `queue` after the first iteration of Step 3

Step 3: Iteration 2: The queue is nonempty. After Step 3.1 executes, the value of u is 9. Step 3.2 stores the value of u, which is 9, in the next available position in the array `topologicalOrder`. Notice that 9 is stored at position 1 in this array. Step 3.3 reduces the predecessor count of all the successors of 9 by 1, and if the predecessor count of any successor node of 9 reduces to 0, that node is added to `queue`. The successor nodes of the node 9 are the nodes 4, 7, and 10. The predecessor count of the node 7 reduces to 0, and the predecessor count of the nodes 4 and 10 reduces to 1. The node 7 is added to `queue`. After the second iteration of Step 3, the arrays `predCount`, `topologicalOrder`, and `queue` are as shown in Figure 11-26.

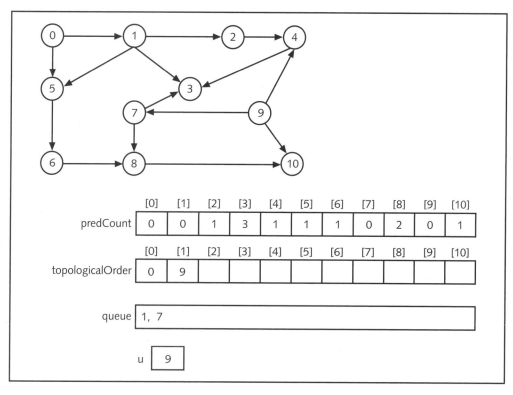

Figure 11-26   Arrays predCount, topologicalOrder, and queue after the second
iteration of Step 3

Step 3: Iteration 3: The queue is nonempty. After Step 3.1 executes, the value of u is 1.
Step 3.2 stores the value of u, which is 1, in the next available position in the array
topologicalOrder. Notice that 1 is stored at position 2 in this array. Step 3.3 reduces the
predecessor count of all the successors of 1 by 1, and if the predecessor count of any successor node of 1 reduces to 0, that node is added to queue. The successor nodes of the node 1
are the nodes 2, 3, and 5. The predecessor count of the nodes 2 and 5 reduces to 0, and the
predecessor count of the node 3 reduces to 2. The nodes 2 and 5, in this order, are added to
queue. After the third iteration of Step 3, the arrays predCount, topologicalOrder,
and queue are as shown in Figure 11-27.

11

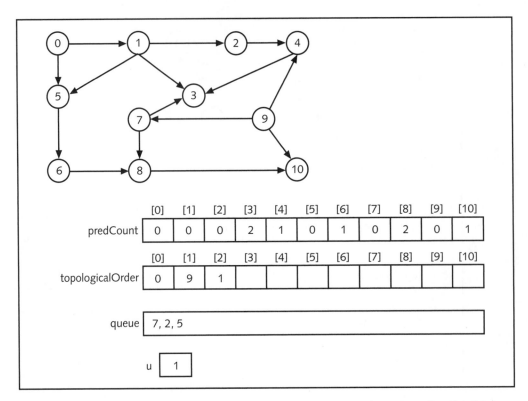

Figure 11-27   Arrays `predCount`, `topologicalOrder`, and `queue` after the third
iteration of Step 3

If you repeat Step 3 eight more times, the arrays `predCount`, `topologicalOrder`, and
`queue` are as shown in Figure 11–28.

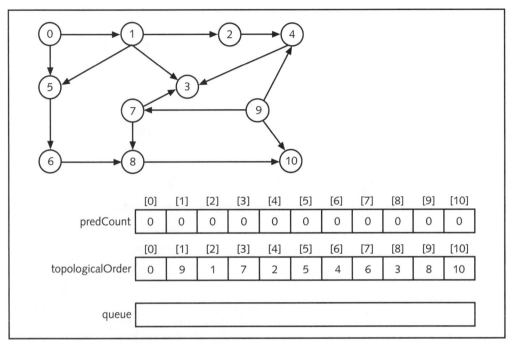

Figure 11-28   Arrays `predCount`, `topologicalOrder`, and queue after Step 3 executes
eight more times

11

In Figure 11-28, the array `topologicalOrder` shows the breadth first topological ordering of the nodes of the graph G_3.

The following Java method implements this breadth first topological ordering algorithm:

```
public void bfTopOrder()
{
    LinkedQueueClass queue = new LinkedQueueClass();

    int u;
    int ind, j;

    int[] topologicalOrder = new int[gSize];

    for(ind = 0; ind < gSize; ind++)
        topologicalOrder[ind] = -1;

    int topIndex = 0;
```

```
    IntElement[] adjacencyList;

    adjacencyList = new IntElement[gSize];

    int alLength = 0;

    int[] predCount = new int[gSize];

    for(ind = 0; ind < gSize; ind++)
        predCount[ind] = 0;

    for(ind = 0; ind < gSize; ind++)
    {
        alLength = graph[ind].getAdjacentVertices(adjacencyList);

        for(j = 0; j < alLength; j++)
            predCount[adjacencyList[j].getNum()]++;
    }

    for(ind = 0; ind < gSize; ind++)
        if(predCount[ind] == 0)
            queue.addQueue(new IntElement(ind));

    while(!queue.isEmptyQueue())
    {
        IntElement temp = (IntElement) queue.front();
        u = temp.getNum();
        queue.deleteQueue();
        topologicalOrder[topIndex++] = u;

        alLength = graph[u].getAdjacentVertices(adjacencyList);
        for(int w = 0; w < alLength; w++)
        {
            int w1 = adjacencyList[w].getNum();
            predCount[w1]--;
            if(predCount[w1] == 0)
                queue.addQueue(new IntElement(w1));
        }
    }//end while

        //output the vertices in breadth first topological order
    for(ind = 0; ind < gSize; ind++)
        System.out.print(topologicalOrder[ind] + " ");
    System.out.println();
}//end bfTopOrder
```

QUICK REVIEW

1. A graph G is a pair, $G = (V, E)$, where V is a finite nonempty set, called the set of vertices of G, and $E \subseteq V \times V$, called the set of edges.

2. In an undirected graph $G = (V, E)$, the elements of E are unordered pairs.

3. In a directed graph $G = (V, E)$, the elements of E are ordered pairs.

4. Let G be a graph. A graph H is called a subgraph of G if every vertex of H is a vertex of G and every edge in H is an edge in G.

5. Two vertices u and v in an undirected graph are called adjacent if there is an edge from one to the other.

6. Let $e = (u, v)$ be an edge in an undirected graph G. The edge e is said to be incident on the vertices u and v.

7. An edge incident on a single vertex is called a loop.

8. In an undirected graph, if two edges e_1 and e_2 are associated with the same pair of vertices, then e_1 and e_2 are called parallel edges.

9. A graph is called a simple graph if it has no loops and no parallel edges.

10. A path from a vertex u to a vertex v is a sequence of vertices $u_1, u_2, ..., u_n$ such that $u = u_1$, $u_n = v$, and (u_i, u_{i+1}) is an edge for all $i = 1, 2, ..., n - 1$.

11. The vertices u and v are called connected if there is a path from u to v.

12. A simple path is a path in which all the vertices, except possibly the first and last vertices, are distinct.

13. A cycle in G is a simple path in which the first and last vertices are the same.

14. An undirected graph G is called connected if there is a path from any vertex to any other vertex.

15. A maximal subset of connected vertices is called a component of G.

16. Suppose that u and v are vertices in a directed graph G. If there is an edge from u to v, that is, $(u, v) \in E$, we say that u is adjacent to v and v is adjacent from u.

17. A directed graph G is called strongly connected if any two vertices in G are connected.

18. Let G be a graph with n vertices, where $n > 0$. Let $V(G) = \{v_1, v_2, ..., v_n\}$. The adjacency matrix A_G is a two-dimensional $n \times n$ matrix such that the (i, j)th entry of A_G is 1 if there is an edge from v_i to v_j; otherwise, the (i, j)th entry is zero.

19. In an adjacency list representation, corresponding to each vertex v is a linked list such that each node of the linked list contains the vertex u, and $(v, u) \in E(G)$.

20. The depth first traversal of a graph is similar to the preorder traversal of a binary tree.

21. The breadth first traversal of a graph is similar to the level-by-level traversal of a binary tree.

22. The shortest path algorithm gives the shortest distance for a given node to every other node in the graph.

11

23. In a weighted graph, every edge has a nonnegative weight.

24. The weight of the path P is the sum of the weights of all the edges on the path P, which is also called the weight of v from u via P.

25. A (free) tree T is a simple graph such that if u and v are two vertices in T, there is a unique path from u to v.

26. A tree in which a particular vertex is designated as a root is called a rooted tree.

27. Suppose T is a tree. If a weight is assigned to the edges in T, T is called a weighted tree.

28. If T is a weighted tree, the weight of T, denoted by $W(T)$, is the sum of the weights of all the edges in T.

29. A tree T is called a spanning tree of graph G if T is a subgraph of G such that $V(T) = V(G)$, that is, if all the vertices of G are in T.

30. Let G be a graph and $V(G) = \{v_1, v_2, ..., v_n\}$, where $n > 0$. A topological ordering of $V(G)$ is a linear ordering $v_{i1}, v_{i2}, ..., v_{in}$ of the vertices such that if v_{ij} is a predecessor of $v_{ik}, j \neq k, 1 \leq j \leq n$, and $1 \leq k \leq n$, then v_{ij} precedes v_{ik}, that is, $j < k$ in this linear ordering.

EXERCISES

Use the graph in Figure 11-29 for Exercises 1 through 4.

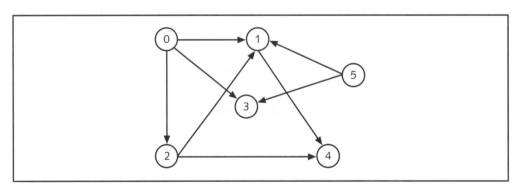

Figure 11-29 Graph for Exercises 1 through 4

1. Find the adjacency matrix of the graph.

2. Draw the adjacency list of the graph.

3. List the nodes of the graph in a depth first traversal.

4. List the nodes of the graph in a breadth first traversal.

5. Find the weight matrix of the graph in Figure 11-30.

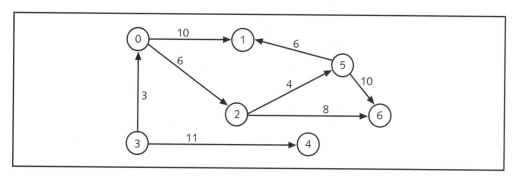

Figure 11-30   Graph for Exercise 5

6. Consider the graph in Figure 11–31. Find the shortest distance from node 0 to every other node in the graph.

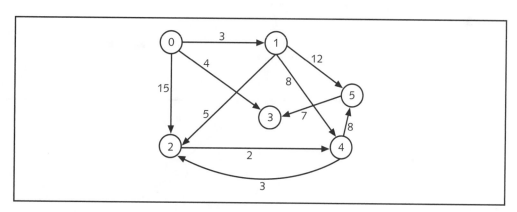

Figure 11-31   Graph for Exercise 6

7. Find a spanning tree in the graph in Figure 11–32.

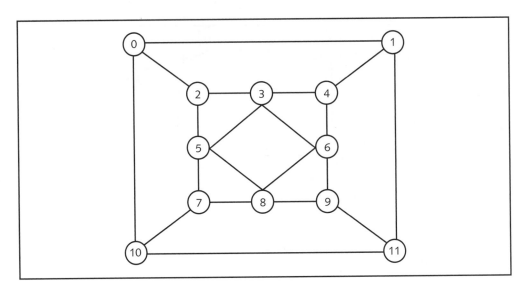

Figure 11-32 Graph for Exercise 7

8. Find a spanning tree in the graph in Figure 11–33.

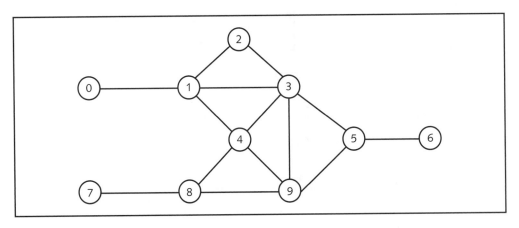

Figure 11-33 Graph for Exercise 8

9. Find the minimal spanning tree for the graph in Figure 11–34 using the algorithm given in this chapter.

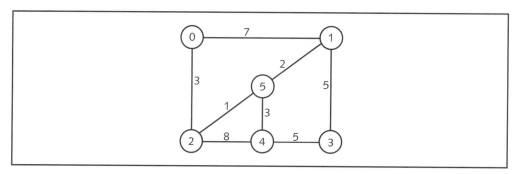

Figure 11-34   Graph for Exercise 9

10. List the nodes of the graph in Figure 11-35 in a breadth first topological ordering.

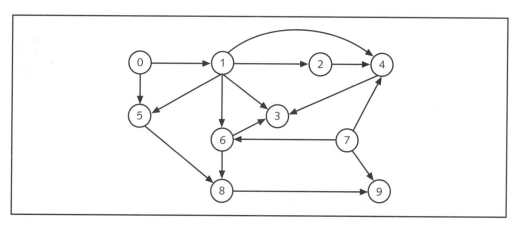

Figure 11-35   Graph for Exercise 10

11

PROGRAMMING EXERCISES

1. Write a program that outputs the nodes of a graph in a depth first traversal.

2. Write a program that outputs the nodes of a graph in a breadth first traversal.

3. Write a program that outputs the shortest distance from a given node to every other node in the graph.

4. Write a program that outputs the minimal spanning tree for a given graph.

5. The algorithm to determine the minimal spanning tree given in this chapter is of the order $O(n^3)$. The following is an alternative to Prim's algorithm that is of the order $O(n^2)$.

   Input: A connected weighted graph $G = (V, E)$ of n vertices, numbered $0, 1, ..., n - 1$; starting with vertex s, with a weight matrix of W

   Output: The minimal spanning tree

```
Prim2(G, W, n, s)
Let T = (V, E), where E = ϕ.

for(j = 0; j < n; j++)
{
    edgeWeight[j] = W[s][j];
    edges[j] = s;
    visited[s] = false;
}

edgeWeight[s] = 0;
visited[s] = true;

while(not all nodes are visited)
{
    Choose the node that is not visited and has the smallest weight, and call it k.

    visited[k] = true;
    E = E ∪ {(k, edges[k])}
    V = V ∪ {k}
    for each node j that is not visited
        if(W(k,j) < edgeWeight[k])
        {
            edgeWeight[k] = W[k][j];
            edges[j] = k;
        }
}

return T.
```

   Write a definition of the method `Prim2` to implement this algorithm, and also add this method to the **class MsTree**. Furthermore, write a program to test this version of Prim's algorithm.

6. Write a program to test the breadth first topological ordering algorithm.

7. Let G be a graph and $V(G) = \{v_1, v_2, ..., v_n\}$, where $n > 0$. Recall that a topological ordering of $V(G)$ is a linear ordering $v_{i1}, v_{i2}, ..., v_{in}$ of the vertices such that if v_{ij} is a predecessor of $v_{ik}, j \neq k, 1 \leq j \leq n$, and $1 \leq k \leq n$, then v_{ij} precedes v_{ik}, that is, $j < k$ in this linear ordering. Suppose that G has no cycles. The following algorithm, a depth first topological, lists the nodes of the graph in a topological ordering.

In a depth first topological ordering, we first find a vertex that has no successors (such a vertex exists because the graph has no cycles), and place it last in the topological order. After we have placed all the successors of a vertex in topological order, we place the vertex in the topological order before any of its successors. Clearly, in the depth first topological ordering, first we find the vertex to be placed in `topologicalOrder[n-1]`, then `topologicalOrder[n-2]`, and so on.

Write the definitions of the Java methods to implement the depth first topological ordering. Add these methods to the **class TopologicalOrder**, which is derived from the **class Graph**. Also, write a program to test your depth first topological ordering.

11

JAVA RESERVED WORDS

abstract	else	interface	super
boolean	extends	long	switch
break	false	native	synchronized
byte	final	new	this
case	finally	null	throw
catch	float	package	throws
char	for	private	translate
class	goto	protected	true
const	if	public	try
continue	implements	return	void
default	import	short	volatile
do	instanceof	static	while
double	int	strictfp	

B

OPERATOR PRECEDENCE

Precedence (highest to lowest)

Operator	Description	Precedence Level	Associativity
.	Object member access	1	Left to right
[ ]	Array subscripting	1	Left to right
(parameters)	Method call	1	Left to right
++	Post-increment	1	Left to right
--	Post-decrement	1	Left to right
++	Pre-increment	2	Right to left
--	Pre-decrement	2	Right to left
+	Unary plus	2	Right to left
-	Unary minus	2	Right to left
!	Logical not	2	Right to left
~	Bitwise not	2	Right to left
new	Object instantiation	3	Right to left
(type)	Type conversion	3	Right to left
*	Multiplication	4	Left to right
/	Division	4	Left to right
%	Remainder	4	Left to right
+	Addition	5	Left to right
-	Subtraction	5	Left to right
+	String concatenation	5	Left to right
<<	Left shift	6	Left to right
>>	Right shift with sign extension	6	Left to right
>>>	Right shift with zero extension	6	Left to right
<	Less than	7	Left to right
<=	Less than or equal to	7	Left to right
>	Greater than	7	Left to right
>=	Greater than or equal to	7	Left to right
instanceof	Type comparison	7	Left to right

Operator	Description	Precedence Level	Associativity
==	Equal	8	Left to right
!=	Not equal	8	Left to right
&	Bitwise AND	9	Left to right
&	Logical AND	9	Left to right
^	Bitwise XOR	10	Left to right
^	Logical XOR	10	Left to right
|	Bitwise OR	11	Left to right
|	Logical OR	11	Left to right
&&	Logical AND	12	Left to right
||	Logical OR	13	Left to right
?:	Conditional operator	14	Right to left
=	Assignment	15	Right to left
Compound Operators			
+=	Addition, then assignment	15	Right to left
+=	String concatenation, then assignment	15	Right to left
-=	Subtraction, then assignment	15	Right to left
*=	Multiplication, then assignment	15	Right to left
/=	Division, then assignment	15	Right to left
%=	Remainder, then assignment	15	Right to left
<<=	Left shift, then assignment	15	Right to left
>>=	Right shift, then assignment	15	Right to left
&=	Bitwise AND, then assignment	15	Right to left
&=	Logical AND, then assignment	15	Right to left
|=	Bitwise OR, then assignment	15	Right to left
|=	Logical OR, then assignment	15	Right to left
^=	Bitwise XOR, then assignment	15	Right to left
^=	Logical XOR, then assignment	15	Right to left

APPENDIX

C

CHARACTER SETS

Unicode (ASCII (American Standard Code for Information Interchange)): The first 128 characters of Unicode

Unicode (ASCII): First 128 characters

	0	1	2	3	4	5	6	7	8	9
0	NUL	SOH	STX	ETX	EOT	ENQ	ACK	BEL	BS	HT
1	LF	VT	FF	CR	SO	SI	DLE	DC1	DC2	DC3
2	DC4	NAK	SYN	ETB	CAN	EM	SUB	ESC	FS	GS
3	RS	US	b	!	"	#	$	%	&	'
4	(	)	*	+	,	-	.	/	0	1
5	2	3	4	5	6	7	8	9	:	;
6	<	=	>	?	@	A	B	C	D	E
7	F	G	H	I	J	K	L	M	N	O
8	P	Q	R	S	T	U	V	W	X	Y
9	Z	[	\	]	^	_	`	a	b	c
10	d	e	f	g	h	i	j	k	l	m
11	n	o	p	q	r	s	t	u	v	w
12	x	y	z	{			}	~	DEL		

The numbers 0–12 in the first column specify the left digit(s); the numbers 0–9 in the second row specify the right digit of each character in the ASCII data set. For example, the character in the row marked 6 (the number in the first column) and the column marked 5 (the number in the second row) is A. Therefore, the character at position 65 (which is the 66th character) is A. Moreover, the character b at position 32 represents the blank character. For more information on the Unicode character set, the reader is recommended to visit the Web site *http://www.unicode.org*.

The first 32 characters, that is, the characters at positions 00–31 and at position 127, are non-printable characters. This table shows the abbreviations of these characters. The meanings of these abbreviations are as follows:

NUL	Null character	VT	Vertical tab	SYN	Synchronous idle
SOH	Start of header	FF	Form feed	ETB	End of transmitted block
STX	Start of text	CR	Carriage return	CAN	Cancel
ETX	End of text	SO	Shift out	EM	End of medium
EOT	End of transmission	SI	Shift in	SUB	Substitute
ENQ	Enquiry	DLE	Data link escape	ESC	Escape
ACK	Acknowledge	DC1	Device control 1	FS	File separator
BEL	Bell character (beep)	DC2	Device control 2	GS	Group separator
BS	Backspace	DC3	Device control 3	RS	Record separator
HT	Horizontal tab	DC4	Device control 4	US	Unit separator
LF	Line feed	NAK	Negative acknowledge	DEL	Delete

EBCDIC (Extended Binary Coded Decimal Interchange Code)

EBCDIC	0	1	2	3	4	5	6	7	8	9
6					b̲					
7						.	<	(	+	|
8	&									
9	!	$	*	)	;	¬	-	/		
10							^	,	%	_
11	>	?								
12		`	:	#	@	'	=	"		a
13	b	c	d	e	f	g	h	i		
14						j	k	l	m	n
15	o	p	q	r						
16		~	s	t	u	v	w	x	y	z
17								\	{	}
18	[	]								
19			A	B	C	D	E	F	G	
20	H	I								J
21	K	L	M	N	O	P	Q	R		
22							S	T	U	V
23	W	X	Y	Z						
24	0	1	2	3	4	5	6	7	8	9

The numbers 6–24 in the first column specify the left digit(s); the numbers 0–9 in the second row specify the right digit of the characters in the EBCDIC data set. For example, the character in the row marked 19 (the number in the first column) and the column marked 3 (the number in the second row) is A. Therefore, the character at position 193 (which is the 194th character) is A. Moreover, the character b̲ at position 64 represents the blank character. This table does not show all the characters in the EBCDIC character set. In fact, the characters at positions 00–63 and 250–255 are nonprintable control characters.

PACKAGES AND USER-DEFINED CLASSES

Chapter 3 defined the class DataElement and its subclasses IntElement and StringElement, and remarked that you can similarly create the classes DoubleElement and so on. This section, in addition to explaining how to use these classes, gives the definitions of these classes.

DataElement AND ITS SUBCLASSES

This section defines the classes DataElement, IntElement, LongElement, CharElement, FloatElement, DoubleElement, BooleanElement, and StringElement.

Class: DataElement

```
public abstract class DataElement
{
    public abstract boolean equals(DataElement otherElement);
      //Method to determine whether two objects contain the
      //same data.
      //Postcondition: Returns true if this object contains the
      //               same data as the object otherElement,
      //               false otherwise.

    public abstract int compareTo(DataElement otherElement);
      //Method to compare two objects.
      //Postcondition: Returns a value < 0 if this element is
      //                   less than otherElement.
      //               Returns 0 if this element is the same as
      //                   otherElement.
      //               Returns a value > 0 if this element is
      //                   greater than otherElement.

    public abstract void makeCopy(DataElement otherElement);
      //Method to copy otherElement into this element.
      //Postcondition: The data of otherElement is copied into
      //                   this object.
```

```
        public abstract DataElement getCopy();
          //Method to return a copy of this object.
          //Postcondition: A copy of this object is created and
          //                 a reference of the copy is returned.
    }
```

Class: IntElement

```
    public class IntElement extends DataElement
    {
        protected int num;

            //default constructor
        public IntElement()
        {
            num = 0;
        }

            //constructor with a parameter
        public IntElement(int x)
        {
            num = x;
        }

            //copy constructor
        public IntElement(IntElement otherElement)
        {
            num = otherElement.num;
        }

            //Method to set the value of the instance variable num.
            //Postcondition: num = x
        public void setNum(int x)
        {
            num = x;
        }

            //Method to return the value of the instance variable num.
            //Postcondition: The value of num is returned.
        public int getNum()
        {
            return num;
        }
```

```
public boolean equals(DataElement otherElement)
{
    IntElement temp = (IntElement) otherElement;

    return (num == temp.num);
}

public int compareTo(DataElement otherElement)
{
    IntElement temp = (IntElement) otherElement;

    return (num - temp.num);
}

public void makeCopy(DataElement otherElement)
{
    IntElement temp = (IntElement) otherElement;

    num = temp.num;
}

public DataElement getCopy()
{
    IntElement temp = new IntElement(num);

    return temp;
}

public String toString()
{
    return String.valueOf(num);
}
}
```

Consider the following statements:

```
IntElement firstNum = new IntElement();       //Line 1
IntElement secondNum = new IntElement(5);     //Line 2
int num;                                      //Line 3
```

The statement in Line 1 creates the object `firstNum` and initializes it to 0. The statement in Line 2 creates the object `secondNum` and initializes it to 5. The statement in Line 3 declares num to be an `int` variable. Now consider the following statements:

```
firstNum.setNum(24);                          //Line 4
num = firstNum.getNum();                      //Line 5
```

The statement in Line 4 sets the value of `firstNum` (in fact, the value of the data member num of `firstNum`) to 24. The statement in Line 5 retrieves the value of the object

firstNum (the value of the data member **num**), and assigns it to **num**. After this statement executes, the value of **num** is 24.

The following statements output the values of **firstNum** and **secondNum** (in fact, the values of their data members).

```
System.out.println("firstNum = " + firstNum);
System.out.println("secondNum = " + secondNum);
```

The following table further illustrates the usage of various methods of the **class IntElement**.

	int	IntElement

Declaration with or without initialization	`int x, y = 5;`	`IntElement x, y;`
		`x = new IntElement();`
		`y = new IntElement(5);`

Assignment	`x = 24;` `y = x;`	`x.setNum(24);` `y.setNum(x.getNum());`
Addition	`x = x + 10;` `x = x + y;`	`x.setNum(x.getNum() + 10);` `x.setNum(x.getNum() + y.getNum());`
Multiplication	`x = x * 10;` `x = x * y;`	`x.setNum(x.getNum() * 10);` `x.setNum(x.getNum() * y.getNum());`
Comparison	`if(x < 10)` `if(x < y)`	`if(x.compareTo(new IntElement(10)) < 0)` `if(x.compareTo(y) < 0)`
	`if(x <= 10)` `if(x <= y)`	`if(x.compareTo(new IntElement(10)) <= 0)` `if(x.compareTo(y) <= 0)`

	`if(x == 10)`
	`if(x == y)`
		`if(x.compareTo(new IntElement(10)) == 0)`
		`if(x.compareTo(y) == 0)`
		or
		`if(x.equals(new IntElement(10)))`
		`if(x.equals(y))`

	`if(x > 10)` `if(x > y)`	`if(x.compareTo(new IntElement(10)) > 0)` `if(x.compareTo(y) > 0)`
	`if(x >= 10)` `if(x >= y)`	`if(x.compareTo(new IntElement(10)) >= 0)` `if(x.compareTo(y) >= 0)`

	`if(x != 10)`
	`if(x != y)`
		`if(x.compareTo(new IntElement(10)) != 0)`
		`if(x.compareTo(y) != 0)`
		or
		`if(!x.equals(new IntElement(10)))`
		`if(!x.equals(y))`

Output	`System.out.print(x);`	`System.out.print(x);`

Class: `LongElement`

```java
public class LongElement extends DataElement
{
    protected long num;

        //default constructor
    public LongElement()
    {
        num = 0;
    }

        //constructor with a parameter
    public LongElement(long x)
    {
        num = x;
    }

        //copy constructor
    public LongElement(LongElement otherElement)
    {
        num = otherElement.num;
    }

        //Method to set the value of the instance variable num.
        //Postcondition: num = x
    public void setNum(long x)
    {
        num = x;
    }

        //Method to return the value of the instance variable num.
        //Postcondition: The value of num is returned.
    public long getNum()
    {
        return num;
    }

    public boolean equals(DataElement otherElement)
    {
        LongElement temp = (LongElement) otherElement;

        return (num == temp.num);
    }
```

D

```java
    public int compareTo(DataElement otherElement)
    {
        LongElement temp = (LongElement) otherElement;

        if(num < temp.num)
            return -1;
        else
            if(num == temp.num)
                return 0;
            else
                return 1;
    }

    public void makeCopy(DataElement otherElement)
    {
        LongElement temp = (LongElement) otherElement;

        num = temp.num;
    }

    public DataElement getCopy()
    {
        LongElement temp = new LongElement(num);

        return temp;
    }

    public String toString()
    {
        return String.valueOf(num);
    }
}
```

Class: CharElement

```java
public class CharElement extends DataElement
{
    protected char ch;

        //default constructor
    public CharElement()
    {
        ch = '\0';
    }
```

```java
    //constructor with a parameter
public CharElement(char x)
{
    ch = x;
}

    //copy constructor
public CharElement(CharElement otherElement)
{
    ch = otherElement.ch;
}

    //Method to set the value of the instance variable ch.
    //Postcondition: ch = x
public void setChar(char x)
{
    ch = x;
}

    //Method to return the value of the instance variable ch.
    //Postcondition: The value of ch is returned.
public char getChar()
{
    return ch;
}

public boolean equals(DataElement otherElement)
{
    CharElement temp = (CharElement) otherElement;

    return (ch == temp.ch);
}

public int compareTo(DataElement otherElement)
{
    CharElement temp = (CharElement) otherElement;

    return ((int)ch - (int) temp.ch);
}

public void makeCopy(DataElement otherElement)
{
    CharElement temp = (CharElement) otherElement;

    ch = temp.ch;
}
```

D

```
    public DataElement getCopy()
    {
        CharElement temp = new CharElement(ch);
        return temp;
    }

    public String toString()
    {
        return String.valueOf(ch);
    }
}
```

Class: FloatElement

```
public class FloatElement extends DataElement
{
    protected float num;

        //default constructor
    public FloatElement()
    {
        num = 0;
    }

        //constructor with a parameter
    public FloatElement(float x)
    {
        num = x;
    }

        //copy constructor
    public FloatElement(FloatElement otherElement)
    {
        num = otherElement.num;
    }

        //Method to set the value of the instance variable num.
        //Postcondition: num = x
    public void setNum(float x)
    {
        num = x;
    }

        //Method to return the value of the instance variable num.
        //Postcondition: The value of num is returned.
    public float getNum()
    {
        return num;
    }
```

```java
    public boolean equals(DataElement otherElement)
    {
        FloatElement temp = (FloatElement) otherElement;

        return (num == temp.num);
    }

    public int compareTo(DataElement otherElement)
    {
        FloatElement temp = (FloatElement) otherElement;

        if(num < temp.num)
            return -1;
        else
            if(num == temp.num)
                return 0;
            else
                return 1;
    }

    public void makeCopy(DataElement otherElement)
    {
        FloatElement temp = (FloatElement) otherElement;

        num = temp.num;
    }

    public DataElement getCopy()
    {
        FloatElement temp = new FloatElement(num);
        return temp;
    }

    public String toString()
    {
        return String.valueOf(num);
    }
}
```

Class: DoubleElement

```java
public class DoubleElement extends DataElement
{
    protected double num;

        //default constructor
    public DoubleElement()
    {
        num = 0;
    }
```

```java
    //constructor with a parameter
public DoubleElement(double x)
{
    num = x;
}

    //copy constructor
public DoubleElement(DoubleElement otherElement)
{
    num = otherElement.num;
}

    //Method to set the value of the instance variable num.
    //Postcondition: num = x
public void setNum(double x)
{
    num = x;
}

    //Method to return the value of the instance variable num.
    //Postcondition: The value of num is returned.
public double getNum()
{
    return num;
}

public boolean equals(DataElement otherElement)
{
    DoubleElement temp = (DoubleElement) otherElement;

    return (num == temp.num);
}

public int compareTo(DataElement otherElement)
{
    DoubleElement temp = (DoubleElement) otherElement;

    if(num < temp.num)
        return -1;
    else
        if(num == temp.num)
            return 0;
        else
            return 1;
}
```

```java
    public void makeCopy(DataElement otherElement)
    {
        DoubleElement temp = (DoubleElement) otherElement;

        num = temp.num;
    }

    public DataElement getCopy()
    {
        DoubleElement temp = new DoubleElement(num);
        return temp;
    }

    public String toString()
    {
        return String.valueOf(num);
    }
}
```

Class: BooleanElement

```java
public class BooleanElement extends DataElement
{
    private boolean flag;

    public BooleanElement()
    {
        flag = false;
    }

    public BooleanElement(boolean f)
    {
        flag = f;
    }

    public boolean get()
    {
        return flag;
    }

    public void set(boolean f)
    {
        flag = f;
    }

    public boolean equals(DataElement otherElement)
    {
        BooleanElement temp = (BooleanElement) otherElement;
```

```
            return (flag == temp.flag);
        }

        public int compareTo(DataElement otherElement)
        {
            BooleanElement temp = (BooleanElement) otherElement;

            if(flag == temp.flag)
                return 0;
            else
                if(flag == true)
                    return -1;
                else
                    return 1;
        }

        public void makeCopy(DataElement otherElement)
        {
            BooleanElement temp = (BooleanElement) otherElement;

            flag = temp.flag;
        }

        public DataElement getCopy()
        {
            BooleanElement temp = new BooleanElement(flag);

            return temp;
        }

        public String toString()
        {
            return (String.valueOf(flag));
        }
    }
```

Class: `StringElement`

```
    public class StringElement extends DataElement
    {
        protected String str;

            //default constructor
        public StringElement()
        {
            str = null;
        }
```

```java
    //constructor with a parameter
public StringElement(String s)
{
    str = s;
}

    //copy constructor
public StringElement(StringElement otherString)
{
    str = otherString.str;
}

    //Method to set the value of the instance variable str.
    //Postcondition: str = x
public void setString(String x)
{
    str = x;
}
public boolean equals(DataElement otherElement)
{
    StringElement temp = (StringElement) otherElement;

    return (str.compareTo(temp.str) == 0);
}

public int compareTo(DataElement otherElement)
{
    StringElement temp = (StringElement) otherElement;

    return (str.compareTo(temp.str));
}

public void makeCopy(DataElement otherElement)
{
    StringElement temp = (StringElement) otherElement;

    str = new String(temp.str);
}

public DataElement getCopy()
{
    StringElement temp = new StringElement(str);

    return temp;
}
```

```
        public String toString()
        {
            return str;
        }
    }
```

USING USER-DEFINED CLASSES IN A PROGRAM

This section describes how to use the classes introduced in the previous section. This discussion also applies to other user-defined classes, such as the classes `ArrayListClass` (Chapter 3), `LinkedListClass` (Chapter 4), and `StackClass` (Chapter 6).

There are two ways to use the class `DataElement` and its subclasses. For illustration purposes, suppose that you want to use the classes `DataElement` and `IntElement`.

First Way

One way to use this class is to create a package and then put the classes `DataElement` and `IntElement` in that package. For example, you can create the package:

`dsuj.ch03.DataElementClasses`

and put these classes in this package. To do so, put the package statement:

`package dsuj.ch03.DataElementClasses;`

before the definition of the classes `DataElement` and `IntElement`.

The definition of the class `DataElement` is in the file `DataElement.java`; the definition of the class `IntElement` is in the file `IntElement.java`. We need to compile these files and place them in the directory `dsuj.ch03.DataElementClasses`.

To do so, for the class `DataElement`, we issue the following command at the command line:

`javac -d c:\j2sdk1.4.0-rc\jre\lib DataElement.java`

and the following command for the class `IntElement`:

`javac -d c:\j2sdk1.4.0-rc\jre\lib IntElement.java`

These classes are now placed in the appropriate subdirectory of `j2dsk1.4.0-rc`.

You can import these classes into a program using the import statement. For example, you can use either of the following statements to use the class `IntElement` in your program:

`import dsuj.ch03.DataElementClasses.*;`

or:

`import dsuj.ch03.DataElementClasses.IntElement;`

Second Way

Another way to use the **class DataElement** and its subclasses is to keep the files **DataElement.java** and **IntElement.java**, and the program, in the same directory. Make sure to remove the package statement:

```
package dsuj.ch03.DataElementClasses;
```

before the definition of these classes.

Compile the files **DataElement.java** and **IntElement.java**, and then compile the program. In this case, we add the following statements to the **autoexec.bat** file:

```
SET PATH = %PATH%;c:\j2sdk1.4.0-rc\bin;
SET CLASSPATH =.; c:\j2sdk1.4.0-rc\jre\lib;
```

Using a Software Development Kit (SDK)

If you are using an SDK such as CodeWarrior, Forte for Java, or J++ Builder, then you can place the file containing the definition of the class in the same directory that contains your program. You do not need to create any package. However, you can create a package. In this case, place the appropriate package statement before the definition of the class and use the compile command provided by the SDK. (In most cases, you do not need to specify any subdirectory.) The compiled file is placed in the appropriate directory. You can now import the class without adding it to the project. (Note that if you have created a package for your classes, to avoid compilation errors, do not add the file containing the definition of the class to the project.)

D

E

JAVA CLASSES

This appendix describes various Java classes, and some of their commonly used members, that are used or mentioned in this text. For a detailed description of all the Java classes, the reader is recommended to visit the web site *http://java.sun.com*.

CLASS: Boolean (PACKAGE java.lang)

Constructors

```
public Boolean(boolean param)
  //Creates a Boolean object initialized with the value specified
  //by param.
public Boolean(String str)
  //Creates a Boolean object initialized to true if the string
  //specified by str is not null and is equal, ignoring case,
  //to the string "true".
```

Methods

```
public boolean booleanValue()
  //Returns true if the value of the object is true,
  //false otherwise.
public int hashCode()
  //Returns the hash code of this object.
public String toString()
  //If the state of the object is true, returns the String
  //object with the value "true"; otherwise, returns the String
  //object with the value "false".
public static Boolean valueOf(String str)
  //Returns a Boolean object initialized to the value
  //specified by str.
```

CLASS: Character (PACKAGE java.lang)

Constructor

```
public Character(char ch)
    //Creates a Character object with the value specified by ch.
```

Methods

```
public static int digit(char ch, int base)
    //Returns the numeric value of ch in radix base
    //specified by base.
public static int forDigit(int digit, int base)
    //Returns the numeric value of digit in radix base
    //specified by base.
public boolean equals(Object obj)
    //Returns true if this object is equal to the object
    //specified by obj, false otherwise.
public static int getNumericValue(char ch)
    //Returns the Unicode representation, as a nonnegative integer,
    //of the character specified by ch. If ch has no numeric
    //representation, -1 is returned; if ch cannot be represented
    //as a nonnegative integer, -2 is returned.
public int hashCode()
    //Returns the hash code of this object.
public static boolean isDigit(char ch)
    //Returns true if ch is a digit, false otherwise.
public static boolean isLetter(char ch)
    //Returns true if ch is a letter, false otherwise.
public static boolean isLowerCase(char ch)
    //Returns true if ch is a lowercase letter, false otherwise.
public static boolean isUpperCase(char ch)
    //Returns true if ch is an uppercase letter, false otherwise.
public static boolean isSpaceChar(char ch)
    //Returns true if ch is the space character, false otherwise.
public static boolean isWhitespace(char ch)
    //Returns true if ch is a whitespace character,
    //false otherwise.
public static char toLowerCase(char ch)
    //Returns the character that is the lowercase equivalent of ch.
    //If ch does not have the corresponding lowercase letter,
    //it returns ch.
public static char toUpperCase(char ch)
    //Returns the character that is the uppercase equivalent of ch.
    //If ch does not have the corresponding uppercase letter,
    //it returns ch.
public String toString()
    //Returns a string representation of the object.
```

CLASS: DecimalFormat (PACKAGE java.text)

Constructors

```
public DecimalFormat()
  //Creates a Decimal Format object with the default pattern.
public DecimalFormat(String str)
  //Creates a Decimal Format object with the pattern specified
  //by str.
public DecimalFormat(String str, DecimalFormatSymbols symbols)
  //Creates a Decimal Format object with the pattern specified by
  //symbols.
```

Methods

```
public void applyPattern(String str)
  //Sets the pattern of the object.
public String toPattern()
  //Returns the pattern of the object as a string.
public object clone()
  //Returns a copy of the object.
public boolean equals(Object obj)
  //Returns true if this object is equal to the object
  //specified by obj, false otherwise.
public String format(double num)
  //Returns a string containing the formatted num.
public String format(long num)
  //Returns a string containing the formatted num.
public DecimalFormatSymbols getDecimalFormatSymbols()
  //Returns the decimal number format symbols of the object.
public void setDecimalFormatSymbols(DecimalFormatSymbols symbols)
  //Sets the decimal number format symbols of this object.
public int hashCode()
  //Returns the hash code of the object.
```

CLASS: Double (PACKAGE java.lang)

Named Constants

```
public static final double MAX_VALUE = 1.7976931348623157E308;
public static final double MIN_VALUE = 4.9E-324;

public static final double NEGATIVE_INFINITY = -1.0/0.0;
public static final double POSITIVE_INFINITY = 1.0/0.0;
```

Constructors

```
public Double(double num)
  //Creates a Double object initialized to the value specified
  //by num.
public Double(String str) throws NumberFormatException
  //Creates a Double object initialized to the value specified
  //by the num contained in str.
```

Methods

```
public byte byteValue()
  //Returns the value of the object as a byte value.
public short shortValue()
  //Returns the value of the object as a short value.
public int intValue()
  //Returns the value of the object as an int value.
public long longValue()
  //Returns the value of the object as a long value.
public double doubleValue()
  //Returns the value of the object as a double value.
public float floatValue()
  //Returns the value of the object as a float value.
public int hashCode()
  //Returns the hash code of the object.
public boolean equals(Object obj)
  //Returns true if the value of this object is equal
  //to the value of the object specified by obj,
  //false otherwise.
public boolean isInfinity()
  //Returns true if the value of this object is positive
  //or negative infinity, false otherwise.
public static boolean isInfinity(double num)
  //Returns true if the value of num is positive or
  //negative infinity, false otherwise.
public static double parseDouble(String str) throws
                                        NumberFormatException
  //Returns the value of the number contained in str.
public String toString()
  //Returns the double value of the object as a string.
public static String toString(double num)
  //Returns the value of num as a string.
public static Double valueOf(String str) throws
                                        NumberFormatException
  //Returns a Double object initialized to the value
  //specified by str.
```

CLASS: Exception (PACKAGE java.lang)

Constructors

```
public Exception()
  //Creates a new instance of the class Exception.
public Exception(String str)
  //Creates a new instance of the class Exception. The
  //parameter str specifies the message string.
```

CLASS: FileReader (PACKAGE java.io)

Constructors

```
public FileReader(FileDescriptor fd) throws FileNotFoundException
  //Creates a FileReader object from a file descriptor.
public FileReader(String fileName) throws FileNotFoundException
  //Creates a FileReader object from a filename.
```

Methods

```
public void close() throws IOException
  //Closes the FileReader.
public int read() throws IOException
  //Returns a single character as an int from the FileReader.
  //Returns -1 if the end of the stream is reached.
public boolean ready() throws IOException
  //Returns true if the object is ready to be read. If the object
  //is nonempty, the state is true.
public void reset() throws IOException
  //Resets the object.
```

CLASS: FileWriter (PACKAGE java.io)

Constructors

```
public FileWriter(String fileName) throws IOException
  //Creates a FileWriter object from a filename.
public FileWriter(String fileName, boolean a)
                                  throws IOException
  //Creates a FileWriter object from a filename.
  //The boolean variable a indicates whether or not to append to
  //the file.
```

```
public FileWriter(FileDescriptor fd)
  //Creates a FileWriter object from a file descriptor.
```

Methods

```
public String getEncoding()
  //Returns the name of the character encoding being used.
public void write(int c) throws IOException
  //Writes a single character.
public void write(char[] cbuf, int off, int len)
                                    throws IOException
  //Writes a part of an array of characters.
public void write(String str, int off, int len)
                                    throws IOException
  //Writes a part of a string.
public void flush() throws IOException
  //Empties the stream.
public void close() throws IOException
  //Closes the stream.
```

CLASS: Float (PACKAGE java.lang)

Named Constants

```
public static final float MAX_VALUE = 3.4028235E38;
public static final float MIN_VALUE = 1.4E-45;

public static final float NEGATIVE_INFINITY = -1.0f/0.0f;
public static final float POSITIVE_INFINITY = 1.0f/0.0f;
```

Constructors

```
public Float(float num)
  //Creates an object initialized to the value specified
  //by num.
public Float(double num)
  //Creates an object initialized to the value specified
  //by num.
public Float(String str) throws NumberFormatException
  //Creates an object initialized to the value specified
  //by the num contained in str.
```

Methods

```
public byte byteValue()
  //Returns the value of the object as a byte value.
```

```
public short shortValue()
  //Returns the value of the object as a short value.
public int intValue()
  //Returns the value of the object as an int value.
public long longValue()
  //Returns the value of the object as a long value.
public double doubleValue()
  //Returns the value of the object as a double value.
public float floatValue()
  //Returns the value of the object as a float value.
public int hashCode()
  //Returns the hash code of the object.
public boolean equals(Object obj)
  //Returns true if the value of this object is equal
  //to the value of the object specified by obj,
  //false otherwise.
public boolean isInfinity()
  //Returns true if the value of this object is positive
  //or negative infinity, false otherwise.
public static boolean isInfinity(float num)
  //Returns true if the value of num is positive
  //or negative infinity, false otherwise.
public static float parseFloat(String str) throws
                                      NumberFormatException
  //Returns the value of the number contained in str.
public String toString()
  //Returns the float value of the object as a string.
public static String toString(float num)
  //Returns the value of num as a string.
public static Float valueOf(String str) throws
                                      NumberFormatException
  //Returns a Float object initialized to the value
  //specified by str.
```

E

CLASS: InputStreamReader (PACKAGE java.io)

Constructors

```
public InputStreamReader(Reader rd)
  //Creates an InputStreamReader object. The object is initialized
  //using rd.
public InputStreamReader(Reader rd, int size)
  //Creates an InputStreamReader object. The object is initialized
  //using rd and to the size specified by size. The default size
  //is 8192 characters.
```

Methods

```
public void close() throws IOException
  //Closes the InputStreamReader.
public int read() throws IOException
  //Returns a single character as an int from the
  //InputStreamReader. Returns -1 if the end of the stream
  //is reached.
public boolean ready() throws IOException
  //Returns true if the object is ready to be read. If the object
  //is nonempty, the statement is true.
public void reset() throws IOException
  //Resets the object.
```

CLASS: Integer (PACKAGE java.lang)

Named Constants

```
public static final int MAX_VALUE = 2147483647;
public static final int MIN_VALUE = -2147483648;
```

Constructors

```
public Integer(int num)
  //Creates an Integer object initialized to the value specified
  //by num.
public Integer(String str) throws NumberFormatException
  //Creates an Integer object initialized to the value specified
  //by the num contained in str.
```

Methods

```
public byte byteValue()
  //Returns the value of the object as a byte value.
public short shortValue()
  //Returns the value of the object as a short value.
public int intValue()
  //Returns the value of the object as an int value.
public long longValue()
  //Returns the value of the object as a long value.
public double doubleValue()
  //Returns the value of the object as a double value.
public float floatValue()
  //Returns the value of the object as a float value.
public int hashCode()
  //Returns the hash code of the object.
```

```
public boolean equals(Object obj)
   //Returns true if the value of this object is equal
   //to the value of the object specified by obj,
   //false otherwise.
public static int parseInt(String str) throws
                                    NumberFormatException
   //Returns the value of the number contained in str.
public static int parseInt(String str, int base) throws
                                    NumberFormatException
   //Returns the value, in radix base, of the int
   //contained in str.

public static String toBinaryString(int num)
   //Returns the string representation of num in binary (base 2).
public static String toHexString(int num)
   //Returns the string representation of num in
   //hexadecimal (base 16).
public static String toOctalString(int num)
   //Returns the string representation of num in octal (base 8).

public String toString()
   //Returns the int value of the object as a string.
public static String toString(int num)
   //Returns the value of num as a string.
public static String toString(int num, int base)
   //Returns the value of num, in radix base, as a string.

public static Integer valueOf(String str) throws
                                    NumberFormatException
   //Returns an Integer object initialized to the value
   //specified by str.
public static Integer valueOf(String str, int base) throws
                                    NumberFormatException
   //Returns an Integer object initialized to the value,
   //in radix base, specified by str.
```

CLASS: JButton (PACKAGE javax.swing)

Constructors

```
public JButton()
   //Creates the JButton object with no text or icon.
public JButton(Icon ic)
   //Creates the JButton object with the icon specified by ic.
public JButton(String str)
   //Creates the JButton object to the text specified by str.
```

```
public JButton(String str, Icon ic)
  //Creates the JButton object to the text specified by str
  //and the icon specified by ic.
```

Methods

```
public String getText()
  //Method to return the text contained in the button.
public void setText(String str)
  //Method to set the text of the button to the string specified
  //by str.
public boolean isSelected()
  //Returns true if the button is selected, false otherwise.
public void setSelected(boolean b)
  //Sets the state of the button to b. This method does not
  //trigger an actionEvent. For that, call doClick.
public void addActionListener(ActionListener obj)
  //Method to register a listener object to the button object.
public void doClick()
  //Programmatically performs a "click".
public void doClick(int msec)
  //Programmatically performs a "click". The button appears
  //pressed for msec milliseconds.
public Icon getIcon()
  //Returns the default icon.
public void setIcon(Icon icon)
  //Sets the default icon.
public Icon getPressedIcon()
  //Returns the pressed icon.
public Icon setPressedIcon()
  //Sets the pressed icon.
public Icon getSelectedIcon()
  //Returns the selected icon.
public void setSelectedIcon(Icon icon)
  //Sets the selected icon.
public Icon getDisabledIcon()
  //Returns the icon used when the button is disabled.
  //If there is no disabled icon, one from the default
  //icon is constructed.
public void setDisabledIcon(Icon icon)
  //Sets the disabled icon.
public int getVerticalTextPosition()
  //Returns the vertical position of the text.
  //Returns one of the following constant values:
  //    SwingConstants.CENTER (the default)
  //    SwingConstants.TOP
  //    SwingConstants.BOTTOM
```

```
public void setVerticalTextPosition(int pos)
  //Sets the vertical position of the text.
  //Possible values are:
  //     SwingConstants.CENTER (the default)
  //     SwingConstants.TOP
  //     SwingConstants.BOTTOM
public int getHorizontalTextPosition()
  //Returns the horizontal position of the text.
  //Returns one of the following constant values:
  //     SwingConstants.RIGHT
  //     SwingConstants.LEFT
  //     SwingConstants.CENTER
  //     SwingConstants.LEADING
  //     SwingConstants.TRAILING (the default)
public void setHorizontalTextPosition(int pos)
  //Sets the horizontal position of the text.
  //Possible values are:
  //     SwingConstants.RIGHT
  //     SwingConstants.LEFT
  //     SwingConstants.CENTER
  //     SwingConstants.LEADING
  //     SwingConstants.TRAILING (the default)
public void setActionCommand(String actionCommand)
  //Sets the action command.
public String getActionCommand()
  //Returns the action command.
public int getMnemonic()
  //Returns the keyboard mnemonic. The mnemonic is the key that,
  //when combined with the meta key (usually Alt), will "click"
  //this button if the focus is within the button's ancestor window.
public void setMnemonic(int mnemonic)
  //Sets the keyboard mnemonic. The mnemonic is the key that,
  //when combined with the meta key (usually Alt), will "click"
  //this button if the focus is within the button's ancestor window.
public void setEnabled(boolean b)
  //Sets the button to enabled if b is true, disabled if b is false.
```

CLASS: JFrame (PACKAGE javax.swing)

Constructors

```
public JFrame()
  //Creates a JFrame object without any title.
public JFrame(String s)
  //Creates a JFrame object with the title specified by s.
```

```
public JFrame(GraphicsConfiguration gc)
  //Creates a JFrame object in the specified
  //GraphicsConfiguration of a screen device with no title.

public JFrame(String t, GraphicsConfiguration gc)
  //Creates a JFrame object in the specified
  //GraphicsConfiguration of a screen device and title.
```

Methods

```
public void setSize(int w, int h)
  //Sets the size of the window.
public void setTitle(String s)
  //Sets the title of the window.
public void setVisible(boolean b)
  //Method to display the window in the program. If the value
  //of b is true, the window is displayed on the screen.
public int getDefaultCloseOperation()
  //Returns the operation that occurs when the user closes
  //this frame.
public void setDefaultCloseOperation(int operation)
  //Method to determine the action to be taken when the user
  //clicks on the window closing button to close the window.
  //Choices for the parameter operation are the named constants:
  //    EXIT_ON_CLOSE — defined in the class JFrame
  //    HIDE_ON_CLOSE — defined in javax.swing.WindowConstants
  //    DISPOSE_ON_CLOSE — defined in javax.swing.WindowConstants
  //    DO_NOTHING_ON_CLOSE — defined in javax.swing.WindowConstants
public void addWindowListener(WindowEvent e)
  //Method to register a window listener object to a JFrame.
public void update(Graphics g)
  //Invokes the method paint(g).
public void setJMenuBar(JMenuBar mbar)
  //Sets the menubar for this JFrame.
public JMenuBar getJMenuBar()
  //Returns the menubar of this JFrame.
public JRootPane getRootPane()
  //Returns the rootPane object for this JFrame.
protected void setRootPane(JRootPane r)
  //Sets the rootPane property.
public Container getContentPane()
  //Returns the contentPane object for this JFrame.
public void setContentPane(Container pane)
  //Sets the contentPane for this JFrame.
public JLayeredPane getLayeredPane()
  //Returns the layeredPane object for this JFrame.
public void setLayeredPane(JLayeredPane layeredPane)
  //Sets the layeredPane for this JFrame.
```

CLASS: JLabel (PACKAGE javax.swing)

Constructors

```
public JLabel()
  //Creates a JLabel object with no text or icons.
public JLabel(String str)
  //Creates a JLabel object with left-aligned text specified
  //by str.
public JLabel(String str, int align)
  //Creates a JLabel object with the text specified by str.
  //The value of align can be any one of the following:
  //      SwingConstants.LEFT
  //      SwingConstants.RIGHT
  //      SwingConstants.CENTER
  //These constants are defined in the class SwingConstants.
public JLabel(Icon icon)
  //Constructs a JLabel with an icon.
public JLabel(Icon icon, int align)
  //Creates a JLabel object with an icon.
  //The value of align can be any one of the following:
  //      SwingConstants.LEFT
  //      SwingConstants.RIGHT
  //      SwingConstants.CENTER
  //These constants are defined in the class SwingConstants.
public JLabel(String t, Icon icon, int align)
  //Constructs a JLabel with both text and an icon.
  //The icon is to the left of the text.
  //The value of align can be any one of the following:
  //      SwingConstants.LEFT
  //      SwingConstants.RIGHT
  //      SwingConstants.CENTER
  //These constants are defined in the class SwingConstants.
```

Methods

```
public Icon GetIcon()
  //Method to return the graphic image (glyph, icon) that
  //the label displays.
public void SetIconTextGap(int IconTextGap)
  //Method to set the gap between the icon and the text properties
  //if both are set.
public int GetIconTextGap()
  //Method to return the gap between the icon and the text
  //properties if both are set.
```

```
public void SetVerticalAlignment(int Align)
  //Method to set the label alignment along the y-axis.
  //The value of align can be any one of the following:
  //     SwingConstants.TOP
  //     SwingConstants.CENTER (default)
  //     SwingConstants.BOTTOM
  //These constants are defined in the class SwingConstants.
public int GetVerticalAlignment()
  //Method to return the label alignment along the y-axis.
public void SetHorizontalAlignment(int Align)
  //Method to set the label alignment along the x-axis.
  //The value of align can be any one of the following:
  //     SwingConstants.LEFT
  //     SwingConstants.RIGHT
  //     SwingConstants.CENTER
  //These constants are defined in the class SwingConstants.
public int GetHorizontalAlignment()
  //Method to return the label alignment along the x-axis.
public void SetVerticalTextPosition(int TextPos)
  //Method to set the vertical text position relative to the icon.
  //The value of align can be any one of the following:
  //     SwingConstants.TOP
  //     SwingConstants.CENTER (default)
  //     SwingConstants.BOTTOM
  //These constants are defined in the class SwingConstants.
public int GetVerticalTextPosition()
  //Method to return the vertical text position.
public void SetHorizontalTextPosition(int TextPos)
  //Method to set the horizontal text position relative to the
  //icon. The value of align can be any one of the following:
  //     SwingConstants.LEFT
  //     SwingConstants.RIGHT
  //     SwingConstants.CENTER
  //These constants are defined in the class SwingConstants.
public int GetHorizontalTextPosition()
  //Method to return the horizontal text position.
```

CLASS: JTextField (PACKAGE javax.swing)

Constructors

```
public JTextField()
  //Creates a JTextField object with 0 columns.
  //The initial text is set to null.
public JTextField(int columns)
  //Creates a JTextField object with the number of columns
  //specified by columns.
```

```
public JTextField(String str)
   //Creates a JTextField object with the text specified by str.
public JTextField(String str, int columns)
   //Creates a JTextField object with the text specified by str,
   //and sets the size of the text field.
```

Methods

```
public void setColumns(int c)
   //Sets the number of columns to c.
public int getColumns()
   //Returns the number of columns.
public void setText(String str)
   //Method to set the text of the text field to the string specified
   //by str.
public String getText()
   //Method to return the text contained in the text field.
public void setEditable(boolean b)
   //If the value of the boolean variable b is false, the user cannot
   //type in the text field.
   //In this case, the text field is used as a tool to display
   //the result.
public void addActionListener(ActionListener obj)
   //Method to register a listener object to a JTextField.
public void removeActionListener(ActionListener obj)
   //Method to remove a registered listener object.
public int getHorizontalAlignment()
   //Returns the horizontal alignment of the text.
   //Valid values are:
   //     JTextField.LEFT
   //     JTextField.CENTER
   //     JTextField.RIGHT
   //     JTextField.LEADING
   //     JTextField.TRAILING
public void setHorizontalAlignment(int a)
   //Sets the horizontal alignment of the text.
   //Valid argument values are:
   //     JTextField.LEFT
   //     JTextField.CENTER
   //     JTextField.RIGHT
   //     JTextField.LEADING
   //     JTextField.TRAILING.
public void setFont(Font font)
   //Sets the current font.
```

E

CLASS: Long (PACKAGE `java.lang`)

Named Constants

```
public static final long MAX_VALUE = 9223372036854775807;
public static final long MIN_VALUE = - 9223372036854775808;
```

Constructors

```
public Long(long num)
   //Creates a Long object initialized to the value specified
   //by num.
public Long(String str) throws NumberFormatException
   //Creates a Long object initialized to the value specified
   //by the num contained in str.
```

Methods

```
public byte byteValue()
   //Returns the value of the object as a byte value.
public short shortValue()
   //Returns the value of the object as a short value.
public int intValue()
   //Returns the value of the object as an int value.
public long longValue()
   //Returns the value of the object as a long value.
public double doubleValue()
   //Returns the value of the object as a double value.
public float floatValue()
   //Returns the value of the object as a float value.
public int hashCode()
   //Returns the hash code of the object.
public boolean equals(Object obj)
   //Returns true if the value of this object is equal
   //to the value of the object specified by obj,
   //false otherwise.
public static long parseLong(String str) throws
                                    NumberFormatException
   //Returns the value of the number contained in str.
public static long parseLong(String str, int base) throws
                                    NumberFormatException
   //Returns the value, in radix base, of the long value
   //contained in str.
public static String toBinaryString(long num)
   //Returns the string representation of num in binary (base 2).
public static String toHexString(long num)
   //Returns the string representation of num in
   //hexadecimal (base 16).
```

```
public static String toOctalString(long num)
   //Returns the string representation of num in octal (base 8).
public String toString()
   //Returns the long value of the object as a string.
public static String toString(long num)
   //Returns the value of num as a string.
public static String toString(long num, int base)
   //Returns the value of num, in radix base, as a string.
public static Long valueOf(String str) throws
                                       NumberFormatException
   //Returns a Long object initialized to the value
   //specified by str.
public static Long valueOf(String str, int base) throws
                                       NumberFormatException
   //Returns a Long object initialized to the value,
   //in radix base, specified by str.
```

CLASS: Math (PACKAGE java.lang)

Methods

```
public static int abs(int x)
   //Returns the absolute value of x.
public static long abs(long x)
   //Returns the absolute value of x.
public static double abs(double x)
   //Returns the absolute value of x.
public static float abs(float x)
   //Returns the absolute value of x.
public static double ceil(double x)
   //Returns a value of the type double, which is the
   //smallest integer value that is not less than x.
public static double exp(double x)
   //Returns eˣ, where e is approximately 2.7182818284590455.
public static double floor(double x)
   //Returns a value of the type double, which is the
   //largest integer value less than x.
public static double log(double x) throws ArithmeticException
   //Returns a value of the type double, which is the
   //natural logarithm of x.
public static int max(int x, int y)
   //Returns the larger of x and y.
public static long max(long x, long y)
   //Returns the larger of x and y.
public static double max(double x, double y)
   //Returns the larger of x and y.
public static float max(float x, float y)
   //Returns the larger of x and y.
```

```
public static int min(int x, int y)
  //Returns the smaller of x and y.
public static long min(long x, long y)
  //Returns the smaller of x and y.
public static double min(double x, double y)
  //Returns the smaller of x and y.
public static float min(float x, float y)
  //Returns the smaller of x and y.
public static double pow(double x, double y)
  //Returns x^y.
public static double random()
  //Returns a random number between 0.0 and 1.0.
public static int round(float x)
  //Returns a value that is the integer closest to x.
public static long round(double x)
  //Returns a value that is the integer closest to x.
public static double sqrt(double x)
  //Returns the positive square root of x; x must be nonnegative.
public static double cos(double x)
  //Returns the cosine of x measured in radians.
public static double sin(double x)
  //Returns the sine of x measured in radians.
public static double tan(double x)
  //Returns the tangent of x measured in radians.
public static double acos(double x)
  //Returns the arc cosine of x measured in radians.
public static double asin(double x)
  //Returns the arc sine of x measured in radians.
public static double atan(double x)
  //Returns the arc tangent of x measured in radians.
```

CLASS: PrintWriter (PACKAGE java.io)

Constructors

```
public PrintWriter(Writer out)
  //Creates a new PrintWriter. No automatic line flushing.
public PrintWriter(Writer out, boolean af)
  //Creates a new PrintWriter. The variable af determines
  //whether automatic line flushing is enabled.
public PrintWriter(OutputStream out)
  //Creates a PrintWriter from an OutputStream. No automatic
  //line flushing.
public PrintWriter(OutputStream out, boolean autoFlush)
  //Creates a new PrintWriter from an existing OutputStream.
```

Methods

```
public void flush()
  //Flushes the stream.
public void close()
  //Closes the stream.
public boolean checkError()
  //Flushes the stream and checks its error state.
protected void setError()
  //Sets an error state.
public void write(int c)
  //Writes a single character.
public void write(char[] b, int offset, int length)
  //Writes a part of an array of characters.
public void write(char[] buf)
  //Writes an array of characters.
public void write(String s, int offset, int length)
  //Writes a part of a string.
public void write(String s)
  //Writes a string.
public void print(boolean b)
  //Prints a boolean value.
public void print(char c)
  //Prints a character.
public void print(int i)
  //Prints an integer.
public void print(long l)
  //Prints a long integer.
public void print(float f)
  //Prints a floating-point number.
public void print(double d)
  //Prints a double-precision floating-point number.
public void print(char[] s)
  //Prints an array of characters.
public void print(String s)
  //Prints a string.
public void print(Object obj)
  //Prints an object.
public void println()
  //Terminates the current line by printing the line
  //separator string.
public void println(boolean x)
  //Prints a boolean value followed by the line separator string.
public void println(char x)
  //Prints a character followed by the line separator string.
public void println(int x)
  //Prints an integer followed by the line separator string.
public void println(long x)
  //Prints a long integer followed by the line separator string.
```

E

```
public void println(float x)
  //Prints a floating-point number followed by the line
  //separator string.
public void println(double x)
  //Prints a double-precision floating-point number followed
  //by the line separator string.
public void println(char[] x)
  //Prints an array of characters followed by the line
  //separator string.
public void println(String x)
  //Prints a String followed by the line separator string.
public void println(Object x)
  //Prints an Object followed by the line separator string.
```

CLASS: Stack (PACKAGE java.util)

Constructors

```
public Stack()
  //Creates an empty Stack object.
```

Methods

```
public boolean empty()
  //Returns true is the stack is empty, false otherwise.
public Object peek() throws EmptyStackException
  //Returns the top element of the stack. It does not remove the
  //top element.
public Object pop() throws EmptyStackException
  //Returns and removes the top element of the stack.
public Object push(Object obj)
  //Pushes the item specified by obj onto the stack.
public int search(Object obj)
  //Returns the relative position of the item specified by obj
  //from the top of the stack. If the item is not in the stack,
  //it returns -1.
```

CLASS: String (PACKAGE java.lang)

Constructors

```
public String()
  //Creates a String object with no characters.
public String(char[] arg)
  //Creates a String object with the string specified by the
  //character array arg.
```

```
public String(char[] arg, int index, int length) throws
                           StringIndexOutOfBoundsException
   //Creates a String object with the string specified by the
   //character array arg, starting at index and of the length
   //specified by length.
public String(String str)
   //Creates a String object and initializes the string
   //object with the characters specified by str.
public String(StringBuffer str)
   //Creates a String object and initializes the string
   //object with the characters specified by str.
```

Methods

```
public char charAt(int index) throws
                              StringIndexOutOfBoundsException
   //Returns the character at the position specified by index.
public int compareTo(String str)
   //Compares two strings character by character.
   //Returns a negative value if this string is less than str.
   //Returns 0 if this string is the same as str.
   //Returns a positive value if this string is greater than str.
public String concat(String str)
   //Returns the string that is this string concatenated with str.
public static String copyValueOf(char[] arg)
   //Returns the string containing the characters of arg.
public static String copyValueOf(char[] arg, int index, int length)
   //Returns the string containing the characters, starting at
   //index and of the length specified by length, of arg.

public boolean endsWith(String str)
   //Returns true if the string ends with the string specified
   //by str, false otherwise.
public boolean equals(String str)
   //Returns true if this string is the same as str, false
   //otherwise.
public boolean equalsIgnoreCases(String str)
   //Returns true if this string is the same as str, wherein cases
   //of the letters are ignored; otherwise, returns false.

public int indexOf(char ch)
   //Returns the index of the first occurrence of the character
   //specified by ch; if the character specified by ch does not
   //appear in the string, it returns -1.
public int indexOf(char ch, int pos)
   //Returns the index of the first occurrence of the character
   //specified by ch; the parameter pos specifies from where to
   //begin the search. If the character specified by ch does not
   //appear in the string, it returns -1.
```

```
public int indexOf(String str)
   //Returns the index of the first occurrence of the string
   //specified by str; if the string specified by str does not
   //appear in the string, it returns −1.
public int indexOf(String str, int pos)
   //Returns the index of the first occurrence of the string
   //specified by str; the parameter pos specifies from where to
   //begin the search. If the string specified by str does not
   //appear in the string, it returns -1.
public int length()
   //Returns the length of the string.
public boolean regionMatches(int ind, String str, int strIndex,
                             int len)
   //Returns true if the substring of str, starting at strIndex,
   //and the length specified by len is the same as the substring
   //of this String object, starting at ind, and has the
   //same length.
public boolean regionMatches(boolean ignoreCase, int ind,
                     String str, int strIndex, int len)
   //Returns true if the substring of str, starting at strIndex,
   //and the length specified by len is the same as the substring of
   //this String object, starting at ind, and has the same length.
   //If ignoreCase is true, then during character comparison,
   //the case is ignored.
public String replace(char charToBeReplaced, char charReplacedWith)
   //Returns the string in which every occurrence of
   //charToBeReplaced is replaced with charReplacedWith.

public boolean startsWith(String str)
   //Returns true if the string begins with the string specified
   //by str, false otherwise.
public String substring(int startIndex)
            throws StringIndexOutOfBoundsException
   //Returns the string that is a substring of this string,
   //starting at startIndex until the end of the string.
public String substring(int startIndex, int endIndex)
            throws StringIndexOutOfBoundsException
   //Returns the string that is a substring of this string,
   //starting at startIndex until endIndex − 1.
public String toLowerCase()
   //Returns the string that is the same as this string, except that
   //all uppercase letters of this string are replaced with
   //their equivalent lowercase letters.
public String toUpperCase()
   //Returns the string that is the same as this string, except
   //that all lowercase letters of this string are replaced with
   //their equivalent uppercase letters.
public char[] toCharArray()
   //Returns the object as an array of characters.
```

```
public char[] toString()
  //Returns the object as a string.
public static String valueOf(boolean b)
  //Returns a string representation of b.
public static String valueOf(char ch)
  //Returns a string representation of ch.
public static String valueOf(int num)
  //Returns a string representation of num.
public static String valueOf(long num)
  //Returns a string representation of num.
public static String valueOf(double decNum)
  //Returns a string representation of decNum.
public static String valueOf(float decNum)
  //Returns a string representation of decNum.
```

Class: StringTokenizer (Package java.util)

Constructors

```
public StringTokenizer(String str)
  //Creates a StringTokenizer object. The object is initialized
  //using the string specified by str. The delimiting characters
  //are the default characters.
public StringTokenizer(String str, String delimits)
  //Creates a StringTokenizer object. The object is initialized
  //using the string specified by str. The string delimits
  //specifies the delimeters.
public StringTokenizer(String str, String delimits, boolean tok)
  //Creates a StringTokenizer object. The object is initialized
  //using the string specified by str. The string delimits
  //specifies the delimeters. If the boolean variable tok
  //is true, the delimeters are treated as words.
```

Methods

```
public int countTokens()
  //Returns the number of tokens in the string.
public boolean hasMoreElements()
  //Returns the value true if there are tokens left in the string,
  //false otherwise.
public boolean hasMoreTokens()
  //Returns the value true if there are tokens left in the string,
  //false otherwise.
public String nextElement() throws NoSuchElementException
  //Returns the next token in the string.
public String nextToken() throws NoSuchElementException
  //Returns the next token in the string.
```

```
public String nextToken(String delimits) throws
                                    NoSuchElementException
   //Returns the next token in the string.
   //The string delimits specifies the delimeters.
```

CLASS: Throwable (PACKAGE java.lang)

Constructors

```
public Throwable()
   //default constructor
   //Creates an instance of Throwable with an empty message string.
public Throwable(String strMessage)
   //constructor with a parameter
   //Creates an instance of Throwable with a message string
   //specified by the parameter strMessage.
```

Variables

```
public String getMessage()
   //Returns the detailed message stored in the object.
public void printStackTrace()
   //Method to print the stack trace showing the sequence of
   //method calls when an exception occurs.
public void printStackTrace(PrintStream stream)
   //Method to print the stack trace showing the sequence of
   //method calls when an exception occurs. Output is sent
   //to the stream specified by the parameter stream.
public void printStackTrace(PrintWriter stream)
   //Method to print the stack trace showing the sequence of
   //method calls when an exception occurs. Output is sent
   //to the stream specified by the parameter stream.
public String toString()
   //Returns a string representation of the Throwable object.
```

CLASS: Vector (PACKAGE java.util)

Variables

```
protected int capacityIncrement;

protected int elementCount;

protected Object[] elementData; //array of references
```

Constructors

```
public Vector()
  //Creates an empty vector of 10 components.
public Vector(int size)
  //Creates an empty vector of the length specified by size.
public Vector(int size, inc increm)
  //Creates an empty vector of the length specified by size and
  //a capacity increment specified by increm.
```

Methods

```
public void addElement(Object insertObj)
  //Adds the object insertObj at the end.
public int capacity()
  //Returns the capacity of the vector.
public Object clone()
  //Returns a copy of the vector.
public boolean contains(Object obj)
  //Returns true if the Vector object contains the object
  //specified by obj, false otherwise.
public void copyInto(Object[] dest)
  //Copies the elements of this vector into the array dest.
public Object elementAt(int index) throws
                              ArrayIndexOutOfBoundsException
  //Returns the element of the vector at the location specified
  //by index.
public void ensureCapacity(int size)
  //Sets the capacity of this vector to size.
public Object firstElement()throws NoSuchElementException
  //Returns the first element of the vector.
public int indexOf(Object obj)
  //Returns the position of the first occurrence of the element
  //specified by obj in the vector. If the item is not in the
  //vector, it returns -1.
public int indexOf(Object obj, int index)
  //Starting at index, this method returns the position of the
  //first occurrence of the element specified by obj in the
  //vector. If the item is not in the vector, it returns -1.
public void insertElementAt(Object insertObj, int index)
                              throws ArrayIndexOutOfBoundsException
  //Inserts the object insertObj at the position specified
  //by index.
public boolean isEmpty()
  //Returns true if the vector is empty, false otherwise.
public Object lastElement() throws NoSuchElementException
  //Returns the last element of the vector.
```

```
public int lastIndexOf(Object obj)
    //Starting at the last element, using a backward search, this
    //method returns the position of the first occurrence of the
    //element specified by obj in the vector. If obj is not in
    //the vector, it returns -1.
public int lastIndexOf(Object item, int index)
    //Starting at the position specified by index and using a
    //backward search, this method returns the position of the
    //first occurrence of the element specified by obj in the
    //vector. If the item is not in the vector, it returns -1.
public void removeAllElements()
    //Removes all the elements of the vector.
public boolean removeElement(Object obj)
    //If an element specified by obj exists in the list, the
    //element is removed and the value true is returned; otherwise,
    //false is returned.
public void removeElementAt(int index) throws
                                ArrayIndexOutOfBoundsException
    //If an element at the position specified by index exists, it is
    //removed from the vector.
public void setElementAt(Object obj, int index) throws
                                ArrayIndexOutOfBoundsException
    //The element specified by obj is stored at the position specified
    //by index.
public int size()
    //Returns the number of elements in the vector.
public void trimToSize()
    //Reduces the length of the vector to the number of elements
    //currently in the vector.
public String toString()
    //Returns a string representation of this vector.
```

F

JAVA FOR C++ PROGRAMMERS

This book assumes that you are familiar with the basic elements of Java such as data types, assignment statements, importing packages, input/output, control structures, methods and parameter passing, and arrays. This appendix reviews these Java programming basics. Moreover, if you have taken C++ as a first programming language, this appendix helps familiarize you with the basic elements of Java. In addition to describing the basic elements of Java, we also compare the various features of Java with C++.

For more details about the Java language, refer to the book, *Java Programming: From Problem Analysis to Program Design* by the authors and listed in the references ([7], Appendix G).

DATA TYPES

Java data types fall into two categories—primitive data types and references. This section discusses the primitive data types. In contrast to C++, the storage of all the primitive data types is independent of the platform. Later in this appendix, we briefly discuss strings, arrays, and references.

The primitive data types are the fundamental data types in Java. There are three categories of primitive data types: integral, floating-point, and `boolean`. Integral data types are further classified into five categories, as shown in Table F-1.

Table F-1 Values and Memory Allocation for the Integral Data Types

Data Type	Values	Storage (in bytes)
char	0 to 65535	2 (16 bits)
byte	−128 to 127	1 (8 bits)
short	−32768 to 32767	2 (16 bits)
int	−2147483648 to 2147483647	4 (32 bits)
long	−9223372036854775808 to 9223372036854775807	8 (64 bits)

The data type `boolean` has only two values: `true` and `false`. In contrast to C++, the `boolean` value `false` cannot be treated as `0`, and the `boolean` value `true` cannot be treated as a non-zero value. The memory allocated for the `boolean` data type is 1 bit.

To represent real numbers, Java uses a form of scientific notation called **floating-point notation**. Table F-2 shows how Java might print a set of real numbers in floating-point notation. In the Java floating-point notation, the letter **E** stands for the exponent.

Table F-2 Examples of Real Numbers Printed in Java Floating-Point Notation

Real Number	Java Floating-Point Notation
75.924	7.592400E1
0.18	1.800000E-1
0.0000453	4.530000E-5
−1.482	−1.482000E0
7800.0	7.800000E3

Java provides two data types to manipulate decimal numbers. The data type `float` represents any real number between −3.4E+38 and 3.4E+38. The memory allocated for the `float` data type is 4 bytes. The data type `double` represents any real number between −1.7E+308 and 1.7E+308. The memory allocated for the `double` data type is 8 bytes. The maximum number of significant digits—that is, the number of decimal places—in `float` values is 6 or 7. The maximum number of significant digits in values belonging to the `double` type is 15. If you use the data type `float` to manipulate floating-point numbers in a program, certain compilers might give you a warning message such as "truncation from double to float" or "possible loss of data." To avoid such warning messages, you should use the `double` data type.

Arithmetic Operators and Expressions

The five arithmetic operators—+, −, *, /, and %—in Java work the same way as in C++. Moreover, arithmetic expressions in Java are formed and evaluated the same as they are in C++. In addition, the increment operator, ++, the decrement operator, −−, and the compound assignment operators, +=, −=, *=, /=, and %=, in Java work the same way as in C++.

The cast operator in Java takes the following form:

```
(dataType) expression
```

NAMED CONSTANTS, VARIABLES, AND ASSIGNMENT STATEMENTS

Named constants in Java are declared using the reserved word `final`. The general syntax of declaring a named constant is:

```
static final dataType identifier = value;
```

For example, the following statement declares CONVERSION to be a named constant of the type double and assigns the value 2.54 to it.

```
final double CONVERSION = 2.54;
```

In Java, variables are declared the same way as they are declared in C++, and the syntax of the assignment statement in both languages is the same.

The general syntax for declaring either one variable or multiple variables is:

```
dataType identifier, identifier, . . .;
```

For example, the following statements declare amountDue to be a variable of the type double and counter to be a variable of the type int.

```
double amountDue;
int     counter;
```

The syntax of the assignment statement is:

```
variable = expression;
```

In an assignment statement, the value of the **expression** should match the data type of the **variable**. The expression on the right side is evaluated, and its value is assigned to the variable on the left side. For example, suppose that amountDue is a variable of the type double and quantity is a variable of the type int. If the value of quantity is 20, then the following statement assigns 150.00 to amountDue:

```
amountDue = quantity * 7.50;
```

Java programmers traditionally use the following rules to name identifiers in order to declare named constants, variables, and classes. An identifier used to declare a named constant is all uppercase. If the identifier is a run-together word, then the words are separated with the underscore character. For example,

```
final int INCHES_PER_FOOT = 12;
```

An identifier used to declare a variable is lowercase. If the identifier is a run-together word, then the first letter of each word, except the first word, is uppercase. For example,

```
int firstNumber;
```

An identifier used to declare a class is all lowercase except the first letter of each word, which is uppercase. For example, Welcome and MakeChange.

Parsing Numeric Strings

A **string** is a sequence of zero or more characters. Strings in Java are enclosed in double quotation marks. The **index**, that is, position, of the first character is 0; the index of the second character is 1; and so on. The length of a string is the number of characters in it.

A string consisting of only integers or decimal numbers is called a **numeric string**. For example, the following are numeric strings.

"6723"

"-823"

"345.78"

"-782.873"

Suppose that we want to process these strings as numbers for addition or multiplication. Then we must first convert them into numeric form. Java provides special methods to convert numeric strings into their equivalent numeric form.

1. To convert a string consisting of an integer to a value of the type `int`, we use the following expression:

   ```
   Integer.parseInt(strExpression)
   ```

   For example,

   ```
   Integer.parseInt("6723") = 6723
   Integer.parseInt("-823") = -823
   ```

2. To convert a string consisting of a decimal number to a value of the type `float`, we use the following expression:

   ```
   Float.parseFloat(strExpression)
   ```

   For example,

   ```
   Float.parseFloat("34.56") = 34.56
   Float.parseFloat("-542.97") = -542.97
   ```

3. To convert a string consisting of a decimal number to a value of the type `double`, we use the following expression:

   ```
   Double.parseDouble(strExpression)
   ```

   For example,

   ```
   Double.parseDouble("345.78") = 345.78
   Double.parseDouble("-782.873") = -782.873
   ```

PACKAGES, CLASSES, METHODS, AND THE IMPORT STATEMENT

Only a small number of operations, such as arithmetic and assignment operations, are explicitly defined in Java. Many of the methods and identifiers needed to run a Java program are provided as a collection of libraries, called packages. A **package** is a collection of related classes, and every package has a name.

In Java, *class* is a broadly used term. The term class is used to create Java programs, applications, or applets; group a set of related operations; and allow users to create their own data types. For example, there are various mathematical operations such as determining the absolute value of a number, determining one number raised to the power of another number, determining the logarithm of a number, and so on. These and other mathematical methods are contained in the **class Math** (see Appendix E). The name of the package containing the **class Math** is **java.lang**.

The package **java.io** contains classes for inputting data into a program and for showing the results of a program. For example, the **class BufferedReader**, contained in this package, includes the method **readLine** for reading a line of characters.

To use the existing classes, methods, and identifiers, you need to tell the program which package contains the appropriate information. You do this with the help of the **import** statement.

The general syntax to import the contents of a package into a Java program is:

```
import packageName.*;
```

For example, the following statement imports the necessary classes from the package **java.io**:

```
import java.io.*;
```

To import a specific class from a package, you can specify the name of the class in place of the *. For example, the following statement imports the **class BufferedReader** from the package **java.io**.

```
import java.io.BufferedReader;
```

The package **java.lang** does not require any import statement in your program.

CREATING A JAVA APPLICATION PROGRAM

The basic unit of a Java program is called a class. A Java application program is, therefore, a collection of one or more classes. One of the classes must have the method called **main**. Moreover, a Java program can have only one method **main**. Thus, if a Java application program has only one class, it must contain the method **main**.

The statements to declare memory spaces (named constants and variables), create input stream objects (such as the object **keyboard**), manipulate data (such as assignments), and input and output data are placed within the class.

The statements to declare named constants and input stream objects are, usually, placed outside of the method **main**; the statements to declare variables are, usually, placed within the method **main**. The statements to manipulate the data and the input and output statements are placed within the method **main**.

The syntax of a class to create a Java application program is as follows:

```
public   class ClassName
{
        classMembers
}
```

where **ClassName** is a user-defined Java identifier, and **classMembers** consists of the data members (such as named constants) and methods (such as the method **main**). In Java, **public** and **class** are reserved words.

The general syntax of the method **main** is:

```
public static void main(String[] args) throws clause
{
     statement1
        .
        .
        .
     statementn
}
```

where the **throws clause** consists of the exceptions thrown by the method **main**. If there is more than one exception, they are separated by commas.

A Java application program might use the resources provided by the SDK, such as the necessary code to input the data, which requires your program to import certain packages. You can, therefore, divide a Java application program into two parts: the import statements and the program. The import statements tell the compiler which packages are being used in the program. The program contains statements (placed in a class) that accomplish some meaningful results. Taken together, the import statements and the program statements constitute the Java **source code**. To be useful, this source code must be saved in a file, called a **source file**, that has the file extension **.java**. Moreover, the name of the class and the name of the file containing the Java program must be the same. For example, if the name of the class to create the Java program is **Welcome**, then the name of the source file must be **Welcome.java**.

The basic parts of the method `main` are the heading and the body. The first line of the method `main`, that is:

```
public static void main(String[] args) throws clause
```

is called the heading of the method `main`.

The statements enclosed between curly braces (`{` and `}`) form the body of the method `main`. The body of the method `main` contains two types of statements:

- Declaration statements
- Executable statements

Declaration statements are used to declare things such as variables. In Java, variables or identifiers can be declared anywhere in the program, but they must be declared before they can be used. Executable statements perform calculations, manipulate data, accept input, create output, and so on. Some executable statements that you have encountered so far are the assignment, input, and output statements.

The following is a simple Java application program that shows where the statements such as import, declaration statements, the method `main`, the executable statements, and so on, typically appear.

```java
import java.io.*;

public class FirstJavaProgram
{
    static final int NUMBER = 12;

    static BufferedReader keyboard = new
            BufferedReader(new InputStreamReader(System.in));

    public static void main(String[] args) throws IOException
    {
        int firstNum;
        int secondNum;

        firstNum = 10;
        System.out.println("firstNum = " + firstNum);
        System.out.print("Enter an integer: ");
        secondNum = Integer.parseInt(keyboard.readLine());
        System.out.println();
        System.out.println("secondNum = " + secondNum);
        firstNum = firstNum + NUMBER + 2 * secondNum;
        System.out.println("The new value of firstNum = "
                        + firstNum);
    }
}
```

F

OBJECTS AND REFERENCE VARIABLES

Consider the following statement:

```
int x;                          //Line 1
```

This statement declares x to be an int variable. Just as you can declare primitive type variables, you can also declare variables using the Java class Integer. For example, consider the statement:

```
Integer num;                    //Line 2
```

This statement declares num to be a reference variable of the Integer type.

The statement in Line 1 allocates memory space to store an int value and calls the memory space x. The variable x can store an int value in its memory space.

The statement in Line 2 allocates memory space for the variable num. However, unlike the variable x, the variable num *cannot* directly store data in its memory space. The variable num stores the memory location, that is, the address of the memory space where the actual data is stored. First, we need to tell the system to allocate memory space to store the data, in our case for an integer. This is accomplished by using the reserved word new. In Java, as in C++, new is an operator and works the same way.

Let Student be a class. In C++ you can create a Student object in two ways:

```
Student studentOne;             //Line 3
```

or:

```
Student  *studentTwo;           //Line 4
studentTwo = new Student();     //Line 5
```

In C++, the statement in Line 3 creates the object studentOne. The statement in Line 4 declares studentTwo to be a pointer (called a reference variable in Java); the statement in Line 5 allocates memory space to store the data, and stores the address of the allocated memory space in studentTwo. Notice the * in Line 4. In C++, pointers are declared using the symbol * as shown in the statement in Line 4.

In Java, you *cannot* declare objects, as shown in the statement in Line 3 (in C++). Statements such as the one in Line 3 in Java only declare studentOne to be a reference variable and it can store the address of any Student object. To store data in a Student object, you must instantiate a Student object as follows:

```
studentOne = new Student();
```

Notice that, in Java, you do not use the symbol * to declare reference variables.

Now suppose that `firstName` is an instance variable of the **class Student**. In C++ or in Java, you can use the following syntax to access the `firstName` of the object **studentOne**:

```
studentOne.firstName
```

In Java, if no reference variable points to an object, then sometimes during program execution, the Java system reclaims the memory space. This is called **garbage collection**. If you do not want to depend on the system for garbage collection, then you can include the statement:

```
System.gc();
```

in your program to instruct the computer to run the garbage collector.

F

class String

The **class String** is one of the most important classes in Java. As inputs to a program, Java accepts only strings. For example, if the input to a program is numeric data, then the numeric data is read as strings of numbers. After reading numeric data into string form, the program converts the strings into numbers for processing. Similarly, before outputting numeric data, it is first converted into strings, which is then output.

Consider the following statement:

```
String name;             //Line 1
name = "Lisa Johnson";   //Line 2
```

The statement in Line 1 declares **name** to be a reference variable of the **String** type. (If there is no confusion, then we also call **name** a **String** variable.) The statement in Line 2 creates the string **"Lisa Johnson"** and assigns it to **name**.

In reality, the statement in Line 2 is equivalent to the following statement:

```
name = new String("Lisa Johnson");
```

The **class String** is so important in Java that it defines the assignment operator for the **class String**. Therefore, while working with **String** variables and objects, you can eliminate the use of the operator **new** and use the assignment operator to instantiate a **String** object.

The **class String** is part of the Java system. That is, the Java system automatically makes the **class String** available for you and so you do not need to import this class. Therefore, in order to use a **String** method you need to know its name, parameters, and what the method does. You also need to know whether the **String** method has the reserved word **static** in its heading. If a method uses the reserved word **static** in its heading, it can be used by including the name of the class and the dot operator. For a list of methods of the **class String**, refer to Appendix E.

The next section discusses input and output (I/O).

INPUT AND OUTPUT

Inputting data and outputting the results of a program is fundamental to any programming language. Because I/O differs significantly in C++ and Java, this section describes I/O in Java in detail.

Input

To put data into variables from the standard input device, we use the Input (Read) statement. In most cases, the standard input device is the keyboard.

To put data into variables from the standard input device, we use the **standard input stream object** `System.in`. The data entered from the standard input device are characters, and the object `System.in` extracts the data in the form of bytes from the input stream. Therefore, using `System.in`, we first need to create another input stream object to read characters from the input stream.

To read characters from the input stream, first we create an object as follows:

```
InputStreamReader charReader =
                new InputStreamReader(System.in);        //Line 1
```

This statement creates the `InputStreamReader` object `charReader`. The object `charReader` is initialized to the standard input device using the object `System.in`.

The object `charReader` can read characters from the input stream, but only one character at a time. To read the entire line of characters, we create another object as follows:

```
BufferedReader keyboard = new BufferedReader(charReader); //Line 2
```

This statement creates the `BufferedReader` object `keyboard`. The object `keyboard` is initialized to the standard input device using the variable `charReader`.

Using the method `readLine` (of the **class BufferedReader**) to read the next line of characters entered from the standard input device, the line of characters can be stored in a `String` variable.

Suppose `inputData` is a `String` variable. The statement in Line 3 then reads and assigns the next line of characters from the input stream to `inputData`.

```
inputData = keyboard.readLine();                         //Line 3
```

 You can combine the statements in Lines 1 and 2, that is:

```
InputStreamReader charReader = new
                InputStreamReader(System.in);
BufferedReader keyboard = new BufferedReader(charReader);
```

into one statement as follows:

```
BufferedReader keyboard = new
        BufferedReader(new InputStreamReader(System.in));
```

Inputting Numeric Data

You've seen how data can be input from the keyboard. Any data you enter from the keyboard (whether numbers, letters, or spaces) is a sequence of characters. Therefore, numeric data is also read as a sequence of characters. Using statements such as the one in Line 3 of the previous section, we can read numbers as a sequence of characters. We then parse the numeric string into an appropriate number. Example F-1 illustrates how to convert a numeric string into a number.

Example F-1

Consider the following statements:

```
String numString1 = "12345";                    //Line 1
int intNum;                                      //Line 2
intNum = Integer.parseInt(numString1);           //Line 3
```

After the statement in Line 3 executes, the value of the variable `intNum` is `12345`.

```
String numString2 = "765.43";                    //Line 4
double doubleNum;                                //Line 5
doubleNum = Double.parseDouble(numString2);      //Line 6
```

After the statement in Line 6 executes, the value of the variable `doubleNum` is `765.43`.

We can now discuss how to read data from the standard input device. Consider the following statement, which declares and initializes the variable `keyboard` to extract data from the standard input device.

```
BufferedReader keyboard = new
        BufferedReader(new InputStreamReader(System.in));
```

Suppose that `numString` is a `String` variable and `miles` is a variable of the type `double`. Suppose that the input is `73.65`. Consider the following statements:

```
numString = keyboard.readLine();
miles = Double.parseDouble(numString);
```

The first statement causes the computer to get the next string, which is `"73.65"`, from the standard input device, and assigns it to `numString`. The second statement converts this string into a value of the type `double`, and places it in the variable `miles`. After the second statement executes, the value of the variable `miles` is `73.65`.

You can combine the preceding two statements into one statement as follows:

```
miles = Double.parseDouble(keyboard.readLine());
```

This eliminates the declaration of the additional `String` variable `numString`.

F

Reading a Single Character

To read a single character, you can use the method **read** (of the **class BufferedReader**). The method **read**, in fact, returns the integer value of the character. For example, if you input A, it returns 65. You need to use the cast operator to convert this integer value into a **char** value. If ch is a **char** variable, the following statement inputs the next character (including a space and the newline character) from the keyboard.

```
ch = (char) keyboard.read();
```

where **keyboard** is a **BufferedReader** object initialized to the standard input device.

Tokenizing a String

The method **readLine** reads the entire line as a string. To break each line into meaningful units of data called **tokens**, Java contains the **class StringTokenizer**, which contains methods to tokenize a string. Tokens are usually delimited with **whitespace** characters. In Java, whitespace characters are the space, tab, newline character, and certain nonprintable characters. You can also specify the delimiting character. The **class StringTokenizer** is contained in the **package java.util**. Therefore, to use this class, the program must import this class from the **package java.util**. To tokenize a string, you first need to create a **StringTokenizer** object and store the string in the created object. For example, consider the following statement:

```
StringTokenizer tokenizer = new StringTokenizer("Hello there!");
```

This statement creates the **StringTokenizer** object **tokenizer** and stores the string "Hello there!" in the object **tokenizer**. There are two tokens in the object **tokenizer**—Hello and there!.

You can now use the method **nextToken** with the object **tokenizer** to retrieve the next token from the string. Suppose that **str1** and **str2** are **String** variables. Consider the following statements:

```
str1 = tokenizer.nextToken();       //Line 1
str2 = tokenizer.nextToken();       //Line 2
```

After these two statements execute, the string assigned to **str1** is "Hello" and the string assigned to **str2** is "there!".

Example F-2

Suppose that we have the following input data:

```
Mickey 97 158.50
```

Also suppose that we have the following statements:

```
BufferedReader keyboard = new
        BufferedReader(new InputStreamReader(System.in)); //Line 1

StringTokenizer tokenizer;                               //Line 2
String inputLine;                                        //Line 3
String name;                                             //Line 4
int num;                                                 //Line 5
double decNum;                                           //Line 6
```

The statement in Line 1 creates the input stream object **keyboard** to input data from the keyboard. The statement in Line 2 declares **tokenizer** to be a reference variable of the type **StringTokenizer**. Consider the following statements:

```
inputLine = keyboard.readline();                         //Line 7
tokenizer = new StringTokenizer(inputLine);              //Line 8
name = tokenizer.nextToken();                            //Line 9
num = Integer.parseInt(tokenizer.nextToken());           //Line 10
decNum = Double.parseDouble(tokenizer.nextToken());      //Line 11
```

The statement in Line 7 reads and assigns the string "**Mickey 97 158.50**" to **inputLine**. If **inputLine** is **null**, then when you execute the program it generates **NullPointerException** and if the program does not handle this exception, the program terminates. Therefore, you should be careful when you tokenize a string. The statement in Line 8 instantiates the object **tokenizer** and stores the string "**Mickey 97 158.50**" in this object. Notice that the object **tokenizer** has three tokens in it. The statement in Line 9 retrieves the next token, which is the string "**Mickey**" and assigns this string to **name**. The next token in the object **tokenizer** is the integer numeric string "**97**". The statement in Line 10 retrieves the integer **97** and stores it in **num**. The next token in the object **tokenizer** is the numeric string "**158.50**". The statement in Line 11 retrieves this number and stores it in **decNum**. Note that the statements in Lines 7 and 8 can be combined into one statement as follows:

```
tokenizer = new StringTokenizer(keyboard.readline());
```

This statement would eliminate the declaration of the variable **inputLine**.

Output

In Java, output on the standard output device is accomplished via the use of the standard output object **System.out**. The object **System.out** has access to two methods, **print** and **println**, to output a string on the standard output device.

The syntax to use the object **System.out** and the methods **print** and **println** is:

```
System.out.print(stringExp);
System.out.println(stringExp);
```

These are called **output statements**. The expression is evaluated, and its value is printed at the current cursor position on the output device. After outputting the `stringExp`, the method `print` leaves the cursor after the last character of the `stringExp`, while the method `println` positions the cursor at the beginning of the next line.

Table F-3 illustrates how the output statements work. In an output statement, a string or an expression involving only one variable or a single value evaluates to itself.

When an output statement outputs `char` values, it outputs the character without the single quotes (unless the single quotes are part of the output statement). For example, suppose `ch` is a `char` variable and `ch = 'A';`. The statement:

```
System.out.println(ch);
```

or:

```
System.out.println('A');
```

outputs:

```
A
```

Similarly, when an output statement outputs the value of a string, it outputs the string without the double quotes (unless you include double quotes as part of the output).

Example F-3

	Statement	Output
1	`System.out.println(29 / 4);`	7
2	`System.out.println("Hello there.");`	Hello there.
3	`System.out.println(12);`	12
4	`System.out.println("4 + 7");`	4 + 7
5	`System.out.println(4 + 7);`	11
6	`System.out.println('A');`	A
7	`System.out.println("4 + 7 = " + 4 + 7);`	4 + 7 = 11
8	`System.out.println(2 + 3 * 5);`	17
9	`System.out.println("Hello \nthere.");`	Hello there.

Formatting the Output of Decimal Numbers

The default output of decimal numbers of the type `float` have up to six decimal places. Similarly, the default output of decimal numbers of the type `double` have up to fifteen decimal places. For example, consider the statements in Table F-4 (the output is shown to the right).

Table F-4 Statements and Output

Statement	Output
`System.out.println(22.0 / 7.0);`	3.142857142857143
`System.out.println(75.0 / 7.0);`	10.714285714285714
`System.out.println((float)(33.0 / 16.0));`	2.0625
`System.out.println((float)(22.0 / 7.0));`	3.142857

Sometimes floating-point numbers must be output in a specific way. For example, a paycheck must be printed to two decimal places, whereas the results of a scientific experiment might require the output of floating-point numbers to six, seven, or perhaps even ten decimal places.

Java provides the **class DecimalFormat** to format decimal numbers in a specific manner. The method **format** of the **class DecimalFormat** is applied to the decimal value being formatted. The following steps explain how to use these features to format decimal numbers.

1. Declare a **DecimalFormat** variable and initialize it to the specific format. Consider the following statement:

    `DecimalFormat twoDecimal = new DecimalFormat("0.00");`

    This statement declares **twoDecimal** to be a **DecimalFormat** variable and initializes it to the string **"0.00"**. Each **0** in the string is a **format flag**. The string **"0.00"** is what specifies the formatting of the decimal number. This string indicates that the decimal number being formatted with the variable **twoDecimal** will have at least one digit to the left of the decimal point and exactly two digits to the right of the decimal point. If the number being formatted does not meet the formatting requirement, that is, it does not have digits at the specified places, they are automatically filled with **0**. Moreover, suppose that the **DecimalFormat** variable is declared as follows:

    `DecimalFormat twoDigits = new DecimalFormat("0.##");`

    The variable **twoDigits** would format the number with two decimal places, but the **##** indicate that the trailing zeros will appear as spaces.

2. Next, use the method **format** together with the **DecimalFormat** variable. (Assume the declaration of Step 1.) For example, the statement:

    `twoDecimal.format(56.379);`

    formats the decimal number **56.379** as **56.38** (the decimal number is rounded). The method **format** returns the string containing the digits of the formatted number.

3. The **class DecimalFormat** is included in the **package java.text**. You must import this class into your program.

F

File Input/Output

The previous sections explained how to get input from the keyboard (standard input device) and send output to the screen (standard output device). This section discusses how to obtain data from other input devices, such as a disk (that is, secondary storage), and how to save the output to a disk. Java allows a program to get data directly from, and save output directly to, secondary storage. A program can use the file I/O and read data from, or write data to, a file. Formally, a **file** is defined as follows:

File: An area in secondary storage used to hold information.

To input data from a file, you use the **class FileReader**; to send output to a file, you use the **class**es **FileWriter** and **PrintWriter**. These classes contain the appropriate methods to read data from a file, and send the output of a program to a file. Both classes are contained in the package **java.io**.

Java file I/O is a four-step process:

1. Import the necessary classes from the package **java.io** into the program.

2. Declare and associate the appropriate variables with the input/output sources.

3. Use the appropriate methods associated with the variables created in Step 2 to input/output the data.

4. Close the output file.

We now describe these four steps in detail. A skeleton program then shows how the steps might appear in a program.

Step 1 requires that the necessary classes be imported from the package **java.io**. The following statement accomplishes this task:

```
import java.io.*;
```

Step 2 requires you to declare and associate the appropriate class variables with the input/output sources. First, we'll describe how to declare and associate class variables for inputting data from a file.

Inputting (Reading) Data from a File

As noted previously, to declare a variable for inputting data you must use the **class FileReader**. Assume that the input is stored in the file **prog.dat** and is stored on the floppy disk **A**. Consider the following statement:

```
FileReader inData = new FileReader("a:\\prog.dat");        //Line 1
```

This statement creates the **FileReader** object **inData** and initializes it to the file **prog.dat**. Notice that there are two \ after **a:** in Line 1. Recall that in Java \ is the escape character. Therefore, to produce a \ within a string, you need \\.

The **class FileReader** contains the method **read** that can be used with **inData** to read the data from the file **prog.dat**. However, the method **read** only reads character by character.

To read the entire line of characters, you can create a **BufferedReader** object and initialize the object to the input source using **inData**. For example, consider the following statement (assume the declaration of the statement in Line 1).

```
BufferedReader inFile = new BufferedReader(inData);      //Line 2
```

This statement creates the **BufferedReader** object **inFile** and initializes it using **inData**. After this statement executes, you can use **inFile** and the method **read** to read the data character by character, or the method **readLine** to read the entire line of characters from the input file **prog.dat**.

The statements in Lines 1 and 2 can be combined into one statement as follows:

```
BufferedReader inFile = new
        BufferedReader(new FileReader("a:\\prog.dat"));    //Line 3
```

 If your Java program and the input file reside in the same directory, you do not need to include **a:** before the file name in statements such as those in Lines 1 and 3. If you need to tokenize the input line, you can use a **StringTokenizer** object.

Storing (Writing) Output to a File

To store the output of a program in a file, you use the **class FileWriter**. First, declare a **FileWriter** variable and associate this variable with the destination, that is, with the file where the output will be stored. Suppose that the output is to be stored in the file **prog.out** on floppy disk **A**. Consider the following statement:

```
FileWriter outData = new FileWriter("a:\\prog.out");      //Line 4
```

This statement creates the **FileWriter** object **outData** and associates it with the file **prog.out** on floppy disk **A**.

Next, to use the methods **print**, **println**, and **flush** to output the data, we create a **PrintWriter** object and initialize this variable using **outData**. The following statement accomplishes this:

```
PrintWriter outFile = new PrintWriter(outData);         //Line 5
```

You can now use the methods **print**, **println**, and **flush** with **outFile** the same way they have been used with the object **System.out**.

For example, the statement:

```
outFile.println("The paycheck is: $" + pay);
```

stores the output—**The paycheck is: $565.78**—in the file **prog.out**. This statement assumes that the value of the variable **pay** is **565.78**.

Of course, you can combine the statements in Lines 4 and 5 into one statement, as follows:

```
PrintWriter outFile = new
                PrintWriter(new FileWriter("a:\\prog.out"));
```

Once the output is completed, Step 4 requires closing the file. You close the output file by using the method `close`. For example, assuming the declarations listed in Steps 2 and 3, the statement to close `outFile` is:

```
outFile.close();
```

Closing the output file ensures that the buffer holding the output is emptied; that is, the entire output generated by the program is sent to the output file.

Step 3 requires that you create the appropriate objects for file I/O. In the case of an input file, the file must exist before the program executes. If the input file does not exist, then the statement to associate the object with the input file fails and it **throws** a `FileNotFoundException` clause. If you do not require the program to handle this exception, the method **main** also **throws** this exception. In this case, the heading of the method **main** contains an appropriate clause to **throw** a `FileNotFoundException`.

An output file does not have to exist before it is opened; if the output file does not exist, the computer prepares an empty file for output. If the designated output file already exists, by default the old contents are erased when the file is opened.

In skeleton form, a program that uses file I/O is usually of the following form:

```
import java.io;
//Add additional packages as needed
class ClassName
{
        //Declare appropriate variables
    public static void main(String[] args) throws
                            FileNotFoundException, IOException
    {
            //Create and associate the stream objects
        BufferedReader inFile =
            new BufferedReader (new FileReader("a:\\prog.dat"));
        PrintWriter outFile =
            new PrintWriter(new FileWriter("a:\\prog.out"));

        //Code for data manipulation

        //Close the files
        outFile.close();
    }
}
```

CONTROL STRUCTURES

C++ and Java have the same six relational operators — ==, !=, <, <=, >, and >= — and they work the same way in both languages. The control structures in C++ and Java are the same. For example, the selection control structures are if, if...else, and switch, and the looping control structures are while, for, and do...while. The syntax for these control structures is the same in both languages. However, there are some differences.

In C++, any nonzero value is treated as true, and the value 0 is treated as false. The reserved word true is initialized to 1, and false is initialized to 0. Logical expressions in C++ evaluate to 0 or 1. On the other hand, logical expressions in Java evaluate to true or false. Moreover, the data type boolean in Java cannot be typecasted to a numeric type, and so its values true and false cannot be typecasted to numeric values.

In C++, the mix-up of the assignment operator and the equality operator in a logical expression can cause serious problems. For example, consider the following if statement:

```
if(drivingCode = 5)
...
```

In C++, the expression drivingCode = 5 returns the value 5. Because 5 is nonzero, the expression evaluates to true. So in C++, the expression evaluates to true, and the value of the variable drivingCode is also changed. On the other hand, in Java, because the value 5 is not a boolean value, it cannot be typecasted to true or false. So the preceding statement in Java results in a compiler error, whereas in C++ it does not cause any syntax error.

METHODS AND PARAMETERS

Methods in C++ are called functions. A Java program is a collection of classes and all methods must be defined in some class. Furthermore, all methods have only definitions, no forward references. There are two types of methods—value-returning and void.

Value-Returning Methods

The syntax of a value-returning method is:

```
modifier(s) returnType methodName(formal parameter list)
{
        statements
}
```

F

In this syntax ,

- `modifier(s)` indicates the visibility of the method, that is, where in a program the method can be used (called). Some of the modifiers are `public`, `private`, `protected`, `static`, `abstract`, and `final`. If you include more than one modifier, they must be separated with spaces. You can select one modifier among `public`, `protected`, and `private`. The modifier `public` specifies that the method can be called outside the class; the modifier `private` specifies that the method cannot be used outside the class. Similarly, you can choose one of the modifiers `static` or `abstract`.

- `returnType` is the type of value that the method calculates and returns. This type is also called the type of the value-returning method.

- `methodName` is a Java identifier, giving a name to the method.

- Statements enclosed between curly braces form the body of the method.

In Java, `public`, `protected`, `private`, `static`, and `abstract` are reserved words.

Formal Parameter List

The syntax of the formal parameter list is:

```
dataType identifier, dataType identifier,...
```

Method Call

The syntax to call a value-returning method is:

```
methodName(actual parameter list)
```

Actual Parameter List

The syntax of the actual parameter list is:

```
expression or variable, expression or variable, ...
```

Thus, to call a value-returning method, you use its name, with the actual parameters (if any) in parentheses.

A method's formal parameter list can be empty. However, if the formal parameter list is empty, the parentheses are still needed. If the formal parameter list is empty, the heading of the value-returning method takes the following form:

```
modifiers(s) returnType methodName()
```

If the formal parameter list is empty in a method call, the actual parameter is also empty. In this case (that is, an empty formal parameter list), in a method call the empty parentheses are still needed. Thus, a call to a value-returning method with an empty formal parameter list is:

```
methodName()
```

In a method call, the number of actual parameters, together with their data types, must match the formal parameters in the order given. That is, the actual and formal parameters must have a one-to-one correspondence.

Once a value-returning method computes the value, the method returns this value via the `return` statement.

F

void Methods

The definition of a **void** method has the following syntax:

```
modifier(s) void methodName(formal parameter list)
{
     statements
}
```

Formal Parameter List

The formal parameter list may be empty. If the formal parameter is nonempty, then the formal parameter list has the following syntax:

```
dataType variable, dataType variable, ....
```

Method Call

The method call has the following syntax:

```
methodName(actual parameter list);
```

Actual Parameter List

The actual parameter list has the following syntax:

```
expression or variable, expression or variable, ...
```

As with value-returning methods, in a method call the number of actual parameters, together with their data types, must match the formal parameters in the order given. Actual and formal parameters have a one-to-one correspondence. A method call causes the body of the called method to execute.

Example F-4

```
public static void funexp(int a, double b, char c, String name)
{
    .
    .
    .
}
```

The method `funexp` has four parameters.

Variables as Parameters

Java has two categories of variables—variables of a primitive type and reference variables. Let us make the following observation about variables of primitive types and reference variables. When a method is called, the value of the actual parameter is copied into the corresponding formal parameter. If the formal parameter is a variable of a primitive data type, then after copying the value of the actual parameter, no connection exists between the formal parameter and the actual parameter. That is, the formal parameter has its own copy of the data. Therefore, during program execution, the formal parameter manipulates the data stored in its own memory space.

On the other hand, suppose that a formal parameter is a reference variable. Here, also, the value of the actual parameter is copied into the formal parameter, but there is a slight difference. A reference variable does not store the data directly in its own memory space. We use the operator `new` to allocate the memory for an object belonging to a specific class, and a reference variable of that class type contains the address of the allocated memory space. Therefore, when we pass the value of the actual parameter to the corresponding formal parameter, after copying the value of the actual parameter, both the actual and formal parameters refer to the same memory space, that is, the same object. Therefore, if the formal parameter changes the value of the object, it can also change the value of the object of the actual parameter.

Reference variables as parameters are useful in three situations:

- When you want to return more than one value from a method.
- When the value of the actual object needs to be changed.
- When passing the address would save time and memory space relative to copying a large amount of data.

ARRAYS

Like C++, in Java, an **array** is a collection of a fixed number of components wherein all of the components are of the same data type. However, in Java, arrays are objects and so they need to be instantiated. Next, we describe how one-dimensional arrays work in Java.

A **one-dimensional array** is an array in which the components are arranged in a list form. The general syntax to declare a one-dimensional array is:

```
dataType[] arrayName;                              //Line 1
```

where `dataType` is the component type.

In Java, an array is an object. Because `arrayName` is an object, `arrayName` is a reference. Therefore, the preceding statement only declares a reference variable. To store data, we must instantiate the array object.

The general syntax to instantiate an array object is:

```
arrayName = new dataType[intExp];                  //Line 2
```

where `intExp` is any expression that evaluates to a positive integer. Also, the value of `intExp` specifies the number of components in the array.

You can combine the statements in Lines 1 and 2 into one statement as follows:

```
dataType[] arrayName = new dataType[intExp];     //Line 3
```

Example F-5

The statement:

```
int[] num = new int[5];
```

creates the array `num` of 5 components. Each component is of the type `int`. The components are `num[0]`, `num[1]`, `num[2]`, `num[3]`, and `num[4]`.

Accessing Array Components

In Java, array components are accessed just like in C++. The general form (syntax) used to access an array component is:

```
arrayName[indexExp]
```

where `indexExp`, called the **index**, is any expression whose value is a non-negative integer. The index value specifies the position of the component in the array. In Java, the array index starts at 0. Consider the following statement:

```
int[] list = new int[10];
```

This statement declares an array `list` of 10 components. The components are `list[0]`, `list[1], ..., list[9]`. The assignment statement:

```
list[5] = 34;
```

stores 34 in `list[5]`, which is the sixth component of the array `list`. Suppose `i` is an `int` variable. Then the assignment statement:

```
list[3] = 63;
```

is equivalent to the assignment statements:

```
i = 3;
list[i] = 63;
```

If `i` is 4, then the assignment statement:

```
list[2 * i - 3] = 58;
```

stores 58 in `list[5]`, because 2 * i - 3 evaluates to 5. The index expression is evaluated first, giving the position of the component in the array.

Next, consider the following statements:

```
list[3] = 10;
list[6] = 35;
list[5] = list[3] + list[6];
```

The first statement stores 10 in `list[3]`, the second statement stores 35 in `list[6]`, and the third statement adds the contents of `list[3]` and `list[6]` and stores the result in `list[5]`.

Array Index Out of Bounds Exception

In Java, if an array index goes out of bounds during program execution, it `throws` an `ArrayIndexOutOfBoundsException`. If the program does not handle this exception, the program terminates with an appropriate error message.

Arrays and the Instance Variable `length`

Recall that an array is an object and so to store data, the array object must be instantiated. Associated with each array that has been instantiated (that is, memory has been allocated to store the data), there is a `public` instance variable `length`. The variable `length` contains the size of the array. Because `length` is a `public` member, it can be directly accessed in a program using the array name and the dot operator.

Consider the following declaration:

```
int[] list = new int[20];
```

This statement creates the array `list` of 20. Here `list.length` is 6.

Arrays as Parameters to Methods

Just like other objects, arrays can be passed as parameters to methods. The following method takes as an argument any `int` array and outputs the data stored in each component:

```
public static void printArray(int[] list)
{
    int index;
    for(index = 0; index < list.length; index++)
        System.out.print(list[index] + " ");
    system.out.println();
}
```

Methods such as this process the data of an entire array. Sometimes the number of elements in the array might be less than the length of the array. For example, the number of elements in an array storing student data might increase or decrease as students add or drop courses. In situations like this, we want to process only the components of the array that hold actual data. To write methods to process such arrays, in addition to declaring an array as a formal parameter, we declare another formal parameter specifying the number of elements in the array, as in the following method:

```
public static void printArray(int[] list, int noOfElements)
{
    int index;
    for(index = 0; index < noOfElements; index++)
        System.out.print(list[index] + " ");
    System.out.println();
}
```

The first parameter of the method `printArray` is an `int` array of any size. When the method `printArray` is called, the number of elements in the actual array is passed as the second parameter of the method `printArray`.

G

REFERENCES

1. G. Booch, *Objected-Oriented Analysis and Design*, Second Edition, Addison-Wesley, Reading, MA, 1995.

2. E. Horowitz, S. Sahni, and S. Rajasekaran, *Computer Algorithms C++*, Computer Science Press, New York, NY, 1997.

3. R. Johnsonbaugh, *Discrete Mathematics*, Fifth Edition, Prentice-Hall, Upper Saddle River, NJ, 2001.

4. D. E. Knuth, *The Art of Computer Programming*, Vols. 1–3, Addison-Wesley, Reading, MA, 1973, 1969, 1973.

5. D. S. Malik, *C++ Programming: From Problem Analysis to Program Design*, Course Technology, Boston, MA, 2002.

6. D. S. Malik, *Data Structures Using C++*, Course Technology, Boston, MA, 2003.

7. D. S. Malik and P. S. Nair, *Java Programming: From Problem Analysis to Program Design*, Course Technology, Boston, MA, 2003.

8. E. M. Reingold and W. J. Hensen, *Data Structures in Pascal*, Little Brown and Company, Boston, MA, 1986.

9. R. Sedgewick, *Algorithms in C*, Third Edition, Addison-Wesley, Reading, MA, Parts 1–4, 1998; Part 5, 2002.

APPENDIX

H

ANSWERS TO SELECTED EXERCISES

Chapter 1

1. a. true; b. false; c. false; d. false; e. false; f. true; g. false; h. false

2. Precondition: The value of **x** must be nonnegative.

   Postcondition: If the value of **x** is nonnegative, the function returns the positive square root of **x**; otherwise, the program terminates.

4. 10

11. a. (i) Constructor at Line 1

    (ii) Constructor at Line 3

    (iii)Constructor at Line 4

    d.
    ```
    public CC(int a, int b)
    {
        u = a;
        v = b;
        w = 0;
    }

    public CC(int a, int b, double d)
    {
        u = a;
        v = b;
        w = d;
    }
    ```

13. ```
    06:23:17
    06:23:17
    ```

14. a. 6

    b. 2

    c. 2

17. Both **aa** and **bb** point to the object **bb**.

18. ```
    06:23:17
    ```

21. ```
    package dsuj.ch01.strangeClasses;
    ```
    ```

Chapter 2

1. a. true; b. false; c. true; d. false; e. true; f. false; g. false; h. true; i. false; j. true; k. true; l. false

4. The `private` members of a class are `private`; they cannot be directly accessed by the member functions of the derived class. The `protected` members of the base class can be directly accessed by the member functions of the derived class.

6. In a constructor of a subclass, and during the overriding of a method in a subclass.

7. The statement:

```
class BClass AClass
```

should be:

```
class BClass extends AClass
```

Also, there is a missing) in the `System.out.println` statement. Moreover, the variables u and v are `private` in `class AClass`, and cannot be accessed directly in `class BClass`.

9.

a.
```
public YClass()
{
    a = 0;
    b = 0;
}
```

b.
```
public XClass()
{
    super(0, 0);
    z = 0;
}
```

c.
```
public void two(int u, int v)
{
    a = u;
    b = v;
}
```

10. `aObject` needs to be initialized.

14. An abstract method is a method that has only the heading with no body. Moreover, the heading of an abstract method contains the reserved word **abstract** and ends with a semicolon.

15. a.
```
Entering the try block.
Exception: Lower limit violation.
After the catch block
```

16. a. Entering the try block.
    Exception: Lower limit violation.
    After the catch block

c. Entering the try block.
    Exiting the try block.
    After the catch block

Chapter 3

1. a. Creates the `UnorderedArrayList` object `intList` of 100 components.

   b. Creates the `UnorderedArrayList` object `stringList` of 1000 components.

   c. Creates the `UnorderedArrayList` object `salesList` of 100 components.

2. Creates the empty `Vector` object `list` of the default length of 10.

3. `list = ["One", "Six", "Two", "Three", "Four", "Five"];`

4. `list = [Goofy, Mickey, Balto]`

5. `[Hello, 10, Happy, 20, Sunny, 30]`
   `[Hello, 10, Joy, Happy, Sunny, 30]`

6. a. `System.out.println(studentFirstName.elementAt(2));`

   b. `System.out.println(studentLastName.elementAt(1));`

   c. `System.out.println(studentFirstName.elementAt(0)`
      `                              + " " +`
      `                          studentLastName.elementAt(0));`

   d.
```
String tempL = (String) studentLastName.elementAt(3);
String tempF = (String) studentFirstName.elementAt(3);
studentLastName.setElementAt(tempF, 3);
studentFirstName.setElementAt(tempL, 3);
```

7. a.
```
String tempOne = (String) studentLastName.elementAt(0);
String tempTwo = (String) studentLastName.elementAt(1);
studentLastName.setElementAt(tempOne, 1);
studentLastName.setElementAt(tempTwo, 0);
```

   b.
```
String tempOne = (String) studentFirstName.elementAt(0);
String tempTwo = (String) studentFirstName.elementAt(1);
studentFirstName.setElementAt(tempOne, 1);
studentFirstName.setElementAt(tempTwo, 0);
```

Chapter 4

1. a. false; b. false; c. false; d. false; e. true

3. a. true; b. true; c. false; d. false; e. true

4. a. valid

   b. valid

   c. valid

   d. valid

   e. invalid (`B` is a reference variable while `A.link.info` is `int`)

   f. valid

   g. valid

   h. valid

6. This is an infinite loop, continuously printing 18.

7. a. This is an invalid code. The statement `s.info = B;` is invalid because `B` is a reference variable and `s.info` is an `int`.

   b. This is an invalid code. After the statement `s = s.link;` executes, `s` is `null` and so `s.info` does not exist.

9. `30 42 20 28`

10.

```
Item to be deleted is not in the list.
18 38 2 15 45 25
```

Chapter 5

1. a. true; b. true; c. false; d. false; e. false

4. A method is called directly recursive if it calls itself.

5. A method that calls another method and eventually results in the original method call is said to be indirectly recursive.

6. A recursive method in which the last statement executed is the recursive call is called a tail recursive method.

9. a. It does not produce any output.

   b. `5 6 7 8 9`

   c. It does not produce any output.

   d. It does not produce any output.

10. a. 15

   b. 6

   Suppose that `low` specifies the starting index and `high` specifies the ending index in the array. The elements of the array between low and high are to be reversed.

   ```
   if(low < high)
   {
      a. swap(list[low], list[high])
      b. reverse elements between low + 1 and high - 1)
   }
   ```

14. b. C(5,3) = 10; C(9,4) = 126

Chapter 6

1. ```
   x = 3
   y = 9
   7
   13
   4
   7
   ```

2. ```
   x = 45
   x = 23
   x = 5
   Stack Elements: 10 34 14 5
   ```

3. a. 26

   b. 45

   c. 8

   d. 29

4. a. AB+CD+*E-

   b. ABC+D*-EF/+

   c. AB+CD-/E+F*G-

   d. ABCD+*+EF/G*-H+

6. Winter Spring Summer Fall Cold Warm Hot

7. 10 20 30 40 50

Chapter 7

1. a. queueFront = 50; queueRear = 0

   b. queueFront = 51; queueRear = 99

3. a. `queueFront = 25; queueRear = 76`

   b. `queueFront = 26; queueRear = 75`

5. 51

7. `Queue Elements: 5 9 16 4 13`

9. The function **mystery** reverses the elements of a queue and also doubles the values of the queue elements.

11.

```
public static void reverseStack(StackClass s, QueueClass q)
{
    DataElement elem;

    while(!s.isEmptyStack())
    {
        elem = s.top();
        s.pop();
        q.addQueue(elem);
    }

    while(!q.isEmptyQueue())
    {
        elem = q.front();
        q.deleteQueue();
        s.push(elem);
    }
}
```

Chapter 8

1. a. false; b. true; c. false; d. false

2. a. 8; b. 6; c. 1; d. 8

3.

   b.

Iteration	first	last	mid	list[mid]	Number of comparisons
1	0	10	5	55	2
2	0	4	2	17	2
3	3	4	3	45	2
4	4	4	4	49	1(found is true)

The item is found at location 4 and the total number of comparisons is 7.

d.

Iteration	first	last	mid	list[mid]	Number of comparisons
1	0	10	5	55	2
2	6	10	8	92	2
3	9	10	9	98	2
4	10	10	10	110	2
5	11	10	the loop stops		

This is an unsuccessful search. The total number of comparisons is 8.

4. There are 30 buckets in the hash table and each bucket can hold 5 items.

9. a. The item with index 15 is inserted at HT[15]; the item with index 101 is inserted at HT[0]; the item with index 116 is inserted at HT[16]; the item with index 0 is inserted at HT[1]; and the item with index 217 is inserted at HT[17].

   b. The item with index 15 is inserted at HT[15]; the item with index 101 is inserted at HT[0]; the item with index 116 is inserted at HT[16]; the item with index 0 is inserted at HT[1]; and the item with index 217 is inserted at HT[19].

10. 101

15. The load factor $\alpha = 850 / 1001 \approx .85$

16. The load factor $\alpha = 500 / 1001 \approx .5$

   a. $(1/2)\{1 + (1/(1-\alpha))\} \approx 1.5$.

   c. $(1 + \alpha/2) = 1.25$

Chapter 9

1. 3

3. 10, 12, 18, 21, 25, 28, 30, 71, 32, 58, 15

6. a. 36, 38, 32, 16, 40, 28, 48, 80, 64, 95, 54, 100, 58, 65, 55

9. During the first pass, 6 key comparisons are made. After two passes of the heap sort algorithm, the list is:

   85, 72, 82, 47, 65, 50, 76, 30, 20, 60, 28, 25, 45, 17, 35, 14, 94, 100

Chapter 10

1. a. false; b. true; c. false; d. false

3. L_A = {B, C, D, E}

4. R_A = {F, G}

5. R_B = {E}

6. D C B E A F G

7. A B C D E F G

8. D C E B G F A

9. 80-55-58-70-79

12.

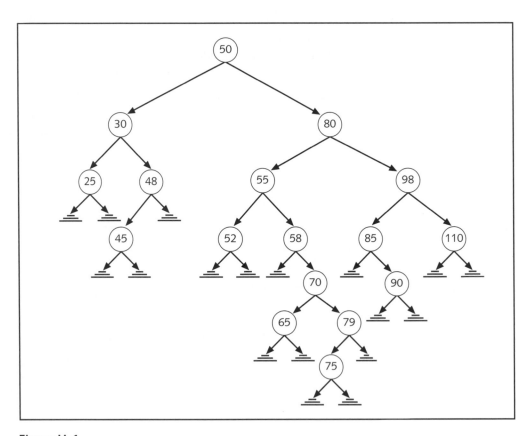

Figure H-1

15.

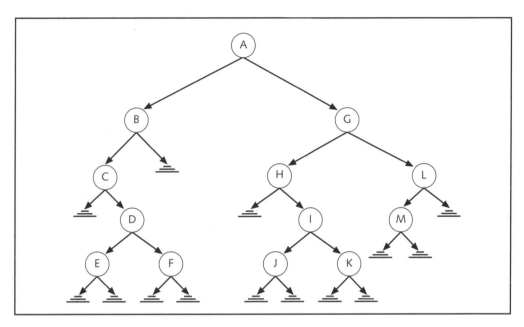

Figure H-2

17. The balance factor of the root node is 0.

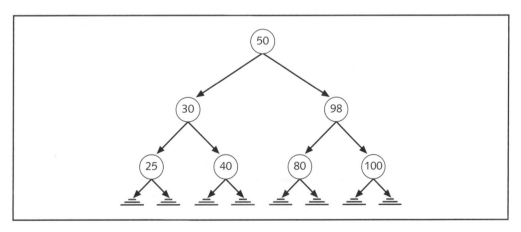

Figure H-3

18. The balance factor of the root node is −1.

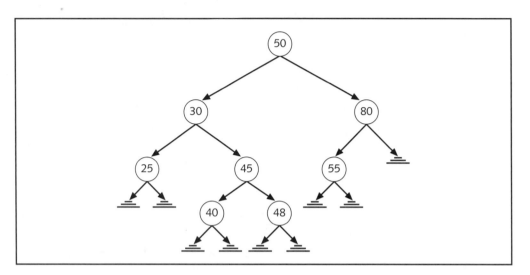

Figure H-4

Chapter 11

2.

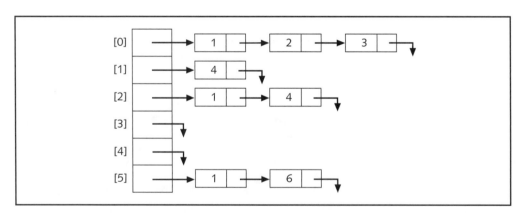

Figure H-5

3. 0 1 4 2 3 5

4. 0 1 2 3 4 5

6.

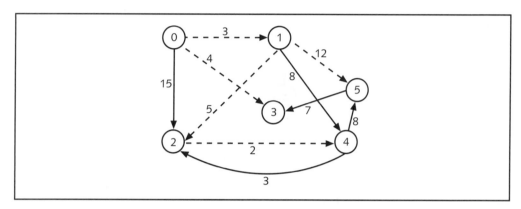

Figure H-6

```
Source Vertex: 0
Shortest Distance from Source to each Vertex
Vertex   Shortest_Distance
   0              0
   1              3
   2              8
   3              4
   4             10
   5             15
```

H

7.

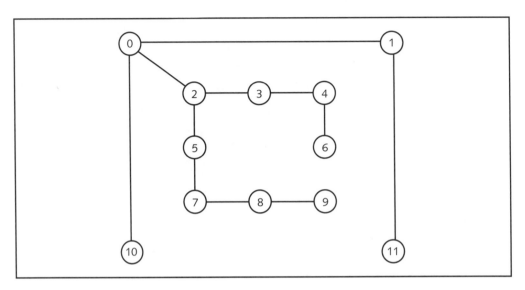

Figure H-7

10. 1, 7, 0, 2, 6, 5, 4, 8, 3, 9

Index